California
Real Property
Sales Transactions

California

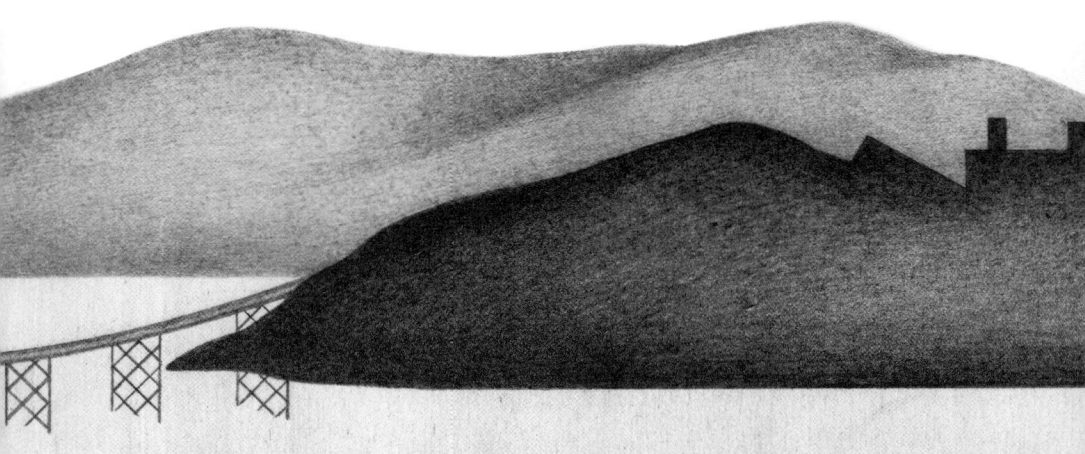

Real Property Sales Transactions

Edited by CEB Attorneys
GORDON GRAHAM
CRAIG H. SCOTT

CALIFORNIA CONTINUING EDUCATION OF THE BAR
Berkeley, California

For supplement information, call (415) 642-6810.

RE-36610

CALIFORNIA CONTINUING EDUCATION OF THE BAR

By agreement between the Board of Governors of the State Bar of California and the Regents of the University of California, Continuing Education of the Bar offers an educational program for the benefit of practicing lawyers. The program is administered by a Governing Committee through University of California Extension in cooperation with local bar associations and the Joint Advisory Committee made up of the State Bar Committee on Continuing Education of the Bar and the Deans of accredited law schools.

Practice books are published as part of the educational program. Authors are given full opportunity to express their individual legal interpretations and opinions, and these obviously are not intended to reflect any position of the State Bar of California or of University Extension. Chapters written by employees of state or federal agencies are not to be considered statements of governmental policies.

California Continuing Education of the Bar publications and oral programs are intended to provide current and accurate information about the subject matter covered and are designed to help attorneys maintain their professional competence. Publications are distributed and oral programs presented with the understanding that CEB does not render any legal, accounting, or other professional service. Attorneys using CEB publications or orally conveyed information in dealing with a specific client's or their own legal matters should also research original sources of authority.

CALIFORNIA CONTINUING

Governing Committee
Daniel W. Crowe, of the Visalia Bar, Chairperson
Warren E. Schoonover, Director of Administrative Services—
Division of Agricultural Sciences, University of California, Vice Chairperson
Jerry Fine, of the Los Angeles Bar
John S. Gilmore, Sacramento
Professor Edward C. Halbach, Jr., University of California
School of Law (Berkeley)
Keith Sexton, Dean, University Extension Programs,
University of California
Professor Stanley Siegel, University of California School of Law (Los Angeles)
Judge Steven J. Stone, of Ventura County
William A. Carroll, Director, Continuing Education of the Bar
Thomas W. Eres, Sacramento, Liaison Governor
William A. Kurlander, San Marino, Liaison Governor

Joint Advisory Committee

State Bar Committee Members
Robert L. Sills, Los Angeles, Chairperson
Stuart D. Buchalter, Los Angeles, Vice Chairperson
Justice Bernard S. Jefferson, Los Angeles, Advisor
Thomas W. Eres, Sacramento, Liaison Governor
John R. Stokes, Jr., Arcata, Liaison Governor
Luther J. Avery, San Francisco
D. Keith Bilter, San Francisco
Hal Bolen II, Fresno
Allan Browne, Beverly Hills
William E. Donovan, San Francisco
Shelly A. Dunfee, San Diego
Robert M. Ferm, Los Angeles
Ima Jean Harvey, Fresno
Margaret S. Henry, Torrance
Sara M. Lake, Walnut Creek
Alvin T. Levitt, San Francisco
Donald N. MacIntosh, San Francisco
Barbara Eiland McCallum, Sacramento
Dixie Moe, Los Angeles
Dennis Montali, San Francisco

EDUCATION OF THE BAR

Mark F. Ornellas, Stockton
C. Delos Putz, Jr., San Francisco
Peter Quon, Jr., San Diego
Robert L. Smith, Huntington Beach
George L. Strasser, Fresno
William G. Van der Mei, Sacramento
Alan Wayte, Los Angeles
Diana M. Wheatley, Los Angeles

Law School Dean Members
Dean Roberta Achtenberg, New College of California School of Law
Dean George J. Alexander, University of Santa Clara
Dean Marvin J. Anderson, Hastings College of the Law
Dean Florian Bartosic, University of California (Davis)
Dean Victor A. Bertolani, Lincoln Law School
Dean Scott H. Bice, University of Southern California Law Center
Dean Maxwell S. Boas, Western State University
Dean Coleman Bresee, San Francisco Law School
Dean Theodore A. Bruinsma, Loyola University
Dean Charles S. Doskow, La Verne College School of Law
Dean Ernest C. Friesen, California Western University
Dean Charles E. Glasser, John F. Kennedy University
Dean Seymour Greitzer, Glendale University
Dean Elwood B. Hain, Jr., Whittier College School of Law
Dean John C. Huffer, University of San Fernando Valley
Dean Sanford H. Kadish, University of California (Berkeley)
Dean Paul L. McKaskle, University of San Francisco
Dean Judith G. McKelvey, Golden Gate University
Dean Charles J. Meyers, Stanford University
Dean Fred J. Olson, Ventura College of Law
Dean Ronald F. Phillips, Pepperdine University
Dean Perry Polski, University of West Los Angeles
Dean Gordon D. Schaber, McGeorge School of Law,
University of the Pacific
Dean Carl R. Sederholm, Northrop University
Dean Leigh H. Taylor, Southwestern University
Dean Oliver Wanger, San Joaquin College of Law
Dean William D. Warren, University of California (Los Angeles)
Dean Donald T. Weckstein, University of San Diego

PREFACE

In 1967 the Continuing Education of the Bar published California Real Estate Sales Transactions. Over the years, changes in this field required CEB to develop new practice books that give a more intensive treatment of special topics. Title insurance, discussed in a chapter of the 1967 sales transactions book, is now the subject of a book, California Title Insurance Practice (Cal CEB 1980). In the near future, CEB is scheduled to publish separate practice books on real property exchanges and on taxation of real property transfers. Both topics were covered in the 1967 sales book, but it was decided that they deserved the fuller development that could be afforded only by separate books.

This publication, California Real Property Sales Transactions, discusses and updates the other subjects of the 1967 book, including agreements with brokers, drafting the purchase and sale agreement, financing the purchase, and closing the sale. The most significant changes affecting real property sales have occurred in the structure of financing. Alternative mortgage instruments have been developed as a result of fluctuating interest rates. Many transactions are now structured to retain existing financing rather than depending on new financing for the entire balance of the purchase price.

The use of common-interest subdivisions (planned developments, condominiums, stock cooperatives, and community apartments) has been growing in both residential and commercial properties. No special attention has been given in this book to sales transactions involving common-interest subdivisions. Subdivision regulation by the California Department of Real Estate is covered in the CEB book, Guide to California Subdivision Sales Law (1974). In the future, CEB plans to publish a separate condominium book covering common-interest subdivisions.

Patricia R. Hersom, now CEB's Program Department Manager, initiated the project, helped plan the book, and worked in the early stages of preparing outlines and obtaining initial draft chapters. Also assisting by serving on the planning committee, recommending authors, and advising on the scope of various chapters were Maxwell J. Fenmore, Beverly Hills; Jarrett S. Anderson, Glendale; Roy H. Aaron, Thomas K. Armstrong, Byron Hayes, Gordon Hunt, Mark Lee Lamken, Jerold L. Miles, Laurence G. Preble, Anthony J. Rossi, Stephen G. Valensi, Richard S. Volpert, and Alan Wayte, Los Angeles.

We are fortunate to have as authors of chapters of this book real property practitioners who gave generously of their time writing, revising, and updating their chapters. They are named on the contents page and at the beginning of their chapters. To all of them we express our profound gratitude.

We are indebted to those lawyers who served as consultants on the various chapters, and list them on the acknowledgments page.

Legal assistance was provided by Margalynne Armstrong, Julie Barreto, Craig Cuden, Michael Fenger, Terri Ellen Gordon, Nathan McClintock, Robert Nakatani, Janice Salter, Carrie Simon, Barry Simons, Cyrian Tabuena, Charles Werner, and Loretta Wider. Ted Francis prepared the index. Rachel Ellis and Dian Duryea handled copyediting and production; they were assisted by Genny Haley. The case table was compiled by Kathleen Andrews, Debra Godin, Cynthia McCartin, and Sandee Sheldon. The book was designed by Elizabeth Weil.

The cutoff dates for this book are February 5, 1981, for statutory and administrative developments and March 12, 1981, for judicial developments. CEB will supplement this book on a regular basis.

WILLIAM A. CARROLL
Director

ACKNOWLEDGMENTS

The following attorneys served as consultants on this book by reviewing and commenting on one or more chapter manuscripts. Their valuable suggestions have made the book more accurate and more reflective of practice throughout the state. To each of them, our special thanks.

Allan L. Alexander
    Agnew, Miller & Carlson, Los Angeles
Professor Roger Bernhardt
    School of Law, Golden Gate University, San Francisco
James E. Burden
    Burden, Aiken & Mansuy, San Francisco
Anthony Canzoneri
    Brown, Winfield & Canzoneri, Los Angeles
William B. Christy IV
    Morrison & Foerster, San Francisco
Michael A. Dean
    Wendell, Lawlor, Rosen & Black, Oakland
Frank E. Feder
    Loeb & Loeb, Los Angeles
Ima Jean Harvey
    Parichan, Renberg, Crossman & Harvey Law Corporation, Fresno
Robert C. Herr
    Pillsbury, Madison & Sutro, San Francisco
John L. Hosack
    Tobin & Tobin, San Francisco
Lawrence H. Jacobson
    Fischer, Shapiro & Krane, Beverly Hills

Faber L. Johnston, Jr.
Johnston, Miller & Giannini, San Jose
Richard J. Kamins
Tyre & Kamins, Los Angeles
Stephen M. Kass
Buchman, Kass, Morgan & Miller, Oakland
John J. McGregor
Thomas, Snell, Jamison, Russell, Williamson & Asperger, Fresno
George I. Nagler
Rosenberg, Nagler, Morson & Weisman, Beverly Hills
J. Ronald Pengilly
Pettit & Martin, San Francisco
W. Jerome Thomas
Chief Legal Officer, Department of Real Estate, Sacramento
Robert A. Thompson
Pettit & Martin, San Francisco
Bruce R. Wallace
Shenas, Robbins, Shenas & Shaw, San Diego
Alan Wayte
Adams, Duque & Hazeltine, Los Angeles

CONTENTS

1

John P. Killeen

The Lawyer's Role in Real Property Sales

JOHN P. KILLEEN, B. Arch., 1952, Ohio State University; J.D., 1963, Loyola University of Los Angeles School of Law. Mr. Killeen is a member of Fine, Perzik & Friedman, Los Angeles.

Sections 1.66-1.78, 1.81-1.82, were adapted by CEB legal staff from material submitted by Burch Fitzpatrick; see biographical footnote to chap 12. Portions of this chapter were derived from chapters 1, 2, and 3 of California Real Estate Sales Transactions (Cal CEB 1967).

I.   THE LAWYER AND REAL PROPERTY PRACTICE

A.   Nature of Real Property Practice

§1.1   1.   Variety of Attorney's Functions

Modern real property practice extends far beyond the classical problems of conveyancing and estates in land. The problems encountered in representing a client in a real property transaction may cover a wide range of statutory enactments and administrative regulations. In conducting a real property transaction, a lawyer may be called on to negotiate and prepare a purchase and sale agreement; evaluate the economic feasibility and tax consequences of the transaction; review proposed financing arrangements; investigate to ensure that the proposed use of the property does not conflict with zoning or other government regulations; review recorded security instruments, covenants, conditions, and restrictions (CC&Rs), easements, and other reserved rights that may affect the property; and generally supervise the transaction to assure a conclusion in conformity with the parties' intentions.

There is a significant increase each year in the extent of state and local regulation affecting real property. The use of land, urban and rural, is ever more closely controlled through the regulations of planning commissions, zoning boards, and other local agencies. See §§1.41-1.54. In addition, the subdivider is experiencing a steady expansion of regulation by the California Department of Real Estate. See §1.53. Much of this increased local and state regulation results from relatively new concepts of land use, such as planned developments, cooperatives, and condominiums, and governments' attempts to deal with air and water pollution, toxic waste, energy and resource scarcity, urban sprawl, and so forth.

The lawyer engaging in modern real property practice finds himself dealing with a highly developed, closely regulated industry in which knowledge of the scope of current regulations, business practices, and administrative attitudes is of major importance.

§1.2   2.   Importance of Legal Counsel

In contrast to the practice in many other states (see, *e.g., Goldfarb v Virginia State Bar* (1975) 421 US 773), most California real property sales are concluded without the participation of attorneys. Although complex legal documents are included in even the simplest real property transaction, the parties are generally unwilling in "routine" transactions to retain counsel to ensure that their respective legal rights are protected.

The need for legal counsel is seldom questioned when a real property transaction is complex or when unusual problems occur; transactions of this nature would not be classed as routine. But no transaction is routine until it has been examined for potentially troublesome areas by someone competent to render legal opinions to the parties. Even after such an examination, a purchase and sale that starts routinely may encounter legal problems. The parties need counsel qualified to watch for trouble areas as the transaction proceeds in order to minimize or avoid them; in other words, to *keep* the transaction routine. The fees incurred for this sort of legal assistance are nominal compared to financial losses that may be sustained if the transaction is not handled properly.

Brokers, title officers, loan officers, and escrow agents play essential roles in any transaction, of course, but the attorney should not rely on them to avoid trouble spots and keep the transaction routine. Only a lawyer is qualified to give the legal advice necessary to protect the parties' respective rights, and only a lawyer is free from a conflicting interest in the transaction (see §1.3).

Among the acts that may be performed only by active members of the State Bar are giving legal advice and preparing documents and contracts by which legal rights are secured. Bus & P C §§6125-6126; *Farnham v State Bar* (1976) 17 C3d 605, 131 CR 661; *Mickel v Murphy* (1957) 147 CA2d 718, 305 P2d 993. Another of these acts is advising a husband and wife what kind of legal document they should execute to secure a real property loan. *People v Sipper* (1943) 61 CA2d Supp 844, 142 P2d 960; see Comment, *California Real Estate Brokers: Conveyancing Forms: The Unauthorized Practice of Law,* 35 S Cal L Rev 336 (1962).

§1.3   3.   Interaction With Lay Real Property Specialists

Even the simplest purchase and sale transaction may require the cooperation of a number of specialists, each concentrating on a particular phase of the transaction. Each operates within a framework of highly developed rules and procedures, and each expects the lawyer to be familiar with and responsive to the requirements of his or her specialty.

Some lay specialists, especially those whose interest is to see the transaction close quickly and without complications, may be found to fear and resist the presence of lawyers. This antagonism often arises because attorneys' unfamiliarity with the nuances of real property transactions may make them more careful than these specialists like, and perhaps more negative than the situation or the client's best interests require. Lawyers dealing with these lay specialists should try to understand this attitude and attempt to allay it, and also understand that a client fully informed of the risks may still want to proceed with a transaction despite the attorney's misgivings concerning legal problems.

The lawyer must recognize the scope and limits of the functions of lay specialists. Each has some degree of self-interest that may not coincide with the interests of buyer or seller. For example, the language sometimes found in escrow instructions giving the buyer the right to approve the preliminary title report is largely meaningless unless a lawyer is consulted for an opinion on the significance of the report and the documents listed in it. Similarly, loan commitments, promissory notes, and deeds of trust are written to protect the lender, and lender and buyer may have conflicting interests concerning these documents.

Brokers earn their commissions by bringing buyers and sellers together and getting them to agree. The broker's interest in early consummation of the transaction may be at odds with the lawyer's interest in protecting the client. Although few lawyers can match the broker's knowledge of the real property market, few brokers can match the lawyer's grasp of the legal implications of the transaction, and no broker (who is not also a lawyer) can give legal advice to the parties or draft legal documents. The broker's role is discussed in chap 2.

Escrow holders also play an important role in real property transactions, but their functions are limited. See chap 11. The escrow holder is not authorized to draft agreements and other legal documents. Attorneys frequently rely on the escrow holder to prepare initial drafts of documents such as deeds, deeds of trust, and escrow instructions, subject to the attorney's review and revision. This practice can save the attorney a good deal of time and thus represent a financial saving for the client, but the attorney must remember that responsibility for protecting the client's rights cannot be left to lay drafters. See §1.12.

Title companies perform useful services in searching and reporting titles, and can be a valuable source of information for the attorney. The attorney cannot, however, rely on title company employees for legal advice nor on a title insurance policy to cure title defects (see §3.78), although endorsements against some risks are sufficient to obtain financing and provide assurance to an informed client. See generally California Title Insurance Practice (Cal CEB 1980). The title insurer, besides its economic interest in limiting its liability under the policy, takes no responsibility for explaining the significance of exceptions noted in the title report or for correcting problems reflected in those exceptions.

In a given transaction, the lawyer may also work with other specialists such as architects, surveyors, and appraisers. He or she may also represent the client before state and local agencies such as planning commissions, various district boards, the Department of Real Estate, and zoning boards. An attorney handling real property matters must understand the functions and limitations of these lay experts and government agencies as well as their requirements so that the client's best interests can be served fully and expeditiously.

§1.4   4.   Permanent Effect of Work

The real property practitioner's work often has a truly permanent effect. Covenants, conditions, and restrictions governing and limiting the use of land may last for many decades; a reversionary interest may become possessory generations after its creation; and a leasehold interest may last longer than a lifetime.

After an interest in real property has been created, its elimination or modification may be beyond the control of the creator. For example, A, the owner of land containing a shopping center, makes a recorded agreement with B, the owner of vacant land nearby, to allow overflow parking on B's land for customers patronizing the shopping center. A has numerous commercial tenants who benefit from the agreements. Later B wants to construct a building and A is willing to obtain his parking elsewhere. Can they simply rescind the agreement or will it be necessary to get the consent of (a) tenants in the shopping center for whose benefit the agreement was created and (b) all lenders with security interests in the parcels? Suppose, instead, that A holds the land under a 99-year lease. Would the owner of the reversion also have to consent to the rescission? The servitude created by the parking agreement may prevent B from developing the proposed building.

The lawyer should never record a document creating an interest in real property without analyzing very carefully the nature of the interest created and its likely immediate and future effects.

5.   Lawyer's Participation in Nonlegal Aspects of Transaction

§1.5   a.   Business Advice

The lawyer must evaluate his or her client so that the nature and extent of the services required can be better understood. The proper approach to counseling a sophisticated real estate developer or investor differs from that indicated for a couple who occasionally purchase income units for investment or for persons entering into their first (and perhaps only) real property transaction.

The experienced client is probably better equipped than the attorney to decide whether the proposed project is sound from a business standpoint and whether it is suitable for its intended purpose. He or she expects and requires less general explanation of documents and concepts, and can usually understand the position, function, and diverse interests of others in the transaction such as the broker, lender, and escrow holder. The procedures of listing, financing, escrow, and title reports are familiar to such a client. The less experienced seller or buyer will, in contrast, require considerably more explanation of the steps to be encountered in the transaction, and their importance.

On the economic and other business features of the project, a person experienced in real estate may be far more expert than the attorney. The attorney should be wary of injecting nonlegal judgments into a relationship that may not require them, but should, at the same time, be sure to be fully informed on the client's economic motivations.

In some instances, however, the attorney's advice on nonlegal problems is actively sought and expected. This is particularly true if the client is a casual dealer in real property, rather than a professional investor. For the casual dealer, the attorney may properly inquire whether the client would welcome an exploration of the suitability of the project for the client in terms of his or her experience, time available, and financial status; evaluation of economic factors including price, value, cash flow projections, long or short term gain, and tax planning; and other considerations such as evaluating the character, integrity, and stability of the parties with whom the client is dealing.

Even when it is appropriate to give advice on the economic and other nonlegal aspects of real property transactions, the attorney should be careful not to exceed the limits of his expertise. The attorney must also be sure that, when business advice is sought, the client has furnished all relevant data as a basis for formulating an opinion. On communication between attorney and client, see §1.20. Unless he or she has substantial background and experience in the real estate market, the attorney's opinion of price, value, and economic feasibility may be unsound and misleading. The attorney should not hesitate to recommend other experts for advice on these kinds of problems. Although often called on to act as a business adviser as well as a legal adviser, the attorney should undertake the former only if qualified by background and training to give sound opinions on the nonlegal questions.

§1.6   b.   Policy Considerations

The lawyer's proper function in modern real estate practice is not only to advise the client on strictly legal matters but also to bring to the client's attention many public policy considerations that may affect the transaction. Land today is thought of not only as a free market commodity but also as a basic community resource that must be conserved. See, *e.g.,* Babcock & Feurer, *Land as a Commodity "Affected With a Public Interest,"* 52 Wash L Rev 289 (1977); Berger, *To Regulate or Not To Regulate—Is That the Question? Reflections on the Supposed Dilemma Between Environmental Protection and Private Property Rights,* 8 Loy LA L Rev 253 (1975); Comment, *Regulation of Land Use: From Magna Carta to a Just Formulation,* 23 UCLA L Rev 904 (1976). Moreover, many social problems stem from inadequate housing, urban blight, crowded neighborhoods, and racial discrimination in housing. See, *e.g.,* Chapman, *The Real Estate Broker and the Unruh Civil Rights Act,* 45 LA B Bull 475 (1970); Comment, *California Lower Income Housing Policy: At Legislative and Judicial Crossroads,* 29 Hastings LJ 793 (1978); Kleven, *Inclusionary Ordinances—Policy and Legal Issues in Requiring Private Developers to Build Low Cost Housing,* 21 UCLA L Rev 1432 (1974); Phillips & Agelasto, *Housing and Central Cities: The Conservation Approach,* 4 Ecology LQ 797 (1975).

Developers and real property investors must consider these problems in terms not only of conscience but also of expense, regulation, and possible government sanctions for failing to recognize the problems and for failing to assume responsibility toward them. Lawyers can and should call these considerations to their clients' attention, just as they raise tax or potential liability questions that the client might not have considered.

For example, a buyer contemplating an urban development must be warned of the risk that the project may be barred under various environmental, zoning, or subdivision laws, and that the right to develop the property becomes vested only when the client has spent substantial sums in reliance on a validly issued building permit.

See, *e.g., Avco Community Developers, Inc. v South Coast Regional Comm'n* (1976) 17 C3d 785, 132 CR 386. A subdivider who promotes "urban sprawl" without regard to the value to society of agricultural and recreational land should be advised that his action could result in economic losses, and that a cooperative approach to state and local planners may enable him to achieve his legitimate commercial objectives without incurring public and government disapproval. Similarly, lawyers for sellers of residential property or landlords who would perpetuate segregated and substandard housing should warn their clients of the illegality and increasing intolerance of local, state, and federal authorities for these business practices.

In all these situations, the lawyer has a unique opportunity not only to protect the client's long term economic interests but also to contribute to the solution of increasingly severe social problems.

B. Lawyer's Role in Different Types of Transactions

§1.7   1. Single-Family Residential

The sale of a single-family home is the type of transaction most commonly completed without participation of an attorney, although it may present a full array of potential legal pitfalls. The absence of attorneys from most of these sales can be accounted for by a number of factors: the fact that sales of family residences are generally viewed as routine and devoid of risk (but see §1.2); the resistance of lay real property specialists to attorneys' participation (see §1.3); and the widespread use of printed forms such as "deposit receipts" (§3.40) and escrow instructions (see §11.35). The attorney's main job (whether acting for buyer or seller, but particularly for the buyer) is to review the purchase and sale agreement to ensure that it is complete and that it adequately describes the transaction as the parties intend. The attorney should also review the other documents (*e.g.,* the preliminary title report, the recorded documents it refers to, and the loan documentation) and be sure that the client understands their contents and import.

As the tight money market makes "creative financing" more prevalent, the lawyer must give the loan documents and security instruments very careful scrutiny. On lawyers' functions, see §§1.26-1.32.

The attorney should also become familiar with the booklet, "Settlement Costs" (published by the United States Department of

Housing and Urban Development (HUD)), which must be given to the borrower when a written loan application is made under the federal Real Estate Settlement Procedures Act of 1974 (RESPA), 12 USC §§2601-2617. For further information about RESPA, see §§1.52, 11.85, 11.89.

§1.8   2. Complex Real Property Transactions

Usually the lawyer will be retained as counsel in real property transactions larger than the purchase and sale of a single-family residence. Participation in such a project can be both challenging and creative.

Planning and completing larger real estate transactions is very much a team effort. Acting toward the common objective, in addition to the attorney, are brokers, architects, mechanical, electrical, civil, and structural engineers, property managers, lenders, appraisers, land planners, contractors, economists, and many others. The attorney must constantly be aware of his or her own capabilities and limitations and those of the other team members.

In larger projects, communication problems can be complex. On communication generally, see §1.20. It is ordinarily impossible or impractical for the attorney to attend every staff meeting, review every document, and be aware of every decision. Decisions may be made and then remade without informing the lawyer. Often the result is legal work wasted in proceeding on an assumption that has been changed. To avoid misunderstanding, the lawyer may have to be specific and insistent about the need to be kept informed. This problem can be alleviated if the client is made aware of it early and designates a knowledgeable staff member to act as liaison, so that the attorney can look to one source for instructions and have a single contact for obtaining and disseminating information. The success of this approach depends on the understanding of the client and the competence of the person designated for liaison. If a capable, experienced person is available, both the client and the attorney will benefit through better over-all communications and the pinpointing of responsibility at an earlier stage.

§1.9   a. Multiple-Unit Residential

The attorney who is counseling a participant in a transaction involving the purchase and sale of an apartment house or other multiple-unit residential property will have matters to consider in addition to those referred to in §1.7 for a single-family residence. These include: the terms, termination dates, and other provisions of existing leases; security deposits; personal property rental agreements; management personnel and management agreements; rent control ordinances; covenants, conditions, and restrictions (CC&Rs); homeowner association bylaws; subdivision regulations; and many similar matters that must be established before a purchaser can take over operation of what is essentially a commercial enterprise. For purchase and sale agreement clauses concerning existing leases, see §§3.106-3.115.

§1.10 b. Commercial and Industrial Properties

Every sale of commercial or industrial property has some of the elements encountered in the sale of a single-family residence (§1.7) and a multiple-unit residential property (§1.9), plus other unique elements of its own.

For example, a shopping center may have leases of varying kinds; common areas to be maintained; a merchants' association; and parking lots to be operated. An industrial property, particularly the newer kind of industrial park, may present problems similar to those of a shopping center, as well as different problems such as compliance with air pollution standards, building codes, and various other types of state and local government regulations. See §§1.41-1.54. The attorney must uncover and evaluate the various elements of the problem, and advise the client on their legal implications.

§1.11 3. Raw Land

Transactions involving "raw" land can be comparatively simple because they may not include many of the problems that arise from past use of the property (see §§1.8-1.10), but can also present difficult problems such as uncertain boundary lines and old, poorly documented easements. In the case of agricultural land there may be leases and water agreements to review. Major problems can arise in purchase of raw land because the historical absence of structures may have allowed the public or particular persons access to or use of the property, creating prescriptive, adverse rights. See, *e.g., County of Los Angeles v Berk* (1980) 26 C3d 201, 161 CR 742; *Gion v City of*

Santa Cruz (1970) 2 C3d 29, 84 CR 162. When prescriptive rights may be a problem, the attorney should order a survey, carefully scrutinize the preliminary title report and underlying documents, and possibly make a visual inspection of the property.

Raw land transactions frequently include problems that arise from the buyer's desire to develop the property and the buyer may want the land only if he or she can obtain permits for its proposed development. See §§3.131-3.141. The buyer's attorney must be alert to environmental restrictions, subdivision regulations, zoning ordinances, possible future zoning changes, building moratoriums, dedication requirements, and other potentially applicable statutes, ordinances, and regulations, which may restrict or completely frustrate the buyer's plans for development of the property. See, *e.g.*, §§1.41-1.49, 3.131-3.150.

§1.12   C.   Possibility of Malpractice

An attorney may be held liable, either in tort or in contract, for failing to perform with the skill, prudence, and diligence lawyers of ordinary skill commonly possess and exercise. See *Neel v Magana, Olney, Levy, Cathcart & Gelfand* (1971) 6 C3d 176, 98 CR 837. Disciplinary proceedings may also be initiated against an attorney who willfully or habitually fails to use reasonable knowledge, skill and diligence in performing legal services. Cal Rules of Prof Cond 6-101. An attorney holding himself or herself out to the public and the profession as specializing in a particular area of the law is held to a duty to perform with the skill, prudence, and diligence exercised by other specialists in the same field. See *Wright v Williams* (1975) 47 CA3d 802, 121 CR 194. Thus, an attorney who purports to be a real property specialist will be judged by the standards of performance of other real property specialists.

An attorney is required to have knowledge of basic legal principles commonly known to well-informed attorneys and to discover additional rules that can be found readily by standard research techniques (*Smith v Lewis* (1975) 13 C3d 349, 118 CR 621), but is not necessarily liable for every mistake made nor an insurer of opinions given (*Lucas v Hamm* (1961) 56 C2d 583, 15 CR 821; but see *Wright v Williams* (1975) 47 CA3d 802, 809 n2, 121 CR 194, 199 n2). An attorney will not be held liable for failing to anticipate the manner in which an area of uncertainty in the law will be resolved, but has an obligation to the client to undertake reasonable research efforts and make an informed decision based on an intelligent assessment of the problem. *Smith v Lewis, supra.*

An attorney representing a party to a real property transaction cannot rely on customary practice in the real estate industry to avoid responsibility for hastily or negligently drafted documents. In *Starr v Mooslin* (1971) 14 CA3d 988, 92 CR 583, an attorney incurred a $42,000 liability for negligently drafting a subordination clause in escrow instructions for the sale of his client's $60,000 home. The subordination provision did not require that the proceeds of the loan to which his client's deed of trust would be subordinated be applied to improvement of the property, and the property was foreclosed on when the buyer failed to meet his obligations under the subordinating loan. Although the attorney produced expert testimony that under proper escrow company practice the subordinating loan should not have been given priority in that situation, the court held that the attorney's failure to include adequate protection in the escrow instructions was the proximate cause of his client's injury and custom in the industry could not be relied on as a defense. On subordination, see §§5.39-5.54.

D.　Ethical Considerations

§1.13　1.　Representing Both Parties

Sometimes, particularly in small transactions, both buyer and seller rely on the same attorney for advice and even drafting. It is improper for an attorney to represent both parties unless their written consent has been obtained after full disclosure to each party of the attorney's representation of the adverse interest. Cal Rules of Prof Cond 5-101—5-102. Violation of these rules may render the attorney civilly liable as well as subject to discipline by the state bar. See *Klemm v Superior Court* (1977) 75 CA3d 893, 142 CR 509.

The safest course is to decline to represent more than one of two or more adverse parties and to suggest that the other party obtain separate counsel. If it appears desirable for the attorney to represent more than one party, and full disclosure is made to each party and the written consent of each obtained, problems may still arise over whether the import of the consent was communicated adequately. See, *e.g., Hawkins v State Bar* (1979) 23 C3d 622, 153 CR 234. It is also good practice for the attorney to send each party represented a letter explaining the major provisions of the agreement as protection against a subsequent claim that one party did not understand a provision.

2. Lawyer Participation in Transaction

§1.14   a.   Duty to Client

An attorney owes a strict fiduciary duty to his or her client. His role is that of agent acting for his principal; he must be neither rival nor competitor. *Sanguinetti v Rossen* (1906) 12 CA 623, 107 P 560. The attorney is held to the standards of conduct required of a trustee toward his beneficiary as set forth in CC §§2228-2239. *Gold v Greenwald* (1966) 247 CA2d 296, 55 CR 660. See also *Neel v Magana, Olney, Levy, Cathcart & Gelfand* (1971) 6 C3d 176, 188, 98 CR 837, 844-845.

Courts give careful scrutiny to agreements entered into between attorney and client. Any agreement giving the attorney an advantage is presumed to have been obtained by undue influence and for insufficient consideration. CC §2235; *Bradner v Vasquez* (1954) 43 C2d 147, 272 P2d 11. The attorney has the burden of rebutting the presumption of undue influence and of proving that the transaction is fair. *Gold v Greenwald, supra.* The presumption does not extend to an agreement concerning employment or compensation of the attorney. *In re Beverly Crest Convalescent Hosp., Inc.* (9th Cir 1976) 548 F2d 817; *Walton v Broglio* (1975) 52 CA3d 400, 404, 125 CR 123, 125. See also Leavitt, *The Attorney as Defendant,* 13 Hastings LJ 1 (1961-1962).

An attorney may not acquire an interest adverse to that of his or her client without making full written disclosure. Cal Rules of Prof Cond 4-101. This rule is designed not only to protect the public from dishonest lawyers, but also to preclude honest lawyers from putting themselves in a position in which they must choose between their duty to their clients and their own self-interest. *Ames v State Bar* (1973) 8 C3d 910, 106 CR 489; *Anderson v Eaton* (1930) 211 C 113, 293 P 788. Participation of a relative or a business associate of the attorney in a transaction with the attorney's client may also subject the attorney to liability for breach of fiduciary duty. See, *e.g., Brown v Critchfield* (1980) 100 CA3d 858, 161 CR 342.

§1.15   b.   Avoiding Conflict of Interest

Attorney participation in a real property transaction as both interested party and lawyer creates a serious conflict of interest. See §§1.14, 1.25. The most favorable position the attorney can assume as an interested participant is to render no legal services of any kind. Even in this situation, because lay persons are accustomed to look to the attorney for advice and counsel, or at least to speak up if anything seems amiss, it should be made clear that legal advice is not contemplated within the arrangement and that the lawyer-participant will be under no duty to make his evaluations or fears available to other participants. Partnership agreements or other articles of association should reflect the fact that one of the participants is an attorney and expressly negate the existence of any attorney-client relationship.

If an attorney enters into a business transaction with a client or knowingly acquires an ownership, possessory, security, or other pecuniary interest adverse to a client, he must disclose fully and transmit in writing to the client the terms of the transaction and the nature of his interest in it, give the client a reasonable opportunity to seek the advice of independent counsel, and obtain the client's written consent. Cal Rules of Prof Cond 4-101.

If, despite these pitfalls, the attorney's role in a transaction includes both equity participation and legal services, the scope of these roles must be carefully delineated. For example, an attorney who undertakes to represent a limited partnership in which he or she will have an interest should not attempt to counsel the limited partners about the partnership agreement he or she has drafted or advise them on the nature of their rights and liabilities if they enter into the partnership. Rather, the partners should be advised that the attorney's representation of the partnership in its relations with the outside world does not include representation of the partners individually. In this situation, the attorney should insist that they retain separate counsel. At the first sign of any dispute arising out of the attorney's financial interest, he or she should also seek legal advice.

E.   Aids to Developing Real Property Expertise

§1.16   1.   Other Lawyers

The attorney who only occasionally handles a real property transaction can often obtain assistance from lawyers who specialize in real property matters. An excellent source of names of real property specialists is the Real Property Law Section of the State Bar of California, which publishes a newsletter, Real Property News, conducts informational programs, and engages in a variety of activities concerning real property law. Inquiries should be directed to the State Bar of California, Department of Sections and Committees, 555 Franklin Street, San Francisco 94102. Local bar associations also frequently have real property committees, and the Martindale-Hubbell Law Directory lists specialties in its biographical section. Inclusion on any of these lists is not assurance of competence and expertise, and careful inquiry should be made by an attorney seeking assistance from a real property expert.

Attorneys employed by title companies, lending institutions, and realty boards may also be an excellent source of help. These lawyers usually devote a substantial part of their time to real property matters and are often willing to discuss specific problems or recommend qualified private practitioners. The attorney may save a great deal of time and effort by making a telephone call to one of these specialists. It is important to remember, however, that lawyers for these institutions owe their first loyalty to their employers and clients; their advice can never be a substitute for the attorney's own research and legal judgment.

Law professors are accustomed to receiving questions from members of the bar, and on difficult, lucrative, or challenging problems may be willing to act as associate counsel.

§1.17   2.   Lay Specialists

Brokers, escrow agents, title officers, appraisers, surveyors, architects and engineers, hydrologists, building contractors, and other nonlawyers are possible sources of expert help at various stages of the transaction.

For example, the broker may contribute experience in property values, terms of sale, and negotiating skill. Attorneys and title specialists employed by title companies can, because of their experience and familiarity with transfers and title litigation, give valuable advice to lawyers. Loan officers are often a source of valuable information about neighborhood trends and values. On services rendered by other lay experts, see §§1.35-1.36.

Some of these occupational specialists may fear and resist the participation of lawyers. See §1.3. The attorney must be sensitive to these fears while at the same time keeping the client's interests paramount over pressure to close the transaction quickly.

The lawyer also may obtain general information about legal requirements from state and local agencies, such as planning commissions, departments of health, flood control districts, zoning boards, and other regulatory bodies. A client's particular problems should not be discussed with public officials unless the attorney has discussed the need for such discussions with the client and obtained the client's consent.

A lawyer handling real estate matters often may use these lay experts and government bodies as sources of information, but must always understand their functions and limitations, so that the client's best interests are served effectively and expeditiously.

§1.18   3. Self-Education

There is no substitute for the lawyer's own research and academic grounding in real property law. Among the books, periodicals, classes, and other sources that are helpful in acquiring understanding of California real estate practice are the following:

(a) California Continuing Education of the Bar (CEB) practice books and attorney's guides on a wide range of real property topics.

(b) Other works on California practice

California Real Estate, Law & Practice, a multivolume, looseleaf series

Miller & Starr, Current Law of California Real Estate (rev ed, 1975, 1977, 1979) 5 vols

Title Insurance & Trust Company, Title Handbook for Title Men (22nd ed 1980)

3 Witkin, Summary of California Law, *Real Property* §§1-605 (8th ed 1973)

American Law of Property (A. J. Casner ed 1952) 7 vols, with pocket parts

Powell, The Law of Real Property (1949–1969) 8 vols, looseleaf

Thompson, Commentaries on the Modern Law of Real Property (5th ed 1980) 14 vols.

(c) Periodicals

The CEB Real Property Law Reporter is a periodical that contains timely articles on real property law topics and summaries of all reported California decisions, legislation, Attorney General opinions, and administrative regulations, as well as significant federal and sister-state decisions and legislation, relating to real property. Real Property News, published by the Real Property Section of the State Bar, contains articles on selected real property topics by leading practitioners.

Articles, Comments, and Case Notes in law reviews are often of great help on particular aspects of real estate law, as are those in the California State Bar Journal and a multitude of local bar bulletins and journals. In addition, the ABA Real Property, Probate and Trust Journal, published quarterly by the ABA Section of Real Property, Probate and Trust Law, and the University of Southern California School of Law Institute on Federal Taxation, published annually, are important resources. Other publications are Real Estate Law Journal and Real Estate Law Report, both published by Warren, Gorham & Lamont, Boston.

(d) Classes

Many lawyers find that lecture programs give information and insights not available elsewhere, as well as emphasizing and reinforcing material available in print. Programs specifically directed to practicing lawyers include California Continuing Education of the Bar lectures and videotapes, programs offered by California law schools and by the American Law Institute. Additional instruction is provided by lectures and panels offered by local bar associations or their real estate committees.

(e) Bar association committees

Opportunities for developing and maintaining competence in real estate matters are afforded by membership in and participation in the activities of the State Bar Real Property Section; the Section of Real Property, Probate and Trust Law of the American Bar Association; and sections or committees on real estate of some local bar associations, such as those of the Los Angeles and San Francisco Bar Associations.

II. ATTORNEY-CLIENT RELATIONSHIP

§1.19   A.   Standards of Courtesy and Efficiency

In addition to meeting standards of competence (see §1.12), lawyers should be aware of those standards of courtesy and efficiency that often make the difference between satisfied and disgruntled clients. Although statutes of limitation are not at issue in the usual real property transaction, time deadlines are nonetheless important, and the attorney must establish and maintain adequate diary, tickler, and file review systems. Whether or not deadlines are actually missed, clients are frequently anxious about the progress of real property transactions and become disillusioned if the appearance of inefficiency is given by the lawyer's failure to return telephone calls or keep them informed of the progress of the transaction. The attorney should also be sure to make adequate file notes of contacts with the client to demonstrate the due care with which the transaction has been handled.

§1.20   B.   Communication With Client

Communication between attorney and client is vital to effective handling of the transaction, and must be a two-way street. An uninformed attorney cannot represent his or her client's interests adequately; a client kept uninformed by his attorney is likely to be unhappy and may embark on his own course of action. Representatives of malpractice carriers report that among the most frequent contributing causes of claims against attorneys is the complaint that "He wouldn't return my calls; I couldn't find out what was going on." Failure to communicate with, and inattention to the needs of, a client are grounds for discipline. See *Spindell v State Bar* (1975) 13 C3d 253, 260, 118 CR 480, 485.

At the first interview the attorney should impress the client with the need to keep the attorney informed. Ideally, all information affecting the problem should be passed to the attorney without screening for relevance. Usually the client does not have the knowledge or ability to make relevancy judgments and should not try to do so. This is true, although to a lesser extent, even if the client is experienced in real property transactions.

The reciprocal duty of the lawyer to keep his or her client informed is dictated by ordinary courtesy, regard for good public relations, the desire to avoid resentments arising from misunderstandings, and recognition that the lawyer's own prompt and frequent reports remind the client to communicate.

Another cause of client complaints is the attorney's delay in completing legal matters as early as promised, or as promptly as the client expects. Sometimes the impression of delay results from the attorney's failure to inform the client about the time that will be necessary, or it may be due to failure to keep the client informed of progress; in other instances, there may be actual delay. But whether the delay is real or only apparent, the attorney who becomes aware of such a circumstance should act immediately to cure the defect.

C. Determining Client's Needs

§1.21   1.   Client's Understanding of Transaction

The attorney should make sure at the initial interview that the client understands the transaction. If documents have been signed before the lawyer is consulted, he or she should analyze and explain the nature of the relationships already created and the rights and duties of the parties. Even though it may be too late to alter the terms of a document already executed, the attorney renders a valuable service by clarifying for the client the meaning and significance of what has been done, and what rights and obligations have been created.

§1.22   2.   Client's Goals

If the client is the buyer, the lawyer will want to know the use the client intends to make of the property. Analysis of a survey and the preliminary title report may depend on the intended purpose.

If the client is the seller, and if tax avoidance or deferral is a major reason for the transaction, the lawyer must tailor the documentation to achieve the client's goals. The structure and terms of the sale may depend on the client's reasons for disposing of the property. For example, under certain circumstances, a tax-deferred exchange for more suitable "like kind" property will better serve the seller's needs than an outright sale and reinvestment of the proceeds.

For either party, the way the transaction is structured (*i.e.,* as an outright sale, option, sale and leaseback, installment sale, etc.) will be important and the lawyer must consider the advantages and disadvantages of each. See §§1.58-1.65

D. Setting Fee

§ 1.23   1. Negotiating Fee Agreement

The initial interview is the best time for fixing the fee, or at least its terms and limits. See, *e.g.*, ABA Code Prof Resp EC 2-19. Because the fee is based, at least in part, on the services to be performed, attorney and client should arrive at an understanding in the initial interview concerning the services to be rendered. The checklists in §§ 1.57, 1.83, and 1.84 may be useful for this purpose. A frank discussion of the probable fee and the elements that go into it is good public relations and may prevent future misunderstandings. The agreement should be flexible enough to allow for reasonable compensation if the attorney renders additional services. See generally ABA, The Lawyers Handbook (1978).

Many lawyers content themselves with oral agreements on fees and services, although this is less than the standard of certainty they would advocate for their clients in the conduct of business. Better practice calls for transcribing the terms of the agreement when it is made. The necessary writing may consist of a formal retainer agreement, a memorandum, or simply a letter confirming the understanding. It is not enough merely to obtain the client's signature on a retainer agreement. See, for example, Cal Rules of Prof Cond 2-107, which permits consideration of the client's consent as a factor in determining the fee only if consent is informed. See also *Mazuran v Stefanich* (1928) 95 CA 327, 272 P 772, noting that clients typically rely on the attorney's draftsmanship, even for the fee agreement.

§1.24   2. Computing Fee

In determining the amount of the fee, it is proper to consider (a) the novelty and difficulty of the issues and the skill required; (b) the likelihood, if apparent to the client, that acceptance of this particular employment will preclude other employment for the lawyer; (c) the amount at stake and the results obtained; (d) the time limitations imposed by the client or the circumstances; (e) the nature and length of the attorney's relationship with the client; (f) the lawyer's experience, reputation, and ability; (g) whether the fee is fixed or contingent; (h) the time and labor required; (i) the client's informed consent to the fee arrangement. Cal Rules of Prof Cond 2-107. See also ABA Code Prof Resp DR 2-106. The client's ability to pay may also be a factor. ABA Code Prof Resp EC 2-16.

Lawyers who call attention to the tax effects of legal fees report that their clients appreciate this attention to their interests. Reasonable fees, if they are ordinary and necessary, are deductible if they fall within the Internal Revenue Code definitions of business expenses (IRC §162), expenses for the production of income or for management, conservation, or maintenance of income-producing property (IRC §§212(1)-(2)); or expenses in connection with the determination, collection, or refund of any tax (IRC §212(3)). Not deductible, however, are expenses paid or incurred in acquiring, defending, or perfecting title, recovering possession, or developing or improving property; these fees are capital expenditures and are added to the cost of the property. Reg §1.212-1(k).

§1.25   3.   Equity Interests

Sometimes a client suggests that the attorney accept an equity interest in the transaction as the fee for performing necessary legal services. Even though the attorney invests no money in the venture, an equity fee arrangement pits the attorney's interest as a participant against the duty to have no interest adverse to the client. See §§1.14-1.15. Real property practitioners recommend strongly that the attorney not become embroiled in this conflict of interest. The arrangement may be unenforceable, and the attorney may be subject to discipline under Cal Rules of Prof Cond 4-101.

Equity compensation arrangements make it more difficult to revise the fee upward if additional services are required; this makes the lawyer feel underpaid and may lead him to shortcut the work. Conversely, if the value of the lawyer's share greatly exceeds the lawyer's work, the client has paid more than a fair price for the legal services, and the attorney has charged what may be held to be a flagrantly excessive fee. Cal Rules of Prof Cond 2-107; ABA Code Prof Resp DR 2-106.

III.   HANDLING MECHANICS OF TRANSACTION

A.   Functions Lawyers Perform in Typical Transactions

§1.26   1.   Examining Documents

If at all possible, the laywer should attempt to influence the transaction while it is still in its formative stages. After the first step in selling the property has been taken (for example, execution of a broker's listing agreement) the seller's bargaining position is diminished. The extent to which the lawyer can protect either buyer or seller decreases as each step of the transaction is reduced to writing without the lawyer's participation.

In some instances it is possible to improve the client's position even though documents have been signed. See §§1.32, 1.80. The broker may be willing to modify listing agreements if the seller did not have the benefit of independent counsel before signing. If the attorney finds terms and conditions in the various documents which are unfavorable to the client, it may be worthwhile to attempt revision through negotiation with the broker, lender, or other party if the consequences to the client are serious.

Even if the attorney is consulted at the very beginning of the transaction, he or she may find that the documents have become so standardized that there is little room for bargaining. This is particularly true of the documents regularly used by lending institutions and the provisions of title insurance policies. The sale of a single-family dwelling is hardly ever important enough to these institutions to warrant a deviation from their established business practices. Nonetheless, the lawyer's obligation is to the client, and the attorney must persist if revisions of form documents are important to the client's position. Even if changes cannot be negotiated, the lawyer can provide a valuable service by giving the client a clear understanding of the rights and duties created by each document.

§1.27   2.   Correcting Errors in Legal Description

The land described in the purchase and sale agreement and title documents must correspond to what the parties believe is being sold. If the description is given in metes and bounds, the lawyer should make sure it was prepared by an expert and take the time to draw an outline from the description to be sure that the perimeter closes. Title companies sometimes err in preparing descriptions and the lawyer's attention to verifying the description is therefore of considerable importance. On descriptions generally, see chap 8.

The lawyer should also question the client closely to be sure that the client is aware of the physical location of the property lines and should, if necessary, accompany the client on a visual inspection of the property to verify the location and extent of the land, buildings, encroachments, rights of way, easements, and so forth.

§1.28   3.   Checking for Illegal Lot Splits and Uses

If the legal description of the property indicates that a partial lot is being conveyed, the lawyer should make sure that the lot split is authorized under local zoning ordinances and the Subdivision Map Act, Govt C §§66410-66499.37. See §1.42. Assume, for example, that a duplex is built on a large lot containing more than the minimum area required by local zoning. Soon after construction, the builder sells the rear third of the lot to the owner of the property behind the duplex. A client who wishes to purchase the duplex consults the lawyer, who discovers on investigation that the lot split was never approved by local authorities and that the remaining portion, on which the duplex is built, is substandard in area. If the client had purchased the property, the municipal authority might have forbidden its use as a multiple-unit dwelling. A CLTA title insurance policy may not provide coverage for an illegal subdivision. See *Nishiyama v Safeco Title Ins. Co.* (1978) 85 CA3d Supp 1, 149 CR 355; California Title Insurance Practice §3.7 (Cal CEB 1980).

§1.29   4.   Explaining Title Report Exceptions

The purchase and sale agreement should condition the buyer's obligation to pay on the seller's being able to convey satisfactory title. See §§3.78-3.115. In most cases a title report and copies of each document listed in the report should be obtained and examined. Copies of title exceptions must be requested specifically when the preliminary title report is ordered; this should be done as a matter of routine practice. When the information is assembled the attorney should review it with the client to be sure that none of the exceptions will interfere with the client's proposed use of the property.

§1.30   5.   Examining Warranties of Conformance

Some listing agreements and purchase agreements contain the seller's warranty that the property conforms with local codes and regulations. See §§3.161-3.163. The problem, particularly with older buildings, is that the seller often does not really know whether the property conforms. Breach of the warranty could result in liability for damages or loss of the sale without corresponding relief from liability for the broker's commission. For both parties, discovering and correcting nonconformance before closing is usually the best course, and the lawyer can play a valuable role in ensuring that this occurs by including conditions to be satisfied or waived by the buyer in the purchase and sale agreement. On preventing liability for the commission, see §2.37; for forms and discussion of conformance with code provisions, see §§3.161-3.163.

§1.31   6.   Explaining Prepayment and Acceleration Clauses

If there is an existing mortgage or deed of trust on the property, the attorney for each party should examine both the note and the security instrument before any agreement is signed. The parties need to know whether prepayment of the loan is permissible or will incur a prepayment penalty, and whether assumption or taking subject to the encumbrance will entitle the creditor to accelerate the obligation and demand the balance. On prepayment and acceleration provisions, see §§5.13, 5.21, 5.24.

§1.32   7.   Coping With Steps Client Has Already Taken

Often the lawyer is not consulted at the beginning of the transaction and a document has already been signed or an understanding given that sets the direction of the transaction. Frequently, too, the lawyer is asked for an opinion or advice about only a part of the over-all transaction. This type of professional employment can lead to problems.

If, for example, the seller comes to the attorney's office after signing a listing agreement with a broker, the attorney's ability to affect the seller-broker relationship is greatly reduced. Later, if a buyer produced by the broker fails to complete the transaction, the broker may sue the client for a commission because the listing agreement entitles him to the commission under those facts. See *Beazell v Kane* (1954) 127 CA2d 593, 274 P2d 224. See also §§2.32-2.36; on desirable provisions for listing agreements, see §§2.37, 2.75.

Similarly, unsophisticated buyers commonly neglect to consult a lawyer until they have signed the so-called deposit receipt (see §§3.39-3.40), and committed themselves to a purchase. On counseling buyer who has already signed deposit receipt, see §1.80.

When handling only part of a transaction, the lawyer should make sure that the client understands the limits of the lawyer's ability to deal with problems outside the scope of his or her employment. A letter to this effect is strongly recommended to inform the client, and protect the attorney.

§1.33   B.   Obtaining the Facts

The lawyer must obtain the client's description of the terms and structure of the proposed transaction and the client's goals and expectations. See §§ 1.21-1.22. The attorney should also have the client list the names of other major participants in the transaction, such as the broker, contractor, architect, or engineer, and the escrow or title company which will be employed. For other frequently valuable sources of information, see §§ 1.34-1.37.

§1.34   1.   Publications

Valuable information about the physical characteristics of the land and its current or permissible use can be obtained from publications available at little or no cost. Some of these are:

Photographs. Ground and aerial photographs are available and can be indispensable in providing a visual perspective of the property and its environs. The United States Department of Agriculture will supply aerial photographs at varying scales from 1 to 4800 (1 inch to 400 feet) to 1 to 20,000 (1 inch to 1667 feet); they may be obtained from the Western Laboratory, Aerial Photography Field Office, P.O. Box 30010, Agricultural Stabilization and Conservation Service, United States Department of Agriculture, Salt Lake City, Utah 84130. The section, township, and range must be given when ordering. Aerial photographs also can be obtained from local aerial photographers.

Topographic and coastal maps. Topographic quadrangle maps may be obtained by mail from the United States Geological Survey, Branch of Distribution, Federal Center, Box 25286, Denver, Colorado, 80225, or from the Geological Survey, United States Department of the Interior, 555 Battery Street, Room 504, San Francisco 94111, or in person at the office of the Geological Survey in the Federal Building, Los Angeles, Custom House, San Francisco, and 345 Middlefield Road, Menlo Park. These maps show natural features and contours of areas covering from 49 to 282 square miles. Although too general to show the precise topographic detail required for subdivision maps, they are useful in checking undeveloped land and its surrounding area.

Navigational maps may be obtained from the National Ocean Survey, C-44 Distribution Division, 6501 Lafayette Avenue, Riverdale, Maryland 20840, and from some of the large map supply houses in metropolitan areas. There are also a number of reputable concerns now engaged in the business of making aerial topographic surveys. Maps showing the California coastal zone line from Oregon to the Mexican border (see Pub Res C §30103) are available from the California Coastal Commission, 1540 Market Street, San Francisco 94102, or from the supplier, Blueprint Service, 149 Second Street, San Francisco 94105.

Local maps. The county assessor's office is a commonly used source of local maps, and title companies usually attach a copy of the assessor's map to the title report (see §1.36).

Many city and county zoning and planning offices have maps that contain information about present zoning and street and highway programs as well as plans for future zoning and development. These maps can be useful in determining the suitability of sites for business and commercial ventures and roadside businesses, such as service stations and motels, but the zoning ordinances themselves must also be checked because the maps may be out of date. Information about highway programs is available from the district engineer of the California Department of Transportation (Caltrans). Maps also may be ordered from title companies.

Zoning ordinances, regulations, and planning studies. Zoning ordinances, regulations, and planning studies are available at local planning agencies, and should be examined to determine whether the buyer can use the property as he wishes, bearing in mind the caveat that there is no vested right to a specific zoning classification until funds have been spent in reliance on a validly issued building permit. See §§1.6, 1.44. Copies of the local general plan (Govt C §§65300-65307), specific plans (Govt C §§65450-65452), and the various plan elements (Govt C §§65302-65303) show contemplated trends and are extremely useful in helping to forecast the future income of the parcel. See also §1.43.

Population and growth studies. Census figures are published periodically and are available in public libraries. Many of the larger public utility companies, financial institutions, chambers of commerce, and government planning agencies have population, growth, and industry trend studies that include valuable information.

Building code requirements. Local ordinances should be checked. Most local government bodies have adopted, with or without amendment, the Uniform Building Code, which contains regulations for the construction, repair, improvement, and enlargement of buildings. The code is published by International Conference of Building Officials, 5360 South Workman Mill Road, Whittier, California 90601. The Uniform Plumbing Code, published by Western Plumbing Officials Association, is available from Reeves Journal, 7555 Blue Bell Avenue, North Hollywood, 91605, and the National Electric Code, published by National Fire Protection Association, 470 Atlantic Avenue, Boston, 02210, also are often adopted locally, with or without revision. See §1.45.

§1.35   2. Experts

Assistance on specific problems can often be obtained from persons expert in their fields. In the purchase of a building, for example, an engineer and a contractor may be helpful in determining whether a building is in good repair, and an architect may advise whether it is suitable for an intended use. In a purchase of raw land, a civil engineer or a land surveyor can point out potential problem areas, such as drainage, compaction, relocation of easements, and defects in soil conditions. Accountants and market research analysts can verify business data submitted or make projections of future income and trends. Appraisers can be used to verify market value.

Many specialties are regulated by the state and practitioners may not claim to be specialists unless they have met the state's standards and been properly licensed. Regulated specialties include accountancy, general contracting (as well as particular contracting fields), civil and structural engineering, and land surveying. Real estate appraisers are not regulated, but many large institutional lenders require appraisals by members of the American Institute of Real Estate Appraisers (identified by the designation MAI), the American Society of Appraisers (ASA), or the Society of Real Estate Appraisers (SREA or SRA).

An attorney has no implied authority to engage assistants at the client's expense. *Cormac v Murphy* (1922) 58 CA 366, 208 P 360. If an attorney needs assistance from another attorney or from an expert, he must be sure that the client agrees to bear the expense, unless the attorney is willing to bear it.

§1.36   3. Title Companies

Many lawyers make it their practice to use the services of a particular title company. These services include examination of title and issuance of preliminary title reports and policies insuring title on closing. Many title companies also handle escrows. For a concise discussion of the title industry, its practices, and the legal issues concerning it, see California Title Insurance Practice (Cal CEB 1980).

For a complete picture of the state of title, the buyer should obtain a current preliminary title report together with copies of all the exceptions at the earliest possible date. The preliminary report contains a description of the property and all exceptions of record, with a map or plat of the property showing the boundaries, location, and extent of all recorded easements and rights of way. These exceptions may include restrictions on the use of the property (§§3.96-3.99), liens and encumbrances (§§3.100-3.104), or other items that impair the buyer's use of the property or affect its value. On unrecorded defects in title that do not appear on a title report, see §§8.6, 8.38-8.43.

The description in the preliminary title report, including all easements and rights of way, should be carefully checked against the map or plat attached to it to assure a complete understanding of any problems. The title company will prepare easement maps and other boundary sketches, as requested.

Usually title companies issuing preliminary reports summarize, by reference to recorded documents, the general nature and extent of exceptions affecting the title, such as easements, tract restrictions, covenants, equitable servitudes, and recorded liens. It is important that the lawyer fully understand the nature and extent of these exceptions, and for this purpose the documents referred to in the title report must be ordered from the title company and read and analyzed. See §1.29. These exceptions may pose problems that require further negotiation with the seller.

§1.37   4. Inspecting the Property

The buyer is charged with constructive notice of matters discoverable by inspection of the property. The usual California Land Title Association policy does not insure the physical location of the parcel or against unrecorded easements or other claims of right that an inspection would reveal. See California Title Insurance Practice §3.8 (Cal CEB 1980).

To guard against these hazards, the buyer should make or have made a physical inspection of the property. Some lawyers experienced in real estate practice believe that the attorney himself should make an inspection, because they believe that few buyers understand the legal implications of what they see in viewing the land.

If there are uncertainties about boundaries, overlapping improvements, or similar problems, inspection may not be enough; a survey and in some cases an extended coverage title insurance policy may be required. A special survey is made in connection with every extended coverage policy, but because of the cost of this coverage, some lawyers prefer to order an ordinary survey and a standard owner's policy. See Title Ins §5.5.

§1.38   C. Negotiation

Each party has interests to protect in a sale of real property. The lawyer's skill and sensitivity can be valuable in helping to negotiate resolutions to those problem areas in which the parties' interests conflict. The essence of negotiation is compromise, and the lawyer must work toward that end by ensuring that the client's interests are protected without becoming so zealous that the other party becomes antagonized and the transaction becomes impossible. In order to be able to negotiate effectively, the lawyer must have a thorough understanding of the client's aspirations for the transaction, and the client's position on the essential elements such as price, time, method of payment, willingness and ability to participate in financing, and the like. The attorney must also determine weaknesses in the client's bargaining position and discuss candidly with client the probable effect of those weaknesses on the negotiations.

Often an element that one party finds unacceptable can be resolved by negotiation. For example, even though the seller is opposed to subordination of his lien (see §§5.39-5.54) as dangerous to his security in the property, he may be willing to consider it in return for a higher price. Similarly, a buyer may be willing to accept a defect in title or a variance in the description if the seller lowers the price or adjusts some other term of the agreement. The lawyer must always be alert, however, to hazards that would make the transaction undesirable to the client at any price.

In short, negotiation is a dynamic process, and the parties must approach the transaction with a willingness to bargain. Each party must consider giving on one point in order to gain on another if he can do so without sacrificing what he considers to be essential.

D. Drafting Considerations

§1.39   1. Use of Forms

The attorney bears a heavy responsibility for drafting documents that effectuate the wishes of the parties. The various types of available forms can be valuable tools in drafting, but caution must be exercised when using them. Forms that lawyers frequently use include (a) printed forms with blanks to be filled in, such as the California Association of Realtors (CAR) form exclusive authorization and right to sell listing agreement (see §2.60) and deposit receipt (see §3.40); (b) forms contained in form books, and books such as this one, which can be adapted for a particular transaction; and (c) form documents retained in the attorney's files or computer bank from previous transactions.

The hazard in using readymade forms instead of tailoring instruments to each situation is that they may be used uncritically and with insufficient attention to the comments that accompany them or to the reasons for using particular language. No readymade form is a substitute for a document designed for the particular client's situation. Nor can any form, however perfect it may have been when originally designed, remain equally dependable in the face of changing times and changing laws.

Nevertheless, there are sound legal and economic reasons why lawyers use forms in drafting instruments. Even if it is supplemented and revised substantially, a good basic form can provide a useful starting point for the drafting process, especially when a lawyer faces a new problem. A checklist of some kind protects against inadvertent omission of necessary or desirable clauses, and each of the basic types of form is a kind of checklist. Moreover, a well-worded form offers protection against ambiguities that may result from drafting done under time pressure. On the economic side, struggling anew with legal problems, organization, and special phrasing can be a waste of productive time, if these things already have been carefully worked out in a good form.

Forms should be used with respect for their constructive uses but with awareness of their shortcomings. The form is an instrument not only for achieving the client's ends in this transaction but also for enhancing the drafter's reputation. The client will talk about the lawyer's work; other lawyers will read documents the lawyer prepares; trial judges and appellate courts may have occasion to review the lawyer's handiwork with a critical eye.

For these reasons, drafted documents should be preserved in the files or computer bank so that they can be retrieved for use in similar situations; forms should be chosen carefully and reviewed critically; annotations should be filed with office forms; drafting should be done only after reading the comments and annotations that accompany the forms; and forms should be adapted in drafting to meet precisely the needs of the new situation.

Finally, the attorney should not adhere slavishly even to forms that appear to meet the situation perfectly. The client may be frightened by an instrument's length, or negotiations may reveal the need to abandon even desirable provisions for the sake of closing a transaction that is otherwise advantageous to the client. An inferior instrument drafted by the other lawyer may still provide adequate protection for the client and be readily acceptable to both parties.

§1.40   2. Interest of Third Parties in Drafting

The lawyer may find that drafting a real property sale document according to his or her client's instructions is not enough to meet the client's own best interests. This is particularly true when the instrument affects the interests or plans of third parties.

For example: If an agreement is drawn to provide that the seller will subordinate a retained security interest to a deed of trust securing a later construction loan, the document is worthless if it is not acceptable to the construction lender. The requirement that both spouses join in a conveyance of community real property (CC §5127) makes the other spouse's desires crucial if one intends to sell; a tenant holding a recorded option to buy the leased premises may be an indispensable party to negotiations between the landlord and another prospective buyer; and third parties owning easements over the land may have to be consulted if the buyer intends to improve the property in any way that might interfere with the easements.

In short, drafting must be based on the needs of all concerned, and difficulty may be expected if through oversight or ignorance those needs are not anticipated and fulfilled. On attorney's standards of care and competence, see §1.12.

§1.41   E.   Ensuring Compliance With Government Requirements

Sales and uses of real property are regulated extensively by government entities and an attorney with a real property practice must keep abreast of these various legal requirements in order to be able to provide effective representation. There is no single fool-proof method for staying current on all statutory and regulatory changes, but the careful attorney should begin by subscribing to services that provide information on pending and recently enacted legislative and administrative developments in his or her primary areas of practice.

Sections 1.42-1.54 are designed to provide a checklist of the more commonly encountered statutory restrictions. For analysis and discussion of these statutes, the attorney will frequently need to undertake a substantial amount of research.

Brokers and title company employees can often be a useful source of information regarding changes in legal requirements, but the attorney will want to read and interpret the applicable ordinance, statute, or regulation personally. Government officials can also be helpful in advising the attorney of changes in the law in their areas of expertise and the attorney should develop relationships of mutual respect with government employees in those areas most germane to his or her law practice. On the local level these may include the city manager's office, the staffs of the local planning and building departments, and the staff of the local agency formation commission (LAFCO). Local architects, engineers, and builders are also useful sources of information regarding changes in local building and zoning ordinances and regulations.

1. Regulation of Development

a. State and Local Controls

§1.42   (1)   Subdivisions

Any time the property to be sold is part of a larger parcel, or the buyer intends to divide the property after the sale, attorneys for both parties must be aware of the requirements of the Subdivision Map Act (Govt C §§66410-66499.37), which gives each local governing entity jurisdiction over subdivisions within its area (Govt C §66411; see *Friends of Lake Arrowhead v Board of Supervisors* (1974) 38 CA3d 497, 113 CR 539), and establishes an approval procedure that must be followed whenever land is subdivided (Govt C §§66451-66472; see, *e.g., Horn v County of Ventura* (1979) 24 C3d 605, 156 CR 718). "Subdivision" as defined in the map act means the division of any unit or units of improved or unimproved lands shown on the latest equalized county assessment roll as a unit or contiguous units, for the purpose of sale, lease, or financing except for leases of agricultural land for agricultural purposes. Govt C §66424.

The attorney needs to be aware of local requirements for subdivision approvals, because failure to meet the requirements of the map act and any local ordinances enacted under it results in disapproval of the subdivision. Govt C §66473; see *Youngblood v Board of Supervisors* (1978) 22 C3d 644, 150 CR 242. Approval is also precluded unless the local agency finds that the subdivision is consistent with the general plan and any applicable specific plans. Govt C §66473.5; *Woodland Hills Residents Ass'n v City Council* (1975) 44 CA3d 825, 118 CR 856. In addition, if a lot split is not authorized, the local building department cannot issue a building permit or other required approval for development of the property. Govt C §66499.34; *Pratt v Adams* (1964) 229 CA2d 602, 40 CR 505. For discussion of map act requirements, see California Zoning Practice §§3.46-3.52 (Cal CEB 1969).

§1.43   (2) General and Specific Plans

Each local jurisdiction must have a general plan adopted under the requirements of Govt C §§65300-65307, and the plan's provisions may have a significant effect on the uses that can be made of real property. The general plan must include elements concerning land use, circulation, housing, conservation, open space, seismic safety, noise, scenic highway, and safety (Govt C §65302), and may include elements regarding recreation, transportation, transit, public services and facilities, public building, community design, redevelopment, and historical preservation (Govt C §65303). Jurisdictions may also have specific plans that have been adopted to implement the provisions of the general plan. Govt C §§65450-65453. Local approval of a proposed subdivision, construction project, or private sale of subdivided lots may be enjoined for inconsistency with the general plan. Govt C §66473.5; *Save El Toro Ass'n v Days* (1977) 74 CA3d 64, 141 CR 282; *Woodland Hills Residents Ass'n v City Council* (1975) 44 CA3d 825, 118 CR 856. Injunctive relief is also proper when a proposed public works project is inconsistent with the general plan. *Friends of "B" Street v City of Hayward* (1980) 106 CA3d 988, 165 CR 514.

On general and specific plan requirements, see California Zoning Practice §§2.21-2.32 (Cal CEB 1969).

§1.44   (3) Zoning

Local jurisdictions are empowered to enact zoning ordinances regulating land use within their territory by Cal Const art XI, §7, and Govt C §§65800-65912. The zoning ordinances of the jurisdiction within which real property proposed to be sold is located will have a substantial impact on the uses to which the property can be put, and the attorney must have a working knowledge of the local ordinances and the procedures to be followed in obtaining zone changes, variances, and conditional use permits. For detailed discussion of zoning, see California Zoning Practice (Cal CEB 1969). For provisions making a sale subject to specific zoning, see §§3.132-3.137. The attorneys for the parties, especially the buyer, must be sure to counsel clients that there is no certainty of being able to obtain a desired zoning change or even that present zoning will continue. A vested right to develop land in a particular way arises only when substantial expenses have been incurred in reliance on a validly issued building permit. See *Avco Community Developers, Inc. v South Coast Regional Comm'n* (1976) 17 C3d 785, 132 CR 386.

§1.45   (4) Building Codes

The parties and their attorneys need to be aware of problems that may arise if an existing structure on the property does not comply with local building codes. Most local jurisdictions have adopted, with varying degrees of amendment and addition, the Uniform Building Code. See §1.34. The provisions of the local code should be checked, as well as the records of the local building department concerning the property. The parties may wish to condition the purchase on compliance with local building ordinances. See §§3.161-3.164. On building codes, see California Zoning Practice §§3.5-3.6 (Cal CEB 1969).

§1.46   (5) Environmental Controls

A buyer who intends to develop the property in a manner that will require issuance of some sort of government permit or approval needs to be aware of the provisions of the California Environmental Quality Act (CEQA), Pub Res C §§21000-21176, which requires preparation of an environmental impact report for any project requiring government approval that may have a significant effect on the environment (Pub Res C §21100). Regulations concerning enforcement of CEQA are published in 14 Cal Adm C §§15000-15203. On environmental impact controls, see §§3.147-3.150; California Zoning Practice §§3.81-3.87 (Cal CEB).

If the property is within the coastal zone (Pub Res C §30103), parties will need to comply with the California Coastal Act, Pub Res C §§30000-30900, which imposes detailed requirements for approval of any development within the protected area. Regulations adopted by the Coastal Commission to implement the coastal act are in 14 Cal Adm C §§13001-13013.5. On the coastal act, see §3.149; California Zoning Practice §§3.88-3.96 (Cal CEB).

§1.47   (6) Local Disclosure Ordinances

Cities and counties are authorized to require by ordinance that an owner of residential real property obtain a report showing the property's authorized use, occupancy, and zoning classification and deliver it to a prospective buyer before selling the property. Govt C §§38780-38785, 25846. An attorney representing one of the parties should be sure to check whether the local entity has enacted an ordinance under these authorizing statutes.

§1.48   (7) Other Statutes

Attorneys representing parties to real property transactions may find any of the following statutes to be applicable to the property involved in a particular sale.

(a) General

(1) Alquist-Priolo Special Studies Zones Act (Pub Res C §§2621-2630) which requires special disclosure form for certain properties within earthquake fault areas;

(2) Porter-Cologne Water Quality Control Act (Wat C §§13000-13998);

(3) Air Pollution Control (Health & S C §§39000-43835);

(4) Williamson Act (Govt C §§51200-51295) which provides property tax incentives for owners of agricultural land who agree with local jurisdictions to maintain agricultural or related uses of land (see California Zoning Practice §§6.15-6.21 (Cal CEB 1969));

(5) Annexation of land through local agency formation commission (LAFCO); Govt C §§35000-35016, 35220-35239, 54773-54863 (see California Zoning Practice §§3.1-3.4 (Cal CEB 1969)).

(b) Regional controls

(1) San Francisco Bay Area: Metropolitan Transportation Commission Act (Govt C §§66500-66522); Bay Area Pollution Control District (Health & S C §§40000-40900); San Francisco Bay Conservation and Development Commission (BCDC) (Govt C §§66600-66661);

(2) Lake Tahoe Basin: Tahoe Regional Planning Compact (Govt C §§66800-66801); California Tahoe Regional Planning Agency (Govt C §§67000-67130).

§1.49   b. Federal Controls

Plans to develop a particular piece of real property might call for knowledge of the requirements of one or more of the following federal acts:

(1) National Environmental Policy Act (NEPA) (42 USC §§4321-4369);

(2) Clean Air Act (42 USC §§7401-7626);

(3) Federal Water Pollution Control Act (33 USC §§1251-1376);

(4) Noise Control Act (42 USC §§7641-7642);

(5) Flood Disaster Protection Act (42 USC §§4001-4128);

(6) Coastal Zone Management Act (16 USC §§1451-1464).

2. Consumer Legislation

§1.50   a. Federal Truth in Lending Act

The federal Truth in Lending Act (15 USC §§1601-1691f), and Regulation Z (12 CFR pt 226, following 15 USC §1693r), promulgated under the act by the Board of Governors of the Federal Reserve System, are aimed at consumer credit protection by requiring disclosure of specified credit information, regulating certain kinds of advertising, and granting the consumer the right to rescission or damages for various violations of its provisions.

Although the Truth in Lending Act applies generally to all real property transactions, regardless of amount (12 CFR §226.3(c), (e)), it usually will not apply to seller-financing of real property because creditors are defined as persons who "in the ordinary course of business regularly" extend credit (12 CFR §226.2(s)).

§1.51   b. Federal Interstate Land Sales Full Disclosure Act

The federal Interstate Land Sales Full Disclosure Act (15 USC §§1701-1720) was enacted to prevent fraud and misrepresentation in the sale of unimproved real property in subdivisions, whose marketing includes the use of transportation or communication in interstate commerce or use of the mails. The regulatory vehicle is a document called a property report, which must be given to every prospective purchaser before an agreement to purchase is executed (15 USC §§1703, 1707). The property report is based on the information in a detailed voluminous registration statement (the Statement of Record), which must be filed for every nonexempt subdivision. 15 USC §§1705, 1706.

The principal exemptions from the act include the sale (1) of fewer than 25 lots in a subdivision; (2) to a builder or for resale to a builder; and (3) of lots on which there is a building, or on which the seller is obligated to erect a building within two years. 15 USC §1702(a). See *Exemptions From the Registration Requirements of the Interstate Land Sales Full Disclosure Act,* 15 Real Prop, Prob & Tax J 334 (1980).

Information on the act and its enforcement can be obtained from the Office of Interstate Land Sales Registration, Department of Housing and Urban Development, 451 Seventh Street, SW, Washington, D.C. 20410.

§1.52   c. Federal Real Estate Settlement Procedures Act (RESPA)

The federal Real Estate Settlement Procedures Act (RESPA), 12 USC §§2601-2617, authorizes the Secretary of Housing and Urban Development to issue regulations, known as Regulation X (24 CFR §§3500.1-3500.14, following 12 USC §2617), for implementation of the act.

The provisions of RESPA apply to every purchase or other transfer of title to residential real property designed principally for occupancy by one to four families, financed in whole or in part by a federal lender who obtains a security interest in the property, or by a loan insured, guaranteed, supplemented, or assisted in any way by any officer or agency of the federal government, or by a loan made in connection with a housing or urban development program administered by any agency of the federal government (24 CFR §3500.5). A "federal lender" is defined in §3500.2(c) to include most lending institutions.

The act requires that   (1) a special information booklet be given to a prospective borrower by the lender within three business days after receipt of a loan application and   (2) that a uniform settlement statement form, HUD Form 1, be given to the borrower in all covered transactions (24 CFR §§3500.6, 3500.8; 12 USC §§2603-2604). The information booklet may be obtained from the United States Government Printing Office, Washington, D.C. 20402. For a discussion of RESPA, see §§11.85-11.89.

§1.53   d. California Subdivided Lands Act

The Subdivided Lands Act (Bus & P C §§11000-11200) which is administered by the California Department of Real Estate (10 Cal Adm C §§2700-3208), is intended to protect the public against fraud and misrepresentation in the sale or lease of subdivided land. It is the counterpart at the state level of the federal Interstate Land Sales Full Disclosure Act. See §1.51.

For detailed discussion of Subdivided Lands Act, see Guide to California Subdivision Sales Law (Cal CEB 1974).

§1.54   e. Equal Credit Legislation

The real property practitioner should be aware of the Equal Credit Opportunity Act (15 USC §§1691-1691f) and the California Credit Protection Act (CC §§1812.30-1812.35), barring discrimination on the basis of sex and marital status in the extension of credit.

IV. COUNSELING SELLER

§1.55   A. Attorney's Role

Before a buyer is found, and preferably before the property is listed with a broker, a seller's lawyer, by skillfull interviewing and counseling, can help shape the transaction to the client's best interests.

The first question is whether the client should sell at all. For example, if both income and market value of the property are increasing, it may be better to refinance the mortgage and obtain additional funds than to sell and reinvest in unknown property. Not all clients welcome these inquiries into their purposes, but a few discreet questions coupled with sensitivity to the client's manner of response may open a line of inquiry that the client will welcome. See §1.5.

The attorney should also inquire into the state of the seller's title. What is the description of the property to be sold? Is the seller's interest encumbered or otherwise limited or impaired? Is execution by anyone other than the client also required for a valid conveyance? Are there impediments to clearing exceptions to title, such as a lock-in loan? See checklist in §1.57. The answers to these questions may reveal impediments of which the client is not aware. Examination of a title report and inspection of the property itself may reveal other impediments and protect the seller against liability for breach of a covenant. See §§3.55, 3.78-3.82.

Few lawyers are qualified to advise the seller on setting the price. They may, however, recommend qualified appraisers or brokers to assist in setting the price.

The lawyer may perform a further service by describing for the client what steps must occur before the transaction closes. The broker's rights under the listing agreement should be explained (chap 2); the range of charges that may be made in the escrow should be anticipated (see §§11.58); escrow instructions should be discussed (see chap 11); and an inexperienced seller should be advised to submit all documents to the attorney before they are signed or accepted. In addition, the kinds of questions that may arise in negotiating the agreement (see chap 3) should be explored, and the seller should be informed of his or her rights and liabilities in case of breach or fraud.

§1.56   B. Use of Checklists

The attorney must learn all he or she can about the purchase or sale the client intends to make, obtain any missing information, and make sure the client understands the implications of the transaction well enough for informed negotiation. The checklists in §§1.57 (seller) and 1.83 (buyer) are intended for that purpose. These checklists are by no means all embracing but are intended as a basis from which an attorney can construct lists meaningful in his or her own practice.

The attorney will not be able to obtain all the information for the checklist during the initial client interview. The manner and sequence in which information is elicited varies. Often, matters such as the client's motives and objectives, experience, financial ability, and resources are best obtained by indirect methods rather than direct questions. The extent to which the client seeks or welcomes the attorney's advice regarding the reasons for selling or purchasing the property in question or on other business matters varies with the client and the attorney. See §1.5. The checklists for seller and buyer help to develop information and point out areas of inquiry that may help the client arrive at necessary decisions.

§1.57   C. Checklist for Interviewing and Counseling Seller

1. Seller's title

a. Is seller the record owner? (§§3.9, 3.78) Establish the sources of information (*e.g.,* deed, title policy, court order or decree, new preliminary title report).

b. Who must sign deed to buyer? (§§3.9-3.26)

c. What interests, if any, should be transferred to others before the sale? (§3.9)

2. Impact on seller's estate

a. What are the tax consequences to seller? (See, *e.g.,* §§5.7, 5.10-5.16, 5.31-5.32.) For tax purposes, the attorney may want to establish some or all of the following:

(1) Date of acquisition

(2) Method of acquisition (*e.g.,* purchase, inheritance, gift, tax-free exchange

(3) Basis at time of acquisition (*e.g.,* cost, fair market value, donor's basis)

(4) Depreciation method used

(5) Adjusted basis of property for tax purposes

(6) Other income of seller

(7) Projection of potential income from sale

(8) Tax effects of method of disposition

b. Will prepayment penalties or assumption fee be payable on existing encumbrances? Is existing financing a "lock-in" loan? (§§5.13, 5.24)

c. What specific facts or circumstances, if any, must seller disclose to avoid fraud or misrepresentation? (§§1.66-1.78)

    d. What will seller's remedies be in the event of a breach by buyer? (See chap 12)

    e. What will buyer's remedies be if seller breaches? (chap 12)

3. The property

    a. Legal description (chap 8)

    (1) Street address

    (2) Most recent survey, date, and surveyor

    (3) Advisability of new survey (§3.118)

    b. Type of property (*e.g.,* residential, income-producing, farm, industrial, commercial, raw land)

    (1) Highest and best use

    (2) Market value and basis of its determination

    (3) Advisability of appraisal

    c. Condition of title

    (1) Liens, encumbrances, easements, and other exceptions (§§3.78-3.115)

    (2) Requirements to produce a marketable title (§§3.78-3.82)

    (3) Covenants and servitudes (§§3.96-3.99, 9.4-9.12)

    d. Method of selling

    (1) Employment of broker (§2.15-2.17)

    (2) Type of listing agreement (§§2.58-2.64)

    (3) Listing period (§2.67)

    (4) Amount of broker's compensation, and when compensation will be deemed earned (§§2.29-2.44)

    (5) Costs required for closing (§11.58)

    e. Types of agreement (*e.g.,* long term lease, lease-option, installment land contract, tax-free exchange, purchase and sale agreement, option) (§§1.59-1.65; chap 3)

    f. Personal property that will be included (§§3.170-3.173)

    (1) Descriptive list

    (2) Sales tax effects

    (3) Bulk sale requirements

4. Proposed terms of sale

    a. Effect of previously signed documents (§1.32)

    b. Type of agreement (preferred or required)

    (1) Lease (*e.g.,* ground lease, net lease)

    (2) Lease with purchase option (§1.63)

    (3) Option to purchase (§1.64, chap 4)

    (4) Straight sale (§1.62)

    (5) Installment sale (§§5.10-5.16)

    (6) "Like kind" exchange (§1.59)

    (7) Installment land contract (§1.65)

(8) Other (§1.58)

c. Price

(1) Amount and method of payment (§§3.47-3.49)

(2) Deposit (§3.47)

(3) Security for deferred amounts (§§5.19-5.20)

(4) Noncash portions

(5) Allocation of price (to land, improvements, and personal property)

d. Escrow (chap 11)

(1) Date of opening and closing

(2) Date of buyer's possession

(3) Proration of insurance, taxes, rents, deposits

(4) Preliminary title report and exceptions to title

(5) Title insurance

(6) Expenses of escrow

e. Leases (§§3.106-3.115)

f. Risk of loss (chap 10)

g. Condemnation

§1.58   D. Shaping Transaction To Meet Seller's Objectives

Sellers have varying reasons for wishing to dispose of real property, and the attorney must be able to structure the transaction in the manner that best suits the seller's needs.

A tax-deferred exchange for more suitable "like kind" property may serve the seller better than an outright sale, particularly when a business property has outlived its usefulness because of inherent inadequacies or changes in the seller's business needs. See §1.59. Conversely, the property itself may be essential for business purposes, but the seller may need the capital it represents in a more liquid form. Refinancing may raise sufficient cash in this situation, but a sale and leaseback (see §1.60) may serve the seller's needs better. A long term lease gives the owner income from the property and also participation in its future appreciation, although the attorney should be sure that an escalator clause is incorporated in a long term lease so that rents will rise with inflation. See §1.61.

The transactions referred to in §§1.59-1.65 are frequently complex and the attorney will need to do a considerable amount of research to be sure of covering all potential ramifications.

The seller may, however, wish to dispose of the property for any of a number of reasons: because its value has reached a plateau, because the seller simply wants a different type of investment, because of a move, etc. The various methods of selling real property (cash sale, deferred payments using deed of trust as security instrument (see chap 5), option, lease-option, and installment land contract) and the advantages and disadvantages of each must be considered. See §§1.62-1.65.

§1.59   1. Tax-Deferred Exchange; Nontaxable Reinvestment

If the seller's aim is to sell currently owned real property and reinvest the proceeds in similar property, consideration should be given to the possibility of exchanging the property for a desired substitute. In an exchange, no tax is incurred on receipt of the exchanged property, and the tax basis for the old property determines the basis for the new property. IRC §1031. The advantages of greater depreciation which would be available on acquisition of a property with a higher market value are lost, however, in a tax-deferred exchange. If part of the exchange consists of cash or other nonlike property ("boot"), the gain represented by this excess is taxed. Sellers have some latitude in structuring exchanges, and may under certain circumstances be able to delay receipt of exchanged property for a reasonable period until suitable property can be found. See *Starker v U.S.* (9th Cir 1979) 602 F2d 1341; Goodman, *The New* Starker *Case: How It Will Revolutionize Tax-Deferred Exchanges,* 3 CEB Real Prop L Rep 1 (1980). Caution must be exercised in delaying receipt of exchanged property because the law in this area remains quite unsettled.

§1.60   2. Sale-and-Leaseback; Need for Liquidity

A seller who needs the property in his trade or business may be able to obtain needed working capital by refinancing, but is then faced with increased payments on the new loan and increased liability on the balance sheet. Another method of obtaining capital is to sell the property with a simultaneous lease back to the seller. If the lease term is 30 years or more, the Internal Revenue Service may treat the transaction as a tax-deferred exchange so that no gain or loss is recognized. IRC §1031; Reg §1.1031(a)-1(c).

Although the seller loses the allowance for depreciation, he or she may deduct reasonable rent paid in connection with a trade or business as a business expense. IRC §162(a)(3). The seller has the use of the property for the term of the lease and ordinarily realizes more cash by this method than by refinancing. See, *e.g.,* Moewe, *Sale and*

Leaseback Financing of Real Estate as Mortgages Under California Law, 48 Cal SBJ 554 (1973).

§1.61 3. Long Term Lease; Production of Income

If the property is appreciating in value, the seller may choose to use a long term lease for continued participation in future growth. Leases for terms of up to 99 years on town and city lots (CC §718), and 51 years for agricultural or horticultural purposes (CC §717), provide income, which generally is adjusted to changing property values or the cost of living. A long term lease usually provides that taxes, insurance, maintenance, and repairs are to be paid by the tenant, giving the landlord what amounts to an annuity for the leasehold term. At the end of the term, the landlord (or his heirs) regains possession of the property, which then will probably be much more valuable. If rent is not prepaid, a lease generates little current cash compared to a sale, and rent is taxable as ordinary income.

On long term leases generally, see Commercial Real Property Lease Practice (Cal CEB 1976); Ground Lease Practice (Cal CEB 1971).

§1.62 4. Purchase and Sale Agreement; Willing Buyer, With or Without Conditions

The most common form of contract for disposition of real property is the purchase and sale agreement (see chap 3), by which the seller undertakes to transfer title to the buyer in consideration of the buyer's payment of the purchase price to the seller. A conditional agreement may be used when performance is contingent on some event, such as the buyer's obtaining financing, or approving the preliminary title report. The seller ordinarily requires some form of deposit when the agreement is executed as evidence of the buyer's good faith and ability to complete the purchase; indeed, a commonly used form of purchase and sale agreement is misleadingly called a "deposit receipt." See §3.40.

On purchase and sale agreements, see chap 3; for remedies on default, see chap 12; on seller's security for deferred payments, see §§5.19-5.20; for buyer's assumption of, or taking subject to, prior encumbrances, see §§3.50-3.51, 5.23-5.25.

§1.63   5. Lease-Option; Buyer Financially Insecure

The seller may be willing to give a prospective buyer a short term lease with an option to purchase at a specified price, particularly when the buyer cannot initially obtain a loan or make an adequate downpayment. Although less advantageous to the seller than an outright sale, and not without risks, the lease-option is superior to an installment land contract (see §1.65) or a sale with a low downpayment, and may be attractive if the property is hard to sell or the seller especially wishes to carry the financing. The seller gets income from the property in the form of rent, and, on default, can evict the tenant through the summary remedy of unlawful detainer (CCP §§1161-1179a). Rent payments are treated as ordinary income for tax purposes, but the seller can depreciate the building during the lease period.

§1.64   6. Option To Purchase; Contingencies or Unwilling Buyer

When the parties reach general agreement on terms but need more time to remove contingencies such as rezoning (see §3.132), or suitability of covenants and restrictions (see §§3.96-3.99), an option to purchase may best achieve the parties' purposes. The option may be a substitute for a conditional purchase and sale agreement, or permit the parties to speculate on the real estate market during the term of the option. See chap 4. Whatever the option's purpose, the seller should demand an option price that provides adequate compensation for removing the property from the market during the option period. An advantage for the seller is the fact that the option price is retained whether or not the option is exercised (see §4.4), without the uncertainties and legal problems that surround retention of the deposit under a purchase and sale agreement (see §§3.179-3.180, 12.26-12.30).

§1.65   7. Installment Land Contract; Buyer Financially Insecure

The installment land contract has occasionally been used as a financing device when the buyer could not qualify for a loan, when the downpayment the buyer could afford was small, or when the parties wanted to avoid a due-on-sale clause (see §5.24). For discussion of installment land contract, see §§5.4-5.7. With this device, the seller retains title, transferring it to the buyer when the purchase price has been paid.

The benefits of using an installment land contract have disappeared, and its use is not recommended. The seller is now subject to regulation (CC §§2985-2985.5; Bus & P C §§10230-10236.1); the remedy of unlawful detainer is not available to evict a recalcitrant buyer (CCP §1161; *Greene v Municipal Court* (1975) 51 CA3d 446, 124 CR 139); there is no advantage in avoidance of a due-on-sale clause in light of *Wellenkamp v Bank of America* (1978) 21 C3d 943, 148 CR 379 (see §5.24); and the tax advantage on repossession was eliminated with the enactment of IRC §1038.

E. Preventing Fraud

§1.66   1. Protections Against Fraud

Most sellers believe themselves innocent of fraud as long as they make no affirmative misrepresentations of fact. As the statutory definitions (see §1.67) demonstrate, however, fraud encompasses a far broader range of conduct. Thus, a party may be liable for failing to disclose a material fact (CC §§1572(3), 1710(3)); for negligently asserting a fact he or she should have known was not true (CC §§1572(2), 1710(2)); or even for the misrepresentations of another person such as a broker (see §§2.118-2.121). The seller's attorney must ensure that the client understands the scope of disclosure and degree of candor required. The expenses, attorneys' fees, and inevitable delay attendant to litigation make the prevention of fraud highly desirable.

The seller must be sure to make disclosure of material facts in a form that makes proof of the disclosure available if litigation ensues. Disclosure of adverse facts should be made part of the purchase and sale agreement (see chap 3), or at least be set forth in a certified or registered letter. If disclosure is not made before the purchase and sale agreement is executed, disclosure before escrow closes coupled with an offer to return the deposit should protect the seller if the buyer elects to consummate the transaction anyway.

§1.67   2. Statutory Definition of Fraud

Actual fraud, which arises from a contractual relationship (CC §1572), consists of essentially the same conduct as "deceit," which arises outside a contractual relationship (CC §1709).

Constructive fraud, which arises from a confidential relationship, is discussed in §§2.86-2.102 in the context of breach of the broker's fiduciary duty to his or her principal. Conduct that may incur liability for actual fraud or deceit includes:

(a) Affirmative misrepresentation, or intentional fraud: representation of a fact as true by one who does not believe it to be true (CC §§1572(1), 1710(1));

(b) Negligent fraud: assertion of a fact as true by one having no reasonable basis for believing it to be true (CC §§1572(2), 1710(2));

(c) Nondisclosure, or concealment: suppression of a fact by one with knowledge of, or belief in, the fact (CC §§1572(3), 1710(3));

(d) Promissory fraud: a promise made without any intention of performing it (CC §§1572(4), 1710(4)); and

(e) Any other conduct "fitted to deceive" (CC §1572(5)).

§1.68   3. Elements of Fraud

In order to impose liability and obtain damages or rescission for fraud (see chap 12), the defrauded party must plead and prove each of the following elements:

(a) Defendant affirmatively misrepresented or concealed a material fact;

(b) If the action is based on a misrepresentation, defendant knew or should have known of its falsity;

(c) The representation or nondisclosure was committed by defendant with intent to induce plaintiff to enter into the transaction;

(d) Plaintiff reasonably relied on the representation, or lack of knowledge of the fact concealed, in entering into the transaction; and

(e) Plaintiff suffered injury or damage as a result of reliance on the representation or concealment.

The absence of any element will defeat the action. *Gonsalves v Hodgson* (1951) 38 C2d 91, 237 P2d 656; *Ach v Finkelstein* (1968) 264 CA2d 667, 70 CR 472. Whether defendant's actions constitute fraud is always a question of fact (CC §1574), and may be proved by direct evidence or inferred from the circumstances. *Palmquist v Mercer* (1954) 43 C2d 92, 272 P2d 26; *Ach v Finkelstein, supra.*

§1.69   4. Nondisclosure

Sellers are usually aware that their affirmative misrepresentations may incur liability for fraud and will exercise caution to avoid making them, but may not be aware that they also are under an affirmative duty to disclose material facts concerning the property. Concealment of a material fact gives rise to a cause of action for fraud (CC §§1572(3), 1710(3)), and concealment may be either the mere nondisclosure, or the active concealment, of a material fact. The seller has a duty to make full disclosure of a fact materially affecting the value of the property of which he or she has actual knowledge if it is not a fact within reach of the attention and observation of the buyer. *Herzog v Capital Co.* (1945) 27 C2d 349, 164 P2d 8; *Lingsch v Savage* (1963) 213 CA2d 729, 29 CR 201.

The seller cannot defend against a claim of concealment of a material fact on the ground that the buyer did not inquire or express concern about the aspect of the property that was not disclosed; the failure to disclose is treated as a representation of the nonexistence of the facts that were not disclosed. *Herzog v Capital Co., supra; Snelson v Ondulando Highlands Corp.* (1970) 5 CA3d 243, 84 CR 806. This duty to disclose extends only to those facts known to the seller and which he or she knows are not reasonably accessible to the buyer. *Burkett v J. A. Thompson & Son* (1957) 150 CA2d 523, 310 P2d 56; *Tatham v Pattison* (1952) 112 CA2d 18, 245 P2d 668. When affirmative misrepresentations are claimed as the basis for the fraud, however, the seller may be liable if he lacks sufficient knowledge to justify the assertion. CC §§1572(2), 1710(2).

The seller has a duty to disclose only those facts that are not known to the buyer and not within the reach of the buyer's diligent attention and observation. *Herzog v Capital Co., supra.* The courts have tended to apply this rule rather strictly, holding buyers to be unaware of facts that could not be discovered from casual observation of the property. *Snelson v Ondulando Highlands Corp., supra* (whether land was cut or fill not apparent from observation); *Piazzini v Jessup* (1957) 153 CA2d 58, 314 P2d 196 (failure to disclose termite infestation although buyer did not order termite report); *Clauser v Taylor* (1941) 44 CA2d 453, 112 P2d 661 (existence of fill not apparent to buyer).

If, in the course of fixing up the property for sale, the seller covers up physical defects, this affirmative concealment will be treated the same as an affirmative misrepresentation of fact. In *Herzog v Capital Co., supra,* the seller was held liable for fraud for painting over structural defects.

For specific examples of situations in which full disclosure must be made, see §§1.72-1.78.

§1.70   5. Partial Disclosure

If the seller makes an affirmative statement or answers the other party's questions, not only must the statement or response be truthful, but the seller then becomes obligated to make full disclosure of all other facts that are material to the subject matter of the statement or answer. *Hale v Wolfsen* (1969) 276 CA2d 285, 81 CR 23. Even though any representation actually made is itself true, the failure to disclose other pertinent facts that condition or modify the representation will constitute fraud. *Hale v Wolfsen, supra* (furnishing two-year-old appraisal required disclosure of decrease in value and fact that property was now vacant); *McCue v Bruce Enterprises, Inc.* (1964) 228 CA2d 21, 39 CR 125 (statement that property "on city utilities" required disclosure that property had septic tank and city did not supply sewage disposal services); *Brady v Carman* (1960) 179 CA2d 63, 3 CR 612 (undertaking to answer buyer's questions about easement creates duty to explain effect of easement on property); *Gilbert v Corlett* (1959) 171 CA2d 116, 339 P2d 960 (seller who furnished buyer with favorable engineer's report had duty to disclose earlier unfavorable report).

§1.71   6. Changed Circumstances

If previously accurate statements become false because of a change in circumstances, the seller must disclose the new circumstances. *Southern Cal. Dist. Council, Assemblies of God v Shepherd of the Hills Evangelical Lutheran Church* (1978) 77 CA3d 951, 144 CR 46 (failure to advise buyer of termination of access easement after representing that access would be available); *Koch v Williams* (1961) 193 CA2d 537, 14 CR 429 (failure to advise buyers of drainage easement granted after purchase agreement executed).

7. Common Fraud Situations

§1.72   a. Structural Defects

The seller has a duty to disclose known structural defects in improvements on the property. *Lingsch v Savage* (1963) 213 CA2d 729, 29 CR 201. If the seller undertakes to make statements about the condition of the property, full disclosure must be made, and the seller is under an additional duty to conduct a reasonable investigation to ensure that the statements made are correct. See, *e.g., Doran v Milland Dev. Co.* (1958) 159 CA2d 322, 323 P2d 792; *Hodgeson v*

Brant (1958) 156 CA2d 610, 319 P2d 684. Efforts to conceal structural defects from view will be treated as affirmative misrepresentations. *Herzog v Capital Co.* (1945) 27 C2d 349, 164 P2d 8.

§1.73   b. Number of Units and Legality of Additions

The seller commits fraud if he or she misrepresents the number of units or their legality. See *Birch v Ciria* (1962) 205 CA2d 1, 22 CR 798 (seller impliedly represented that basement apartment was legal unit by listing property as multiple dwelling and stating income from unit would make it easy to pay off mortgage). If the units are illegal, or if the seller knows of an illegal conversion, these facts must be disclosed to the buyer. *Gulke v Brock* (1963) 222 CA2d 459, 35 CR 200.

If the seller has knowledge of illegal work done on the premises, he must disclose it. *Unger v Campau* (1956) 142 CA2d 722, 298 P2d 891; *Curran v Heslop* (1953) 115 CA2d 476, 252 P2d 378; *Tatham v Pattison* (1952) 112 CA2d 18, 245 P2d 668. There is no liability for fraud, however, when the seller has no knowledge of the illegality of the work. *Corbett v Otts* (1962) 205 CA2d 78, 22 CR 849.

The safest course for both parties is to condition the purchase agreement on a physical inspection to verify the number of units and check for possible illegal add-ons, and on confirmation by the local health or building department of the legality of the structures (see §§3.120-3.122, 3.161-3.163).

§1.74   c. Presence of Fill

The presence of fill must be disclosed when raw land is being sold. *Massei v Lettunich* (1967) 248 CA2d 68, 56 CR 232; *Clauser v Taylor* (1941) 44 CA2d 453, 112 P2d 661. If the property is already improved, failure to disclose that the buildings stand on filled ground is also actionable. *Central Mut. Ins. Co. v Schmidt* (1957) 152 CA2d 671, 313 P2d 132.

Conditioning the purchase agreement on an inspection to determine the existence of fill (§3.170) may prove costly, and the parties must weigh its desirability against the added cost and delay. In some instances, the seller's warranty on this point may be a better solution (see §3.121).

§1.75   d. Termite Infestation

The seller's knowledge of termite infestation is a fact that must be disclosed. *Orlando v Berkeley* (1963) 220 CA2d 224, 33 CR 860; *Piazzini v Jessup* (1957) 153 CA2d 58, 314 P2d 196.

The fact that the buyer was not diligent enough to order a termite inspection will not excuse the seller's nondisclosure of termite infestation. *Piazzini v Jessup, supra.* Requiring a termite inspection is commonplace in the sale of woodframe structures, and its cost is low enough to make it advisable even when the likelihood of infestation is remote. See §3.125-3.127.

§1.76   e. Area and Boundaries

An owner is presumed to know the boundaries of the property being sold, and a misrepresentation of the quantity of land or its geography is fraud. *Wilbur v Wilson* (1960) 179 CA2d 314, 3 CR 770. The seller has a duty to inform himself of the boundary lines when selling the property (*Edwards v Sergi* (1934) 137 CA 369, 30 P2d 541), and is not excused from an erroneous representation by evidence that he relied on information from the previous owner (*Wilbur v Wilson, supra*). See also *Williams v Marshall* (1951) 37 C2d 445, 235 P2d 372 (number of acres of citrus trees); *Soderling v Tomlin* (1959) 170 CA2d 169, 338 P2d 946 (location of boundaries); *Piazzini v Jessup* (1957) 153 CA2d 58, 314 P2d 196 (length of lot); *Mills v Hellinger* (1950) 100 CA2d 482, 224 P2d 34 (number of acres). For warranty provision concerning acreage, see §3.124.

A misrepresentation of the location of a boundary line is not fraud, if the seller relies in good faith on a misplaced surveyor's mark. *Roland v Hubenka* (1970) 12 CA3d 215, 90 CR 490. Although a survey will eliminate boundary and area problems from the transaction, the parties are often unwilling to bear its cost. The standard title insurance policy does not insure the boundaries, and a survey will be required before the title insurer will extend coverage. See California Title Insurance Practice §§3.8, 3.32 (Cal CEB 1980).

§1.77   f. Value

Statements concerning the property's value are generally held to be expressions of opinion and not actionable as fraud, even though exaggerated. *Craig v Wade* (1911) 159 C 172, 112 P 891; *Finch v McKee* (1936) 18 CA2d 90, 62 P2d 1380. However, a representation of the property's value based on a factual statement known to be false constitutes fraud. *Friedberg v Weissbuch* (1955) 135 CA2d 750,

287 P2d 785. If a misrepresentation of value is not honestly held it is also actionable. *Feckenscher v Gamble* (1938) 12 C2d 482, 85 P2d 885; *Salvati v Cusolito* (1950) 98 CA2d 582, 220 P2d 800. Negligent misrepresentations of value, if made in the context of a confidential relationship such as that between seller and broker, are also actionable. *Schoenberg v Romike Properties* (1967) 251 CA2d 154, 59 CR 359; see §2.100.

§1.78   g. Income

A seller who misrepresents the income that the property produces commits fraud even though the buyer could have discovered the truth by a more careful investigation. *Pearson v Norton* (1964) 230 CA2d 1, 40 CR 634. A buyer should ask to see the income and expense statement on the property, but even if one is obtained, there is no way of guaranteeing its veracity. In *Ach v Finkelstein* (1968) 264 CA2d 667, 70 CR 472, the seller was held liable for fraud when none of the leases shown the buyer included rent concessions the seller had made to tenants to induce them to move in. Failure to disclose material facts regarding rental income may also render the seller liable. In *Daniels v Oldenburg* (1950) 100 CA2d 724, 224 P2d 472, the seller's representation that a motel could be kept fully rented in the future was held actionable because the seller failed to disclose that the existing occupants were from a temporary construction project. On the other hand, mere statements of opinion about probable potential income are viewed as expressions of opinion and do not constitute fraud. *Pacesetter Homes, Inc. v Brodkin* (1970) 5 CA3d 206, 85 CR 39.

V. COUNSELING BUYER

§1.79   A. Attorney's Role

The lawyer's function is to guide and counsel the buyer, and frequently to supervise the work performed by brokers, appraisers, title companies, and lenders. For further discussion of attorneys' functions see, *e.g.,* §§1.26-1.32. Problems will inevitably arise because of the complexities of modern business; the lawyer's role is to reduce those problems to a minimum and solve them when they do arise. Besides this negative, protective function, attorneys are also frequently concerned with the client's affirmative purposes for acquiring the property. If the attorney, out of an excess of zeal to secure every possible contractual advantage for the client, succeeds only in driving off the other party, the client's best interests may not have been served.

The attorney must ascertain the client's purposes, explain the legal and contractual elements of the transaction, and determine in advance of negotiations what the client is willing to risk or sacrifice to obtain what he or she wants. If the client is inexperienced in business matters, the lawyer may feel obligated to determine whether the client has considered all the business risks that may flow from the transaction. Even experienced clients may not be aware of tax implications, zoning difficulties, and similar problems.

The attorney should ascertain whether he or she is expected to negotiate all the terms and conditions or merely to render guidance. The seller may be reluctant to negotiate with the buyer's lawyer, and many buyers prefer to handle active negotiations themselves or through the broker.

For these reasons, the initial interview may consist as much of finding out about the parties as of learning about the transaction. Counsel may need to know such things as what business experience the client has; what experience the client has in the particular kind of transaction; what the client's attitude is toward lawyers in general; what the client expects of the lawyer in the transaction, and whether the client has thoroughly analyzed his or her reasons for acquiring real property.

For a checklist of information to be obtained and advice to be given in counseling the buyer, see §1.83. For a checklist from the seller's viewpoint, but which contains many matters common to the parties, see §1.57. For points to consider in preparing the purchase agreement, see chap 3.

§1.80   B. Dealing With Unfavorable Agreement Buyer Has Already Signed

Occasionally an attorney is faced with a client who seeks counsel only after signing an agreement (often a deposit receipt; see §3.40) on unfavorable terms. Even though the parties have signed an "agreement," there may be no mutual assent as, for example, when an offer or counteroffer is not accepted according to its terms. *Krasley v Superior Court* (1980) 101 CA3d 425, 161 CR 629; *Conley v Fate* (1964) 227 CA2d 418, 38 CR 680. Thus, the attorney must find out if the buyer has indeed signed a contract, and, if so, acquaint the buyer with available defenses. On defenses to an action for breach, see §§12.93-12.107; on remedies for fraud, see §§12.31-12.38, 12.60. Even though a purchase agreement has been executed, the attorney may find it worthwhile to attempt to renegotiate with the seller or the lender, especially if defenses are available to the buyer.

If there are no defenses to an action for breach and attempts at renegotiating the agreement have failed, the buyer must weigh the consequences of breaching the agreement. See §12.7. On the buyer's breach, the seller's recovery of money damages under CC §3307 may be minimal, especially if the contract price is close to the property's market value. On seller's measure of damages, see §§12.19-12.30. The attorney should also determine whether the agreement contains a valid liquidated damages provision that will enable the seller to retain the deposit. See §§3.179-3.180, 12.27-12.30. Rather than risking liability for breach, the buyer may be able to resell the property on terms that tend to make him whole.

Generally, it is neither simple nor inexpensive to avoid valid contracts, and even invalid ones may present problems. The buyer should either make a thorough investigation before signing, or include conditions in the purchase and sale agreement, or both. See §§3.1-3.3, 3.64-3.76. The buyer might also consider using an option rather than a purchase agreement as a means of avoiding some of these problems. See chap 4.

C. Avoiding Fraud

§1.81   1. Of Seller

The buyer's best protection against fraud by the seller is to provide (through conditions in the purchase agreement, or use of an option) for adequate investigation of the condition of the property, the state of title, financing constraints, and so forth. If circumstances prohibit investigation of every feature of the transaction in as thorough a manner as a prudent attorney would advise, the buyer's lawyer should insist that all representations be put in writing, preferably as warranties in the purchase agreement which survive closing (see §§3.65-3.67). Insistence on written representations should have a deterrent effect on any thoughts the seller may have about committing fraud, and a refusal to comply should put the buyer on notice that further investigation is called for.

§1.82   2. Of Buyer

Although fraud by the seller is more common because of the seller's greater knowledge of the property, buyers have been held liable for fraud, particularly when the buyer is experienced and the seller is not. In some instances, sellers have recovered when they have been misled by some misrepresentation or nondisclosure into selling the property for less than its value. *Seeger v Odell* (1941) 18 C2d 409, 115 P2d 977; *Palm v Smither* (1942) 52 CA2d 500, 126 P2d 428. A seller may also be defrauded concerning the value of the security being offered by the buyer. *Banville v Schmidt* (1974) 37 CA3d 92, 112 CR 126. A buyer who obtains the seller's consent to a subordination agreement (see §§5.39-5.54) may be liable to the seller for fraud, if in addition to other claims, the loan funds are used for purposes other than those specified in the subordination agreement, or if the amount of the loan is larger than was represented to the seller. *Joanaco Projects, Inc. v Nixon & Tierney Constr. Co.* (1967) 248 CA2d 821, 57 CR 48.

As with the seller (see §1.66), the buyer must be advised to make disclosure of all material facts and to do so in a form that makes proof of disclosure available should litigation ensue. Preferably, disclosure of adverse facts should be contained in the purchase and sale agreement itself; if disclosure is not made before the agreement is executed, disclosure by certified or registered letter should be made before escrow closes to protect the buyer if the seller wishes to proceed anyway.

§1.83   D. Checklist for Interviewing and Counseling Buyer

On use of checklist, see §1.56.

1. Buyer's title
   a. Who will take title and in what form? (§§3.27-3.31)
   (1) Husband and wife: community property, joint tenancy, other (§3.30)
   (2) Joint buyers: joint tenancy, tenancy in common; partnership; corporation; joint venture; other (§§3.28, 3.29, 3.30)
   b. Will buyer use a nominee or agent? (§§3.19-3.21)
2. Impact on buyer's estate
   a. Purpose of the acquisition (*e.g.*, residence, investment, income, speculation, tax shelter)
   b. Buyer's relevant experience in acquisition, ownership, development, and operation of real property

    c. Tax purposes and consequences (chap 5)

    d. Buyer's program for payment

    (1) Source of deposit

    (2) Source of balance

    (3) Source of deferred payments

    (4) Source of operating expenses

    e. Buyer's remedies if seller breaches (chap 12)

    f. Seller's remedies if buyer breaches (chap 12)

3. The property

    a. Location and description, boundaries and size, source of information (§§8.5-8.9)

    b. Condition of seller's title

    (1) Is seller the record owner?

    (2) Interests held by others

    (3) Covenants, conditions, restrictions, easements, rights of way, servitudes

    (4) Other encumbrances (*e.g.,* judgment liens, mechanics' liens)

    (5) Sources of information

    c. Land

    (1) Inspection of physical condition and extent

    (2) Employment of experts (*e.g.,* civil engineers, soil and water engineers, geologists, well drillers, hydrologists)

    d. Improvements

    (1) Type, description, and size

    (2) Inspection of physical condition

    (3) Employment of experts (*e.g.,* structural engineers, architects, contractors)

    e. Personal property and fixtures

    f. Facilities and appurtenances

    (1) Utilities (*e.g.,* water, gas, electricity, sewage disposal) and the extent of any charge for installation or connection of service

    (2) Community services (*e.g.,* schools, churches, shopping centers, medical facilities)

    (3) Public services (*e.g.,* fire and police protection) and their effect on fire, theft, and casualty insurance rates

    (4) Transportation (*e.g.,* buses, industrial spur, public transportation, highways)

    g. Access to the property

    h. Use for a particular purpose

    i. Future trends and projections, and the employment of experts (*e.g.,* market researchers, accountants, appraisers)

    j. Prior history of the property in seller's hands (*e.g.,* filled land, violations of building codes or zoning ordinances, lot splits)

k. Miscellaneous potential problems
(1) Flooding (FHA, VA, and Flood Control Commission requirements) and use of civil engineers
(2) Possibility of condemnation for redevelopment or other purposes
(3) Seismic (location of faults and fault zones) (§1.48)
4. Proposed terms of purchase
a. Effect of previously signed documents (§§1.32, 1.80)
b. Type of agreement (preferred or required)
(1) Lease (*e.g.*, ground lease, net lease) (§1.61)
(2) Lease with purchase option (§1.63)
(3) Option to purchase (chap 4)
(4) Straight sale (chap 3)
(5) Installment sale (chap 5)
(6) "Like kind" exchange (§1.59)
(7) Installment land contract (§1.65)
(8) Other (§1.58)
c. Purchase price (§§3.47-3.51)
(1) Amount
(2) Method of payment
(3) Security for deferred amounts
(4) Noncash consideration
(5) Allocation of price (to land, improvements, and personal property)
d. Escrow (§3.53; chap 11)
(1) Date of opening and closing
(2) Date of possession
(3) Proration of insurance, taxes, rents, deposits
(4) Name of title company
(5) Preliminary title report and exceptions to title
(6) Title insurance
(7) Expenses of escrow
e. Approval of leases (§§3.106-3.115)
f. Risk of loss (chap 10)
g. Condemnation
Note: For detailed checklist for preparation of purchase and sale agreement, see §§3.42-3.62, 3.72-3.191.
5. Economic factors
a. Financing
(1) Availability of financing in the amount and type needed (*e.g.*, construction, long term (takeout) financing) and at terms desired (*e.g.*, interest rate, amortization, loan fee, prepayment penalties) (chaps 5-6)
(2) Analysis by prospective lender revealing advantages and defects of proposed purchase (§§6.20-6.37)

(3) Items not covered by financing (*e.g.,* profit, overhead)

b. Estimated income

(1) Current rental income

(2) Vacancy factor

(3) Fixed expenses

(4) Allowance for maintenance and repairs

(5) Effect of increases in taxes

c. Intangibles affecting value

(1) Neighborhood trends

(2) Single-purpose property (*e.g.,* garage, warehouse)

(3) Proximity to airfields or noisy highways, hazards, availability of services, future government action, zoning, recorded restrictions

d. Plans for depreciation

(1) Allocation of cost between improvements (depreciable) and land (not depreciable)

(2) Method of depreciation

(3) Anticipated holding period

6. Additional factors (depending on type of property or intended use)

a. Residential property

(1) Financing (chaps 5-6)

  (a) Availability of veteran loan (VA or Cal Vet) (§§5.25, 6.17)

  (b) Mortgage insurance

  (c) Taxes

  (d) Effect of recorded restrictions and zoning on neighborhood trends and buyer's intended use (§§3.96-3.99)

(2) Personal property included in sale (§§3.170-3.173)

b. Agricultural lands

(1) Fertility and productivity

  (a) Production history obtainable from farm cooperative or government agency

  (b) Government crop allotments

  (c) Effect of past practices on future production

  (d) Condition of trees, vines, or other perennial crop producers

(2) Production costs

(3) Water availability and cost

(4) Leases, tenants in possession, and expiration dates of leases (§§3.106-3.115)

c. Subdivision development

(1) Subdivision requirements affecting lot size, recreational facilities, street pattern, dedications, setback requirements, etc.

(2) Zoning and annexation

(3) Availability of tentative map

(4) Offsite improvement costs, including street improvement costs, city fees, connection fees, underground utility fees, and engineering costs

(5) Availability of public services (*e.g.*, police, fire department)

(6) Availability of community services (*e.g.*, school, shopping)

(7) Compliance with environmental requirements, availability and cost of an environmental impact report, availability of a "negative declaration" (§1.46)

(8) Necessity of Coastal Commission approval (§1.46)

(9) Possibility of community resistance

(10) Availability of VA or FHA approval

(11) Possibility of partial condemnation (*e.g.*, freeway, park, school)

d. Commercial, recreational, and industrial property

(1) Market analysis of economic factors

(2) Highway programs, present and anticipated, and population trends

(3) Local market area and its competitive business

(4) Local labor market

(5) Parking facilities available

(6) Existing leases and terms

(7) Zoning

(8) Licenses and permits needed

(9) Use of accountants, market research analysts, and appraisers

(10) Pollution considerations (air, water) (§§1.48, 1.49)

§1.84   VI. SAMPLE INTERVIEWING CHECKLIST FOR PURCHASE OR SALE OF REAL PROPERTY

The checklist in this section is a sample of a form that might be kept in the attorney's office and used in interviewing a client who wishes to buy or sell a parcel of real property. When filled in, it serves both as a source of information about the property and transaction and a reminder of tasks to be completed as the transaction progresses. The attorney should develop his or her own checklists to meet specific office or transaction requirements, perhaps adding relevant items from the buyer and seller checklists in §§1.57 and 1.83. This sample is intended for use when the parties have already decided on a purchase and sale agreement as the format of the transaction; different forms should be developed for exchanges, leases, options, and so forth.

Client: _____ Date: _____

--[Name of property; city and state]--

1. Parties
   a. Buyer _____
   b. Seller _____
   c. Title holder (if different from seller)
      _____

2. Description of property
   a. Name _____
      Location: Street Address _____
                  _____
                  City   _____
                  County   _____
                  State   _____
   b. Type
      Office building _____ Square feet
      Shopping center _____ Square feet
      Apartment _____ Units
      Mobile home park _____ Spaces
      Industrial building _____ Square feet
      Other _____
   c. Legal description (attach)

3. Condition of title
   a. Interests held by others than seller _____
   b. Title exceptions
      (1) Easements, rights of way, servitudes _____
      (2) Covenants, conditions, and restrictions (CC & Rs) _____
      (3) Other encumbrances (*e.g.,* judgment liens, lis pendens, mechanics' liens)

4. Construction
   a. Status
      (1) Completed new _____ (Date)
          Completed used _____ (Date)
      (2) Under construction, to be completed
          Before closing _____ (Date)
          After closing _____ (Date)
      (3) Construction not started _____
          To start
          Before closing _____ (Date)
          After closing _____ (Date)

b. Construction plans and specifications (important in all cases except used property)

    Architect _____

    Title _____

    Page nos. and dates _____

c. General contractor _____

    Name and address _____

    Subcontractors _____

    Names and addresses _____

    (Make separate list)

d. Building Permit—Dated _____

e. Use Permit—Dated _____

5. Purchase and loan terms

  a. Deposit: Amount _____

           When paid _____

           To whom paid _____

  b. Purchase price _____

    Payable _____ First loan

            _____ Second loan

            _____ Third loan

            _____ Cash at closing

            _____ Deposit application

            _____ Other

  c. Other consideration

    Prepaid interest _____

    Points _____

    Prepaid expenses _____

    Other _____

  d. Allocation

            _____ Land

            _____ Buildings

            _____ Personal property

  e. Third party loan details

    (1) Existing first loan

        Lender

        Name _____

        Branch _____

        Address _____

        Loan number _____

        Attention _____

        Amount _____

        Note—Date _____

Deed of trust—Date _____
                   Book _____
                   Page _____
Acceleration clause
                   Yes _____
                   No _____
To be: ☐ Assumed
       ☐ Taken subject to _____
       ☐ Paid off
Monthly payments _____
Term and due date _____

(2) Existing second, third, etc., loan (furnish same data as for first)

_____
_____

(3) New loans—third party lenders
Lender
Name _____
Branch _____
Address _____
Attention _____
Loan number _____
Written commitment dated _____
Verbal commitment received
from _____ on _____ by _____
Terms
   Amount _____
   Points _____
   Fees _____
      (Borrower usually pays title insurance premiums and coun-
      sel fees)
   Points and fees paid by
      ☐ Seller
      ☐ Buyer
   Loan constant _____
   Term _____
   Interest rate _____
   Monthly payments _____
f. Seller loan details
(1) Status (second, third, wraparound) _____
   Amount _____
   Interest rate _____
   Payments _____
   Offset rights (against lease) _____

Earn-out provisions _____

(Use separate sheet if necessary)
(2) Status (second, third, wraparound) _____
   Amount _____
   Interest rate _____
   Payments _____

Offset rights (against lease) _____

Earn-out provisions _____

(Use separate sheet if necessary)
6. Warranties of seller
Operating statements correct _____
Projections based on best knowledge _____
Building permit, zoning, use permit, environmental report all proper
_____
Construction meets all codes _____
Construction in accord with plans and specifications _____
Rent roll accurate _____
Tenant leases all in effect according to terms _____
Seller's financial statements correct and no material adverse changes to
   date or anticipated _____
Title in name of seller _____
No outside brokers or finders _____
Condition of building
   Roof watertight _____
   Mechanical _____
   Foundation _____
   Other _____
Personal property free and clear, all onsite _____
7. Conditions of buyer's obligation
Item: Time to satisfy:
   Physical inspection   _____
   Operating income/expenses   _____
   Seller's financial condition   _____
   Plans and specifications   _____
   Title exceptions   _____
   Tenant leases   _____
   Loan assumable   _____
   Financing available   _____
   Acquisition committee approval _____

8. Escrow
   a. Holder
      Name _____
      Address _____
      _____

   b. Title insurer
      Name _____
      Address _____
      _____

9. Closing
   Time _____
   Place _____
   Title insurance premiums: Seller/Buyer
   Escrow fee: Seller/Buyer
   Transfer tax: Seller/Buyer
   Prorate taxes, rents, as of _____

2

Robert D. Lynch

The Broker

ROBERT D. LYNCH, A.B., 1966 University of California (Los Angeles); J.D., 1972, Loyola University of Los Angeles School of Law. Mr. Lynch (1943-1978) was a member of the firm of Agnew, Miller & Carlson, Los Angeles.

I. REGULATION OF BROKERS

§2.1   **A. Statutory Requirements**

The California real property brokerage industry is regulated by statute (Bus & P C §§10000-10602, commonly known as the Real Estate Law) and by administrative regulations adopted by the Real Estate Commissioner (10 Cal Adm C §§2700-2785; 2830-3013). Under this regulatory scheme, it is unlawful for any person to act as a real estate broker or salesperson without first obtaining a license from the Department of Real Estate (Bus & P C §10130). See §§2.2-2.6 for a discussion of activities that require a broker's license. A violation of these license requirements can be prosecuted by the district attorney of the county in which it occurs (Bus & P C §10130) and is punishable as a misdemeanor (Bus & P C §10139). In addition, a person seeking to recover compensation for services as a broker must plead and prove the existence of a valid license at the time the services were rendered. Bus & P C §10136; *Fellom v Adams*

(1969) 274 CA2d 855, 79 CR 633. See §2.30 for a discussion on license as a prerequisite to recovery of the broker's commission.

§2.2   B. Activities Requiring a License

A real estate broker within the meaning of the licensing laws is a person who performs any of the following acts for another for compensation:

(1) Sells or offers to sell, or buys or offers to buy, real property (Bus & P C §10131(a));

(2) Solicits prospective sellers or buyers, solicits or obtains listings, or negotiates for the purchase, sale, or exchange of real property (Bus & P C §10131(a));

(3) Leases or rents, offers to lease or rent, solicits listings of places to rent or prospective tenants, collects rents, or negotiates the sale, purchase, or exchange of leases of real property (Bus & P C §10131(b));

(4) Assists or offers to assist in filing an application for purchase or lease of lands owned by the state or federal government (Bus & P C §10131(c));

(5) Charges an advance fee in connection with various specified activities relating to the sale or lease of real property (Bus & P C §10131.2);

(6) Engages in various categories of activities relating to the sale of mobile homes (Bus & P C §§10131.6, 10131.7);

(7) Collects payments or performs other services for borrowers, lenders, or note owners in connection with loans secured by liens on real property (Bus & P C §10131(d); see also §2.3 on loan brokering activities);

(8) Sells or offers to sell, buys or offers to buy, or exchanges or offers to exchange, real property sales contracts or promissory notes secured by real property, either as agent or principal (Bus & P C §§10131(e), 10131.1).

In addition, a number of related types of brokering activities require a real estate broker's license. These activities are discussed in §§2.3-2.6.

A person need not be in the business of real estate brokering, nor have completed even one transaction, to be subject to the licensing requirements of the Real Estate Law. Anyone who offers, sells, negotiates, or does any of the other acts described in Bus & P C

§10131 in expectation of compensation must be licensed. *Rench v Harris* (1947) 79 CA2d 125, 179 P2d 341; *Kornman v Nelson* (1927) 83 CA 616, 257 P 150.

C. Specialized Licensees

§2.3   1. Mortgage Loan Brokers

A real estate broker's license is required for any person who solicits borrowers or lenders for or negotiates loans secured directly or collaterally by liens on real property. Bus & P C §10131(d). In addition to the requirement that mortgage loan brokers obtain a real estate broker license, their activities are regulated under the Real Property Loan Law (Bus & P C §§10240-10248.9) and regulations adopted by the Real Estate Commissioner (10 Cal Adm C §§2840-2849.7).

The Real Property Loan Law protects the borrower by limiting the fees which may be charged on covered loans and by requiring detailed and specific disclosure of loan charges. Most of its provisions are applicable only to loans of less than $20,000 secured by first deeds of trust of less than $10,000 if secured by junior liens. Bus & P C §10245. The charge that can be imposed for brokerage costs and expenses including appraisal fees, escrow, title, notary, recording, and credit investigation in a mortgage loan subject to regulation is limited to the greater of 5 percent of the principal amount of the loan or $195 and in no event may exceed $325. Bus & P C §10242(a). The law also requires that the broker deliver to the borrower a detailed mortgage loan disclosure statement in the form prescribed by the Department of Real Estate which discloses the amount of commissions and all other costs charged to the borrower in making the loan. Bus & P C §§10240, 10241; 10 Cal Adm C §2840. Because mortgage loan brokers are required to be licensed real estate brokers (Bus & P C §10131(d)), the Real Estate Commissioner has jurisdiction over their operations and can suspend or revoke a license for violations of the law or the regulations. Statutes and regulations also impose special limitations on advertising (Bus & P C §§10248.7-10248.9; 10 Cal Adm C §§2847.1-2848), interest (Bus & P C §10242(c)), balloon payments (Bus & P C §§10244, 10244.1), and the commissions brokers may charge on covered loans (Bus & P C §10242(b)).

A mortgage loan broker owes a fiduciary duty to the borrower, including a duty to draw the attention of an unsophisticated borrower to the fact that provisions of the loan may be unfavorable. *Wyatt v Union Mortgage Co.* (1979) 24 C3d 773, 157 CR 392. In *Wyatt,* the broker failed to make an affirmative disclosure of unfavorable terms regarding interest, late charges, and the size of the balloon payment, and the borrowers were awarded punitive damages of $200,000 for this breach of the broker's duty. In *Realty Projects, Inc. v Smith* (1973) 32 CA3d 204, 108 CR 71, the borrowers sought loans within the coverage of the Real Property Loan Law, but were persuaded by the broker to borrow above the applicable regulated loan limit. The court held that the brokers were required to disclose to the borrowers that the commissions and other charges would have been substantially lower if the loans had been within the coverage of the Real Property Loan Law.

Under Proposition 2, adopted in 1979 as an amendment to California Constitution art XV, §1, real estate brokers who make or arrange loans secured by real property are exempt from usury limitations. How this amendment will be interpreted legally is unclear, but most of the activities of mortgage loan brokers would seem to fit within almost any definition of arranging loans. See, *e.g.,* Bosko & Larmore, *Practice Under the New California Usury Law,* 55 Cal SBJ 59, 63 (1980). Note that the amendment exempts loans arranged by any brokers, not just mortgage loan brokers.

§2.4   2. Business Opportunity Brokers

Although formerly separately licensed, business opportunity brokers are now required to obtain a real estate broker license. Bus & P C §10131. As defined in the Real Estate Law, the term "business opportunity" includes the sale or lease of the business and goodwill of an existing business enterprise. Bus & P C §10030. A sale of all or substantially all of the assets of a corporation, partnership, or sole proprietorship is considered a business opportunity and the sale of all or substantially all the shares of a corporation may also be considered one. *Meisner v Reliance Steel & Aluminum Co.* (9th Cir 1959) 273 F2d 49.

§2.5   3. Real Property Securities Dealers

A real property securities dealer must have a real estate broker license with a special endorsement by the Real Estate Commissioner. Bus & P C §10237.3. A person comes within this requirement who, acting as either principal or agent, engages in the business of (a) selling real property securities as defined in Bus & P C §10237.1(a), or (b) offering to accept, or accepting, funds for continual reinvestment in real property securities, or for placement in a plan under which the dealer implies that a return will be derived from a real property sales contract or a promissory note secured by a lien on real property when the terms of the note or contract do not so provide. Bus & P C §10237. For specific securities, the detailed definition in Bus & P C §10237.1 should be reviewed. The distinctive feature of a real property security is that its sale includes an agreement by either dealer or principal to guarantee or pay the obligation in the event of default, in addition to the secured note or contract itself. Bus & P C §10237.1(a). Like mortgage loan brokers, real property securities dealers are required to make detailed disclosures of relevant information regarding the instrument being sold and the real property security. Bus & P C §10237.5. The Real Estate Commissioner has issued regulations concerning the activities of real property securities dealers. 10 Cal Adm C §§2975-2980.

§2.6   4. Real Estate Syndicate Securities Dealers

A real estate broker license is required for any person who, for compensation, issues or sells, solicits prospective sellers or buyers of, solicits or obtains listings of, or negotiates the purchase, sale, or exchange, of any interest in a general or limited partnership, joint venture, or unincorporated association, owned by no more than 100 persons and formed for the sole purpose of, and engaged solely in, investment in real property. Bus & P C §10131.3; Corp C §25206. A person dealing in such securities normally would be subject to licensing requirements as a "broker-dealer" by the Commissioner of the Department of Corporations (Corp C §§25210-25220), but is exempt if licensed as a broker under the Real Estate Law (Corp C §25206). Conversely, a broker-dealer licensed under the Corporate Securities Law of 1968 (Corp C §§25000-25804) is exempted from the requirement of obtaining a real estate broker license for dealing in real estate syndicate securities. Bus & P C §10131.3.

§2.7   D. Exemptions From Licensing Requirements

A person who performs any of the activities described in §§2.3-2.4 and §2.6 with respect to his or her own property is exempt from the licensing requirements of the Real Estate Law; generally, a real estate broker license is required only for activities undertaken on behalf of others. Bus & P C §§10131, 10133(a); see, *e.g., Robinson v Murphy* (1979) 96 CA3d 763, 158 CR 246; *McGaughey v Fox* (1979) 94 CA3d 645, 156 CR 593. Caution must be exercised, however, because a few specifically enumerated activities require a license even when the individual is acting as principal. For example, a person who engages as a principal in the business of buying, selling, or exchanging with the public real property sale contracts or notes secured by liens on real property, must be licensed as a broker. Bus & P C §10131.1; see §2.2. The term "in the business" is defined to mean the acquisition for resale, or the sale or exchange with the public of eight or more sale contracts or notes during a calendar year. Bus & P C §10131.1. A real property securities dealer (see §2.5) is required to be licensed, even for activities undertaken as principal. Bus & P C §10237.

All of the following are also specifically exempted from licensing requirements:

(1) A corporate officer who functions as broker with respect to the corporation's property without receiving any special compensation (Bus & P C §10133(a));

(2) An attorney acting as such (Bus & P C §§10133(c), 10133.1(f));

(3) A receiver, trustee in bankruptcy, or any person acting under a court order (Bus & P C §10133(d));

(4) A trustee selling under a deed of trust (Bus & P C §10133(e));

(5) A person holding a power of attorney from the owner (Bus & P C §10133(b));

(6) Resident managers of apartment buildings, managers of hotels, motels, or trailer parks, and their employees, with respect to the rental activities specified in Bus & P C §10131(b) (Bus & P C §10131.01);

(7) A stenographer, bookkeeper, receptionist, telephone operator, or other clerical worker, while functioning as such (Bus & P C §10133.2).

The following are exempt from broker licensing requirements in connection with their activities in lending and in purchasing and selling promissory notes and real property sales contracts:

(1) Banks, trust companies, savings and loan companies, pension trusts, credit unions, and insurance companies, and their employees (Bus & P C §§10133.1(a), 10133.1(j));

(2) A lender making a loan guaranteed or insured by a federal agency (Bus & P C §10133.1(b));

(3) Agricultural cooperatives and marketing entities (Bus & P C §§10133.1(c), 10133.1(d));

(4) A corporation securing credit or money from a federal intermediate credit bank (Bus & P C §10133.1(e));

(5) A licensed personal property broker (Bus & P C §10133.1(g));

(6) A cemetery authority (Bus & P C §10133.1(h)).

A finder is also exempt from broker licensing requirements. See §2.10.

§2.8   E. Licensing Qualifications

Brokers and salespersons must pass a written examination in order to obtain a real estate license. Bus & P C §10153. An applicant for a broker's license must also meet an experience qualification in one of two ways: (1) by holding a salesperson's license for at least two years and having qualified for renewal within a five-year period preceding the application; or (2) by having the equivalent of at least two years of general real estate experience or having a degree from a four-year college or university course with a specialty in real estate. Bus & P C §10150.6. In addition, the broker applicant must meet certain specific educational requirements (Bus & P C §§10153.2, 10153.4, and 10153.5), and may also be required to submit proof of his or her honesty and truthfulness. Bus & P C §10152.

Licenses for both brokers and salespersons are issued for a four-year period, subject to renewal on payment of the required fee. Bus & P C §§10153.6, 10153.7. After January 1981, brokers and salespersons seeking license renewals will have the additional requirement of completion of 45 hours of continuing education courses, seminars, or conferences. Bus & P C §§10170-10171.6.

§2.9   F. Corporations and Partnerships as Licensees

A corporation can be a real estate licensee, and the license issued to it entitles one designated officer to act as a broker on behalf of the corporation without payment of any further fee. Bus & P C §10211. If it desires more than one of its officers to act as a broker, it must secure an additional license for each (Bus & P C §10158), and each officer through whom the corporation acts as a licensee must pass the commission's written examination (Bus & P C §10153). Each officer through whom a corporation is licensed may act as a broker as long as employed under the license, but only on behalf of the corporation. Bus & P C §10159.

Under regulations of the Real Estate Commissioner, an officer or director of a corporation shall not be issued a salesperson's license to act on behalf of the corporation. 10 Cal Adm C §2741. In addition, no salesperson's license will be issued to a shareholder to act on behalf of the corporation if (a) the shareholder controls, directly or indirectly, a majority of the outstanding shares of the corporation; or (b) if the aggregate of the shares controlled by the shareholder, and the shares controlled, directly or indirectly, by all other salesperson licensees constitute a majority of the corporation's outstanding shares. 10 Cal Adm C §2741. Notwithstanding these provisions, a corporate officer or employee may be licensed as a salesperson provided that the corporation is licensed as a broker and its chief executive officer is licensed to act as a broker on the corporation's behalf. 10 Cal Adm C §2741.5.

There is no provision for a broker license to be issued to a partnership, but two licensed brokers can form a partnership. Bus & P C §10137.1. A salesperson can act on behalf of a partnership if his or her employing broker is a partner. 10 Cal Adm C §2755.

A broker license may be issued in a fictitious name provided that the broker has first qualified to do business under the fictitious name. Bus & P C §10159.5. A licensee cannot do business under a fictitious name unless the license was issued in that name. 10 Cal Adm C §§2731, 2732.

§2.10   G. Brokers Distinguished From Finders

The finder exception to broker licensing requirements has long been recognized by the California courts. The terms "finder" and "middleman" are used interchangeably to refer to one whose role in a transaction is limited to introducing the parties, leaving it to them to negotiate the terms. *McConnell v Cowan* (1955) 44 C2d 805, 285 P2d 261. A broker, on the other hand, actually plays a role in bringing about a meeting of the minds between the parties (*Eaton v Yount* (1920) 48 CA 221, 191 P 1009). An intermediary who engages in any activity beyond merely arranging an introduction of seller and buyer will be classified as a broker. *Zappas v King Williams Press, Inc.* (1970) 10 CA3d 768, 89 CR 307; *Hasekian v Krotz* (1968) 268

CA2d 311, 74 CR 410; *Abrams v Guston* (1952) 110 CA2d 556, 243 P2d 109. The distinction between broker and finder is important because the finder does not have the fiduciary duty toward the principal that is imposed on the broker. *Batson v Strehlow* (1968) 68 C2d 662, 68 CR 589; *Spielberg v Granz* (1960) 185 CA2d 283, 8 CR 190. See §§2.86-2.102 for a discussion of brokers' fiduciary duties. Moreover, an intermediary who acts as a finder without having a broker license will be able to recover a fee (*Tyrone v Kelley* (1973) 9 C3d 1, 106 CR 761) but one who performs as a broker without being licensed will not (*Hasekian v Krotz, supra*). See §2.30 on a license as a prerequisite to compensation. Because a finder has no fiduciary obligations, courts are reluctant to find that an intermediary is not acting as a broker. *Batson v Strehlow, supra; Zappas v King Williams Press, Inc., supra*. It is hazardous, therefore, to participate as an intermediary in a real property transaction in reliance on being considered a finder rather than a broker.

A further restriction on an intermediary's ability to collect a finder's fee is found in the Real Estate Settlement Procedures Act (RESPA) (12 USC §§2601-2617). Referral fees and fee-splitting are barred in transactions involving four or fewer units that are financed by loans secured by first trust deeds obtained from federally insured lending institutions. 12 USC §2607. Exempted from this prohibition are fees for services actually performed (12 USC §2607(b)) and payments under cooperative broker and referral arrangements or agreements between real estate agents and brokers (12 USC §2607(c)(3)). The latter exemption has yet to be interpreted by the courts, and it is not known whether it exempts any finder's fee paid to a licensed broker or exempts only referrals between brokers in different geographical areas. See 1 Miller & Starr, Current Law of California Real Estate §6:6 (rev ed 1975). See §§11.85-11.89 for a discussion of RESPA.

H. Broker's Relationship With Salespersons

§2.11 1. Salesperson License and Employment Requirements

A natural person employed by a licensed real estate broker to perform any act that requires a broker license is defined as a "salesman" by the Real Estate Law (Bus & P C §10132), and must be licensed by the Department of Real Estate (Bus & P C §10130). Under a 1977 amendment, "salesman" means "salesperson" wherever it is used in the Real Estate Law, and a licensee may refer to the licensed status as salesman, saleswoman, or salesperson. Bus & P C §10017. A salesperson can be employed only by a licensed broker and cannot deal with the public except through that broker. Bus & P C §§10132, 10137; *Grand v Griesinger* (1958) 160 CA2d 397, 325 P2d 475.

A broker cannot employ a person who is not a licensed broker or licensed salesperson to perform acts that require a license. Bus & P C §10137. A salesperson cannot be employed by, or accept compensation from, anyone other than the broker under whom he or she is licensed at the time. Bus & P C §10137; *Hoar v Tuley* (1970) 12 CA3d 344, 90 CR 559. It is also unlawful for a salesperson to pay compensation to any real estate licensee for acts requiring a license, except through the employing broker. Bus & P C §10137.

§2.12 2. Employee or Independent Contractor

A broker must supervise his or her salespersons, and is subject to disciplinary action by the Real Estate Commissioner for failure to do so. Bus & P C §10177(h). This duty to exercise supervisory control over salespersons makes them employees of the broker, and not independent contractors, for purposes of the Real Estate Law (*Gipson v Davis Realty Co.* (1963) 215 CA2d 190, 30 CR 253), and may make them employees for other purposes also. For example, in *Resnik v Anderson & Miles* (1980) 109 CA3d 569, 167 CR 340, the court held that a salesperson was an employee in determining that the Labor Commissioner had jurisdiction under Lab C §98(a) to adjudicate the salesperson's claim for a commission owed him by the broker. Although it is common practice in the real estate industry to identify a salesperson as an independent contractor in the contract of employment (1 Miller & Starr, Current Law of California Real Estate §4:10 (rev ed 1975), this contractual characteristic is not controlling and the salesperson may still be considered an employee. See *Resnik v Anderson & Miles, supra.* The parties' characterization of the relationship is not determinative (*Brown v IAC* (1917) 174 C 457, 163 P 664; *Anderson v Badger* (1948) 84 CA2d 736, 191 P2d 768); the decisive test is generally whether the broker has responsibility for supervision and control (*Baugh v Rogers* (1944) 24 C2d 200, 148 P2d 633; *Burlingham v Gray* (1943) 22 C2d 87, 137 P2d 9).

(a) *Unemployment compensation.* Brokers and real estate salespersons are excluded from the coverage of the California unemployment insurance system if they are paid solely by commission. Un Ins C §650. If a salesperson is paid a salary, coverage turns on whether he or she is an independent contractor or an employee under Un Ins C §601, and this determination depends on the degree of control the employer is able to exercise. See, *e.g., Grant v Woods* (1977) 71 CA3d 647, 139 CR 533. In light of the broker's duty to supervise (Bus & P C §10177(h)), a salaried salesperson would almost certainly be considered an employee for unemployment insurance purposes.

(b) *Workers' compensation.* The status of a real estate salesperson under the California Workers' Compensation Act has not been clearly settled but it seems almost certain that as a general rule, the common law test (existence of the right of control) is also applicable to worker's compensation claims. *Flickenger v IAC* (1919) 181 C 425, 184 P 851; *Esquer v Teresi* (1951) 105 CA2d 89, 232 P2d 895. Under this test, the broker's duty to supervise (Bus & P C §10177(h)) would seem to compel the conclusion that the salesperson would be considered an employee. The only two cases to consider the issue held real estate salespersons to be employees for workers' compensation purposes under the facts presented (*Brown v IAC, supra; Cameron v Pillsbury* (1916) 173 C 83, 159 P 149), but these cases were decided before enactment of the Real Estate Law.

(c) *Income and social security taxes.* There has also been no definitive ruling on the status of a California salesperson with respect to the employer's obligation to withhold income and social security taxes. These payments must be withheld from compensation paid employees, but not independent contractors. IRC §§3121(d)(2), 3306(i)(1). In 1976, the IRS issued two revenue rulings which provided guidelines for making this determination, and which would have treated the salesperson as an employee if the broker had the right and duty to exercise supervision and control over the details of the salesperson's work. Rev Rul 76-136, 1976-1 Cum Bull 312; Rev Rul 76-137, 1976-1 Cum Bull 313. These rulings were revoked in 1978 by Rev Rul 78-365, 1978-2 Cum Bull 254, however, and the IRS's earlier position (Mim 6566, 1951-1 Cum Bull 108) was reinstated. Under Mim 6566, the fact that brokers are under a duty to supervise salespersons under statutory requirements and established custom and practice in the industry is not sufficient to establish the status of salespersons as employees: each case is examined on its merits to determine whether close supervision and control in fact exist. The Revenue Act of 1978, § 530 (Pub L 95-600, 92 Stat 2885 (1978), as amended by Pub L 96-167, 93 Stat 1278 (1979)) imposes a moratorium on IRS regulations and rulings regarding employee status through December 31, 1980. It is expected that Congress will extend the moratorium and eventually adopt legislation clarifying factors for determining employee status for withholding purposes.

See also 59 Ops Cal Atty Gen 369 (1976) which concluded that Bus & P C § 10177(h) probably imposes a sufficient measure of control on the broker to make the salesperson an employee for income and social security tax purposes.

(d) *Tort liability.* Under the common law doctrine of respondeat superior, brokers are liable for torts committed by their salespersons within the course and scope of their employment. Tort liability turns not on a determination that the salesperson is an employee as opposed to an independent contractor, but rather on the holding that, for tort purposes, a salesperson is the broker's agent as a matter of law. *Gipson v Davis Realty Co., supra.*

I. Broker as Escrow Agent

§2.13   1. License Requirements

Escrow agents are regulated by the California Escrow Law (Fin C §§ 17000-17654), and are required to obtain a license from the Corporations Commissioner (Fin C § 17200). Real estate brokers are exempt from these requirements while performing acts in the course of or incidental to a real estate transaction in which the broker is an agent or a party and performs an act for which a license is required. Fin C § 17600(d). A broker may act as an escrow agent without an escrow license in a transaction in which he or she is also acting as a broker (54 Ops Cal Atty Gen 13 (1971)) but must obtain a license in order to act as an escrow agent in a transaction in which he or she is not providing broker services (43 Ops Cal Atty Gen 284 (1964)). When acting under Fin C § 17006(d), the broker may charge a separate fee for the escrow services. 44 Ops Cal Atty Gen 105 (1964). The Real Estate Commissioner has issued regulations concerning a broker's handling of funds as an escrow agent (10 Cal Adm C § 2833), and a broker's action in handling an escrow (10 Cal Adm C § 2950).

§2.14   2. Decision To Use

The decision whether to use a broker-affiliated escrow company must be carefully weighed. Generally, the escrow departments of banks or large title companies have greater resources and can provide a wider range of ancillary services than are available at a smaller, broker-owned escrow company. A smaller escrow holder, on the other hand, may be able to provide more individualized and prompter service. Counsel generally advise against permitting brokers to act as both broker and escrow agent in the same transaction because of the difficulty in differentiating between the broker's fiduciary obligation to his or her principal (see §§2.86-2.102) and the escrow holder's fiduciary duties to both parties (see *Colonial Sav. & Loan Ass'n v Redwood Empire Title Co.* (1965) 236 CA2d 186, 46 CR 16; *Spaziani v Millar* (1963) 215 CA2d 667, 30 CR 658).

(Attorneys are also exempted from the licensing requirements of the Escrow Law (Fin C §17006(b)), but should exercise caution about the conflicting duties which would arise from acting as both escrow agent and attorney in the same transaction.)

II. RETAINING A BROKER

§2.15   A. Advantages

The primary advantage in engaging a broker in a real property sales transaction is the addition of the broker's professional skill and expertise to the pursuit of prospective buyers or sellers. Because of his or her knowledge of the local market, the broker is in a singular position to provide accurate information on current real property values and advice on how best to offer a seller's property or locate property to meet a buyer's needs. Brokers perform many routine functions such as obtaining title reports and distributing documents for review and execution. They also generally provide advice and assistance to the parties in negotiating the terms of the transaction. Depending on the circumstances of the particular transaction, the broker may also offer highly sophisticated services, such as:

(1) Preparing, or arranging for preparation of, reports, surveys, and other compilations of data to assist the parties in evaluating the physical condition of the property;

(2) Compiling business and financial information, such as cash flow analysis data, to facilitate evaluation of the income potential of the property;

(3) Assisting in evaluating the state of title and in clearing defects or removing existing encumbrances;

(4) Suggesting various financing methods to enhance the property's marketability or to meet special needs of the parties;

(5) Working out the details of real property exchanges as an alternative to cash purchases.

§2.16   B. Disadvantages

The obvious disadvantage of including a broker in a transaction is that the broker's commission, although subject to negotiation, will always be a significant expense of the sale. See §2.41 on the amount of the commission. Even though the seller usually pays the commission, the amount will affect the buyer to the extent that it is a factor in the seller's calculation of an acceptable sale price.

For some properties, the existence of a large group of potential buyers and the simplicity of the transaction may make the broker's commission a needless expense. When attractive property is offered, market values are known, the seller's price expectations are realistic, and there is no time pressure, the seller's attorney might suggest that the seller attempt to market the property without a broker.

§2.17   C. Selecting a Broker

The services brokers offer, and their expertise, experience, knowledge of the market, and charges, vary greatly. A prospective buyer or seller should look for a broker who will be able to fulfill his or her specific needs. In selecting a broker, a buyer or seller should consider the following factors:

(1) Whether the broker is familiar with the area in which the property is located. A local broker is likely to be well informed regarding prospective buyers or sellers in the area, the advantages and disadvantages of the area and of a particular parcel, local real property values, and available sources of financing;

(2) Whether the broker is experienced in handling the type of property under consideration (e.g., industrial, commercial, subdivision) and the type of transaction contemplated (e.g., a commercial lease, or an exchange). A broker who specializes in particular kinds of properties will probably know of prospective buyers or sellers and of available financing for that type of property. If the transaction will be complex or unusual, it is important that the broker have sufficient expertise in that type of transaction to be able to understand and meet the principal's needs;

(3) Whether a large or small brokerage office would better suit the principal's needs. A large brokerage office may be able to provide specialized expertise and may have branch offices which enable it to have greater familiarity with a number of geographic areas. The staff of a small office may be able to provide more individualized attention to the principal's needs, and to make a more personal and energetic effort. Multiple listing services (see §2.26) enable even small offices to disseminate listing information widely.

The attorney should advise buyer or seller clients that the range of services provided and the broker's compensation are subject to negotiation. Principals frequently want to retain as much flexibility as possible through short term and nonexclusive listings, but this consideration must be weighed against the likelihood that a broker with an exclusive or long term listing will put more effort into the transaction. In commercial transactions, oral understandings and nonexclusive listings are not uncommon. For residential properties, however, brokers generally insist on a written, exclusive, listing agreement, and multiple listing services (see §2.26) generally will not accept anything but an exclusive listing. See §§2.59-2.64 on types of listing agreements; see §§2.46-2.57 on the requirements for a writing.

D. Appointment of an Agent

§2.18   1. Agency Versus Contract Law

The broker-principal relationship is governed by both agency and contract law, and the distinction is one that must be kept in mind by all parties to a transaction. Although the broker's right to compensation depends on the existence of a written agreement (CC §1624(5); see §§2.46-2.57), an agency relationship may be created without either consideration (CC §2308; *Leno v YMCA* (1971) 17 CA3d 651, 95 CR 96) or a writing (*Steiner v Rowley* (1950) 35 C2d 713, 221 P2d 9; *Beeler v West Am. Fin. Co.* (1962) 201 CA2d 702, 20 CR 190). Thus, a broker without an enforceable contractual claim for a commission may still be subject to the fiduciary duties of the principal-agent relationship, breach of which may render the broker liable in damages (*Steiner v Rowley, supra; Beeler v West Am. Fin. Co., supra*) or subject to disciplinary action by the Real Estate Commissioner (*Buckley v Savage* (1960) 184 CA2d 18, 7 CR

328). Moreover, the actions of the agent may bind the principal even though there is no written contract of employment. See §§2.20-2.22.

§2.19   2. Creation of the Agency

The agency relationship can be created in three ways: (1) by agreement of the parties, express or implied (§2.20); (2) by ratification of previously unauthorized acts of the agent (§2.21); or (3) by estoppel (or ostensible agency) (§2.22). California's statutory provisions substantially codify common law agency principles. CC §§2295-2369.

§2.20   a. Agency by Express or Implied Agreement

An agency is generally created by an express agreement, sometimes referred to as precedent authorization. CC §§2299, 2307. No special formalities are required for the creation of an agency, however, and the existence of an agency relationship may be inferred from the actions of the parties. *Zander v Texaco, Inc.* (1968) 259 CA2d 793, 66 CR 561; *Vargas v Ruggiero* (1961) 197 CA2d 709, 17 CR 568; *Whiteman v Leonard Realty Co.* (1961) 189 CA2d 373, 11 CR 211. Although no formalities are required, the parties must intend that the relationship exist and this intent must be disclosed either by their express agreement or their actions. *Nizuk v Gorges* (1960) 180 CA2d 699, 4 CR 565.

Written authorization is generally not required for the creation of an agency relationship (CC §2309), but under the equal dignities rule an agent must be authorized in writing to enter into a contract that is itself required to be in writing (CC §2309). Brokers are rarely authorized by their principals to enter into real property purchase agreements or to execute conveyances or other documents that are required to be in writing under the statute of frauds.

The existence of an agency is a question of fact for the trial court. *Skopp v Weaver* (1976) 16 C3d 432, 128 CR 19; *Leno v YMCA* (1971) 17 CA3d 651, 95 CR 96. California courts have demonstrated an inclination to find the existence of an agency relationship when protection of the seller against injury necessitates imposition of a fiduciary obligation on the broker. *Skopp v Weaver, supra*; *Hale v Wolfsen* (1969) 276 CA2d 285, 81 CR 23; *Weber v Tonini* (1957) 151 CA2d 168, 311 P2d 132; *Baker v Van Dolzer* (1956) 142 CA2d 428, 298 P2d 86. In *Skopp v Weaver, supra*, 16 C3d at 440, 128 CR at 24, the supreme court observed that: "No California decision has held a realtor exempt from fiduciary obligation to the seller when the realtor has in fact acted to the seller's detriment."

§2.21   b. Agency by Ratification

An agency may also be created when the principal ratifies previously unauthorized actions. CC §2307. Ratification results when the purported agent has held himself out as representing the principal (*Anderson v Fay Improvement Co.* (1955) 134 CA2d 738, 286 P2d 513), and the principal then accepts the benefits of the purported agent's actions (CC §2310; *Rakestraw v Rodrigues* (1972) 8 C3d 67, 104 CR 57). The third party is bound only when ratification occurs and may withdraw at any prior time. 1 Witkin, Summary of California Law, *Agency and Employment* §82 (8th ed 1973).

The equal dignities rule (CC §2309) applies to ratification (CC §2310); when the purported agent's act comes within the statute of frauds, ratification must be in writing. *Moore v Hoar* (1938) 27 CA2d 269, 81 P2d 226. Although a principal can ratify any act that he could have authorized in the first instance, he cannot ratify a void contract or one that is against public policy. *Davis v Chipman* (1930) 210 C 609, 293 P 40.

§2.22   c. Ostensible Agency

Agency by estoppel, or ostensible agency, results when the principal either intentionally or negligently causes a third party to believe that another person is his agent. CC §2300. The California courts have always treated ostensible agency as resting on estoppel principles. *Lee v Helmco, Inc.* (1962) 199 CA2d 820, 19 CR 413; *Keppelman v Heikes* (1952) 111 CA2d 475, 245 P2d 54.

Unlike agency by ratification (§2.21), ostensible agency rests on statements or acts of the principal that lead a third party to believe that the agency relationship exists. CC §2300; *Lee v Helmco, Inc., supra*; *Hill v Citizens Nat'l Trust & Sav. Bank* (1937) 9 C2d 172, 69 P2d 853. Ostensible agency theory has been invoked to permit a seller to recover from a brokerage firm for the actions of a nonmember broker who occupies space in the firm's offices and shares commissions. *Peterson v Ryan* (1951) 108 CA2d 41, 238 P2d 117; *Vigli v Davis* (1947) 79 CA2d 237, 179 P2d 586.

§2.23   3. Special or General Agent

A special agent is one who is retained only for a specific act or transaction; all others are general agents. CC §2297. A real estate broker is generally retained only for a particular transaction, and is thus generally a special agent. *Rhode v Bartholomew* (1949) 94 CA2d 272, 210 P2d 768. A broker who represents the same principal in a number of transactions does not become a general agent if the authority conferred in each transaction is limited. *Kruger v Vernon* (1925) 73 CA 476, 238 P 1062.

§2.24   4. The Problem of Dual Agency

Although the broker's commission is generally paid by the seller, he may be the buyer's agent for some purposes (*Wolf v Price* (1966) 244 CA2d 165, 52 CR 889; *Bonaccorso v Kaplan* (1963) 218 CA2d 63, 32 CR 69), and this dual role is the source of many disputes and potential breaches of fiduciary duty (see §2.90). Normally the broker is the agent of the party first employing him. *Stephens v Ahrens* (1919) 179 C 743, 178 P 863. Frequently, however, a real estate transaction involves two principals and just one broker who was originally retained by one of the parties but who works with both in attempting to complete the sale. In this situation, the broker may be the seller's agent for one purpose, and the buyer's agent for another purpose. *Bonaccorso v Kaplan, supra; Sartern v Pomatto* (1961) 192 CA2d 288, 13 CR 588. When one party has retained the broker, an agency relationship between the broker and the other party may arise from the broker's acceptance of duties and responsibilities to that party. See, *e.g., Wright v Lowe* (1956) 140 CA2d 891, 296 P2d 34 (broker's agreement to convey buyer's counteroffer to seller made him buyer's agent for that purpose); *Wolf v Price, supra* (seller's broker held to be buyer's agent for purpose of approving title exceptions); *Whiteman v Leonard Realty Co.* (1961) 189 CA2d 373, 11 CR 211 (buyer's broker held to be seller's agent in undertaking to transmit escrow instructions). In the absence of other factors, payment of a commission is strong evidence of the existence of an agency relationship between the broker and the one who pays him. *Standard Realty & Dev. Co. v Ferrera* (1957) 151 CA2d 514, 311 P2d 855; *Angus v London* (1949) 92 CA2d 282, 206 P2d 869.

5. Broker's Authority To Appoint Subagents

§2.25   a. Statutory Authority

An agent cannot employ subagents to act on behalf of the principal except in the following instances:

(1) When the subagent's act is purely mechanical;

(2) When the agent cannot, and the subagent can, lawfully perform an act (*e.g.*, notarization);

(3) When local usage permits delegation of the subagent's act;

(4) When the principal specially authorizes delegation of the power to do the act in question. CC §2349.

Thus, the listing agreement will generally be the key factor in determining whether a broker is authorized to employ subagents. See §2.74 for a form provision giving the broker this authority.

§2.26   b. Subagents Through Multiple Listing Services

Many listing agreements contain a provision authorizing the broker to appoint other brokers or salespersons as subagents through the device of a multiple listing service. See §2.74. Multiple listing services are products of regional agreements among brokers in which each agrees to refer multiple listings to other real estate licensees through a central information exchange. The service compiles and publishes listings submitted by participating brokers. If the buyer is procured by a subagent, or cooperating broker, the commission is divided.

Multiple listing services traditionally limited access to their listings to their members or those of their sponsoring boards of realtors, but recent case law has held that restrictions on access to the service violate the Cartwright Anti-Trust Act (Bus & P C §§16700-16758). *Marin Bd. of Realtors v Palsson* (1976) 16 C3d 920, 130 CR 1; *Glendale Bd. of Realtors v Hounsell* (1977) 72 CA3d 210, 139 CR 830. See Comment, *Exclusion from Real Estate Multiple Listing Services as Anti-Trust Violations*, 14 Cal W L Rev 298 (1978). The precise impact of these holdings on multiple listing agreements is yet to be determined, but they seem, at a minimum, to broaden the category of potential cooperating brokers to include all those licensees with access to the multiple listing service, rather than just its members.

§2.27   c. Conflict of Interest

All those persons involved, including the listing and cooperating brokers, need to be aware of the potential problems in the subagency situation. If the seller has authorized his broker to use the services of another broker, when the broker finds a buyer an agency relationship may be created between the seller and the buyer's broker, the subagent. As a result, the subagent owes fiduciary obligations to the seller, and the seller may incur liability to third persons for the acts of the subagent. CC §2351. See §2.118. A subagent's knowledge will be imputed to the seller who is responsible for the acts of the subagent toward a prospective purchaser. *Granberg v Turnham* (1958) 166 CA2d 390, 333 P2d 423; *Johnston v Seargeants* (1957) 152 CA2d 180, 313 P2d 41.

This situation raises serious problems: the subagent identifies much more closely with the buyer, but stands in a fiduciary relationship to the seller; the seller may be liable for the acts of a subagent he has never met. The subagent may, in fact, be an agent of the buyer at the same time that an agency relationship exists with the seller. *Walters v Marler* (1978) 83 CA3d 1, 147 CR 655. See §2.24. This dual relationship, often unperceived, can easily lead to violations of the fiduciary duty owed by the broker to one or the other of the principals in the transaction. *Skopp v Weaver* (1976) 16 C3d 432, 128 CR 19; *Hale v Wolfsen* (1969) 276 CA2d 285, 81 CR 23; see §§2.86-2.102 regarding broker's fiduciary obligations.

Questions remain regarding the liability of an innocent listing broker to either buyer or seller for the misconduct of a subagent. Language in cases in which the listing broker had some involvement in the misconduct suggests that liability might be incurred by an innocent listing broker as well. In *Granberg v Turnham, supra,* a seller was permitted to recover from a listing broker who had herself been negligent, but the court noted that since the subagents were the listing broker's agents, any misrepresentations they made would be imputed to the listing broker. Civil Code §2351 expressly insulates the original agent from liability to a third party (*i.e.,* a buyer) for the acts of a subagent. In *Johnston v Seargeants, supra,* a buyer recovered from a broker and subagent who jointly made misrepresentations on the theory that the representations of one became the representations of both. It has been suggested that this rationale might extend liability to an innocent listing broker for misconduct by a subbroker despite the language of CC §2351. 1 Miller & Starr, Current Law of California Real Estate §4:8 at 20, n10 (rev ed 1975).

§2.28   6. Extent of Broker's Authority

A real estate broker's authority is limited to that actually or ostensibly conferred by the principal. CC §2315. The listing agreement should specify the extent of the broker's authority because an agent is authorized by statute to do everything "necessary or proper and usual" to carry out the purpose of the agency. CC §2319. This very broad implied authority invites disputes about what is proper and usual.

Generally, the broker's authority is limited to negotiating the terms of the transaction and does not include the authority to bind the seller contractually, even if the buyer makes an unconditional offer on all the terms and conditions required by the listing agreement. *Mason v Mazel* (1947) 82 CA2d 769, 187 P2d 98; *Holland v McCarthy* (1916) 173 C 597, 160 P 1069. Thus, the broker may not deliver the seller's deed to the buyer without specific authority (*Keele v Clouser* (1928) 92 CA 526, 268 P 682), or sign a contract of sale on behalf of the principal (*Lyne v Bonner* (1954) 129 CA2d 743, 277 P2d 941). Only the principal, and not a third party, can raise the broker's lack of authority. *Mitchell v Locurto* (1947) 79 CA2d 507, 179 P2d 848.

A broker is almost never given express authority to accept the purchase price, as distinguished from the deposit (see §2.70), on behalf of the seller. *Sarten v Pomatto* (1961) 192 CA2d 288, 13 CR 588. Even when the broker is expressly authorized to negotiate the sale, a court will not imply authorization to collect the purchase price. *Ernst v Searle* (1933) 218 C 233, 22 P2d 715. However, if the seller has led the buyer to believe that the agent can receive the purchase price, then ostensible authority exists (see §2.22), and the seller will not be able to recover from the buyer if the broker misappropriates the funds. *Hicks v Wilson* (1925) 197 C 269, 240 P 289; *Sarten v Pomatto, supra*; *Gaine v Austin* (1943) 58 CA2d 250, 136 P2d 584; *Smeade v Rosen* (1932) 121 CA 79, 8 P2d 507. If a broker should receive the purchase price for the seller, he or she must be careful to comply with provisions of the Real Estate Law and regulations of the Real Estate Commissioner regarding brokers' handling of clients' funds. Bus & P C §10145; 10 Cal Adm C §§2830-2835.

E. Broker's Compensation

§2.29   1. Prerequisites to Broker's Right to Commission

In order to recover the commission, a broker must show that he or she: (a) is licensed as required by Bus & P C §10130 (§2.30); (b) is authorized in writing by the principal (CC §1624(5); see §§2.46-2.57); and (c) has rendered the services required under the listing agreement (see §§2.31-2.37).

Under all types of listings, the broker must show, at a minimum, the procurement of a buyer "ready, willing, and able" to purchase the property on the terms specified in the listing agreement, unless the seller accepts a nonconforming offer. See §§2.33-2.36. The listing agreement may impose additional requirements that must be met before the broker is entitled to the commission. See §2.31.

Under an open listing (see §2.62), the broker must be the "procuring cause" of the contract between seller and buyer to earn the commission. Under an exclusive agency listing (§2.61), the broker is entitled to the commission unless the seller was the procuring cause. Under the exclusive right to sell listing (see §2.59), the broker need not be the procuring cause. See §2.32 for a discussion of procuring cause.

The buyer's broker in the usual transaction, often called a "cooperating broker" (see §2.26), has to satisfy additional requirements in order to recover compensation. He can sue the seller's (or listing) broker for his share of any commission already paid, and for a declaratory judgment that he is entitled to share in future payments, but he cannot recover from the listing broker any portion of the commission that remains unpaid. *Iusi v Chase* (1959) 169 CA2d 83, 337 P2d 79. The buyer's broker's right to recover from the seller is less clear. At least one case has held that a cooperating broker who procures a ready, willing, and able buyer can recover from the seller directly if the seller refuses to consummate the transaction. *Smith v Wright* (1961) 188 CA2d 790, 10 CR 675.

§2.30   a. Not Recoverable if Unlicensed

An agreement to employ an unlicensed person to perform services that require a real estate license is void and unenforceable. *Fellom v*

Adams (1969) 274 CA2d 855, 79 CR 633. The purpose of the licensing requirements is to protect the public from incompetent and untrustworthy practitioners (*Schantz v Ellsworth* (1971) 19 CA3d 289, 96 CR 783), and, in furtherance of this policy, an unlicensed agent will not be permitted to recover a commission even though the services were rendered and rendered competently (*Davis v Chipman* (1930) 210 C 609, 293 P 40; *Firpo v Murphy* (1925) 72 CA 249, 236 P 968).

In order to recover the commission, a broker must be licensed at the time the services are actually performed (Bus & P C §10136), but it is not necessary that he or she be licensed when the listing is executed (*Wise v Radis* (1925) 74 CA 765, 242 P 90) or when the commission is due (*Cline v Yamaga* (1979) 97 CA3d 239, 158 CR 598; *Page v Principe* (1963) 220 CA2d 151, 33 CR 836; *Koeberle v Hotchkiss* (1935) 4 CA2d 252, 40 P2d 911). If the broker is unlicensed when the services are performed and the commission is paid in the form of a promissory note, the broker cannot recover on the note. *Hoar v Tuley* (1970) 12 CA3d 344, 90 CR 559. If the services are performed by two people, one of whom is licensed and one of whom is not, neither person can recover compensation. *Estate of Prieto* (1966) 243 CA2d 79, 52 CR 80. A mere finder or middleman can recover a fee without being licensed. See §2.10.

§2.31   b. Provisions of Contract Govern

When a valid listing agreement exists, it is the governing document: the broker's rights and duties arise from it (*Seck v Foulks* (1972) 25 CA3d 556, 102 CR 170), and the broker's right to compensation must be found within its terms (*Blank v Borden* (1974) 11 C3d 963, 115 CR 31; *Seck v Foulks, supra;* see §2.37).

The many reported decisions involving brokers' attempts to collect their commissions underscore the importance of specifying unambiguously in the listing agreement the circumstances under which the commission will be earned. A number of issues are commonly generated in the brokerage situation, and the courts have developed rules for interpreting listing agreements and for determining when the commission is due in the absence of specific provisions in an agreement. The usual issues are: (1) whether the broker was the procuring cause in producing the buyer (§2.32); (2) whether the buyer procured is ready, willing, and able (§§2.33-2.36); (3)

whether payment of the commission is dependent on some event such as the closing (§2.37); (4) whether the commission is due if the seller withdraws the property from the market (§2.38); and (5) whether the commission is due if the sale occurs after the expiration of the listing agreement (§§2.39-2.40). Careful drafting of the listing agreement to specify the conditions that must be satisfied for the commission to be earned should avoid disputes over these issues. See §§2.75-2.77 for sample provisions regarding broker compensation.

§2.32   c. Procuring Cause

Whether a broker is the procuring cause is a question of fact. *Sessions v Pacific Improvement Co.* (1922) 57 CA 1, 206 P 653. "Procuring cause" has been defined as the cause originating a series of events that, without a break in their continuity, result in the contemplated transaction. *Rose v Hunter* (1957) 155 CA2d 319, 317 P2d 1027; *Bail v Glantz* (1926) 78 CA 49, 248 P 258. The broker must set in motion a chain of events that proximately cause the buyer and seller to come to terms. *Nelson v Mayer* (1954) 122 CA2d 438, 265 P2d 52.

Merely being the first person to contact the eventual buyer does not in itself satisfy the procuring cause requirement (*Rose v Hunter, supra*); once the broker has introduced buyer and seller, however, the seller's efforts to exclude the broker from negotiations will not be grounds for denying him the commission (*Justice v Ackerman* (1960) 183 CA2d 649, 6 CR 921; *Vidler v De Bell* (1954) 125 CA2d 326, 270 P2d 120). If seller and buyer agree to delay execution of the purchase agreement until after the listing period has expired with the intent of defeating the broker's claim to being the procuring cause, each may be liable, the seller under the listing agreement, and the buyer in tort. *California Auto Court Ass'n v Cohn* (1950) 98 CA2d 145, 219 P2d 511; see §2.44.

A broker is not the procuring cause, even though he exhibits the property to the buyer, if the eventual buyer is already aware of the property's availability, and the broker is not instrumental in closing the sale. *Fitzpatrick v Underwood* (1941) 17 C2d 722, 112 P2d 3. If there is a good faith break in the continuity of the negotiations that prevents the broker from showing that the buyer and seller came to terms as a proximate result of his efforts, the broker then would not be the procuring cause. *Nelson v Mayer, supra,* 122 CA2d 438, 265 P2d 52.

If the listing agreement provides that the commission will be paid only on completion of the sale, the fact that the broker is the procuring cause of an acceptable buyer is not sufficient to entitle him to compensation. See §2.37. Unless there is such a condition in the listing agreement, however, the conclusion of a sale is not necessary; the broker is considered the procuring cause, and entitled to compensation, if he brings the parties together so that they can enter into a contract whether or not the sale occurs. *Woodbridge Realty v Plymouth Dev. Corp.* (1955) 130 CA2d 270, 278 P2d 713.

If a broker has an exclusive right to sell listing (see §2.59), a sale to any party, even if to one procured by the seller, entitles the broker to compensation. In an exclusive agency listing (see §2.61), the broker must prove that someone other than the seller was the procuring cause of the sale. Under an open listing agreement (see §2.62), the broker must prove that he alone, and no other party including the seller or any other broker, brought buyer and seller together. Thus, being the procuring cause is particularly important for a broker under an open listing or comparable situation in which several brokers may be showing the property and a prospective buyer may be contacted by other brokers. If more than one broker has contributed to completing the sale, the broker seeking the commission must prove that his activities were the predominant cause in bringing about the transaction. *Sessions v Pacific Improvement Co., supra.* When procuring cause may be an issue, as in an open or exclusive agency listing, broker should immediately notify seller, in writing, names of prospective buyers whom he has contacted.

d. Ready, Willing, and Able Buyer

§2.33   (1) Basic Considerations

The basic condition that must be satisfied by the broker under any listing agreement is the procuring of a buyer who is ready, willing, and able to purchase the property on the terms provided in the listing agreement. The agreement may require that further conditions be met before the commission is earned. See §§2.31, 2.37.

Satisfaction of the ready and willing requirements turns on whether the buyer's offer meets all of the material terms and conditions of the listing agreement (see §2.34). *Prather v Vasquez* (1958) 162 CA2d 198, 327 P2d 963. A buyer is able when he or she has the legal capacity and financial ability to purchase the property. The broker has the burden of proving the buyer's ability to purchase the property under the listing agreement's terms. *Herring v Fisher* (1952) 110 CA2d 322, 242 P2d 963. Financial ability means that the buyer has sufficient resources available to conclude the sale. *Russell v Ramm* (1927) 200 C 348, 254 P 532; *Merzoian v Kludjian* (1920) 183 C 422, 191 P 673. The buyer need not have cash on hand when the offer is made, but must have sufficient property, credit, or other assets to be able to obtain the necessary funds at the prescribed time. *Ramsdell v Krehmke* (1928) 95 CA 195, 272 P 333.

§2.34   (2) Offer Rejected by Seller

If the seller refuses to sell the property to a ready, willing, and able buyer, the procuring broker normally will still be entitled to the commission (*Collins v Vickter Manor, Inc.* (1957) 47 C2d 875, 306 P2d 783; *Martin v Culver Enterprises, Inc.* (1966) 239 CA2d 924, 49 CR 149; *Williams v Gaither* (1962) 202 CA2d 308, 20 CR 779), but the broker must be able to prove that the buyer's offer comports with the terms of the listing agreement. If the offer differs materially from the listing agreement, the broker will not be able to recover a commission. *Dea v Davy* (1957) 150 CA2d 435, 309 P2d 894. This test emphasizes the need for a listing agreement that sets forth precisely the important terms of the sale.

Whether an offer differs materially from the listing agreement is a question of fact to be decided in each case. *Rylee v DeFini* (1955) 134 CA2d Supp 877, 285 P2d 115. Provisions of the buyer's offer which have been considered sufficiently at variance with the listing terms to justify rejection by the seller include: a different method of paying the deposit *(Dea v Davy, supra);* a different time for possession (*Adams v Angelich* (1964) 231 CA2d 258, 41 CR 728); inclusion of a liquidated damages provision giving the buyer an inexpensive alternative to performance (*California Land Sec. Co. v Ritchie* (1919) 40 CA 246, 180 P 625); and the inclusion of the right to assume an existing loan against the property (*Cottingham v Smith* (1938) 28 CA2d 345, 82 P2d 479). Whether or not a deviation will be considered material will depend on the intentions and expectations of the parties. *Andrews v Waldo* (1928) 205 C 764, 272 P 1052. The facts of each case must be evaluated; it is risky to rely on past holdings to determine whether certain terms are or are not material.

§2.35   (3) Offer Accepted; Sale Not Completed

Absent a provision in the listing agreement conditioning the commission on consummation of the sale (see §2.37), the broker's commission is earned on execution of an unconditional purchase agreement, even if the sale later fails. *Deeble v Stearns* (1947) 82 CA2d 296, 186 P2d 173. If the offer differs materially from the listing (see §2.34) and the seller's acceptance of the offer is conditional, the conditions must be satisfied before the commission is earned. *Cochran v Ellsworth* (1954) 126 CA2d 429, 272 P2d 904. Similarly, mere execution of a conditional purchase agreement will not entitle the broker to the commission; the conditions must first be satisfied or waived. *Kopf v Milam* (1963) 60 C2d 600, 35 CR 614.

If the transaction fails because of the seller's breach or inability to perform, after acceptance of a conforming offer, the broker is entitled to the commission. For example, sellers have been held liable for the commission when they are unable to deliver marketable title (*Coulter v Howard* (1927) 203 C 17, 262 P 751), and when a spouse or joint tenant refuses to join in the transfer (*McAlinden v Nelson* (1953) 121 CA2d 136, 262 P2d 627; *Contant v Wallace* (1923) 62 CA 768, 217 P 1081). On the broker's right to the deposit in the event of the buyer's failure to perform, see §2.42.

§2.36   (4) Nonconforming or Conditional Offer Accepted

If the parties execute a purchase agreement on terms different from those in the listing agreement, the seller is presumed to have consented to the variance in terms. *Lathrop v Gauger* (1954) 127 CA2d 754, 274 P2d 730. If the offer was unconditional or the conditions have been satisfied, the broker is no longer required to prove the readiness, willingness, or ability of the buyer in order to earn the commission (*Caine v Briscoe* (1926) 78 CA 660, 248 P 774) unless fraud by broker or buyer was used in inducing the seller's acceptance (*Wright v Buzzine* (1960) 180 CA2d 426, 4 CR 482). Unless the listing agreement specifies consummation of the sale as a condition to payment of the commission, a seller who accepts a nonconforming, unconditional offer is liable for the commission if the buyer refuses to perform. *Jauman v McCusick* (1913) 166 C 517, 137 P 254; *Beazell v Kane* (1954) 127 CA2d 593, 274 P2d 224.

If the purchase agreement is subject to conditions, the broker is not entitled to compensation until the conditions have been satisfied or waived. *Kopf v Milam* (1963) 60 C2d 600, 35 CR 614. If a condition for the benefit of the buyer is waived or satisfied, the seller becomes liable for the commission whether or not he is willing to complete the transaction with the buyer. *Wesley N. Taylor Co. v Russell* (1961) 194 CA2d 816, 15 CR 357. If the condition is for the benefit of both buyer and seller, the seller does not become liable for the commission until the conditions are either satisfied or waived by both parties. *Yoakum v Tarver* (1967) 256 CA2d 202, 64 CR 7. If the condition is inserted solely for the benefit of the seller, it must be satisfied or waived by the seller, before the seller becomes liable to the broker for the commission. *Kopf v Milam, supra*; *Devereaux v Harper* (1962) 210 CA2d 519, 26 CR 837; *Wiseman v Ross* (1962) 202 CA2d 138, 20 CR 565. When all conditions have been satisfied or waived the broker becomes entitled to the commission even if the parties subsequently abandon or rescind the agreement (*Weber v Ross* (1958) 159 CA2d 77, 323 P2d 465), unless the listing agreement has conditioned payment of the commission on consummation of the transaction (*Cochran v Ellsworth* (1954) 126 CA2d 429, 272 P2d 904; see §2.37).

§2.37   e. Conditional Commission Provision

The broker's right to a commission is dependent on the terms of the listing agreement (§2.31), and the parties are free to impose conditions that must be satisfied before the commission is earned. *Blank v Borden* (1974) 11 C3d 963, 115 CR 31. Care must be taken in drafting the listing agreement to state the seller's intention that the event which must occur for the commission to be earned is a condition for payment (*Seck v Foulks* (1972) 25 CA3d 556, 102 CR 170; *Shepherd-Teague Co. v Hermann* (1910) 12 CA 394, 107 P 622) and not a mere limitation on the time and manner of payment, which will not defeat the broker's right to the commission (*Miller v Lerdo Land Co.* (1921) 52 CA 662, 199 P 1073).

Even under such a provision the seller is liable for the commission if he or she unreasonably prevents the occurrence of the condition on which payment of the commission depends (*Collins v Vickter Manor,*

Inc. (1957) 47 C2d 875, 306 P2d 783; *Swanson v Thurber* (1955) 132 CA2d 171, 281 P2d 642) or acts in bad faith in failing to complete the transaction (*Stromer v Browning* (1966) 65 C2d 421, 55 CR 18). The purpose of the condition is to protect the seller against the buyer's failure to perform; the commission cannot be recovered if the buyer refuses to perform or to satisfy the condition. *Cochran v Ellsworth* (1954) 126 CA2d 429, 272 P2d 904. Moreover, the broker cannot compel the seller to sue the buyer for breach as a means of recovering the commission. *Dunne v Colomb* (1923) 192 C 740, 221 P 912.

The primary purpose of including conditions in listing agreements is to protect the seller against having to pay the commission if no proceeds are actually realized. See 1 Miller & Starr, Current Law of California Real Estate §2:19 (rev ed 1975). Conditions that have been used successfully for this purpose include the following:

(1) providing for payment only on consummation of the transaction, *e.g.,* when the purchase price is paid and title is transferred (*Cochran v Ellsworth, supra,* 126 CA2d 429, 272 P2d 904; *Peak v Jurgens* (1935) 5 CA2d 573, 43 P2d 569);

(2) requiring that the commission be paid out of proceeds received from escrow (*Dale v Raines* (1953) 115 CA2d 309, 252 P2d 22);

(3) providing that the commission will be paid out of funds received from the buyer (*Cannon v Selmser* (1927) 85 CA 783, 260 P 332).

The exclusive authorization and right to sell form (see §2.60) issued by the California Association of Realtors (CAR) provides that the commission is due when the property is "sold." This language has not been interpreted in any appellate decision, but it would appear to encompass more than mere production of a ready, willing, and able buyer as a prerequisite to the commission. Moreover, the CAR real estate purchase contract and receipt for deposit (see §3.40) provides that the commission is to be paid on recordation of the deed, on the seller's breach, if completion of the sale is prevented by the seller, or on the seller's recovery of damages in the event of the buyer's breach.

§2.38   2. Broker's Rights Under a Withdrawal-From-Sale Clause

Some listing agreements contain a provision that the broker will be entitled to the commission if the seller withdraws the property from sale or otherwise renders it unmarketable during the listing period. See, *e.g.,* the CAR exclusive right to sell agreement form at

§2.60. The California courts have enforced withdrawal-from-sale provisions, albeit somewhat reluctantly. *Alderson v Houston* (1908) 154 C 1, 96 P 884; *Baumgartner v Meek* (1954) 126 CA2d 505, 272 P2d 552. In *Ertell v Lloyd's Food Prods., Inc.* (1953) 115 CA2d 615, 252 P2d 683, the validity of such provision was recognized, but the court held that the seller's act of leasing a portion of the property enhanced the property's value for sale and thus did not reduce its marketability. In *Blank v Borden* (1974) 11 C3d 963, 115 CR 31, the supreme court concluded that withdrawal provisions are enforceable on the rationale that they constitute a true option for the seller rather than a penalty for forfeiture. If the withdrawal-from-sale provision is enforced, the broker recovers the entire agreed-on commission, even though the seller has had a change of heart regarding the sale and has, in fact, realized nothing. Recovery is not limited to amounts actually expended by the broker. *Blank v Borden, supra.*

A seller's repudiation of a listing agreement may also entitle the broker to sue for the commission without first producing a ready, willing, and able buyer, on a theory of anticipatory breach of contract. *Daum v Superior Court* (1964) 228 CA2d 283, 39 CR 443.

3. Sale After the Listing Period

§2.39   a. When Broker Can Recover Commission

In order to earn the commission, a broker must perform the services contracted for within the term of the listing agreement or any extensions granted by the seller. *Lawrence Block Co. v Scholer* (1958) 166 CA2d 608, 333 P2d 396; *Ridgway v Chase* (1954) 122 CA2d 840, 265 P2d 603. This general rule is subject to two judicially created exceptions which arise when the broker procures a buyer ready, willing, and able to meet the terms of the listing but a binding purchase agreement is not executed during the listing period.

The first exception is based on a waiver rationale and occurs when the seller encourages the broker to continue his efforts beyond the listing period, and the broker does so with the seller's knowledge. *Kraemer v Smith* (1960) 179 CA2d 52, 3 CR 471; *Filante v Kikendall* (1955) 134 CA2d 695, 286 P2d 448. If the broker subsequently procures an acceptable buyer, the requirement of performance within the listing period is considered waived, and the statute of frauds is not a bar to such a waiver. *Lewis v Foppiano* (1957) 150 CA2d 752, 310 P2d 658.

The second exception allows a broker to recover the commission if, during the listing period, he procures a buyer who meets all the terms of the listing agreement, but the purchase agreement is not actually executed until after the period has expired. *De La Questa v Armstrong Holdings Co.* (1920) 48 CA 487, 192 P 135. Under some safety clauses (§2.40), the broker need not prove that he is the procuring cause of the eventual transaction.

§2.40   b. The Safety Clause

Listing agreements frequently provide that the broker will be entitled to the commission if a sale is made within a specified time after the listing period expires to a buyer with whom the broker had contact during the listing period. A safety clause form is set out in §2.77. The extent of the broker's activity required varies: some listing agreements require only that the buyer have been "introduced" to the property by the broker (*Korstad v Hoffman* (1963) 221 CA2d Supp 805, 35 CR 61); others that the broker have "negotiated" with the buyer (*Delbon v Brazil* (1955) 134 CA2d 461, 285 P2d 710; see, *e.g.,* the CAR standard form in §2.60); still others that the buyer be "procured" by the broker (*E.A. Strout W. Realty Agency, Inc. v Lewis* (1967) 255 CA2d 254, 62 CR 918). See §2.32 for a discussion of procuring cause. As discussed below, the performance specified has a significant bearing on the broker's right to the commission. Generally, the safety clause also requires that the broker give the seller written notice of the names of potential buyers he has contacted during the listing period.

If the safety clause requires only introduction or negotiation by the broker, then the broker can recover the commission without proving that he was the procuring cause of the eventual sale. *Leonard v Fallas* (1959) 51 C2d 649, 335 P2d 665; *Delbon v Brazil, supra,* 134 CA2d 461, 285 P2d 710. Courts have, however, required that the broker demonstrate some activity in some connection with the ultimate sale beyond simply having contacted the prospective buyer. *Hobson v Hunt* (1922) 59 CA 679, 211 P 242; *Wright & Kimbrough v Dewees* (1921) 52 CA 42, 197 P 957. In *Simank Realty, Inc. v DeMarco* (1970) 6 CA3d 610, 86 CR 212, a broker with an exclusive right to sell listing containing a safety clause was denied a commission when the owner sold the property one day after expiration of the listing, because the broker did not show the buyer the property or negotiate with him, although the broker's sign had "flagged" the buyer's interest in the property. If the safety clause provides that the commission will be earned only if the broker actually procures a sale, it will be enforced according to its terms and the broker will have to establish that he was the procuring cause. *E.A. Strout W. Realty Agency, Inc. v Lewis, supra.*

Under a safety clause that does not require that the broker be the procuring cause in order to recover the commission, the seller might be liable for two commissions on the same sale. See, *e.g., Delbon v Brazil, supra,* in which the listing broker recovered a commission even though a second broker was actually the procuring cause of the sale. One way for the seller to avoid this problem is to provide in the second listing agreement that no commission will be earned for sales to prospective buyers named in the notification given by the first broker. A form for this purpose is set out in §2.76. The CAR exclusive right to sell agreement form avoids this problem by waiving the safety clause for a sale that occurs during the protection period if a valid listing agreement has been entered into with another broker. See §2.60. The rules of many multiple listing service boards (see §2.26) provide that when there is a second listing either the first broker earns no commission, or the commission is divided. 1 Miller & Starr, Current Law of California Real Estate §2:21 (rev ed 1975).

§2.41   4. Amount of Commission

The amount of the commission is governed by the listing agreement negotiated by the parties. See §2.31. If the listing agreement does not fix the amount of compensation, a reasonable commission will be allowed. *Beazell v Schrader* (1963) 59 C2d 577, 30 CR 534.

Commissions vary according to the broker, the region, the type of property, and the relative bargaining positions of the parties to the listing agreement. The usual range in percentage commissions for improved urban property is 5 to 6 percent of the sale price. It is not uncommon for brokers to charge a lower percentage or even a flat fee.

In large transactions, brokers may prefer a schedule of declining percentages, such as 5 percent on the first $500,000 of the sale price and 2-1/2 percent on the balance. (In long term leasing arrangements, brokers may charge a declining percentage of each year's rentals for a prescribed period.) For sales or exchanges of rural properties, commissions range from 5 percent to about 10 percent. For the sale of furnishings, fixtures, equipment, and stock in trade, declining percentages are often charged, *e.g.*, 10 percent on the first $3,000 to $5,000, 5 percent on the balance, minimum $50.

The commission due under a percentage arrangement is generally computed on the total sale price regardless of the amount of the encumbrance. In installment sales (see §5.10), sellers usually try to receive enough in the first installment to cover the commission, or provide in the listing agreement that the commission is to be paid in installments.

Brokers' ability to fix the amount of the commissions they will charge is subject to several legal constraints. Agreements among brokers to fix commission rates may constitute violations of federal or state antitrust laws. In *McLain v Real Estate Bd., Inc.* (1980) 444 US 232, the Supreme Court held that plaintiffs in a private action had sufficiently alleged and proved that defendant realtors' brokerage activities had a substantial effect on interstate commerce to establish jurisdiction under the Sherman Antitrust Act (15 USC §§1-7). Local realty boards have also been held subject to the Cartwright Anti-Trust Act (Bus & P C §§16700-16760), although not in the context of price-fixing (see §2.26). *Marin Bd. of Realtors v Palsson* (1976) 16 C3d 920, 130 CR 1; *Glendale Bd. of Realtors v Hounsell* (1977) 72 CA3d 210, 139 CR 830.

California statutes and regulations further restrict broker activity in setting commission rates. For example, Bus & P C §10147.5 requires that any printed listing agreement form contain a provision advising that the rate of the commission is not fixed by law and may be negotiable between seller and broker, and that the rate of compensation shall not be printed in any printed or form listing agreement. Regulations of the Real Estate Commissioner subject the broker to discipline for stating or implying to the seller that the broker is precluded by law, regulation, or the rules of an organization, from charging less than the commission the broker has quoted. 10 Cal Adm C §2785(a)(2).

§2.42   5. Buyer's Breach; Broker's Right to Deposit or Damages

Many real property purchase agreements, including the CAR real estate purchase contract and receipt for deposit form (see §3.40), limit the broker's commission to not more than one-half of any damages the seller is able to recover, minus expenses, in the event of a breach by the buyer. This provision in an executed purchase agreement binds the broker regardless of the terms of the listing agreement and limits the commission to one-half of any amounts actually recovered by the seller. If no funds are retained or recovered by the seller, the broker is entitled to nothing. *Chapman v Gilmore* (1963) 221 CA2d 506, 34 CR 515; *Swanson v Thurber* (1955) 132 CA2d 171, 281 P2d 642. Moreover, the seller has no obligation either to retain the deposit (*Huttlinger v Far W. Enterprises, Inc.* (1955) 131 CA2d 808, 281 P2d 554; *Kritt v Athens Hills Dev. Co.* (1952) 109 CA2d 642, 241 P2d 606) or to bring an action against the buyer for damages (*Lipton v Johansen* (1951) 105 CA2d 363, 233 P2d 648). An executed purchase agreement, however, constitutes compliance with the statute of frauds and entitles the broker to one-half of the deposit or damages, despite the absence of a listing agreement. *Beazell v Kane* (1954) 127 CA2d 593, 274 P2d 224.

The obvious source of recovery for both seller and broker in the event of the buyer's breach is the deposit. The seller's right to retain the deposit as liquidated damages is now strictly circumscribed by statute. CC §§1671-1681. A liquidated damages provision in an agreement to purchase real property must be printed in 10 point bold type or in contrasting red print in at least 8 point bold type and must be separately initialed by both buyer and seller. CC §1677. In a sale of residential property (defined as a dwelling containing not more than four units in which the buyer intends to reside) the provision is valid only if the deposit is actually paid and does not exceed 3 percent of the purchase price. CC §1675. If the seller retains the deposit under a purchase agreement that contains a valid liquidated damages provision and a provision that the broker recover one-half of any funds recovered by the seller, then the broker's commission will be one-half of the deposit. If the seller elects to return the deposit to a breaching buyer despite a valid liquidated damages provision, the broker would appear to have no right to compensation under the CAR real estate purchase contract and receipt for deposit form and the cases cited above. See §2.75. If more than one payment is to constitute liquidated damages, a separate liquidated damages clause meeting the requirements of CC §§1675 and 1677 must be executed for each payment. CC §1678.

6. Recovery of Commission From Buyer

§2.43   a. Implied Covenant To Complete Purchase

Under both listing and purchase agreements, the prevalent practice is to require that the seller pay whatever commissions are due. If the broker is retained by a buyer, however, and the broker locates property which the owner agrees to sell at the price offered, the law implies a promise by the buyer to complete the transaction and treat the broker as third party beneficiary of the purchase agreement between buyer and seller. If the buyer then breaches the purchase agreement he becomes liable to the broker for the commission. *Donnellan v Rocks* (1972) 22 CA3d 925, 99 CR 692; *Herman v Savage* (1936) 17 CA2d 238, 61 P2d 1195; *Traxler v Katz* (1931) 116 CA 226, 2 P2d 553. Moreover, the broker's recovery is not limited to one-half of the deposit (§2.42); he is entitled to the commission he would have earned if the buyer had performed.

This rule is applicable only when broker and buyer stand in the relationship of agent and principal. When the broker is employed by the seller, courts have not permitted recovery of the commission from the buyer on the implied promise rationale. *Hunter v Vernon* (1948) 85 CA2d 525, 193 P2d 139; *Steinberg v Buchman* (1946) 73 CA2d 605, 167 P2d 207.

§2.44   b. Interference With Prospective Economic Advantage

Brokers may be able to utilize the cause of action for tortious interference with prospective economic advantage to recover the commission from the buyer when the seller has a technical defense such as failure to comply with the statute of frauds. *Buckaloo v Johnson* (1975) 14 C3d 815, 122 CR 745; *Keely v Price* (1972) 27 CA3d 209, 103 CR 531; *Friedman v Jackson* (1968) 266 CA2d 517, 72 CR 129; *Zimmerman v Bank of America* (1961) 191 CA2d 55, 12 CR 319. These cases arise when a buyer, who is originally contacted by the broker, goes to the seller directly and induces the seller to close the sale without involving the broker, discounting the sale price by the commission that would otherwise be paid. Occasionally, buyers purchase the property through dummies in an attempt to conceal this conduct. *Golden v Anderson* (1967) 256 CA2d 714, 64 CR 404; *California Auto Court Ass'n, Inc. v Cohn* (1950) 98 CA2d 145, 219 P2d 511.

The broker need not plead and prove the existence of a contract in order to recover under a tortious interference theory, because it is interference with an economic relationship, not a contract, that is the gravamen of the action. In *Buckaloo v Johnson, supra,* the supreme court identified the elements of the cause of action: (1) an economic relationship between broker and seller containing the probability of future economic benefit to the broker; (2) the defendant's knowledge of the existence of the relationship; (3) intentional acts by the defendant designed to disrupt the relationship; (4) actual disruption of the relationship; and (5) damages proximately caused by the defendant's actions.

Although the leading cases, which all arose on demurrers, hold that a cause of action for tortious interference can be stated, the problems of proof remain substantial. Under the test announced in *Buckaloo v Johnson, supra,* the broker must prove that the economic relationship was one which included the *probability* of future economic benefit, that the defendant knew of the relationship, and that the defendant proposed to the seller that the parties deal directly in order to obtain a lower price for the property.

F. Contracting With the Broker

1. Elements Applicable to Both Sellers and Buyers

§2.45   a. Essentials of Contract

Although an agency can be created without a written contract and need not impose bilateral obligations on principal and agent, the broker-principal relationship is generally governed by a negotiated agreement granting limited agency authority to the broker and imposing contractual obligations on the principal to compensate the broker if specified conditions are fulfilled.

As with any other contract, an agreement with a broker requires: (1) parties capable of contracting, (2) their consent, (3) a lawful object, and (4) a sufficient consideration. CC §1550. In addition, a contract must have an ascertainable object to be enforceable. CC §1598. These elements are elaborated on in CC §§1556-1615. Contracts with real estate licensees are subject to peculiar requirements, in addition to general contract requirements. For example, a copy of any agreement authorizing or employing a real estate licensee must be delivered to the person signing it when the signature is obtained. Bus & P C § 10142; 10 Cal Adm C § 2902; see § 2.81. In addition, the broker's right to a commission depends on written authorization (see §§ 2.46-2.57). Other requirements are discussed in connection with forms for listing agreement provisions that satisfy those requirements. See §§ 2.66-2.82.

b. Statute of Frauds

§2.46 (1) Writing Required

Although an agent can be appointed without a writing, CC § 1624(5) requires that a contract employing a person to purchase or sell real property, to lease real property for a period longer than one year, or to procure a purchaser, seller, lessee or lessor of real property, must be in writing.

Courts have applied the statute to broker-principal relationships in virtually all categories of real property transactions, including options (*Pacific S.W. Dev. Corp. v Western Pac. R.R.* (1956) 47 C2d 62, 301 P2d 825), assignments of interests in real property (*King v Tilden Park Estates* (1958) 156 CA2d 824, 320 P2d 109), and exchanges (*Zimmerman v Bank of America* (1961) 191 CA2d 55, 12 CR 319).

The words "or any other person" in CC § 1624(5) mean that even a finder or middleman (see § 2.10) must have a written agreement in order to recover a fee in a real property transaction. *Zappas v King Williams Press, Inc.* (1970) 10 CA3d 768, 89 CR 307. See also *Zalk v General Exploration Co.* (1980) 105 CA3d 786, 164 CR 647, in which a finder was able to enforce an oral agreement, but for locating a company to be acquired rather than real property.

In the absence of a writing, the broker is not permitted to recover the value of his services even if the principal has taken advantage of the services and has received a substantial benefit from them. *Augustine v Trucco* (1954) 124 CA2d 229, 268 P2d 780. The broker may be able to recover a commission for the sale of personal property (*Marks v Walter G. McCarty Corp.* (1949) 33 C2d 814, 205 P2d 1025) or for various nonbrokering services (*Carey v Cusack* (1966) 245 CA2d 57, 54 CR 244), without a writing, but these services must be separable from real estate brokering services. *Carey v Cusack, supra.*

§2.47 (2) Exceptions

The courts have recognized a very limited number of exceptions to the requirement that the broker's authorization be in writing. An agreement between two brokers who cooperate in the sale of real property need not be in writing. *Holland v Morgan & Peacock Properties Co.* (1959) 168 CA2d 206, 335 P2d 769. The cooperating broker can recover his share of the commission from the listing broker if the listing broker has a written contract with the seller, or if the entire commission has already been paid to the listing broker. *Iusi v Chase* (1959) 169 CA2d 83, 337 P2d 79; *Daft v Enos* (1957) 155 CA2d 315, 318 P2d 66. If the broker is acting as a member of a joint venture, he is a principal rather than an agent, and his authority to bind his coadventurers in a real property transaction need not be in writing. *Foote v Posey* (1958) 164 CA2d 210, 330 P2d 651.

§2.48 (3) Contents of the Writing

To satisfy the statute of frauds the writing need not contain all the elements of a binding contract. See §2.45. It must, however, establish the broker's appointment to act for the principal (§2.49), identify the real property (§2.50), and be executed by the principal (§2.51).

§2.49 (a) Employment of Broker

The writing must establish the employment of the broker by the principal in language that clearly authorizes the appointment. CC §1624(5). Because the courts have interpreted this requirement rather strictly, a prudent broker should make certain that any memorandum on which he intends to rely uses words that have typically denoted an employment relationship, such as "appoint," "employ," or "authorize." (Other language that has been held sufficient to show the existence of an employment relationship includes: "You may have the listing with one or two other realtors" (*Rogers v Grua* (1963) 215 CA2d 1, 30 CR 39); "go ahead" (*Spitler v Avery* (1961) 189 CA2d 811, 11 CR 724); "take it up" (*Bruner v Van's Mkts.* (1951) 103 CA2d 135, 229 P2d 56.)

Cases have generally held that writings that set forth the terms on which the principal is willing to sell or buy, without specific language appointing the broker, do not comply with CC §1624(5).

Franklin v Hansen (1963) 59 C2d 570, 30 CR 530; *Pacific S.W. Dev. Corp. v Western Pac. R.R.* (1956) 47 C2d 62, 301 P2d 825. Even a letter indicating the terms of sale and the commission that would be paid has been held insufficient. *Morrill v Barneson* (1939) 30 CA2d 598, 86 P2d 924. On the other hand, it has been held that the statute of frauds was satisfied when the broker jotted down the terms of the sale, including the commission, on the back of one of his business cards and had the seller date and sign it, despite the fact that there was no specific language of appointment used. *Seck v Foulks* (1972) 25 CA3d 556, 102 CR 170.

§2.50   (b) Identity of the Property

The property that is the subject of the agency relationship must be described with sufficient clarity to permit reasonable identification. See, *e.g., Wolf v Price* (1966) 244 CA2d 165, 52 CR 889. An exact legal description is not required and parol evidence may be admitted to explain the meaning of the written description. A description such as "my house," when the principal owned only one house in the state, has been held sufficient. *Pray v Anthony* (1929) 96 CA 772, 274 P 1024. Courts have not, however, admitted extrinsic evidence to prove the identity of the property, when the memorandum contains no description at all. *Proulx v Sacramento Valley Land Co.* (1912) 19 CA 529, 126 P 509.

§2.51   (c) Execution

The writing need not be signed by both parties but it must be subscribed by or on behalf of "the party to be charged." CC §1624. The signature of an authorized agent of a corporation is sufficient to bind the corporation. *Marks v Walter G. McCarty Corp.* (1949) 33 C2d 814, 205 P2d 1025.

Because the purpose of the statute of frauds is to establish the existence of a contract (and not all of its terms), the writing can be signed after the services are rendered and even after the sale has closed and title has been transferred. *Estate of Rule* (1944) 25 C2d 1, 152 P2d 1003; *Hillman v Koch* (1949) 92 CA2d 163, 206 P2d 434.

In commercial and industrial transactions, there may be no memorandum on which the broker can rely until the contract of sale or escrow instructions have been executed. Both escrow instructions

(*Beazell v Schrader* (1963) 59 C2d 577, 30 CR 534) and a deposit receipt (*Mitchell v Johnston* (1956) 140 CA2d Supp 982, 298 P2d 170) have been held to be sufficient writings, but the broker's rights in this situation are contingent on completion of the sale, and the requirements of CC §1624(5) will not be considered to have been met if the sale is not consummated because of mutual rescission or the buyer's breach (*Paulsen v Leadbetter* (1968) 267 CA2d 148, 72 CR 819; *Mitchell v Johnston, supra*). A promissory note for the broker's commission, which the seller signed after closing, has been held to comply with the statute of frauds. *Fellom v Adams* (1969) 274 CA2d 855, 79 CR 633.

§2.52   (4) Commission Need Not Be Specified

The statute of frauds does not require that the writing indicate the amount of the broker's commission or even the broker's entitlement to compensation. *Barcelon v Cortese* (1968) 263 CA2d 517, 69 CR 657. If a writing demonstrates that the principal authorized the agent to act on his behalf, other provisions of the agreement, including the commission, may be proved by parol evidence. *Bruner v Van's Mkts.* (1951) 103 CA2d 135, 229 P2d 56. If the court can find no evidence concerning the amount of the commission in the writing or by parol evidence, it will infer an agreement to pay reasonable compensation. *Beazell v Schrader* (1963) 59 C2d 577, 30 CR 534; *Cramer v Lee Wa Corp.* (1952) 109 CA2d 691, 241 P2d 550.

§2.53   (5) Modification of Listing Agreements

Contracts required to be in writing generally cannot be modified by oral agreements. CC §1698. An exception to this rule is that an executed oral modification is enforceable. CC §1698. Thus, a party is permitted to enforce an oral modification to a listing agreement if both parties have carried out the terms of the modification. *Bard v Kent* (1940) 37 CA2d 160, 99 P2d 308; *Realty Corp. of America, Inc. v Burton* (1958) 162 CA2d 44, 327 P2d 948. For example, if a broker agrees to reduce his commission, and the owner then agrees to accept a lower sale price, the broker is bound by the oral modification. *Fidler v Schiller* (1963) 212 CA2d 569, 28 CR 48; *Lawrence Block Co. v Scholer* (1958) 166 CA2d 608, 333 P2d 396. A broker's oral agreement to receive his commission from the proceeds of the buyer's installment payments was enforced when the broker accepted partial payments out of the downpayment and first installment, but demanded full payment when the buyer defaulted on a later installment. *Waldteufel v Sailor* (1944) 62 CA2d 577, 144 P2d 894.

§2.54   (6) No Recovery of Commission Without a Writing

With very few exceptions, courts have strictly enforced the statute of frauds against brokers seeking to recover commissions from sellers without a writing. A broker may be able to recover from the buyer on a theory of tortious interference with prospective economic advantage, despite the absence of a written listing agreement with the seller (see §2.44). The quasi-contract, misrepresentation, and estoppel theories considered in §§2.55-2.57 have been raised by brokers and, for the most part, rejected by the courts. The prudent broker will not render services or expend funds in reliance on oral assurance that the commission will be paid.

§2.55   (a) Quasi-Contract Theory

A broker cannot recover against the seller on a quasi-contract theory regardless of the amount of time, expense, or effort expended and regardless of the substantial benefit conferred on the seller. *Beazell v Schrader* (1963) 59 C2d 577, 30 CR 534; *Wm. E. Doud & Co. v Smith* (1967) 256 CA2d 552, 64 CR 222; *Ford v Palisades Corp.* (1950) 101 CA2d 491, 225 P2d 545. This theory of recovery has been so roundly rejected by the courts that many recent attempts by brokers to recover commissions do not even raise it.

(Brokers have, however, been allowed to recover under oral agreements on a quasi-contractual basis for nonbrokering expenditures such as survey costs, costs of locating suitable sites, subdivision costs, and other indirect selling expenses. *Carey v Cusack* (1966) 245 CA2d 57, 54 CR 244; *Owen v National Container Corp.* (1952) 115 CA2d 21, 251 P2d 765. These nonbrokering services must be clearly separable from brokering services for which no recovery is allowed without a writing. *Carey v Cusack, supra.*)

§2.56   (b) Principal's Misrepresentation Theory

The broker's claim for recovery based on the principal's alleged misrepresentation has not been accepted by the courts. The theory of this cause of action is that the principal has defrauded the broker because he had no intention of paying the commission when he orally promised to do so. Courts have looked on this cause of action as a technical device to avoid the intent of the statute of frauds and have rejected it because of the important public policy behind the statute of frauds. *Keely v Price* (1972) 27 CA3d 209, 103 CR 531; *Kroger v Baur* (1941) 46 CA2d 801, 117 P2d 50.

§2.57 (c) Estoppel Theory

Estoppel theory provides very limited help to real estate brokers in collecting commissions without a written contract. Many seller-broker disputes would appear to present a prima facie case for invoking equitable estoppel doctrine to prevent a reneging principal from raising the defense of the statute of frauds (see 7 Witkin, Summary of California Law, *Equity* §132 (8th ed 1974)). *Domarad v Fisher & Burke* (1969) 270 CA2d 543, 76 CR 529. Generally, however, courts have been unwilling to apply estoppel theory because to do so would be to permit precisely what the statute of frauds was designed to prevent: the oral assertion of a promise with no easily available countervention other than denial. *Pacific S.W. Dev. Corp. v Western Pac. R.R.* (1956) 47 C2d 62, 301 P2d 825; *Hicks v Post* (1908) 154 C 22, 96 P 878; *Augustine v Trucco* (1954) 124 CA2d 229, 268 P2d 780.

Principals have been estopped from raising the statute of frauds as a defense when the broker has given up an *enforceable* commission right based on an oral promise to pay a commission. *LeBlond v Wolfe* (1948) 83 CA2d 282, 188 P2d 278. Estoppel is not available, however, when the broker waives the seller's oral promise to pay the commission because the buyer orally promises to pay it. *Keely v Price* (1972) 27 CA3d 209, 213, 103 CR 531, 534; *King v Tilden Park Estates* (1958) 156 CA2d 824, 320 P2d 109. Estoppel doctrine has been invoked to prevent an undisclosed principal from relying on the statute of frauds against a broker who had a written exclusive listing agreement with the principal's agent. *Fleming v Dolfin* (1931) 214 C 269, 4 P2d 776. A principal will also be estopped from defending on the basis of the statute of frauds if he has represented to the broker that written authorization exists, and the broker has changed position in reasonable reliance on that representation.

Owens v Foundation for Ocean Research (1980) 107 CA3d 179, 165 CR 571.

§2.58   2. Seller-Broker Agreements

A listing agreement is simply an employment contract between seller and broker, and the parties are free to negotiate any terms that are lawful. *Blank v Borden* (1974) 11 C3d 963, 115 CR 31. The performance required of the broker, and the conditions under which the seller will become obligated to pay the broker's compensation, must be found within the listing agreement. *Blank v Borden, supra*; *Seck v Foulks* (1972) 25 CA3d 556, 102 CR 170; see §2.31. Three stylized, commonly used types of listing agreements have evolved in the industry: the exclusive right to sell (§2.59), the exclusive agency listing (§2.61), and the open listing (§2.62). See, *e.g.*, *Tetrick v Sloan* (1959) 170 CA2d 540, 339 P2d 613. The three listings are distinguished by the conditions that must be fulfilled under each for the broker to earn the commission. None of these common types of listing agreements need be used; the rights of the parties are determined by the provisions actually included in their contract. It is the contents of the agreement and not its title that will be considered controlling by the courts. See, *e.g.*, *Tetrick v Sloan, supra*; *Coleman v Mora* (1968) 263 CA2d 137, 69 CR 166.

Any one of the common listing agreements, or any hybrid agreement negotiated by the parties, may include a net listing arrangement (see §2.63) or an option listing (see §2.64), and may either allow or require the broker to refer the listing to the local multiple listing service (see §2.26).

a. Types of Listing Agreements

(1) Exclusive Right To Sell

§2.59   (a) General Characteristics

The agreement's title is misleading; the listing does not empower the broker to sell the property or to execute a purchase agreement or deed on behalf of the seller. Under an exclusive right to sell listing, the broker is entitled to the commission if the property is sold during the listing period by anyone, including the seller. *Lowe v Loyd*

(1949) 93 CA2d 684, 209 P2d 851. The broker need not be the procuring cause (see §2.32) and need not even have contacted the prospective buyer. *Berzon v U.L.C. Corp.* (1969) 274 CA2d 690, 79 CR 277; *Rankin v Miller* (1960) 179 CA2d 133, 3 CR 496.

Listing agreements are strictly construed against the broker, and courts will not find an exclusive right to sell agreement unless it is expressly so designated. *E.A. Strout W. Realty v Gregoire* (1950) 101 CA2d 512, 225 P2d 585. An exclusive right to sell agreement must contain a definite termination date; if it does not, the broker will be subject to disciplinary action by the Real Estate Commissioner if he seeks compensation under the agreement. Bus & P C §10176(f).

Provisions in many exclusive right to sell agreements entitle the broker to the full commission if the seller withdraws the property from the market (*Baumgartner v Meek* (1954) 126 CA2d 505, 272 P2d 552), or does something to the property that makes it unmarketable or substantially reduces its marketability (*Alderson v Houston* (1908) 154 C 1, 96 P 884). In *Blank v Borden* (1974) 11 C3d 963, 115 CR 31, the validity of such a commission-on-withdrawal clause was upheld. See §2.38.

Many exclusive right to sell listing agreements also contain a safety clause that entitles the broker to the commission if the property is sold within a stated period after expiration of the listing to a buyer contacted by the broker. See §2.40 on the safety clause.

The CAR exclusive right to sell standard form agreement is set out in §2.60. It contains a commission-on-withdrawal clause, and a limited safety clause.

§2.60   (b) Form: CAR Exclusive Authorization and Right To Sell Listing Agreement

The CAR Exclusive Authorization and Right To Sell Listing Agreement is reproduced on pages 114–115.

EXCLUSIVE AUTHORIZATION AND RIGHT TO SELL

THIS IS INTENDED TO BE A LEGALLY BINDING AGREEMENT—READ IT CAREFULLY.

CALIFORNIA ASSOCIATION OF REALTORS® STANDARD FORM

1. **Right to Sell**. I hereby employ and grant _____ hereinafter called "Agent," the exclusive and irrevocable right commencing on _____, 19 _____, and expiring at midnight on _____, 19 _____, to sell or exchange the real property situated in _____, County of _____, California described as follows:

_____

_____

_____

_____

2. **Terms of Sale**. The purchase price shall be $ _____, to be paid in the following terms:

_____

_____

_____

(a) The following items of personal property are to be included in the above-stated price:

_____

_____

_____

(b) Agent is hereby authorized to accept and hold on my behalf a deposit upon the purchase price.

(c) Evidence of title to the property shall be in the form of a California Land Title Association Standard Coverage Policy of Title Insurance in the amount of the selling price to be paid for by _____

(d) I warrant that I am the owner of the property or have the authority to execute this agreement. I hereby authorize a FOR SALE sign to be placed on my property by Agent. I authorize the Agent named herein to cooperate with sub-agents.

3. **Notice: The amount or rate of real estate commissions is not fixed by law. They are set by each broker individually and may be negotiable between the seller and broker.**

Compensation to Agent. I hereby agree to compensate Agent as follows:

(a) _____ % of the selling price if the property is sold during the term hereof, or any extension thereof, by Agent, on the terms herein set forth or any other price and terms I may accept, or through any other person, or by me, or _____ % of the price shown in 2, if said property is withdrawn from sale, transferred, conveyed, leased without the consent of Agent, or made unmarketable by my voluntary act during the term hereof or any extension thereof.

(b) the compensation provided for in subparagraph (a) above if property is sold, conveyed or otherwise transferred within _____ days after the termination of this authority or any extension thereof to anyone with whom Agent has had negotiations prior to final termination, provided I have received notice in writing, including the names of the prospective purchasers, before or upon termination of this agreement or any extension thereof. However, I shall not be obligated to pay the compensation provided for in subparagraph (a) if a valid listing agreement is entered into during the term of said protection period with another licensed real estate broker and a sale, lease or exchange of the property is made during the term of said valid listing agreement.

4. If action be instituted to enforce this agreement, the prevailing party shall receive reasonable attorney's fees and costs as fixed by the Court.

5. In the event of an exchange, permission is hereby given Agent to represent all parties and collect compensation or commissions from them, provided there is full disclosure to all principals of such agency. Agent is authorized to divide with other agents such compensation or commissions in any manner acceptable to them.

6. I agree to save and hold Agent harmless from all claims, disputes, litigation, and/or judgments arising from any incorrect information supplied by me, or from any material fact known by me concerning the property which I fail to disclose.

7. This property is offered in compliance with state and federal anti-discrimination laws.

8. Other provisions:

9. I acknowledge that I have read and understand this Agreement, and that I have received a copy hereof.

Dated _____ , 19 _____ , California

_____   _____
OWNER   OWNER

_____   _____
ADDRESS   CITY—STATE—PHONE

10. In consideration of the above, Agent agrees to use diligence in procuring a purchaser.

_____   _____
AGENT   ADDRESS—CITY

By _____
              PHONE   DATE

FORM A-11

EQUAL HOUSING OPPORTUNITY

For these forms address California Association of Realtors*
505 Shatto Place, Los Angeles 90020. All rights reserved
Copyright 1978 by California Association of Realtors.* Revised 1980

NO REPRESENTATION IS MADE AS TO THE LEGAL VALIDITY OF ANY PROVISION OR THE ADEQUACY OF ANY PROVISION IN ANY SPECIFIC TRANSACTION. IF YOU DESIRE LEGAL ADVICE, CONSULT YOUR ATTORNEY.

Reprinted by permission, CALIFORNIA ASSOCIATION OF REALTORS®

§2.61   (2) Exclusive Agency

Under an exclusive agency listing, the broker is the only agent authorized to procure offers for the purchase of the property, and is entitled to a commission even if the property is sold by another broker. *Fleming v Dolfin* (1931) 214 C 269, 4 P2d 776; *Carlsen v Zane* (1968) 261 CA2d 399, 67 CR 747. If the owner independently procures a buyer and sells the property the broker is not entitled to the commission. *Faith v Meisetschlager* (1919) 45 CA 7, 187 P 61. But see *Coldwell, Banker & Co. v Pepper Tree Office Center Assocs.* (1980) 106 CA3d 272, 165 CR 51, in which the broker was denied a commission under an exclusive agency listing despite the absence of a finding that the owner was the procuring cause.

If the broker presents the offer of a ready, willing, and able buyer before a purchase agreement is actually executed by a buyer independently procured by the seller, the broker is entitled to the commission. *Houston v Williams* (1921) 53 CA 267, 200 P 55. Conversely, if the seller procures a buyer and enters into a purchase agreement before the broker procures a buyer, the broker's right to the commission is defeated. *California Land Sec. Co. v Ritchie* (1919) 40 CA 246, 180 P 625.

If the owner sells to a prospective buyer who had already been contacted by the listing broker, the broker must show that he was the procuring cause. *Nelson v Mayer* (1954) 122 CA2d 438, 265 P2d 52. For a discussion of procuring cause, see §2.32. Sale of the property by the owner automatically terminates an exclusive agency listing even if the broker is given no notice. *E.A. Strout W. Realty v Gregoire* (1950) 101 CA2d 512, 225 P2d 585.

As with the exclusive right to sell agreement, courts will not find the existence of an exclusive agency in the absence of clear and specific language (*Summers v Freeman* (1954) 128 CA2d 828, 276 P2d 131); moreover, an exclusive agency listing must contain a definite termination date (Bus & P C §10176(f)).

§2.62   (3) Open Listing

Under an open (or general) listing, a broker must be the procuring cause (see §2.32) of a buyer who is ready, willing, and able (see §2.33) to purchase the property on the terms of the listing. An owner can employ a number of brokers to sell the same property under open listing agreements, and the first broker to procure a buyer earns the commission. *Marks v Rowley* (1951) 102 CA2d 619, 228

P2d 29. If the owner sells the property without the assistance of a broker, all open listings are terminated, and no commission is owed. *Edens v Stoddard* (1954) 126 CA2d 56, 271 P2d 610. Brokers do not favor open listings because of the risks and are not usually willing to expend time or money under them.

An open listing agreement need not contain a definite termination date, unlike either of the exclusive listings. Bus & P C §10176(f); *Summers v Freeman* (1954) 128 CA2d 828, 276 P2d 131. An open listing without a specified duration may be revoked by the owner at any time before the broker produces a buyer, regardless of the efforts the broker may have expended prior to termination. *Tetrick v Sloan* (1959) 170 CA2d 540, 339 P2d 613; *Heffernan v Merrill Estate Co.* (1946) 77 CA2d 106, 174 P2d 710. The only limitation on the owner's right seems to be that the revocation must be made in good faith. *Tetrick v Sloan, supra.*

§2.63   (4) Net Listing Provisions

Under a net listing provision, the commission is earned in any manner the parties agree on, *e.g.,* any one of the listing agreements in §§2.59-2.62, but the amount of the commission is the amount by which the actual sale price exceeds a stated net price. See *Smith v Zak* (1971) 20 CA3d 785, 98 CR 242. If the property is sold for the specified net sum or a lesser amount, the broker does not earn a commission. *Haigler v Donnelly* (1941) 18 C2d 674, 117 P2d 331. Although legal, a net listing provision provides an obvious opportunity for abuse by brokers, and its use will be scrutinized closely by the Real Estate Commissioner under the authority of Bus & P C §10176(g).

Both brokers and owners should be cautious about using net listing arrangements. A broker should explain the nature and effect of a net listing to the principal and should ensure that the net sale price is determined by the owner. The broker will bear a heavy burden in trying to prove the fairness of the transaction and his good faith in advising the seller regarding the net price. Any facts tending to indicate that the broker influenced the fixing of the price may subject the broker to civil liability for secret profits (see §§2.99, 2.105) and disciplinary action by the commissioner (§2.110).

A broker ordinarily must disclose to the seller any amounts he will receive as a result of the sale (see §§2.94, 2.99) and any interest, direct or indirect, he has in the purchase of the property (§§2.95-

2.98). There is some authority for relaxation of these disclosure requirements when the property is sold under a net listing (§2.63) (*Pascal v Cotton* (1962) 205 CA2d 597, 23 CR 357; *Allen v Dailey* (1928) 92 CA 308, 268 P 404), but the continuing vitality of this exception is open to question, and in any event it is very strictly limited to sales in which the net price has been determined by the seller without any influence from the broker (*Sierra Pac. Indus. v Carter* (1980) 104 CA3d 579, 163 CR 764; *Smith v Zak, supra*; *Loughlin v Idora Realty Co.* (1968) 259 CA2d 619, 66 CR 747). Courts have held the broker to a strict duty to disclose the fact that the purchaser under a net listing is a relative of the broker, when the broker has influenced the setting of the net price. *Sierra Pac. Indus. v Carter, supra; Smith v Zak, supra; Loughlin v Idora Realty Co., supra.*

§2.64 (5) Option Listing Provisions

An option listing provides for the commission to be earned in any manner the parties agree on (*e.g.*, any one of the listing agreements described in §§2.59-2.62), but contains an added clause giving the broker an option to purchase the property at the listing price. When the option is exercised, the broker must give the seller written notice of the full amount of his profit and obtain the principal's written consent to the amount of the broker's profit. Bus & P C §10176(h). Because the broker is still a fiduciary of the seller when he exercises the option, he also must disclose all outstanding offers and any other material information about the property (see §2.98). *Rattray v Scudder* (1946) 28 C2d 214, 169 P2d 371.

Brokers should be cautious about accepting option listings because of the conflict between the fiduciary relationship with the seller and the broker's role as purchaser of the property. If the option price approximates the fair market value of the property, the option is of no great benefit to the broker; if the option price is less than fair market value when the option is exercised, the broker will be unable to retain any subsequent profits that have not been fully disclosed to the seller and approved in writing. Bus & P C §10176(h).

b. Provisions in Listing Agreements

§2.65 (1) Format and Use

The listing agreement may be prepared in any format acceptable to seller and broker. Usually the needs of the parties can be adequately met by use of one of the standard form listing agreements in common use, although every form should be reviewed carefully by the seller's attorney, especially those provisions specifying when the commission is earned. The exclusive right to sell form agreement distributed by the California Association of Realtors is set forth in §2.60. All standard listing agreements tend to favor brokers, and the seller's attorney may feel it necessary to make changes or include additional provisions by use of an addendum, or rider, attached to a form listing agreement. Alternatively, the attorney may feel it preferable to draft the listing agreement in the form of a letter agreement employing the broker or a formally prepared and executed contract of employment.

Circumstances will dictate which format should be used for a given transaction. Brokers often prefer to use their own forms, and more readily accept riders to those forms. Riders present some risk of contradiction between the agreement and riders and both should be carefully reviewed to ensure consistency. The form agreement should include a notation that it is made subject to the provisions of the attached rider. Seller and broker should initial the notation and also execute the addendum.

The provisions in §§2.66-2.81 are intended to enable the seller's attorney to draft a complete listing agreement, or a letter agreement, or a rider to a standard form agreement. Some of the provisions are found in standard listing agreements; others are generally omitted from standard agreements but ought to be added by addendum or separate agreement when needed to serve the needs of the parties. Many of the provisions are not essential to every listing agreement, but might be included to cover a situation in a particular transaction.

§2.66   (2) Form: Employment of Broker

Form 2.66-1 (By Letter Agreement)

_____, 19__

____[Name and address of broker]____

Dear _____:

____[I / We]____ employ you as broker

Form 2.66-2 (By Employment Contract)

_____, 19__

____[I / We]____ employ ____[name of broker]____ as broker

Comment: The need to use language indicating employment of the broker is discussed in §2.49. Many form and drafted agreements specify at this point that the broker is employed under an open, exclusive agency, or exclusive right to sell listing. These characterizations, however, really define the conditions under which the commission is earned and are placed in the form provision in §2.75. There is no reason to specify the type of listing in this clause because the title used is not determinative (*Tetrick v Sloan* (1959) 170 CA2d 540, 339 P2d 613; see §2.58) and may be misleading (§2.59).

§2.67   (3) Form: Listing Period (Termination Date)

Form 2.67-1

for the period beginning _____, 19__, and ending at midnight on _____, 19__, called the listing period

Comment: An exclusive agency or exclusive right to sell listing agreement must contain a definite termination date. See §§2.59-2.61. A broker is subject to discipline under Bus & P C §10176(f) if he attempts to collect compensation under either of these exclusive listings if it does not have a termination date. The broker may be able to recover the commission if he has performed fully under an exclusive listing agreement without a termination date and the seller has received the benefit of his services. *Babcock v Houston* (1973) 33 CA3d 858, 109 CR 454. If the broker has not performed, however, the owner can rescind the agreement and the broker cannot enforce it. *Lewis & Queen v N.M. Ball Sons* (1957) 48 C2d 141, 308 P2d 713; *Nichols v Boswell-Alliance Constr. Corp.* (1960) 181 CA2d 584, 5 CR 546.

The termination date need not be a calendar date, but it must be determinable from the listing agreement itself without reference to some external event. *Dale v Palmer* (1951) 106 CA2d 663, 235 P2d 650. Listing agreements that provide for the listing to continue until revoked by the seller, but in no event later than a definite calendar date, have been upheld. *Lowe v Loyd* (1949) 93 CA2d 684, 209 P2d 851. Thus, if the principal wishes termination of the listing to relate to some activity such as construction, the listing should specify termination some period after commencement of the activity, but not later than a specified future date.

§2.68   (4) Form: Property To Be Sold

Form 2.68-1

for the sale of ____[my / our]____ [*specify, e.g., fee interest / undivided inter-est / leasehold interest / fee interest subject to leasehold*]____ in the real prop-erty in the City of _____, County of _____, described as follows: _____

Comment: The statute of frauds does not require that the listing agreement contain an exact legal description of the property. CC §1624(5); see §2.50. Whether a street address or legal description is used, accuracy is vital. The purchase agreement will most likely describe the property as it is shown in the listing agreement, and the buyer may have a defense against performing if the description in the purchase agreement is not correct. See §§12.93-12.107 on the buyer's defenses.

§2.69   (5) Form: Purchase Price

Form 2.69-1 (Minimum Total Price)

The minimum total price for sale of the property shall be $ _____ ____ [*cash to seller / in installments as follows:* _____ / *other consideration*]____.

Form 2.69-2 (Net Listing)

The total price of the property shall be not less than $ _____, net to seller after deduction of any and all expenses and costs of sale payable by the seller, except ____[*specify expenses seller will bear*]____ .

Comment: The listing price should be the product of discussion and negotiation between broker and seller in order to meet the seller's objectives and still be competitively attractive on the market. Occasionally brokers overstate the value of the property in order to obtain the listing and eliminate competition. This practice is unethical and may subject the broker to discipline under 10 Cal Adm C §2785(a)(1). See California Department of Real Estate, Real Estate Bulletin, *Freeze-Out,* Fall, 1979, p 7.

For a discussion of net listings, see §2.63.

Unless the transaction is to be an exchange or installment sale, the listing agreement generally need not specify the terms of payment in any greater detail than "cash to seller." The commission will then be earned when the broker produces a buyer who can pay cash or the seller accepts some other arrangement, such as the buyer's assumption of an existing loan or the seller's acceptance of the buyer's note. See §§2.34-2.36 on when the commission is earned. See chapters 5 and 6 on financing terms in the purchase and sale agreement. In most instances, these details can be left to the negotiations between the seller and a potential buyer. Occasionally, the seller may want to specify details of payment of the purchase price in the listing agreement, and the form can be modified for that purpose.

With slight alterations, this provision can be utilized for exchanges. If the broker is to be paid a percentage of the value of the exchange property, that value must be specified in the listing agreement. Because of valuation problems and the possibility of the listing seller or the buyer receiving some cash in the exchange, exchange listing agreements often state a dollar amount for the commission. When an exchange may not generate any cash, the seller may prefer that the listing agreement provide for payment of the commission in installments. See chap 5 on exchanges.

If the seller wishes the transaction to be an installment sale under IRC §453, the listing agreement should specify the maximum downpayment the seller will accept, the amounts of future installments, their payment dates, and the interest rate. See chap 5 on installment sales.

(6) Buyer's Deposit

§2.70 (a) Form: Authority To Accept Deposit Only as Buyer's Agent

Form 2.70-1

You are authorized to accept buyer's deposit only as buyer's agent until seller's acceptance; the deposit is to be considered accepted only when seller accepts buyer's offer. The purchase and sale agreement shall provide that the deposit is at buyer's risk until seller's acceptance of buyer's offer.

Comment: The purpose of this provision is to protect the seller against the broker's loss or misappropriation of the deposit. Most form listing agreements (see, *e.g.,* CAR form in §2.60) authorize the broker to accept the deposit on the seller's behalf. The distinction is critical. An express authorization to accept the deposit for the seller renders the broker the seller's agent in holding the deposit and thus shifts the risk of loss to the seller. *Hicks v Wilson* (1925) 197 C 269, 240 P 289; *Warshauer v Bauer Constr. Co.* (1960) 179 CA2d 44, 3 CR

570. In the absence of express authorization, the broker holds the deposit as the buyer's agent and the risk of loss remains with the buyer. *Clark v Patterson* (1931) 213 C 4, 300 P 967.

Deposits are a cause of more disputes than is justified by their importance. See also §2.71. Sellers sometimes feel that the buyer will be under a greater psychological compulsion to complete the sale because of the deposit, but it is not essential to the formation of the purchase agreement. In many instances there is no reason to require a deposit with the offer, and the deposit could instead be made when the offer is accepted.

§2.71   (b) Form: Handling of Deposits

Form 2.71-1

Buyer's deposit shall be acceptable only ____[*specify, e.g., in cash or cashier's check or a combination*]____ . All checks must be made to the order of ____[*specify, e.g., seller or name of escrow holder*]____ and all deposits must be delivered by broker to ____[*specify, e.g., seller or escrow holder*]____ by the next business day following receipt.

Comment: Lawyers frequently require that payments be made in cash or by cashier's check because payment on personal checks, even certified checks, can be stopped. See §3.47. If payment on a check is stopped, neither party may be sure of his rights respecting the property until the dispute over the check is resolved, and the effect may be to remove the property from the market for a considerable period.

If both buyer and broker (as seller's agent) intend a check itself to be held as the desposit without being cashed, the broker's receipt of the check will be treated as payment of the deposit. *Beazell v Kane* (1954) 127 CA2d 593, 274 P2d 224. If it is not expressly agreed that the check is to be held without being cashed, the check does not constitute payment of the deposit until it is honored by the drawee bank. *Mendiondo v Greitman* (1949) 93 CA2d 765, 209 P2d 817. This provision does not authorize receipt of promissory notes for the deposit, because a promissory note will be of little value to the seller in the event of the buyer's failure to perform. See 1 Miller & Starr, Current Law of California Real Estate §2:7 (rev ed 1975). A broker must disclose to the seller the fact that the deposit is in the form of a promissory note, and is subject to discipline under Bus & P C §10176(a)(i) for failing to do so. *de St. Germain v Watson* (1950) 95

CA2d 862, 214 P2d 99. Some purchase agreements provide for the buyer to make the deposit by means of a promissory note and to substitute cash in an equal amount prior to closing.

This provision requires immediate delivery of any deposit, and this is in the best interests of both seller and broker. It minimizes the chances for loss or misappropriation by the broker, and reduces the time in which the buyer can change his decision and stop payment. The broker is required to place the deposit into an escrow depository or broker's trust account the next business day after receipt, or to inform the seller when the offer is presented that the broker is holding the offeror's check. Bus & P C §10145; 10 Cal Adm C §2832. The buyer retains title to the deposit, and is entitled to its return, until the offer is accepted unconditionally by the seller. *Norris v San Mateo County Title Co.* (1951) 37 C2d 269, 231 P2d 493; *Sartern v Pomatto* (1961) 192 CA2d 288, 13 CR 588.

Attorneys disagree concerning who should hold the deposit: an escrow company, the broker, or the seller. An escrow holder is not satisfactory because if there is a dispute between buyer and seller, it will almost invariably refuse to release the deposit to either, preferring to interplead the funds in the buyer-seller litigation. Custody of the deposit by broker or seller exposes the buyer to the risk of loss or misappropriation by either. One solution favored by some attorneys is to have the deposit be a check made out to the escrow holder but to specify that it be held by the broker until the seller accepts the buyer's offer.

Whatever methods of payment and custody of the deposit are used, the deposit never becomes the property of the broker. The broker holds the deposit as agent, escrow holder, and trustee for the respective parties. *Savage v Mayer* (1949) 33 C2d 548, 203 P2d 9; *Holloway v Thiele* (1953) 116 CA2d 68, 253 P2d 131.

§2.72 (7) Form: Designation of Escrow Holder

Form: 2.72-1

Escrow shall be held by ____[give name and title of escrow holder]____ , and shall close on _____, 19__. Broker shall deliver any deposits broker then holds under the terms of this listing agreement to the escrow holder on execution by both buyer and seller of a purchase and sale agreement.

Comment: Some sellers wish to designate a particular escrow holder in the listing agreement. The seller's right to select the escrow holder is somewhat constrained by CC §2995, which bars a developer from requiring use of an escrow holder in which it has a financial interest, and by the Real Estate Settlement Procedures Act (RESPA) (12 USC §§2601-2617), which prohibits most sellers from conditioning the sale on the use of a particular title company (12 USC §2608). Whether or not an escrow holder is named, the seller may wish to set out the closing date in order to prevent closing before he can deliver possession, or to ensure closing by a particular date, or to specify a closing date within a particular tax year.

§2.73   (8) Form: Possession

Form 2.73-1

Buyer shall have possession of the property____[at close of escrow / on _____, 19__]____.

Comment: If the date of delivery of possession is important to the seller, it should be a condition of the listing agreement. Close of escrow is commonly given as the time for delivering possession, but an owner-occupant may need additional time in order to move; unless provided for, he may be in violation of the buyer's right to possession if he cannot vacate at the close of escrow.

§2.74   (9) Form: Right To Appoint Subagents; Multiple Listing Service

Form 2.74-1 (Broker Authorized To Appoint)

Broker is authorized to appoint and cooperate with subagents.

Form 2.74-2 (Broker Not Authorized To Appoint)

Broker is not authorized to appoint or cooperate with subagents.

Form 2.74-3 (Multiple Listing Service Authorized)

Broker ____[may / shall]____ refer the listing to the ____[name]____ multiple listing service, and is authorized to cooperate with any of its members in securing a purchaser.

Comment: The first alternative provision, which approximates the language of many standard form listing agreements, gives the broker the maximum amount of flexibility and discretion regarding the use of subagents.

If the seller does not want subagents used, it is good practice to so specify in the listing agreement, because CC §2349 provides that an agent can employ subagents when local usage permits, and it could be argued that reference to a multiple listing service is authorized when the listing agreement is silent but local practice is to refer listings to the service. On subagents and multiple listing services, see §§2.25-2.27.

In some instances, the seller may want to require that the listing be referred to a multiple listing service, while the broker may want to attempt to sell the property without the services of a cooperating broker to avoid having to split the commission but to have the right to cooperate with a subagent if necessary. The provision for use of a multiple listing service can be either permissive or mandatory.

(10) Broker's Compensation

§2.75   (a) Form: Entitlement to Commission

Form 2.75-1

Seller agrees to pay broker as a commission
[Simple percentage]
_ _ _ _ _ _ _ _ percent of the selling price, if during the listing period of any extension of it
[Graduated percentage]
_ _ _ _ _ _ _ _ percent of the first $ _ _ _ _ _ _ _ _ of the selling price plus _ _ _ _ _ _ _ _ percent of the selling price in excess of $ _ _ _ _ _ _ _ _, if during the listing period or any extension of it
[Flat fee]
the total sum of $ _ _ _ _ _ _ _ _ regardless of the selling price _ _ _ _*[or the type or value of any property accepted in exchange for the property]*_ _ _ _ , if during the listing period or any extension of it
[Balance over net to seller]
the balance of the selling price in excess of a net of $ _ _ _ _ _ _ _ _ to seller after payment of all other costs in escrow except the following which shall be paid by seller out of seller's net: _ _ _ _*[list expenses to be paid by seller]*_ _ _ _ , if during the listing period or any extension of it

[Add appropriate statement]
[Open listing]
broker procures a buyer on the terms stated in this listing agreement or any other terms acceptable to seller.
[Exclusive agency listing]
any broker procures a buyer on the terms stated in this listing agreement or any other terms acceptable to seller.

[*Exclusive right to sell listing*]
anyone procures a buyer on the terms stated in this listing agreement or any other terms acceptable to seller.

[*Add appropriate statement*]
[*Commission conditioned on closing*]
The commission shall be payable on close of escrow and recording of a deed to the buyer or on failure to close if failure to close is due to seller's default or lack of good faith.

[*Commission not conditioned on closing*]
If buyer defaults, the commission shall be payable only if and when seller collects damages from the buyer, by suit or otherwise, and in an amount not to exceed one-half of the damages recovered after first deducting title and escrow expenses and any expenses of collection.

[*Optional withdrawal-from-sale clause*]
A commission of _____ percent of ____[*state price*]____ shall be payable if seller withdraws the property from sale, encumbers it, leases it, or otherwise renders it unmarketable during the listing period.

[*Add if a printed or form agreement is used; set words below in 10-point bold type to comply with Bus & P C §10147.5*]
Notice: The amount or rate of real estate commissions is not fixed by law. They are set by each broker individually and may be negotiable between the seller and broker.

Comment: On the differences among open listings, exclusive listings, and exclusive right to sell listings, see §§2.59-2.62; on net listings, see §2.63. Regardless of which listing is used, the seller should insist that the commission be payable only if the sale is consummated. See §2.37. Otherwise, the seller may be liable for the commission if the broker produces a buyer who makes an unconditional offer under the listing terms, even though the sale never goes through. See §§2.33-2.36.

Even when the commission is conditioned on closing, the seller cannot avoid the commission by unreasonably preventing the closing and will be liable for the commission if the failure to close is due to his or her lack of good faith. *Stromer v Browning* (1966) 65 C2d 421, 55 CR 18. See §2.37. Nevertheless, the broker may want to make this inherent obligation explicit by including the optional language at the end of the commission-on-closing clause.

If the commission is not to be conditioned on closing, the broker should seek inclusion of a provision that the commission will be one-half of any damages recovered for the buyer's breach. Language in this form is similar to that in the CAR real estate purchase contract and receipt for deposit form. See §3.40. The purchase agreement may contain such a provision even if the listing agreement does not, and if so, the purchase agreement will control regardless of the broker's rights under the listing agreement. If the amount retained or recovered by the seller is nominal, the broker's recovery will be reduced to an inconsequential amount. *Chapman v Gilmore* (1963) 221 CA2d 506, 34 CR 515.

In many instances, the only funds really at issue as damages will be the deposit, and the seller's right to retain the deposit is governed by code provisions regarding liquidated damages. CC §§1671-1681; see §2.42. If the purchase agreement contains a valid liquidated damages provision and either the listing or purchase agreement contains a provision that the broker recover one-half of any funds recovered by the seller, then the broker will be entitled to one-half of the retained deposit.

An interesting question arises when the seller elects to return a deposit to which he or she is entitled. Does the provision that the broker receive one-half of any funds recovered by the seller entitle the broker to a commission equal to one-half of the deposit? In *Kritt v Athens Hills Dev. Co.* (1952) 109 CA2d 642, 241 P2d 606, the listing agreement provided that the commission should be one-half of any deposit retained, but did not obligate the seller to retain the deposit. It was held that the seller had no obligation to retain deposits to which it was otherwise entitled and the broker recovered nothing for units on which deposits were returned. Thus, a broker seeking protection regarding this problem should attempt to negotiate a provision obligating the seller to retain the deposit and split it with the broker. Even under the standard provision, the broker might be able to argue that the seller cannot simply elect to return the deposit without first consulting the broker. In *Huttlinger v Far W. Enterprises, Inc.* (1955) 131 CA2d 808, 281 P2d 554, the broker was unable to recover one-half the value of the deposit because he had urged its return to the buyer and the court held that this action constituted a waiver of the broker's rights. Implicit in the finding of a waiver is the notion that the broker's consent to return of the deposit would otherwise have been required.

The language in the last paragraph is required by Bus & P C §10147.5, effective July 1, 1980. It must be included in any printed or form agreement for the sale of a mobile home or residential real property containing four or fewer residential units; moreover, Bus & P C §10147.5 provides that the amount or rate of compensation shall not be printed in the agreement. See also §2.41.

§2.76   (b) Form: Buyers Excluded From Agency

Form 2.76-1

Broker shall not be entitled to the commission for any sale, lease, exchange or other transfer to any of the following persons: ____[names]____.

Comment: When the seller signs a listing agreement with a particular broker, he may already have brought the property to the attention of one or more prospective buyers, or he may be under obligation to another broker under a safety clause. See form in §2.77; for discussion, see §2.40. This provision enables the seller to eliminate any claim by the present broker for a commission on a sale to such a buyer. The safety clause contained in the CAR standard exclusive authorization and right to sell form provides an exemption for a sale procured during the protection period under a valid licensing agreement with another licensed broker. See §2.60.

Under an exclusive right to sell listing (see §2.59) this provision is essential to protect the seller in the event of a sale to a buyer with whom the seller or previous broker had negotiated. It is also useful under an open listing (see §2.62) or exclusive agency listing (see §2.61) to prevent disputes about who procured a particular buyer.

§2.77   (c) Form: Sale After Termination of Listing Agreement (Safety Clause)

Form 2.77-1

If, within ____ days after the termination of the listing period or any extension of it, seller sells ____[leases / transfers / exchanges]____ the property ____ [to / with]____ any person with whom broker negotiated concerning a possible purchase of the property during the listing period or any extension of it, broker shall be entitled to a commission in the amount and on the terms specified in the listing agreement. Seller shall have no obligation to pay broker any commission under this provision unless, not later than ____ days after the expiration of the listing period or any extension of it, broker provides to seller a written list of all parties with whom broker has negotiated for a possible sale. This provision shall have no application if seller terminates this agreement because of broker's failure to perform, or breach of duty, or if, during the period specified in this provision, a sale of the property is procured by a licensed real estate broker under a valid listing agreement.

Comment: A safety clause as set out above is reasonable, and a seller should not object to its inclusion in a listing agreement as long as the protection period is reasonably short, and the broker is required to notify the owner in writing of parties with whom he or she has negotiated. Under this safety clause, the broker must actually have negotiated with the buyer regarding the property (*Simank Realty, Inc. v DeMarco* (1970) 6 CA3d 610, 86 CR 212), but need not be the procuring cause of the eventual sale (*Leonard v Fallas* (1959) 51 C2d 649, 335 P2d 665; *Delbon v Brazil* (1955) 134 CA2d 461, 285 P2d 710). According to their wishes, seller and broker can require that the broker be the procuring cause of any subsequent sale, or only that the eventual buyer be introduced by the broker. See §2.40 for a discussion of various safety clauses and the broker's right to recovery under each. If the safety clause includes leases as well as sales, the broker will be able to recover if the owner executes a lease during the protection period with a person contacted by the broker. *Al Herd, Inc. v Isaac* (1969) 271 CA2d 749, 76 CR 697.

§2.78 (11) Form: Condition of Title; Title Insurance

Form 2.78-1

Title shall be marketable, subject only to ____[*list known exceptions to unencumbered title*]____ . Evidence of title shall be a California Land Title Association standard policy of title insurance to be paid for by ____[*buyer / seller*]____ .

Comment: The seller is obligated to deliver marketable title subject to stated exceptions. See §3.78. Title exceptions must be stated in the purchase agreement to protect the seller against liability to the buyer for breach of the implied agreement to deliver marketable title. This provision puts the broker on notice of title exceptions that must be included in the purchase agreement.

The most common way to determine the condition of record title is to order a title report. On the preparation and contents of a title report, see §3.80. If no title report is available, title should be made subject at least to "all matters of record." This language is probably sufficient for the listing agreement, but would not provide adequate protection to the buyer if it were the only provision concerning title in the purchase agreement. Whether buyer or seller pays for title insurance is generally determined by customs that vary from place to place in California (see §11.58), though this may be altered by agreement. On the various kinds of title insurance see California Title Insurance Practice (Cal CEB 1980).

§2.79   (12) Form: Broker's Duties

Form 2.79-1

In accepting this listing, broker agrees to exercise due diligence to procure a buyer and promptly and diligently to do the following: ____[state broker's duties, e.g., to advertise, show premises, post signs, protect occupant against annoyance]____ .

Comment: Services performed may vary widely from broker to broker, but printed listing agreements rarely spell out the broker's duties. Promotion of a particular property may require services beyond those ordinarily performed by the broker selected. The agreement should specify the services to be provided so that the owner can revoke the listing if the broker fails to perform.

The broker's failure to exercise due diligence may enable the owner to revoke the listing. *Coleman v Mora* (1968) 263 CA2d 137, 69 CR 166; see §2.101 for discussion of the owner's right to revoke. Whether the broker has performed with due diligence is a question of fact that depends on the circumstances of each case (*Whitney Inv. Co. v Westview Dev. Co.* (1969) 273 CA2d 594, 78 CR 302), and the standards for determining whether the duty has been breached are thus rather imprecise. Accordingly, the seller should list the services expected of the broker in as much detail as possible. The seller may, for example, want the agreement to specify marketing services such as advertising (names of newspapers, frequency, appearance of advertisements, emphasis of special features), signs (size, design, location, wording), photographs, and limitations on showing the premises. A broker's failure to advertise and offer the property to members of the public in a nondiscriminatory fashion might breach the duty to exercise due diligence by failing to reach a market that would otherwise be available. *Crowell v Isaacs* (1965) 235 CA2d 755, 45 CR 566.

§2.80 (13) Form: Printed Form Subordinate to Drafted Provisions

Form 2.80-1 (Rider to Printed Form)

This rider constitutes an integral part of the agreement between seller and buyer and supersedes inconsistent provisions of the printed listing agreement to which it is attached.

Comment: Brokers often prefer to use standard listing agreement forms even when the terms are substantially altered; these altered terms are set out in a specially drafted rider. See §2.65. To make it clear that the printed form is part of a broader agreement, the rider should refer to the printed form, which should contain a clause such as the following:

The rider containing ____[*pages / provisions*]____ numbered_____ through _____, executed concurrently with this agreement and appended to it, constitutes an integral part of this agreement and supersedes inconsistent provisions in it.

§2.81 (14) Form: Acknowledgment of Receipt; Broker's Acceptance

Form 2.81-1 (Letter Agreement Mailed to Broker)

Please sign and return the enclosed copy of this letter as evidence of your agreement to its terms.

Form 2.81-2 (Listing Agreement)

Seller acknowledges receipt of a copy of this listing agreement.

Comment: These provisions are designed to protect the broker, who is required to give a copy of the agreement to the person signing it (Bus & P C §10142), and is subject to discipline for failing to do so (Bus & P C §10177). The broker's right to the commission under a valid listing agreement, however, is not affected by the failure to deliver a copy. *Summers v Freeman* (1954) 128 CA2d 828, 276 P2d 131.

If the agreement takes the form of a letter to the broker, acknowledgment by the seller is unnecessary and the second alternative should be used to show the broker's assent to the terms of the listing agreement.

§2.82 (15) Execution

Under the statute of frauds, a broker's listing agreement must be executed by the person to be held responsible in a given situation.

CC §1624(5). The issue of proper execution typically arises in the context of the broker's attempt to recover a commission; consequently the primary question is generally whether the seller has executed the listing agreement. Sound practice, however, calls for both seller and broker to sign the agreement; if a letter agreement is used, the broker should be required to sign and return a copy to the seller. See form in §2.81.

If amendments are appended to a printed form, both the form and the final page of drafted provisions should be dated and executed, and the other pages should be initialed. See Comment to the form in §2.80 for a provision in which the number of pages or provisions of the addenda are stated.

3. Buyer-Broker Agreements

§2.83   a. General Considerations

The number of transactions in which brokers earn their commissions from buyers instead of sellers is relatively small. Even when the broker is employed by the buyer, it is frequently understood that the commission will be paid by the seller. In many buyer-broker agreements the principal is a substantial commercial client interested in locating sites for new ventures, and broker and principal have worked together over a period of time and developed a relationship of mutual trust. For these reasons, their agreement is often not reduced to writing until a purchase agreement is executed. In this less formal atmosphere it is important that the terms of the broker's employment be clearly expressed and understood by both buyer and broker. Oral understandings should be reduced to writing as soon as possible, even if only in the form of a confirming letter, to avoid disputes and misunderstandings.

The various listing agreement provisions set forth in §§2.66-2.81 can be readily adapted for use in a buyer-broker agreement as appropriate, whether a letter or employment contract format is followed. Provisions which might be desired by buyer or broker include: employment of the broker (§2.66); term of the agency (§2.67); characteristics of the property sought; conditions under which the commission will be earned, and by whom it will be paid (§2.75); a safety clause (§2.77); and the broker's duties (§2.79).

A broker should notify the seller that he or she is the buyer's broker (§2.84), and obtain an acknowledgment (§2.85) for protection against possible disciplinary action and civil liability.

§2.84   b. Notifying Seller of Buyer-Broker Relationship

The broker owes various fiduciary duties to the principal (see §§2.86-2.102), and in some situations, the buyer's broker may be considered a subagent of the seller (see §§2.24, 2.27). See also California Department of Real Estate, Real Estate Bulletin, *Dilemma of the Cooperating Agent,* Fall, 1979, p 1. To avoid the problem of dual representation and possible discipline under Bus & P C §10176(d), the buyer's broker should give the seller written notice of his or her position as buyer's agent. In addition, the buyer's broker might want to obtain the seller's written acknowledgment, as set forth in §2.85.

§2.85   c. Form: Seller's Acknowledgment of Buyer-Broker Agency

Form 2.85-1

Seller acknowledges that ____[name of broker]____ is acting in this transaction as the agent and broker for buyer.

Form 2.85-2 (Compensation To Be Paid by Buyer)

Broker's compensation in connection with this transaction shall be paid by buyer rather than seller.

Form 2.85-3 (Compensation To Be Paid by Seller)

Compensation to be paid to broker by seller in connection with this transaction is part of the consideration for seller's agreement with buyer and does not arise out of any agency relationship between seller and broker.

Comment: This acknowledgment is frequently made a part of the first paper to be signed by the seller, whether an acceptance of the buyer's offer or a counteroffer. The reasons for giving notice to the seller that the broker is the agent of the buyer are discussed in §2.84.

III. DUTIES AND LIABILITIES

A. Broker to Principal

§2.86   1. Broker's Fiduciary Duty

The real estate broker owes strict fiduciary obligations to his or her principal. *Batson v Strehlow* (1968) 68 C2d 662, 68 CR 589; *Ward v Taggart* (1959) 51 C2d 736, 336 P2d 534; *Earle v Lambert* (1962) 205 CA2d 452, 23 CR 79. The broker's duties are quite similar to those owed by a trustee to the beneficiary of a trust (CC §§2228-2240) and he is held to a standard of utmost good faith in dealings with his principal. The Real Estate Law (Bus & P C §§10000-10602) condemns all acts of the broker that would constitute breach of this fiduciary duty under general agency law, and also subjects the broker to discipline for particular activities even though these might not result in civil liability. Bus & P C §§10176-10177; *Buckley v Savage* (1960) 184 CA2d 18, 7 CR 328; *de St. Germain v Watson* (1950) 95 CA2d 862, 214 P2d 99. See §2.110. Commencement and termination of the broker's fiduciary duty are discussed in §§2.87-2.88.

§2.87   a. Duty Arises When Agency Created

The broker's fiduciary obligations arise at the creation of the agency relationship, and the agency may precede the execution of a formal employment contract (see §2.18). Fiduciary duties may arise even before creation of the agency, however, if the principal relies on the broker on the basis of past dealings between them. See *Darrow v Klein & Co.* (1931) 111 CA 310, 296 P 566. Because the agency relationship can be created with little or no formality and need not meet the requirements of the statute of frauds (see §2.20), an oral agreement or authorization signals the commencement of the broker's fiduciary duties, and the broker has a duty to preserve the confidentiality of information he obtains from the seller before execution of the listing agreement. *Beeler v West Am. Fin. Co.* (1962) 201 CA2d 702, 20 CR 190.

§2.88   b. Expiration May Survive Closing

Although the sale of the property terminates the agency relationship, the broker's fiduciary duties include postclosing obligations related to the sale. *Menzel v Salka* (1960) 179 CA2d 612, 4 CR 78. For example, after expiration of the agency, a broker is bound to preserve the confidentiality of information obtained during the term of the agency relationship. *Beeler v West Am. Fin. Co.* (1962) 201 CA2d 702, 20 CR 190. The Real Estate Law imposes at least two separate postclosing duties on brokers. A broker must: (1) inform both seller and buyer in writing of the sale price within one month after the transaction closes (Bus & P C §10141), and (2) record or deliver to the beneficiary any deed of trust executed in the transaction (Bus & P C §10141.5).

§2.89   2. Duty To Disclose

The broker is obligated to make full and complete disclosure to his principal of all facts material to the pending transaction. CC §2020; see *Zikratch v Stillwell* (1961) 196 CA2d 535, 16 CR 660. Material facts include those which the broker should realize might influence the principal regarding the transaction and his willingness to sell or buy. *Rattray v Scudder* (1946) 28 C2d 214, 169 P2d 371; *Fisher v Losey* (1947) 78 CA2d 121, 177 P2d 334. Matters which must be disclosed are discussed in §§2.90-2.94.

§2.90   a. Dual Representation

A broker may not act as an agent for more than one party to a transaction without full disclosure to all parties and their consent. Bus & P C §10176(d). Similarly, he cannot participate in a transaction in which he has an interest adverse to that of his principal unless he obtains his client's consent after full disclosure. CC §§2230, 2322(3). Disclosure must be made, and consent obtained, when a broker represents both buyer and seller and intends to receive two separate commissions. *Ohanesian v Watson* (1953) 118 CA2d 386, 257 P2d 1022. Potential conflicts are inherent in multiple listing situations in which a cooperating or buyer's broker may find himself representing the buyer, while also acting as a subagent of the seller. See §§2.24-2.27. Brokers also face conflicting fiduciary obligations in offer and counteroffer situations. See *Timmsen v Forest E. Olson, Inc.* (1970) 6 CA3d 860, 86 CR 359.

b. Disclosures Concerning Price

§2.91   (1) Offers To Buy

The broker must inform the principal of all offers received, whether or not they conform to the terms of the listing agreement and whether or not the broker considers them attractive. Failure to disclose an offer is equivalent to a representation to the principal that no offers were received. *Simone v McKee* (1956) 142 CA2d 307, 298 P2d 667. This duty exists whether the offer is oral or written. *Duin v Security First Nat'l Bank* (1955) 132 CA2d Supp 904, 283 P2d 790. Sound business practice calls for the broker to advise the seller of serious preliminary negotiations or anticipated offers even before actual receipt of an offer.

§2.92   (2) Best Price Obtainable

The broker's advice concerning the best price obtainable for the property is an important service, particularly for the unsophisticated seller. The broker must disclose all material facts relating to the value or price of the property, including the possibility that a higher price might be obtained at a later time or by marketing the property in another way. *Smith v Zak* (1971) 20 CA3d 785, 98 CR 242; *Kinert v Wright* (1947) 81 CA2d 919, 185 P2d 364; *Vigli v Davis* (1947) 79 CA2d 237, 179 P2d 586; *Fisher v Losey* (1947) 78 CA2d 121, 177 P2d 334; *Troendle v Clinch* (1932) 125 CA 147, 13 P2d 852.

§2.93   (3) Statements to Buyers About Price

The broker's role in transmitting offers and counteroffers may require that he make an estimate for his client regarding a purchase price that will be acceptable to the other party. If the seller's broker suggests to a prospective buyer that the seller is willing to accept less than the listed sales price, he may be committing a breach of his fiduciary duty to the seller. *Bate v Marsteller* (1959) 175 CA2d 573, 346 P2d 903; *Mitchell v Gould* (1928) 90 CA 647, 266 P 565. Multiple listing arrangements place the buyer's broker in a position in which he is expected to suggest counteroffers and estimate the firmness of the seller's listing price, at the risk of breaching his duty to the seller. See §§2.24-2.27.

§2.94   c. Speculative Purchases and Resales

Brokers may be subjected to litigation by sellers when the property is resold at a substantially higher price by a speculator, although the law regarding the extent of the broker's duty in the area of speculative resales is not settled. Speculation in residential real property is a matter of public concern because of the fear that it contributes to inflated prices for residential property.

If the broker is aware that a prospective buyer intends to resell the property shortly at a significantly higher price, disclosure to the seller might be required. CC §2020; *Rattray v Scudder* (1946) 28 C2d 214, 169 P2d 371; see §§2.91-2.92. The mere existence of a price differential probably would not suffice to establish either negligence (§2.100) or breach of fiduciary duty, because the price might be the result of inflationary increases in property values. On the other hand, an immediate price differential might suggest that the broker had not diligently represented his principal's interest in obtaining the best price for the property.

The seller's broker would almost certainly be required to disclose any discussions with the buyer regarding the possibility of relisting the property with the broker for resale. *Menzel v Salka* (1960) 179 CA2d 612, 4 CR 78; *McPherson v Real Estate Comm'r* (1958) 162 CA2d 751, 329 P2d 12. In *Bay Shore Homes, Inc. v San Diego Trust & Sav. Bank* (1969) 276 CA2d 108, 80 CR 849, a broker was denied recovery of his commission because of his failure to disclose that he had agreed to turn over his commission to the buyer in exchange for a listing on resale of the property. But see *Moody v Osborne* (1953) 120 CA2d 598, 261 P2d 783, holding that failure to disclose the broker's loan to the buyers to enable them to complete the transaction did not violate the broker's fiduciary duty.

3. Broker's Purchase of Principal's Property

§2.95   a. Disclosure Requirements

Whenever the broker purchases the listed property, it will be presumed that the principal entered the transaction without sufficient consideration and under undue influence, and the broker will have the burden of proving the fairness of the transaction. CC §§2235, 2322(3); *Smith v Zak* (1971) 20 CA3d 785, 98 CR 242. The broker may purchase the listed property provided this fact is disclosed to all parties. CC §2230; *Donnellan v Rocks* (1972) 22 CA3d 925, 99 CR 692. If the required disclosure is not made, however, the fact that the broker paid a fair price for the property will not be a defense to liability for nondisclosure. *Bate v Marsteller* (1959) 175 CA2d 573, 346 P2d 903. On the broker's purchase of the principal's property generally, see Comment, *Unprofessional Conduct by Real Estate Brokers: Conflict of Interest and Conflict in the Law,* 11 Pac LJ 821 (1980).

Any fact which might conceivably be material must be disclosed by the purchasing broker. In *Skopp v Weaver* (1976) 16 C3d 432, 128 CR 19, for example, the seller's allegations that the broker had failed to disclose that the listed property had been sold to the state for taxes and that the broker had then acquired the property for himself were held sufficient to state a cause of action for breach of the broker's fiduciary duty.

The broker's duty to disclose all facts relating to the best price obtainable (§2.92) poses particularly acute problems for the broker who purchases his principal's property for resale. See, *e.g., Smith v Zak, supra,* 20 CA3d 785, 98 CR 242. Resale at a substantial profit will make it difficult for the broker to meet his burden of demonstrating that full disclosure was made. *Smith v Zak, supra.* The prudent broker should carefully document all disclosures to the principal and hold the property for a substantial period of time before resale.

§2.96   b. Indirect Sales

The broker's duty to disclose his purchase of the listed property extends to purchases by his relatives, friends, and employees and to entities in which he has an interest. In *Batson v Strehlow* (1968) 68 C2d 662, 68 CR 589, a broker's disclosure to the seller that he was president of the purchasing corporation was held inadequate because he did not also disclose that he and his wife were its sole shareholders and had paid the entire price out of their own pockets. Concealed from the principal in this case was the fact that the broker was really dealing for himself as principal yet attempting to earn a commission as well. A broker should always disclose to the seller his relationship with a buyer corporation or partnership, even if he is only a limited partner or minority shareholder.

Brokers will also be held to a duty to disclose that the purchaser is a relative or employee. *Smith v Zak* (1971) 20 CA3d 785, 98 CR 242 (buyer was broker's salesperson); *Loughlin v Idora Realty Co.* (1968) 259 CA2d 619, 66 CR 747 (buyer was broker's mother-in-law).

§2.97   c. Net Listings

A narrow exception to the requirement of full disclosure of the broker's interest in, and profit from, the sale may arise if the property is sold under a net listing (§2.63). *Allen v Dailey* (1928) 92 CA 308, 268 P 404. The underlying rationale is that the net price is all that the seller has bargained for and the amount of the broker's profit is thus irrelevant. Brokers have not prevailed in any recent cases under this exception, however, because it is very strictly limited to situations in which the net price has been freely determined by the seller without the broker's participation. *Sierra Pac. Indus. v Carter* (1980) 104 CA3d 579, 163 CR 764; *Pascal v Cotton*

(1962) 205 CA2d 597, 23 CR 357. If the broker has influenced the setting of the net price, then even indirect sales to the broker must be disclosed (see §2.96). *Smith v Zak* (1971) 20 CA3d 785, 98 CR 242; *Loughlin v Idora Realty Co.* (1968) 259 CA2d 619, 66 CR 747.

§2.98   d. Option Listings

A broker who has an option to purchase the property under the listing agreement (see §2.64) will be held to a strict fiduciary obligation and a duty to disclose all outstanding offers and other material information. *Rattray v Scudder* (1946) 28 C2d 214, 169 P2d 371. A broker with an option cannot wait until someone makes a higher offer and then exercise his option without disclosing the higher offer to the principal. *Zikratch v Stillwell* (1961) 196 CA2d 535, 16 CR 660. If the option is exercised, the broker must give the seller written notice of the full amount of his profit and obtain the seller's written consent. Bus & P C §10176(h).

§2.99   4. Secret Profits

The broker is liable to the principal for any secret profits, gratuities, or other benefits obtained in the transaction. See *Menzel v Salka* (1960) 179 CA2d 612, 4 CR 78. The broker will not be permitted to retain any benefit derived from the transaction unless the nature and amount of the benefit have been fully disclosed to the principal. It is immaterial that the transaction is otherwise fair to the principal or that the principal receives exactly the price he wants for his property or pays no more for it than he intended. *Menzel v Salka, supra*; *Thompson v Stoakes* (1941) 46 CA2d 285, 115 P2d 830.

The broker must disgorge all secret profits regardless of whether the principal has suffered any actual damages (see §2.105). *Savage v Mayer* (1949) 33 C2d 548, 203 P2d 9. The principal may recover from the broker and from all others who have knowingly shared in the receipt of the secret profits (*Crogan v Metz* (1956) 47 C2d 398, 303 P2d 1029), and a fiduciary is liable for secret profits which he causes to flow to a third party even though he personally does not share in the secret profits (*St. James Armenian Church v Kurkjian* (1975) 47 CA3d 547, 121 CR 214).

If the broker expends money to repair or improve property obtained as a secret profit he will not be entitled to offset these expenses against the principal's claim for recovery of the secret profits even though they have increased the value of the property. *Rempel v Kells* (1923) 62 CA 81, 215 P 1042.

The requirement that all benefits be fully disclosed also applies when the broker is agent for the buyer. A broker is required to disgorge any profits he realizes if he fails to disclose his interest in property that is purchased by his principal. *Kroeker v Hurlbert* (1940) 38 CA2d 261, 101 P2d 101.

Brokers are subject to discipline by the Real Estate Commissioner for taking undisclosed profits as part of a transaction. Bus & P C §10176(g). In *Rylander v Karpe* (1976) 60 CA3d 317, 131 CR 415, it was held that the broker did not violate Bus & P C §10176(g) by accepting loan origination fees from the lender without the sellers' knowledge.

Kickbacks, referral fees, and other unearned fees from title companies, escrow holders, and the like, are prohibited under federal law, whether disclosed by the broker or not. Real Estate Settlement Procedures Act (RESPA) §8(a)-(b) (12 USC §2607(a)-(b); see §§11.85-11.89 for a discussion of RESPA. Violation of the act's ban on kickbacks could render a broker subject to criminal penalties as well as liable civilly for three times the amount of the referral fee. RESPA §8(d) (12 USC §2607(d)).

§2.100   5. Duty To Exercise Reasonable Care

A broker or salesperson must exercise reasonable skill and care for the benefit of the principal (*Schoenberg v Romike Properties* (1967) 251 CA2d 154, 59 CR 359), and is liable for any damages suffered by the principal as a result of delay or negligence (see *Wilson v Hisey* (1957) 147 CA2d 433, 305 P2d 686).

The cases on breach of the broker's duty of care are somewhat difficult to analyze because they generally include allegations of intentional misrepresentation or failure to disclose as well as negligence, and the actual grounds of liability are often difficult to pinpoint. See, *e.g.*, *Ford v Cournale* (1973) 36 CA3d 172, 111 CR 334. The cases discussed below demonstrate that courts have held brokers to a duty to advise the principal correctly and to investigate certain details of the property and the transaction, especially when the principal is unskilled and is relying on the broker's expertise.

The area in which brokers are most commonly held liable for

breach of their duty of care is that of advising the principal regarding the financial soundness of the other party or the security offered. See, *e.g., Timmsen v Forest E. Olson, Inc.* (1970) 6 CA3d 860, 86 CR 359 (negligent recommendation of sale to buyer who was financially unsound); *Banville v Schmidt* (1974) 37 CA3d 92, 112 CR 126 (negligent misrepresentation of the value of the security under a deed of trust and the financial strength of the obligor on the note); *Pepper v Underwood* (1975) 48 CA3d 698, 122 CR 343 (negligent misrepresentation that the seller's income tax returns were consistent with his financial statements); *Tackett v Croonquist* (1966) 244 CA2d 572, 53 CR 388 (exchange property incorrectly valued due to broker error regarding location).

A broker must investigate the value of exchange or security property, and cannot simply rely on an appraisal supplied by the other party. *Schoenberg v Romike Properties, supra,* 251 CA2d 154, 59 CR 359. When the income that the property will produce is important to his buyer-principal, the broker must investigate the reliability of the seller's income reports and explain them to his client. See *Ford v Cournale, supra.*

Brokers may also breach their duty of care for failing to investigate, or failing to advise the principal to investigate, matters relating to title. In *Brady v Carman* (1960) 179 CA2d 63, 3 CR 612, a broker was held liable for erroneously advising a buyer that an easement across the property did not affect its value. Failure to recommend a title search was the basis for finding a broker negligent when he had erroneously stated that there was only one encumbrance on the property. *Wilson v Hisey* (1957) 147 CA2d 433, 305 P2d 686. In *Pepitone v Russo* (1976) 64 CA3d 685, 134 CR 709, a broker was held liable for failing to advise his principal of a due-on sale clause in a second deed of trust on exchange property.

A broker may be liable for failing to verify the existence and location of an easement as represented by his principal, but may also be entitled to indemnification from the principal if his transmittal of the representation to the other party is innocent. *Gardner v Murphy* (1975) 54 CA3d 164, 126 CR 302; see §2.117.

Brokers may incur liability if they undertake to advise principals regarding tax considerations, and do so incorrectly. In *Santos v Wing* (1961) 197 CA2d 678, 17 CR 457, a broker escaped liability for his alleged failure to give advice regarding the tax consequences of a transaction because he had advised his principal to seek the advice of counsel on the question.

A broker is a professional agent who represents himself to the public as having particular knowledge and skill in the real estate field, and is under a corresponding obligation to exercise greater care and skill than is within the capacity of the ordinary citizen. *Richards Realty Co. v Real Estate Comm'r* (1956) 144 CA2d 357, 300 P2d 893. Brokers must meet certain educational requirements (Bus & P C §§10153.4, 10153.5), and must update their professional knowledge through continuing professional education (Bus & P C §§10170-10171.6). In addition, they must pass an examination prepared and administered by the state which tests, among other things, their knowledge of real property law and legal principles. Bus & P C §10153. Although the courts have yet to rule on the extent of legal competence required of brokers, it seems likely that a broker will incur liability for negligently giving legal advice to his principal or for negligently drafting legal documents for the transaction. See, *e.g., Biakanja v Irving* (1958) 49 C2d 647, 320 P2d 16, in which a notary public was held liable for negligence in drafting a will. In a questionable situation, a prudent broker should probably follow the example of the broker in *Santos v Wing, supra,* and recommend that the principal seek the advice of an attorney or other expert, as appropriate.

§2.101   6. Duty To Perform With Diligence

The seller can revoke an exclusive agency or exclusive right to sell listing if the broker fails to carry out the terms of the agency diligently. *Coleman v Mora* (1968) 263 CA2d 137, 69 CR 166. An open listing is generally characterized as a unilateral offer and can be revoked by the seller whether or not the broker has exercised diligence. See §2.62. Under either of the exclusive listings the broker's lack of dilgence will constitute a defense to his action for the commission if the seller revokes the listing before accepting an offer procured by someone other than the broker. In *Coleman v Mora, supra,* the court of appeal held that a listing agreement may be revoked by the principal for any of the reasons for which contracts generally may be revoked (see CC §1689), including failure to perform. The broker's breach does not of itself terminate the listing agreement, however, and to avoid liability for the commission the seller should clearly exercise his right to revoke before the property is sold. See *Whitney Inv. Co. v Westview Dev. Co.* (1969) 273 CA2d 594, 73 CR 302.

Whether the broker has performed with diligence is a question of fact to be determined in light of the circumstances of each case. *Whitney Inv. Co. v Westview Dev. Co., supra.* If the seller terminates the listing without adequate cause, and if the listing agreement contains a withdrawal-from-sale clause, then the broker would become entitled to the commission without any further performance under the terms of the listing (see §2.38). *Blank v Borden* (1974) 11 C3d 963, 115 CR 31. This underscores the importance for the seller of including in the listing agreement a provision specifying exactly what services the broker is to perform. See §2.79. Establishing the broker's breach will be facilitated if the duties have been stated in detail.

§2.102   7. Duty To Account

The broker must account for all funds held on behalf of the principal, and is not permitted to commingle the principal's funds with his own. Bus & P C §10176(e); *Brown v Gordon* (1966) 240 CA2d 659, 49 CR 901. The broker holds the principal's funds as trustee and is responsible for their disposition in accordance with the principal's directions. *Holloway v Thiele* (1953) 116 CA2d 68, 253 P2d 131.

The broker may be called on to receive and hold the buyer's deposit as agent for the buyer, as agent for the seller, or as escrow holder under written instructions contained in the offer or contract. See §§2.70-2.71. The Real Estate Law and regulations adopted by the Real Estate Commissioner limit the circumstances under which a broker may receive and hold a deposit check before acceptance of the offer, and generally require that the deposit be placed in escrow or the broker's trust account on the next business day after receipt. Bus & P C §10145; 10 Cal Adm C §2832. One of the shortcomings of the commonly used CAR real estate purchase contract and receipt for deposit form (see §3.40) is its implied requirement that a deposit accompany the initial offer. Many brokers and prospective buyers interpret this form as requiring delivery of a check to the broker long before the parties have reached agreement, although the seller's interest would be adequately protected by a deposit at the time the purchase agreement is executed. See §2.70.

The Department of Real Estate regulates brokers' trust funds generally and imposes various recordkeeping requirements on brokers. Bus & P C §10145, 10 Cal Adm C §§2830-2835. Under Bus & P C §10146, a broker is required to render quarterly accountings to the principal of any advance fees which he holds for the principal. In *Burch v Argus Properties, Inc.* (1979) 92 CA3d 128, 154 CR 485, the principal was permitted to recover the amount of fees advanced, as punitive damages, for the broker's failure to render quarterly accountings as required by Bus & P C §10146, even though the funds had been returned to the principal before the action was commenced.

§2.103   8. Remedies Against Broker

The broker is subject to two separate and distinct areas of liability for violation of his fiduciary duties. He may incur civil liability to his principal under various causes of action (§§2.82-2.102) and he is subject to disciplinary proceedings before the Real Estate Commissioner under Bus & P C §§10175-10185. See §2.110.

A broker who breaches the contract with his principal is liable under general contract law, entirely apart from the law of agency. *Anderson v Badger* (1948) 84 CA2d 736, 191 P2d 768. In addition to his contractual rights against the broker, the principal may also be able to avail himself of the following remedies: (a) damages for losses suffered as a result of breach of the broker's fiduciary duty (§2.104); (b) recovery of secret profits realized by the broker (§2.105); (c) recovery of the commission (§2.106); (d) punitive damages (§2.107); and (e) indemnity for damages recovered from the principal by third parties (§2.108).

§2.104   a. Damages for Breach of Fiduciary Duty

A broker who has breached his or her fiduciary duty, intentionally or negligently, will be liable to the principal for damages caused by the breach. See §§2.86-2.102 on breach of fiduciary duty. There is disagreement concerning the appropriate measure of damages for breach of the fiduciary duty, however, and the principal's recovery may vary a great deal depending on which measure is used. Confusion exists because the cases have used terms such as "benefit of the bargain" with imprecision, and because rules articulated in cases involving breach of contract, fraud, and unjust enrichment have been applied to inappropriate fact situations. See *Overgaard v Johnson* (1977) 68 CA3d 821, 137 CR 412, for analysis of these conflicting rules. Naturally, the principal will want to frame a lawsuit for breach of fiduciary duty in terms that will bring the case under the broadest possible measure of damages, while the broker will seek to invoke the most restrictive measure.

Under a benefit of the bargain standard, the principal would be entitled to recover the difference between the actual value of the property and the value he expected to receive, while an out-of-pocket measure would permit recovery only of the difference between the actual value of the property and the amount paid. Somewhere in between is the "loss of profits" measure, recognized by the California Supreme Court in *Stout v Turney* (1978) 22 C3d 718, 150 CR 637, which permits recovery of incidental costs and expenses in addition to out-of-pocket loss. Also at issue in closely related cases is recovery of secret profits which the broker had obtained in the course of the transaction. See, *e.g., Ward v Taggart* (1959) 51 C2d 736, 336 P2d 534; *Simone v McKee* (1956) 142 CA2d 307, 298 P2d 667. See §§2.99 and 2.105 regarding secret profits.

For breach of contract actions, the measure of damages is governed by CC §3300, which authorizes recovery under a true benefit of the bargain standard. In fraud cases recovery is limited to out-of-pocket loss plus various expenses incurred in reliance on the fraud, plus lost profits if the principal acquired the property for profit or gain. CC §3343. Lost profits would not be available if the property had been purchased for residential purposes. See *Stout v Turney, supra,* 22 C3d at 728 n12, 150 CR at 643 n12. For breach of fiduciary duty, the tort measure of damages of CC §3333 applies. Civil Code §3333 provides for recovery of an amount that will "compensate for all the detriment proximately caused" by the breach, but does not include the benefit of the bargain language of CC §3300. *Overgaard v Johnson, supra.*

Disagreement arises regarding the recovery formula to be applied under CC §3333. Some courts have held that the measure of damages under CC §3333 is the benefit of the bargain rule applicable to actions for breach of contract under CC §3300. *Pepitone v Russo* (1976) 64 CA3d 685, 134 CR 709; *Pepper v Underwood* (1975) 48 CA3d 698, 122 CR 343; *Walsh v Hooker & Fay* (1963) 212 CA2d 450, 28 CR 16; *Simone v McKee, supra,* 142 CA2d 307, 298 P2d 667. A benefit of the bargain standard for breach of fiduciary duty is provided for in BAJI 12.57. Other courts have held that CC §3333 limits the principal's recovery to the extent of the financial injury actually sustained and is not a benefit of the bargain measure. *Ward v Taggart, supra,* 51 C2d 736, 336 P2d 534; *Gagne v Bertran* (1954) 43 C2d 481, 275 P2d 15; *Walters v Marler* (1978) 83 CA3d 1, 147 CR 655; *Overgaard v Johnson, supra.* See also California Attorney's Damages Guide §2.33 (Cal CEB 1975). In *Overgaard v Johnson, supra,* the seller listed some farm property for sale at $250,000. The broker obtained a buyer at that price, but negligently failed to advise the buyer that the acreage for sale was less than that stated in the sale documents. The buyer recovered from the seller the difference between the sale price and market value, and the seller then sued the broker for that amount plus attorneys' fees. The court of appeal held that under CC §3333 the seller was entitled to recover brokerage fees on the price differential and attorneys' fees but not the price differential itself because CC §3333 does not provide for a benefit of the bargain standard.

§2.105   b. Recovery of Secret Profits

A broker who obtains secret profits is required to return them to the principal on the theory that all profits in the transaction, absent full disclosure and specific agreement to the contrary, belong to the principal. *Menzel v Salka* (1960) 179 CA2d 612, 4 CR 78; *Ramey v Myers* (1952) 111 CA2d 679, 245 P2d 360. See §2.99.

The broker must disgorge all secret profits whether or not the principal has actually been injured. *Savage v Mayer* (1949) 33 C2d 548, 203 P2d 9. The remedy generally utilized to recover secret profits is the imposition of a constructive trust. *St. James Armenian Church v Kurkjian* (1975) 47 CA3d 547, 121 CR 214. However, when the funds have been dissipated, an award of money damages is proper. *St. James Armenian Church v Kurkjian, supra; Alexandrou v Alexander* (1974) 37 CA3d 306, 112 CR 307.

If the broker himself has received no secret profits, but through his breach of fiduciary duty secret profits have flowed to a third party, the broker is liable to the principal for those profits. *St. James Armenian Church v Kurkjian, supra.*

§2.106   c. Recovery of Commission

If the breach of the broker's fiduciary duty is willful, the principal may be entitled to recover any commission paid. See also *Robson v*

Hahn (1929) 98 CA 671, 277 P 507; *Menzel v Salka* (1960) 179 CA2d 612, 4 CR 78. When the breach is merely negligent, however, the broker is entitled to retain the commission. *Tackett v Croonquist* (1966) 244 CA2d 572, 53 CR 388.

§2.107   d. Punitive Damages

Punitive damages may be awarded if the broker's misconduct has been oppressive, fraudulent, or malicious. CC §3294; *Haigler v Donnelly* (1941) 18 C2d 674, 117 P2d 331; *Simone v McKee* (1956) 142 CA2d 307, 298 P2d 667; *Hartzell v Myall* (1953) 115 CA2d 670, 252 P2d 676. Punitive damages are not available for breach of contract, even if the breach is willful and even if the contract creates the fiduciary obligation. CC §3294; *Crogan v Metz* (1956) 47 C2d 398, 303 P2d 1029. They may, however, be available for breach of fiduciary duty, a noncontract claim, on proof of oppression, fraud, or malice. CC §3294. It is not clear whether the standard for broker misconduct is the same as that for a party not in a fiduciary relationship with the plaintiff. It seems likely, however, that imposition of punitive damages against a broker could be based on behavior less flagrant than would justify their award against either a nonprofessional or a nonfiduciary. See, *e.g., Ward v Taggart* (1959) 51 C2d 736, 336 P2d 534.

§2.108   e. Indemnity

The principal is entitled to indemnity from the broker for damages recovered by third parties because of the broker's actions. *Walsh v Hooker & Fay* (1963) 212 CA2d 450, 28 CR 16; *Kruse v Miller* (1956) 143 CA2d 656, 300 P2d 855. See *Overgaard v Johnson* (1977) 68 CA3d 821, 137 CR 412, discussed in §2.104, regarding the measure of damages in an indemnity situation.

§2.109   f. Recovery of Unsatisfied Judgments From the Real Estate Fund

The Real Estate Law provides for a special fund out of which any aggrieved person may satisfy a judgment against a real estate licensee for fraud, misrepresentation, deceit, or conversion. Bus & P C §§10470-10483. Until 1977, this fund was maintained separately as the real estate education, research and recovery fund, but is now simply a special account of the real estate fund. Bus & P C §10450.6.

A principal who has reduced his claim to judgment may apply to the court in which the judgment was entered for an order directing payment of the claim out of the real estate fund. Bus & P C §10471. Application must be made within one year after the judgment becomes final, and the applicant must show that he has made reasonable attempts to levy on the assets of the judgment debtor. Bus & P C §10472. The defendant must have been licensed as a broker or salesperson under the Real Estate Law at the time the misconduct occurred. Bus & P C §10471; see *Powers v Fox* (1979) 96 CA3d 440, 158 CR 92. In order for the fund to be liable, the transaction that gave rise to the plaintiff's claim must have been one for which a real estate license is required (Bus & P C §10471); recovery is not permitted if the broker was acting on his own behalf (*Robinson v Murphy* (1979) 96 CA3d 763, 158 CR 246; *McGaughey v Fox* (1979) 94 CA3d 645, 156 CR 593).

Recovery is limited to $20,000 per transaction ($10,000 if the cause of action arose before January 1, 1980, regardless of the amount of the judgment and the number of creditors (Bus & P C §10471), and a plaintiff can recover only this amount even if a broker commits more than one fraudulent act under one listing agreement. *Dombalian v Fox* (1979) 88 CA3d 763, 152 CR 86. The liability of the fund is limited to $100,000 for any one licensee; $40,000 if the cause of action arose before January 1, 1980. Bus & P C §10474. When the total of the claims exceeds the maximum limitations, the funds available must be distributed proportionately among the claimants. *Shirai v Karpe* (1976) 57 CA3d 276, 127 CR 549. Within these statutory limits, the claimant is entitled to recover the amount of his judgment which cannot be satisfied from the licensee's assets, including prejudgment and postjudgment interest and costs. *Antonio v Hempel* (1977) 71 CA3d 128, 139 CR 309; *Nordahl v Department of Real Estate* (1975) 48 CA3d 657, 121 CR 794.

On payment from the fund, the license of the broker or salesperson is automatically suspended until the fund has been reimbursed with interest. Bus & P C §10475.

g. Disciplinary Proceedings by the Real Estate Commissioner

§2.110 (1) Grounds for Imposing Discipline

Under the Real Estate Law, the commissioner is given substantial authority to bring disciplinary proceedings against brokers and salespersons. Bus & P C §§10071, 10176-10177. The grounds for disciplining licensees are very broad, and include all breaches of fiduciary duty under general agency law. Bus & P C §§10176, 10177; *Rhoades v Savage* (1963) 219 CA2d 294, 32 CR 885. In addition, the Real Estate Law specifies a number of actions which are not breaches of fiduciary duty, but which nonetheless may subject the broker to license suspension or revocation. Additional actions prohibited by statute include:

(a) Engaging in a continued and flagrant course of misrepresentation or making of false promises through real estate agents or salespersons (Bus & P C §10176(c));

(b) Commingling the broker's own money or property with that of others (Bus & P C §10176(e));

(c) Failing to inform the principal in writing of the full amount of the profit a broker will realize from the exercise of an option given to him by his principal and failing to obtain the principal's written approval of the amount of the profit (Bus & P C §10176(h); for further discussion of option listings, see §§2.62, 2.98);

(d) Claiming or receiving compensation under an exclusive agreement employing him to sell, buy, or exchange real estate for compensation or commission if the agreement does not contain a definite termination date (Bus & P C §10176(f); see §§2.59, 2.61, 2.67);

(e) If a broker, failing to exercise reasonable supervision over the activities of his salespersons (Bus & P C §10177(h); see *Norman v Department of Real Estate* (1979) 93 CA3d 768, 155 CR 715). The broker's license is not subject to suspension or revocation solely for the activities of an employee, however, unless the broker had guilty knowledge of the violation (Bus & P C §10179);

(f) Entering a plea of guilty or nolo contendere to, or having been convicted of, a felony or crime involving moral turpitude if the crime is substantially related to the qualifications, functions, or duties of a real estate licensee (Bus & P C §§490, 10177(b); see *Arneson v Fox* (1980) 28 C3d 440, 170 CR 778).

(g) Soliciting or inducing the sale of residential property on the ground of loss in value, increase in crime, or decline in quality of the schools, due to the present or prospective entry into the neighborhood of persons of another race, color, religion, ancestry, or national origin. Bus & P C §10177(*l*). See also 10 Cal Adm C §§2780-2782. See also §2.116 on other fair housing violations.

Standards for broker conduct are also found in the Code of Ethics and Professional Conduct promulgated by the Real Estate Commissioner. 10 Cal Adm C §2785. Subdivision (a) of §2785 lists specific acts and omissions that violate Bus & P C §§10176 and 10177 and constitute grounds for discipline. Subdivisions (b) (unethical conduct) and (c) (beneficial conduct) contain guidelines that are not intended to be statements of duties imposed by law or grounds for discipline, but are standards for upgrading the performance of the real estate industry.

If the broker's activities constitute a violation of the Real Estate Law, neither his good faith nor the absence of any injury to the principal will shelter him from the commissioner's disciplinary proceedings. *Abell v Watson* (1957) 155 CA2d 158, 317 P2d 159; *de St. Germain v Watson* (1950) 95 CA2d 862, 214 P2d 99. The absence of injury to the principal, of advantage to the broker, or of intent by the broker to act in a fraudulent or dishonest manner may, however, be taken into account by the commissioner in mitigating the penalty. *de St. Germain v Watson, supra.*

§2.111   (2) Procedures and Remedies

Disciplinary proceedings often originate with complaints filed with the Department of Real Estate, although the commissioner has the power to initiate disciplinary actions without receiving a private complaint, and even when the principal is fully satisfied with the licensee's performance. *McPherson v Real Estate Comm'r* (1958) 162 CA2d 751, 329 P2d 12. The broker is subject to disciplinary action regardless of his contractual relationship with his principal and regardless of whether he has an enforceable claim for compensation. *Buckley v Savage* (1960) 184 CA2d 18, 7 CR 328.

Disciplinary proceedings for violations of the Real Estate Law most commonly take the form of license suspensions or revocations under Bus & P C §10175. With limited exceptions (see Bus & P C §10177.1), the commissioner must hold a hearing before suspending or revoking a license (Bus & P C §10100). Hearings must be conducted in accordance with the Administrative Procedure Act (Bus & P C §10100; Govt C §§11370-11528), and are subject to judicial review by means of administrative mandamus proceedings (Govt C §11523; CCP §1094.5; see California Administrative Mandamus (Cal CEB 1966).

The commissioner is empowered to bring a civil action to enjoin violations of the Real Estate Law. Bus & P C §10081. The commissioner is also authorized to issue desist and refrain orders to any person, including a licensee, who violates the Real Estate Law. Bus & P C §10086. A licensee affected by a desist and refrain order is entitled to an administrative hearing regarding the commissioner's order. If the licensee files a verified request for a hearing alleging that the order precludes him from engaging in a substantial portion of his business, the commissioner must initiate a civil action to enforce the desist and refrain order. Bus & P C §10086.

The Real Estate Law also provides criminal sanctions for various actions by real estate licensees, including willful violations of the law's provisions. Bus & P C §10185. The district attorney of the county in which the violation occurs has jurisdiction to prosecute such actions, although the commissioner may participate in the proceedings. Bus & P C §10130.

B. Broker to Third Parties

§2.112   1. Secret Profits

The broker owes no fiduciary duty to a person who is not his principal, but he has a general duty under the Real Estate Law to deal fairly and honestly with all parties to any real estate transaction. Bus & P C §10176(i). A broker can be held liable to a third party for secret profits he receives through fraud or misrepresentation, and can be compelled to disgorge his secret profit whether or not the third party has suffered any actual loss. *Ward v Taggart* (1959) 51 C2d 736, 336 P2d 534. See §2.99 for a discussion of the broker's liability to the principal for secret profits.

§2.113   2. Misrepresentation and Failure To Disclose

Because the broker is the principal's agent, his dealings with a third party to the transaction are generally measured by the same obligations the principal owes to that party. The broker has the same affirmative obligation as the seller to disclose material facts concerning the value and desirability of the property that are not apparent to the buyer on investigation. *Lingsch v Savage* (1963) 213 CA2d 729, 29 CR 201. On the seller's duty to disclose, see §§2.89-2.94. For example, the seller and the broker must disclose illegal construction on the property (*Unger v Campau* (1956) 142 CA2d

722, 298 P2d 891); known termite infestation (*Orlando v Berkeley* (1963) 220 CA2d 224, 33 CR 860; *Saporta v Barbagelata* (1963) 220 CA2d 463, 33 CR 661); the existence of fill soil on raw land (*Massei v Lettunich* (1967) 248 CA2d 68, 56 CR 232); and that improvements have been built on filled ground (*Central Mut. Ins. Co. v Schmidt* (1957) 152 CA2d 671, 313 P2d 132). Whether a particular fact concerning the property is sufficiently material to require affirmative disclosure depends on the particulars of each case. *Saporta v Barbagelata, supra.*

If no disclosure is made, the broker and the seller are jointly and severally liable for the full amount of the buyer's damages. If the broker is aware of misrepresentations being made by the seller directly to the buyer, he is probably under an obligation to correct the misrepresentations; the broker has no duty to conceal the fraudulent or dishonest acts of his principal. *Willig v Gold* (1946) 75 CA2d 809, 171 P2d 754. If the broker misrepresents a material fact to the buyer, the seller will be liable along with the broker under a respondeat superior theory. See §§2.118-2.121.

§2.114   3. Negligence

A broker who renders service in a negligent manner will generally be liable to any third person within the zone of foreseeable risk who is injured by the negligent act. *Merrill v Buck* (1962) 58 C2d 552, 25 CR 456; *Gipson v Davis Realty Co.* (1963) 215 CA2d 190, 30 CR 253. The broker will be held liable to third parties for the negligence of salespersons in his or her employ. Bus & P C §10177(h); CC §2343(3); *Merrill v Buck, supra.*

§2.115   4. Breach of Contract

A broker may also be held liable to a third party for breach of an agreement that is ancillary to the contract to convey. In *Barr v Rhoades* (1969) 274 CA2d 852, 79 CR 505, both seller and broker were held liable for damages when they breached their agreement with the buyer to secure tenants and financing in connection with the sale of an apartment building.

§2.116   5. Housing Discrimination

Brokers who participate in discriminatory practices in the housing market may incur liability under any of a number of fair housing statutes. Brokers have been held to be covered by California's Unruh Civil Rights Act (CC §§51-53; *Lee v O'Hara* (1962) 57 C2d 476, 20 CR 617; *Vargas v Hampson* (1962) 57 C2d 479, 20 CR 618), and the fact that a broker was merely following instructions from his principal will not constitute a defense to an Unruh act suit (*Wagner v O'Bannon* (1969) 274 CA2d 121, 79 CR 44). Moreover, a realty board or multiple listing service might also incur liability under the Unruh act if it accedes to a seller's wish to market property in a discriminatory manner. *Wagner v O'Bannon, supra.*

The federal Fair Housing Act of 1968 (42 USC §§3601-3631) and Civil Rights Act of 1866 (42 USC §§1981-2000h-6) are also potential bases for imposing liability for damages on brokers who participate in discriminatory practices. Private actions alleging that brokers engaged in the practice of steering blacks into, and whites out of, certain neighborhoods were upheld in *Gladstone, Realtors v Bellwood* (1979) 441 US 91, and *Broadmoor Improvement Ass'n v Stan Weber & Assoc.* (5th Cir 1979) 597 F2d 568.

Other possible avenues for imposing liability on brokers for discriminatory practices include California Fair Employment and Housing Act (Govt C §§12900-12996); administrative action under the Real Estate Law to revoke the broker's license (Bus & P C §10177(*l*); 10 Cal Adm C §§2780-2782); and tort causes of action for fraud or interference with business opportunity. See Chapman, *The Real Estate Broker and the Unruh Civil Rights Act,* 45 LA B Bull 475 (1970). A broker who supplies information regarding the race, color, sex, religion, ancestry, or national origin of a prospective buyer, even when requested by the seller, commits a violation of the Rumford Fair Housing Act. 53 Ops Cal Atty Gen 196 (1970).

§2.117   C. Principal to Broker; Indemnification

The broker's duty to disclose defects in the property is coextensive with the seller's (see §2.113). *Lingsch v Savage* (1963) 213 CA2d 729, 29 CR 201. Generally broker and seller will be held jointly and severally liable for misrepresentations made to a buyer by the broker. *Saporta v Barbagelata* (1963) 220 CA2d 463, 33 CR 661. If a broker merely relays a misrepresentation from seller to buyer, and is unaware of its falsity, he may escape liability for fraud but still be liable for negligence, although the basis of the seller's liability would be fraud. *Gardner v Murphy* (1975) 54 CA3d 164, 126 CR 302.

In this situation, the broker may be entitled to indemnification from the principal for any liability he incurs. *Gardner v Murphy, supra.* The right to equitable indemnity (as opposed to contractual indemnity) arises when the misconduct of the party seeking indemnity is secondary or passive, and that of the party against whom indemnity is sought is primary or active. *Aerojet Gen. Corp. v D. Zelinsky & Sons* (1967) 249 CA2d 604, 57 CR 701. In *Gardner,* the court characterized the broker as the negligent transmitter and the principal as the intentional originator of the misrepresentation, and concluded that the primary-secondary test was met. The court indicated that the result would have been different if the broker had independently endorsed the misrepresentation, known it to be false, or added to it in a manner that made the principal's misrepresentation his own. See, *e.g., Schoenberg v Romike Properties* (1967) 251 CA2d 154, 59 CR 359, in which the brokers were found to have engaged in their own misrepresentations regarding the property and were denied indemnity.

It should be noted that the listing agreement may provide for contractual indemnity. The CAR exclusive authorization and right to sell listing agreement, for example, contains a clause in which the principal agrees to hold the broker harmless for liability incurred because the principal supplies incorrect information or fails to disclose a material fact. See §2.60. Apparently the broker's right to indemnity under such a provision would not depend on a finding that the broker's conduct was passive and the principal's active as would be required to impose equitable indemnity. *Gardner v Murphy, supra,* 54 CA3d 164, 126 CR 302.

D. Principal to Third Parties for Broker's Acts

§2.118   1. Misrepresentations

Under general rules of agency law, a principal is liable to third parties for the agent's actions undertaken on the principal's behalf whether or not the principal was aware of or authorized the agent's actions. CC §2338; *Warshauer v Bauer Constr. Co.* (1960) 179 CA2d 44, 3 CR 570. In real property transactions this rule is applied to impose liability on the principal for misrepresentations made by the broker whether the principal has knowledge of the misrepresentation (*Burkett v J.A. Thompson & Son* (1957) 150 CA2d 523, 310 P2d 56), or is innocent of it (*Miller v Wood* (1961) 188 CA2d 711, 10 CR

770). The principal is held liable for the broker's misrepresentations even when the broker is acting as the disclosed agent for both parties to the transaction. *Owens v Schneider* (1938) 29 CA2d 593, 85 P2d 198.

The broker's negligent, as well as intentional, misrepresentations will subject the principal to liability, whether or not the principal knew of or consented to the statements. Thus, the principal may incur liability if the broker should have known that his statement was false but had no actual knowledge of its falsity. *Richard v Baker* (1956) 141 CA2d 857, 297 P2d 674. See also *Gagne v Bertran* (1954) 43 C2d 481, 275 P2d 15.

The principal's liability also extends to misrepresentations made to the other party by a subagent. *Johnston v Seargeants* (1957) 152 CA2d 180, 313 P2d 41. This rule is of particular concern to sellers because of the common use (in the real property market) of multiple listing services and cooperating brokers. See §§2.24-2.27.

§2.119   2. Failure To Disclose

Both broker and seller have an affirmative obligation to disclose defects in the property which would not be apparent to the buyer (see §2.113). *Lingsch v Savage* (1963) 213 CA2d 729, 29 CR 201. A seller without actual knowledge of a defective condition of the property is liable if the broker knows of the defects and fails to disclose them on the theory that the broker's knowledge is imputed to the seller. *Rothstein v Janss Inv. Corp.* (1941) 45 CA2d 64, 113 P2d 465. The broker's knowledge is not imputed to the seller, however, if the broker is acting in a dual capacity and thus has an interest adverse to the seller's. *Herdan v Hanson* (1920) 182 C 538, 189 P 440; *Owens v Schneider* (1938) 29 CA2d 593, 85 P2d 198.

§2.120   3. Effect of Exculpatory Provision

An "as is" or exculpatory provision in a purchase agreement will not immunize a seller of real property from liability for his own failure to disclose hidden defects (*Lingsch v Savage* (1963) 213 CA2d 729, 29 CR 201; see *Katz v Department of Real Estate* (1979) 96 CA3d 895, 158 CR 766), nor from liability for fraudulent acts of his broker of which he has knowledge (*Lingsch v Savage, supra; Herzog v Capital Co.* (1945) 27 C2d 349, 164 P2d 8). An innocent principal, however, is protected by an exculpatory provision from liability for damages for the affirmative acts of misconduct of his agent; the injured party's remedy is limited to rescission. *Speck v Wylie* (1934) 1 C2d 625, 36 P2d 618; *Kett v Graeser* (1966) 241 CA2d 571, 50 CR 727.

The unanswered question is whether an exculpatory provision will protect an innocent principal from liability for damages for the broker's failure to disclose defects. See *Lingsch v Savage, supra.* Because the broker's knowledge of defects is imputed to the principal (see §2.119), and because an exculpatory clause will not protect a seller who fails to disclose defects of which he knows, it could be argued that the rule of *Speck v Wylie, supra,* is limited to misrepresentations, and would not apply to the broker's nondisclosure of defects. See 1 Miller & Starr, Current Law of California Real Estate §4:30 (rev ed 1975).

§2.121   4. Liability to Subsequent Purchasers

The seller's liability to third persons for either his or his agent's fraudulent misconduct may extend to subsequent purchasers of the property. If the original purchaser has a legally enforceable claim for damages for fraud by the seller or the seller's broker, a person who acquires the property from the original purchaser can enforce the claim against the seller. *Burkett v J.A. Thompson & Son* (1957) 150 CA2d 523, 310 P2d 56. Apparently the original buyer must assign his claim to the subsequent buyer in order for the subsequent buyer to recover. *Cohen v Citizens Nat'l Trust & Sav. Bank* (1956) 143 CA2d 480, 300 P2d 14.

3

John F. Soukup

The Purchase and Sale Agreement

JOHN F. SOUKUP, A.B., 1970, J.D., 1973, University of Southern California. Mr. Soukup practices in Beverly Hills, California. Mr. Soukup acknowledges the assistance of Richard J. Kamins of Tyre & Kamins, Los Angeles, in the preparation of his manuscript and in supplying certain forms.

Portions of this chapter are based on material written by Richard S. Jensen, A.B., 1966, Stanford University, J.D., 1969, Hastings College of the Law. Mr. Jensen is a partner in the San Francisco firm of Skjerven, Morrill, Jensen, MacPherson & Drucker.

Some material in this chapter was derived from chapters 4 and 6 of California Real Estate Sales Transactions (Cal CEB 1967).

I. DRAFTING CONSIDERATIONS

§3.1   A. Interplay Between Negotiating and Drafting

The negotiating process cannot be completely separated from the drafting of the purchase and sale agreement; both tasks are linked. The goal of negotiations is the creation of an agreement that meets the desire of the parties; conversely, the clauses agreed to represent the results of negotiations that have taken place. The discussion of negotiating techniques is therefore generally combined with the discussion of drafting the particular clauses designed to carry out the terms that have been negotiated.

§3.2   B. Meeting the Expectations of the Parties

The care with which an agreement for the sale or exchange of real property is drafted largely determines whether the parties' expectations will be realized or frustrated. If the intentions of the parties to the agreement are to be realized, it must be enforceable and clear. It must also anticipate reasonably foreseeable events and should reflect the drafter's alertness to modern language and a respect for the client's essential need to understand and to be able to use the agreement he or she has signed.

To draft an effective agreement, the drafter must first obtain all relevant facts. See §§1.21, 3.3 on interviewing to obtain these facts. The agreement itself must satisfy the legal requirements for contracts respecting real property (these requirements are discussed in §§3.8-3.38) and must be molded to the client's purposes (see §§1.58-1.79). The lawyer must do more than choose effective provisions; the proper type of agreement, *e.g.*, exchange, sale-and-leaseback, or installment sale, must be drafted with an awareness of the tax effects of various types of agreements.

§3.3   C. Resolving Conflicting Interests of the Parties

The lawyer's skill and sensitivity are crucial in negotiating resolutions when the interests of the parties conflict. The client's purpose is to enter into a transaction that he considers desirable, if this can be done without disadvantages that outweigh the advantages. The lawyer's first goal should be to make certain that his client properly understands the legal and business effects and risks of the proposed transaction so that the client makes his decision with full awareness of the advantages and disadvantages. For example, a seller who takes back a purchase money note secured by a deed of trust on the property sold must understand that, under CCP §580b, his sole recourse for nonpayment is foreclosure. Once the client has made an informed decision to proceed, the lawyer's role should be to create conditions that enable the client to enter into a desired transaction. In negotiating for that result, he or she must inform the client of the legal implications of the transaction as presented, and should try to obtain every possible protection. If, however, out of zeal to protect the client, the lawyer antagonizes the other party or otherwise makes achieving an advantageous transaction impossible, he has failed in his duty.

Often, an unacceptable element in the transaction can be resolved by compromise. For example, even though the seller may oppose subordination as dangerous to his security, he may be willing to consider it if the buyer offers a higher price. Similarly, a buyer may be willing to accept a defect in title or a variance in description if the seller lowers the price or adjusts some other term of the agreement. On the other hand, the lawyer must be alert to hazards that would make the transaction undesirable to the client at any price. In the final analysis, the lawyer should provide the client with an objective analysis of the degree of risk associated with the various points which cannot be negotiated in his favor, and in this way assist the client in assessing the transaction's net economic worth.

Provisions which may be useful in resolving various problems that separate parties are set out in §§3.63-3.191.

D. Preparation and Format of the Agreement

§3.4   1. Who May Prepare

In most real property transactions, the lawyer is only one of the participants acting for the parties. Usually, he finds himself in the company of a real estate broker, a title company representative, and in southern California perhaps an escrow company representative. During the transaction the attorney may be confronted with documents he has not prepared, ranging from standard forms with blanks to be filled in to deposit receipts with elaborate interlineations and addenda. The lawyer, however, is the only person authorized to practice law, draft legal documents, and advise parties on the legal implications of a transaction. See §1.2. He has an obligation to his client to review carefully documents prepared by others and to recommend changes in the forms if necessary to protect the client's interests or to reflect accurately the agreement of the parties. Printed forms prepared by nonattorneys should be reviewed carefully to make certain they accurately reflect the understanding of the parties and to see if additional provisions should be added for the client's protection.

§3.5   2. Language of the Agreement

Lawyers may shorten the agreement and make it more intelligible by eliminating archaic and unimportant legal jargon and unnecessary words. For example, outmoded language such as "situate, lying and located" should be eliminated whenever possible. The search for brevity and clarity is a continuing one and is advanced by each lawyer who finds an effective way to eliminate redundant wording or to clarify obscure expressions. See Wydick, Plain English for Lawyers (1979). (This book is an expansion of an article by the author in 66 Calif L Rev 727 (1978).)

§3.6   3. Format of the Agreement

The agreement is more readable when it is divided into numbered paragraphs, each dealing with one subject. All provisions dealing with one subject should be grouped together, and cross-references to related provisions should be supplied so that all material on a particular point can be quickly located. Although no particular order is required, a common organization is to identify the parties, describe the property, state the purchase price and manner of payment, define the condition of title required at closing, set forth special provisions tailored to meet the requirements of the transaction, specify the division of various expenses, and conclude with general provisions.

The attorney preparing a purchase and sale agreement has an opportunity to free the document from outmoded customs. For example, letter-size rather than legal-size paper may be preferable because few clients have legal-size filing cabinets, and time and money may be saved if boiler plate provisions are duplicated or typed from word processing equipment memory storage.

§3.7   4. Use of Printed Forms

Whether printed forms provided by brokers, title companies, escrow agents, and stationery stores should be used must be decided after careful consideration. It may be advantageous to use some of these forms, e.g., deposit receipts. Most clients accept them readily, assuming the printed form has a certain authority, and the typing required to amend a form may be less than is required to prepare an entire agreement. Many of these forms, however, contain provisions that may be objectionable, e.g., a provision that title is to be taken by buyer "subject to covenants, conditions, and restrictions of record" or "subject to any state of facts an accurate survey would reveal." If the lawyer uses any printed forms, they should be read carefully to determine the propriety and adequacy of their provisions for a particular transaction and their compatibility with the addenda so that the agreement as a whole is consistent and unambiguous. On provisions common to various agreements, see §§3.41-3.62. For provisions reconciling inconsistencies between printed provisions and addenda, see §2.80. See §3.40 for California Association of Realtors printed form of real estate purchase contract and receipt for deposit.

II. ESSENTIAL ELEMENTS OF THE AGREEMENT

§3.8   A. Requisites for Enforceability

The essential elements of an enforceable contract are: parties capable of contracting, mutual consent, a lawful object, and a sufficient consideration. CC §1550. Agreements for the sale of real property must meet the additional requirement that the agreement, or memorandum of it, must be in writing and signed by the party to be bound. CC §1624(4). The buyer's agreement "to pay an indebtedness secured by a mortgage or deed of trust upon the property" is also required to be in writing. CC §1624(7). To obtain specific performance, the agreement must also be sufficiently certain. CC §3390(5). This requires designating the parties, the purchase price, the method of payment, and the description of the property. See 3 Witkin, California Procedure, *Pleading* §645 (2d ed 1971). The form at §§3.41-3.62 contains all of the common provisions that should be included for even the simplest transaction.

B. Parties

§3.9   1. Necessary Parties as Sellers

Before preparing a purchase and sale agreement, counsel must know who has to sign it. To determine this, he must know who has an interest in the property. (It is preferable to do this preliminary title work before the agreement is signed, to be sure that all persons who have an estate in the property are made parties to the agreement.) A party who signs an agreement for sale of an interest greater than he owns is liable not only for specific performance for the interest that he has but also in damages to the buyer if he cannot deliver title to the interests sold. *Armstrong v Sacramento Valley Realty Co.* (1921) 52 CA 110, 115, 198 P 217, 219.

Seller's counsel should be familiar with the condition of title not only to determine who must sign the agreement as sellers, but also to assure that title can be delivered free of all encumbrances other than those to which the buyer will take subject to under the agreement. (For example, the seller may be unable to remove easements or restrictive covenants; if so, the agreement must provide that the buyer take subject to them.) If the seller is to deliver title free and clear of any existing deed of trust, counsel should make certain that there is no lock-in provision in the note preventing early repay-

ment. See §5.13. If the buyer is to assume existing financing, seller's counsel should determine if the existing financing is, in fact, assumable. See California Mortgage and Deed of Trust Practice §§2.34-2.35 (Cal CEB 1979) for a discussion of the validity and enforceability of due-on clauses. See also §§3.50, 5.23-5.24.

Buyer's counsel should also satisfy himself about the seller's title. Even though the agreement states the buyer's title requirements as a prerequisite to its enforceability (see §§3.55, 3.80), the buyer may waste time and money on plans, engineer's reports, etc., before learning that these requirements cannot be met.

One should begin title work with the most recent existing title insurance policy or report, or with the deed or judgment by which the owner acquired title. If title was derived by gift or inheritance, some earlier title policy may exist. The preferred practice is to obtain a new preliminary title report, and to review copies of all documents shown on the schedule of exceptions or as reservations in the legal description.

To determine who holds title and to make sure that the seller can deliver the agreed title, counsel must consider these questions:

(a) Was the seller married when the property was acquired? Has a marriage taken place since? (In either event, the spouse should also sign the agreement or execute a waiver such as the one at §3.16.) See §3.15.

(b) Has the property been declared as a homestead? All owners of homestead rights should join in the agreement. The spouse of an owner declaring a homestead on the owner's own separate property for their joint benefit has an interest in the property. CC §§1242, 1265. After a property settlement judgment, a spouse may not claim a homestead in property of the other spouse. *Wiltrakis v Wiltrakis* (1966) 244 CA2d 257, 53 CR 97.

(c) If the property was held in joint tenancy, has any joint tenant died? If so, the vesting of title in the survivor requires certain formalities, including release of the state's lien for inheritance taxes.

(d) Is record title held by anyone who is deceased? If so, it is generally necessary to obtain court approval of any conveyance by the administrator or executor. See 1 California Decedent Estate Administration, chap 14 (Cal CEB 1971).

(e) Is the property held in cotenancy by several people? If so, they all must participate in the agreement and deed.

(f) If the property is held in the name of a general partnership, has a statement of partnership been recorded? If held in a limited partnership, has a certificate of limited partnership been recorded? If so, does the statement or certificate reflect who the current partners are? See §§3.22-3.23.

(g) If the property is held in the name of a corporation, are officers available who can sign the deed on behalf of the corporation? Are there corporate formalities, *e.g.,* directors' vote or shareholders' vote, that will have to be observed? See §3.26.

§3.10   2. Capacity To Contract

It is essential to the existence of an enforceable contract that the parties be capable of contracting. CC §1550. All persons are capable of contracting except minors, persons of unsound mind, and persons deprived by law of civil rights. CC §1556. The word "person" includes a corporation as well as a natural person. CC §14. Under Corp C §15008, a partnership may also contract in the firm's name concerning property. See §3.22.

§3.11   a. Minors

An individual under 18 years of age is a minor (CC §25), and cannot make a contract relating to real property, or any interest in real property (CC §33). Such contracts are absolutely void and thus need not be disaffirmed (*Sparks v Sparks* (1950) 101 CA2d 129, 225 P2d 238). Not only are such contracts void from their inception but it has been held that the minor need not even return the consideration. *Sparks v Sparks, supra.* (It would appear that the only protection even a bona fide purchaser has against any conveyance by a minor is a claim against the title insurance policy or a claim to the property by adverse possession if the buyer, or his predecessors in interest, has held the property for at least five years after the minor reached majority.)

A minor can hold title to real property because the law presumes acceptance of a beneficial grant. *People v Fujita* (1932) 215 C 166, 8 P2d 1011; *Estate of Yano* (1922) 188 C 645, 206 P 995. A transfer of title to real property held by a minor requires the appointment of a guardian. See §3.13. An emancipated minor does have the power to buy and sell real property. CC §63(g). An emancipated minor is one

who has entered into a valid marriage, whether or not such marriage was terminated by dissolution, or who is on active duty with the United States Armed Forces, or who has received a declaration of emancipation under CC §64. CC §62.

§3.12   b. Persons of Unsound Mind

Persons of unsound mind are classified in two categories: those entirely without understanding (CC §38) and those of unsound mind but not entirely without understanding (CC §39). The former have no power to make a contract and contracts made by them are void. *Estate of McConkey* (1939) 33 CA2d 554, 92 P2d 456. Contracts of people defined in CC §39, made before judicial determination of their incapacity, are subject to rescission. CC §§39, 1689(b)(7). After incompetence is judicially determined, no conveyance or other contract is valid unless made after the incompetent was held to be restored to capacity. CC §40; *Carroll v Carroll* (1940) 16 C2d 761, 108 P2d 420.

§3.13   c. Guardianship or Conservatorship for Persons Under Disability

Although minors and incompetents do not have the capacity to convey property, a guardian or conservator may do so for them if properly authorized. Prob C §2420(b); *Estate of Kay* (1947) 30 C2d 215, 181 P2d 1. The California guardian and conservatorship law is in Prob C §§1400-3803. See also California Conservatorships §§5.43-5.60 (Cal CEB 1968) for a discussion of conservatorship procedures with respect to real property.

§3.14   d. Prisoners

Under a 1975 amendment to the Penal Code, civil rights of persons incarcerated in a state prison may be subject to suspension during the period of imprisonment, but are not forfeited. Pen C §2600. A prisoner has the right to own, sell, or convey real property but the Department of Corrections may restrict or prohibit sales or conveyances that are made for business purposes. Pen C §2601(a). If one of the parties to the agreement is imprisoned in a state prison, the other party should first verify that the prisoner has a right to enter into the agreement.

3. Married Persons as Sellers

§3.15   a. Buyer's Need for Certainty

The buyer wants to be sure that good title to the property being purchased will be transferred, free from challenges to the transaction by a spouse. To protect the buyer, counsel should inquire about the seller's marital status and determine whether the property to be sold is community or separate property. See §3.30 for a discussion of community property. If there has been a dissolution of the marriage, the property settlement agreement should be reviewed to verify the status of the property.

Both spouses must execute any instrument by which the community real property is leased for longer than one year, or is sold, conveyed, or encumbered. CC §5127. If that is not possible, the spouse who cannot execute should appoint the other spouse as agent by a power of attorney. The power of attorney must be in recordable form (*i.e.,* acknowledged) so that it can be recorded with the deed. The language in the power of attorney should also be cleared with any title company asked to insure title. (A power of attorney cannot be used if a declaration of homestead has been recorded on the property; instead, the deed must be personally executed and acknowledged by each spouse. CC §1242.) A spouse who does not execute a conveyance may file an action to void it within one year after its recordation. CC §5127. An instrument executed by one spouse in favor of a lessee, purchaser, or encumbrancer, in good faith without knowledge of the marriage is presumed to be valid with respect to property standing in the name of that spouse alone. CC §5127. If the selling spouse claims the property is separate property, the buyer should obtain a waiver or a quitclaim deed from the other spouse. See waiver by spouse form at §3.16. The waiver estops a spouse from setting aside the transaction at a later date. Many title companies require a quitclaim deed before insuring title.

§3.16   b. Form: Waiver by Spouse for Sale of Separate Property

Form 3.16-1

____[Name of spouse]____ acknowledges that ____[he / she]____ is the spouse of ____[name of seller]____ who executed the attached purchase and sale agreement and further acknowledges that the real property described in

the attached agreement is seller's separate property and waives any requirement that ____[he / she]____ join in the execution of any other document required for the transaction set forth in the attached agreement, and agrees to
execute a quitclaim deed if necessary so that buyer can obtain title insurance.
Dated: _____

[Signature of spouse]

Comment: If the property to be sold is separate property this form of
waiver or a quitclaim deed should be obtained by the buyer.

§3.17   4. Trustees

A trustee has the power to sell or lease real property held in trust
when necessary or appropriate to carry out the purposes of the trust,
unless he is expressly forbidden to do so by the trust instrument or it
appears from the terms of the trust that the property was to be retained in specie in the trust. *Church v Church* (1940) 40 CA2d 696,
105 P2d 640. A trust affecting real property must be in writing. CC
§852. Counsel should inspect the document authorizing the trustee
to act and verify that the trustee has the power to sell or buy real
property. If the trustee is acting in breach of the trust and the buyer
is not a bona fide purchaser for value without notice of the breach,
the beneficiary can recover the property from the buyer. CC §2243;
Firato v Tuttle (1957) 48 C2d 136, 308 P2d 333; *Ruth v Lytton Sav. &
Loan Ass'n* (1968) 266 CA2d 831, 72 CR 521.

If the record buyer takes title as trustee, but the deed does not
name the beneficiary, the trustee's subsequent conveyance creates a
rebuttable presumption of its validity in favor of his grantee, which
becomes conclusive if the grantee establishes that he is a bona fide
purchaser. CC §869a; *Hansen v G & G Trucking Co.* (1965) 236
CA2d 481, 46 CR 186. The fact that the deed to the grantor designated him as "trustee" does not prevent his grantee from being a
bona fide purchaser.

§3.18   5. Sales by Agents and Attorneys-in-Fact

The typical listing agreement with a real estate broker empowers
the broker to act as the seller's agent to find a buyer, and to
negotiate, on the seller's behalf, the terms of the sale. The broker
rarely is authorized to execute the purchase and sale agreement or
the grant deed. This is true even if the broker is given an exclusive

right to sell listing. Such a listing merely entitles the broker to a commission if the property is sold during the term of the listing without regard to who procured the buyer. See §2.59.

Sometimes, however, the seller may actually authorize another to sell the property. This often occurs if the seller is located some distance from the property. The agent's authority to act is usually in the form of a written power of attorney. The power of attorney must be carefully drafted to make certain it authorizes the particular acts to be performed by the attorney-in-fact, and is satisfactory to the title company insuring title. For example, it should contain a power to "sell and convey." A power to "sell" alone would not authorize the execution of the deed. *Delano v Jacoby* (1892) 96 C 275, 31 P 290. A power to execute a mortgage might not include the power to execute a deed of trust unless the words "to mortgage or otherwise encumber" are used. A power to "sell and convey" is not a power to exchange property. See 1 Bowman, Ogden's Revised California Real Property Law §3.72 (TI Corp-CEB 1974) for the rules of title practice regarding the interpretation of powers of attorney.

A power of attorney to convey or mortgage real property must be recorded in the county where the real property is located. Govt C §27322; CC §2933. A recorded power of attorney can be revoked only by recording a revocation in the same county. CC §1216.

Usually it is best to draw a power of attorney as narrowly as possible, limiting it to the specific transaction and recording a revocation as soon as the transaction is closed. Otherwise the principal would be exposed to possible liability for the agent's acts as long as the recorded power of attorney remains unrevoked. Another method of limiting the power of attorney is to set out an expiration date in the instrument itself.

Agreements, deeds, and other documents executed by an attorney-in-fact must be executed by first subscribing the name of the principal and then the agent's name as attorney-in-fact. CC §1095. For example, "A, by B, his attorney-in-fact" and not "B, attorney-in-fact for A."

It is also important for the agent to be protected from inadvertently assuming personal liability. For example, the agent is personally liable when the document does not disclose the principal, even if the other party knows of the agency relationship. *Otis Elevator Co. v Berry* (1938) 28 CA2d 430, 82 P2d 704. Even if the existence of the agency is disclosed, if the identity of the principal is

not disclosed the agent is personally liable unless the parties agree otherwise. *Cline v Atwood* (1966) 241 CA2d 108, 50 CR 233.

§3.19   6. Buyer's Use of Agents or Nominees

A buyer may use an agent to purchase property in the buyer's name, to take title in the agent's name, or may designate in the purchase and sale agreement a nominee to take title for the buyer. If the buyer wishes to take title in his own name, but to designate an agent to execute the necessary documents (*e.g.,* the purchase agreement, note, deed of trust, and escrow instructions), the buyer will need to give the agent a power of attorney. See §3.18. Sometimes the buyer wishes to have the agent execute all the documents in the agent's name and to take title in the agent's name. See §3.20. A nominee is sometimes designated in the purchase agreement when the agreement is to be assigned, before the closing, to the ultimate buyer, but the practice of designating a nominee should always be avoided. See §3.21.

§3.20   a. Agents as Buyers

A buyer may wish to have an agent execute the purchase agreement in the name of the agent alone and also to have title taken in the name of the agent. Often this is done because the buyer does not wish to disclose his identity. The buyer, for example, may be assembling a large number of contiguous parcels and the buyer's identity could cause an increase in the value of the other parcels the buyer is seeking.

A buyer may arrange for a title company to hold title in its name, under a holding agreement, until all parcels have been acquired. (Title companies are now refusing to do this unless they are also trust companies.) The use of an agent to take title and then convey to the actual buyer raises some important questions:

(1) Is there a danger of liens? If the agent is to take title at the closing and thereafter convey to the actual buyer, it is important that no liens attach to the property because of any personal debts of the agent. The actual buyer may be adversely affected because judgments or tax liens will attach as soon as the agent acquires title; the seller may be adversely affected if the real buyer delays closing to prevent liens from attaching. In *Majewsky v Empire Constr. Co.* (1970) 2 C3d 478, 85 CR 819, a speculator purchased the property

and immediately resold it at a profit. The buyer ended up holding the property subject to $50,000 in judgment liens which attached during the instant the title passed through the speculator. To minimize this danger, the buyer should know his agent's circumstances and run a search of the record to discover any recorded judgment liens or tax liens and, preferably, should obtain title insurance. The transfer from the agent to the actual buyer should be made as soon as possible after title vests in the agent to minimize the time during which new liabilities of the agent may affect title.

(2) Will the transfer from the agent cause loan charges to accrue? If the agent is to take title at the closing and thereafter convey to the actual buyer, the papers representing the obligation and encumbrance should be read in advance to make certain that this retransfer can be made without acceleration of the debt or imposition of prepayment penalties. For a discussion of due-on provisions see §§3.50, 5.24.

(3) Will the transfer from the agent cause a new reassessment for property taxes? See Cal Const, art XIIIA; Rev & T C §§60-67. This may present a problem if the property has been held for any length of time in the agent's name and has appreciated in value during that time. Note, however, the exception from reassessment for the transfer of "bare legal title." State Board of Equalization Rule 462(*l*), 18 Cal Adm C §462(*l*).

(4) Is the principal protected from contractual liability? The execution of the agreement by an agent of an undisclosed principal will not insulate the principal from contractual liability; the general rule is that the third party may elect to hold either the agent or the undisclosed principal. See 1 Witkin, Summary of California Law, *Agency and Employment* §§147-149 (8th ed 1973). It is possible to insulate the principal from liability only when a negotiable instrument is executed by the agent, because the general rule does not apply to negotiable instruments. See 2 California Commercial Law §2.7 (Cal CEB 1965).

§3.21   b. Use of Nominees

If the agreement is executed by one whose rights are to be conveyed to the actual buyer before closing, the agreement should be drafted to allow for the transfer. See provision in §3.184. The use of a provision allowing the party signing as buyer to designate a

nominee is not a satisfactory solution to the problem of facilitating a transfer to the actual buyer, because the actual buyer, even after being designated nominee by the party signing the agreement, is not entitled to specific enforcement of the agreement against the seller. In *Cisco v Van Lew* (1943) 60 CA2d 575, 141 P2d 433, the court concluded that the agreement was uncertain in that no memorandum signed by the seller identified the buyer. The court also decided that mere designation of a nominee without a formal assignment did not vest in the nominee (in this case the principal) any right to enforce the agreement and that without an assumption by the assignee of the buyer's obligations under the agreement, the agreement lacked the mutuality of obligation required for specific performance. See also *Ott v Home Sav. & Loan Ass'n* (9th Cir 1958) 265 F2d 643 ("nominee" not a synonym for "assignee"); *Rivadell, Inc. v Razo* (1963) 215 CA2d 614, 30 CR 622. But see *JMR, Inc. v Hedderly* (1968) 261 CA2d 144, 148, 67 CR 742, 745, in which the court concluded that a corporate nominee should have the opportunity to present evidence "to show that the contract was made in the contemplation of the formation of the plaintiff corporation, and for its benefit, and that it adopted and ratified the contract after its formation." On taking title in the name of an entity to be formed, see §3.31. The preferred practice is to avoid the term "nominee"; instead, make the agreement assignable and use a formal assignment to the assignee. See §3.184 for a provision for assignment.

§3.22   7. Partnerships

Partnerships may hold title to real property in the partnership name. Corp C §15008. It is usually advisable to hold title in the partnership name and not in the name of the individual partners. See 1 Bowman, Ogden's Revised California Real Property Law §6.73 (TI Corp-CEB 1974). Any partner of a general partnership, or a general partner of a limited partnership, can bind the partnership or convey partnership property. Corp C §§15009-15010. However, the other partners can attack a conveyance if it is beyond the authority of the signing partner and the buyer knows that the signing partner exceeded his authority. Corp C §§15009(1), 15010(1). See 6 Witkin, Summary of California Law, *Partnership* §34 (8th ed 1974). Corporations Code §15010.5 provides that recording a statement of partnership in the county where the real estate is located creates a conclusive presumption in favor of a bona fide purchaser for value that those named in the statement are all of the partners.

Title insurers will usually require that the statement of partnership be recorded before the conveyance, and the prudent buyer should at least examine it to verify the authority of the signing partner. In order to obtain insurable title when selling real property in a partnership name, all parties must sign or the partnership agreement, signed by all partners, must expressly authorize the partners who did sign. See 1 Bowman, Ogden's Revised California Real Property Law §6.75 (TI Corp-CEB 1974). Title insurers may be willing to accept a statement in a recorded statement of partnership that certain partners or fewer than all partners may convey if the statement is signed by all the partners. See Advising California Partnerships §3.113 (Cal CEB 1975). See also §3.43.

§3.23   8. Limited Partnerships

A limited partnership comes into existence only when the certificate of limited partnership is recorded (Corp C §15502), and recordation creates the same presumption as the statement of partnership (Corp C §15502(4); see §3.22). The certificate must be recorded in the county where the limited partnership has its principal place of business and wherever it owns real property. Corp C §15502(1) (b)-(3). If the certificate has not been recorded, the agreement may bind only the individual signing for the partnership but not the limited partnership itself. Putative limited partners would probably be treated as joint venturers or general partners subject to personal liability unless they renounced their interest in the profits of the partnership and took advantage of the "escape clause" contained in Corp C §15511. See 6 Witkin, Summary of California Law, *Partnership* §§53-59 (8th ed 1974).

For forms useful in drafting a limited partnership, see Advising California Partnerships, chap 4 (Cal CEB 1975).

§3.24   9. Joint Ventures

The provisions of Corp C §15008 permitting partnerships to hold title in the partnership's name are not clearly applicable to a joint venture. Prior to 1970, it was generally believed that a joint venture could not hold title in its own name but, instead, must hold title in the names of the individual venturers. The preferred method of holding title would be either "*A, B,* and *C,* doing business as *X* Company, a joint venture" or "*X* Company, a joint venture composed of *A, B,* and *C.*" See 1 Bowman, Ogden's Revised California Real Property Law §6.89 (TI Corp-CEB 1974). However, because of the 1970 amendment to Corp C §20001 permitting unincorporated associations to hold title in their own names, it *may* be possible for a joint venture to hold title in its own name. This may depend on whether the members choose to identify themselves as a joint venture or as an unincorporated association. See 1 Ogden's Real Property §6.88. See also §3.25 on unincorporated associations.

The distinction between a joint venture and a partnership has never been sharply drawn. In most respects, other than ability to hold title, a joint venture is treated like a partnership and the courts freely apply the provisions of the Uniform Partnership Act when appropriate. *MacIsaac v Pozzo* (1945) 26 C2d 809, 161 P2d 449; *Orlopp v Willardson Co.* (1965) 232 CA2d 750, 43 CR 125.

In most transactions the designation "joint venture" should be avoided. A so-called joint venture is, in fact, usually either a partnership or an unincorporated association, both of which can hold title in their own name. See §§3.22, 3.25.

§3.25   10. Unincorporated Associations

Before November 23, 1970, the only unincorporated associations that could hold title in their own name were benevolent or fraternal societies or associations, labor organizations, organized medical societies, and religious associations. Effective November 23, 1970, any unincorporated association may, subject to its bylaws and regulations, own and deal with real property for the business purposes of the organization. Corp C §20001. Property not necessary for business purposes may be held for ten years. Corp C §§20001-21200. Conveyances by such an organization must be executed by its president, or other head, and the secretary, or other comparable officer, and must be authorized by resolution of the organization. An unincorporated association may record a statement in the county where it owns real property, listing those officers authorized to execute conveyances on its behalf. Corp C §20002. A bona fide purchaser or encumbrancer for value is entitled to rely on a conveyance executed by the listed persons unless a member of the association has recorded a statement that the previously recorded statement is not authorized. Corp C §20002.

§3.26 11. Corporations

If one of the parties is a corporation, the other party must be assured that the transaction has been properly authorized by the corporation. Corporations Code §313 provides that any conveyance signed by the chairman of the board, the president or any vice-president, and the secretary, assistant secretary, chief financial officer or any assistant treasurer is not invalid for lack of authority, provided that the buyer did not have actual knowledge of the lack of authority. Further protection for the buyer is obtained by requiring that the statement set forth in CC §1190.1 be added to the acknowledgment. That section provides that a certificate of acknowledgment of an instrument executed by a corporation by its president or vice-president and secretary or assistant secretary may also contain a statement that the corporation executed the instrument pursuant to its bylaws or a resolution of its board of directors. Such a recital is prima facie evidence of authority and conclusive evidence in favor of a bona fide purchaser, lessee, or encumbrancer.

Assurance that a sale of real property is authorized can also be provided by a corporate secretary's certifying that the transaction has been approved by the board of directors and stating either (a) that the property transferred is less than substantially all of the assets of the corporation, or (b) that the transfer is in the usual or regular course of business of the corporation, or (c) if the transfer is of substantially all of the assets of the corporation, that the transaction has been approved by a majority of the outstanding shares as required by the Corporations Code. Corp C §1002.

A corporation comes into existence by filing its articles with the Secretary of State. An inquiry to that office will determine whether a corporate party has filed its articles and is in good standing. Under Corp C §207(a), a corporate seal is no longer required to show corporate authority, so there is no longer any need to demand that a document bear a corporate seal.

12. Manner of Holding Title

§3.27 a. Importance of Ownership Form

Title to real property may be held by one or more persons. Depending on their purposes and relationships to one another, several persons may hold property together in joint tenancy, tenancy in common, partnership, or community interest. CC §682. A corporation may also be formed to hold title. Important tax and estate consequences flow from the form of ownership chosen, and buyers must be counseled to consider their choice carefully. On probate consequences, see California Will Drafting §§2.43-2.57 (Cal CEB 1965).

§3.28   b. Cotenancies

Co-owners of equal interests may be either tenants in common or joint tenants. Tenants in common may have unequal undivided interests, but the interests of joint tenants must be equal. CC §§683, 685.

There are other differences between tenancies in common and joint tenancies. Surviving joint tenants take the entire interest on the death of a joint tenant. See 3 Witkin, Summary of California Law, *Real Property* §§203-204 (8th ed 1973). Because of survivorship rights, a joint tenant's interest is not subject to his testamentary disposition or, after his death, to his debts. But see *Rupp v Kahn* (1966) 246 CA2d 188, 55 CR 108 (survivor's entire interest, resulting from conveyance by insolvent without consideration, subject to decedent's debts). The interest of a tenant in common forms part of his probate estate. A joint tenancy terminates on death or when a joint tenant conveys his interest to a third party, who then becomes a tenant in common. *Delanoy v Delanoy* (1932) 216 C 23, 13 P2d 513. One case held that a conveyance by a joint tenant to herself also terminates the joint tenancy. *Riddle v Harmon* (1980) 102 CA3d 524, 162 CR 530. If there are three or more joint tenants, and one conveys his interest to a third party, the third party becomes a tenant in common with the others, whose interests continue to be held as joint tenants among themselves. *Shelton v Vance* (1951) 106 CA2d 194, 234 P2d 1012. The joint tenant's conveyance may be voluntary (*i.e.,* by deed) or involuntary (*e.g.,* through sale in execution of judgment or on foreclosure). *Young v Hessler* (1945) 72 CA2d 67, 164 P2d 65. A conveyance to another joint tenant also terminates the joint tenancy (*Hiltbrand v Hiltbrand* (1936) 13 CA2d 330, 56 P2d 1292), even when the transfer occurs through an installment land contract with the selling joint tenant retaining title until all payments are made (*Smith v Morton* (1972) 29 CA3d 616, 106 CR 52). Execution of a lease by one joint tenant, however, does not terminate the joint tenancy, and the surviving joint tenant takes sole ownership of the property free of the leasehold. *Tenhet v Boswell*

(1976) 18 C3d 150, 133 CR 10. Moreover, a judgment or mortgage lien alone is insufficient to sever the joint tenancy; the joint tenant's interest, acquired at the time of original acquisition of the property, terminates at his death, and the lien, which attached only to this interest, does not survive the debtor's death. See *Hamel v Gootkin* (1962) 202 CA2d 27, 20 CR 372 (lien of deed of trust); *People v Nogarr* (1958) 164 CA2d 591, 330 P2d 858 (mortgage lien); *Zeigler v Bonnell* (1942) 52 CA2d 217, 126 P2d 118 (judgment lien); Comment, *Severance of a Joint Tenancy in California,* 8 Hastings LJ 290 (1957).

A corporation may own land as a tenant in common. Under common law, it could not be a joint tenant with an individual or another corporation. In *American Bible Soc'y v Mortgage Guar. Co.* (1932) 217 C 9, 17 P2d 105, the court refused to decide whether the common law still applied, and held that the joint tenancy created a trust in favor of the charitable corporation named as joint tenant in the gift deed.

Of particular importance in cotenancies is an agreement that the entire property will be used to the mutual advantage of all and that none of the cotenants will partition the property (thus destroying the overall development or investment plan) without the consent of all cotenants. Although the right of a cotenant to partition is absolute rather than discretionary with the courts, the right may be modified or waived in advance either expressly or by implication. *Penasquitos, Inc. v Holladay* (1972) 27 CA3d 356, 103 CR 717; *Thomas v Witte* (1963) 214 CA2d 322, 29 CR 412; *Asels v Asels* (1919) 43 CA 574, 185 P 419.

§3.29   c. Partnership Compared With Tenancy in Common

It may be possible to avoid partnership income tax status when property is acquired in cotenancy for passive investment, even though its management may constitute a trade or business for purposes of IRC §§1221, 1231. If a partnership does not exist, partnership tax returns need not be filed; one owner may elect the installment method of reporting his gain on the sale without concurrence of the other owners. He may also treat the asset as a capital asset, without regard to the dealer status of the other co-owners.

Mere co-ownership of property does not establish a partnership.

Corp C §15007(2); Reg §1.761-1(a). In the absence of an intention to become partners, the mere holding of business property as tenants in common does not make the owners partners for tax purposes. *Gilford v Commissioner* (2d Cir 1953) 201 F2d 735. However, cotenants who actively carry on a trade or business and divide the profits may be treated as partners for tax purposes. For example, co-owners who both lease space and provide services to tenants are treated as partners. See Reg §1.761-1(a). If no active business is carried on and one of the owners is a dealer for tax purposes, a tenancy in common may afford some protection against an assertion by the Internal Revenue Service that the entire interest should be considered held by the partnership as a dealer and that any gain on the sale of the property should be subjected to ordinary income rather than capital gains tax treatment. *U.S. v Rosebrook* (9th Cir 1963) 318 F2d 316; *Charles E. Tibbals* (1958) 17 CCH TCM 228, 27 P-H TCM ¶58,044.

Despite these advantages, a partnership form would usually be preferable to a tenancy in common except possibly in a small investment with very few owners. A disadvantage to consider with a tenancy in common is that a transfer of ownership will normally cause a reassessment for property tax purposes under Cal Const art XIIIA, but a transfer of a partnership interest may not. See Rev & T C §64.

§3.30   d. Husband and Wife as Buyers

When property is acquired by husband and wife, it may be taken (1) as separate property of either spouse, (2) as their community property, (3) in joint tenancy, or (4) in tenancy in common. CC §5104. They may also form a partnership or corporation to take title. When property is acquired by a married couple as joint tenants each spouse is presumed to own an undivided one-half interest as his or her separate property. The character of property acquired as tenants in common is determined by the source of funds used for purchase or the understanding of the spouses. See California Marital Termination Settlements §§4.16, 4.45 (Cal CEB 1971); *Tax, Legal, and Practical Problems Arising From the Way in Which Title to Property Is Held by Husband and Wife,* USC Tax Inst 35 (1966). The purchase agreement and the deed should specify the exact nature of the holding. The same interest or estate cannot be both joint tenancy and community property. *Siberell v Siberell* (1932) 214 C 767, 7 P2d 1003.

The community property provisions of the Family Law Act (CC §§5100-5138) apply only to valid marriages. *Marvin v Marvin* (1976) 18 C3d 660, 134 CR 815. All property of either spouse owned before marriage or acquired after marriage by gift or inheritance, and the rents and profits of that property, are the separate property of that spouse. CC §§5107, 5108. Property acquired during marriage with separate property or the proceeds of separate property remains separate property, unless there is an agreement to the contrary. *Rosenthal v Rosenthal* (1963) 215 CA2d 140, 30 CR 49. If the buyer is married, the character of the property purchased as community or separate will be the same as the property given in exchange for it. CC §§5107, 5108, 5110. If the property is purchased with separate property assets, it retains its character as separate property, and the same is true of property acquired with community assets.

The above rule is, however, subject to modification if a married couple takes title by a deed specifying that they hold as joint tenants or as holders of community property. This creates a presumption that they intended an equal ownership regardless of the source of funds (separate or community) used for the purchase. *Marriage of Lucas* (1980) 27 C3d 808, 166 CR 853. An attorney representing a married couple in the purchase of real property needs to be aware of the implication of this rule if the downpayment is going to be contributed from one spouse's separate property. Under *Lucas,* if the form of ownership is specified as either community property or joint tenancy, a separate property investment can be recouped only if an agreement to that effect can be proven.

Real property acquired by a married couple by an instrument in which they are described as husband and wife is also presumed to be community property. CC §5110. However, property otherwise acquired before 1975 by a married woman in her own name is presumed to be her separate property; and if acquired with another person, the married woman's interest is presumed to be that of a tenant in common except when acquired by a husband and wife by an instrument in which they are described as such. CC §5110. The manner in which title appears of record is not conclusive of the nature of the actual holding. See California Marital Termination Settlements §4.15 (Cal CEB 1971). Property acquired under joint tenancy deeds, for example, may be shown to be community property (*Tomaier v Tomaier* (1944) 23 C2d 754, 146 P2d 905) and, in fact, is presumed to be community property for purposes of division on dissolution of marriage (CC §5110). Because joint tenancy can be created only by an instrument expressly declaring the estate to be a joint tenancy (CC §683), property held in another form may not be shown to be joint tenancy property. *Dalton v Keers* (1931) 213 C 204, 2 P2d 355. When drafting the deed, it is important that it correctly state the nature of the holding rather than try to cure the defect later.

See §3.16 for a form for acknowledgment by a spouse that the property being sold is the other spouse's separate property; see §3.15 for a discussion of conveyances by married persons.

§3.31   e. Entity To Be Formed

In many instances the purchase agreement is executed by one of the promoters or by an agent in the expectation that an entity, *e.g.*, a general or limited partnership or a corporation, will be formed to take title. If there is no misrepresentation by the signator, it appears that the seller is bound to perform. But see discussion at §3.21 on avoidance of the use of the term "nominee." However, if the agreement is executed in the name of a corporation that has yet to be formed rather than in an agent's name, the seller can probably withdraw from the transaction before the corporation is formed. See *Macy Corp. v Ramey* (Ohio CP 1957) 144 NE2d 698. This may also be true if the agreement is executed by a limited partnership that is not yet in existence because of a failure to comply with the requirements of Corp C §15502. However, if the unformed limited partnership is considered to be a general partnership, the seller may be bound because a general partnership can be formed without formalities. In any event, the agreement should include an appropriate assignment provision to facilitate the transfer to the entity being formed. See §3.184.

When the actual buyer is an entity to be formed, it is generally preferable to complete its formation before the close of escrow for the following reasons:

(1) The entity can take title as grantee and execute any notes and trust deeds required;

(2) If the promoter or agent takes title and later conveys to the new entity, the property is exposed to personal creditors of the promoter or agent;

(3) Under IRC §1551 it is possible to lose the surtax exemption if the entity ultimately chosen is a corporation and the individuals making the transfer control the new corporation and meet the other tests of that section;

(4) Title in the name of the promoter or an agent for a period of time may convert new property into used property and prevent the ultimate grantee entity from using accelerated tax depreciation methods under IRC §167 or from being entitled to investment tax credit under IRC §38;

(5) Transfer of title might trigger a due-on-sale clause in an encumbrance (see §3.50); and

(6) Transfer of title could cause a property tax reassessment (see §3.20).

On the use of agents to take title see §3.20; on designating nominees in the purchase agreement to take title see §3.21.

§3.32   C. Consent

The consent of the parties to a contract must be free, mutual, and communicated by each to the other. CC §1565. Consent that is not free can be rescinded. CC §1566. See §§12.58-12.76 on rescission. Consent is not real or free if it is obtained through duress, menace, fraud, undue influence, or mistake, and would not have been given if that cause had not existed. CC §§1567-1568; see §§12.31-12.38, 12.60 on remedies for fraud. Mutual assent is also lacking if the contract is so ambiguous that the parties' intentions cannot be determined. See §§12.95-12.98.

Mistake may, in rare instances, prevent a contract from coming into existence. For example, if both parties have a different understanding of the subject matter, and if neither is at fault or both are equally at fault, there is no contract. See *Barfield v Price* (1871) 40 C 535. Usually, however, mistake does not prevent the formation of a contract but makes it voidable. On reformation, see §3.38.

§3.33   D. Description of Property

The description of the property in the agreement must be sufficiently certain to satisfy the statute of frauds (CC §1624(4);

CCP §1971) and to make the agreement specifically enforceable (CC §3390). For certainty in descriptions generally, see §§8.10-8.12. For certainty in partial releases of land from deeds of trust, see §5.59. On uncertainty as a defense to an action for breach, see §12.98.

§3.34   E. A Lawful Object

The object of a contract must be "lawful" at the time the contract is made. CC §§1550, 1596. A contract's object is the performance which the party receiving the consideration agrees to provide. When a contract has but one object, and that object is unlawful, the contract is void (CC §1598), but when a contract has several objects it is void only to the extent that a particular object is unlawful (CC §1599). Unlawfulness is defined as that which is: "(1) contrary to an express provision of law; (2) contrary to the policy of express law, though not expressly prohibited; or (3) otherwise contrary to good morals." CC §1667.

§3.35   F. Consideration

To support a claim in damages for breach or an assertion that the buyer is a bona fide purchaser, an agreement must be based on good, *i.e.,* valuable, consideration. See *Horton v Kyburz* (1959) 53 C2d 59, 346 P2d 399. Any benefit conferred or detriment suffered (or agreed to be conferred or suffered) is a good consideration if it is more than nominal. CC §1605. If, however, the agreement is to be specifically enforced, the consideration must also be adequate, *i.e.,* just and reasonable. CC §3391. In both situations, the value or adequacy of the consideration is fixed as of the time the agreement is executed. *O'Connell v Lampe* (1929) 206 C 282, 274 P 336; *Henderson v Fisher* (1965) 236 CA2d 468, 46 CR 173.

In a bilateral contract, in which mutual promises are exchanged by the parties, both must assume a legal obligation. If mutuality of obligation is lacking, the agreement is illusory and, in its executory stage, may not be enforced by either party. See *Kowal v Day* (1971) 20 CA3d 720, 98 CR 118; *Black Light Corp. v Ultra-Violet Prods., Inc.* (1961) 195 CA2d 473, 15 CR 852. For effect on conditional agreements, see §§3.68-3.70; for effect on provisions for subordination, see §5.42; for effect on provisions for partial releases, see §5.59. For rule in options, see §4.6. On consideration for amending a signed agreement, see §3.37.

G. Writing

§3.36 1. General Rules

A contract for the sale of an interest in real property must be evidenced by a writing subscribed by the party to be charged. CC §1624(4); CCP §1971. If the writing is subscribed by an agent, written authority must be subscribed by the principal. CC §1624(4). The signature does not have to be handwritten but may be typed, printed, or stamped, and it may be initials or any other form, as long as it is intended as the execution. *Weiner v Mullaney* (1943) 59 CA2d 620, 140 P2d 704. The agent's authority to sign need not be in writing when the act is purely clerical or ministerial, *e.g.*, when he is directed by the principal to sign the document for the principal. *Murphy v Munson* (1949) 95 CA2d 306, 212 P2d 603.

To satisfy the statute of frauds, the writing need not be a formal agreement but may be in the form of a letter, memorandum, or telegram. It must contain the essential elements of a contract, *i.e.*, the names of the buyer and the seller and their identification (see §§3.42-3.45), the description of the property (see §3.46), the price to be paid, and the time and manner of payment (see §§3.47-3.52). *Corona Unified School Dist. v Vejar* (1958) 165 CA2d 561, 332 P2d 294. It is best to reduce the agreement to a formal document to avoid ambiguities and inadequacies.

A distinction must be made between the statutory requirement that the agreement be signed by the person to be charged and the effect of the parties' understanding that no agreement is to come into existence until a formal agreement is signed by both parties. *Stromer v Browning* (1966) 65 C2d 421, 55 CR 18; *Apablasa v Merritt & Co.* (1959) 176 CA2d 719, 1 CR 500. In the event of the latter, both parties must sign and the agreement must take the form intended by the parties before an enforceable contract exists. See also *Fugate v Cook* (1965) 236 CA2d 700, 46 CR 291 (husband's signature to agreement ineffective if given on condition that wife's signature also necessary). But see *Angell v Rowlands* (1978) 85 CA3d 536, 149 CR 574 (husband bound on contract of sale not signed by wife absent a showing that the contract was not intended to be complete until signed by all parties named in it).

Despite the somewhat contrary language of CC §1624, it has been uniformly held that noncompliance with the statute of frauds renders a contract unenforceable rather than void. An oral contract subject to the statute is effective until its invalidity is urged as a defense to an attempt to enforce it. 1 Witkin, Summary of California Law, *Contracts* §199 (8th ed 1973). Thus, the statute's use is primarily defensive. It cannot be invoked by a buyer to recover payments made under an oral contract to sell land if the seller remains ready and able to perform. *Walbridge v Richards* (1931) 212 C 408, 298 P 971; *Thompson v Schurman* (1944) 65 CA2d 432, 437, 150 P2d 509, 512. Moreover, part performance of an oral contract may be sufficient to overcome even defensive use of the statute of frauds. CCP §1972. In some cases a party may be estopped to assert the statute of frauds as a defense.

Some contracts concerning real property do not require a writing. Examples include: an agreement to share the profits of a sale of real property; a partnership agreement to deal in real property; a license to use real property; an agreement settling a disputed boundary; a fully executed partition agreement; and a sale of growing crops or mining rights. 1 Witkin, Summary, *Contracts* §235.

§3.37   2. Changing Signed Documents

Adding interlineations or addenda or otherwise changing the terms of a purchase agreement, escrow instructions, or other instrument already signed by one or both parties is a dangerous practice.

Acceptance of an offer must be unqualified; a qualified acceptance is a new offer. CC §1585. A purchase agreement signed by one party is an offer; interlineations or addenda by the other party constitute a new proposal and prevent the formation of a contract. *Angus v London* (1949) 92 CA2d 282, 206 P2d 869. The changes reject the original offer and bar its subsequent acceptance. *Niles v Hancock* (1903) 140 C 157, 73 P 840. To form a contract, the new proposal with the interlineations or addenda must in turn be accepted by the original offeror.

An attempt to change the terms of an agreement already signed by both parties also creates problems. A written contract may be modified only by: (a) a written contract; (b) an oral agreement to the extent that it is performed by the parties; (c) an oral agreement supported by new consideration unless the original contract expressly provides otherwise. CC §1698.

A promise to do what one is already legally bound to do is not consideration for the new contract. CC §1605. Frequently it is difficult to find additional consideration for the amendment, which then is ineffective unless the parties have rescinded the original agreement and entered into a new one. *Bush v Vernon* (1955) 135 CA2d 33, 286 P2d 903. See also *Godbey & Sons Constr. Co. v Deane* (1952) 39 C2d 429, 246 P2d 946 (permitting oral amendment with consideration when performed by one party). However, a written instrument is at least presumptive evidence of consideration. CC §1614. See §3.191 for form for amending an agreement.

§3.38   3. Reformation

If a written instrument, because of mistake or fraud, does not express the agreement of the parties, it can be reformed on application of the aggrieved party. It will not be reformed if to do so prejudices rights acquired by third persons in good faith and for value. CC §3399. See *Stafford v California Canning Peach Growers* (1938) 11 C2d 212, 78 P2d 1150; *Demetris v Demetris* (1954) 125 CA2d 440, 270 P2d 891; *Nunes v De Faria* (1951) 107 CA2d 794, 238 P2d 106. However, the right to reformation may be waived if it is not asserted at the proper time. For example, if the aggrieved party, with knowledge of the mistake, accepts performance according to the terms of the unreformed agreement, he cannot thereafter have the agreement reformed. See *Burnand v Nowell* (1948) 84 CA2d 1, 189 P2d 796. The court will not make a new contract for the parties (*Bailard v Marden* (1951) 36 C2d 703, 227 P2d 10); therefore, a contract wholly void for illegality (*Ainsworth v Morrill* (1916) 31 CA 509, 160 P 1089) or lacking consideration (see *Enos v Stewart* (1902) 138 C 112, 70 P 1005) cannot be reformed. But if an illegal term is mistakenly inserted in an otherwise valid contract, reformation is proper (see *Strauss v Bruce* (1934) 139 CA 62, 33 P2d 71), and a contract unenforceable under the statute of frauds can be reformed by adding omitted terms to make it a sufficient writing (see *Oatman v Niemeyer* (1929) 207 C 424, 278 P 1043).

Reformation is designed to correct a mistake in reducing the agreement to writing and must be distinguished from rescission. The latter is granted when the contract would not have been entered except for the mistake or fraud. See §3.32.

Reformation is permitted not only for mutual mistakes but also for unilateral mistake known or suspected by the other party. See *Baines v Zuieback* (1948) 84 CA2d 483, 191 P2d 67.

On reformation generally, see 1 Witkin, Summary of California Law, *Contracts* §§304-312 (8th ed 1973).

III. DRAFTING THE BASIC PURCHASE AND SALE AGREEMENT

A. California Association of Realtors Real Estate Purchase Contract and Receipt for Deposit

§3.39   1. Major Revisions

In 1967, pursuant to an accord with the State Bar, the California Association of Realtors (CAR) (then called the California Real Estate Association) copyrighted and published a new purchase contract to supplant its deposit receipt. One purpose of the 1967 form was to emphasize the fact that the form, when properly filled out and executed by the parties, became a legally binding contract and not merely a receipt for the buyer's deposit. The accord further stated that the purpose and desire of the two organizations was that the new form be used in all real property transactions in California for which it is appropriate. For further details of the accord, see *Real Estate Purchase Contract and Receipt for Deposit,* 42 Cal SBJ 487 (1967).

Substantial revisions were made in the form in 1978 to reflect current real property laws and practices. The latest revised form is reprinted in §3.40. A major purpose in the 1978 revision was to revise the form to comply with the changes in the liquidated damages law which became effective July 1, 1978. See CC §§1675-1681.

Paragraph 12 of the 1978 form is intended to reflect these new statutory changes. Civil Code §1677(b) requires that such a clause in a printed agreement be either in 10-point bold type or in contrasting red, 8-point bold type. In the first printing of the revised CAR form paragraph 12 was printed in IBM Univers 10-point bold. The IBM Univers 10-point bold is smaller than the 10-point typefaces of some other composing equipment manufacturers. Paragraph 12 in the second printing is set in IBM Univers 11-point bold and is clearly larger than the type in paragraphs 11 and 13 (see §3.40). To avoid any possible question of compliance with CC §1677(b), a seller using the CAR form who wants a liquidated damages provision should not use the first printing of that form. The CAR is of the opinion that because of CCP §1019 (enacted effective January 1, 1981) even the first printing is in compliance with CC §1677(b).

Another significant change in the 1978 form is the language in paragraph 7 concerning the condition of title. Under the pre-1978 form, the seller was obligated to deliver title free and clear of all liens, encumbrances, easements, and other restrictions except for those matters specifically mentioned in the agreement. In the 1978 form the buyer agrees to take subject to all covenants, conditions, restrictions, and public utility easements of record that do not adversely affect the continued use of the property unless reasonably disapproved by the buyer in writing within an agreed number of days after receipt of a current preliminary title report. The 1978 form is more advantageous to the seller because he is no longer required to list all exceptions to title in the agreement at the time it is signed. The buyer, however, may find himself obligated either to take title subject to matters of which he was unaware when signing the agreement or to permit the seller to withdraw from the agreement. A buyer would be better protected under the pre-1978 form in which the seller is contractually obligated to deliver title free and clear of all matters except those specifically set forth in the agreement.

In addition to the above changes, the 1978 form includes a provision for incorporation of supplemental forms (paragraph 4), an arbitration provision (paragraph 13), and an attorney's fee provision (paragraph 14). The CAR has prepared forms, or will do so, for the supplemental forms. It has not sought State Bar approval for the supplemental forms, as it did for the basic form. Care should be exercised, if non-CAR forms are incorporated by reference, to make certain that the language of the supplemental form is consistent with the basic agreement.

The arbitration clause (paragraph 13) refers only to a controversy arising out of the disposition of the buyer's deposit. Because the paragraph does not require arbitration, instead providing that it be at the election of the parties, it is difficult to see any legal effect to paragraph 13.

The risk-of-loss provisions (paragraph 7 in the pre-1978 form) have been deleted in the 1978 revision (leaving risk of loss to be determined under the Uniform Vendor and Purchase Risk Act (CC §1662)). See chap 10 on risk of loss.

The CAR form, or any other printed form of purchase agreement should be used only in a simple transaction for which extensive riders are not needed. Although some lawyers are convinced that laymen are less suspicious of a printed form that has been altered than they are of an agreement entirely typewritten, it is generally preferable, whenever possible, to prepare a typewritten agreement tailored to the specific transaction. For simple transactions, the essential provisions in the form in §§3.42-3.62 should be sufficient. For more complex transactions, counsel should consider the appropriateness of the other provisions in §§3.72-3.190. See also §§3.4 and 3.7 for a discussion of the use of printed forms.

§3.40   2. Form: CAR Real Estate Purchase Contract and Receipt for Deposit

The CAR Real Estate Purchase Contract and Receipt for Deposit is reproduced on pages 194-197.

CALIFORNIA ASSOCIATION OF REALTORS® STANDARD FORM

REAL ESTATE PURCHASE CONTRACT AND RECEIPT FOR DEPOSIT

THIS IS MORE THAN A RECEIPT FOR MONEY. IT IS INTENDED TO BE A LEGALLY BINDING CONTRACT. READ IT CAREFULLY.

_____, California._____ , 19 ____

Received from _____

herein called Buyer, the sum of _____ Dollars $ _____

evidenced by cash ☐, cashier's check ☐, or _____ ☐, personal check ☐ payable to _____

_____ , to be held uncashed until acceptance of this offer, as deposit on account of purchase price of

_____ Dollars $ _____

for the purchase of property, situated in _____ , County of _____ , California,

described as follows: _____

1. Buyer will deposit in escrow with _____ the balance of purchase price as follows:

_____

_____

_____

_____

_____

_____

_____

_____

_____

_____

_____

_____

_____

_____

_____

_____

_____

_____

Set forth above any terms and conditions of a factual nature applicable to this sale, such as financing, prior sale of other property, the

matter of structural pest control inspection, repairs and personal property to be included in the sale.

2.   Deposit will ☐ will not ☐ be increased by $_____ to $_____ within_____ days of

acceptance of this offer.

3.   Buyer does ☐ does not ☐ intend to occupy subject property as his residence.

4.   The supplements initialed below are incorporated as part of this agreement.

_____ Structural Pest Control Certification Agreement   _____ Occupancy Agreement   _____ Other

_____ Special Studies Zone Disclosure   _____ VA Amendment

_____ Flood Insurance Disclosure   _____ FHA Amendment

5.   Buyer and Seller acknowledge receipt of a copy of this page, which constitutes Page 1 of _____ Pages.

X_____
    B U Y E R

X_____
    B U Y E R

X_____
    S E L L E R

X_____
    S E L L E R

A REAL ESTATE BROKER IS THE PERSON QUALIFIED TO ADVISE ON REAL ESTATE. IF YOU DESIRE LEGAL ADVICE CONSULT YOUR ATTORNEY.

THIS STANDARIZED DOCUMENT FOR USE IN SIMPLE TRANSACTIONS HAS BEEN APPROVED BY THE CALIFORNIA ASSOCIATION OF REALTORS® AND
THE STATE BAR OF CALIFORNIA IN FORM ONLY. NO REPRESENTATION IS MADE AS TO THE APPROVAL OF THE FORM OF SUPPLEMENTS. THE LEGAL
VALIDITY OF ANY PROVISION, OR THE ADEQUACY OF ANY PROVISION IN ANY SPECIFIC TRANSACTION. IT SHOULD NOT BE USED IN COMPLEX
TRANSACTIONS OR WITH EXTENSIVE RIDERS OR ADDITIONS.

D-11-1 NCR SETS

For these forms, address California Association of Realtors®
505 Shatto Place, Los Angeles, California 90020
(Revised 1978)

REAL ESTATE PURCHASE CONTRACT AND RECEIPT FOR DEPOSIT

The following terms and conditions are hereby incorporated in and made a part of Buyer's Offer

6.   Buyer and Seller shall deliver signed instructions to the escrow holder within _____ days from Seller's acceptance which shall provide for closing within _____ days from Seller's acceptance. Escrow fees to be paid as follows:

_____

_____

7.   Title is to be free of liens, encumbrances, easements, restrictions, rights and conditions of record or known to Seller, other than the following: (1) Current property taxes, (2) covenants, conditions, restrictions, and public utility easements of record, if any, provided the same do not adversely affect the continued use of the property for the purposes for which it is presently being used, unless reasonably disapproved by Buyer in writing within _____ days of receipt of a current preliminary title report furnished at _____ expense, and (3) _____

Seller shall furnish Buyer at _____ expense a standard California Land Title Association policy issued by _____ Company, showing title vested in Buyer subject only to the above. If Seller (1) is unwilling or unable to eliminate any title matter disapproved by Buyer as above, Seller may terminate this agreement, or (2) fails to deliver title as above, Buyer may terminate this agreement; in either case, the deposit shall be returned to Buyer.

8.   Property taxes, premiums on insurance acceptable to Buyer, rents, interest, and _____ shall be pro-rated as of (a) the date of recordation of deed; or (b) _____ Any bond or assessment which is a lien shall be _paid_ by _____ : _____ shall pay cost of _assumed_ transfer taxes, if any.

9.   Possession shall be delivered to Buyer (a) on close of escrow, or (b) not later than _____ days after close of escrow or (c) _____

10.   Unless otherwise designated in the escrow instructions of Buyer, title shall vest as follows: _____

_____

(The manner of taking title may have significant legal and tax consequences. Therefore, give this matter serious consideration.)

11.   If Broker is a participant of a Board multiple listing service ("MLS"), the Broker is authorized to report the sale, its price, terms, and financing for the information, publication, dissemination, and use of the authorized Board members.

12.   **If Buyer fails to complete said purchase as herein provided by reason of any default of Buyer, Seller shall be released from his obligation to sell the property to Buyer and may proceed against Buyer upon any claim or remedy which he may have in law or equity; provided, however, that by placing their initials here Buyer: ( ) Seller: ( ) agree that Seller shall retain the deposit as his liquidated damages. If the described property is a dwelling with no more than four units, one of which the Buyer intends to occupy as his residence, Seller shall retain as liquidated**

damages the deposit actually paid, or an amount therefrom, not more than 3% of the purchase price and promptly return any excess to Buyer.

13. If the only controversy or claim between the parties arises out of or relates to the disposition of the Buyer's deposit, such controversy or claim shall at the election of the parties be decided by arbitration. Such arbitration shall be determined in accordance with the Rules of the American Arbitration Association, and judgment upon the award rendered by the Arbitrator(s) may be entered in any court having jurisdiction thereof. The provisions of Code of Civil Procedure Section 1283.05 shall be applicable to such arbitration.

14. In any action or proceeding arising out of this agreement, the prevailing party shall be entitled to reasonable attorney's fees and costs.

15. Time is of the essence. All modifications or extensions shall be in writing signed by the parties.

16. This constitutes an offer to purchase the described property. Unless acceptance is signed by Seller and the signed copy delivered to Buyer, in person or by mail to the address below, within _____ days, this offer shall be deemed revoked and the deposit shall be returned. Buyer acknowledges receipt of a copy hereof.

Real Estate Broker_____ Buyer_____

By_____

Address_____ Address_____

Telephone_____ Telephone_____

ACCEPTANCE

The undersigned Seller accepts and agrees to sell the property on the above terms and conditions. Seller has employed _____ as Broker(s) and agrees to pay for services the sum of _____ Dollars ($_____), payable as follows:

(a) On recordation of the deed or other evidence of title, or (b) if completion of sale is prevented by default of Seller, upon Seller's default or (c) if completion of sale is prevented by default of Buyer, only if and when Seller collects damages from Buyer, by suit or otherwise and then in an amount not less than one-half of the damages recovered, but not to exceed the above fee, after first deducting title and escrow expenses and the expenses of collection, if any. In any action between Broker and Seller arising out of this agreement, the prevailing party shall be entitled to reasonable attorney's fees and costs. The undersigned acknowledges receipt of a copy and authorizes Broker(s) to deliver a signed copy to Buyer.

Dated:_____ Telephone_____ Seller_____

Address_____ Seller_____

Broker(s) agree to the foregoing. Broker_____ Broker_____

Dated:_____ By_____ Dated:_____ By_____

For these forms, address California Association of Realtors®   D-11-2 NCR SETS
505 Shatto Place, Los Angeles, California 90020 (Revised 1978)   Page_____ of_____ Pages

Reprinted by permission, CALIFORNIA ASSOCIATION OF REALTORS®

§3.41 B. Basic Purchase and Sale Agreement

The clauses at §§3.42-3.62 contain the basic provisions common to all purchase and sale agreements. These provisions are sufficient for simple transactions. In more complex transactions, counsel will want to consider the use of the various forms contained in §§3.72-3.190.

§3.42 1. Form: Opening Clause; Parties

Form 3.42-1

Purchase and Sale Agreement

This agreement is made on _____, 19__, between ____[name and capacity, e.g., a general partnership]____ ("Seller") and ____[name and capacity]____ ("Buyer").

Comment: The opening clause names the parties, states their status and capacity, and gives them short titles for ease of drafting and reading. It is important to specify the capacity and status of the parties (see §§3.42-3.45), *i.e.,* the parties should be identified as, *e.g.,* a California corporation, a general partnership, a limited partnership, a trustee acting under a designated trust agreement, and the like, as appropriate.

Short titles ease drafting by reducing the length of names and important terms which are used many times in the agreement. However, brevity must not sacrifice clarity; the drafter should avoid the use of so many short titles that the reader must continually return to the introduction in order to understand the agreement. Clarity can be improved by using terms that explain their referant, for example "Buyer" or a shortening of buyer's name to refer to the buyer rather than such terms as "party of the first part." Use of standardized terms permits an office form to be modified easily to fit each transaction. (Care should be used in exchange transactions to avoid using "buyer" and "seller" or similar terms because the transaction is an exchange, not a purchase and sale.)

See §3.9 for a discussion of parties necessary to the agreement.

§3.43 a. Form: Warranty of Partnership Authority

Form 3.43-1

____[Buyer / Seller]____ warrants that it is a ____[general / limited]____ partnership organized and existing under the laws of the State of _____ with its principal place of business in _____ County. ____[*Names of authorized partners*]____ are general partners authorized to execute this agreement. The attached ____[*statement of partnership / certificate of limited partnership*]____ was recorded on _____, 19__ as Instrument _____ in book _____, page _____ of ____[*official book*]____, in the Office of the County Recorder of _____ County and is now, and at the closing will be, in full force and effect.

Comment: The recital of the recording information gives the parties an opportunity to check the record and satisfy themselves that the warranties are correct. If there is, in fact, no partnership as warranted, the warrantor is liable in damages. If there is any doubt about the authority of one partner to bind the partnership, all partners should join in the agreement. When both the seller and the buyer are partnerships, a separate warranty should be used for each party. The title insurer will insist that the statement or certificate be recorded before it will issue a title policy when the seller is a partnership and title is in the partnership name. A limited partnership does not come into existence until the certificate of limited partnership is recorded. See §§3.22 and 3.23 on general and limited partnerships.

§3.44   b. Form: Warranty of Corporate Authority

Form 3.44-1

____[*Buyer / Seller*]____ warrants that it is a corporation organized and existing under the laws of the State of _____; that ____[*names and titles of authorized officers*]____ are authorized to execute this agreement on its behalf;

[*Add when seller is California corporation*]
that this transaction ____[*is / is not*]____ a transfer of substantially all of Seller's assets;

[*Add when sale by a California corporation is
of substantially all the corporation's assets*]
that this transaction has been approved by a majority of the outstanding shares as required by the California Corporations Code;

[*Continue*]
and that this transaction has been approved by resolution of its board of directors and a certified copy of that resolution which remains in effect ____[*is attached / will be delivered to escrow holder before the close of escrow*]____.

Comment: There are specific corporate formalities necessary to bind a corporation (see discussion in §3.26). This provision gives a

cautious buyer a warranty that the property does or does not constitute substantially all the corporation's assets and a document complying with the corporate formalities. See §3.26 and Corp C
§§1001-1002. If documents required are not forthcoming, the parties signing would be liable for breach of this warranty. Corporate
officers are agents of the corporation and would be liable under an
implied warranty of authority if they, in fact, did not have the authority they represented. If a foreign corporation is transferring
substantially all of its assets, the laws of the jurisdiction where it is
incorporated should be checked concerning any requirements for
shareholder approval.

§3.45　　　c. Form: Warranty of Authority To Bind Unincorporated Association

Form 3.45-1

____[Seller / Buyer]____ warrants that it is an unincorporated nonprofit association and that ____[name of president or other head]____ and ____[name
of secretary or comparable officer]____ are its ____[title]____ and ____
[title]____ respectively; that they were authorized by ____[Seller / Buyer]____
to execute this agreement on its behalf pursuant to a resolution adopted on
_____, 19__, in accordance with its bylaws; and that the resolution has
not been amended or rescinded and continues in force. A copy of the resolution, certified by the secretary of the association, is attached to this agreement.

Comment: The president or other head and the secretary or other
comparable officer of an unincorporated nonprofit association are
authorized by Corp C §20002 to execute deeds after a sale has been
authorized by the association. Presumably they or any other officer
or person could be authorized to act for the association for other
purposes, *e.g.,* acquiring property or signing agreements.

On the capacity of an unincorporated association to hold and convey property, see §3.25.

§3.46　　　2. Form: Agreement To Sell and To Purchase; Description of Property

Form 3.46-1

Seller agrees to sell and Buyer agrees to purchase the property located at
____[street address or nearest intersection]____ ____[city]____, ____
[county]____, State of California and described ____[as follows: / in Exhibit
_____attached]____ .

Comment: The description of the real property may be incorporated by reference, avoiding inclusion of a lengthy legal description in the body of the agreement. Making the description an exhibit allows it to be prepared separately or to be photocopied from seller's deed or a title insurance policy or preliminary title report. This saves time and reduces the chance of error from retyping the description. It is best to use the legal description so that there can be no ambiguity about what property is the subject of the agreement. It is also wise to refer to a street address, if available, in case the seller supplies the wrong legal description. The attorney should carefully check that descriptions prepared by title companies are accurate.

If the legal description is not available, the property to be transferred should be described in the agreement as accurately and completely as possible. To survive judicial scrutiny, the property must be identifiable with certainty from the description (see §8.10). A street address may be sufficient for the sale of a single family home or other improved property if no ambiguity would exist. In all cases, counsel should verify that the description refers solely to the property to be transferred without ambiguity.

If the property is not described by reference to a recorded subdivision map, the buyer should inquire with the city or county in which the property is located about its compliance with the Subdivision Map Act (Govt C §§66410-66499.37). Virtually every division of property, even for purposes of leasing or financing, is regulated by that act. See §3.143. All personal property included in the sale should also be described. See §§3.170-3.173. See chap 8 on description of property.

3. Purchase Price

§3.47   a. Form: Fixed Price and Deposit

Form 3.47-1

The purchase price for the property is $_____ payable as follows:

(1) $_____ by ____[*personal / certified / cashier's*]____ check, on execution of this agreement, payable to ____[*name of broker or escrow holder*]____ as a deposit to be applied to the price at close of escrow;

[*Add applicable provisions as set out at §§3.49, 3.51-3.52*]

Comment: The provision set out above is intended as the beginning clause, to which are to be added additional provisions for price and terms, such as those concerning payment of balance at close of escrow (see §3.49), assumption of encumbrances (see §3.51), and installment payments (see §3.52).

The agreement should clearly and completely define the consideration to be delivered by each party and the method of payment, including amounts paid outside escrow, amounts paid through escrow, and the terms of any notes, to the extent those terms are known.

The purpose of the deposit is to demonstrate the buyer's good faith and to provide a fund from which the seller's damages may be recovered. (This latter may be of little immediate help to the seller, however, because escrow holders are generally unwilling to release funds in their possession without authorization from the parties after the alleged breach.) The nature and amount of the deposit is for the parties to determine, subject to the restrictions on liquidated damages discussed in §3.179. It should, at a minimum, cover all escrow charges, and generally be large enough to cause a buyer who may later contemplate backing out considerable discomfort at the prospect of having funds tied up for a long period of time. Deposits usually consist of cash but may take the form of documents readily converted to cash such as the assignment of a savings account or a letter of credit with instructions to the escrow holder to draw against it under specified circumstances. The use of a note as a deposit has been criticized as being of little value to the seller, because the seller's remedy if the buyer defaults is to sue on the note. In the absence of a liquidated damages provision (see §3.179) the seller would be required to prove actual damages rather than simply suing for the face value of the note. See 1 Miller & Starr, Current Law of California Real Estate §2:7 n15 (rev ed 1975).

(The parties should consider instructing the escrow holder to place the deposit in an interest-bearing account, unless the size of the deposit and the length of the escrow are such that the return would be too small.) If cash passes outside of escrow, this fact should be stated in the agreement, including a statement whether the cash applies against the purchase price and, if the transaction fails, who gets the funds.

If the deposit is to be in the form of a check payable to the broker, rather than to the escrow holder, the agreement should state whether the deposit is to be transferred to the escrow holder, held by the broker, or delivered to the seller outside of escrow. See also §2.71 on handling deposits.

§3.48   b. Form: Unit Price and Deposit; Computation of Units

Form 3.48-1

The purchase price for the property shall be $_____ per ____[state unit, e.g., gross acre]____ ____[excluding ____[describe exclusions]____ / without exception]____ to the nearest ____[e.g., 1/1000 of an acre]____ as determined by a survey prepared by a licensed land surveyor or a civil engineer no later than _____. The survey shall be obtained and paid for by ____[Buyer / Seller]____ and approved by ____[Seller / Buyer]____.

The purchase price shall be paid as follows:

(1) $_____ by ____[personal / cashier's / certified]____ check on execution of this agreement, payable to ____[name of broker or escrow holder]____ as a deposit to be applied against the price at close of escrow;

[Add applicable provisions set out at §§3.49, 3.51-3.52]

Comment: When the price is by unit, *e.g.,* so much per acre, it is essential that the total number of acres or other units be definitely determined. Because a surveyor cannot certify to the precise number of acres or other units within the property, the degree of certainty should be specified, *e.g.,* to the nearest 1/1000 of an acre. On the need for a survey and matters to consider in determining gross or net area, see §§3.118, 8.12. The buyer may wish to pay only for land that he can use. If the purchase price is stated at a rate per acre of "usable land" or rate per "net acre," misunderstandings are very likely to arise unless these terms are defined. If the buyer cannot determine how much of the land can be used and its value to him, the agreement should include an explicit definition of what constitutes "usable land" or "net acres," by description, by contour or contour changes, or by excluding portions of the property such as those portions dedicated or to be dedicated for streets.

An alternative frequently used is to compute the purchase price based on the development density eventually approved for the property by applicable governmental agencies. For example, if the property is to be developed with apartment units, the purchase price might be based on the number of units to the acre permitted to be developed on the property. The seller may establish a minimum purchase price and require that the buyer apply for governmental approvals permitting development with a specified number of units per acre.

§3.49 c. Form: Balance in Escrow

Form 3.49-1

[Precede with form at §3.47 or §3.48]

(2) Buyer's deposit of the balance of the price in escrow in cash or by cashier's check during business hours at least one business day before close of escrow.

Comment: This provision is intended to be used with the form at §3.47 (fixed price) or §3.48 (unit price) when the balance of the purchase price is to be paid into escrow without deduction for existing encumbrances and without any seller financing. If the buyer is to assume or take subject to existing encumbrances, the provision at §3.51 should be used. If the seller is to provide any of the financing, the provision at §3.52 should be used. If the buyer will have to obtain new financing in order to raise the necessary cash to be paid to seller at the close of escrow, the buyer will probably want to include a condition regarding financing. See §§3.151-3.152.

d. Effect of Taking Subject to Encumbrances

§3.50 (1) General Considerations

When a buyer acquires real property subject to an encumbrance, he usually receives a credit against the purchase price in an amount equal to the unpaid principal balance of the secured obligation plus the accrued interest on the obligation prorated through the date of close of escrow. Taking title subject to an existing encumbrance may permit the buyer and seller to avoid prepayment penalties and refinancing costs and to keep in effect an existing encumbrance with a favorable interest rate. The terms of the underlying deed of trust and the interest rate on the secured promissory note should be examined by the buyer and compared with those available with new financing. (For a more sophisticated device involving an existing encumbrance, see the discussion of wraparound deeds of trust and all-inclusive notes at §§5.26-5.37. See form at §3.101 for approval of note and deed of trust.) If the buyer merely takes subject to an existing encumbrance he is not burdened with personal liability for the underlying obligation (*Cornelison v Kornbluth* (1975) 15 C3d 590,

125 CR 557), but the property remains as security for payment of the obligation. Subject to the effect of CCP §580b, the maker or guarantor of the note or the person who had previously assumed liability remains liable (see *Ward v DeOca* (1898) 120 C 102, 52 P 130); if that person subsequently pays the liability, he acquires no rights against the buyer but is subrogated to the mortgagee's right to foreclose against the property (*Vincent v Garland* (1936) 14 CA2d 726, 58 P2d 1320). See also CC §§2848, 2849; *Sanders v Magill* (1937) 9 C2d 145, 70 P2d 159; Rintala, *California's Anti-Deficiency Legislation and Suretyship Law: The Transversion of Protective Statutory Schemes,* 17 UCLA L Rev 245, 284 n116 (1969). A non-assuming buyer, however, will be personally liable for waste resulting from his intentional or reckless conduct, and, in the absence of a CCP §580b defense, possibly for waste resulting from negligent conduct. *Cornelison v Kornbluth, supra*; Leipziger, *The Mortgagee's Remedies for Waste,* 64 Calif L Rev 1086, 1129 (1976).

The buyer may assume a loan by a written agreement with either the lender or the seller. In the latter case, a recital in the deed constitutes a sufficient writing (CC §1624(7)), and the assuming buyer becomes personally liable to the beneficiary for repayment of the loan under a theory of equitable subrogation (*Braun v Crew* (1920) 183 C 728, 192 P 531). Assumption of the debt does not release the seller from liability, but the seller's liability becomes that of a surety. *Everts v Matteson* (1942) 21 C2d 437, 132 P2d 476; *Birkhofer v Krumm* (1935) 4 CA2d 43, 40 P2d 553. Generally, the suretyship principles of law are applicable. See *Woodward v Brown* (1897) 119 C 283, 51 P 542 (effect of release of part of encumbered property); *Wise v Clapper* (1968) 257 CA2d 770, 65 CR 231 (extension of time for payment). A seller who incurs liability for a deficiency may seek indemnification from the assuming grantee. *White v Schrader* (1921) 185 C 606, 198 P 19; *Robson v O'Toole* (1919) 45 CA 63, 187 P 110.

These rules are modified if the original loan comes under the anti-deficiency provisions of CCP §580b. See generally California Mortgage and Deed of Trust Practice §§4.53-4.58 (Cal CEB 1979). If the loan was initially a purchase money loan under CCP §580b, the assuming grantee will be entitled to the antideficiency protection of CCP §580b, whether the original loan was made by the vendor (*Jackson v Taylor* (1969) 272 CA2d 1, 76 CR 891; see also *Cornelison v Kornbluth supra,* 15 C3d 590, 125 CR 557), or a third party lender

(*Kistler v Vasi* (1969) 71 C2d 261, 78 CR 170). If the original obligation is a nonpurchase money loan, the grantee will not be entitled to section 580b protection if it is assumed under circumstances that would make a new loan a nonpurchase money loan (*Brown v Jenson* (1953) 41 C2d 193, 259 P2d 425). This is probably also true even if a new loan to the buyer would come under CCP §580b (*Jackson v Taylor, supra;* see Mortgage & Deed of Trust §4.55 (Cal CEB 1979)).

A due-on-sale (or due-on) clause in the existing note and deed of trust may restrict the ability of the new buyer to take subject to or to assume the existing obligation. A due-on clause permits the secured lender to accelerate the loan in the event of a sale or other specified transfer or transaction affecting the property. See California Mortgage and Deed of Trust Practice §§2.32-2.45 (Cal CEB 1979).

Historically, institutional lenders have included due-on-sale provisions in their deeds of trust, in part to ensure that, on a sale of the real property security, the rate of interest on the loan can be adjusted to the then current market rate. The enforcement of due-on-sale clauses, however, has been limited by the courts.

In a series of decisions, the California Supreme Court has found enforcement of due-on clauses to constitute unreasonable restraints on alienation, and has limited the situations in which lenders will be entitled to automatic acceleration. In *La Sala v American Sav. & Loan Ass'n* (1971) 5 C3d 864, 97 CR 849, the court ruled that the beneficiary under a deed of trust could not automatically accelerate when the trustor further encumbered the property by imposing a second mortgage on it. In *Tucker v Lassen Sav. & Loan Ass'n* (1974) 12 C3d 629, 116 CR 633, the court ruled that a due-on clause does not permit automatic acceleration when the trustor executes an installment land contract for the sale of the property. In *Wellenkamp v Bank of America* (1978) 21 C3d 943, 148 CR 379, the court held that automatic acceleration by an institutional lender was not permitted under a due-on clause even when there is an outright sale of the property by the trustor with title passing to the purchaser.

Despite this judicial limitation on the enforceability of due-on clauses, there are situations in which they may be used with expectation of being enforced. Lenders will continue to employ due-on clauses because even under *Wellenkamp* an institutional lender can refuse to permit assumption of its loan if it can show that the security would be impaired by the proposed transfer of the property. Thus, acceleration may be permitted if the sale is to an uncreditworthy buyer or to a buyer who makes no personal investment in the property.

Federally chartered savings and loan associations are also permitted automatic acceleration under due-on clauses. On June 8, 1976, the Federal Home Loan Bank Board adopted a regulation permitting federal associations to enforce due-on clauses. It has been held that this federal regulation preempts state law regarding due-on clauses, and that federally chartered lenders may thus enforce due-on clauses contained in loan instruments executed after June 8, 1976. *Glendale Fed. Sav. & Loan Ass'n v Fox* (CD Cal 1978) 459 F Supp 903.

Before close of escrow, the buyer should obtain a beneficiary's statement under CC §2943 or perhaps even a more complete estoppel certificate (see California Mortgage and Deed of Trust Practice §§3.26, 3.29 (Cal CEB 1979)), indicating the state of the account on the prior encumbrance. The buyer should be credited for interest on the obligation which accrues through the close of escrow. The agreement should also allocate liability between the parties for any other charges of the lender.

§3.51   (2) Form: Balance in Escrow; Retaining Prior Encumbrances

Form 3.51-1

[Precede with form at §3.47 or §3.48]

(2) ____*[Buyer's assumption in form satisfactory to lender of / Buyer's purchase subject to]*____ **the following encumbrances:** ____*[list encumbrances, e.g., Form 351-2 if encumbrance is first deed of trust]*____

Form 3.51-2 (First Deed of Trust Encumbrance)

First deed of trust, dated _____**, 19__, in favor of** ____*[name of lender]* ____ **recorded on** _____**, 19__, as Instrument** _____ **in book** _____**, page** _____ **of** ____*[official book]*____**, in the Office of the County Recorder of** _____ **County.**

[Continue]

Buyer shall be credited with the balance of principal due the lender(s) at the date of the close of escrow ____*[plus any other charges, e.g., interest not prorated to seller or charges asserted by the lender to reinstate a note with due-on-sale provisions]*____**;**

(3) The balance of the price in escrow in cash or by cashier's check during business hours at least one business day before close of escrow.

Comment: This form is intended to be used with the form at §3.47 (fixed price) or §3.48 (unit price) when the balance of the purchase price to be paid into escrow is subject to credit for encumbrances which the buyer takes subject to, or obligations that he assumes. See also §5.18-5.20 for forms when existing encumbrances are retained.

§3.52　e. Form: Seller To Provide Financing

Form 3.52-1

[Precede with form at §3.47 or §3:48]

(2) ____[$ _____ / *an amount that, together with the deposit of* $ _____ *equals* _____ *percent of the purchase price*]____ **in escrow in cash or by cashier's check during business hours at least one business day before close of escrow;**

(3) **Buyer's promissory note in the form attached as Exhibit** _____, **for the balance of the purchase price bearing interest at** _____ **percent per year from close of escrow, payable** _____*[e.g., in monthly]____ __***installments of** $_____ ____*[or more]____* **beginning** ____[_____, *19__ / one month after close of escrow]____* **and continuing** ____*[until paid / with final payment due* _____, *19__ unless sooner paid]____.*

The note is to be secured by _____*[e.g., first deed of trust]*_____**on the property** ____*[in the form used by ____[name of title company or lender]____ / in the form attached as Exhibit__]____ .*

Comment: This provision is intended to be used with the form at §3.47 (fixed price) or §3.48 (unit price) when the seller is to provide some of the financing.

When the buyer is to take subject to or to assume an existing encumbrance, information sufficient to identify the loan is all that need be recited. When the seller is to provide financing, however, a fuller description must be set forth so that no further negotiations are necessary on the terms of the loan. If possible, the form of the note should be attached as an exhibit. If this is not done, the agreement should specify its essential terms, *i.e.*, interest rate, principal sum, maturity date, number and amount of installment payments, and state if any special provisions such as late charges, prepayment restrictions, or due-on clauses are to be included. See also §§5.19-5.20 on seller financing.

§3.53　4. Form: Escrow

Form 3.53-1

This sale shall be consummated through an escrow established with ____ *[name of escrow holder]____ ____[address]____,* **California. The closing date**

for the escrow will be _____, 19__. Escrow shall be considered closed when the grant deed to the property is recorded.

Within ____ days after execution of this agreement, each party shall execute and deliver to the escrow holder its written instructions consistent with the terms of this agreement and shall provide the escrow holder with such other information, documents, and instruments as the escrow holder may reasonably require to enable it to close the transactions on the closing date.

If the designated escrow holder should be unable or unwilling to act, ____ [Buyer / Seller]____ shall designate another escrow holder subject to the ____[Seller's / Buyer's]____ approval, which shall not be unreasonably withheld.

Comment: A timely close of escrow may be critical to either party. Most title companies record their documents at the commencement of a business day after checking them over the day or evening before. It is often difficult to complete the necessary recording on the date scheduled for the close of escrow if all of the papers are not in the hands of the escrow holder no later than the day before the scheduled date for the close of escrow. See chap 11 on escrows and closing.

§3.54   5. Form: Vesting Title; Individuals

Form 3.54-1

On close of escrow, title shall vest in

Form 3.54-2 (Community Property)

____[name]____ and ____[name]____ , husband and wife, as their community property.

Form 3.54-3 (Separate Property)

____[name]____, a ____[married man / married woman / widower / widow] ____ as separate property.

Form 3.54-4 (Joint Tenancy)

____[names]____, as joint tenants.

Form 3.54-5 (Tenancy in Common)

____[names]____ , as tenants in common, in undivided ____[equal interests / interests as follows: _____]____ .

Comment: For discussion of nature of holding between husband and wife, see §3.30; on cotenancies, see §3.28. It is preferable that the manner in which title is to be taken be specified in the agreement and the escrow instructions, and thus carried into the deed. By so doing, the buyers are given an opportunity to discuss the subject and arrive at an informed decision rather than accepting a vesting routinely determined or recommended by an employee of a broker or escrow agent.

Often, however, the buyer is not certain, at the time the agreement is signed, how title is to vest. In those instances the agreement should state that buyer will advise escrow holder of the desired vesting before close of escrow.

Because the interests of tenants in common need not be equal, each fractional interest should be stated explicitly. If the interests are unequal, the provision might be completed in this way: "*A*, an undivided three fifths, *B*, an undivided two fifths."

See also §§7.27-7.30 for a discussion of language in the grant deed.

§3.55   6. Form: State of Title Evidenced by Title Insurance

Form 3.55-1

Seller shall by grant deed convey to Buyer a fee simple interest free and clear of all title defects, liens, encumbrances, deeds of trust, and mortgages except real property taxes ____[*and assessments*]____, a lien not delinquent and ____[*specify all other exceptions*]____.

Seller shall procure a California Land Title Association standard policy of title insurance in the amount of $_____ with ____[*specify any endorsements*]____ to be paid by ____[*Seller / Buyer*]____ and to be issued by ____ [*name of title insurance company*]____ of ____[*office or location*]____ showing title vested in ____[*state name of buyer and manner in which title to be held or indicate, e.g., as shown in paragraph* ____[*see §3.54*]____]____.

Comment: This form requires the conveyance of a fee simple interest. If a different interest is being sold, the provision should so state. On the right to marketable title generally and maintaining the seller's obligation to deliver it, see §3.78.

If the parties are able to agree that title shall remain subject to exceptions known to them, such as "exceptions shown in preliminary title report attached to this agreement" or "deed of trust described in paragraph 3 of this agreement," that understanding may be stated in the clause. (The buyer should examine the documents referred to in title reports before approving an exception. See

§§3.79, 11.63.) Unrecorded interests, such as existing tenancies, should be listed as an exception. If the seller intends to take back a deed of trust, reserve an easement, or otherwise encumber the property, that fact should be stated. The lien for current taxes should usually be listed as an exception. See §3.83. The seller should also see that any other exceptions that will not be removed, such as easements and restrictive covenants, are included in the list of exceptions. For provisions allowing buyer a period of time after execution of the agreement in which to examine and approve title, see §3.79.

There is no implied obligation of the seller to furnish title insurance (see *Easton v Montgomery* (1891) 90 C 307, 27 P 280; *Seymour v Shaeffer* (1947) 82 CA2d 823, 187 P2d 95); the agreement should expressly provide for it. On the available forms of title insurance, see California Title Insurance Practice chap 3 (Cal CEB 1980). The amount of coverage is customarily the purchase price of the property, although this may vary. On endorsements, see Title Ins §§3.26-3.32. For other agreement provisions concerning title insurance, see §§3.79-3.80 below.

The buyer should specify the name of the title company that is to issue the policy; it is in his interest to obtain coverage from a financially responsible company. Moreover, the buyer may have a long term working relationship with one particular company. Occasionally, the seller prefers to name the company because of his relations with it, especially when it is to be the trustee under a deed of trust to the seller. The designation of the title company may be a matter of negotiation between the parties, although the Real Estate Settlement Procedures Act of 1974 (RESPA), 12 USC §§2601-2617, as amended, provides that no seller of real property subject to the act may directly or indirectly require a particular title company as a condition to selling the property. 12 USC §2608. (The act is discussed in §§11.85-11.89.)

For a discussion of the manner in which title ought to be held, see §§3.27-3.31.

§3.56   7. Form: Proration of Taxes, Insurance, and Interest

Form 3.56-1

Real property taxes, interest on assessments assumed by Buyer, rents, insurance premiums on hazard insurance assigned to Buyer, and interest on any indebtedness secured by any deed of trust to remain on the property shall all be prorated as of the closing date on the basis of a 30-day month. All security deposits and prepaid rents held by Seller shall be credited to Buyer. Any balance in any tax and insurance impound account shall be credited to Seller. Assessments of record shall be ____[*paid by Seller / assumed by Buyer*]____.

Comment: Traditionally taxes, rents, insurance, and all other costs or income items transferred from the seller to the buyer are computed on a daily basis and divided between the buyer and the seller as of the closing date. The adjustments are usually made in cash through the escrow.

If there is no current tax bill and the previous year's bill does not afford a reasonable basis for estimating the current year's bill, the parties may agree on a specified daily amount pending receipt of the future tax bill. This problem occurs only if the closing occurs between July 1 and October 31 of a given year because the tax bill is not available during this period. See Rev & T C §2610.5. Alternatively, the agreement could provide that a specified sum is to be adjusted outside of escrow when the bill is received. Such a procedure, however, complicates the transaction by requiring that a calculation be made after the close. A 30-day month is specified as the basis for prorations to ease computations.

Because of the provisions of Cal Const art XIIIA (the Jarvis-Gann initiative), the possibility exists of a change in the assessed valuation if there has been a change in ownership or new construction occurring before the lien date (the previous March 1st) for the current tax fiscal year (year of sale). If the assessor was unaware of such previous change of ownership or of new construction at the time the original assessment was made, a supplemental tax bill may be issued when the change is noted by the assessor, based on an escape assessment. The prorations provision above (and the escrow instructions, see §§11.51 and 11.70) are sufficient for the proper proration of any supplemental tax bill issued before the close of escrow. Any prorations based on a supplemental tax bill issued after the close of escrow will have to be handled between the buyer and seller, by agreement outside of escrow. If the possibility of such a supplemental tax bill exists, the purchase agreement should provide that any supplemental tax bill be prorated between the parties outside of escrow with the seller being responsible for any additional taxes assessed for any period before close of escrow and the buyer responsible for any period after the close of escrow. With respect to liability for payment of taxes based on escape assessments, see Rev & T C §531.2. That section is discussed in California Taxes §4.70 (Cal CEB 1978).

Insurance premiums are prorated only if the seller's insurance can be transferred and the buyer and the seller desire to transfer it. See §3.174.

Rent should be prorated. The amount of the rent and deposits is set out in the seller's rent statement, which should be subject to the buyer's approval. The buyer can confirm the accuracy of the rent statement from the tenants' estoppel certificates. See §3.112. The seller should be required to warrant the accuracy of the rent statement if it is not feasible to obtain estoppel certificates. If rent for the month in which the closing occurs has not been paid, the parties must decide if the rent due should be prorated or not and state in the escrow instructions how the item is to be handled. If rents are delinquent for more than the current month, see §3.115.

Other items that may be prorated include installment payments on personal property being transferred with the real property, homeowner's association assessments in planned developments and condominiums, and interest on loans assumed by the buyer. If a loan being assumed has an impound account, the account should be assigned to the buyer and the seller credited with the balance. Interest is not prorated on an underlying note when an all-inclusive note or wraparound deed of trust is used.

§3.57   8. Form: Closing Costs

Form 3.57-1

Seller shall pay all costs and expenses of clearing title, preparing, executing, acknowledging, and delivering the grant deed, ____[the premium for the title insurance policy]____ and shall pay any transfer taxes.

Buyer shall pay all recording fees (except those in connection with clearing title), ____[the premium for the title insurance policy]____ , and all fees and costs for any new financing.

Buyer and Seller shall each pay one half of the escrow fee.

Comment: The division of costs is subject to negotiation and can be made on any terms to which the parties agree. Once the division is determined, it should be clearly stated to avoid disputes. Almost without exception the seller pays for all costs of clearing title and delivering the grant deed; the buyer pays for all costs in connection with any new financing. Customarily, the seller pays the documentary transfer tax, but customs differ with respect to payment of city or other local transfer taxes. Often local taxes are split between buyer and seller. Generally, in Bay Area counties the buyer pays both the escrow fee and the title insurance premium; in Southern California the seller commonly pays the title insurance premium and the escrow fees are divided. Elsewhere, both charges may be divided. The provision in this form and the form in §3.55 should be consistent regarding which party pays the title insurance premium. See §11.58 on closing costs.

Other costs that might be specified in this provision are the additional cost of an American Land Title Association policy above CLTA coverage, the cost of any special title policy endorsements and the cost of any survey that might be required.

§3.58   9. Form: Notices

Form 3.58-1

All notices and demands shall be given in writing ____[either by personal service or]____ by registered or certified mail, postage prepaid, and return receipt requested. Notice shall be considered given ____[when mailed / when received / ____ hours after mailed / on date appearing on the return receipt, but if the receipt not returned within ____[e.g., 5]____ days, then ____[e.g., 48 hours after deposit in mail]____. Notices shall be addressed as appears below for each party, provided that if any party gives notice of a change of name or address, notices to the giver of that notice shall thereafter be given as demanded in that notice.

To Seller	To Buyer
____[Name]____	____[Name]____
____[Address]____	____[Address]____

Comment: All notices should be required to be in writing to ensure that there is a record of them and to avoid disputes about their contents. Registered or certified mail with a return receipt is useful, and even superior to personal service, to establish that the party to whom the notice was sent received it, and to verify the date of receipt. Notice by telegram or mailgram can be provided, with the date of service considered to be the following day or the date of delivery confirmed by the telegraphic agency.

§3.59   10. Form: Signature Lines

Form 3.59-1

Executed on the day and year first above written.

Seller	Buyer
[Signature]	_[Signature]_
____[Typed name]____	____[Typed name]____
[Signature]	_[Signature]_
____[Typed name]____	____[Typed name]____

Comment: See §3.36 for a discussion of the requirements for a contract to be signed by the party to be charged.

This form may also be used when the agreement is to be executed by both parties at a meeting held for such purpose. See §3.36 for a discussion of the requirements concerning signatures.

§3.60   11. Form: Offer and Acceptance

Form 3.60-1

Buyer's signature constitutes an offer to Seller to purchase the property on the terms and conditions set forth. This offer shall remain irrevocably open until ____[time]____ on ____[date]____. If it is not accepted by Seller by that date, it shall be considered revoked, and broker shall return the deposit to Buyer on the demand of Buyer. If Seller accepts this offer within the time specified, communication of the acceptance to Buyer shall be satisfied if broker orally notifies Buyer of the acceptance by that date and delivers to Buyer within ____[e.g., 48 hours]____, in person or by United States mail, one copy of this agreement executed by Seller.

Comment: In a complex transaction it is generally best to have the parties review the document and execute it at a meeting of the parties called for such purpose. Often, however, the buyer prepares the agreement and submits it to the broker for submission to the seller. In such event, the above form may be used with the forms in §§3.61-3.62; it provides that the buyer's signature constitutes an offer to purchase the property on the terms and conditions set forth in the agreement, gives the seller a certain amount of time within which to accept the offer, and provides for the procedure to communicate the acceptance of the offer to the seller. Even though the form states that the offer shall remain irrevocably open for a period of time, an offer generally is not irrevocable unless the offeree has paid consideration for it. CC §1586; *Thomas v Birch* (1918) 178 C 483,

489, 173 P 1102, 1104; *Prather v Vasquez* (1958) 162 CA2d 198, 327 P2d 963. See §4.10 on options.

§3.61 12. Form: Signature of Buyer

Form 3.61-1

The undersigned Buyer offers and agrees to buy the property on the terms and conditions stated in this agreement and acknowledges receipt of a copy of the agreement.
Dated: _____

Buyer
__[Signature]__
____[Typed name]____

Comment: If the offer and acceptance provision in §3.60 is used, this signature and the form in §3.62 should also be used. Under Bus & P C §10142 the broker has an obligation to deliver a copy of the document signed by the buyer to the buyer. In this provision, the buyer not only offers to buy the property but agrees to buy the property under the terms and conditions stated in the agreement and acknowledges receipt of a copy of the agreement.

§3.62 13. Form: Acceptance; Broker Commission

Form 3.62-1

The undersigned Seller accepts the foregoing offer to purchase the property and agrees to sell the property to Buyer on the terms and conditions specified. In consideration of real estate brokerage services rendered by ____ [name of broker]____, to Seller, the undersigned Seller agrees to pay the broker ____[only on condition that the escrow closes]____ a real estate brokerage fee in a sum equal to ____ percent of the purchase price. ____[No commission or other fee is payable to the broker if escrow fails to close]____. Seller acknowledges receipt of a copy of this agreement and authorizes broker to deliver a signed copy to Buyer.
Dated: _____

Seller
__[Signature]__
____[Typed Name]____

Broker consents to commission provision.

__[Signature of broker]__
____[Typed name of broker]____

Comment: This form may be used in lieu of form at §3.59 whether or not the parties are signing the agreement simultaneously. It should always be used with the form at §3.61. The seller accepts the offer of the buyer and agrees to sell the property to the buyer on the terms and conditions set forth in the agreement. The name of the broker should be filled in and in this form the seller agrees to pay the broker a specified percentage of the purchase price. The language in brackets should be used if the seller's obligation to pay the broker is to be conditioned on the transaction closing. This may be a matter of concern to the seller. See §§2.37, 2.75. The broker should sign the agreement to confirm his acceptance of the commission provisions. See also provision at §3.175 relating to broker's commission.

IV. POTENTIAL PROBLEMS AND CONTRACTUAL SOLUTIONS

§3.63   A. Creating a Checklist of Potential Problems

The clauses in §§3.72-3.190 represent possible solutions to common problems that are likely to arise in a real property sales transaction. Not all of the clauses are applicable to every transaction nor are all those that are applicable indispensable to a given agreement; each party may yield on some points in order to obtain concessions on others. A particular sale may have problems pertinent to it that are not covered in this chapter; each transaction is different, and the lawyer must be alert to the unique elements in the situation presented to him.

The various topics discussed in §§3.72-3.190 and the forms set out can serve as a convenient checklist of other provisions that should be included in the agreement, depending on the nature of the transaction. Matters dealing with the condition of title are in §§3.78-3.115; physical condition of the property in §§3.116-3.130; use and development of the property in §§3.131-3.150; and business operations on the property in §§3.157-3.169. Provisions on other subjects are found in §§3.78-3.190.

For a checklist of the items that should be included in every purchase and sale agreement, see the basic form headings in §§3.42-3.62.

If the seller is to provide some of the financing, the provisions in chapter 5 should be considered. For more general checklists to be used when representing buyer or seller, see §§1.57 and 1.83-1.84.

§3.64   B. Kinds of Solutions

Contractual solutions to common problems are classed generally as warranties and covenants (see §§3.65-3.67), conditions (see

§§3.68-3.75), and options (see §3.77). Whether one or more of these solutions are to be applied to a particular problem and which are to be used depends on the nature of the problem, the remedies that the solutions afford, and the negotiating process in which the desires of the respective parties are balanced against each other.

Whatever the reason for acquiring property, the buyer must have some assurance that the property is suitable for his purpose. It is common practice to sign an agreement that allows the buyer to withdraw if the property does not meet his needs. One way to do this is to sign an option. See §3.77, and chap 4. Another way is to sign a purchase agreement that is subject to conditions precedent, warranties, covenants, or combinations of these devices. The agreement is consummated if the conditions are met, the warranties prove true, and the covenants are performed. If not, the party for whose protection the clause was inserted has a remedy, usually either withdrawal from the agreement or damages against the other party. The nature of the remedy depends on the kind of protection drafted into the agreement. Those protections are compared in §§3.65-3.77.

§3.65   1. Warranties

A warranty is an affirmation by the seller of a fact or facts relating to the property. See generally 2 Witkin, Summary of California Law, *Sales* §§48-70 (8th ed 1973). Failure of a condition in the agreement generally excuses a party's performance, but breach of a warranty will entitle a party to damages, and possibly rescission. Unless a warranty is also a condition, its breach will not relieve the buyer from the duty to perform, although any damages might be offset against any sums owed by the buyer. See 1 Witkin, Summary, *Contracts* §§56, 58.

In any major acquisition, the buyer should always obtain warranties from the seller that there is no litigation arising out of or affecting the property (see form at §3.164), that there are no known violations of codes or other regulations, and no pending zoning changes (see form at §3.137), and that the seller has disclosed to the buyer all leases, amendments to leases, building service contracts, and other similar documents affecting the property (see forms at §§3.110, 3.165).

The forms at §§3.73-3.75 give the buyer the right to terminate if a breach of a warranty exists at the time for close of escrow.

§3.66   a. Merger of Warranties Into Deed

Absent fraud, mistake, and other special circumstances, the buyer's acceptance of the deed at closing results in a merger of prior negotiations and agreements, and discharges the seller's obligations. The buyer's rights are then measured solely by the deed. *Bryan v Swain* (1880) 56 C 616; *Burnand v Nowell* (1948) 84 CA2d 1, 189 P2d 796. Both *Bryan* and *Burnand* appear to be based on the buyer's intent in accepting the deed. However, matters collateral to the conveyance (*i.e.*, those that ordinarily do not become part of the deed) are not merged (*Stiles v Bodkin* (1941) 43 CA2d 839, 111 P2d 675 (agreement to put in streets)) and, because they survive, may sometimes support an action for damages (*Christensen v Slawter* (1959) 173 CA2d 235, 343 P2d 341 (agreement relating to time of delivery)).

Usually the merger diminishes the seller's obligations because the ordinary grant deed is accepted without covenants or warranties although the prior agreement contained them. For covenants of title implied in a grant deed, see §§9.5-9.7. The obvious solution to the problem of merger is to make certain that the deed contains the necessary covenants and warranties, but the use of warranty deeds has not been common in California. To prevent any inadvertent diminution of his rights, the buyer may insist that the agreement provide that the covenants and warranties survive delivery of the deed. When warranties would not survive the closing, the buyer should use conditions instead and rely on investigation before the sale closes.

§3.67   b. Form: Warranties To Survive Delivery of Deed

Form 3.67-1

All warranties, covenants, and other obligations contained in ____[*this agreement / paragraphs ____ of this agreement*]____ shall survive delivery of the deed.

Comment: The effect of the deed in merging and discharging certain covenants and warranties is discussed in §3.66. This provision is intended to continue the effect of covenants, warranties, and other obligations even after delivery of the deed. It is effective between the parties but will not benefit subsequent purchasers. The preferred practice is to include the covenants and warranties that are to survive in a warranty deed (see §3.66).

In negotiating, the buyer may be concerned that only certain warranties survive the closing. In that event, the provision may be drafted to include only those obligations on which there is agreement, or this clause can be eliminated and each warranty to survive can so state (see, *e.g.*, §3.82).

2. Conditions

§3.68   a. Function of Conditions as Contingencies

The great majority of real property sales agreements in California contain at least one provision under which the buyer's obligation to perform is conditioned on the occurrence or nonoccurrence of some event, the existence or nonexistence of some fact, or on someone's approval or disapproval of something. Commonly called "conditions" or "contingencies," these so-called out clauses allow a party to execute promptly and to withdraw from the transaction if the necessary precondition cannot be realized.

Typical of these conditions are those requiring (1) the approval of a third party, *e.g.*, a planning commission, lending institution, or the FHA (see §§3.126, 3.136, 3.144); (2) the buyer's satisfaction about physical conditions that are discoverable only after time-consuming tests, *e.g.*, soil tests or engineering studies (see §3.120); and (3) the buyer's satisfaction with the condition of title, *e.g.*, the terms of deeds of trust or leases or covenants, conditions, and restrictions (see §§3.79, 3.101). Frequently in the transfer of income properties, buyers demand and sellers concede that the sale be subject to the results of an accounting analysis of seller's operations or an application for a license. See §§3.138-3.159.

If the execution of the agreement were postponed until all of these factors could be properly checked by the buyer, the seller would be required to keep his property off the market without any commitment from the buyer, or the buyer would be required to spend time and money checking out property that might be sold to another at any time. In many cases, an option could solve these problems more effectively than conditional agreements. From the buyer's standpoint the advantage of the conditional agreement is that he obtains a return of his deposit if the condition fails.

In drafting an agreement with conditions to performance by either party, the attorney should include the following: (1) the content of the report or instrument (*e.g.*, preliminary title report showing specified title as in §3.79) or the nature of the act (*e.g.*, granting of zoning as in §3.136) required to fulfill the condition; (2) the liability of each party if the condition is not fulfilled (see §3.73); (3) the party for whose benefit the condition exists and how he may waive it (see §3.72); (4) who bears any expenses incurred, such as title work and escrow costs to the time of failure, if the condition fails (see §3.75); and (5) the time limit within which the condition must be satisfied.

b. Problems Raised by Conditions

§3.69   (1) Mutuality

In a bilateral contract the promises of the parties must be mutual in obligation, *i.e.*, for the contract to bind either party, both must have assumed some legal obligations. See §3.35. If one of the parties is left free to perform or not to perform at his sole option, without even the requirement of good faith, his promise is illusory and affords no consideration; it is a free and therefore revocable option. See *Shortell v Evans-Ferguson Corp.* (1929) 98 CA 650, 277 P 519. However, in *Mattei v Hopper* (1958) 51 C2d 119, 330 P2d 625, a sale conditioned on obtaining leases "satisfactory" to the buyer was held to be binding because the buyer's satisfaction is not unfettered but must meet the legal standard of reasonableness or good faith, depending on the nature of the performance. Subsequent decisions have upheld contracts conditioned on the buyer's satisfaction with results of a test of a well (*Lyon v Giannoni* (1959) 168 CA2d 336, 335 P2d 690) and on the buyer's satisfaction with a subdivision map as finally approved (*Rodriguez v Barnett* (1959) 52 C2d 154, 338 P2d 907). If the condition can be measured by an objective standard, as in the case of financial or structural considerations, the party's satisfaction must meet the reasonable person test. *Mattei v Hopper, supra; Kadner v Shields* (1971) 20 CA3d 251, 97 CR 742. If the party's satisfaction entails matters of taste or judgment, however, the courts require that the party act in good faith. *Kadner v Shields, supra.*

Nevertheless, it is still possible that the use of conditions in an agreement, without an affirmative obligation to attempt to obtain performance of the condition, may either be held to lack mutuality (in a future case distinguishing those cited above) or may lead to litigation on the point. Such a result may be avoided if the agreement (a) obligates the buyer or seller to perform certain acts in trying to obtain performance of the condition (see *White & Bollard, Inc. v Goodenow* (Wash 1961) 361 P2d 571; Note, *Contracts: Consideration: Effect of Clauses in Real Estate Contracts Conditioning Buyer's Promise,* 47 Calif L Rev 753 (1959)) or (b) imposes standards of reasonableness on the exercise of any approval rights. The agreement, however, should protect buyer or seller by negating any implied obligation on his part to *obtain* the condition's performance rather than just to *attempt* to obtain it. See Friedman, Contracts and Conveyances of Real Property §1.5 (3d ed 1975). A condition, such as the availability of financing, may be held to include an implied covenant that the party it was intended to benefit will use due diligence in attempting to fulfill the condition. *Abrams v Motter* (1970) 3 CA3d 828, 83 CR 855; *Fry v George Elkins Co.* (1958) 162 CA2d 256, 327 P2d 905. It is the seller's burden to prove the buyer's lack of due diligence, but when the buyer admits a lack of diligence, the burden shifts to him to prove that the condition could not have been fulfilled in any event. *Abrams v Motter, supra.* In certain instances, the seller might want to retain the right to obtain performance of the condition if the buyer is unable to do so.

§3.70   (2) Waiver of Condition

The general rule is that a party may waive a condition that is solely for his benefit and obtain performance of the agreement. *Doryon v Salant* (1977) 75 CA3d 706, 142 CR 378. Such a party may be deprived of the right to waive the condition under certain circumstances, *e.g.,* automatic termination. Automatic termination takes place if the agreement provides that it is "void" or that it "ceases and terminates" on the failure of performance of a condition. *Nikora v Mayer* (2d Cir 1958) 257 F2d 246. Parties who wish to reserve the right to waive conditions included for their benefit should provide that they may terminate or proceed at their discretion on the happening or failure of the condition. See forms at §§3.73-3.75.

Another situation in which one party cannot waive unless the agreement expressly permits a waiver arises when the condition is for the benefit of both buyer and seller. An example is a condition calling for FHA approval for development, which would enhance the value of the property as security for the seller's purchase money deed of trust. See *Spangler v Castello* (1956) 147 CA2d 49, 304 P2d

752. When the rights of a tenant with an option to purchase are to be eliminated, waiver of that condition by the buyer alone does not suffice because the seller would be liable to the tenant. *Britschgi v McCall* (1953) 41 C2d 138, 257 P2d 977.

In some instances, action by the seller may deprive the buyer of his election to waive. When the buyer inserts a condition that the contract be subject to his ability to obtain financing, without indicating the source, the seller may be able to bind the buyer by agreeing to take back a purchase money deed of trust on the same terms. This could be disadvantageous to the buyer because the seller may be more difficult as a creditor than a third party, such as an institution with established practices. To avoid this result, see the provisions in §§3.74, 3.152 giving the buyer the sole option with respect to third party financing.

§3.71   c. Consequences of Failure To Meet Condition

When the buyer objects to the title, condition, or use of the property within his approval period, a number of questions arise, and the agreement should be clear on each point:

(1) Does the objection terminate the agreement automatically, or does it give the buyer an option to terminate? The disadvantage of an automatic termination clause is discussed in §3.70. If the agreement does not provide for automatic termination, the party for whose benefit the condition exists may be given an election to waive the defect. See §§3.70-3.75.

(2) Does the agreement give one of the parties an obligation or election to cure the defect? For a provision obligating the seller to remove defects in title, see §3.73. For provisions giving the seller an election to remove defects (except buyer's failure to obtain financing), see §§3.74-3.75.

(3) If the defect cannot be cured, what course of action is open to each party? For a provision giving the buyer a fairly wide range of options, see §3.73; for a provision more favorable to the seller, see §3.74; for a possible compromise provision, see §3.75.

(4) If the agreement is to be terminated, how does the buyer get his money back? This, too, should be spelled out in the agreement. See §3.76.

The same question should be asked if the condition is for the seller's benefit. The discussion and provisions at §§3.72-3.75 concern conditions made part of the agreement for the buyer's benefit but they are also applicable to those needed for the seller's benefit.

§3.72 (1) Form: Subject to Conditions

Form 3.72-1

Buyer's obligation to perform this agreement is subject to the satisfaction of ____[conditions in Schedule _____ / the following condition(s)]____ which ____[are / is]____ for Buyer's benefit only:

Comment: This provision uses the drafting suggestions contained in §§3.69-3.70 and satisfies the requirements discussed in §12.100. In creating a checklist of conditions to which the buyer may want to qualify his commitment, see §3.63. For forms establishing various conditions, see §3.79 (title matters), §§3.154-3.156 (other transactions), §3.120 (survey and engineering report), §3.144 (map approval), §3.126 (termite report), §3.159 (business data). Other provisions (*e.g.,* §§3.101 and 3.111), obligate seller to deliver materials to facilitate buyer's approval.

The words "subject to" indicate that the promise is conditional. See *Rodriguez v Barnett* (1959) 52 C2d 154, 338 P2d 907; *Humes v Walker* (1931) 116 CA 599, 3 P2d 33. This interpretation is rendered certain by the use of the word "condition" and the express election given to the buyer in the above form. If the standard is subjective (*e.g.,* the buyer's satisfaction or approval), the agreement should specifically require that his acceptance not be withheld unreasonably. See §3.69. With an objective standard there is no need for the form to mention reasonable approval; whether the standard has been met can be determined from objective facts, without approval by either party.

The manner of giving notice need not be spelled out in this provision if the agreement contains a provision defining notice (see §3.58), and if (as in the provisions in this chapter) the clause for each condition states the time and the effect of the buyer's notice or failure to give notice. The agreement should also state the rights and obligations of each party if the condition is not satisfied; for those provisions, see §§3.73, 3.75.

This form is for use when the condition is inserted for the buyer's benefit. It should be modified for use when the condition is for the seller's benefit.

§3.73   (2) Form: Seller Required To Remove Defects;
             Buyer's Elections

Form 3.73-1

[Precede with form at §3.72]

If Buyer notifies Seller that Buyer disapproves any matter set out in ____*[spec-ify, e.g., paragraph _____ concerning title / paragraph _____ concern-ing termite reports]____* or if there is a breach of Seller's warranty set out in ____*[specify, e.g., paragraph _____ concerning zoning]____* discovered by Buyer before close of escrow, Seller shall diligently attempt to correct those matters at Seller's expense within _____ days after Buyer's notice of objec-tion. If all those matters are not corrected within that time, Buyer has the elec-tion within _____ days after Seller's time for correcting has expired of: (a) terminating the agreement without liability on Buyer's part; (b) completing the purchase, in which event the purchase price shall be reduced by an amount equal to the reduction in market value resulting from the uncorrected matters; or (c) removing the defect, in which event the purchase price shall be reduced by an amount equal to Buyer's cost of correcting those matters. If Buyer makes no election, Buyer's silence shall be considered an election of option (a).

If Buyer elects option (b), the reduction in market value caused by a lien or encumbrance securing a liquidated dollar amount shall be considered to be the unpaid principal balance of that amount plus accrued interest not charged to Seller in escrow. Other reductions in market value, if not mutually agreed on by Buyer and Seller, shall be arbitrated under the provisions of paragraph ____*[see §3.183]____* of this agreement. Seller shall bear the cost of arbitra-tion. The reduction in price shall first be applied to the downpayment and sec-ond to the purchase money note.

If Buyer elects option (c), the closing shall be extended for no more than _____ days. If Buyer does not remove the defects within that time, Buyer shall still be entitled to exercise option (a) or option (b) within that time. If Buyer does not remove the defects within that time and fails to elect either option (a) or (b), Buyer's silence shall be considered an election of option (a).

If the agreement is terminated by Buyer's election or failure to elect under this paragraph, all funds or other things deposited by Buyer shall be returned to Buyer immediately on demand, and Seller shall pay all title company and es-crow charges.

Comment: In addition to making the agreement subject to condi-tions (see §3.72) and stating those conditions clearly, the agree-ment should provide what is to happen if the buyer disapproves a condition or discovers the seller's breach of covenant or warranty before close of escrow. For breach discovered after close of escrow, see chap 12.

The above provision, used with the provision at §3.72, gives the buyer the right to choose among several courses of action. One of these is the right to buy the property at a lower price. This option is not appropriate for all conditions, *e.g.*, a condition that the buyer be able to obtain a change from agricultural to residential zoning. If a buyer cannot obtain rezoning of agricultural land, the farmer might prefer to retain and work the land than to sell it at the lower price obtainable for farmland. Recognizing this difference among conditions, the provision is limited to conditions designated in it.

If the agreement is subject to additional conditions not designated in this provision, the drafter should provide for action to be taken on the failure or disapproval of those conditions as well, perhaps by combining this provision with provisions such as those in §3.74 or §3.75. Instead of combining, however, a seller in a strong bargaining position may prefer to use §3.74 alone, because it is more favorable to him. (Section 3.75 represents a compromise.) The provisions at §§3.73-3.75 by no means exhaust the variants that may be demanded or agreed on in the course of bargaining, nor should any provision be considered to be invariable.

In using any of the three provisions at §§3.73-3.75, the buyer's attention should be called to the effect of his silence in terminating the agreement. Arbitration provisions are found at §3.183; provisions for serving notices are found at §3.58.

§3.74   (3) Form: Seller's Election To Remove Defects

Form 3.74-1

[Precede with provision at §3.72]

If Buyer notifies Seller that Buyer disapproves any matter ____*[on which this agreement is conditioned for Buyer's benefit / set out in* ____*[specify paragraph of agreement]*____]____ or if there is a breach of ____*[any covenant or warranty by Seller / Seller's warranty or covenant set out in* ____*[specify paragraph of agreement]*____]____ discovered by Buyer before closing of escrow, Seller may at Seller's election correct those matters, except third party financing, and shall for this purpose be entitled to postpone close of escrow for no more than ____ days. If Seller elects not to correct or fails to correct all those matters within the extended escrow period, Buyer has the election of (a) terminating the agreement without any liability on the part of either party or (b) accepting the property without reduction of the price for the uncorrected matter and without any liability on Seller's part. Seller's election to correct those matters shall be evidenced by notice within _____ days after receipt of Buyer's notice specifying the item breached or disapproved; Buyer's failure to give notice shall be construed as an election of option (b). If Buyer terminates this agreement by electing or failing to elect under this paragraph, all funds or other things deposited by Buyer shall be returned to Buyer immediately on demand, less obligation for title company and escrow charges.

Comment: The agreement should provide what is to happen if the buyer disapproves any matter to which he has a right to object under conditions stated in the agreement. The Comment at §3.73 contrasts this provision with those in §§3.73 and 3.75. This provision is more favorable to the seller. For a possible compromise provision, see §3.75.

On the manner of serving notices required by this provision, see §3.58.

This provision may be altered by changes in language. For example, if the buyer elects to terminate the agreement, he may be relieved of all expenses of escrow; if he accepts the property subject to the defect there may be a reduction of price or some other compromise may be negotiated.

§3.75   (4) Form: Compromise on Removal of Defects

Form 3.75-1

[Precede with provision at §3.72]

If Buyer notifies Seller that Buyer disapproves any matter ____*[on which this agreement is conditioned for Buyer's benefit / set out in* ____*[specify paragraph of agreement]* ____]____ or if there is a breach of ____*[any covenant or warranty by Seller / Seller's warranty or covenant set out in* ____*[specify paragraph of agreement]* ____]____ discovered by Buyer before close of escrow, Seller shall diligently attempt to correct those matters, except third party financing, within _____ days after Buyer's notice. If all those matters are not corrected within that time, Buyer has the election of (a) terminating this agreement without liability on Buyer's part, or (b) accepting the property without reduction of the price for the uncorrected matter and without any liability on the part of either party except that, if the only matters are either defects in title resulting from encumbrances in liquidated dollar amounts that can be removed by paying them or matters requiring the expenditure of funds under ____*[specify, e.g., paragraph* _____*concerning termite reports]* ____, and if the total cost of correcting these matters does not aggregate more than $_____, Seller shall be required to pay those amounts, or, at Seller's election, they may be paid from escrow out of Seller's proceeds. Buyer's election shall be evidenced by notice within _____ days after Seller's time for correction has expired. Buyer's failure to give notice shall be construed as an election to terminate this agreement. If Buyer terminates this agreement by electing or failing to elect under this paragraph, all funds or other things deposited by Buyer shall be returned to Buyer immediately on demand without liability on Buyer's part, and Seller shall pay title company and escrow charges.

Comment: There are many ways to compromise; this provision illustrates one way. It obligates the seller to try to remove the defect, as does the provision in §3.73, but it does not give the buyer all the elections provided in that section. However, it does not charge the buyer with escrow charges, as does the form in §3.74, and it provides an automatic method of paying off encumbrances below a stated maximum. The need for a clause providing what is to happen if a warranty is breached or if the buyer disapproves under a condition made for his benefit is explained in Comment to §3.73. That section offers a form favorable to the buyer. For a form favorable to seller, see §3.74.

§3.76 d. Recovery of Buyer's Deposit

If the agreement and the escrow, if any, are to be canceled because of the buyer's disapproval of some item or failure of performance of some condition, the buyer's primary concern is the speedy return of his deposit or downpayment. For this purpose, the agreement normally should provide for repayment to the buyer. See §§3.73-3.75. This is more readily achieved if the downpayment has been placed in escrow. A provision for repayment may not, however, operate effectively in practice. If a dispute arises, the escrow holder may be unwilling to release the funds without cancellation instructions from both parties and may interplead the funds, creating an unfavorable situation from the buyer's viewpoint. On the interpleader of disputed funds by escrow holder, see §11.22. To avoid the possibility that a dispute will prevent or delay a refund to the buyer when an agreement is canceled for failure of a condition, the buyer should attempt to make a minimal deposit at the time of executing an agreement (perhaps just enough to cover costs), with a more substantial deposit to be made on approval of the conditions of the agreement. Such an arrangement postpones the buyer's outlay of funds until the agreement becomes unconditional and protects the buyer from having funds tied up in a disputed escrow. For a discussion of deposits by personal check, see §3.47.

If, in addition to getting his deposit back, the buyer desires to reserve his right to damages or specific performance, he should make this right explicit in the agreement. Otherwise, the provision for the return of his deposit is likely to be regarded as terminating the agreement. See §§12.26-12.30. If the agreement is regarded as terminated, the buyer is prevented from waiving the defect and buying at a reduced price. For a provision in which the buyer's right to waive is expressly reserved, see §3.73.

§3.77   3. Options

A number of California lawyers advocate options to enable buyers to tie up property while investigating it without being bound to buy it. The option also serves to permit retention of the deposit by the seller as the price for the option if it is not exercised, thus avoiding problems of liquidated damages. Options are discussed in more detail in chapter 4. On requirements for liquidated damages provisions, see §§3.179-3.180.

§3.78   C. Marketable Title

Under California law a buyer of real property is entitled to "marketable title" as an implied condition of the bargain. *King v Stanley* (1948) 32 C2d 584, 197 P2d 321. Marketable title must "embrace both the legal and equitable estates, must be free from any encumbrance, [and] must be defensible and salable." *Palos Verdes Corp. v Housing Auth.* (1962) 202 CA2d 827, 838, 21 CR 225, 233. Title must be sufficiently free from doubt that a reasonable purchaser, well informed about the facts and their legal effect, and exercising ordinary business prudence, would be willing to accept it. *Hocking v Title Ins. & Trust Co.* (1951) 37 C2d 644, 234 P2d 625; *Wilson v Pacific Coast Title Ins. Co.* (1951) 106 CA2d 599, 602, 235 P2d 431, 433. A visible encumbrance, such as a road, is not considered to render title unmarketable because the parties are considered to have contracted with the encumbrance in mind. *Evans v Faught* (1965) 231 CA2d 698, 42 CR 133. The general rule is that restrictions imposed by law, such as local zoning ordinances, do not impair marketability because the parties are considered to have contracted in light of applicable law. *Hartman v Rizzuto* (1954) 123 CA2d 186,

266 P2d 539. Examples of defects that render title unmarketable include easements of record unless they are visible, judgment liens, deeds of trust and mortgages, covenants, conditions and restrictions, tax and assessment liens, mechanics' liens, adverse possession, and leases. See 1 Miller & Starr, Current Law of California Real Estate §2:44 (rev ed 1975) for a discussion of encumbrances that render title unmarketable.

Title insurance has become customary as a way of protecting the buyer against defects in title. A title insurance policy does not remove a defect in title (*Frabotto v Alencastre* (1960) 182 CA2d 679, 6 CR 536), but it does provide the buyer with a means of recovery of loss or damage if title turns out to be unmarketable. Special endorsements are available from title companies to solve some of the more frequent title problems. The buyer may also be able to negotiate with the title company to eliminate an exception from the policy. Elimination of an exception may not, however, remove the defect, because there is still the risk that a subsequent purchaser might not be able to obtain the same policy coverage. See California Title Insurance Practice, chap 3 (Cal CEB 1980) for a detailed discussion of title insurance.

The usual procedure is to obtain a preliminary title report which summarizes the exceptions to marketable title that the title company has found. The buyer, or his attorney, must examine the documents evidencing the exceptions and make a determination whether the property, so impaired, is unacceptable. Title companies do not ensure the accuracy of their preliminary reports, so counsel should discuss possible unlisted exceptions to title with the title officer in order to avoid later difficulties. The preliminary title report may include exceptions that can be eliminated, such as expired leases or liens that have been paid. Counsel should investigate each exception and discuss with the title officer those that can be eliminated.

Buyer's counsel should look beyond marketability of title because the courts have held that some matters that affect the use of the property do not impair title even though they do reduce the value of the property. For example, in *Nishiyama v Safeco Title Ins. Co.* (1978) 85 CA3d Supp 1, 149 CR 355, the court held that the fact that the property had been divided in violation of the Subdivision Map Act and that the owner might be required to comply with conditions that could have been imposed had the property been subdivided in compliance with the law, did not render title unmarketable. See also *Hocking v Title Ins. & Trust Co., supra,* 37 C2d 644, ¦ 625.

See also provision and Comment at §3.55.

1. Approval of Condition of Title

§3.79   a. Form: Condition; Approval of Title as a Condition to Closing (Subject to Buyer's Review of Preliminary Title Report)

Form 3.79-1

[Insert in provision for conditions at §3.72]

____*[Name of title company]*____ to be able to issue its standard California Land Title Association owner's policy of title insurance dated as of the closing date, on its usual form, with liability not less than the purchase price, covering the property, showing title vested in Buyer, and showing as exceptions any current real property taxes, not yet delinquent, and those exceptions to title which have been approved by Buyer.

Form 3.79-2

[Insert Form 3.104-1, 3.104-2 or 3.104-3, if applicable]

[Continue]

Form 3.79-3

Seller will furnish Buyer within _____ days of this agreement a preliminary title report and the documents reported as exceptions in it ("title documents"). Buyer shall notify Seller in writing within _____ business days after receipt of the report and the title documents of Buyer's disapproval of any exception therein.

[Add if insurance is desired to cover off-record risks not insured by standard coverage]

If Buyer so elects, Buyer may order ____*[at Buyer's expense]*____ an American Land Title Association title report (ALTA report), provided that the right to disapprove any exception shown on an ALTA report shall expire unless Buyer shall have ordered an ALTA report before _____, 19__. If an ALTA survey is required by title company, Buyer shall order such survey not later than _____, 19__. Buyer shall notify Seller in writing within _____ business days after receipt of the ALTA report, or any supplemental report for ALTA coverage, of Buyer's disapproval of any exception in it.

[Continue]

Failure to so notify Seller shall conclusively be considered ____*[disapproval / approval]*____. If Buyer disapproves any item referred to in this paragraph, the provisions of paragraph ____*[see §§3.73-3.75]*____ shall apply.

Comment: This provision is to be used when the agreement is executed before the buyer has had an opportunity to examine the seller's title. It allows the buyer to examine and approve the exceptions reported by the title company. The seller usually wishes to have the conditions eliminated as quickly as possible, and will therefore urge a short period of time for review of title. The time for approval should run only from receipt of all documents referred to in the title report, not from receipt of the report itself. Sufficient time should be allowed for the elimination of objectionable exceptions.

The agreement should set out what is to happen if buyer disapproves an exception reported by the title company. The above form refers to the provisions in §§3.73-3.75; either one of those or some other provisions must cover this matter.

Whether this provision or that at §3.80 is used, the buyer will usually wish to specify the title company because he will want to obtain coverage from a financially responsible company. The choice of title company may, however, be a matter for negotiation if either party has reasons for specifying a particular title company. See also §3.53 on choice of escrow holder and §3.55 on choice of title insurance company. In Northern California the title company chosen will usually also be the escrow holder; in Southern California it is not uncommon for the escrow holder to be a different entity from the title insurance company.

There is no implied obligation of the seller to furnish title insurance (see *Easton v Montgomery* (1891) 90 C 307, 27 P 280; *Seymour v Shaeffer* (1947) 82 CA2d 823, 187 P2d 95); the agreement should expressly provide for it. On the available policies and the endorsements, see California Title Insurance Practice, chap 3 (Cal CEB 1980). The amount of coverage is customarily the purchase price of the property, though this may vary. In Northern California the buyer generally pays for title insurance, but Southern California custom calls for the seller to pay this charge. See §§11.31, 11.58.

This provision gives the buyer an option to purchase ALTA coverage. The advantage to ALTA coverage is that it provides protection against visible easements and other off-record matters. See §3.92. To accommodate the seller's desire to eliminate conditions quickly, the provision sets deadlines for ordering the coverage and any survey required in connection with the ALTA coverage.

The effect of the buyer's failure to respond should be specified. The seller will want the buyer's silence to mean approval while the buyer will prefer to have it signify disapproval. See §§3.73-3.75 concerning the seller's right to cure a disapproved exception. The parties should settle who is to pay the extra cost of ALTA coverage. See §3.57 for a form generally covering allocation of closing costs. See also discussion of ALTA coverage in §11.44.

§3.80   b. Form: Condition; Approval of Condition of Title (Subject to Stated Exceptions)

Form 3.80-1

[Insert in provision for conditions at §3.72]

_ _ _ _[Name of title company]_ _ _ _ to be able to issue its standard California Land Title Association owner's policy of title insurance dated as of the closing date, on its usual form, with liability not less than the purchase price, covering the property, showing title vested in Buyer, and showing as exceptions only real property taxes for the tax fiscal year 19_ _-19_ _, a lien not yet payable, and the following: _ _ _ _[specify all other exceptions]_ _ _ _ _.

Form 3.80-2

[Insert Form 3.104-1, 3.104-2 or 3.104-3, if applicable]

Comment: This form does not provide time for the buyer to inspect title. Instead it sets forth the exceptions to which title will be subject. This form should be used only when the buyer has reviewed the title exceptions and approved them before the agreement is executed. Before signing the agreement the buyer, or his counsel, should examine the actual documents referred to in the list of exceptions to determine whether any of the exceptions may prohibit or interfere with some intended use of the property.

See also Comment at §3.79. See also form and Comment at §3.55.

c. Title Warranties

§3.81   (1) Supplement to a Condition

The buyer might want to include a warranty as well as a condition regarding the state of title because standard CLTA title insurance does not cover matters that do not appear on the public record but could be ascertained by an inspection of the property. See §3.92. A warranty is a supplement to a condition regarding title, but is not a substitute.

If the parties intend that a warranty survive the close of escrow, language should be included to express that intent. See §§3.66, 3.67. Preferred practice is to include the covenants of title that are to survive in a warranty deed. See chapter 9 on title covenants. Only a limited covenant of title is implied under CC §1113 by the use of a grant deed. See §9.6. See generally Freshman, *The Warranty Deed: Where and When to Use It,* 51 LA BJ 186 (1975).

§3.82   (2) Form: Warranty; Status of Title

Form 3.82-1

As a covenant that will survive the close of escrow, Seller warrants that Seller is the sole owner of the property, free and clear of all liens, claims, encumbrances, easements, encroachments on the property from adjacent properties, encroachments by improvements or vegetation on the property onto adjacent property, or rights of way of any nature, other than: ____*[list exceptions including any off-record items such as unrecorded leases or month-to-month tenancies]*____.

Comment: In this warranty, the seller covenants that there are no off-record items that would affect title. This provision prevents the seller from remaining silent about title defects of which he is aware. The warranty also extends to defects of which the seller may be unaware. This provision is important because title insurance does not cover matters that would be disclosed by inspection of the land or inquiry of those in possession. Moreover, defects such as encroachments are difficult to detect without a survey of the property, and the buyer may not want to incur the expense of a survey. See §3.94 for a warranty against unrecorded easements.

2. Exceptions to Marketable Title

a. Taxes

§3.83   (1) Real Property Taxes

The state and federal governments secure the payment of various taxes by placing liens on real property. Such liens make the title unmarketable. In addition, the lien for real property taxes is superior to earlier recorded private liens. Rev & T C §2192.1. See also 2 Miller & Starr, Current Law of California Real Estate §§11:133-11:153 (rev ed 1977). Tax liens will normally be reflected on the preliminary title report, and the buyer will have an opportunity to approve or disapprove the item, if he has reserved the right to approve title (see §3.79).

The most commonly encountered tax lien is that for real property taxes for local government general revenue. The tax fiscal year begins on July 1st and the tax lien attaches to property the preceding March 1st. Rev & T C §2192. The tax is payable in two equal installments which are delinquent if not paid by the following December 10th and April 10th. Rev & T C §§2617-2618. If real property taxes are not paid when due, the property securing them is "sold to the state" for the unpaid taxes in June following the delinquency date. Rev & T C §§3351, 3436. If the property is not redeemed within five years, the state sells the property at public auction. Rev & T C §§3511, 3691. See generally 2 Miller & Starr, Current Law §§11:133-11:135.

Real property taxes are usually prorated to the date of closing, unless the parties agree otherwise. See §3.56 for a provision for prorating taxes. When a buyer requests a seller to extend the closing date of escrow, the seller may insist that the original closing date be used as the date for prorations. Delinquent taxes should be paid at or before closing to protect the buyer's title.

§3.84   (2) Personal Property Taxes

Personal property is also subject to taxation under California law (Rev & T C §§201, 401) and a personal property tax is a lien on real property belonging to the owner of the personal property if the personal property is located on the real property on the lien date. Rev & T C §2189. If the personal property or improvement on a parcel is owned by someone other than the fee owner, a statement can be filed with the assessor before the lien date attesting to the separate ownership. In that case, the real and personal property will be assessed on separate bills. Rev & T C §2188.2. When a segregated tax bill is issued, the lien for the tax on the personal property does not attach to the land. However, the personal property tax lien can attach to other real property owned by the owner of the personal property.

If the title report shows a lien for personal property taxes, buyer's counsel should determine who owns the property. If the sale does not include the personal property, the buyer should request a separate assessment under Rev & T C §2188.2. The buyer should either receive the amount of the personal property tax from the seller or some security for payment of the tax if the personal property is owned by someone other than the seller. Personal property tax should be prorated as follows:

(a) If the buyer is not purchasing the personal property, the phrase "all personal property taxes shown on the tax bill shall be paid by Seller through escrow" should be added to the proration provision in §3.56;

(b) If the buyer is purchasing all the personal property, "personal property taxes" should be added to the items to be prorated in the provision at §3.56;

(c) If the buyer is purchasing only some of the personal property, the parties should agree on the value of the personal property transferred, and the following should be added to the proration provision in §3.56.

Buyer shall pay _____ percent of the personal property taxes coming due after the close of escrow.

§3.85   (3) Federal Tax Liens

In addition to liens for property taxes (see §§3.83-3.90), which are usually prorated between buyer and seller, there may also be liens for federal taxes, such as income, withholding, estate, and gift taxes; these are usually not borne by the buyer. The seller, however, may be given an opportunity to remove the lien at or before closing without impairing the agreement. For alternative provisions, see §§3.73-3.75 on giving seller an opportunity to remove.

On assessment, federal taxes become a lien against all the taxpayer's property or rights to property. IRC §6321. Federal tax lien procedures that do not provide for preattachment hearings have been upheld in the face of challenges contending that they deny property owners due process. *Baldassari v U.S.* (1978) 79 CA3d 267, 144 CR 741. The lien is not valid against a purchaser of real property unless notice of the lien is filed with the recorder of the county where the property is located and a public index of the lien is maintained at the IRS district office in the district where the property is located. IRC §6323.

A special lien for estate and gift taxes exists without assessment and includes tax not paid when due. IRC §6324. In addition, there are special lien provisions for estate tax deferred (IRC §§6166-6166A) and for additional estate tax attributable to farm or closely held business valuation (IRC §§6324A-6324B). If unassessed estate tax appears as a possible lien on the preliminary title report, written application for its release should be made to the IRS district director under Reg §301.6325-1(c). If a notice of tax lien has been filed, and the tax has been paid or will be paid out of escrow, arrangements can be made for the release of the lien.

A federal tax lien is not filed against specific property of a taxpayer; it is filed against a named taxpayer and becomes a lien by operation of law. When the taxpayer has a common name, some confusion occurs if others of the same name own real property in the same county. On showing the facts, a certificate of nonattachment of federal tax lien (ROWR Form 2333) may be obtained (from the district director's office, chief of special procedures staff), certifying that the filed lien does not attach to a particular parcel of property. When a taxpayer against whom a federal tax lien is filed is refinancing or purchasing property through third party financing, he may obtain a similar certificate. This certificate permits the taxpayer to complete the transaction by certifying that the lien does not attach to the lender's interest in the property.

Inquiries concerning discharging property from the effects of a federal tax lien should be directed to the Special Procedures Section of the District Director of Internal Revenue in San Francisco or Los Angeles. The balance due on a notice of lien can be determined by writing to the district director, identifying the property, the particular lien, and stating the reason for the request. The owner or intended purchaser may obtain this information even when he is not the taxpayer against whom the lien is filed. Reg §301.6323(i)-1(c). If federal tax lien problems are suspected, the parties should provide in the purchase and sale agreement sufficient time before closing to resolve them.

(4) Special Assessments

§3.86   (a) General Considerations

The lien of a special assessment to pay for the construction or maintenance of some public improvement, such as a lighting district, a road, or a sewer, arises when a notice of assessment is recorded. Str & H C §§3114, 3115. An assessment lien generally affects only the parcels benefited by the improvement. Assessment liens have priority over private liens (Rev & T C §2192.1) and, if not paid when due, the property may eventually be sold by the tax collector (Rev & T C §3691). Problems can arise when an improvement has been completed, but the government has not yet levied an assessment. In that case, the lien would not be listed as an exception on the preliminary title report because it would not be a lien of record. The buyer would be liable for such assessments and would have no recourse against the title insurance policy. This is a typical matter to be covered by a seller's warranty that will survive close of escrow. See §3.88 for a warranty provision.

The treatment of assessments is a point to be negotiated. The seller usually feels that the buyer should bear the burden of the assessment due because the buyer will reap the benefits of the improvement. The buyer will argue that the improvements have increased the value of the property and were taken into consideration in arriving at the purchase price and should therefore be paid off by the seller at closing.

§3.87   (b) Form: Assessments Paid by Seller

Form 3.87-1

All assessments against the property ____[except for _____]____ including all installments of those assessments that shall become due after the closing, shall be paid in full by Seller before the close of escrow, or, at Buyer's option, the assessments may remain a lien against the property and Buyer shall receive a credit against the purchase price in the amount of the assessments.

Comment: This provision is to be used if the seller is to pay off the assessment before close of escrow, or the buyer is to take title subject to the assessment but with a credit against the purchase price; it should not be used if the buyer is to take title subject to the assessment without any credit against the purchase price. In that case, the assessment should be listed as a title exception. See provisions at §§3.79 and 3.80. Interest on the assessment should be prorated to the closing date if assumed by the buyer.

§3.88   (c) Form: Seller's Warranties Regarding Assessments

Form 3.88-1

Seller warrants and represents that the property is not and at the close of escrow shall not be the subject of any proposed assessments or assessment liens, other than those specifically excepted in this agreement, by reason of any work or improvement completed or installed at or before the close of escrow.

Form 3.88-2 (Seller Responsible for Improvements Proposed But Not Completed at Close of Escrow)

Seller warrants and represents that the property is not and at the close of escrow shall not be the subject of any proposed assessment for work or improvements to be completed after the close of escrow.

Form 3.88-3 (Buyer Responsible for Improvements Proposed But Not Completed at Close of Escrow)

Proposed assessments against the property for work or improvements to be completed after the close of escrow shall be borne by Buyer and are not the responsibility of Seller.

Comment: The provisions in 3.88-1 and 3.88-2 are intended to protect the buyer when a work of improvement may have been started or completed but the government has not yet levied an assessment. See discussion in §3.86.

5. Segregation When Part of Assessed Parcel Sold

§3.89   (a) Separate Problems

When the real property being sold is part of a parcel under one assessment, the periods before and after closing present separate problems.

For the period before closing, because segregation of taxes is not possible before ownership is transferred, the division must be made by agreement to prorate. For discussion and provisions, see §11.51.

For the period after closing, all taxes should be separately assessed to each of the parcels resulting from the sale. For a provision, see §3.90. Segregation is authorized by Rev & T C §2821. The application and affidavit of interest must be made during the current fiscal year. A county may prohibit applications during the ten-day period preceding each tax installment delinquent date (December 10 and April 10) and during the ten-day period prior to June 30 of each year.

§3.90   (b) Form: Segregation of Taxes

Form 3.90-1

Before the close of escrow the parties shall deposit in escrow all documents necessary to accomplish a segregation of the property from the larger tax parcel of which it is now a part. As an agreement that shall survive the close of escrow, Buyer and Seller agree that if any installment of tax becomes due before the segregation is made, the following proportion of the tax due shall be allocated to the property:

(1) _____ percent of taxes attributable to land;

(2) _____ percent of taxes attributable to improvements on the land;

(3) The percentage of personal property tax equal to the proportion that the value of Buyer's personal property bears to the value of all personal property assessed;

[Add if applicable]

(4) _____ percent of the assessment for ____[*e.g., street*]____ improvements shown as item _____ on the preliminary title report.

If the taxes on the property on segregation differ from the foregoing values, except for differences arising from revaluation of the property, the parties shall adjust the difference between themselves.

Comment: The initial allocation between the property sold and the remaining part of the seller's land must be made on the basis of an agreed valuation when the agreement is executed. This allocation may not be borne out by the assessor's valuations on segregation. The parties may either let their own values stand or adjust to a ratio determined from the assessor's valuations. The last paragraph of the provision does the latter. The provision for taxes on improvements and personal property takes into account changes and additions made by either party. Assessed values of each improvement and article of personal property are readily available in the assessor's records.

In some instances, special district taxes (such as school districts) or special assessments for sidewalk repair and other current maintenance are assessed and collected with the regular tax bill. These should be included in the segregation. To avoid any confusion between this type of assessment and improvement assessments (see §3.88), the agreement should differentiate between the two types if they both affect the property.

§3.91 b. Reservations and Exceptions

An exception or reservation is a withholding by the grantor of an estate or a use less than a fee (*e.g.*, a life estate or an easement) or a portion of the property in fee. The distinction between an exception and a reservation "is so slight and shadowy that in common parlance they are used interchangeably." *Van Slyke v Arrowhead*

Reservoir & Power Co. (1909) 155 C 675, 680, 102 P 816, 818. The essential distinction is that a seller who excepts property from the deed does not pass title to the excepted portion, but a seller who reserves an interest passes fee title to the buyer but takes back some interest less than a fee. 3 Miller & Starr, Current Law of California Real Estate §18:18 (rev ed 1977). A reservation may be made for the benefit of someone other than the grantor. CC §1085; *Willard v First Church of Christ, Scientist* (1972) 7 C3d 473, 102 CR 739. Any reservation or exception of record should be carefully examined to determine its effect on the buyer's intended use of the property. If made in a prior grant in the chain of title, the reservation should appear in the title report. If the property is to be developed in connection with adjacent property retained by the seller, the parties should consider whether reciprocal parking, utility and access easements, and related agreements should be executed as part of the purchase transaction. Buyer's counsel should at least obtain a commitment from the seller to join in any necessary grants of easement over the seller's adjacent land, and an agreement on the division of the costs of any required improvements affecting both parcels should also be reached. See also discussion in §8.34 on distinction between reservations and exceptions.

§3.92   c. Easements

In most cases the existence of an encumbering easement destroys marketability of title. *Zlozower v Lindenbaum* (1929) 100 CA 766, 281 P 102. Counsel for the buyer must ascertain what easements exist, obtain and review the documents pertaining to the easements, and explain their significance to the buyer. The buyer must then decide if the property is suitable for his use.

Ascertaining easements requires more than just a review of the preliminary title report and the underlying documents. Standard form title insurance protects the insured from losses resulting from easements disclosed from the public record only. CLTA Form, Schedule B, Part I, §3 (1973). It excludes interests which are not shown by public record but which are ascertainable by inspection of the property or by inquiring of persons in possession. CLTA Form Schedule B, Part I, §2 (1973). An ALTA policy provides further protection by insuring against defects that are discoverable from an inspection of the property. ALTA Owner's Policy Form B-1970. Both the CLTA and ALTA policies exclude defects known to the insured party but unknown to the title company. On coverage of title insurance policies, see California Title Insurance Practice, chap 3 (Cal CEB 1980).

If the buyer does not wish to incur the expense of ALTA coverage, the premises must be inspected and those in possession questioned about rights of others to use the property. Protection may also be obtained by including in the purchase and sale agreement the seller's warranty against easements not of record. See §3.94.

§3.93   (1) Effect of Visible Easements

An easement that is evidenced by visible effects sufficient to create a prescriptive or implied easement will bind subsequent purchasers, even if not shown on the record. *Ocean Shore R.R. v Spring Valley Water Co.* (1933) 218 C 86, 21 P2d 588; *Lindsay v King* (1956) 138 CA2d 333, 292 P2d 23. Examples of visible effects include: portions of a railroad grade and trestle (*Ocean Shore R.R. v Spring Valley Water Co., supra*); stand pipes for a water pipeline (*Johnson v Cella* (1953) 122 CA2d 72, 264 P2d 98); and a paved portion of property used for access to an adjacent gas station (*Amerco, Inc. v Tullar* (1960) 182 CA2d 336, 6 CR 71).

Such visible evidence puts the buyer on inquiry and he can neither assume that the use is abandoned nor be satisfied with the owner's opinion that the easement will not be used. The buyer is charged with constructive knowledge of those facts that would be disclosed if reasonable inquiry were made. *Ocean Shore R.R., supra.*

A visible easement is not treated as a breach of the covenant to sell free of encumbrances (CC §1113) because the parties are presumed to have contracted with it in mind. *Rustigan v Phelps* (1923) 190 C 608, 213 P 957; *McCarty v Wilson* (1920) 184 C 194, 193 P 578.

§3.94   (2) Form: Warranty Against Easements Not of Record

Form 3.94-1

Seller warrants to Buyer that the title conveyed to Buyer will not be encumbered by any easements, licenses, or other rights not disclosed by the public record other than ____[*list unrecorded leases, tenancies, easements or other interests*]____.

Comment: The implied covenant against encumbrances under CC §1113 is not breached by the existence of visible easements that are a physical burden on the land (see §3.92); therefore this warranty should be included among those that survive delivery of the deed (see §§3.67, 3.82). The preferred practice is to include this warranty in the deed as well. See §3.81. If the seller intends to encumber the property with an easement, deed of trust, or otherwise, that fact should be stated. Unlike the rule with respect to visible easements, unrecorded leases, even when known to the buyer, constitute encumbrances within the meaning of CC §1113. *Evans v Faught* (1965) 231 CA2d 698, 42 CR 133. See §3.82 for a broad warranty concerning status of title.

§3.95   d. Party Walls

If a structure on the property has a wall in common with a structure on adjoining property, the situation concerns the buyer in at least three ways: (1) It may affect title (even rendering it unmarketable), (2) it may limit the buyer's use, and (3) it may subject the buyer to expenses and obligations in connection with the wall. On the other hand, a party wall may give the buyer an easement on the adjoining property.

The right to use a party wall is an easement. CC §801(12). It may not render title unmarketable when the party wall stands equally or partly on the adjoining land and mutual rights and obligations exist, but it may render title unmarketable when the wall stands entirely on the subject property. 3 American Law of Property §11.49 at p 137 (A.J. Casner ed. 1952); Anno, *Marketable Title—Party Walls,* 81 ALR2d 1020 (1962).

In addition to affecting title, a party wall may limit the buyer's uses of the property. For example, the right to demolish an existing structure is subject to the buyer's obligation to maintain the party wall. *Nippert v Warneke* (1900) 128 C 501, 61 P 96.

A party wall also subjects the owner to rights that the adjoining owner may exercise. For example, in the absence of an agreement to the contrary, each owner is entitled to increase the height and width of the wall as long as no damage is done to the other structure or to the wall itself. *Tate v Fratt* (1896) 112 C 613, 44 P 1061. In addition, either owner may use his part of the wall for advertising, may deepen the foundation, and may rebuild a dilapidated wall. Injury to the wall is actionable (*McCarthy v Mutual Relief Ass'n* (1889) 81 C 584, 22 P 933) as is removal (*Nippert v Warneke, supra,* 128 C 501, 61 P 96).

A wall may stand entirely on one parcel and still be a party wall. See *Tate v Fratt, supra,* 112 C 613, 44 P 1061. If it is a party wall, the use of each parcel must not impair the cross-easements of support and beam rights (CC §801(12)) in favor of the adjoining owner.

If the buyer regards the party wall as an asset, he should be aware that destruction by fire or other casualty terminates the easements and related rights and duties unless they are preserved by agreement. 5 Powell, The Law of Real Property §691 (1968).

In view of these risks, any wall that appears to support a structure on adjoining land as well as one on the subject property is a signal to the buyer to determine: (1) whether the wall does indeed support both structures; (2) the exact location of the boundary line in relation to the wall (normally fixed by a survey); and (3) the existence and provisions of any express or implied agreement between the seller or his predecessor and the adjoining property owner or his predecessor. On implied agreements, see *Bank of Escondido v Thomas* (1895) 5 CU 94, 41 P 462; *Guttenberger v Woods* (1876) 51 C 523; *Nippert v Warneke, supra,* 128 C 501, 61 P 96.

If no express agreement exists, it may be possible to negotiate and execute one before the close of escrow. For provision for party wall agreements, see Belsheim, Modern Legal Forms §§6482-6495 (1958).

e. Covenants, Conditions, and Restrictions

§3.96   (1) As Impairments of Title

If there is no agreement to the contrary, the existence of covenants, conditions, or restrictions (CC&Rs) in the chain of title generally renders title unmarketable and entitles the buyer to withdraw from the transaction. *Tandy v Waesch* (1908) 154 C 108, 97 P 69. Restrictions imposed by law, however, do not impair title, because the parties are considered to have contracted in the light of applicable law. See *Hartman v Rizzuto* (1954) 123 CA2d 186, 266 P2d 539 (holding, nevertheless, that facts in the case relieved the buyer of the consequences of the rule). Not all enforceable restrictions impair the value of the property; some enhance value by preventing objectionable use of neighboring parcels.

Covenants are promises, and if they are not performed, give rise to an action for breach. See 2 Bowman, Ogden's Revised California

Real Property Law §§23.5-23.12 (TI Corp-Cal CEB 1975). For remedies on breach, see chap 12. Conditions are limitations on the full and unqualified enjoyment of the right or estate granted. *Zlozower v Lindenbaum* (1929) 100 CA 766, 281 P 102. If they are enforceable their violation terminates the estate or gives a right of termination. 2 Ogden's Real Property §§23.1-23.2. Easements are not included in the term "restrictions" (see *Zlozower v Lindenbaum, supra*), except in the sense that restrictions are considered to be either "negative" easements or equitable servitudes (*Sackett v Los Angeles City School Dist.* (1931) 118 CA 254, 5 P2d 23).

Not all purported restrictions are enforceable. Some restrictions are unenforceable on constitutional or public policy grounds. See, *e.g., Shelley v Kraemer* (1948) 334 US 1, and *Cumings v Hokr* (1948) 31 C2d 844, 193 P2d 742 (refusing to enforce racial restrictions).

Enforcement of CC&Rs will not be made against a buyer of a subdivision lot if the buyer's deed is recorded before recordation of the declaration of restrictions and the deed does not contain the restrictions. *Riley v Bear Creek Planning Comm.* (1976) 17 C3d 500, 131 CR 381. Similarly, a buyer at a trustee's sale foreclosing a lien senior to the declaration of restrictions is not bound by the CC&Rs because the sale extinguishes the junior restrictions. *Sain v Silvestre* (1978) 78 CA3d 461, 144 CR 478. For further discussion of the enforceability of CC&Rs, see 2 Ogden's Real Property, chap 23.

(In order to make title marketable within the needs of the buyer, the agreement should give the buyer the right to determine within a reasonable time whether the restrictions are enforceable and tolerable for his purposes. The provision for buyer's approval of title at §3.79 gives the buyer this right.)

§3.97   (2) Uses for Covenants, Conditions, and Restrictions

The orderly development of subdivisions usually requires recording of the restrictions on the use of each lot. See generally Guide to California Subdivision Sales Law §§4.5-4.6, 4.22 (Cal CEB 1974). In a condominium, the use of common areas and of the individually owned parcel is also controlled by this means. CC §1355. Frequently, participation in a mutual water company or in a community recreation center, with its attendant financial responsibility, is founded on some provision in recorded restrictions. Some lawyers, however, believe that zoning ordinances are preferable to CC&Rs,

because they are more flexible and adaptable to changing conditions.

In addition to the use of CC&Rs in the development of large parcels of land, covenants are useful in resolving many problems affecting small parcels, adjoining owners, or lot splits. Adjoining owners may by agreement provide for a common right-of-way and for its maintenance; in the absence of any agreement, cost of maintenance is borne by the owners proportionately to their use. CC §845.

Drafting requires the usual care that should be given to any technical document intended to define rights and obligations of parties over an extended period of time.

§3.98   (3) Examination of Record

To protect the buyer against having to purchase before examining the record, his lawyer should either condition the agreement on the buyer's right to approve (as in §3.79) or employ the option device (as in chap 4). If neither can be done, the buyer should examine the condition of title before executing any agreement.

Protection is essential if printed forms are used for the purchase and sale agreement (or deposit receipt) or for escrow instructions. Many printed forms contain the clause, "subject to covenants, conditions, restrictions . . . of record." The California Association of Realtors form of deposit receipt adopted in 1978 provides that the buyer take subject to CC&Rs of record with limited right to disapprove. See §3.40. (Any printed escrow instructions that provide that title is to be taken subject to any matters of record not specified should always be modified. A preliminary title report should be received before closing and the escrow instructions should specifically mention all exceptions to title to which the buyer has agreed. See §11.44 (Form 11.44-2) on escrow instructions.)

In addition to examining the title report, the lawyer should read the documents referred to in the report. For this reason, when a preliminary report is ordered, the title company should be instructed to provide a copy of all the documents referred to in the exceptions at the time the preliminary report is issued and delivered. The attorney should compare these documents with entries in the report to make certain that they are copies of the right documents. When it is appropriate, documents should also be shown to the buyer's architect, engineer, and contractor for analysis, *e.g.*, if there are improvements planned, and to a title company attorney if title problems appear (see example in §§8.8-8.9).

§3.99 (4) Inquiry Beyond Record

If examination of the record reveals restrictions, the following questions arise:

(a) Are the restrictions objectionable in the light of the buyer's purposes? Restrictions limiting the property to residential uses, for example, ordinarily are not objectionable if the buyer's purpose is residential use. However, if they set minimum sizes or require the approval of an architectural committee, they may be objectionable.

(b) Have the restrictions been violated? If so, the title may be subject to an action for defeasance or may, in fact, have reverted automatically. See 2 Bowman, Ogden's Revised California Real Property Law, chap 23 (TI Corp-CEB 1975). Their violation does not appear of record except by lis pendens or by a judgment determining whether title has been affected; for this reason the inquiry must proceed beyond the record.

(c) Are the restrictions enforceable? A condition of record, even though violated, does not affect title unless it can be enforced. (Enforceability is discussed in 2 Ogden's Real Property, chap 23.)

(d) Is there a defense against the enforcement of the restriction? If a restriction has been violated and can be enforced, there may still be a defense against it. A written release from all parties concerned, supported by consideration, is a defense. If the restriction is an equitable servitude, a material change in conditions since the restriction was created may bar its enforceability. *Downs v Kroeger* (1927) 200 C 743, 254 P 1101; *Robertson v Nichols* (1949) 92 CA2d 201, 206 P2d 898.

(e) Can title insurance be obtained in view of the restrictions? Seeking title insurance is helpful in two ways: (1) If the title company refuses to insure without showing the restriction as an exception, the buyer's suspicions are confirmed and the reasonableness of his disapproval is established; and (2) if the title company agrees to insure, the buyer is protected against the defect (subject to the limitations discussed in §3.78). Sometimes, when new improvements are planned, the title company will agree to insure against violation of building restrictions once construction is completed; usually, the buyer must agree to bear litigation costs if any arises.

f. Existing Deed of Trust and Note

§3.100 (1) Importance of Examining Documents

Problems that may be encountered in consummating the transaction and solutions that should be covered in the agreement are pinpointed below. The existence of a mortgage or deed of trust (both are referred to as a "deed of trust" in this section) against the real property and the question whether the buyer will assume or take subject to it are covered in §§5.23-5.25.

One way of protecting the buyer is to provide in the agreement for his right to approve the preliminary title report and documents referred to in it. See §3.79. The deed of trust is one of these documents if it is of record, but such a provision in the purchase and sale agreement may not alone give the buyer access to the note or entitle him to approve it in spite of the fact that certain of its provisions, such as prepayment penalties, may be discoverable only by an examination of the note. (The beneficiary statement that the beneficiary is obligated to provide under CC §§2943 and 2954 does not include prepayment information.) Therefore, a provision for approval of the deed of trust and note should be part of the agreement.

If any existing deed of trust will not be removed of record (e.g., paid off by the seller or refinanced by the buyer at the closing), the buyer, for his protection, must have an opportunity to examine both the promissory note and the deed of trust securing it. For example, the balance may accelerate on sale of the property or on the buyer's violation of some covenant; prepayment may not be permitted or the prepayment penalty may be too costly; destruction of existing improvements or removal of trees and vegetation may be prohibited or result in acceleration; there may be restrictions on use; the borrower may be obligated to make improvements; release clauses may be nonexistent or unrealistic; or the deed of trust may cover additional real property exposing the buyer to acceleration or foreclosure for a breach over which he has no control. (Regarding enforceability of due-on-sale clauses, see *Wellenkamp v Bank of America* (1978) 21 C3d 943, 148 CR 279; *California Mortgage and Deed of Trust Practice* §§2.32-2.45 (Cal CEB 1979). See also §3.50.) If the agreement merely provides that the buyer takes subject to or assumes the existing deed of trust, the buyer has no opportunity to approve it.

§3.101   (2) Form: Approval of Deed of Trust and Note

Form 3.101-1

Seller shall deliver to ____[Buyer / Buyer's attorney, ____[name and address]____]____ within _____ days after the date of this agreement for Buyer's approval under paragraph ____[see §3.79]____ of this agreement the following items:

[If encumbrances not yet known]

(1) all encumbrances that may be shown by a preliminary title report.

[If particular encumbrances to be delivered]

(1) the encumbrance(s) ____[shown in preliminary title report dated _____ 19__ / evidenced by deed of trust recorded on _____, 19__, as Instrument _____ in book _____, page _____ of ____[official book] ____]____, in the Office of the County Recorder of _____ County,

[Continue]

(2) the note(s) or other agreements secured by ____[that / those]____ encumbrance(s),

(3) beneficiary statement(s) showing balance(s) and last payment date(s),

(4) ____[lender's / lenders']____ statement(s) that no unremedied default exists,

(5) ____[lender's / lenders']____ unconditional assent to Buyer's taking subject to the encumbrance, and ____[lender's / lenders']____ consent to the sale if lender(s) ____[has / have]____ the right to object.

Seller warrants and represents that the foregoing note(s) and the encumbrance(s) securing it are not in default in any respect.

Comment: This provision protects the buyer against the consequences discussed in §3.100. It is intended to implement the provisions set out in §3.79 that conditions the buyer's obligations on his approval of title.

Generally it is preferable to refer to "all encumbrances that may be shown by a preliminary title report," because the reference to particular encumbrances leaves the buyer unprotected against unspecified encumbrances, unless the agreement elsewhere specifies that the seller is to convey free and clear of all other encumbrances.

This provision also refers to the notes secured by those encumbrances and to beneficiary statements. The value of studying the notes is explained in §3.100.

Beneficiary statements may serve a number of purposes. Because they are signed by the lender (the mortgagee or beneficiary) statements may estop the lender from asserting a different balance later (see Anno, 90 ALR 1432 (1934)); because the last payment date is given, they may furnish a clue to possible defaults; if the creditor has a right to object to the sale, his consent is essential; and if the buyer intends to leave any encumbrance in existence, the creditor's insistence on the buyer's assuming the debt rather than taking subject to it (see §3.50) may be crucial to the transaction.

Frequently seller's payments on the loan include prepayments, called "impounds," to cover taxes, insurance, and other items. The parties should determine them and fix their disposition. The lender may require an assignment or other document to effect the agreement. For escrow instructions concerning impounds, see §11.57.

§3.102   g. Adverse Possession

Title by adverse possession may confront the parties either as (1) an attempt by the seller to base his title on adverse possession or (2) an interest in a third party adverse to the interest the buyer expects to acquire from the seller.

In California, a title by adverse possession is apparently not considered marketable and need not be accepted by a buyer. See *Gwin v Calegaris* (1903) 139 C 384, 73 P 851; *Benson v Shotwell* (1890) 87 C 49, 25 P 249. The practice of requiring "marketable record title" in the agreement, while it would oblige the seller to reduce his adverse interest to record title, may have the undesired effect of waiving record defects. The provisions in §§3.55, 3.79, and 3.80 do not refer to "marketable" fee simple title but do commit the seller to procure title insurance. The requirement of title insurance in effect obligates the seller to reduce his title to judgment and record it.

Ordinarily adverse interests will not appear on the preliminary report unless they appear in a recorded judgment or lis pendens in a quiet title action by or against the adverse interests. Moreover, the buyer is considered to have taken subject to these interests if an examination of the premises would have revealed them (see §§3.92, 3.106); he should, therefore, make a physical inspection of the property.

On title insurance protection against adverse interests, see California Title Insurance Practice §3.29 (Cal CEB 1980); on covenants of title, see chap 9.

h. Mechanics' Liens

§3.103   (1) General Considerations

Those who supply labor or materials to improve real property are entitled to a mechanics' lien against the property to secure payment. CC §§3109-3153. See generally California Mechanics' Liens and Other Remedies (Cal CEB 1972). Such a lien makes title unmarketable. The lien takes its priority as of the date work commenced on the project. The contractor must record a lien claim within 90 days after completion of the work if no notice of cessation or completion is filed, or 30 days after recordation of a notice of completion or cessation (60 days if original contractor). CC §§3115-3116. An action to foreclose the lien must be brought within 90 days after recording the claim of lien unless the time is extended by a recorded grant of credit. CC §3144.

If the title report shows any mechanics' liens or an action to foreclose a mechanics' lien, the seller should be required to clear the lien from the title report. Standard form title insurance covers only matters disclosed by the public record. A buyer, therefore, should obtain a warranty from the seller that no work has been or will be performed during the 90-day period before the close of escrow, and that the seller knows of no mechanics' liens other than those shown on the record. If improvements have been completed within 90 days before close of escrow, unrecorded mechanics' liens may exist. In that case, a notice of completion should be recorded immediately and the close of escrow delayed until the 30-day period for filing claims of lien has expired. The CLTA Indorsement Form 101.1 insures the buyer against any liens arising out of work referred to in the notice of completion.

If it is not possible to delay the closing for 30 days or if construction is continuing up to the closing date, other devices are needed to protect the buyer from claims of lien. Assuming that the contractor did not post a completion bond for the job prior to commencement, the buyer can be given some protection by requiring the remainder of the construction funds to be deposited in escrow, with the escrow holder instructed to pay only on receipt of paid bills and partial or complete lien waivers. See §11.47. Another choice is to leave a fund in escrow for a period after closing to be used to clear any liens that may appear. The lender and buyer, respectively, are protected for work under construction or completed as of the date of the title policy by CLTA Indorsements 101.3 and 101.4. The title company may, however, require an indemnity agreement or bond to ensure payment of any claims that may arise. 2 Miller & Starr, Current Law of California Real Estate §12:44 (rev ed 1977). Other endorsements are available that give more limited coverage or apply to unusual situations. See provision in §3.104. See also California Title Insurance Practice §§3.28, 3.32 (Cal CEB 1980).

In policies insuring one-to-four, owner-occupied family residences, title companies often include, at no additional charge, an endorsement insuring against unrecorded mechanics' liens arising out of any work in progress or completed at the date of the policy, except work for which the insured owner has agreed to be responsible.

§3.104 (2) Form: Title Insurance Endorsement Regarding Mechanics' Liens

[Add to provision in §3.79 or §3.80 as Form 3.79-2 or Form 3.80-2]

Form 3.104-1 (When Notice of Completion Has Been Recorded)

Title insurance policy to include CLTA Indorsement 101.1 insuring Buyer against any loss from the enforcement of any mechanics' liens for the work referred to in the Notice of Completion filed on _____, 19__ as Instrument _____ in book _____, page _____ of ____[official book]____ in the Office of the County Recorder of _____ County,

Form 3.104-2 (When for Coverage for Lender for Work in Process)

Title insurance policy to include CLTA Indorsement 101.3 insuring Buyer's lender against any loss by reason of any mechanics' liens arising out of any work of improvement under construction or completed on the closing date,

Form 3.104-3 (When for Coverage for Buyer for Work in Process)

Title insurance policy to include CLTA Indorsement 101.4 insuring Buyer against any loss by reason of any mechanics' liens arising out of any work of improvement under construction or completed on the closing date,

§3.105 i. Form: Seller's Work To Be Performed After Closing

Form 3.105-1

Seller has entered into a contract with ____[specify contractor]____ for ____[describe work to be done]____ for the sum of $ _____.

(a) Seller shall pay $ _____ and Buyer shall pay $ _____ of that sum.

Buyer shall deposit Buyer's share in escrow before close of escrow. Seller's share of costs shall be retained by escrow holder from Seller's proceeds, less any of contractor's bills delivered to escrow holder before the close with (1) a written statement signed' by Seller stating that each such bill has been paid and (2) contractor's partial lien waiver. Any amounts in excess of Seller's $_____ share paid by Seller to contractor shall be reimbursed to Seller by Buyer through escrow at the close.

(b) Seller shall administer the contracts, and Buyer shall do all acts and execute all documents necessary or convenient to Seller's administration of those contracts.

(c) Escrow holder shall be instructed to disburse funds: (1) to contractor on receipt of a bill approved by Seller, and contractor's partial lien waiver, or, in the case of a final bill, contractor's full lien waiver conditioned only on payment of the amount approved by Seller; or (2) to Seller on receipt from Seller of contractor's bill, a written statement signed by Seller stating that each such bill has been paid, and an unconditional lien waiver. Any amount remaining after the above-mentioned contract has been paid in full shall be disbursed by escrow holder's check payable to Buyer.

Comment: This provision covers certain work to be performed after the close of escrow by the seller. Funds are held by the escrow holder to ensure the payment of all bills, and lien waivers are required to ensure that the work will be completed free of liens. In this provision, the parties agree to share the cost of the work. If the seller is paying for all of the work, the provision can be simplified. The buyer may also wish to modify the form to provide that contractor's bills also be approved by the buyer before payment is made by escrow holder. This would be appropriate if the buyer is sharing the cost of the work or wishes control over the contractor's performance.

§3.106   j. Leases Affecting the Property

Unless there is an agreement to the contrary, an outstanding lease of all or part of the property renders title unmarketable. *Dennis v Overholtzer* (1960) 178 CA2d 766, 3 CR 193. Unrecorded leases do not appear on a preliminary title report. Inquiries, therefore, must be made of those in possession to determine the identity of the tenants and their rights vis-a-vis the owner. See §3.112 for form of tenant's estoppel certificate. In all cases, the buyer's counsel must carefully study the leases to determine the respective rights of the parties. Oil and gas leases are not considered to be leases but rather unrecorded easements. *Wolf v Price* (1966) 244 CA2d 165, 52 CR 889.

(1) Purchase Free From Leases

§3.107   (a) Tenant Leases

If the seller is to deliver the property free of tenants, and a tenant's lease is expiring, the lease must be reviewed to determine when the term ends; whether the tenant has an option to extend, right of first refusal, or option to purchase the property; and what the tenant can remove on departure. If the seller has, or plans to enter into, a lease termination agreement with the tenant, that agreement should also be reviewed.

Timing problems arise if the property is to be acquired free of tenants. Regarding eviction procedures generally, see California Eviction Defense Manual (Cal CEB 1971). If the tenants are on a month-to-month basis, a 30-days prior notice is required. CC §1946. If the term of a lease has expired, no notice is needed. CCP §1161(1). If the tenants do not leave, unlawful detainer proceedings (CCP §1161) must be instituted, and such proceedings may be time consuming. The seller will not want to begin forcing out tenants without assurance that the buyer will perform. The buyer, on the other hand, will want possession as soon after closing as possible. Possible solutions include: (1) placing a sufficient deposit in escrow and removing all other conditions to closing so that the seller feels secure that buyer will perform, and if not, an adequate fund to pay damages exists (see §§3.179-3.180 concerning liquidated damages); (2) closing escrow with the tenants in possession and retaining some of the seller's proceeds to pay the buyer's liquidated damages if the tenants do not vacate on time; or (3) closing escrow immediately with the buyer assuming the problem of removing the tenants in return for an adjustment in the purchase price. If the tenants remain after the closing, rents should be prorated (see §3.56), and security deposits should be transferred to buyer. See §3.115 for treatment of unpaid back rent. The possibility that local rent control or condominium conversion ordinances may contain eviction controls should not be overlooked.

§3.108   (b) Form: Seller's Duty To Eliminate Leases

Form 3.108-1

Seller shall deliver possession of the property to Buyer on the closing date free of all tenants and shall indemnify and hold Buyer harmless from the claims of any tenants claiming a right to possession arising before the closing date. If a tenant remains in possession on the closing date, Buyer may (1) terminate this agreement without liability on Buyer's part, or (2) extend the time for close of escrow for 60 days to allow Seller to remove the tenant(s) from the property, or (3) instruct escrow holder to retain $ _____ in escrow until Buyer advises Seller and escrow holder that all tenants have been removed from the property. Seller shall then be entitled to the retained sum, less rent at the rate of $_____ for each day from the closing until all tenants vacate the premises and all of Buyer's costs in removing tenants, as set forth in Buyer's statement delivered to Seller and escrow holder.

Comment: This provision allows the buyer a choice of remedies in the event tenants are still present at the time of closing. It should be changed to fit the agreement actually bargained for.

§3.109 (2) Purchase Subject to Leases

Unless a lease provides to the contrary, the landlord may sell the property to another. The buyer succeeds to the seller's position in relation to the tenant without the necessity for the tenant's attornment. See CC §1111; *Diepenbrock v Luiz* (1911) 159 C 716, 115 P 743. However, assignments of leases merit more than a perfunctory preparation by escrow holders. For example, the seller may have a cause of action for waste that should be assigned to the buyer along with the lease (see *Hill v Pinque* (1922) 56 CA 245, 204 P 1097), or he may have rights on the land that will not pass without express assignment (see *Chipman v Emeric* (1855) 5 C 49). Moreover, because the buyer is bound by the seller's interpretation of the leases and by any waivers that the seller has made (*Doll v Maravilas* (1947) 82 CA2d 943, 187 P2d 885), the buyer may need the protection of the seller's warranties or the tenants' estoppel certificates. See provision in §§3.111; 3.112. For these reasons, the buyer should reserve the right either to prepare the assignments or to approve them. The right of approval is reserved in §3.111.

If the present tenants are to remain in possession, the buyer should review all of the leases, and any other related documents such as amendments and correspondence. Counsel should examine and outline the following provisions of each lease: term; rent; renewal rights; inflation adjustment provisions; landlord's right to pass increased taxes and operation costs on to the tenant; options to lease additional space; and any options to purchase. An estoppel certificate (see §3.112) should be obtained from each tenant to confirm that there are no other agreements between landlord and tenant, and to estop the tenant from claiming otherwise after the closing. The buyer should also obtain a letter from the seller to be delivered after the closing instructing the tenants to pay rent to the buyer. On considerations applicable in commercial leasing situations, see generally Commercial Real Property Lease Practice (Cal CEB 1976).

If the transaction pertains to agricultural land, the buyer should be advised that a tenant holding under an expired lease cannot always be ousted in a short time. If a tenant of agricultural land holds over more than 60 days after expiration of the term without demand for possession or notice to quit, the tenant can continue in possession for another year on the same terms as the prior year. CCP §1161(2).

If the buyer is purchasing a ground lease interest, counsel should verify that: the seller can transfer the tenant's interest in the lease; there are no defaults under the lease or, if there are, that they have been waived; there are no provisions that could cause early termination of the lease; and that there are no provisions calling for removal of improvements from the property at the end of the term. The nature of any restrictions on the use or subleasing of the property should also be reviewed. Counsel should also determine if the ground lease contains the necessary provisions to enable the tenant to obtain financing on the leasehold. See Nellis, *Drafting or Reviewing a Ground Lease to Make It "Mortgageable"* 1 CEB Real Prop L Rep 49 (1978). The seller must also deliver an assignment approved by the ground lessor (if such approval is required by the lease) before the closing. For considerations relating specifically to ground leases, see Ground Lease Practice (Cal CEB 1971).

§3.110   (a) Form: Buyer's Approval of Previously Reviewed Leases

Form 3.110-1

Buyer acknowledges that Buyer has received and hereby approves the following documents: ____*[list all leases, modifications and amendments, management agreements, etc., which buyer has approved]*____.

Comment: If the buyer has approved the leases before signing the purchase and sale agreement, the approval should be recited and the leases and other documents sufficiently described to identify them. If the documents are numerous, they should be listed as an exhibit and incorporated by reference. The provision on the condition of title at closing should refer to the approved leases. See §§3.55, 3.79, 3.80.

§3.111   (b) Form: Buyer's Right To Approve Leases; Seller's Warranty

Form 3.111-1

Seller shall within _____ days after the date of this agreement deliver to ____[Buyer / Buyer's attorney, ____[name and address]____]____ for Buyer's approval under terms of paragraph ____[see §3.79]____ the following:

(1) Originals or true copies of all leases and amendments within _____ days after execution of this agreement.

(2) Proposed form of assignment of Seller's rights under the leases.

(3) A certificate executed by ____[each / the]____ tenant within _____ days after execution of this agreement, in the form attached as Exhibit ____[see §3.112]____. Seller warrants and represents that at this time and as of the closing no other leases of the property are or will be in force; no one else has a right of possession; no rent concessions were given ____[state exceptions]____; no other agreements were made with the tenant(s) ____[or any of them]____; and neither Seller nor any tenant is in default under any lease.

Comment: See §3.109 on the desirability of this provision if the buyer intends to take subject to existing leases.

§3.112   (3) Form: Estoppel Certificate

Form 3.112-1

To: ____[Buyer's name and address]____

The undersigned hereby certifies that:

1. I am the tenant and present occupant of ____[describe legal premises] ____ ("premises"), ____[address]____

[Add if leased premises are a portion of a larger building]
which constitutes a portion of the property ("the building") located at: ____ [description of property containing building]____.

2. The premises are leased under a lease dated _____, 19__, as amended by documents dated _____, 19__ and _____, 19__. A copy of the lease and all amendments (collectively called "the lease") are attached. The lease contains all of the agreements between me and the landlord.

3. Rent of $ _____ per month has been paid through _____, 19__.

4. The lease provides option(s) to extend or renew the lease term for _____ years each. (If no option exists insert "None.")

5. I have no option or right of first refusal to purchase the premises or the building. My only interest in the premises or the building is my lease.

6. The sum of $ _____ was paid to the landlord as a security deposit and the sum of $ _____ was paid for the last month's rent. (If none paid insert "None.")

7. All work required of the landlord by the lease has been completed in accordance with the terms of the lease, and I have accepted, and I am now in possession of, the premises.

8. No person or firm other than myself is in possession and to the best of my knowledge no other person or firm other than the landlord has a future right to the premises. (If anyone else has such rights, state name, address, and explain such rights.) _____

9. I have not assigned or entered into any subleases of the lease, except as follows: _____

10. I claim no offset against the landlord, and the landlord is not in default under the lease or in connection with the premises or the building. (If there is any claim, offset, or default, please explain.) _____

11. The statements in this letter may be relied on by the landlord, the purchaser of the building, and any lender who extends credit in connection with the purchase of the building. I agree that on receipt of notice of the name and address of any lender who holds a mortgage or deed of trust on the building, I will give such lender notice of any default by the landlord during the term of the lease and a reasonable period after the default within which such lender may cure the default.

12. I have been advised that the landlord is selling the building to ____ [name of buyer]____. After receipt of notice from the landlord that the sale has been completed, I will honor the assignment of the landlord's interest in the lease.

This certificate was executed on _____, 19__.

[Signature of tenant]
____[Typed name]____

Comment: The certificate prevents the tenant from contradicting the statements made in it if litigation arises under the lease. Evid C §623. The underlying theory is that of equitable estoppel, and is limited to present or past facts, not mere promises or expressions of opinion about the future. *Berverdor, Inc. v Salyer Farms* (1950) 97 CA2d 459, 218 P2d 138.

§3.113   (4) Form: No New Leases

Form 3.113-1

After the execution of this agreement, Seller shall not enter into any new leases or options to lease or negotiate extensions or modifications of any existing leases without Buyer's prior written consent.

Comment: The buyer does not want to be bound by a last-minute lease negotiated by the seller but, on the other hand, may not want to lose existing tenants seeking to renew their leases or prospective new tenants. This provision offers one solution: the seller may lease or negotiate, but the buyer must approve in writing. The seller might also limit the buyer's veto by requiring it to be exercised within a certain number of days after receipt of the proposed lease and considering the buyer's silence to be approval. See §3.108 for a form in which seller is to terminate tenancies by close of escrow.

§3.114   (5) Form: Condition; Obtaining New Leases

Form 3.114-1

[Insert in provision for conditions at §3.72]

Buyer has obtained before _____, 19__, leases on terms acceptable to Buyer and Buyer's lender from ____*[list tenants by name or general description, e.g., a chain supermarket with not less than 25 stores]*____ for portions of the property. Buyer shall advise Seller in writing no later than _____, 19__ that the leases have been obtained. Buyer's failure to give such notice shall be considered ____*[satisfaction / failure]*____ of this condition.

Comment: If the buyer is putting together an investment, the buyer will want to obtain leases from the key tenants before being committed to purchase the property. The seller may not wish to agree to such a condition without some consideration. In that case an option may be a way for the buyer to tie up the property while negotiating other aspects of the investment. See chap 4 on options.

§3.115   (6) Form: Unpaid Rent

Form 3.115-1

Seller will retain the right to collect from ____*[name]*____, a tenant of the property, the unpaid rent tenant owes Seller, and Buyer agrees to cooperate at no expense to Buyer with Seller's efforts to collect such rent. All sums paid by that tenant to Buyer after the closing shall be applied first by Buyer against sums due from tenant under the lease for periods following the closing date, and the remainder, if any, shall be paid over to Seller until such unpaid rent is paid.

Comment: A common problem with the sale of leased property is that one or more tenants may be behind in the payment of rent. The buyer does not want to inherit the tenant's rent arrearage, and the seller fears that without the leverage of being landlord the sum will never be collected. This provision is a compromise: the seller retains the right to the rent from the tenant, and the buyer agrees to co-operate with the seller to collect it.

§3.116 D. Physical Condition of the Property

Of equal importance with the state of title is the physical condition of the property and its suitability for the buyer's intended use. Discovering the property's condition may require that time-consuming work be done, such as soil tests, engineering studies, surveys, and termite inspection; it is important that some provision be made for the buyer's approval of the results of this work. If numerous tests and studies are necessary, it may be wiser for the buyer to obtain an option and conduct tests during the option period. On options, see chap 4. The buyer will usually want to avoid purchasing property on an "as is" basis; the seller will usually prefer to sell on that basis. How this conflict is resolved depends on the needs and negotiating strengths of the parties.

A first step in determining the physical condition is to obtain all plans, specifications, and reports that have already been completed and are in the seller's possession. These may disclose conditions that will cause the buyer to decide against purchasing; if not, the buyer should have professionals review the reports and determine if updated information is needed. For example, although generally the soil does not change, the soil tests previously conducted may not be conclusive for the particular buyer because the tests may have been made of the property for a different use, on a building at a different location on the property, or in consideration of a different set of building codes.

§3.117 1. Engineering Studies and Reports

The nature of the property and its intended use will dictate the studies needed. For example, if the property is a used home, a termite report and an inspection by a home inspection service will disclose if there are defects of which the home buyer would not be aware, such as the existence of dry rot, the condition of the roof, electrical system, plumbing, cesspool, and so forth. For commercial property, the buyer should retain a structural engineer and such other professionals as the engineer suggests to check not only the structure of the building, but also the roof; electrical, plumbing, heating, air-conditioning and ventilation systems; the elevators, and all other components of the building. The engineer should survey the building to determine how it conforms to present or proposed codes, and outline the work and expense necessary to bring the building up to code. On agricultural land, well tests may be needed in addition to the above-mentioned inspections of any improvements on the property.

Engineering studies for the development of urban land affecting the flow of surface waters are especially important in view of the holding in *Keys v Romley* (1966) 64 C2d 396, 50 CR 273, that the upper landowner who changes a natural drainage system may be strictly liable to a lower landowner even if his actions are reasonable. The issue of reasonable or unreasonable use is a question of fact, after considering the relevant circumstances including such factors as the amount of harm caused, the ability of the person making the change to foresee the harm caused, and the purpose with which he acted. See also, *Ellison v City of San Buenaventura* (1976) 60 CA3d 453, 131 CR 433; *Sheffet v County of Los Angeles* (1970) 3 CA3d 720, 84 CR 11; *Western Salt Co. v City of Newport Beach* (1969) 271 CA2d 397, 76 CR 322; *Burrows v State* (1968) 260 CA2d 29, 66 CR 868.

§3.118   2. Land Surveys

It is desirable and frequently necessary for the buyer to obtain a current survey of the property by a licensed surveyor or civil engineer. A survey is necessary in order to determine exact acreage, existence of encroachments and party walls (see §3.95), boundaries of the property (see chap 8), and compliance with setback requirements.

When the sale price is set at a unit rate, rather than a specific amount for the entire parcel, a survey of the property is particularly important. Gross acreage generally includes property, such as roads, which revert to the fee owner if abandoned; net acreage excludes such reversionary interests. The seller will generally demand a gross acreage sale, but the buyer, having no immediate use for the easement, may prefer a net price. This issue is usually resolved by adjusting the price to the parties' satisfaction during negotiations. The parties should be certain, however, that the fee interest under the roads is transferred in order to avoid future disputes on this point. If agricultural land is being sold, an accurate survey is needed, especially if the property is being sold at a per acre price. Counsel should be careful to define whether the price is based on gross or net acreage. See §3.48 for clause on unit price.

An accurate survey will disclose the existence of any encroachments. An encroachment will render title unmarketable whether it is by or on the property in question. See 7 Witkin, Summary of California Law, *Equity* §56 (8th ed 1974). An encroachment on the subject property not only limits the buyer's use of the property, but may also ripen into a prescriptive easement (*Jones v Harmon* (1959) 175 CA2d 869, 1 CR 192); moreover, an encroachment by the subject property exposes the purchaser to possible liability for its removal or damages (*Brown Derby Hollywood Corp. v Hatton* (1964) 61 C2d 855, 40 CR 848).

§3.119   3. Form: Condition; Buyer's Approval of Reports and Surveys in Seller's Possession

Form 3.119-1

[Insert in provisions for conditions at §3.72]

Buyer's approval, within _____ days after the date of this agreement, of ____*[specify report]*____ report that ____*[state purpose of report, e.g., that property is suitable for construction of a single-family residence]*____. ____ *[Prior to execution of this agreement, Seller has delivered / Concurrently with the execution of this agreement, Seller will deliver / Within _____ days after execution of this agreement, Seller will deliver]*____ to Buyer copies of all plans and specifications for improvements on the property, all surveys, soil tests, engineering studies, and any other test results or reports in Seller's possession or under Seller's control concerning the property and, if so requested by Buyer, will instruct those who prepared the reports to divulge any other information they may have about the property to Buyer, provided that Buyer pays any additional costs incurred. Buyer shall have until _____, 19__, to deliver to Seller a disapproval notice stating that Buyer's review of such reports and studies has disclosed a defect in the property and describing the defect with reasonable particularity. Failure to so notify Seller shall conclusively be considered ____*[approval / disapproval]*____.

Comment: Most engineers and other professionals will not release data or discuss their reports with anyone other than the party who ordered the report originally; therefore, it is important to obtain the seller's commitment to aid the buyer in getting the assistance of such professionals. All of the documents and data called for should be reviewed by appropriate professionals selected by the buyer and at his expense; only then can the buyer determine whether the property will be satisfactory for his needs.

§3.120   4. Form: Condition; Buyer's Approval of Onsite Investigation and Tests

Form 3.120-1

[Insert in provision for conditions at §3.72]

Buyer's approval, within _____ days after the date of this agreement, of inspections, tests, surveys and other studies to be conducted by Buyer. Buyer, Buyer's representatives, or authorized agents may enter on the property to make tests, surveys, or other studies of Seller's property, provided that Buyer pays for all such tests and studies, keeps Seller's property free and clear of any liens, repairs all damage to the property, and indemnifies and holds Seller harmless from and against all liability, claims, demands, damages, or costs of any kind whatsoever (including attorneys' fees) arising from or connected with the tests, surveys, or studies. Buyer shall have until _____, 19__ to deliver to Seller a disapproval notice stating that Buyer's inspection of the property has disclosed a defect in the property and describing the defect with reason-able particularity. Failure to so notify Seller shall conclusively be considered ____[approval / disapproval]____ . If escrow should fail to close for any rea-son, the refundable portion of Buyer's deposit shall not be released to Buyer until escrow holder has received valid mechanics' lien waivers from all contrac-tors who worked on the property at Buyer's request as identified to escrow holder by Seller.

[Add if seller to give warranties]

Buyer's approval of any such inspection of the property, however, shall not alter or diminish Seller's representations or warranties under this agreement, and Seller acknowledges and agrees that Buyer is nonetheless relying on Sell-er's representations and warranties made herein, unless such representation or warranty is specifically waived in whole or in part by the Buyer.

Comment: The buyer may need to inspect and test the property for any unusual conditions that might make the development of the property economically unfeasible. The seller should not object to such studies because, if a defect were discovered after the closing, the buyer's argument that he relied on the seller's representations concerning the property would be weaker.

The seller should, however, be protected from any liability for costs of such tests as well as damages that may arise, *e.g.,* injury to persons or property arising out of the entry onto the seller's property. This provision gives some protection. The seller may wish to have the buyer's obligations secured by a performance bond to ensure that any mechanics' liens arising from the buyer's work will not become the seller's problem and require liability insurance. In any case, the seller should post and record notices of nonresponsibility within ten days after work is commenced, as provided by CC §3094. The seller should also insist that the buyer's deposit in escrow be large enough to cover possible mechanics' liens. If the sale does not close, the seller should require delivery of valid lien waivers executed by the contractors who worked on the property before the buyer's deposit is returned. The seller can determine which of those contractors have lien rights from the preliminary notices contractors are required to give under CC §3097.

The seller may wish to approve the dates and times of tests to minimize interference with the seller's use of the property. The requirement of a notice of disapproval describing the alleged defect with particularity is to allow the seller an opportunity to cure the defect, if possible.

Often the buyer will agree to deliver copies of any studies in his possession to the seller if the transaction does not close. The reports may be useful to the seller and to future buyers, and the data is of no further use to the buyer.

The buyer should require that contractors retained to study the property are adequately insured and that they hold the buyer harmless from any damage or injury they may cause.

If a survey is needed, the parties may agree to split the cost or that one party will bear the entire cost. This item should be specified in the agreement.

§3.121   5. Form: Warranty; Condition of Property

Form 3.121-1

Seller warrants and represents that as of the close of escrow the property will ____[specify, e.g., not contain any fill]____.

Comment: This warranty may be used instead of or in addition to a provision such as that in §3.120 which conditions the agreement on the buyer's approval of engineering studies. Without an express warranty, the buyer takes the risk of defects in the condition of soil and improvements except in those situations in which the seller's suppression of the facts is actionable as fraud. See §§1.66-1.78. This warranty uses "as of the close of escrow" to give the seller time to correct existing defects. See also §3.122 for a warranty covering material defects.

§3.122   6. Form: Warranty; Material Defects

Form 3.122-1

Seller has no knowledge, actual or constructive, of any material defect in the property, other than ____[as follows / as set forth in Exhibit _____ attached]____.

Comment: The seller is obligated to inform the buyer of any facts materially affecting the value or desirability of the property that would not be apparent to the buyer on inspection. *Lingsch v Savage* (1963) 213 CA2d 729, 29 CR 201. Whether a defect is discoverable on inspection is often a difficult question of fact. The above provision requires disclosure of any material defect known to the seller regardless of whether it would be apparent on an inspection. Because the seller is usually in the best position to know the condition of the property, the buyer may insist that the seller disclose the defects in the property, whether apparent or not, and give a warranty against the existence of any defects other than those disclosed. However, the older the improvements on the property, the more likely it is that defects do exist, and the seller may insist that the buyer make his own inspection and purchase the property "as is" in reliance on his own inspection. Even an "as is" clause does not relieve the seller of the obligation to disclose material defects of which he is aware. *Lingsch v Savage, supra.* See §3.123 for an "as is" clause form.

§3.123   7. Form: "As Is" Clause; No Warranties Given by Seller

Form 3.123-1

Buyer acknowledges that Buyer is purchasing the property solely in reliance on Buyer's own investigation, and that no representations or warranties of any kind whatsoever, express or implied, have been made by Seller, Seller's agents, or brokers. Buyer further acknowledges that as of the close of escrow Buyer will be aware of all zoning regulations, other governmental requirements, site and physical conditions, and other matters affecting the use and condition of the property and agrees to purchase the property in the condition that it is in at close of escrow, subject, however, to Buyer's right to terminate under the risk-of-loss provision of this agreement at paragraph ____[see §§3.129-3.130]____.

Comment: If the seller does not want to make any warranties regarding the condition of the property and if market conditions allow that advantage, this provision which puts the entire burden of determining the condition of the property on the buyer may be used. Even if warranties are given by the seller, the buyer and the buyer's counsel should investigate the warranted items. It is always preferable to investigate rather than to rely on the seller's warranty because the seller may have left the area or be judgment proof when a breach is discovered.

An "as is" clause does not excuse a seller from disclosing hidden material defects known to the seller. Failure to disclose such matters is fraud, and the "as is" provision applies only to visible and observable matters. *Lingsch v Savage* (1963) 213 CA2d 729, 29 CR 201. See also *Katz v Department of Real Estate* (1979) 96 CA3d 895, 158 CR 766.

§3.124   8. Form: Warranty; Area of Property

Form 3.124-1

Seller warrants that the property contains not less than _____ ____ [*square feet / acres*]____ not including ____[*specify exceptions*]____.

Comment: Care must be taken to avoid ambiguities about what is included or excluded in the area. The provision above therefore states the area of the property and defines what is excluded in computing the area. If the purchase price is not computed using a formula based on area, and there is no representation setting out the area of the property, the buyer who discovers after the closing that the size of the property is less than he believed has no cause of action against the seller. CCP §2076.

§3.125   9. Structural Pest Control Inspection

The damage caused by termites, dry rot, or fungus can be expensive to repair, and there is no implied warranty that the property will be free of latent defects unknown to the seller. *Murphy v Sheftel* (1932) 121 CA 533, 9 P2d 568. The buyer, therefore, should insist on an inspection of the property by a structural pest control operator before close of escrow.

If the property has had a pest control inspection within the preceding two years, certified copies of the inspection report can be obtained from the Structural Pest Control Board for a nominal fee. Bus & P C §8614. Civil Code §1099 requires the seller to furnish the buyer with a copy of any report obtained by the seller if such a report or a certificate is a condition of the contract or a requirement for financing.

§3.126   a. Form: Condition; Structural Pest Control Inspection

Form 3.126-1

[Insert in provisions for conditions at §3.72]

Buyer's approval of the report issued under Business and Professions Code §8516 of a licensed structural pest control operator, dated _____, 19__ or later, certifying that the operator inspected the property and that no accessible areas of the property are infested by termites, dry rot, fungi, or other wood-destroying pests or organisms. ____[Seller / Buyer]____ shall pay the cost of such inspections.

If the structural pest control operator's report discloses any infestation of or damage to the property caused by wood-destroying pests or organisms, Seller shall cause the necessary corrective work to be done and shall deliver to the escrow holder and Buyer before the close of escrow a certificate or a Notice of Work Completed under Business and Professions Code §8519(b) signed by the operator stating that the required corrective work has been completed and that the property is now free of evidence of active infestation or infection. The cost of such corrective work shall be paid from funds accruing to Seller at the close of escrow. If the operator's report also indicates that preventive work is recommended, Buyer shall have the option of having such work done at the same time as the corrective work by delivering a notice in writing to escrow holder and Seller within ____[e.g., five]____ days after Seller advises Buyer in writing of the recommended preventive work. Buyer shall pay for such preventive work through escrow.

Comment: Which party will choose the pest control operator, bear the cost of the report, and bear the cost of any remedial or preventive work, are all subject to negotiation. This provision embodies the usual practice of having the seller pay for corrective work. Preventive work is a benefit to the new owner, however, and this form provides that the buyer is to pay for such work if the buyer elects to have it done.

If the buyer bears the cost of corrective work, or if the seller is to pay and fears that the cost of such work will be great, a provision might be inserted allowing the party paying for the repairs to terminate the transaction if the estimated cost of repairs exceeds a certain sum. The seller should always either obtain a report and a price quotation for any corrective work before executing a purchase and sale agreement, or insert a provision limiting the amount of his liability for any such work. Even if the seller is willing to pay for the repairs, the buyer may wish to retain the right to terminate if the report indicates that extensive corrective work is required, because the corrective work may not eliminate the problem.

If the work is to be completed before the close of escrow (as this form provides), it may be necessary to include a provision extending the closing date if repairs are extensive. An alternative is to provide that if repairs are not completed by the closing date, an amount equal to the cost of the repairs (or balance due the pest control operator) shall be held in escrow to be released when the escrow holder has received a notice of work completed under Bus & P C §8519(b) and the buyer has indicated that the work was performed to his satisfaction. See also provision at §3.105 on seller's work to be performed after closing.

If preventive work is to be paid for by the seller, a lien waiver from the pest control operator should be obtained in order that title insurance can be issued. See §11.47.

§3.127　　b. Form: Warranty; Structural Pests

Form 3.127-1

Seller warrants that, as of the date of closing, the property will be free of any damage from or infestation by wood-destroying pests and organisms, including but not limited to termites, dry rot, and fungi.

Comment: This provision is an alternative to the condition contained in §3.118. The buyer should have the premises inspected as soon as possible following the close of escrow. Delay increases the likelihood that the infestation will be found to have occurred after closing.

§3.128　　10. Risk of Loss

Unless the agreement provides otherwise, the risk of loss to the property after the execution of the purchase and sale agreement is governed by the Uniform Vendor and Purchaser Risk Act (CC §1662). This act provides generally that if all or a material part of the property is destroyed, the seller cannot enforce the contract, and the buyer is entitled to recover any portion of the price paid if neither legal title nor possession has been transferred. If either legal title or possession has been transferred all loss falls on the buyer. See chap 10 on risk of loss and property insurance.

§3.129   a. Form: Code Governs Except as Expressly Agreed

Form 3.129-1

Except as expressly provided in ____[designate any paragraphs relating to risk of loss or right to enforcement after destruction or condemnation]____, this agreement shall be governed by the provisions of California Civil Code section 1662 in effect at the date of this agreement.

Comment: At least one court has held that any provision relating to risk of loss makes the entire Uniform Vendor and Purchaser Risk Act inapplicable in that the parties had "provided otherwise." *World Exhibit Corp. v City Bank Farmers Trust Co.* (App Div 1946) 61 NYS2d 889 (construing a statute similar to CC §1662). To meet this problem it is desirable to state that the act will apply to the extent it is not in conflict with the provisions of the contract.

§3.130   b. Form: Buyer's Assumption of Risk

Form 3.130-1

Buyer shall not, by reason of eminent domain or the destruction of all or any part of the property without Seller's fault, be relieved of the obligation to complete the purchase. Buyer shall bear the risk of all losses by destruction without fault of the Seller or by eminent domain.

Comment: This provision requires the buyer to purchase notwithstanding any loss covered by CC §1662(a). Its utility is discussed in §10.6. For an additional caveat, see §3.129.

E. Use and Development of Property

§3.131   1. Form: Condition; Buyer's Approval of Property for Buyer's Intended Operation

[Insert appropriate clause in provision for conditions at §3.72]

Form 3.131-1 (When Broad Discretion Given)

Buyer has notified Seller in writing before _____, 19__ that the property meets Buyer's requirements for use as a ____[state proposed use]____. Failure to so notify Seller shall ____[waive this condition / terminate this agreement]____.

Form 3.131-2 (When Report of Professional Is Basis)

Buyer has notified Seller in writing before _____, 19__ that Buyer has ____[specify action taken, e.g., that buyer has received reports from the architect, contractor, and other professionals that property fits Buyer's intended *use]____.* **Failure to so notify Seller shall ____**[*waive this condition / terminate this agreement*]____.

Comment: The buyer needs to ensure that the property is suitable for its intended use. This may require study by a space planner or architect, and the results of such a study may not be apparent at the time of signing the purchase and sale agreement. The first alternative is very broad; if included in the agreement, it should be limited in time so that the property is not tied up longer than necessary. The second alternative attempts to define the matters the buyer must approve, narrowing the scope of the buyer's discretion. To further limit the buyer, the seller could require that a copy of the opinions from the listed professional advisors supporting the buyer's termination of the agreement be delivered to the seller.

§3.132   2. Zoning

If the buyer believes the present zoning permits his intended use of the property, he should confirm it with the zoning authorities and attempt to obtain a warranty from the seller. See §3.137. Ordinarily, the seller will resist any such warranty, leaving to the buyer the burden of satisfying himself about zoning and other governmental approvals that may be required for the buyer's intended use. The buyer may, however, desire to use the property in a way that requires a change in the present zoning restrictions. A change can be obtained in one of three ways: by amendment to the zoning ordinance, by a variance from current zoning, or by a conditional use permit. On the distinctions among these devices, see California Zoning Practice, chap 7 (Cal CEB 1969). Because the rezoning procedures are time-consuming and expensive, the buyer must either use an option or enter into the purchase agreement before the desired change has been obtained. If an agreement is used, it should protect the buyer by conditioning closing on a zoning change to meet the buyer's needs being obtained. Even a change in zoning will not give the buyer a vested right to develop the property in accordance with the change. See §3.134.

Zoning ordinance amendments are considered to be legislative in character, and must be accomplished by an ordinance approved by the local legislative body. A proposal to adopt a zoning amendment triggers the applicability of the California Environmental Quality Act. Pub Res C §21080. See also §3.147. Under the state zoning law, amendments to zoning laws follow the same procedures applicable to the adoption of zoning ordinances (Govt C §65853) *i.e.,* the planning commission must hold a noticed public hearing and submit a recommendation to the legislative body (Govt C §§65854-65855). See *People v County of Kern* (1974) 39 CA3d 830, 115 CR 67. The legislative body must also normally hold a hearing. Govt C §§65855-65856. In addition, cities and counties are required to amend their zoning ordinances when they become inconsistent with the applicable general plan, and such amendment must be accomplished within a reasonable time. Govt C §65860(c). See Higginbotham, *The Compatibility of Economic and Environmental Objectives in Governmental Decision Making,* 5 Pac LJ 92 (1974).

Some jurisdictions have special requirements concerning zoning. The city of Los Angeles, for example, requires the seller, with a confirmation from the sale or exchange or during escrow, to provide the buyer with a confirmation from the city of the property's zoning classification, authorized occupancy, and a statement of assessments against the property, repair notices, and brush abatement orders of record. Los Angeles Mun Ct R §96.302. Counsel should check local ordinances for similar requirements.

§3.133   a. Conditional Use Permits and Variances

On a proper showing, existing restrictions on use imposed by zoning ordinances may be modified under variances or conditional use permits. On the distinction between the two, see *Van Sicklen v Browne* (1971) 15 CA3d 122, 92 CR 786 and *Tustin Heights Ass'n v Board of Supervisors* (1959) 170 CA2d 619, 339 P2d 914. Both are issuable, not as a matter of right, but as a matter of grace within the discretionary power of the granting authority. *Tustin Heights Ass'n v Board of Supervisors, supra.*

Conditional use permits are provided for in most zoning ordinances. They are typically a method of allowing different uses to coexist in a zone on a decision by the appropriate zoning body that the use for which the permit is sought will not be inconsistent with the public health, morals, safety, or welfare. Conditional use permits are administrative in nature, but differ from a variance in that a conditional use permit allows uses that are conditionally permitted under the zoning ordinance. See, *e.g., Essick v City of Los Angeles* (1950) 34 C2d 614, 213 P2d 492. Government Code §65901 requires the board of zoning adjustment or a zoning administrator to hear and decide applications for conditional use permits.

In general, variances can be granted only when, because of special circumstances that are applicable to the particular property (including size, topography, location, and shape), strict application of the zoning ordinance would unfairly deprive the subject property of the same type of privileges that are enjoyed by other properties in the area that are subject to identical zoning classifications. Govt C §65906. The granting of variances authorizing a use or activity that is not otherwise authorized by the zoning ordinance is specifically prohibited by Govt C §65906. This section, however, apparently does not apply to charter cities. See California Zoning Practice §7.49 (Cal CEB 1969).

The requirement that special circumstances be shown has led to substantial litigation over the years regarding the approval or denial of variances. See, *e.g., Broadway, Laguna, Vallejo Ass'n v Board of Permit Appeals* (1967) 66 C2d 767, 59 CR 146; *Siller v Board of Supervisors* (1962) 58 C2d 479, 25 CR 73; *Zakessian v Sausalito* (1972) 28 CA3d 794, 105 CR 105; *Hamilton v Board of Supervisors* (1969) 269 CA2d 64, 75 CR 106. In addition, it is now clear that the special circumstances claimed to justify the variance must be such that make the property different from other property in the same zone. *Topanga Ass'n for a Scenic Community v County of Los Angeles* (1974) 11 C3d 506, 113 CR 836. As noted above, the statutory standards for a variance also require that the strict application of the zoning ordinance would deprive the property of privileges that are enjoyed by other property in the same area having the same zoning classification. This requires that the court must find that unnecessary hardship would be created if a variance were not granted. See *Zakessian v Sausalito, supra.*

§3.134　　b. Future Zoning Changes

The buyer's attorney should consider the effect of possible future zoning changes in or enlargement of zoning classifications. The general pattern of zoning changes in recent years has been to increase the nature and extent of regulations. New bases for the zoning power, such as aesthetics, have raised additional risks of future zoning changes. See *Bohannon v San Diego* (1973) 30 CA3d 416, 106

CR 333; *Van Sicklen v Browne* (1971) 15 CA3d 122, 92 CR 786; *Burk v Municipal Court* (1964) 229 CA2d 696, 40 CR 425; Anno, *Aesthetic Objectives or Considerations as Affecting Validity of Zoning Ordinance,* 21 ALR3d 1222 (1968).

Local planning maps and general plans contain information on projected changes but do not assure there will be no other changes. The purchase of property for a valid consideration does not confer on the purchaser a vested right in present zoning or against future moratoriums or changes in zoning. *Avco Community Developers, Inc. v South Coast Regional Comm'n* (1976) 17 C3d 785, 132 CR 386; *Morse v County of San Luis Obispo* (1967) 247 CA2d 600, 55 CR 710. In general, a landowner acquires a vested right in zoning only when he has obtained a building permit and, relying on the permit, has incurred obligations or expended funds for actual onsite improvements. *Avco Community Developers, supra*; *Raley v California Tahoe Regional Planning Agency* (1977) 68 CA3d 965, 137 CR 699.

For further discussion of zoning, see generally California Zoning Practice (Cal CEB 1969).

§3.135   (1) Form: Condition; Approval of Zoning

Form 3.135-1

[Insert in provision for condition at §3.72]

The local zoning authorities have confirmed to Buyer in writing that the property is finally and validly zoned to permit the ____*[present use of the property / use of the property as a _____]*____. If Buyer is unable to obtain such confirmation, or if Buyer is advised that the proposed use does not conform to the present zoning, Buyer shall so notify Seller within ____*[e.g., five]*____ days after the local authority's refusal to confirm or unfavorable confirmation ("disapproval"), or by _____, 19__, whichever is sooner, of Buyer's inability to obtain satisfaction of this condition. Failure to so notify Seller shall ____*[waive this condition / terminate this agreement]*____.

Comment: Zoning can be critical to the value of the property to the buyer. Therefore, the zoning should be confirmed before escrow is closed. If the zoning report is unfavorable, the parties may wish to provide for an extension of the closing to allow either the buyer or the seller to apply for a permit as a nonconforming use or for a variance. See §3.136. The buyer should also confirm that the proposed sale will not affect the zoning or proposed zoning.

§3.136   (2) Form: Condition; Change in Zoning

Form 3.136-1

[Insert in provision for conditions at §3.72]

Buyer secures the right, under applicable zoning and land use laws, regulations, and ordinances, to ____*[state use]*____. Buyer shall file the documents and pay the fees necessary to obtain the change. Seller agrees to cooperate with Buyer provided Seller shall have to bear no expense. If Buyer has proceeded with diligence but has not obtained a final determination by the close of escrow, on Buyer's written notice to Seller, the closing shall be extended

[If extended to final determination]

until final determination. However, Seller may terminate this agreement on _____ days' notice if Buyer is not diligent in pursuing a determination. If the final determination is adverse, Buyer may elect within _____ days after final determination either to terminate this agreement or to waive this condition

[If extended for a stated time]

for _____ days. If the final determination has not been obtained by the end of that period, Buyer may elect before the expiration of the extended time either to terminate this agreement or to waive this condition

[Conclude]

by delivering a notice to that effect to Seller. Buyer's failure to so notify Seller shall ____*[waive this condition / terminate this agreement]*____. A determination shall be final when all nonjudicial appeal rights from an administrative determination have lapsed or been exhausted.

Comment: This provision avoids technical designations of the kinds of zoning changes which might be obtained (*e.g.,* amendment, variance, or conditional use permit (see §§3.132-3.133)), and focuses instead on the use which the buyer intends to make of the property. Sometimes it is necessary for the buyer to obtain some change in the zoning or land use designation of the property for it to be suitable for the buyer's needs. Because the property will be of little value to the buyer if the change is not obtained, the buyer will want to obtain the change before escrow is closed. This provision conditions the purchase on obtaining the needed change. It can be modified to deal with other types of governmental actions, such as annexation of the property to a city or special district (see §3.142) or obtaining a subdivision map (see §§3.143-3.144). The form may be modified to allow the buyer to terminate if the local agency's requirements for approval are too onerous or the change as approved is otherwise not satisfactory to the buyer.

The time required to obtain the change may be lengthy, and the seller may require a large deposit as a condition for extending the closing date, or may refuse to agree to such an extension. In such cases, an option should be considered. See chap 4. Another possibility is to have the buyer "purchase" an extension. The seller may be concerned that the sale might fail, but the zoning change be granted. To limit the chances of being bound by an unwanted change, the seller may require that the applications for the change be worded so that the change will not become effective if the sale does not close. For example, the agreement might provide that a subdivision map will not be recorded until after close of escrow.

The buyer's commitment to file documents and pay fees fortifies the element of mutuality discussed in §3.69. If time expires before a determination is made or the determination proves to be adverse, this provision gives the buyer an option to cancel or waive the condition. This is more favorable to the buyer than automatic termination (see §3.70). See *Isaacson v G. D. Robertson & Co.* (1948) 85 CA2d 71, 192 P2d 486, in which an automatic termination clause prevented the buyer from waiving the benefit of a zoning provision.

Generally this provision is favorable to the buyer. A compromise clause less favorable to the buyer would (a) require the application to be filed within a certain number of days after execution, (b) put a time limit on each step of the proceeding, (c) eliminate the buyer's unilateral right to extend the closing, and (d) provide for automatic cancellation on failure to rezone. If an option is used, this clause would not be necessary because the option permits the seller to retain the deposit if the option is not exercised because of failure to obtain rezoning.

§3.137   c. Form: Warranty; Zoning

Form 3.137-1

Seller warrants that at this time and as of the close of escrow the property is and will be zoned ____[state zoning classification]____, under the laws of ____[city / county]____.

Comment: A seller is rarely willing to broaden the warranty to describe the specific uses covered by the zone classification. The buyer's attorney should examine the zoning law and confer with the applicable zoning department to satisfy himself concerning available uses, bearing in mind the possibility of future zoning changes. This provision places the risk of zoning changes on the seller until the close of escrow.

3. Necessary Permits

§3.138   a. Form: Condition; Obtaining Necessary Permits

Form 3.138-1

[Insert in provision for conditions at §3.72]

Buyer has obtained, subject only to those conditions ____*[reasonably]*____ acceptable to Buyer ____*[in Buyer's sole and absolute discretion]*____, all permits, approvals, certificates, and licenses (collectively "permits") necessary for the construction, maintenance, and operation of ____*[describe what is to be built]*____ on the property. Buyer shall, at Buyer's sole expense, initiate and diligently pursue to completion proceedings to obtain such permits. Buyer shall notify Seller within _____ days after the date of this agreement if Buyer is unable to obtain the necessary permits. Failure to so notify Seller shall ____*[waive this condition / terminate this agreement]*____.

Comment: If the buyer's use of the property is dependent on obtaining a governmental approval, such as a liquor license or a building permit, he will want to obtain it before the close of escrow. This provision provides that the permits must be acceptable to the buyer to protect him from being required to close if the permit contains conditions that seriously impair the intended use of the property.

Issuance of a permit or license does not guarantee that the buyer will be able to develop the property as planned. The mere issuance of a building permit does not vest a buyer's right to build the improvements for which it was issued. The buyer must be able to show detrimental reliance on the permit for his rights to vest. A permit holder without a vested right will be subject to any changes in the law, including changes subsequent to the date of the permit. Even if the buyer's rights vest, those rights are limited to the terms and conditions of the permit and do not go beyond the project described in the approval. 59 Ops Cal Atty Gen 641, 655 (1976). For example, a grading permit does not vest rights to obtain a building permit for a project even though a grading permit is a precondition to obtaining the building permit. *Avco Community Developers, Inc. v South Coast Regional Comm'n* (1976) 17 C3d 785, 797, 132 CR 386, 394. Usually, obtaining a permit is as far as a buyer can go during escrow because the seller generally will not allow the buyer to commence construction before the close of escrow.

§3.139   b. Form: Seller's Cooperation in Securing Permits

Form 3.139-1

Seller agrees to cooperate with Buyer by executing applications for governmental permits or approvals affecting the property, provided that Seller shall not bear any expense for that purpose; and provided further that such applications shall be limited so that the status of the property will not be changed before the close of escrow.

Comment: Often, governmental agencies require the property owner to sign any applications for governmental permits or changes of the status of the property, such as rezoning or subdivision applications. Therefore, the buyer who wishes to determine if the permits and other governmental actions required for the buyer's project are obtainable before the close of escrow needs the seller's cooperation. The seller, however, must be certain that no change that might affect future development of the property becomes final before the close of escrow.

4. Approval of Access

§3.140   a. Form: Condition; Approval of Access

Form 3.140-1

[Insert in provision for condition at §3.72]

Buyer has delivered to Seller a notice of approval of access to the property, of traffic signals, and traffic flow on all adjoining and nearby streets within _____ business days after date of this agreement. Failure to so notify Seller shall ____[waive this condition / terminate the agreement]_____.

Comment: If the property is to be used for commercial purposes, access is extremely important. The buyer will want to check the ease of ingress and egress to the property and the capacity and traffic flow of nearby streets. The buyer will also want to check with local officials to determine what plans exist to improve, change, or abandon the adjacent streets. For example, the addition of a median in a street can have a significant impact on a commercial development because access to the property from one direction is cut off or limited to specific openings in the divider. The buyer will also want to check access from nearby major traffic arteries. Traffic planners generally limit the number of curb cuts for access in an attempt to avoid impairment of the traffic flow by cars entering at many points along the highway. Such limitations may or may not be compatible with the buyer's intended use.

Even if the property is not to be used for commercial purposes, the buyer should be certain that access to the property is adequate. Local governmental requirements regarding emergency access must be complied with, otherwise a building permit may be denied.

§3.141   b. Form: Warranty; Access

Form 3.141-1

Seller warrants that there are no restrictions on entrance to or exit from the property from the adjacent public streets.

Comment: The buyer will want the protection of a warranty; the seller will prefer that the buyer make an independent investigation. See §3.140 for a provision making approval of access a condition to closing.

§3.142   5. Annexation

When the property is in an unincorporated area, its annexation to a city is often essential to the buyer who will want to be certain that services are available for his intended use. In some counties, water, sewer, and other services are provided by special districts to which the property must be annexed to obtain the services.

Annexation may be a problem in areas where the local agency formation commission (LAFCO) is attempting to prevent urban sprawl. Govt C §54774. Annexation applications usually require the signature of the record owner or his agent; the seller may be liable for unpaid annexation fees if the buyer defaults after annexation has begun. The buyer may find that additional conditions to annexation require the annexing party to finance new or parallel facilities (such as pipelines), to pay a retroactive prorata share of taxes, and to share otherwise in the city or district financial burdens. Because annexation conditions vary widely, the buyer's attorney should confer with the executive officer of the local agency formation commission and the city attorney or district counsel before negotiating the agreement to determine the scope and nature of conditions likely to be imposed.

Factors to be considered by LAFCOs in reviewing proposals are specified in Govt C §54796 and include, among other elements, population, population density, land area, land use, assessed value, topography, natural boundaries, likelihood of significant growth in the area, need for organized community services and their cost and adequacy, conformity with appropriate city or county general and specific plans, and the sphere of influence applicable to the proposal being reviewed. See *Meyers v Local Agency Formation Comm'n* (1973) 34 CA3d 955, 110 CR 422.

Procedures required by LAFCO include the submission of an application before proceedings can be initiated and a hearing on the application by the commission (Govt C §§54791, 54793), except that the commission may approve an annexation to or a detachment from a city without a notice or hearing when all the owners of land within the territory proposed to be annexed or detached have consented to such annexation or detachment. Govt C §54797.1. Notice and description requirements by LAFCO on annexation are discussed in *Bookout v Local Agency Formation Comm'n* (1975) 49 CA3d 383, 122 CR 668.

6. Subdivision

§3.143   a. Need for Map and Related Approvals

When land is purchased for subdivision, the buyer usually wants to be assured that the appropriate governmental agency will approve a subdivision map permitting the land's economic development. Cities and counties are granted the power by the Subdivision Map Act (Govt C §§66410-66499.37) to regulate and control the design and improvement of subdivisions, and each city or county is required to adopt an ordinance regulating and controlling subdivisions whenever state law requires the preparation of a tentative, final, or parcel map. Govt C §§66411-66411.1. See *Friends of Lake Arrowhead v Board of Supervisors* (1974) 38 CA3d 497, 113 CR 539, on local supplemental ordinances.

The term "subdivision" is defined to mean the division of any improved or unimproved land that is shown on the latest equalized county assessment roll as a unit or as contiguous units for the purpose of sale, lease, or financing, whether immediate or future. However, this definition does not operate to prevent a division of land before the time an equalized county assessment roll has been completed that reflects the unit to be subdivided. Govt C §66424.1. The term specifically includes a condominium project, community apartment project, or a stock cooperative, and specifically excludes agricultural leases. Govt C §66424.

The terms "design" and "improvement," which are the elements of subdivisions that may be regulated by cities and counties, are defined broadly. "Design," for example, includes street alignments, grades and widths, drainage and sanitary facilities, easements and rights of way, fire roads, lot size and configuration, access, grading, land to be dedicated for park or recreational purposes, and any other specific requirements as may be "necessary or convenient" to ensure conformity to or implementation of the local agency's general plan or any adopted specific plan. "Improvement" includes street work and utilities to be installed by the subdivider, highways, easements, and any other specific improvements or types of improvements whose installation is necessary or convenient to ensure conformity to or implementation of the local agency's general or specific plans. Govt C §§66418-66419.

As with other conditions to the agreement, delaying execution of the agreement until approval is obtained requires the buyer to spend money and the seller to withhold his property from the market without assurance to either party that an agreement will eventually be signed. Conditioning the agreement on approval by the governmental agency of a subdivision map acceptable to the buyer permits him to seek that approval before completing the purchase. The buyer may not unreasonably withhold acceptance of the approved map. *Rodriguez v Barnett* (1959) 52 C2d 154, 338 P2d 907. Obtaining approval of a subdivision map often is very time-consuming, and a seller may be unwilling to wait. For use of options, see chap 4.

§3.144   b. Form: Condition; Subject to Map and Related Approvals

Form 3.144-1

[Insert in provision for conditions at §3.72]

Buyer's acceptance of the requirements of ____[county / city]____ for development of ____[e.g., residential]____ subdivision on the property, approval by ____[e.g., the planning commission]____ and ____[Board of Supervi-

sors / Council]____ of ____[*county / city*]____ of a tentative subdivision map showing lot size and general design acceptable to Buyer, and site approval of the property ____[*e.g., for single-family residences by the Department of Housing and Urban Development or Veterans Administration*]_____. Buyer shall notify Seller before _____, 19__, if the approvals and acceptances required by this paragraph have been obtained. Failure to so notify Seller by that date shall ____[*waive this condition / terminate the agreement*]____ ____[*in which event Buyer shall deliver to Seller copies of all engineering and planning reports, plans, and documents relating to map approval*]_____.

Comment: This provision conditions buyer's obligation on governmental approval of a tentative subdivision map (Govt C §§66452-66452.7) rather than recordation of the final map (Govt C §§66456-66462). The final map may not be recorded until performance and surety bonds for street improvements have been filed or the streetwork has been completed (Govt C §§66499-66499.10), and its recordation requires the consent of the record owner (Govt C §66430). A final map can be disapproved only for failure to meet or perform the requirements or conditions applicable to the subdivision at the time the tentative map was approved. *Youngblood v Board of Supervisors* (1978) 22 C3d 644, 150 CR 242.

It is extremely difficult to fix objective standards for approval, such as the minimum number of lots, linear feet of curb and gutter, and square footage for streets. At this early stage, the developer ordinarily does not have sufficient information on these engineering elements to make an intelligent decision. In fixing a time limit within which the buyer must determine whether the condition has been satisfied, the seller limits the buyer's ability to use the condition as an escape hatch; the seller also has the buyer's increasing investment in engineering expenses in preparation of the subdivision map and other studies as an added factor.

§3.145   c. Form: Warranty; Subdivision Map Act

Form 3.145-1

Seller warrants that the property complies with the Subdivision Map Act, and no final subdivision map, parcel map, or division of land is required to transfer the property validly to Buyer.

Comment: This provision warrants that the property as it is being sold is in compliance with the Subdivision Map Act (Govt C

§§66410-66499.37) (the provision in §3.144 pertains to the buyer's concern about future subdivision). The act requires a final subdivision map or a parcel map for any division of land. A sale, lease, or encumbrance of only a portion of a larger parcel triggers the provisions of the act. Govt C §66499.30. If the property is described by a lot number on a recorded final map or parcel map, it conforms to the Subdivision Map Act. Govt C §66499.35(d). If the property is described in any other manner, further investigation is required to determine if the property conforms to the act.

The standards for compliance differ from jurisdiction to jurisdiction. Some local agencies require formal compliance with subdivision procedures regardless of the time when the actual division occurred; others have "grandfathered" all lot splits before a certain date.

A certificate of compliance may be obtained under Govt C §66499.35(c) from the local agency which approves maps. The procedures for issuing certificates also vary from one jurisdiction to another.

If the Subdivision Map Act has not been complied with, the buyer may void the transaction or sue for damages within one year after discovering the violation (Govt C §66499.32), and local agencies are barred from issuing any permit or granting any approval necessary to develop the property (Govt C §66499.34). Failure to comply with the act does not, however, render title unmarketable, and a buyer probably will have no right of recovery under a standard policy of title insurance. *Nishiyama v Safeco Title Ins. Co.* (1978) 85 CA3d Supp 1, 149 CR 355.

Because the seller is in the better position to know the history of the property, the buyer will want a warranty that the property complies with the Subdivision Map Act. The seller, on the other hand, will prefer that the buyer rely on a certificate of compliance.

§3.146   7. Form: Warranty; No Pending Governmental Action

Form 3.146-1

Seller warrants that there is not now, and as of the close of escrow there will not be, any violation of any law, ordinance, rule, or administrative or judicial order affecting the property, nor is there any condemnation, zoning change, or other proceeding or action (including legislative action) pending, threatened, or contemplated by any governmental body, authority, or agency that will in any way affect the size of, use of, improvements on, construction on, or access to the property.

Comment: In addition to the seller's warranty concerning the state of the property on the date of sale, the buyer will want to know if any steps are being taken by any governmental agency that would affect the property in the future. The seller is in the best position to know of such actions because the owner of the property must be notified at some stage of the proceeding. The seller will not want to give a warranty as broad as the one above because the seller may not know of such matters or, if the seller has received notice of a proceeding, he may have forgotten or misplaced the notice. One way of reducing the scope of the warranty is to limit it to the seller's actual knowledge. See also §3.163.

8. Environmental Requirements

§3.147   a. California Environmental Quality Act

The California Environmental Quality Act (CEQA) (Pub Res C §§21000-21176) was enacted in 1970 to enhance the environmental quality of the state by requiring all governmental agencies to consider qualitative factors and long term benefits and costs as well as economic and technical factors in connection with proposed projects which the agency intends to carry out or approve. Pub Res C §§21000-21001. Governmental agencies are barred from approving a project as proposed if there are feasible alternatives or mitigating measures that would substantially lessen the adverse environmental effects of such project. However, if specific economic, social, or other conditions make the proposed alternative infeasible, an agency may approve the proposed project. Pub Res C §21002.

Projects and alternatives are identified by CEQA, primarily through the environmental impact report (EIR). Pub Res C §§21002.1, 21061. Developers are discovering that preparation of an EIR is required for a broad range of proposed projects, and must be considered at a very early stage in development planning.

All state and local agencies must prepare an EIR on any project they propose to carry out *or approve* that may have a significant effect on the environment. Pub Res C §§21100, 21151. "Project" includes (a) activities directly undertaken by any public agency, (b) activities which are supported in whole or in part through contracts, grants, subsidies, loans, or other forms of assistance from one or more public agencies, and (c) activities involving the discretionary issuance of a lease, permit, license, certificate, or other entitlement for use by a public agency. Pub Res C §21065.

An EIR need not be prepared for a project that will not have a significant effect on the environment (14 Cal Adm C §15060); in that case a negative declaration must be prepared (Pub Res C §21064). Emergency projects to maintain, repair, demolish or replace property, facilities, or services damaged by a disaster are exempted from the requirement that an EIR be prepared. Pub Res C §21172; 14 Cal Adm C §§15071(b), (c). The Administrative Code contains numerous exemptions for small projects, replacement of existing structures, minor lot line adjustments, minor land use changes, and the like. See 14 Cal Adm C §§15100-15124 for specific exemptions.

Only projects that entail an exercise of discretion or judgment by the agency require an EIR; CEQA does not apply to ministerial acts. Pub Res C §21080; 14 Cal Adm C §15100.1. Ministerial acts include those that are required by law on the occurrence of a certain contingency, such as issuance of a building permit or a business license, approval of a final subdivision map, or a utility connection or disconnection. 14 Cal Adm C §15073. The issuance of a grading permit, on the other hand, is not a ministerial act (*Day v City of Glendale* (1975) 51 CA3d 817, 124 CR 569) nor is the enactment of a rezoning ordinance (56 Ops Cal Atty Gen 404 (1973)).

"Significant effect on the environment" means a substantial or potentially substantial change in the physical conditions that exist within the area that will be affected by the proposed project, including land, air, water, minerals, flora, fauna, ambient noise, and objects of historic or aesthetic significance. Pub Res C §§21068, 21060.5.

Whether a project will have a significant effect on the environment is a question of fact dependent on many factors, some of which are enumerated in 14 Cal Adm C Div 6, chap 3, App G. The courts have held that an EIR should be prepared whenever an agency perceives "some substantial evidence that a project may have a significant effect environmentally" or that the project "*arguably* will have an adverse environmental impact." *No Oil, Inc. v City of Los Angeles* (1974) 13 C3d 68, 85, 118 CR 34, 45.

Any project for which discretionary governmental approval is required, and any that entail more than a minimal amount of construction, may require study under CEQA. Such a study does not necessarily mean an EIR will be required. Before an EIR is begun, the agency makes a preliminary investigation and can issue a notice of exemption if the property is statutorily exempt from CEQA (14 Cal Adm C §§15035.5; 15074) or issue a negative declaration if it finds that the project will have no significant effect on the environment (14 Cal Adm C §§15033; 15083). Such determinations are subject to judicial review.

The law concerning CEQA is still evolving, and, if an EIR may be required for a project, counsel should review the case law and the Administrative Code provisions interpreting and implementing CEQA. If it appears that some study of the project will be required under CEQA, counsel should discuss with the buyer the potential costs and delays. The buyer may not wish to proceed with the purchase without assurance that the project can be built. An option or a long escrow period may be agreed on to allow the buyer to comply with the EIR process and obtain an agency ruling on the project before becoming committed to purchase the property. The buyer should remember that obtaining the necessary governmental approvals does not guarantee the buyer's right to develop, because the approval is subject to challenge in the courts by those who feel they will be harmed by the project.

§3.148   b. National Environmental Policy Act

The National Environmental Policy Act (NEPA) (42 USC §§4321-4369) directs all agencies of the federal government to prepare an environmental impact statement (similar in purpose to the EIR discussed in §3.147) as part of every proposal for major federal action significantly affecting the quality of the human environment. 42 USC §4332(2)(c).

Courts have interpreted the term "federal action" literally (see, e.g., *National Wildlife Fed. v Andrus* (D DC 1977) 440 F Supp 1245) and if the proposed project involves the federal government in any way or is to receive federal grant money, counsel for the buyer should carefully inquire whether the project falls under NEPA. If so, the buyer may not know for a long period of time whether the project will be approved. The buyer may wish to purchase an option on the property rather than buy it outright if the property's value to the buyer might be severely impaired by environmental constraints. See chap 4 on options.

§3.149 c. California Coastal Act

A coastal development permit may be required for any improvement or modification of property within the coastal zone. California Coastal Act (Pub Res C §§30000-30900). The coastal zone extends seaward to the state's jurisdictional limit, includes all offshore islands, and generally extends inland 1000 yards from the mean high tide line. In certain coastal estuarine, habitational, or recreational areas, however, it may extend up to five miles inland. Pub Res C §30103. If the property is situated within five miles of the shoreline, the prospective buyer should check the map on file with the county clerk to determine whether the property falls within the coastal zone. If so, development of the property will be subject to stringent controls under the act. To be assured that the property can be developed, the buyer should insist that closing be conditioned on issuance of a coastal development permit and approval of any conditions contained in it. The provision in §3.138 can be adapted for this purpose. Issuance of the permit does not ensure that the project can be built, because the permit can be challenged in the courts by those who feel they will be harmed by the project. See Comment in §3.138 for a discussion of the vesting of rights under a permit.

§3.150 d. Form: Special Studies Zone

Form 3.150-1

The property ____[is / may be]____ situated in a special studies zone as designated under the Alquist-Priolo Special Studies Zones Act, Public Resources Code sections 2621-2630, and the construction or development on the property of any structure for human occupancy may be subject to the findings of a geologic report prepared by a geologist registered in the State of California, unless such report is waived by the city or county under the terms of that act.

Comment: The broker, or the seller if acting without a broker, is obligated to disclose to the buyer that the property is located in a special studies zone as designated under the Alquist-Priolo Special Studies Zones Act. Pub Res C §2621.9. Special studies zones include all "potentially and recently active" earthquake faults, and can be identified from an index map prepared by the State Division of Mines and Geology. Pub Res C §2622. The California Association of Realtors (CAR) has published Special Studies Zone Disclosure Form SSD-11 for disclosure that property is or may be within a special studies zone, and it may be used as an addendum to the purchase agreement in place of this provision.

F. Financing Conditions

§3.151   1. Requirements in Drafting Financing Conditions

When the buyer is willing to purchase only if acceptable financing can be obtained, the agreement must be conditioned on his success in obtaining that financing. The condition must be clearly stated to avoid uncertainty. On uncertainty as a defense, see §12.98. To avoid uncertainties the following points should be observed in drafting conditions relating to financing:

(a) Amount. The buyer should state the minimum loan he expects to obtain. The seller should place a realistic maximum on the amount to be borrowed, especially if he is taking back a subordinate note.

(b) Interest. Failure to state the interest rate may amount to a fatal uncertainty. The buyer generally states a maximum.

(c) Amortization and term of loan. With the loan amount and interest rate determined, the amortization period fixes the term of the loan (unless there is a balloon payment at the end of the term) and the size of the periodic payment. See *Bruggeman v Sokol* (1954) 122 CA2d 876, 265 P2d 575. To avoid ambiguity, the parties should be careful that the periodic payments, duration, amount, and interest rate of the loan are consistent. Loan officers at lending institutions are usually willing to furnish this information. The parties may consider the possibility of an alternative to the conventional fixed rate note. See §§6.47-6.52.

(d) Penalties and fees. Loan fees and penalties for late payment or prepayment may be costly and should be made part of the condition. Loan fees are often expressed in points. One "point" is one percent of the loan amount, *e.g.*, 5 points on $50,000 is $2,500. The loan fee effectively reduces the amount of new financing the buyer is obtaining, whether deducted from the loan or paid by the buyer when he obtains the loan. See §6.38.

(e) Identity of lender. Buyers generally prefer to borrow from institutional lenders rather than from private lenders and include the condition that the loan is to come from an institutional source. Otherwise a seller might be able to put the buyer in default by showing that the loan could be obtained from a private source. The seller may seek to limit the choice to a specific type of institutional lender, *e.g.,* banks or insurance companies, or to a specific institutional lender. On sources of financing, see chap 6.

(f) Buyer's efforts required. The requirement, express or implied, of a good faith effort to obtain financing is not satisfied when the buyer unsuccessfully applies to only two banks or when he fails to apply to a mortgage company after being advised that the financing is probably available from the latter. *Fry v George Elkins Co.* (1958) 162 CA2d 256, 327 P2d 905. To obviate litigation on whether the buyer has satisfied his obligation to seek financing, it may be wise to spell out the precise steps the buyer is expected to take.

(g) Time in which to obtain financing. If no time limit is stated, a reasonable time is implied. CC §1657. However, because "reasonable" time may have to be fixed by litigation, it is generally better to set a time within which the buyer believes he can obtain the necessary funds.

(h) Type of commitment required from the lender. See §6.60.

(i) Subordination and release provisions. Lack of particularity in spelling out intended subordination and release provisions may make the sales agreement unenforceable or lead to litigation after the sale is completed. On these provisions, see §§5.38-5.67.

§3.152 2. Form: Condition; Subject to Financing Condition

Form 3.152-1

[Insert in provision for conditions at §3.72]

Buyer's obtaining from a ____*[designate name or type of lending institution]*____ within _____ days of execution of this agreement ____*[a written commitment for]*____ a loan of not less than $ _____, secured by ____*[state nature of security, e.g., a first deed of trust]*____ on the property on terms no less favorable to Buyer than the following: Interest at _____ percent per year, principal and interest payable in equal monthly installments of $ _____ per month, term of _____ years, privilege of prepayment at any time____ *[without penalty / with penalty not exceeding _____ month's interest]*____, loan fees and costs of not more than _____ percent, acceleration provisions to be approved by Buyer, ____*[guaranty by ____[name of guaranteeing agency]____]*____ ____*[add release when appropriate; see Comment]*____

[Add when conditioned on loan rather than on commitment]

and the deposit in escrow of documents by Buyer and lender that will permit the recordation, concurrently with the recordation of the deed from seller to Buyer under this agreement, of the security instrument for the loan.

[Continue]

Buyer shall give Seller notice within _____ days after execution of this agreement if the condition is satisfied. If Buyer fails to give notice, Buyer's silence shall waive the condition; if Buyer gives notice that the condition is not satisfied, the agreement shall be terminated, and all funds and other documents deposited by either party shall be returned to each of them, less one half of escrow and title company costs.

[Add for seller's benefit]

Buyer shall make diligent application to ____*[state number if to more than one]*____ lending institution(s) and execute and furnish documents and supply all information reasonably requested by the lending institution(s) in connection with Buyer's application(s). Within _____ days after notice from Buyer to Seller of Buyer's inability to satisfy this condition or after the expiration of the period provided for Buyer to obtain it, without notice from the Buyer that it has been obtained, Seller may obtain the financing for Buyer and Buyer agrees to supply all information and execute all documents reasonably required by the lender to apply for and close the loan.

Comment: This provision includes the elements listed in §3.151 except for a subordination and release clause (see §§5.38-5.67). Provision for guaranty by FHA may be included when a guaranty can be obtained before closing, as in resales of single-family homes. When land is sold for subdivision, however, it may not be possible to obtain FHA or VA commitments within these time limits.

By making the agreement conditional on obtaining a commitment rather than on the loan itself, the buyer runs the risk that the lender will breach the loan commitment and refuse to close the loan. See *Patterson v Marchese* (1960) 196 NYS2d 903. Many commitments are subject to numerous conditions, and some lenders have breached their commitment when interest rates have increased. The loan itself cannot be made until closing, because the buyer must have title to be able to give the required security of a deed of trust. Construction loans usually require that a map be on record and that building plans be submitted. See §§6.14-6.15. Whether the agreement is conditioned on obtaining the loan or on obtaining the commitment may be a matter for negotiation.

The seller may wish to limit the buyer to particular types of lending institutions to avoid speculative loans at high interest rates or inflated appraisals. This may be controlled to an extent by the interest rates, loan fee, and other agreed terms. The seller may also want assurance that the buyer cannot use the financing condition as an escape clause. The additional provisions for his benefit may satisfy this desire.

On requiring buyer's efforts, see §3.69; on waiver of the financing condition, see §3.70.

The provision can be modified to include a release clause, *i.e.,* a provision that portions of the property are to be released from the deed of trust on payment of agreed on amounts. If so, a schedule showing the release price(s) might be added, and language such as the following be included at the end of the first paragraph:

, the note and deed of trust ____[or other security devices]____ to provide for release from the lien of the deed of trust of lots _____, _____, and _____ as designated on Map No. _____, recorded on _____, 19__, as Instrument _____ in book _____, page _____ of ____[official book] ____, in the Office of the County Recorder of _____ County, on the payment of $_____ per lot.

See also §§5.38-5.67 on subordination and release.

G. Sale Subject to Another Transaction

§3.153   1. Nature of Problem

A very troublesome contingency problem arises when the buyer's purpose in purchasing the subject property can be fully realized only if other property is also acquired. The buyer requires that the sale contract give him the right to rescind the subject sale if he is unable to acquire the other property. The same problem occurs when all record owners do not sign one agreement and the purchase of each interest must be conditioned on the purchase of the others.

This condition is objectionable to most sellers but in many situations the sale can proceed on no other basis. The seller can protect himself somewhat by requiring the buyer (a) to determine as promptly as possible whether he will be able to acquire adjacent property on satisfactory terms and then (b) to either eliminate the contingency or reject the present sale. The use of an option may be desirable, especially if the buyer desires to avoid all publicity regarding his plans. See §4.3.

Often the buyer agrees to purchase property he does not want because the owner of the property he wishes to purchase will not sell but will exchange it for the parcel being purchased. Similarly, the buyer may expect the closing of another escrow to provide the funds for the particular purchase. In both situations, the agreement should be conditioned on the occurrence of these events; otherwise the buyer may find himself obligated to a purchase he did not intend to make. For provisions, see §§3.154-3.156.

§3.154   2. Form: Condition; Subject to Buyer's Other Acquisitions

Form 3.154-1

[Insert in provision for conditions at §3.72]

Close of escrow, simultaneously with close of escrow under this agreement, for the Buyer's purchase of the property described in this paragraph on the following terms:

(a) Price not to exceed $ _____ ____*[describe unit, e.g., per acre]*____;

(b) Payable, not more than ____*[$* _____ / _____ *percent]*____ at close of escrow, balance by note in _____ equal ____*[annual / monthly]* ____ installments, bearing interest of not more than _____ percent per year, due no earlier than _____, 19__;

(c) Subject to the same conditions set forth in paragraph _____ of this agreement.

[Add other terms appropriate to the acquisition]

[Describe property to be acquired]

If this condition is not satisfied, Buyer may, at Buyer's election, waive the condition or terminate the agreement. Buyer's waiver or termination shall be evidenced by Buyer's notice to Seller. If Buyer gives no notice at least one business day before close of escrow, Buyer's silence shall ____*[waive the objection / terminate the agreement]*____.

Comment: This provision, which is part of the provision at §3.72, conditions the buyer's liability on simultaneous close of escrow for properties not yet subject to an agreement for purchase. Specific terms of the agreement are set as standards for other purchases; this may be changed, but some standard is needed to avoid a situation in which the buyer can use the condition as a means of withdrawing from the transaction. The provision may also be used when other undivided interests in the same property are being purchased under other agreements.

If the condition is not satisfied, the buyer may, by notice to the seller, waive the condition or terminate the agreement. The buyer should be advised of the effect of his failure to give the seller notice of his election. The time limit of one business day before closing may be extended. Generally, however, the interests of both parties are served by giving the buyer every reasonable opportunity to close his other transaction.

A different approach is to condition the buyer's liability only on the signing of an agreement for other purchases, with a definite date for the condition to be fulfilled or notice of disapproval given. Another approach is to have the seller include the additional parcel in his agreement with the buyer and add the provision in §3.155.

§3.155 3. Form: Buyer's Acquisition Through Seller

Form 3.155-1

The parties understand that Seller does not now have title to Parcel ____ [specify, e.g., A / 1]____ and will incur no liability to Buyer if Seller is unable to acquire title by close of escrow. Seller will make diligent efforts to obtain title by close of escrow. If Seller is unable to deliver title to Parcel ____[e.g., A / 1]____ under the terms of this agreement, Buyer shall have the right to elect either (a) to terminate this agreement and to obtain the return of all funds or moneys deposited by him without any deduction whatever, and without liability on his part, or (b) to perform and require performance of the agreement as it affects Parcel(s) ____[e.g., B / 2 and B / 3]____.

Comment: The seller may believe that the buyer is unable or unwilling to complete the purchase of the additional parcel and would use the provision in §3.154 as a means of avoiding performance. The seller may also be in a better position than the buyer to make the purchase, *e.g.,* have better personal relations with the other owners. For either reason, the seller may include the other parcel in the agreement and attempt to acquire it before closing.

If that is done, this provision protects the seller against liability if he fails to deliver title. Because the buyer does not want the seller to use this provision to avoid completing the sale, the provision gives the buyer the right in any event to purchase the seller's parcel.

If this approach is used, the agreement will have to state the purchase price separately for each parcel so an adjustment can be made if only the seller's parcel is acquired.

§3.156   4. Form: Condition; Subject to Another Transaction

Form 3.156-1

[Insert in provision for conditions at §3.72]

[If conditioned on exchange for another property]

Close of escrow for exchange of the property received by Buyer under this agreement for ____*[describe real property to be received]*____ under an agreement with _____ dated _____, 19__,

[If conditioned on sale of another property]

Close of escrow for sale of ____*[describe real property]*____ under an agreement with _____ dated _____, 19__,

[Continue]

simultaneously with close of escrow under this agreement.

If the condition is not satisfied, Buyer may, at Buyer's election, waive the condition or terminate the agreement. Buyer's waiver or termination shall be evidenced by Buyer's notice to Seller. If Buyer gives no notice at least one business day before close of escrow, Buyer's silence shall ____*[waive the condition / terminate the agreement]*____.

Comment: When the buyer bases the purchase on the closing of another transaction, the agreement should be conditioned on that occurrence. If the other transaction is an additional purchase by the buyer, the provision in §3.154 should be used. If it is a transfer by the buyer, whether by sale or exchange, the above provision is appropriate.

In a three-way exchange, the buyer makes one purchase solely to exchange it for another parcel. In other situations, the buyer may intend the purchase to be financed from the proceeds of sale of another property.

§3.157   H. Business Operations on Property

In purchasing real property, the buyer may be doing so as part of the purchase of a going business. If the seller's business (and personal property) is being transferred as a part of the purchase of real property, the buyer will be concerned with business operations on the property. This concern may include the continuance of the business operations by the seller until close of escrow (§3.158), the buyer's right to verify and approve the seller's income statements

(§3.159), and the approval or rejection of contracts relating to the business operations on the property (§§3.165-3.168). Matters dealt with in §§3.158-3.169 are those that may be of concern to a buyer purchasing real property with the intent of continuing the present business operations on the property. (If a going business is being purchased without purchase of the real property at which the business is located, the purchase and sale agreement for the business would not be in the form contained in this chapter. See Drafting Agreements for the Sale of Businesses (Cal CEB 1971) for forms of agreements when the business is acquired through the transfer of stock or assets rather than as a part of the purchase of real property.)

The provisions in §§3.131-3.150 dealing with the buyer's intended use of or development of the property (rather than the continuation of its present business operations) should also be reviewed by the drafter because there is some overlap between provisions dealing with present operations on the property and those dealing with the buyer's intended use and development of the property. Provisions dealing with the physical condition of the property (§§3.116-3.130) are also relevant to the buyer's intended use of the property.

§3.158   1. Form: Seller To Continue Normal Operation

Form 3.158-1

Seller shall diligently continue the normal management and operation of the property and the business conducted on it and shall maintain the property until close of escrow in as good repair as it was when buyer inspected it on _____, 19__. Seller shall make books and records pertaining to the business available for Buyer's inspection on reasonable notice.

Comment: When income property is being purchased, the economics of the operation may be as important as its physical condition. The buyer may require that the seller remain open for business, continue to collect the rents, or otherwise continue to operate in the manner that gave the property its value to the buyer. The seller usually has no objection to maintaining the property until the sale closes and his interest in it ends. Consideration might also be given to placing some limitation on the seller's right to make new leases without the buyer's consent. See provision at §3.113.

§3.159   2. Form: Condition; Buyer's Approval of Business Data

Form 3.159-1

[Insert in provision for conditions at §3.72]

Buyer's approval of the following documents: ____*[enumerate items; see suggested checklist in Comment]*____, delivery of the documents to be made by Seller to Buyer within _____ days of execution of this agreement. If the condition is not satisfied, Buyer may at his election terminate the agreement or waive the condition. Buyer's termination or waiver shall be evidenced by Buyer's notice to Seller within _____ days after delivery of all of the above documents. If Buyer gives no notice, Buyer's silence shall ____*[waive the condition / terminate the agreement]*____.

Comment: Many aspects of the operation may seriously affect its attractiveness to the buyer. The list below is not exhaustive; the variety of businesses and variables among them make comprehensiveness impossible. Aspects the buyer should approve include:

management agreements

employment agreements

collective bargaining
    agreements

books of account

installment purchase
    agreements

equipment or service rental
    agreements

guard service contracts

guaranties on appliances

maintenance contracts

subscriptions

liability insurance policies

casualty insurance policies

income statements

The buyer may also wish to examine the seller's books to see what the seller's costs have been. Such an examination may expose items such as a balky boiler that needs repeated repair or other unexpected continuing expenses.

On buyer's use of reasonable standards in approving, see §3.69.

Under this provision the buyer must indicate his approval or disapproval within a time limit, which prevents his using these items as a device to withdraw from the sale. On combined sale of personal and real property, see §8.64.

§3.160   3. Business Assets and Liabilities

The name under which the operation is conducted may be of value to the buyer in continuing the operation. The same may be true of signs, fixtures, rented equipment, goodwill, and many other items of personal property, both tangible and intangible. Some fixtures, improvements, and appliances may carry valuable guaranties or warranties. The lawyers for both parties should consider whether these should be acquired by the buyer, whether in the same agreement or in a separate agreement, and whether the price should be separately stated. See §8.64 on personal property descriptions in the sale agreement.

Because the seller may have incurred liabilities in the course of his operation, the buyer may validly require an agreement by the seller to defend and indemnify the buyer against all debts and liabilities incurred by the seller or claimed against him by reason of his operations before the close of escrow. The seller may also be required to comply with the provisions of Com C §§6101-6111 covering bulk sales. See 1 California Commercial Law, chap 15 (Cal CEB 1966). See also CC §3440 on fraudulent transfers of personal property.

For sellers' tax treatment of proceeds on sale of a business, see Rev Rul 55-79, 1955-1 Cum Bull 370. For tax aspects of selling a business, see generally Business Buy-Out Agreements (Cal CEB 1976); Drafting Agreements for the Sale of Businesses, chap 2 (Cal CEB 1971).

§3.161 4. Contractual Protection Against Legal Violations

Existing uses are no assurance to the buyer that he can continue those uses. For example, nonconforming uses that were in existence when the zoning ordinance was passed may be permitted for only a limited time after enactment of the legislation. See Comment, *The Elimination of the Nonconforming Use in California,* 8 Hastings LJ 64 (1956); Comment, *The Elimination of Nonconforming Uses,* 7 Stan L Rev 415 (1955). Sometimes the recording of a new conveyance is the signal for a building inspector to investigate possible violations of building or zoning regulations. Because municipal action to abate these uses is ordinarily instituted only after the buyer has completed his purchase and taken possession, the consequences to him may be grave.

In California, the seller's failure to disclose to the buyer the existence of violations that are known to the seller may be actionable. See, *e.g., Hartman v Rizzuto* (1954) 123 CA2d 186, 266 P2d 539 (rescission); *Barder v McClung* (1949) 93 CA2d 692, 209 P2d 808 (damages). It is better, however, for the buyer to discover violations before closing, if possible, because the seller may have been unaware of the violations or may be unable to respond in damages should there be a judgment.

If the buyer cannot recover on the ground of nondisclosure, he may have no remedy in the absence of contractual protections; an existing violation of a zoning law or building code may not be an encumbrance rendering title unmarketable. *Hartman v Rizzuto, supra.* Nor can the buyer rely on title insurance to protect against violations in the absence of a special endorsement. See California Title Insurance Practice §3.32 (Cal CEB 1980).

An inspection of the premises by an experienced engineer familiar with zoning and building regulations is one way to ascertain if there are violations; another way is to confer with the staff of the appropriate building and health departments. Additional protection is afforded by the provisions offered in §§3.162-3.163.

A seller who is selling part of a larger parcel or taking back multiple trust deeds may be unknowingly violating the Real Estate Law. On subdivision sales, see §3.143.

§3.162   a. Form: Warranty Against Violations

Form 3.162-1

Seller warrants and represents that at present and as of close of escrow no violation of any statute, ordinance, regulation or administrative or judicial order or holding, whether or not appearing in public records, exists or will exist, with respect to the property or any improvements on the property.

[*Add curative or indemnity provisions acceptable to both parties*]

Comment: The need for contractual protections against violations of law is discussed in §3.161. One kind of protection is a warranty that no violations exist. On remedies for breach, see chap 12.

There can be many variables in negotiating this provision. A provision more favorable to the buyer might, for example, require the seller to cure all violations or indemnify the buyer against claims, liabilities, damages, legal fees, and expenses incurred by the buyer because of violations.

The seller might modify those provisions by (1) conditioning seller's obligation on the buyer's notice, within a limited time after discovering the violation; (2) limiting seller's obligation to violations officially noted in governmental records; (3) limiting the warranty to violations in existence at the time of execution, rather than at closing, to prevent buyer from bringing an enforcement action as a defense to the contract; (4) obligating seller only to have the violation dismissed of record rather than curing it; (5) limiting the warranty to violations known to seller; (6) requiring buyer to share the expense of curing violations; or (7) limiting the cost of curing violations to a fixed amount or to the damage that would otherwise result. See also alternative provisions at §§3.146, 3.163.

§3.163   b. Form: Warranty; Seller's Knowledge of Government Orders or Directives

Form 3.163-1

Seller has no knowledge of any order or directive of ____[specify agency, e.g., Department of Building and Safety]____, or any other city, county, state, or federal authority, that any work of repair, maintenance, or improvement be performed on the property. Seller has received no notice from any municipal, state, or other statutory authority, or from any board of fire underwriters or any improvement association or architectural committee relating to defects in the improvements on the property or relating to noncompliance with any applicable building code or restriction that has not been corrected, or relating to any threat of impending expropriation or condemnation.

Comment: This is an alternative to the provision at §3.162. The buyer will want assurances that the property is not under an order of an applicable governmental authority requiring performance of any repair or improvement. This provision does not warrant against such an order, but merely that the seller has no knowledge of any such order (see §3.162 for a warranty). The buyer will usually not want to purchase any property that is subject to a threat of expropriation or condemnation. This paragraph warrants only that the seller has not received any notice of expropriation or condemnation. Occasionally a seller receives a notice from a governmental agency or a board of fire underwriters that the property does not comply with current codes or building standards; this form warrants that the seller has not received such a notice. This provision also covers possible covenants, conditions, and restrictions (CC&Rs; see

§§3.96-3.99) in its reference to notice from any improvement association or architectural committee. The phrase "that has not been corrected" is intended to limit the warranty to those matters that are outstanding and unremedied. Title insurance does not provide protection against the defects warranted against in this provision and they might not be discoverable on visual inspection of the property. See also §3.146.

§3.164　5. Form: Warranty Against Litigation Concerning the Property

Form 3.164-1

To Seller's knowledge, there is no litigation pending respecting the use or operation of the property.

Comment: The buyer needs to know if he stands to inherit litigation that is pending. Such litigation would include, *e.g.,* mechanics' lien foreclosure actions, unlawful detainer actions (if the seller is transferring a tenant's interest in a ground lease), and actions by governmental agencies concerning violations on the premises. If a notice of pending action (lis pendens) has been recorded concerning litigation affecting the property, that fact should be disclosed by a preliminary title report. The buyer's knowledge of all such actions is critical.

6. Contracts Affecting Property

§3.165　a. Form: Warranty Against Contracts Concerning the Property

Form 3.165-1

Seller warrants that at the close of escrow there will be no contracts, licenses, commitments, or undertakings respecting maintenance of the property or equipment on the property, or the performance of services on the property, or the use of the property or any part of it ____*[other than contracts approved pursuant to paragraph* ____*[see §3.167]*____]____ by which Buyer would become obligated or liable to any person.

Comment: The buyer needs to know if he will succeed to any contractual obligations by purchasing the property. By this warranty, the buyer is assured that if any agreements exist that are not disclosed, the seller will be required to compensate the buyer for any liability incurred under them.

§3.166　　b. Form: Warranty; Seller Not in Default Under Contracts

Form 3.166-1

To the best of Seller's knowledge, Seller is not in default under any contract, transaction, agreement, lease, encumbrance, or instrument pertaining to the property.

Comment: The buyer will want to know whether the seller is in default under any lease or under any other agreements, such as easements, deeds of trust, management or maintenance contracts, or agreements for providing utilities. The seller's default under a lease may entitle the tenant to terminate the lease or withhold rent. A default by seller under a deed of trust may entitle the lender to accelerate the loan. A requirement that the document be inspected might be enough to satisfy and protect the buyer. See §§3.159, 3.167.

§3.167　　c. Form: Condition; Buyer's Approval of Contracts

Form 3.167-1

[Insert in provision for conditions at §3.72]

Buyer's approval of contracts pertaining to the property. Seller shall furnish buyer with copies of contracts pertaining to the property within _____ days after execution of this agreement and Buyer shall notify Seller within _____ days after receipt of such copies of Buyer's approval or disapproval of each contract. Seller shall terminate in accordance with paragraph ____*[see §3.168]*____ any contracts disapproved by Buyer. Buyer's failure to notify Seller shall conclusively be considered ____*[approval / disapproval]*____.

Comment: The owner may have contractual arrangements for management, maintenance, security, and other matters pertaining to the property which the buyer will want to examine and have the right to approve or disapprove. Contracts for services to the property and collective bargaining agreements affecting persons employed by the seller should be examined to ensure that such agreements are acceptable to the buyer or cancellable within a reasonable time after the close of escrow. If not, the buyer may wish to have the seller arrange to terminate such agreements or adjust the purchase price. See alternative form at §3.165.

§3.168   d. Form: Termination of Existing Contracts

Form 3.168-1

Seller shall give notices of termination, at the written request of Buyer, to all persons and companies under contractual agreements with Seller to provide goods and services to the property ____[other than contracts approved by Buyer under paragraph ____[see §3.167]____]____. All such notices shall be given in sufficient time to effect the full termination of such contractual agreements not later than the close of escrow.

Comment: Existing agreements, for example, management and maintenance agreements, may include provisions that they are binding on heirs, successors, and assigns of the owner of the property. The buyer will ordinarily want to make his own arrangements for the management of the property for its maintenance and security. These agreements should be terminated prior to the close of escrow by the seller if the buyer so requests, even though the buyer does not become the seller's "successor or assigns" merely by buying the property.

§3.169   7. Form: Assignment of Warranties

Form 3.169-1

Seller shall assign to Buyer all warranties and all of Seller's rights against the contractors, subcontractors, suppliers, and materialmen involved in the construction or operation of the property.

Comment: If the building is a new construction or if improvements have been recently added to the property, there may be warranties which run in favor of the seller and which may be assignable to the buyer. These rights may have considerable value and the buyer will usually want a specific assignment of them.

§3.170   I. Transfer of Personal Property

Real property includes improvements which are "affixed" to the land or are "fixtures" (CC §658), and fixtures pass to the buyer with transfer of the fee interest. *Southern Pac. Co. v Riverside County* (1939) 35 CA2d 380, 95 P2d 688. Personal property does not pass to the buyer with the transfer of title to real property. However, the parties frequently want to include personal property as part of the sale and the agreement should specify exactly what items of personal property are to be included. If only a few items are to be transferred they can be listed in the agreement itself; otherwise, an inventory should be prepared and referred to in the agreement.

§3.171 1. Form: Personal Property To Be Included

Form 3.171-1

Included in the sale as personal property to be transferred from Seller to Buyer shall be: ____[describe items or indicate the items inventoried and list in exhibit attached]____

Comment: In residential sales, items such as stoves, refrigerators, and drapes may be included. In some commercial transactions, the personalty may consist of no more than janitorial equipment and electrical supplies. The items to be transferred should be specified to avoid uncertainty. If the property is an industrial building or small commercial building, there may be no personal property; this clause would then be omitted.

§3.172 2. Form: Transfer With Warranties

Form 3.172-1

The personal property described in ____[Exhibit _____ / paragraph ____[see §3.171]____]____ shall be transferred by a bill of sale in which Seller will covenant that at the time of execution of the bill of sale, Seller is lawfully possessed of good title to the personal property and that Seller has the right and authority to sell it, and that the personal property is free of all encumbrances, except for current taxes, a lien not yet payable

[Add if warranty concerning condition to be included]

and that the personal property is in good operating condition and repair, ordinary wear and tear excepted, and will be kept in such condition to the close of escrow.

Comment: When personal property is transferred, the buyer is concerned about liens on the personal property. The buyer can be protected by searching the Uniform Commercial Code Financing Statements filed with the Secretary of State. See Com C §§9302, 9401. A search will disclose any encumbrances of record and the seller is then required to clear them so that the foregoing warranty will be correct at the closing. See §3.173. If no major items of personal property are transferred and if the buyer is confident that there are no encumbrances, the use of this warranty without a search may suffice.

§3.173   3. Form: UCC Financing Statement Search by Escrow Holder

Form 3.173-1

The escrow holder shall be instructed to order a Uniform Commercial Code Financing Statement search covering the personal property described in ____[Exhibit _____ / paragraph ____[see §3.171]____]____. The escrow holder will be instructed to pay any encumbrances disclosed by the UCC search and approved by Seller from funds accruing to Seller so that at the closing the personal property is transferred to Buyer free and clear of any encumbrances. At the close of escrow Seller shall deliver to Buyer through escrow a bill of sale for the personal property and an assignment of all warranties and guaranties of any kind Seller may have concerning the personal property.

Comment: If buyer believes there are a significant number of encumbrances, this provision should be used; it calls for a UCC search as part of the escrow, and for the escrow holder to pay encumbrances. It can be used with the warranty in §3.172. If the majority of the assets of the seller are being sold, the bulk transfer requirements of Com C §§6101-6111 may have to be satisfied.

§3.174   J. Form: Cancellation or Assumption of Insurance

Form 3.174-1 (When Seller Will Cancel)

Seller's ____[specify, e.g., fire and casualty]____ insurance on the property shall be cancelled as of the closing, and Buyer shall be responsible for obtaining insurance coverage at the closing.

Form 3.174-2 (When Buyer Will Assume)

Within _____ days after execution of this agreement, Seller shall deliver copies of Seller's ____[specify, e.g., fire and casualty]____ insurance policies on the property to Buyer. Buyer shall inform escrow holder and Seller _____ days before closing whether Buyer wishes to take an assignment of Seller's insurance or to terminate it and secure insurance for the property.

Comment: It is important that the parties understand what will happen to the insurance on the property. Usually the fire insurance can be transferred to the buyer; transfer of liability insurance may be more difficult, especially if the buyer's intended use of the property differs from the seller's. Transferring insurance is easier if the property is income property and the same tenant is remaining in possession because then the insurer's risk is not changed. If the seller has a blanket policy covering the property being sold and other properties, a transfer may not be possible. If the seller has no objection to transferring the insurance, the assumption provision gives the buyer the option of assuming the seller's insurance of getting his own. The buyer should be required to elect a sufficient number of days before the closing to permit the insurance agent to handle the necessary paperwork. If a loan is being obtained, the lender will not fund the loan until it is satisfied that adequate fire insurance exists for the property. If the seller is taking back a note for part of the purchase price, the agreement should set forth the seller's insurance requirements.

K. Brokers

§3.175   1. Form: Broker's Commission

Form 3.175-1

Seller shall pay through escrow at the close and conditioned on the close of escrow a total broker's commission of $ _____, payable $ _____ to ____[name and address of broker]____; $_____ to ____[name and address of second broker, if any]____; and $_____ to ____[name and address of any finder entitled to fee]____. Buyer and seller hereby acknowledge that no other broker's commission or finder's fee is payable with regard to this transaction; and the Buyer and Seller each ("Indemnitor") agrees to indemnify and hold the other harmless from and against all liability, claims, demands, damages, or costs of any kind arising from or connected with any broker's or finder's fee or commission or charge claimed to be due any person arising from Indemnitor's conduct with respect to this transaction, other than the commissions authorized in this paragraph.

Comment: Both parties wish to avoid claims for commissions or finder's fees after the closing. This provision states the commissions to be paid and provides that each party indemnify the other against any claims that any other fee or commission is due because of that party's acts.

The broker's commission is determined by the broker's written agreement with the client. See chap 2. Usually this takes the form of a listing agreement. If none is executed, the broker must rely, as a third party beneficiary, on the purchase and sale agreement or escrow instructions to supply the writing required by CC §1624(5). To avoid difficulties, the drafter should ascertain who is to receive what commission or fee, who is to pay, and when the commission is to be considered earned. Then all of the parties, including the broker, should confirm this information in writing. Without the broker's written acknowledgment, confusion will arise about which document controls, the original commission agreement signed by the broker or the later purchase and sale agreement. If this provision is included in the sale agreement, each broker should sign the agreement on the signature page. See §3.62. Payment of the commission should be conditional on closing the transaction; thus, no commission is due if the sale is not completed. See also form at §3.62 on broker's commissions.

§3.176   2. Form: Disclosure of Licensee's Status

Form 3.176-1 (When Licensee Is Buyer or Seller)

Buyer and Seller acknowledge that ____[name of party]____ **is a licensed real estate** ____[broker / salesperson]____.

Form 3.176-2 (When Licensee Holds Interest in Buyer or Seller)

Buyer and Seller acknowledge that ____[name of licensee]____ **is a licensed real estate** ____[broker / salesperson]____ **and that** ____[he / she] ____ **holds** ____[specify, e.g., partnership interest, stock ownership]____ **in** ____[Buyer / Seller]____.

Comment: If a licensed real estate broker or salesperson acting as an agent in the transaction is also a party to the agreement, or holds a direct or indirect interest in one of the parties, the licensee must disclose that fact. 10 Cal Adm C §2785(a)(11). It is immaterial that the transaction is otherwise fair to the parties. *Batson v Strehlow* (1968) 68 C2d 662, 68 CR 589; *Smith v Zak* (1971) 20 CA3d 785, 98 CR 242.

L. Remedies

1. Time of Essence Clause

§3.177   a. Value

A printed time is of the essence clause may have little value. Some deposit receipts contain language permitting the broker to extend time, and escrow instructions often state that the escrow agent should close escrow as soon after the closing date as can be done. Courts have usually held that the parties have waived the time is of the essence clause by other provisions of the agreement or escrow instructions. *Katemis v Westerlind* (1953) 120 CA2d 537, 261 P2d 553, appeal after new trial (1956) 142 CA2d 799, 299 P2d 383.

Either party may waive strict performance by the other by failing to insist on it. *Johnson v Goldberg* (1955) 130 CA2d 571, 279 P2d 131.

In light of holdings such as *Britschgi v McCall* (1953) 41 C2d 138, 257 P2d 977 and *Pike v Von Fleckenstein* (1962) 203 CA2d 134, 21 CR 390, the clause might not excuse the aggrieved party from tendering his own performance and demanding strict performance by the other before he can put the other into default. At best the clause seems to permit a party to insist on the contract date and, after timely tender and notice, to reject belated attempts at performance by the other. See *McCown v Spencer* (1970) 8 CA3d 216, 87 CR 213. Absent the clause, tardy performance might have to be tolerated if it were done within a "reasonable" time. When either party wants to be automatically released if escrow does not close on time, the contract should state this specifically and unequivocally. See *Nash v Superior Court* (1978) 86 CA3d 690, 150 CR 394.

§3.178 b. Form: Clause Requiring Timely Performance

Form 3.178-1

Time is of the essence of this agreement and failure to comply with this provision shall be a material breach of this agreement. Unless previously extended in writing by Buyer and Seller, the escrow shall close at _____, 19__, ____[except as expressly provided in paragraph(s) _____ of this agreement, but not later than _____ , 19__]____. If the escrow fails to close as provided above, Buyer or Seller may at any time thereafter give written notice to the escrow holder to cancel the escrow and return all money and documents in escrow to their respective depositors. The escrow holder shall comply with the notice without further consent from any other party to the escrow or from the broker. Cancellation of escrow as provided here shall be without prejudice to whatever legal rights Buyer and Seller may have against each other.

Comment: The provision's effectiveness in permitting one party to withdraw from escrow against the will of the other depends on the attitude of the escrow holder, which is traditionally cautious. Escrow holders tend to refuse to return money and documents in escrow unless all parties consent in writing after the alleged breach. To obtain the escrow holder's cooperation, a similar provision requiring the return of money and documents if escrow fails to close by a certain date should be included in the escrow instructions. As a condition to accepting such an instruction, the escrow holder may require the buyer and the seller to execute an indemnity agreement holding him harmless against any loss or liability he may incur in complying with the instruction. See §§11.23-11.28.

The reference in this provision to other time limits expressly given in the agreement is to provisions such as those in §§3.73-3.75 (giving time for successive acts that could extend beyond the date otherwise set for closing) or §§3.108, 3.136 (giving express rights to extend).

2. Liquidated Damages

§3.179   a. Code Revisions

Effective July 1, 1978, CC §§1671 and 1675-1681, which govern liquidated damages provisions, were extensively revised. See generally, Guggenhime, *California's New Liquidated Damages Law,* 1 CEB Real Prop L Rep 17 (1978). Under the revised law, liquidated damages provisions generally are valid unless the party seeking to invalidate the provision establishes that the provision was unreasonable under the circumstances existing at the time the contract was made. CC §1671(b). Factors that can be considered include: the relative bargaining power of the parties, whether the parties were represented by counsel, whether the parties anticipated that proving actual damages would be costly or inconvenient, and whether the liquidated damages provision was part of a form contract. 13 Cal L Rev'n Commn Reports 1750 (1976) Commission Comment to CC §1671.

In real property transactions, a provision liquidating damages to the seller for the buyer's breach is subject to the additional requirements that it must be separately signed or initialed by each party to the contract (CC §1677(a)); and if printed, it must be set out in at least 10 point bold type or in contrasting red print in at least 8 point bold type (CC §1677(b)). These liquidated damages provisions apply only when the seller's damages for the buyer's failure to complete the purchase of real property is at issue. All other situations are governed by CC §1671. The revised statutes do not limit either party's rights to seek specific performance, nor do they affect installment land sale contracts controlled by CC §2985. A clause liquidating damages is in §3.180.

If the property is residential property of four or fewer units, and if at the time of the sale the buyer intends to occupy the dwelling or one of its units as the buyer's residence, CC §1675 imposes further requirements: (1) the liquidated damages clause is valid only up to the amount of the cash or check which is actually paid as deposit (CC §1675(b)); (2) if the amount actually paid as liquidated damages does not exceed 3 percent of the purchase price, the provision is presumed valid to the extent payment is made unless the buyer shows that that amount is unreasonable as liquidated damages (CC §1675(c)); (3) if the amount paid exceeds 3 percent, the provision is presumed invalid unless the party seeking to uphold the provision establishes that the amount paid is reasonable as liquidated damages (CC §1675(d)). In determining reasonableness, the circumstances existing at the time the contract was made and the price and other terms and circumstances of any subsequent sale or contract for sale of the same property made within six months of the buyer's default are taken into account. CC §1675(e). If more than one payment is made by the buyer as liquidated damages, the total of all of the payments must satisfy the requirements discussed above, and a separate liquidated damages statement must be initialed by all parties for each such subsequent payment. CC §1678. This provision would apply, for example, when the buyer gives a check for a deposit to the broker when making the offer and then augments that check on opening of escrow.

Even under the revised law, the seller, as a practical matter, will have difficulty enforcing liquidated damages provisions if the buyer resists because escrow holders will probably continue to require both parties to consent in writing *after* the breach before they release the buyer's funds to the seller. Failing such agreement, the escrow holder may interplead the funds into court. The seller would be in a stronger position if the earnest money deposit were paid directly to the seller outside escrow. The seller then would have the deposit in hand, and the buyer would have to sue to recover any amount claimed to be in excess of the sums allowed by law.

Under pre-1978 law, it was exceptionally difficult, no matter what words were used in the agreement, to draft an enforceable liquidated damages clause. See, *e.g., Cook v King Manor & Convalescent Hosp.* (1974) 40 CA3d 782, 115 CR 471. The revised law has yet to be thoroughly tested in the courts, and so it is difficult to predict whether this provision would result in an enforceable liquidated damages provision. If the parties desire to have an enforceable liquidated damages clause, it is important that the parties openly discuss it before the execution of the agreement and agree that the dollar amount set forth in the agreement truly comports with their mutual understanding of what the damages to the seller would be if the buyer should default. See *Cook v King Manor & Convalescent Hosp.*, *supra*.

§3.180   b. Form: Liquidated Damages

Form 3.180-1

If ____[Buyer / Seller]____ fails to complete the transaction contained in this agreement, the parties agree that ____[Seller / Buyer]____ shall retain the sum of $ _____ as liquidated damages, which sum the parties agree is a reasonable sum considering all of the circumstances existing on the date of this agreement, including the relationship of the sum to the range of harm to ____[Seller / Buyer]____ that reasonably could be anticipated and the anticipation that proof of actual damages would be costly or inconvenient. In placing their initials at the places provided, each party specifically confirms the accuracy of the statements made above and the fact that each party was represented by counsel who explained the consequences of this liquidated damages provision at the time this agreement was made.

| Seller | Buyer |
| Initial here: _____ | Initial here: _____ |

Comment: This provision has been drafted to comply with the 1978 revision of the liquidated damages law. See §3.179. It is also important from the buyer's standpoint in drafting a liquidated damages clause that it not be construed as a continuing option, *i.e.*, as a clause that gives the buyer the option of either buying the property or forfeiting a stated sum of money. If the clause is construed as a continuing option, it may preclude the buyer from obtaining specific performance against the seller, if the seller defaults, notwithstanding the provisions of CC §3389 permitting specific performance even though the contract provides for liquidated damages. See *People v Ocean Shore R.R.* (1949) 90 CA2d 464, 203 P2d 579; *California Land Security Co. v Ritchie* (1919) 40 CA 246, 180 P 625. Civil Code §3389 was unchanged by the 1978 revision of the liquidated damages law. Therefore, in order to avoid the result of these cases, it is still important that the clause not provide that the retention of liquidated damages relieves the buyer from any further liability. Such a provision could be construed as making the liquidated damages clause a continuing option. Civil Code §1671 also permits the provision to be drafted to liquidate the buyer's damages for the seller's breach.

Because of the availability of specific performance as a remedy for the buyer, parties rarely provide for liquidation of damages for a seller's breach.

§3.181 3. Form: Attorneys' Fees

Form 3.181-1

If either party files any action or brings any proceeding against the other arising out of this agreement, or is made a party to any action or proceeding brought by the escrow holder, then as between Buyer and Seller, the prevailing party shall be entitled to recover as an element of its costs of suit, and not as damages, reasonable attorneys' fees to be fixed by court. The "prevailing party" shall be the party who is entitled to recover its costs of suit, whether or not suit proceeds to final judgment. A party not entitled to recover its costs shall not recover attorneys' fees. No sum for attorneys' fees shall be counted in calculating the amount of a judgment for purposes of determining whether a party is entitled to its costs or attorneys' fees.

Comment: This provision, in addition to providing for attorneys' fees as between the parties, also provides for attorneys' fees for the prevailing party when the escrow holder interpleads funds. In the absence of a provision for attorneys' fees, the cost to the aggrieved party of enforcing his rights may equal or exceed the damages to which he is entitled under CC §3306, particularly if the seller's breach is not in bad faith. Attorneys' fees are not recoverable by the prevailing party in a contract action unless the contract expressly so provides. CCP §1021. They may, however, be awarded to the prevailing party even if the contract purports to award them only to one party. CC §1717. This provision is based on a suggested provision in Brutocao, *Attorneys fees: Who prevails?* 55 Cal SBJ 300 (1980).

See also §11.28 for a discussion of attorneys' fees under an indemnity agreement.

§3.182 4. Form: Effect of Waiver of Provision on Remedy

Form 3.182-1

No waiver by a party of any provision of this agreement shall be considered a waiver of any other provision or any subsequent breach of the same or any other provision, including the time for performance of any such provision. The exercise by a party of any remedy provided in this agreement or at law shall not prevent the exercise by that party of any other remedy provided in this agreement or at law.

Comment: Unless otherwise provided, the law may imply waiver when a party entitled to performance accepts partial or defective performance. 1 Witkin, Summary of California Law, *Contracts* §593 (8th ed 1973). Similarly, because many of the remedies available in case of a breach are inconsistent, the law may find that the injured party has elected to pursue one remedy to the exclusion of others. The parties can modify or nullify the doctrine of election of remedies by contract. 2 Witkin, California Procedure, *Actions* §129 (2d ed 1970). To avoid a broader waiver than was intended or an early election of remedies, this provision should be included in the agreement.

§3.183   5. Form: Arbitration

Form 3.183-1

Any controversy arising from this agreement or its breach shall be determined by three arbitrators appointed as set out below:

(a) Within _____ days after a notice by either party to the other requesting arbitration and stating the basis of the party's claim, one arbitrator shall be appointed by each party. Notice of the appointment shall be given by each party to the other when made.

(b) The two arbitrators shall immediately choose a third arbitrator to act with them. If they fail to select a third arbitrator within _____ days of their appointment, on application by either party the third arbitrator shall be promptly appointed by the then presiding judge of the Superior Court of the State of California in and for the County of _____, acting as an individual. The party making the application shall give the other party _____ days' notice of the application.

The arbitration shall be conducted under Code of Civil Procedure sections 1280 through 1294.2. Hearings shall be held in _____ County, California. All notices, including notices under Code of Civil Procedure section 1290.4, shall be given as provided in paragraph ____[see §3.58]____.

Comment: The parties may agree to arbitrate any disputes arising under the agreement (CCP §1281) and can seek to have the arbitrator's award enforced in court (CCP §1285). The arbitration agreement may: (a) provide for the county in which hearings are to be held (CCP §1282.2) and thus determine the venue of any proceeding to compel arbitration (CCP §1292) or to confirm the award (CCP §1292.2); (b) specify the manner of service of notice of judicial proceedings (CCP §1290.4); (c) determine whether rules of evidence and procedure are to apply (CCP §1282.2(c)); and (d) bind a defaulting party to the arbitrator's determination (*Brink v Allegro Builders, Inc.* (1962) 58 C2d 577, 25 CR 556).

Although some attorneys favor arbitration, the costs often outweigh the benefits, especially if the parties must resort to court action to enforce or challenge the arbitration award.

§3.184   M. Form: Assignment by Buyer

Form 3.184-1

Buyer may not assign this agreement without prior written consent of Seller

[Add if buyer to be given limited rights of assignment]

except that Buyer shall have the right to assign this agreement and all of Buyer's rights under it ____*[to an entity in which Buyer has at least a _____ percent interest]*____, subject to the terms and provisions of this agreement, provided that the assignee assumes all obligations of Buyer and agrees to execute all documents and to perform all obligations imposed on Buyer as if the assignee were the original buyer in this agreement.

[Add if assignment is to relieve buyer of liability]

On the assignee's assumption of Buyer's obligations ____*[and the close of escrow]*____, Buyer shall be relieved of liability under this agreement.

Comment: If the buyer intends to form a corporation, partnership, or other entity to take title, or if the buyer wishes to sell to another, the buyer wants the right to assign the agreement without further consent of the seller. Merely stating "Buyer or nominee" in the agreement is insufficient because this description of the buyer is not sufficiently certain. See §3.21. If the seller wants a more restrictive clause, provisions requiring the buyer to hold a specified interest in the assignee and providing that the buyer will not be relieved of the obligations of the agreement until escrow closes can be inserted. The seller may also require that the seller approve the assignee. The seller will want this right when taking back a note for part of the purchase price because the seller wants to know who the buyer is and what the buyer's credit standing is.

An agreement is assignable by law unless it was intended to be nonassignable or assignment would impair the seller's chances of obtaining the buyer's performance. *Farmland Irrigation Co. v Dopplmaier* (1957) 48 C2d 208, 308 P2d 732. If the parties wish to limit the agreement's assignability, the agreement should so state. An assignor is not relieved of liability unless the agreement so specifies. CC §1457. Therefore, unless the assigning buyer is specifically released, the seller can look to the assigning buyer if the assignee fails to perform.

A formal written assignment should be executed between the buyer and the assignee to ensure that the rights to specific enforcement of the agreement are transferred to the assignee.

§3.185   N. Form: Time for Possession

Form 3.185-1 (When Buyer To Take Possession on Close of Escrow)

On close of escrow, Seller shall deliver the property to Buyer in substantially the same condition, reasonable wear and tear excepted, as on the date of this agreement.

Form 3.185-2 (When Seller To Retain Possession After Close of Escrow)

As an agreement that will survive the close of escrow, Buyer agrees that Seller may remain as a tenant on the property until _____, 19__ at a ____ [*daily / monthly*]____ rent of $_____. Escrow holder shall be instructed to withhold from Seller's proceeds and deliver to Buyer at the closing the sum of $_____ ("rent deposit"), consisting of $_____, to pay the anticipated ____[*daily / monthly*]____ rent, and $ _____ as a security deposit to ensure Seller's timely vacation of the property and delivery of the property in substantially the same condition, reasonable wear and tear excepted, as on the date of this agreement. When Seller vacates the property, Buyer shall deliver the unapplied portion of the rent deposit to Seller. If Seller has incurred liability in excess of the rent deposit, Seller shall promptly pay the excess to Buyer on demand. If Seller holds over after _____, 19__, Seller shall be a tenant at sufferance.

Comment: If the seller wishes to remain in possession after the closing date, the parties should agree to a daily rental rate. A sum sufficient to pay the anticipated rent, plus a security deposit, should be delivered to the buyer pending the seller's delivery of possession. Civil Code §1950.5 limits the amount of the security deposit for residential property. The security deposit is to protect the buyer if the seller holds over, damages the property, or if the buyer must bring an unlawful detainer action to obtain possession. The provision states that the agreement survives the close of escrow so that it cannot be argued that the agreement merged with the deed. An unlawful detainer action can be initiated against a tenant who holds over after the expiration of a fixed rental term (CCP §1161(1)) without prior service of notice, and this provision clarifies that situation by making the seller a tenant at sufferance after expiration of the term of the tenancy.

O. Interpretation of the Agreement

§3.186   1. Form: Integration Clause

Form 3.186-1

This agreement constitutes the entire agreement between the parties and supersedes all prior discussion, negotiations, and agreements whether oral or written. Any amendment to this agreement, including an oral modification supported by new consideration, must be reduced to writing and signed by both parties before it will be effective.

Comment: In the absence of fraud, lack of consideration, and similar defenses, this provision terminates all agreements not set forth in the document and eliminates the claim that there are other agreements outside the document. Requiring all amendments to be in writing satisfies the statute of frauds, and also establishes a record of the amendments made. For a discussion of the requirements for an effective modification, see §3.37. For a form for amendments, see §3.191. This provision makes extrinsic evidence to vary its terms inadmissible. CCP §1856.

It should be noted, however, that notwithstanding such a provision, courts have been lenient in admitting extrinsic evidence to interpret ambiguities. See Witkin, California Evidence §732 (2d ed 1966).

§3.187   2. Form: Counterparts

Form 3.187-1

This agreement and all amendments and supplements to it may be executed in counterparts, and all counterparts together shall be construed as one document.

Comment: Often the parties are in a hurry to execute the agreement. Counterparts allow simultaneous execution without the need for all parties to meet. Counterparts, however, increase the possibility of unauthorized alteration of the document because all parties do not sign the same document at the same time. To reduce the chances of such alteration, each party should execute a complete agreement, not just the signature page, and initial each page. This procedure makes it more difficult to substitute pages, and if the counterparts are later found not to match, it will establish which party signed what form of the document.

§3.188   3. Form: Binding on Successors

Form 3.188-1

This agreement inures to the benefit of, and is binding on, the parties, ____[and except as limited by paragraph ____[see §3.184]____]____ their respective heirs, personal representatives, successors and assigns.

Comment: This provision ensures that the agreement survives the death of any of the parties or the assignment of the agreement. The usual rule is that a contract obligation survives the death of the promisor except in the case of a contract calling for personal services by the promisor. 1 Witkin, Summary of California Law, *Contracts* §606 (8th ed 1973). Depending on the details of a particular agreement, a court might or might not find a purchase and sale agreement to be for personal services. See, *e.g., Central Contra Costa Sanitary Dist. v National Sur. Corp.* (1952) 112 CA2d 61, 246 P2d 150. The clause should be limited if the agreement is not freely assignable. For a discussion of assignments, see §3.184.

§3.189   4. Form: Captions, Joint and Several Liability, Controlling Law

Form 3.189-1

[Add if captions used in the agreement]

The captions heading the various paragraphs of this agreement are for convenience and shall not be considered to limit, expand, or define the contents of the respective paragraphs.

[Continue]

Masculine, feminine, or neuter gender and the singular and the plural number, shall each be considered to include the other whenever the context so requires. If either party consists of more than one person, each such person shall be jointly and severally liable. This agreement shall be interpreted under California law and according to its fair meaning, and not in favor of or against any party.

Comment: This provision sets out the agreed rules of interpretation to be used in construing the agreement. The provision for interpretation according to the document's fair meaning is intended to negate the usual rule (CC §1654) that a document is interpreted against the party who caused the uncertainty to exist.

The provision also provides for joint and several liability if more than one person is signing for a party.

§3.190 5. Form: No Representation Regarding Legal Effect of Document

Form 3.190-1

No representation, warranty, or recommendation is made by ____[Seller / Buyer]____ or their brokers, their respective agents, employees, or attorneys regarding the legal sufficiency, legal effect, or tax consequences of this agreement or the transaction, and each signatory is advised to submit this agreement to his respective attorney before signing it.

Comment: This provision may be added when there are many parties and some are not represented by counsel. The provision should be placed near the signature line and prominently set forth so that the signing parties will see it. Its purpose is to put all parties not represented by counsel on notice that they should not rely on the attorney who drafted the agreement to protect their interests.

§3.191 P. Form: Amendment to the Agreement

Form 3.191-1

____[First]____ Amendment to Purchase and Sale Agreement
The purchase and sale agreement dated _____, 19__ between ____ [name of seller]____, and ____[name of buyer]____, is amended as follows:
____[Specify nature of amendment, e.g., at page _____, line _____ ____, the date "September 21, 1979" is deleted and the date "November 28, 1979" is inserted in its place]____

Except as set forth above, the purchase and sale agreement shall remain in full force and effect.

Dated: _____

Seller:
__[Signature]__
____[Typed name]____

Buyer:
__[Signature]__
____[Typed name]____

Comment: In complex transactions it is often necessary to amend the agreement before the sale finally closes. This form provides a simple way to do so. The material deleted should be clearly identified or quoted and the new language set forth. To avoid confusion, the amendments should be consecutively numbered. An amendment must be executed in the same manner as the original document. See also §3.37 on changing signed documents.

4

Bruce W. Hyman
James A. Moewe

Options

BRUCE W. HYMAN, B.S., 1954, University of California (Berkeley); J.D., 1957, University of California School of Law (Berkeley).

JAMES A. MOEWE, B.S., 1968, University of California (Los Angeles); J.D., 1972, University of California School of Law (Los Angeles).

Mr. Hyman and Mr. Moewe are members of the firm of Landels, Ripley & Diamond, San Francisco.

319

I. ANALYSIS OF OPTIONS

A. Definition and Characteristics of Options

§4.1   1. Definition of an Option

An option is a contract by which the owner of property (the op-tionor) gives a potential buyer (the optionee) the exclusive right to purchase at a stipulated price within a limited or reasonable time in the future. *Caras v Parker* (1957) 149 CA2d 621, 626, 309 P2d 104, 107. Typically, the optionor offers to sell the property on stipulated terms and conditions, and promises to leave the offer open for a certain period of time. In return for granting an exclusive right to purchase during that specified time period, the optionor usually receives consideration from the optionee. If no time period is stated for exercise of the option, a "reasonable" time is inferred. *Auslen v Johnson* (1953) 118 CA2d 319, 257 P2d 664. When consideration is given for the option, a unilateral irrevocable promise by the optionor to perform according to his offer is created. *Caras v Parker, supra.* Unlike a purchase and sale agreement, under an option the optionee incurs no corresponding obligation, but rather may choose to purchase or not. *Warner Bros. Pictures Inc. v Brodel* (1948) 31 C2d 766, 192 P2d 949.

If an ostensible option agreement appears to bind the optionee to future performance under the agreement, a court will look beyond form and find the agreement imposed mutuality of obligation on the parties and was thus in reality a purchase and sale agreement rather than an option. *Scarbery v Bill Patch Land & Water Co.* (1960) 184 CA2d 87, 7 CR 408 (purchaser allowed to cure default and avoid forfeiture).

§4.2   2. The Two Agreements in an Option Contract

Much of the confusion between contractual rights and property interests arises from the fact that an option is in fact two separate agreements. The first agreement arises on the execution of the option contract; it concerns the option itself, its duration, the way it may be exercised, and the consideration paid for it. The second agreement, arising on the exercise of the option by the optionee, consists of a complete purchase and sale agreement that is to take effect if the optionee chooses to exercise the option. *Caras v Parker* (1957) 149 CA2d 621, 309 P2d 104.

The provisions in §§4.24-4.41 are for the option agreement only. The purchase and sale agreement, arising on the exercise of the option, is to be attached to the option as an exhibit. See §§3.42-3.62 for a form of purchase and sale agreement.

B. Purpose of Options

§4.3   1. Advantages for the Buyer-Optionee

The option, if properly recorded (see §4.42), provides the buyer-optionee with assurances that during the option period no one else can buy the property free and clear of the buyer-optionee's rights and that the price will not rise within that time (unless the option contract provides for increases in price during the option period). The buyer-optionee may use the option period to investigate the suitability of the property for his needs, to determine the availability of financing, or to seek any permits or approvals that would be needed for the buyer's proposed use or development of the property. If progress in one of these areas proves unsatisfactory, the buyer-optionee, having no obligation to purchase the property, is free to continue his search for property suitable for his purposes. The use of an option eliminates the need to include, in the purchase and sale agreement, extensive conditions to the buyer's obligation to purchase. See §§3.68-3.70 on the use of conditions.

An option may also give the buyer-optionee an opportunity to speculate on an increase in the property's value. If the property appreciates during the option period, the seller must still accept the agreed price; if the value declines, the buyer has no obligation to purchase.

Although to some extent the recordation of an option increases the likelihood of discovery by third parties of the existence of the option, a buyer-optionee may use an option to secure the right to acquire property without undue publicity. During the option period, the buyer may conduct investigations in relative secrecy without alerting adjoining land owners, or negotiate the transfer of other property on which the decision to purchase may depend.

§4.4   2. Advantages for the Seller-Optionor

The seller-optionor usually demands sufficient consideration for assuming the risks associated with keeping the property off the market during the option period. The chief risk is that the purchase will not be consummated (*e.g.*, because the market value of the property falls, building permits are unobtainable, or unavailability of other property sought by the buyer).

However, in spite of this risk the seller may be willing to agree to an option. For example, although an option never obligates the optionee to purchase, the consideration for the option, if sufficiently large, may constitute an investment which motivates the optionee to consummate the sale, especially when the option consideration is applied as a partial payment of the purchase price. (However, if the consideration is too large, a court may find that the option was merely a disguised security device to induce the buyer to consummate the purchase. See discussion in §4.7.)

One advantage to the seller in the use of an option agreement is that it allows the seller to avoid the possibility of a complicated action for breach of contract if the buyer decides not to purchase. Under a valid option contract, the seller-optionor retains the consideration paid for the option, whether or not the buyer-optionee exercises the option. *Sheveland v Reed* (1958) 159 CA2d 820, 324 P2d 633. The seller need not justify the option consideration as liquidated damages. See §§3.179, 12.26-12.30 for a discussion of liquidated damages.

§4.5   3. The Option as a Financing Device

Occasionally, an option is created as part of a method of financing real property by the seller through the use of an outright sale of the property, coupled with a leaseback to the seller with an option to repurchase. The effect of such a transaction is to provide the seller with financing equal to 100 percent of the value of the property, while he maintains control of the property through the leaseback and option to repurchase. However, the parties must be careful in drafting the documents for such a transaction, because under certain circumstances, sale and leaseback financing with repurchase options constitutes disguised security devices. For a more complete discussion of the advantages of sale-leaseback financing, and the associated pitfalls, see Moewe, *Sale and Leaseback Financing of Real Estate as Mortgages under California Law,* 48 Cal SBJ 554 (1973).

§4.6   C. Requisites for Enforceability

In order to be enforceable, an option contract must comply with the statute of frauds (CC §1624(4)). *Woods v Bradford* (1967) 254 CA2d 501, 62 CR 391; *Bovo v Abrahamson* (1929) 100 CA 373, 280 P 191.

In addition to being in writing, an enforceable option agreement must set forth all terms material to the contract. It cannot leave any important terms to future agreement by the parties. *Roven v Miller* (1959) 168 CA2d 391, 335 P2d 1035. The agreement must comply with all the usual requirements for a real property sales contract. It must

(1) identify both seller and buyer (*Malerbi & Assoc. v Seivert* (1961) 191 CA2d 760, 12 CR 852);

(2) specify the price of the property (*Stockwell v Lindeman* (1964) 229 CA2d 750, 40 CR 555);

(3) indicate the time and manner of payment, including any terms of subordination (*Roven v Miller, supra,* 168 CA2d 391, 335 P2d 1035); and

(4) describe the property with reasonable certainty (*Calvi v Bittner* (1961) 198 CA2d 312, 17 CR 850 (property described sufficiently to obviate resort to parol evidence); *Best v Wohlford* (1904) 144 C 733, 78 P 293 (description must be such that the property can be identified and located on the ground); *Ganiats Constr., Inc. v Hesse* (1960) 180 CA2d 377, 4 CR 706 (phrase "next contiguous thirty acres" was insufficient description); *Ontario Downs, Inc. v Lauppe* (1961) 192 CA2d 697, 13 CR 782 (optionee to make choice of specified amount of acreage subject to optionor's good faith approval)).

It is not necessary to provide for a definite period of time for the exercise of the option in order for the agreement to be enforceable, although it is recommended that the term be specific in order to avoid judicial intervention in the determination of the term.

See also §3.8 for a discussion of the requirements for the enforceability of purchase and sale agreements.

In addition to the above requirements, an option must also be supported by consideration to be irrevocable. See §4.7.

D. Consideration for the Option

1. Consideration Paid

§4.7   a. Value of Consideration for Option

If the optionee has given "valuable" consideration, the optionor cannot revoke the offer to sell, except as the terms of the option agreement provide, or unless consent of the optionee is obtained. *Kowal v Day* (1971) 20 CA3d 720, 98 CR 118; *Prather v Vasquez* (1958) 162 CA2d 198, 327 P2d 963; *Stough v Hanson* (1941) 46 CA2d 504, 116 P2d 77.

The consideration need not be proportionate to the property's value. California courts have held that any consideration, however small, will bind the optionor to the option agreement. *Kowal v Day, supra,* 20 CA3d 720, 98 CR 118 (use of a car constituted sufficient consideration); *Wheat v Morse* (1961) 197 CA2d 203, 17 CR 226 ($1 consideration sufficed); *Marsh v Lott* (1908) 8 CA 384, 97 P 163 (payment by optionee of 25 cents for an option to purchase land for $100,000).

Nevertheless, some authorities suggest that consideration must be more than nominal, even to support an action for damages. See case cited in 1 Miller & Starr, Current Law of California Real Estate §1:37 at 43 n8 (rev ed 1975). Even though case law does not support the view that consideration must be more than nominal, the better practice would still be to provide for more than just a nominal consideration. In most cases, the seller-optionor will demand sufficient consideration to cover costs during the option period, or to compensate for the likelihood of an increase in the property's value.

If the value of the consideration given for the option constitutes a large percentage of the eventual purchase price, a court may interpret the option as a hidden security device, intended to force the optionee to exercise. *Scarbery v Bill Patch Land & Water Co.* (1960) 184 CA2d 87, 7 CR 408 (option consideration amounted to more than 75 percent of purchase price). See discussion in §4.5.

§4.8   b. Services as Consideration for Option

When the optionee performs services as consideration for an option, they must be services bargained for by the parties. *Kelley v Rouse* (1961) 188 CA2d 92, 10 CR 235; *Prather v Vasquez* (1958) 162 CA2d 198, 327 P2d 963. Activities merely detrimental to the optionee will not suffice, unless the optionee promised them as an inducement for the option. *Kelley v Rouse, supra* (optionee's activities, after execution of option, to determine whether to exercise option not bargained for consideration); *Spielberg v Granz* (1960) 185 CA2d 283, 8 CR 190 (illegal services were not good consideration); see *Prather v Vasquez, supra* (efforts by proposed purchaser to obtain rezoning not bargained for consideration for option allegedly contained in escrow instructions).

§4.9   c. The Significance of Adequate Consideration

To ensure the right to sue for specific performance of an option, the contract must be "just and reasonable." CC §3391. However, in determining if the consideration is adequate a court generally looks only to the adequacy of the purchase price for the property, not the adequacy of the consideration for the option. See §4.7. In *Marsh v Lott* (1908) 8 CA 384, 97 P 163, the court stated that any consideration (in that case 25 cents) was sufficient to support an option because the court is not able to determine what would constitute a fair consideration for an option. In contrast, a court can ascertain a just consideration for the purchase of the real property. (In *Marsh* the court refused to enforce the option agreement, not because the 25-cent option consideration was inadequate, but because the terms for payment of the purchase price for the real property were inadequate.)

A court will determine the just and reasonable price for the property subject to the option as of the time the option agreement is entered into rather than as of the date of exercise (*Stough v Hanson* (1941) 46 CA2d 504, 116 P2d 77) but any consideration, no matter how small, is sufficient to make the option irrevocable.

In assessing the fairness of the purchase price, the court will look at the option agreement in its entirety. Thus, although the purchase price for the property might, by itself, be insufficient, the price might, when viewed together with the consideration given for the option, be sufficient to obtain specific enforcement of the agreement. *Crocker v Grandi* (1961) 189 CA2d 431, 11 CR 330; *Denbo v Senness* (1953) 120 CA2d 863, 262 P2d 31.

§4.10   2. No Consideration Paid

In addition to the requirements discussed in §4.6, an option agreement must be supported by consideration in order to be irrevocable. *Torlai v Lee* (1969) 270 CA2d 854, 76 CR 239. If the optionee gives no consideration, the option agreement is merely an offer that the optionor can revoke at any time before acceptance by the optionee. *Kelley v Rouse* (1961) 188 CA2d 92, 10 CR 235; *Prather v Vasquez* (1958) 162 CA2d 198, 327 P2d 963. When an option contract provides that the optionor must return the consideration paid if the optionee fails to exercise the option, a court may view the payment as no consideration at all. *Torlai v Lee, supra,* 270 CA2d 854, 895, 76 CR 239, 242.

§4.11   E. The Rule Against Perpetuities

Because courts have held an option to be a future interest which vests on exercise, parties to an option contract should be aware of the effect of the Rule Against Perpetuities. Civil Code §715.8, enacted in 1963, defined an interest in real or personal property as vested if there was a person or persons who, irrespective of the nature of their respective interests, could together convey a fee simple title. Because an optionor and an optionee could always agree to convey the optioned property in fee simple, an option to a living person entered into prior to 1970 did not violate the Rule Against Perpetuities.

Civil Code §715.8 was repealed in 1970; options are now subject to CC §§715.2 and 715.6. Civil Code §715.2 codifies the common law Rule Against Perpetuities, providing that an interest in the property must vest, if at all, no more than 21 years after a life in being at the creation of that interest. Civil Code §715.6 simplifies the rule somewhat: It provides that an interest which must vest within 60 years of its creation will not violate CC §715.2. Thus, an option agreement providing for exercise within 60 years will not violate the Rule Against Perpetuities. One which provides no termination date, and therefore creates an option for a "reasonable" time, will not violate the Rule Against Perpetuities if it meets the reasonableness standards set forth in *Wong v Di Grazia* (1963) 60 C2d 525, 35 CR 241 (lease to begin "on completion" of building not violative of Rule Against Perpetuities).

F. Effect of Exercise of Option

§4.12   1. Relation Back on Exercise

The exercise of an option creates a real property sales contract that relates back to the date the option was signed. The contract had bound the optionor to its terms on that date; acceptance merely removes the conditions, and makes the contract mutually binding. *Seeburg v El Royale Corp.* (1942) 54 CA2d 1, 128 P2d 362.

§4.13   2. Priority of Option on Exercise

An exercised option may raise questions concerning the priority of third party interests in the property. Because the optionee's interest relates back to the date of signing, the optionee's interest (and any lien or encumbrance on the optionee's interest) has priority over any interest acquired from the owner-optionor by a third party between the time the option agreement is signed and the time it is exercised, provided that the third party either has knowledge, actual or constructive, of the existence of the option, or failed to record his interest first. See §4.42. Thus, the exercise of an option which was created before the creation of a lien on the optionor's property will terminate the lien.

California courts have held that an option to purchase contained in a lease constitutes a covenant running with the land. *Andrade v Casteel* (1947) 81 CA2d 729, 185 P2d 51. Subsequent purchasers with notice of the option take subject to the option holder's rights. *Chapman v Great W. Gypsum Co.* (1932) 216 C 420, 14 P2d 758; *Andrade v Casteel, supra.* A mortgage or other lien on an option contained in a lease will burden the property, once the mortgagor-optionee exercises the option. *Chapman v Great W. Gypsum Co., supra.*

§4.14 G. Termination of Options

The most frequent cause of termination of an option is the expiration of its term. See Comment in §4.35 for a discussion of the effect of termination. An option may also terminate as a result of the exercise of a prior right (§4.15), or the expiration of a lease containing an option (§4.16). The death of the optionor does not usually cause the option to terminate (§4.17).

§4.15 1. Exercise of Rights That Are Prior to an Option

The foreclosure of a lien on the optioned property will terminate the option if the lien was given prior to the creation of the option and provided the optionee had notice of the existence of the lien or failed to record his interest first. See §4.42. Correspondingly, an option can be terminated by the exercise of a prior option, or by the acquisition of title to the optioned property by a purchaser under a prior contract to purchase the property assuming the optionee had notice of such rights or failed to record his interest first.

On exercise of the option, the optionee takes title subject to all matters and exceptions which were enforceable against the optionor as of the date the option was created. Thus, even if the optionee exercises the option before the acquisition of title by a party claiming an interest superior to that of the optionee, the rights of the optionee will still be terminated.

§4.16 2. Options Contained in Leases

If the option is in a lease, it may terminate on termination of the lease. Whether a default in a lease containing an option terminates the option depends on the agreement and the intent of the parties. If the option to purchase is conditioned on the performance of the lease terms, a breach of the lease can be treated by the lessor as the occurrence of an event that terminates the option. However, when the lessor accepts rent after the breach of the lease, a court may find a waiver of the default occurred, and that the option remains in effect. *Soon v Beckman* (1965) 234 CA2d 33, 44 CR 190. See also Anno, 115 ALR 376 (1938). See §4.18 for a discussion of assignability of options contained in leases.

§4.17   3. Death of Optionor Does Not Terminate Option

If the optionor dies before the exercise of the option by the optionee, or before the completion of the contract of sale after exercise, the option remains enforceable by the optionee on exercise against the estate of the optionor. *Bewick v Mecham* (1945) 26 C2d 92, 156 P2d 757; *O'Donnell v Lutter* (1945) 68 CA2d 376, 156 P2d 958.

However, with contracts to convey real or transfer personal property when remedy of specific performance is available (and there is no real controversy about the obligations of the parties), it is possible to avoid the expense and delay of a separate legal action against the optionor's estate. Probate Code §850 empowers the court to issue a decree authorizing and directing the executor or administrator to convey the property in accordance with the terms of a written contract with the decedent. This section authorizes such transfer without joining the beneficiaries of the estate to whom the title has passed at the death of the decedent (Probate Code §300) when the right of the petitioner in the property is free from doubt. If it appears, however, that the question of the optionee's right to the property is complex and the right is contested by other parties, or when monetary damages are sought rather than specific performance, it may be wiser to bring a legal action in a court of general jurisdiction. It is then possible to resolve all competing claims and to determine the appropriate legal or equitable relief, if any, to be granted to the optionee. *Messer v Hibernia Sav. & Loan Soc'y* (1906) 149 C 122, 84 P 835; *Estate of Corwin* (1882) 61 C 160.

H. Assignability of Options

§4.18   1. When Optionee May Assign

As long as the option contains no provisions regarding personal trust and requires only the payment of money, it is assignable. *Mas-*

terson v Sine (1968) 68 C2d 222, 65 CR 545; *Mott v Cline* (1927) 200 C 434, 253 P 718. Generally, an option for purchase on credit is not assignable unless it expressly so provides. *Prichard v Kimball* (1923) 190 C 757, 214 P 863.

In the absence of a provision making the exercise of an option contained in a lease personal to the lessee, the option may be separated from the lease and transferred by the lessee independently of the leasehold interest. *Spaulding v Yovino-Young* (1947) 30 C2d 138, 180 P2d 691. If the option cannot be separated from the lease, and the lease prohibits assignment without the lessor's permission, the optionee may not assign the option without permission from the lessor-optionor. *Prichard v Kimball, supra,* 190 C 757, 214 P 863. Since an option in a lease which is part of the lease is a covenant running with the land, an assignment of the lease is also an assignment of the option. *Bewick v Mecham* (1945) 26 C2d 92, 156 P2d 757. See §4.16 for a discussion of whether a default under a lease terminates an option contained in the lease.

§4.19   2. Rights and Obligations of Assignee of Optionee

When the optionee assigns the option without any reservation, all benefits under it are assigned. *Tatum v Levi* (1931) 117 CA 83, 3 P2d 963. Thus, if the optionor breaches, the assignee may recover the money paid by the optionee-assignor on the option. *Tatum v Levi, supra.* If the option provides that the optionee shall be the exclusive judge of the title and the consideration paid for the option shall be returned if the title is rejected, this right passes to the assignee. *Simmons v Zimmerman* (1904) 144 C 256, 79 P 451. The assignee takes the option subject to any reservation of interest in the property by the optionee-assignor. *Mulligan v Wilson* (1949) 94 CA2d 286, 210 P2d 526 (absolute assignment in which assignors reserved certain interests in profits or income on sale or lease of property).

An assignee takes the option subject to any obligations imposed on the optionee-assignor in the option agreement (CC §1589), although a mere assignment generally does not create a personal liability on the part of the assignee for the obligations imposed by the contract on the assignor absent an express assumption by the assignee. *Griffin v Williamson* (1955) 137 CA2d 308, 290 P2d 361. It has been held, however, that a clause binding successors and assigns eliminates the necessity for an express assumption of burdens.

Weidner v Zieglar (1933) 218 C 345, 350, 23 P2d 515, 517; *Citizens Suburban Co. v Rosemont Dev. Co.* (1966) 244 CA2d 666, 53 CR 551; *Brady v Fowler* (1920) 45 CA 592, 188 P 320. But see *Lisenby v Newton* (1898) 120 C 571, 52 P 813, in which the court held there was no personal liability to pay arising from an assignment of a contract with a successors and assigns clause because the promise to pay was only the personal covenant of the promisor.

§4.20   3. Optionor's Successors and Assigns

A party to whom the property has been conveyed, with notice of the option, takes subject to the optionee's right to exercise the option. *Walter G. Reese Co. v House* (1912) 162 C 740, 124 P 442. See also *Chapman v Great W. Gypsum Co.* (1932) 216 C 420, 14 P2d 758 (subsequent purchaser).

§4.21   I. Effect of Bankruptcy on Option

Under California law, an option contract is considered to be executory until both the option has been exercised and the contract for the acquisition of the optioned property has been completed. *Title Ins. & Trust Co. v King Land & Improvement Co.* (1912) 19 CA 458, 126 P 372. Thus, if bankruptcy proceedings are filed by or against the optionor either before the exercise of the option or before the completion of the contract after exercise, the option may be either assumed or rejected by the bankruptcy trustee under the trustee's powers to reject executory contracts. 11 USC §365(a); see *Gulf Petroleum, S.A. v Collazo* (1st Cir 1963) 316 F2d 257; *In re New York Investors Mut. Group, Inc.* (SD NY 1956) 143 F Supp 51 (both cases decided under §70(b) of former Bankruptcy Act of 1878).

If the bankruptcy trustee chooses to reject the option, the optionee then has a cause of action for damages against the bankrupt estate as an ordinary creditor. The optionee does not have any preference over other creditors of the estate. *Gulf Petroleum, S.A. v Collazo, supra.* However, if the option consideration is on deposit in an escrow at the time the trustee rejects the option, the optionee will be entitled to a refund of the consideration because under such circumstances the funds were never really delivered to the bankrupt and commingled with other funds. *Gulf Petroleum, S.A. v Collazo, supra.*

§4.22 J. Remedies

If the optionee pays value to the optionor for the option, the seller cannot revoke the option. *Jonas v Leland* (1947) 77 CA2d 770, 176 P2d 764. However, if no consideration is paid, the seller may revoke the option at any time before the exercise of the option; the optionee then has no recourse against the optionor under the agreement. See discussion at §4.10.

Generally, an optionee cannot enforce the option agreement unless and until he exercises the option in strict compliance with the terms of the contract, and is otherwise in strict compliance with all other terms and conditions of the option contract. *Briles v Paulson* (1915) 170 C 408, 149 P 804. If, however, when the time to exercise the option occurs, it is clear that the optionor cannot perform, then the optionee can sue to recover the option consideration without tendering performance or formally rescinding the contract, because to do so would be an idle act. *Tatum v Levi* (1931) 117 CA 83, 3 P2d 963. If the inability to perform is temporary, however, the optionee must tender performance. *Seeburg v El Royale Corp.* (1942) 54 CA2d 1, 128 P2d 362.

When the optionor can perform but does not, and the optionee tenders full performance, the optionee has various remedies:

(1) The optionee can bring a declaratory relief action to have the court declare the option unrevoked. *Diggs v El Royale Corp.* (1944) 67 CA2d 341, 154 P2d 444.

(2) Once the option is exercised, a bilateral executory contract is created which is specifically enforceable. *Schomaker v Osborne* (1967) 250 CA2d 887, 58 CR 827. To be specifically enforceable, the purchase price to be paid must be "just and reasonable." *Marsh v Lott* (1908) 8 CA 384, 97 P 163. The fairness of the consideration is measured at the time the contract was entered into rather than the time of breach. *Cushing v Levi* (1931) 117 CA 94, 3 P2d 958. Thus, if the value of the land rises after the date of the contract, it is still specifically enforceable if the consideration was fair and reasonable at the time the contract was entered into. *O'Connell v Lampe* (1929) 206 C 282, 274 P 336. See §§4.7-4.9 on adequate consideration. In bringing an action for specific performance, the optionee must allege with particularity the satisfaction of all express conditions necessary to enforce the option. *Estes v Hardesty* (1944) 66 CA2d 747, 152 P2d 772. In order to be specifically enforced, all terms of the

option contract must be clearly expressed. *Wilson v Ward* (1957) 155 CA2d 390, 317 P2d 1018.

(3) If the optionee is entitled to maintain an action for breach of the agreement without exercising the option, the optionee is entitled to the recovery of only actual damages under CC §3300. Such damage would not include the value of the property itself, but rather the value of the right to purchase the property less the amount agreed to be paid for the property. *Schmidt v Beckelman* (1960) 187 CA2d 462, 9 CR 736. If the optionee must tender full performance under the option agreement in order to maintain an action, and specific performance is neither available nor desired by the optionee, damages are governed by CC §3306. *Cushing v Levi, supra,* 117 CA 94, 3 P2d 958. In the latter situation, the optionee is entitled to recover an amount equal to the price paid under the option agreement, plus expenses incurred in examining title and preparing necessary papers, with interest, and, when bad faith is shown, the recovery will be an amount equal to the difference between the price agreed to be paid and the value of the estate at the time of breach, plus expenses incurred in preparing to enter on the land. See §§12.13-12.18.

§4.23   K. Effect on Option of Damage or Destruction to Improvements Located on the Optioned Property

Although California law is unclear, the general rule in other jurisdictions appears to be that, despite the fact that the optionor bears the risk of loss arising from damage or destruction occurring to improvements located on optioned property if the optionee does not exercise the option, the optionee cannot force a conveyance of the premises on payment of the option price less the value of the improvements destroyed or damaged. See Anno, 23 ALR 1225 (1923). The refusal of the optionor to repair damage to or destruction of the improvements is not a breach of the option contract; furthermore, the optionee is not entitled to a refund of the option consideration since there has not been a total failure of consideration. (The parties should consider a provision for risk and loss during the option period, *e.g.,* against fire or condemnation. See §4.37 on condemnation; chap 10 on risk of loss. The provision should be in the option agreement itself, because the provisions in the purchase and sale agreement attached as an exhibit will not take effect until the option is exercised.)

II. THE OPTION AGREEMENT

§4.24   A. Form: Introduction; Parties

Form 4.24-1

Option Agreement

This option agreement is made on _____, 19__, between _____ ("Owner") and _____ ("Optionee").

Comment: The same considerations pertain to naming parties to an option agreement as to a purchase and sale agreement. See §§3.9-3.31. See also provision at §4.31 for a warranty that the optionor owns the property and has a right to grant the option and convey the property.

§4.25   B. Form: Grant of Option

Form 4.25-1

Owner grants to Optionee an option to purchase the real property (the "Property") described in the purchase and sale agreement attached to this option as Exhibit _____, on the terms and conditions set forth in this option agreement and in the purchase and sale agreement attached.

Comment: The option agreement and the terms of the purchase and sale, if the option is exercised, may be combined in one agreement, or a separate purchase and sale agreement may be drafted and attached to the option agreement as an exhibit (as is set out in this provision). In the latter case, the option agreement contains only those provisions concerning the grant of the option and its exercise; the terms of the sale, in the event the option is exercised, are contained in the exhibit. See §§3.42-3.62 for provisions for the purchase and sale agreement. When an option is used, the purchase and sale agreement will seldom need to contain extensive conditions to the buyer's obligation. See §§3.68, 4.3.

§4.26   C. Form: Option Consideration

Form 4.26-1

Concurrently with the execution of the option, Optionee has paid to Owner the sum of $_____ as consideration for the option, which sum ____ [shall / shall not]____ be applied to or credited against the purchase price of the Property in the event the option is exercised.

Comment: This paragraph sets forth the consideration paid for the option. The consideration to be paid for the property, in the event the option is exercised, is set forth in the purchase and sale agreement to be attached as an exhibit to the option agreement. See §§4.7-4.10 for a discussion of the requirement that the option be supported by consideration in order to create an irrevocable offer to sell. The consideration for the option may, however, be applied to the purchase price in the event the option is exercised. See §4.4.

§4.27   D. Form: Term of Option

Form 4.27-1

The term of the option shall commence on the date of this option agreement and shall expire at _____ p.m. on _____, 19__.

Comment: California courts have enforced option agreements that failed to specify the term or duration of the option. See, *e.g., Hughes v Heffner* (1938) 29 CA2d 382, 84 P2d 540. In such cases, the court looks to the intent of the parties to determine a time period which is reasonable under the circumstances of the particular case. *Auslen v Johnson* (1953) 118 CA2d 319, 257 P2d 664; *Murfee v Porter* (1950) 96 CA2d 9, 214 P2d 543. To avoid disputes, however, the parties should set forth the term of the option with precision. The option may run for a specific period of time. The parties may instead tie its termination to a specific future event (see, *e.g., Auslen v Johnson, supra* (option to run until preliminary title report completed); *Fabares v Benjamin* (1960) 180 CA2d 264, 4 CR 359 (option to run two years from closing of escrow in another sale)), although this should be avoided because it creates problems of proof of occurrence of factual events. See §4.28 for provisions extending the option term.

§4.28   E. Form: Extensions of Option Term

Form 4.28-1

Optionee may extend the term of this option for a first extension period of _____ months by paying to Owner additional option consideration in the amount of $_____, and Optionee may further extend the term of this option for _____ additional extension periods of _____ month(s) each by paying to Owner additional option consideration of $_____, for each of the _____ extensions, each such payment to be delivered before the expiration of this option or the expiration of any extension period of this option which may then be in effect, and by providing to Owner written notice of Optionee's intent to extend the term of this option.

Comment: Parties to an option contract may agree to extend its term. The optionee must give new consideration for the extension in order for the extension to be binding. See, *e.g., Auslen v Johnson* (1953) 118 CA2d 319, 257 P2d 664. (Although the court tacitly upheld an oral extension agreement in *Auslen,* extensions of the option term should be in writing, signed by all parties.)

§4.29   F. Form: Manner of Exercising Option

Form 4.29-1

Provided Optionee is not in default under any term or provision of this option, the option may be exercised by Optionee's delivering to Owner, before the expiration of the option term, written notice of such exercise (the "exercise notice"), which exercise notice shall state that the option is exercised without condition or qualification. The exercise notice must be accompanied by (a) two copies of a purchase and sale agreement identical to the form of purchase and sale agreement attached as Exhibit _____ executed by Optionee and with the blank in paragraph ____[*specify provision designating closing date*]____ of the purchase agreement completed by insertion of a date which is not less than _____ nor more than _____ days following the date the exercise notice is given, and (b) Optionee's check payable to ____[*name of escrow holder*]____ in the amount of the deposit set forth in paragraph ____ [*specify provision stating deposit*]____ of the purchase agreement.

Comment: To avoid disputes, the parties should set forth precisely the actions that will constitute exercise. The optionee should take particular care to comply with these terms in exactly the order and manner specified.

The form of option agreement set out in this chapter is designed to include, as an exhibit, the form of purchase and sale agreement to be entered into by the parties on exercise of the option. For this reason, after the option is exercised the parties are to execute the purchase and sale agreement in duplicate. See §4.30. If any dates in the purchase agreement are to run from the date of exercise of the option (*e.g.,* the closing date), this provision should state which dates are to be filled in before the purchase agreement is submitted to the seller-owner and the manner of their completion. (An alternative is to draft the purchase agreement to refer to the date the option is exercised, *e.g.,* "the close of escrow shall be ____ days after the exercise of the option granted for the purchase of the property.")

If the purchase and sale agreement calls for an initial deposit (in addition to the consideration for the option itself) at the time of its execution, the deposit should be made at the time the option is exercised. Courts will not require tender of payment in the exercise of an option if the option agreement does not require tender of payment as a part of the method of exercise. *Erich v Granoff* (1980) 109 CA3d 920, 167 CR 538. When tender is not required for exercise, the optionee need tender only payment for the property as performance of the bilateral sales contract created by exercising the option. *Cates v McNeil* (1915) 169 C 697, 147 P 944. When the contract does include tender of payment, such payment should be made in precisely the form required in order to properly exercise the option. See, *e.g., Bourdieu v Baker* (1935) 6 CA2d 150, 44 P2d 587. The optionee must take care not to attach any new conditions to such payment. See *Cummings v Bullock* (9th Cir 1966) 367 F2d 182 (contract required exercise by the payment of $4000; optionee failed to exercise when he put $4000 in escrow and conditioned payment on receipt of an agreement and a warranty deed). An optionee who attempts to exercise an option in a manner inconsistent with the provisions specified in the agreement is considered to have made a counteroffer rather than an exercise of an option. *Pruitt v Fontana* (1956) 143 CA2d 675, 300 P2d 371; *Bourdieu v Baker, supra.*

If the option agreement does not set forth the method of exercise, the optionee may exercise the option by using any reasonable means of communication calculated to notify the optionor of acceptance, before the time for exercise expires. *Cates v McNeil, supra,* 169 C 697, 147 P 944; *Murfee v Porter* (1950) 96 CA2d 9, 214 P2d 543.

§4.30   G. Form: Completion of Sale

Form 4.30-1

On receipt by Owner before the expiration of the option term of the exercise notice and two copies of the purchase agreement executed by Optionee, Owner shall execute the purchase agreement and deliver an executed copy to Optionee. Owner's failure to execute and deliver a copy of the purchase agreement in accordance with this paragraph shall not affect the validity of the purchase agreement. The purchase agreement shall be immediately effective and binding on both Owner and Optionee without further execution by the parties, on exercise of the option in accordance with paragraph ____[see §4.29]____ of the option agreement.

Comment: On exercise of the option, an executed bilateral purchase and sale agreement is created, the terms of which then govern the rights and obligations of the parties in the completion of the transaction. The option agreement should be clear that the terms of the purchase agreement become binding on both parties on exercise of the option without further execution of the purchase agreement by the optionor. Some attorneys prefer to combine the purchase agreement with the option agreement in order to avoid any dispute concerning whether the purchase agreement must be separately executed to be binding. The requirement in this provision that the optionor execute and return a copy of the purchase agreement is only for the convenience of the parties; execution and delivery by the optionor is not necessary to create a binding purchase and sale agreement.

§4.31 H. Form: Representations and Warranties

Form 4.31-1

Owner warrants that it is the owner of the Property and has marketable and insurable fee simple title to the Property free of restrictions, leases, liens, and other encumbrances. In the event this Option is exercised by Optionee, Owner will convey title to the property to Optionee by grant deed subject only to (a) taxes for the current year which are not then due and payable, and (b) only those exceptions which Optionee has approved in writing in accordance with paragraph ____[see §4.32]____ of this document. Owner covenents and agrees that during the option term and until the Property is conveyed to Optionee in the event this option is exercised, Owner will not encumber the Property in any way nor grant any property or contract right relating to the Property without the prior written consent of Optionee.

Comment: Before paying the option consideration, the optionee will want some assurance that the optionor either owns the property, or is otherwise able to acquire it, in order to be able to convey the property in the event the option is exercised. This provision should be modified if the optionor does not own the property (but has some other right to acquire it) at the time the option is granted. The clause should also be consistent with the provision in §4.32 concerning the state of title at the time of conveyance of the property.

§4.32   I. Form: Condition of Title

Form 4.32-1

Within ____[e.g., 10]____ days after execution of this option by both parties, Owner shall deliver to Optionee a preliminary report of the condition of title to the Property. From the date of receipt by Optionee, Optionee shall have _____ days in which to approve or disapprove of any and all exceptions shown on the report.

If Optionee disapproves any exception to title, as provided above, Owner shall notify Optionee within _____ days of notice of disapproval from Optionee if Owner is unwilling to clear the disapproved exceptions. If Owner elects not to clear any such exceptions, Optionee may elect, by giving notice to Owner within _____ days of receipt of Owner's notice, to terminate this Option and receive a refund of the option consideration paid to Owner, or to waive this condition and this Option shall then remain in full force and effect. Failure of Optionee to give notice shall ____[waive this condition / terminate this Option]____.

Comment: This provision is included in the option agreement when the optionee wishes to conclude an agreement with the optionor concerning the state of title before a decision is made whether to exercise the option. For this reason, the time limits in this provision should not extend beyond the time provided in §4.27 for the exercise of the option. If this provision is included in the option agreement, the purchase and sale agreement should make reference to this provision and provide that title is to be conveyed at the closing in accordance with this provision.

An alternative to the use of this provision is to include a provision in the purchase and sale agreement concerning the examination of a preliminary report and the state of title at closing (see, *e.g.,* provisions in §§3.55, 3.79 and 3.80). A third approach is to specify in the option agreement the state of title to be conveyed if the option is exercised. This approach, when feasible, is the most favorable to the optionee.

§4.33   J. Form: Right of Entry on Property

Form 4.33-1

During the option term, Optionee and its designated agents and independent contractors shall have the right to enter on the Property to the extent necessary for the purpose of ____[state purpose and limitation, e.g., conducting soil tests and engineering studies]____. Optionee agrees to repair any damages it or its agents or independent contractors shall cause to the Property, and further agrees to indemnify and hold Owner harmless from any and all costs, expenses, losses, attorneys' fees and liabilities (including, but not limited to, claims of mechanics' liens) incurred or sustained by Owner as a result of any acts of Optionee, its agents, or independent contractors pursuant to the right granted by this paragraph.

Comment: A provision concerning the optionee's right of entry on the property should usually be included in the option agreement because the right to examine the property before being committed to purchase is often a significant reason for the use of an option.

§4.34   K. Form: Owner's Cooperation in Seeking Permits and Approvals

Form 4.34-1

Owner agrees to execute any and all documents or to join in any applications that may be required to obtain approval of the development plan proposed by Optionee by any municipal or other agency having jurisdiction. Optionee agrees to hold Owner harmless from any costs and expenses arising in connection with gaining approval of the Optionee's development plan.

Comment: Frequently, the potential buyer uses an option in order to determine if the necessary approvals for the proposed development can be obtained before making a commitment to purchase the property. Governmental regulations often require that the owner execute or join in applications for permits and approvals.

§4.35   L. Form: Time of Essence; Failure To Exercise Option

Form 4.35-1

Time is of the essence of this option agreement. If the option is not exercised in the manner provided in paragraph ____[see §4.29]____ before the expiration of the option term, Optionee shall have no interest whatever in the Property and the option may not be revived by any subsequent payment or further action by Optionee

[*Add if appropriate*]

and Optionee agrees to deliver to Owner all soil tests, engineering and marketing studies, and the like respecting the Property in Optionee's possession or under Optionee's control.

Comment: Option agreements may terminate under CC §1587(2), which provides for automatic revocation of the offer to sell if the optionee fails to exercise the option during the option term. Notice is unnecessary; the burden of proof falls on the optionee to show that the option remained in effect at time of exercise. *Auslen v Johnson* (1953) 118 CA2d 319, 257 P2d 664.

In California, time is automatically assumed to be of the essence of an option that has a specific term. *Rosenaur v Pacelli* (1959) 174 CA2d 673, 345 P2d 102. "The rule that in equity time is not of the essence of a contract does not apply to a mere offer to make a contract." 174 CA2d at 677, 345 P2d at 105. In an option contract, the offer automatically terminates at the end of the specified time period. *Auslen v Johnson, supra,* 118 CA2d 319, 257 P2d 664. Unless the parties specifically recite that time is *not* of the essence (see *Hughes v Heffner* (1938) 29 CA2d 382, 84 P2d 540), courts will strictly enforce option deadlines. *Scarbery v Bill Patch Land & Water Co.* (1960) 184 CA2d 87, 7 CR 408; *Sheveland v Reed* (1958) 159 CA2d 820, 324 P2d 633.

In the strict construction of time for performance, California courts distinguish between the *exercise* of the option and the *performance* of the bilateral contract created by the exercise of the option. *Murfee v Porter* (1950) 96 CA2d 9, 214 P2d 543. The assumption by the court that time is of the essence applies only to those activities required for exercise.

§4.36   M. Form: Recording Quitclaim Deed on Termination of Option

Form 4.36-1

If this option is terminated, Optionee agrees, if requested by Owner, to execute, acknowledge, and deliver a quitclaim deed to Owner within _____ days after termination and to execute, acknowledge, and deliver any other documents required by any title company to remove the cloud of this option from the Property.

Comment: A recorded option or memorandum of option acts as a cloud on optionor's title for one year after it has expired, whether it has expired by operation of law or by the terms of the option itself. CC §1213.5. (See §4.43 for a provision for a memorandum of option.) The most effective method for removing the cloud is to record a quitclaim deed executed by the optionee. Instead of merely agreeing to deliver a quitclaim deed if the option expires, the parties may provide that the optionee will, at the time the option is signed, deposit with the optionor, or a third party, a quitclaim deed executed by the optionee that contains instructions for its recording on lapse or default of the option. Because, in this procedure, the quitclaim deed would be recorded without the optionee's further consent, a determination would first need to be made whether the optionee is in default or has failed to exercise the option. Many title companies will not make these determinations and it may be difficult to find a third party who will assume the risks of these decisions if the optionee refuses to agree. Moreover, such instruction can always be effectively revoked by optionee in the event of dispute.

A third possibility is for the parties to include a clause in the option that provides that the option will have no effect against bona fide purchasers unless a memorandum extending the option period is recorded before a certain date. Many title companies will exclude the option as an exception under these circumstances, but may require an additional premium. Some title companies, however, still require the optionee's agreement that the option is no longer in effect.

If the option does not provide for the removal of the option from the record, the optionor's remedy is a quiet title action. See *Krobitzsch v Middleton* (1946) 72 CA2d 804, 165 P2d 729.

§4.37 N. Form: Condemnation

Form 4.37-1

If before the close of escrow, either Owner or Optionee receives notice of any condemnation or eminent domain proceeding, or any proceeding in lieu of condemnation being initiated against the Property, the party receiving the notice shall promptly notify the other party of that fact. Optionee may elect to either proceed with the purchase contemplated by this option or to terminate this option within ____[e.g., 15]____ days from the date the notice is received. If Optionee elects to so terminate, Owner shall refund to Optionee all option consideration (cash or notes) within ____[e.g., 5]____ days of the date of such termination. If Optionee proceeds with the purchase in accordance with all of the terms of this option, all condemnation proceeds shall be paid to Optionee (or assigned if not yet collected).

Comment: California courts formerly treated an optionee under an option agreement for the purchase of real property as the owner of a contract interest rather than a property interest. *People v Ocean Shore R.R.* (1949) 90 CA2d 464, 203 P2d 579. Thus, under earlier cases, the optionee was not entitled to share in a condemnation award arising out of eminent domain proceedings against the real property when such proceedings were commenced before the exercise of the option. In *County of San Diego v Miller* (1975) 13 C3d 684, 119 CR 491, the court held that, based on the view that compensability in condemnation proceedings depends on concepts of fairness and public policy rather than traditional common law concepts of property, an optionee has a compensable property right. The measure of damage to the optionee is the excess, if any, of the total condemnation award above the exercise price under the option.

This provision gives the optionee the right to receive the entire condemnation award by electing to purchase the property from the optionor in accordance with the option agreement. An alternative would be to provide that the optionor has the right to terminate the option agreement (and receive the full amount of the award) in the event of condemnation. In the absence of an agreement to the contrary the matter would be left to case law (with the expectation that optionee would receive the amount of the award over the exercise price under the option). See also §4.23 for a discussion of risk of loss due to fire or other causes.

§4.38   O. Form: Notices

Form 4.38-1

All notices, demands, requests, and exercises under this option by either party shall be hand-delivered or sent by United States mail, registered or certified, postage prepaid, addressed to the other party as follows:

Owner: ____[name]____
____[address]____
Optionee: ____[name]____
____[address]____

Notices, demands, requests, and exercises served in the above manner shall be considered sufficiently given or served for all purposes under this option at the time the notice, demand, or request is hand-delivered or postmarked to the addresses shown above.

Comment: The manner of giving notice is crucial to determining whether the option has been exercised in accordance with its terms. See §4.29 on the method of exercising the option.

§4.39 P. Form: Assignment of Option

Form 4.39-1

Optionee ____[*may / may not*]____ assign this option and the rights under it

[*Add if limited right to assign*]

except under the following limitations: ____[*list limitations*]____.

Comment: It is important that the agreement specifically state whether the option is assignable; if there are conditions to its assignment, these conditions should be stated. See §§4.18-4.20 for a discussion of the assignability of options.

§4.40 Q. Form: Attorneys' Fees

Form 4.40-1

If it becomes necessary for either party to take any action to enforce this option, or any of its terms, the prevailing party shall be entitled to reasonable attorneys' fees and all costs.

Comment: The attorneys' fees clause, if used, should be included in both the option agreement and in the purchase and sale agreement attached as an exhibit. See §3.181 for another provision for attorneys' fees and a discussion of that provision.

§4.41 R. Form: Entire Agreement; Signatures

Form 4.41-1

This option contains the entire agreement between the parties respecting the matters set forth, and supersedes all prior agreements between the parties respecting such matters.

Executed on the day and year first above written.

By __[*Signature; typed name below*]__
Owner
By __[*Signature; typed name below*]__
Optionee

Comment: To be enforceable, the option agreement must be signed by the party who will convey the property if the option is exercised. See §3.9 for a discussion of the necessary parties to a purchase and sale agreement and §3.36 for a discussion of the requirement that the agreement be in writing.

III. RECORDING THE OPTION

§4.42   A. Reasons for Recording Memorandum of Option

If, in violation of the option agreement, the optionor transfers the property to a purchaser or encumbrancer who records first and who has no notice of the optionee's right to buy, the optionee's ability to acquire the property under the option agreement is lost. CC §1214. See §11.90 on priority. To protect against this result, the optionee may give constructive notice to subsequent purchasers and encumbrancers by recording the option agreement or a short form of memorandum of it. See §4.36 for a provision for recording a quitclaim deed on termination when a memorandum of option is to be recorded.

Recordation statutes are designed to protect bona fide purchasers for value in disputes that arise from the priorities of several competing interests in a parcel of real property. In California, every conveyance of real property (except a lease for a term not to exceed one year) is void against subsequent bona fide purchasers, mortgagees, or judgment creditors who are without notice of the conveyance *and* who record their interest first. CC §1214; see §11.90. Notice, for this purpose, can be either actual notice of the conveyance or interest in the real property or constructive notice. Under California law, the recordation of an option acts as constructive notice of its contents to subsequent purchasers and mortgagees for one year after it has expired by its terms, or by operation of law, or for a longer period if a document has been recorded that shows the option has been exercised or extended. See CC §1215 (conveyance defined), §1213.5 (termination of notice after expiration of recorded option to purchase), and §1213 (recorded conveyance as notice of contents). See also Govt C §27280 (instruments and judgments recordable) and §27288 (party required to execute and acknowledge or prove agreement or other document affecting interest in real property).

If a party acquires an interest in property after an option has been given, even if acquired before the option is exercised, and that party has either actual or constructive notice of the existence of the option, or being without notice fails to record first, the optionee's exercise of the option will extinguish the intervening party's interest. *Smith v Bangham* (1909) 156 C 359, 104 P 689. This holds because under such circumstances the title that the optionee receives when he exercises the option relates back to the date the option was given. *Smith v Bangham, supra.* See also *Anthony v Enzler* (1976) 61 CA3d 872, 132 CR 553. See §4.12.

In order to impart constructive notice, an option or a memorandum of it must be properly recorded. An option that is improperly acknowledged is not entitled to be recorded and therefore does not give constructive notice of its contents (*Hale v Pendergrast* (1919) 42 CA 104, 183 P 833) until one year after its recordation. CC §1207. Moreover, when an option is recorded outside the chain of title, it is not constructive notice to subsequent purchasers, mortgagees, or judgment creditors. *Ludy v Zumwalt* (1927) 85 CA 119, 259 P 52.

§4.43   B. Form: Memorandum of Option

Form 4.43-1

Recording requested by	)
	)
	)
After recording, return to	)
	)
	)
	)

Memorandum of Option Agreement

By this memorandum of option, made ＿＿＿＿＿＿＿＿＿＿, 19＿＿, concurrently with an option agreement between the same parties covering the same property, ＿＿＿＿[name of optionor]＿＿＿＿, optionor, and ＿＿＿＿[name of optionee]＿＿＿＿, optionee, agree:

1. Optionor grants to optionee the right, on the terms and conditions stated in that agreement, to purchase the property described ＿＿＿＿[in Exhibit ＿＿＿＿＿＿＿＿ / as follows:]＿＿＿＿, provided the option is exercised before ＿＿＿＿[date option expires]＿＿＿＿.

2. ＿＿＿＿[Set forth other provisions from option agreement that parties consider necessary to protect their rights]＿＿＿＿.

Comment: If the parties desire, for reasons discussed in §4.42, to record a short form of the option, this form may be suitable. On the data at the top of the form and on the requirements for recordation, see §§11.90-11.93. To be recorded, the memorandum must be executed and acknowledged by the party whose real property is affected. Govt C §27288.

Some title officers express doubt about the effect of a document stating "This is an abstract of an agreement," but they express no doubt about an abstract that purports, by its own terms, to transfer the interest in question. Therefore, this form uses the language, "Optionor grants to optionee . . . ."

This form is not suitable for successive options or options that may be extended. In those situations, the optionee needs to give constructive notice of the full extent of his option right, but the optionor must avoid a continuing cloud on his title if the optionee fails to exercise any option or extension that is a prerequisite to later rights.

It is no solution to require that the optionee's notice of exercise or extension be recorded, because the document must be executed by the party whose property is affected. Govt C §27288. To request the optionor to execute in advance a series of documents evidencing the extensions as they are made is generally unsatisfactory, because neither party has complete assurance that the other will record or retain the documents as agreed, and title companies almost never agree to exercise what is essentially a trust function without having formal trust authorization and compensation. Under a properly drawn trust instrument and with title vested in the trustee, title company reluctance might be overcome, but few sellers are willing to make such transfers in trust, and many clients begrudge the additional legal fees required for this solution. The alternative method of recording a quitclaim deed from the optionee is discussed in §4.36; see Comment in §4.36 for a discussion of the fact that recording an option creates a cloud on title.

5

Richard P. Sims

Seller Financing

RICHARD P. SIMS, B.S., 1965, San Diego State University; LL.B., 1968, Columbia University. Mr. Sims is a member of Rutan & Tucker, Newport Beach.

Portions of this chapter were adapted by CEB legal staff from chapters 2 and 9 of California Real Estate Sales Transactions (Cal CEB 1967).

I. INTRODUCTION

§5.1   A. Why Seller Financing?

Few buyers of real property pay the purchase price entirely from their own funds. Most finance the purchase by borrowing from an institutional, governmental, or individual lender; by acquiring the property subject to existing encumbrances; by having the seller defer payment of at least a portion of the price; or by a combination of these devices. The indebtedness resulting from financing is usually secured by withholding title to the property until payment has been made, by encumbering title to the property, or by encumbering some other property. In addition, the seller has a lien on the property for as much of the price as remains unpaid, to the extent that the property is otherwise unsecured. CC §3046.

Although most funds for real property financing come from institutional lenders, such as savings and loan associations and banks (see §6.1), seller financing plays an important role in the real property market. Each party to a sale may have reasons for wanting to defer payment of all or part of the purchase price. The seller may want the tax advantages of installment reporting (§5.10), or be able to negotiate a higher purchase price in exchange for deferring its receipt. For the buyer, seller financing provides the protections of antideficiency legislation (CCP §580b; but see *Spangler v Memel*

(1972) 7 C3d 603, 102 CR 807, discussed in §5.39), and may enable the buyer to acquire property for which he does not have cash and cannot obtain third party financing.

If the seller defers part of the price and encumbers the property, he may also be asked to participate in the buyer's financing by subordinating the priority of his lien to liens for financing obtained by the buyer from third parties or by agreeing to release his lien from portions of the property as the property is developed or sold. Subordination is discussed in §§5.39-5.54; release in §§5.55-5.67.

B. Lawyer's Role in Financing

§5.2   1. Functions

The lawyer's role in the financing aspects of a sale transaction may be crucial. He or she may be called on to perform a wide range of functions, beginning with negotiating the purchase price and the extent to which the seller will participate in financing the buyer's development of the property. Counsel may be required to structure the financing to minimize adverse tax consequences to the seller or to satisfy the requirements of title insurance companies, lenders, and governmental agencies. The lawyer must either draft the purchase and sale agreement or evaluate one that someone else has drawn. If the buyer needs time to arrange financing for the purchase, his lawyer must ensure that the agreement affords the necessary time. The seller's lawyer must make certain that the buyer is not allowed to postpone the sale unreasonably and that, if the delay is to be substantial, the seller is protected against possible fluctuations in value. See §§3.151-3.152 for a discussion of conditions to protect buyers and sellers in these situations.

The attorney must be ready to furnish advice concerning the kind of financing to be provided. If the seller is to provide financing, the type of financing and the security arrangement must be considered carefully because they may have significantly different tax consequences and differences concerning the remedies available on breach and default.

§5.3   2. Standard of Care

The need for the attorney to demonstrate a high degree of care, skill, and diligence in advising clients and drafting documents relating to real property financing cannot be overemphasized. Different methods of financing present different drafting problems. For example, a purchase agreement with an improperly drafted subordination or partial release clause may be unenforceable or subject the completed sale to rescission. See §§5.42, 5.59.

To the extent that the seller releases land from the lien or subordinates the lien, the security for the note is reduced, but the buyer may be unable to purchase the land or complete the development without subordination or releases. The extent to which subordination or release provisions are used and their effect on the price are problems that vary in each transaction, and the attorney must be able to anticipate possible problems and draft provisions that effectuate and protect the client's interests.

The attorney is held to a duty to possess knowledge of plain and elementary legal principles, and to perform sufficient research to be able to make informed and intelligent decisions. *Smith v Lewis* (1975) 13 C3d 349, 118 CR 621. If he holds himself out as an expert in a particular field, the standard applied in determining whether he has performed negligently will be the degree of skill exercised by other experts in the field. *Wright v Williams* (1975) 47 CA3d 802, 121 CR 194. Of particular interest is *Starr v Mooslin* (1971) 14 CA3d 988, 92 CR 583, which pertained to a transaction in which the seller agreed to take back a promissory note for the balance of the purchase price and to subordinate her lien to a construction loan. The seller recovered a substantial damage award against her attorney for his negligence in drafting escrow instructions that failed to provide adequate protection against the possibility of the buyer's default on the purported construction loan, despite the attorney's reliance on custom and practice of local escrow holders. See also §1.12 concerning the attorney's duty of care.

II. SELLER FINANCING DEVICES

A. The Installment Land Contract

§5.4   1. Defined; Distinguished From Purchase and Sale Agreement

Rather than securing the unpaid portion of the purchase price by a conventional security instrument such as a deed of trust (see §5.9), the parties may agree that the seller will retain legal title to the property until the buyer completes payment of the purchase price.

Under such an agreement, commonly referred to as an installment land contract, equitable title vests in the buyer, who has the right to acquire legal title on completion of the contract, and the contract encumbers the seller's legal title. Normally, possession is transferred to the buyer on delivery of the contract, as are the risks of ownership. Although the seller does not receive a security interest in the property, retention of title operates as the security and the installment land contract is therefore treated as a security device. *Venable v Harmon* (1965) 233 CA2d 297, 43 CR 490.

The installment land contract used as a security device must be distinguished from the purchase and sale agreement (see chap 3) also known as a marketing contract, under which legal title and possession are transferred to the buyer concurrently with payment of the purchase price through escrow. On closing, any deferred balance of the purchase price under a marketing contract will then be secured by a deed of trust, mortgage, or other security device. Further compounding the confusion over terminology, an installment land contract is called a "real property sales contract" in the Civil Code and is defined as an agreement to convey title on satisfaction of specified conditions, "which does not require conveyance of title within one year from the date of formation of the contract." CC §2985. Note that this definition could include a marketing contract which does not require closing within one year, even though the parties have no intention that the marketing contract function as a security device.

§5.5   2. Periods of Usage; Disadvantages

The installment land contract was widely utilized in the early 1960s as an inexpensive and expedient financing vehicle, especially for lower priced developments. It enjoyed some popularity in the 1970s as a device for circumventing due-on-sale clauses based on the decision in *Tucker v Lassen Sav. & Loan Ass'n* (1974) 12 C3d 629, 116 CR 633. When the California Supreme Court extended the holding of *Tucker* to sales of property whose financing was evidenced by notes secured by deeds of trust in *Wellenkamp v Bank of America* (1978) 21 C3d 943, 148 CR 379, this rationale for utilizing installment land contracts disappeared. See §5.24 for a discussion of due-on-sale clauses.

Before its brief resurgence in the 1970s, the installment land contract had gradually fallen into disuse because of a long series of court decisions that eliminated any legal advantage the form offered sellers over the use of a note secured by a deed of trust. See California Mortgage and Deed of Trust Practice §1.7 (Cal CEB 1979) for a discussion of judicial erosion of seller's rights under installment land contracts.

Disadvantages of the installment land contract include:

(a) The applicability of CCP §580b, barring deficiency judgments (*Venable v Harmon* (1965) 233 CA2d 297, 43 CR 490);

(b) The existence of the right to reinstatement of the contract, even for a willfully defaulting buyer (*MacFadden v Walker* (1971) 5 C3d 809, 97 CR 537; *Newhouse v Upchurch* (1971) 22 CA3d 204, 99 CR 436; *Barkis v Scott* (1949) 34 C2d 116, 208 P2d 367);

(c) The defaulting buyer's right to recover, as restitution, any amounts paid to the seller in excess of the seller's actual damages (*Freedman v The Rector* (1951) 37 C2d 16, 230 P2d 629);

(d) The seller's inability to utilize an unlawful detainer action to evict a defaulting buyer who refuses to vacate the premises (*Greene v Municipal Court* (1975) 51 CA3d 446, 124 CR 139; CCP §1161).

These disadvantages support the conclusion that the installment land contract is becoming obsolete as a security device in California and ordinarily should not be recommended as a financing method. Despite its disadvantages and formidable legislative, judicial, and administrative hurdles, some sellers, including developers, continue to use the installment land contract. Because of this continued use, and because many contracts executed in the 1960s and 1970s are still in existence, installment land contracts are discussed in this chapter. Forms for installment land contracts are not presented, however, because their use is not recommended.

§5.6   3. Protective Statutory and Regulatory Provisions

A real property sales contract is defined in CC §2985 as an agreement to convey title on satisfaction of specific conditions, which does not require conveyance within one year of the agreement's formation. See §5.4. Civil Code §§2985.1-2985.6 regulate the use of these contracts and prohibit certain acts that might prejudice the seller's ability to convey unencumbered legal title to the buyer on completion of the contract. For example, CC §2985.4 restricts the seller's use of impound payments for insurance and taxes, and CC §2985.5

requires that the contract contain certain information regarding tax payments and the contract term. Civil Code §2985.6 permits the buyer's prepayment of the balance due under a contract for sale of land subdivided into a residential lot or lots which contain a dwelling for not more than four families, except that the seller may prohibit prepayment for up to 12 months following sale. When applicable, CC §2985.6 may make use of the real property sales contract inappropriate for the seller who wishes to limit payments in future years by reporting the sale on an installment basis under IRC §453. See §5.10.

Regulations of the California Department of Real Estate applicable to the use of real property sales contracts in subdivision offerings are discussed in Guide to California Subdivision Sales Law §§3.31-3.32 (Cal CEB 1974). These regulations (10 Cal Adm C §§2814-2814.8) require that the seller deposit the buyer's payments in an impound account until various specified conditions for the buyer's protection have been complied with.

§5.7   4. Income Tax Reporting by Seller

A seller who utilizes an installment land contract as a security device instead of a note and deed of trust can qualify for installment reporting (see §5.10) as long as the sale complies with the requirements of IRC §453. See generally §§5.10-5.14. Before enactment of the Installment Sales Revision Act of 1980, Pub L 96-471, 94 Stat 2247 (1980), the installment land contract afforded the seller an advantage in sales of property subject to an obligation which exceeded the seller's basis in meeting the requirement that payments in the year of sale not exceed 30 percent of the total selling price. Because the Installment Sales Revision Act eliminated the 30-percent requirement, however, the installment land contract no longer provides this advantage in qualifying for installment reporting.

A seller who employs an installment land contract instead of a note and deed of trust may, however, be able to defer reporting gain under the deferred payment method (see §5.16), also sometimes referred to as "cost recovery" reporting. Under this method, the seller reports no gain until payments received equal his or her basis in the property. A sale will qualify for deferred payment reporting only if the security instrument is not marketable because it does not have a readily determinable sale price. See *Burnet v Logan* (1931) 283 US 404. In the Installment Sales Revision Act, Congress extended installment reporting to sales in which the selling price is subject to a contingency (Act §2(a), IRC §453(i)(2)), and in doing so expressed its intention that deferred payment reporting would now be "limited to those rare and extraordinary cases involving sales for a contingent price where the fair market value of the purchaser's obligation cannot reasonably be ascertained." SR No. 96-1000, 96th Cong, 2d Sess (1980), reprinted in 1980 US Code Cong & Ad News 8340, 8363.

When the security instrument is a note secured by a deed of trust, a present dollar value can almost always be determined, and the seller will be required to report that value in the year of sale for tax purposes unless the transaction qualifies for installment reporting (see §§5.10-5.15). In some installment land contracts, however, the sale price is neither stated nor readily determinable, and such sales may qualify for deferred payment reporting. An illustration is an installment land contract under which the buyer assumes some nonmonetary obligation in addition to, or in place of, the obligation to pay money. See Anderson, Tax Factors in Real Estate Operations 147 (6th ed 1980). The presence of the nonmonetary factor may make the sale price incapable of being ascertained. In the past, the tax court frequently held that installment land contracts qualified for deferred payment reporting if they were not the "equivalent of cash"; that is, if they were not freely negotiable (see *Childers v U.S.* (DC Iowa 1965) 66-1 USTC ¶9183, 17 AFTR2d ¶621; *Estate of Coid Hurlbut* (1956) 25 TC 1286, nonacq 1956-2 Cum Bull 10; *Estate of Clarence W. Ennis* (1955) 23 TC 799, nonacq 1956-1 Cum Bull 6), but the federal courts had limited this cash equivalency theory and cast doubt on its continuing vitality. See *Warren Jones Co. v Commissioner* (9th Cir 1975) 524 F2d 788; *Heller Trust v Commissioner* (9th Cir 1967) 382 F2d 675. Under the Installment Sales Revision Act, installment reporting, rather than deferred payment reporting, must be used if the installment land contract contains a stated or ascertainable sale price. See US Code Cong & Ad News 8340, 8363. Deferred payment reporting would presumably still be available for a sale such as that in *Burnet v Logan, supra,* 283 US 404, in which there was no price stated and consideration for the sale was not determinable in the year of sale.

§5.8   B. Lease With Option To Purchase

A prospective buyer can acquire possession but defer payment of the purchase price by using a lease with an option to purchase (lease-option). This form of transaction is often used when (1) a buyer, usually of a home, is unable to meet a lending institution's standards for a loan, (2) a commercial lessee wants the right to purchase the property during the tenancy or at its end, (3) institutional lenders have insufficient funds available for real property loans or (4) interest rates currently charged by institutional lenders are high and are expected to decline during the term of the option.

The typical option to purchase can be exercised at any time during the lease term. Because the market value of the property on the sale date is likely to be higher than at the beginning of the lease term, the value of the option increases as its duration lengthens. To take account of inflation, the sales price may be determined by an appraisal or by a formula using the consumer price index.

A lease-option may actually be a security device for a sale with retention of title in the seller, rather than a lease with an option to purchase. Buyers and sellers have used the lease-option as a hidden security device (1) to avoid exercise of a due-on-sale clause in an existing loan at a favorable interest rate (see §5.24); (2) to avoid subordinating the seller's interest to the buyer's construction financing (see §§5.39-5.54); (3) to obtain favorable tax treatment (see Commercial Real Property Lease Practice §§4.65-4.66; 5.22-5.25 (Cal CEB 1976); and (4) to avoid the effects of government regulation (*Frank Lyon Co. v U.S.* (1978) 435 US 561).

In determining whether a lease-option is a hidden security device, courts will look to the intent of the parties as evidenced by the agreement's provisions and the economic realities of the transaction. See Moewe, *Sale and Leaseback Financing of Real Estate as Mortgages under California Law,* 48 Cal SBJ 554 (1973). An important factor in determining the existence of a security device is a disparity between the purchase price, when the option is exercised, and the property's value. *In re San Francisco Indus. Park, Inc.* (ND Cal 1969) 307 F Supp 271. A security device rather than a lease-option will also be found when (1) the rent payments are too high to be economically realistic and (2) the payments plus the option price closely approximate the fair market value of the property at the time of the agreement. *Robinson v Elliot* (9th Cir 1958) 262 F2d 383;

Haggard v Commissioner (9th Cir 1956) 241 F2d 288; *Oesterreich v Commissioner* (9th Cir 1955) 226 F2d 798; Frank, *Lease With Purchase Option May Be Deemed Disguised Purchase If Caution Not Used*, 21 J Tax 66 (1964). Apparently the courts will accept the parties' characterization of the transaction as a lease-option if the format is compelled by business or regulatory realities and not solely by tax-avoidance considerations. *Frank Lyon Co. v U.S., supra.* If the transaction is treated as a true lease, the lessor is entitled to deduct depreciation, interest on construction and permanent loans, and other ordinary and necessary expenses of leasing the property *(Frank Lyon Co. v U.S., supra),* and rent payments are treated as ordinary income to the lessor, even though they may be applied to the purchase price on exercise of the option *(Joseph A. Harrah* (1958) 30 TC 1236). If the transaction is treated as a sale, the owner may be able to defer gain until the payments exceed basis *(Truman Bowen* (1949) 12 TC 446) if the price is not ascertainable (see §5.7). The owner would not then be entitled to deduct depreciation and other amounts deductible by a lessor *(Frank Lyon Co. v U.S., supra).*

§5.9   C. Promissory Note Secured by Mortgage or Deed of Trust

The most common seller financing device, in fact, the most common financing device generally, is one in which the buyer gives the seller a promissory note for the purchase price and secures the note by creating a lien which enables the seller to foreclose and reach the property's value if the buyer defaults. In many jurisdictions, the security instrument is called a mortgage, but in California it is commonly called a deed of trust. See generally California Mortgage and Deed of Trust Practice (Cal CEB 1979). All financing devices have the primary purpose of protecting the lender (in this instance, the seller) if the buyer fails to pay the purchase price. The installment land contract (§§5.4-5.7) and the lease with option to purchase (§5.8) achieve this protection by retaining title to the property in the seller until the price is paid. In contrast, under the note and security instrument method, the buyer receives title to the property, but gives the seller a recordable instrument that encumbers the property and enables the seller to sell it in case of default.

There are various aspects of seller financing by the encumbrance method, as opposed to the installment land contract and lease-option. The seller may accept the entire purchase price on a deferred

basis, but more commonly defers a portion of the price in conjunction with a new third party loan or existing encumbrance, and accepts back from the buyer a second deed of trust. On institutional
financing see chap 6; on seller financing with existing encumbrances, see §§5.18, 5.23-5.37. Important federal income tax benefits may inure to the seller who defers payment of the purchase price
to subsequent years. See §§5.10, 5.66. If the property is to be developed, the buyer may need the seller's participation in financing the
development by subordination of the seller's security interest to
that of construction lenders (see §§5.39-5.54), or by releasing portions of the property from the seller's lien as development progresses (see §§5.55-5.67), or both.

California regulates mortgages and deeds of trust extensively. On
creation and form of security instruments, see CC §§2920-2944,
2947-2955. See CCP §§580a-580d, 725a-730; CC §§2924-2924.6
on foreclosure of security instruments.

III. POSTPONING SELLER'S INCOME TAX LIABILITY

§5.10   A. Installment Method of Reporting Gain; IRC §453

When payment is deferred, the seller will want to avoid reporting
and paying tax on the entire gain realized on the sale in the year the
property is transferred, because he or she receives only a fraction of
the purchase price from the buyer in that year. Even if the
downpayment is sufficient to cover the tax payment, most sellers
want to postpone their tax payments on the sale as long as possible
for a variety of reasons: because tax treatment may be more favorable in a later year; because of a desire to invest the funds; because
of a desire to avoid paying tax on the entire gain before it has been
realized; or because of fears that the buyer will not perform.

Under IRC §453, the seller may report gain as if a prorata portion
of the total gain were realized on receipt of each of the buyer's payments, spreading tax treatment of the gain over the life of the purchase agreement. The installment method of reporting gain has a
number of advantages: only a portion of the downpayment will be
needed for tax payments due for the year of sale; payment of tax due
on gain received in later years is postponed; and there may be some
tax savings if realization of gain is spread over a number of years,
especially if the gain is taxed as ordinary income. Installment sales

under IRC §453 must be distinguished from deferred payment sales under which no gain is reported until the property's basis has been recovered, at which point all future payments are reported as gain. See §5.16.

§5.11   1. Statutory Requirements

The gain from a disposition of real property may be reported on the installment method whenever at least one payment is to be received after the close of the taxable year in which the disposition occurs. Installment Sales Revision Act of 1980, §2(a); IRC §453(b)(1). Under the installment method, the taxpayer recognizes gain to the extent of the proportion of payments received in a given taxable year which the gross profits realized from the sale bear to the total contract price (selling price minus existing encumbrances). IRC §453(c); see §5.12 on computation of gain. Before enactment of the Installment Sales Revision Act, the seller could qualify for installment reporting only if payments received in the tax year of sale totalled less than 30 percent of the total selling price. Because it included noncash items such as interest imputed under IRC §483 and the amount by which existing encumbrances exceeded the seller's basis in the property, the initial payment could exceed 30 percent despite the parties' intention that the sale qualify for installment reporting. If the initial payment exceeded 30 percent, the entire gain had to be recognized in the year of sale even though the amount received might not suffice to cover the seller's tax liability. This rule led to a substantial amount of litigation, frequently caused sellers to devise elaborate schemes to ensure qualification, and constituted a trap for the unwary seller. Elimination of the requirement greatly simplifies installment reporting; under new IRC §453, any time payment is to be received after the year of sale, installment reporting is automatically available to the seller. (Legislation to repeal the 30-percent limitation in California's installment sales statute (Rev & T C §17578) is anticipated but had not been enacted as of the cutoff date for this book.)

Another qualifying hurdle which sellers previously had to clear was the IRS requirement that payments be made in two or more taxable years. Rev Rul 69-462, 1969-2 CB 107; Rev Rul 71-595, 1971-2 CB 223. Under the Installment Sales Revision Act's definition of installment sales, installment reporting is available any time payment is to be made after the taxable year of the sale even if made in the form of one lump sum payment. IRC §453(b)(1).

Treatment of a sale in which payment is to be made after the taxable year of sale as an installment sale is automatic (IRC §453(d)(1)), and the seller must make a timely election in order not to have the sale treated as an installment sale (IRC §453(d)(2)). This reverses the treatment from that of the pre-1980 IRC §453, under which the seller was required to elect installment reporting and lost the right to do so unless election was made in a timely fashion.

The provisions of the Installment Sales Revision Act eliminating the 30-percent and two-payment requirements of the previous law are effective for transactions occurring in taxable years ending after October 19, 1980. Installment Sales Revision Act, §6(a)(7). Thus, calendar year 1980 taxpayers may take advantage of the repeal of the 30-percent and two-payment limitations.

§5.12   2. Computation of Gain

The percentage of each payment received which must be reported by the seller as gain is the ratio determined by dividing the gross profit realized, or to be realized, by the contract price. IRC §453(c). The contract price consists of the payments due the seller (price minus encumbrances) plus the amount by which any encumbrances exceed the seller's basis in the property. Reg §1.453-4(c).

Example: A sells real property with a tax basis of $30,000 to B for $100,000. B assumes, or takes subject to, a $40,000 deed of trust. A's gain is $70,000 ($100,000 selling price minus $30,000 basis), and the entire amount of each payment would have to be reported as gain because the contract price is also $70,000 ($100,000 selling price minus $40,000 encumbrance plus $10,000 excess of encumbrance over basis). If, however, the basis had been $50,000, the gain on a sale for $100,000 would have been $50,000. The contract price would have been $60,000 (only payments due seller, because encumbrance ($40,000) would not exceed basis ($50,000)). The ratio of gain ($50,000) to contract price ($60,000) makes five-sixths of each payment the seller receives reportable as gain.

§5.13   3. Seller's Ability To Limit Prepayments

Frequently the seller will want to limit the amount received in the year of sale (even after repeal of the 30-percent qualification requirement; see §5.11), and in future years. The seller's ability to limit the buyer's payments is subject to restrictions under California law and these must be carefully considered when structuring an installment sale. There is no right to prepay a note unless expressly permitted by either the note itself or a statute (see California Mortgage and Deed of Trust Practice §§2.46-2.50 (Cal CEB 1979)), but California statutes create such a right in many real property sales. Civil Code §2954.9 permits prepayment at any time of a loan for residential property of four units or less secured by a deed of trust, mortgage, or other lien on real property. However, a seller who takes back a security interest can restrict payments in the calendar year of sale under CC §2954.9(a)(3), provided that the seller does not take back four or more such security instruments during the same calendar year. Thus, CC §2954.9's restrictions on prepayments may defeat plans to spread income over a number of years, but should still permit a seller to limit payments during the year of the sale. A taxpayer using an accounting year other than the calendar year should note that CC §2954.9(a)(3) allows the seller to restrict prepayments only in the *calendar year* of sale. If, for example, a seller on a July 1st to June 30th taxable year sells property in December, he can restrict prepayments only until the end of that calendar year, but his taxable year extends another six months. Timing the sale to close in January would enable this seller to restrict prepayments for the remainder of his taxable year.

Under Bus & P C §10242.6, the buyer of an owner-occupied, single-family dwelling is permitted to prepay at any time, but this section has little impact on seller financing because it applies only to loans negotiated by mortgage loan brokers (Bus & P C §10248.3).

An alternative to barring prepayments altogether is to impose a monetary penalty on prepayments. Prepayment charges are permitted for loans for residential property of four units or less (CC §2954.9(a)(2)), but limited in amount (CC §2954.9(b)). If the property is not residential property of four or fewer units, the only limitation on the prepayment charge is that it not be exorbitant or unconscionable. In sales of such property, the seller can calculate the additional tax liability that a prepayment would entail and impose a penalty adequate to cover it. *Williams v Fassler* (1980) 110 CA3d 7, 167 CR 545 (penalty of 50 percent of any prepayment upheld on showing that additional tax amounted to 41 percent of prepayment).

§5.14   4. Disposition of Installment Obligations

The seller who contemplates selling or borrowing on an installment note must be aware that a subsequent disposition will generally result in recognition of gain. Unless exempted by statute or regulation every disposition of an installment obligation results in recognition of gain to the holder of the obligation that is equal to the amount realized on disposition less the basis of the installment obligation. IRC §453B. Because any transaction, including a second installment sale, may be considered a disposition, careful analysis of the proposed transaction must be made if recognition of gain is to be avoided. Transfers, such as outright sales, gifts, transfers in trust, etc., will generally be considered dispositions. However, neither the seller's death, nor various categories of liquidations and corporate reorganizations, are considered dispositions. See generally Anderson, Tax Factors in Real Estate Operations 139–142 (6th ed 1980).

Cancellation of an installment obligation by the seller had not been treated as a disposition as a result of the decision in *Miller v Usry* (DC La 1958) 160 F Supp 368, although an outright gift was treated as a disposition. The Installment Sales Revision Act of 1980, §2(a), IRC §453B(f)(1), provides that if an installment obligation is cancelled or otherwise becomes unenforceable, the cancellation or lapse must be treated as a disposition, and the seller realizes gain measured by the difference between the fair market value of the installment obligation and its basis. The rule is applicable to installment obligations that become unenforceable after October 19, 1980, the date of enactment. Installment Sales Revision Act, §6(a)(5).

A pledge of installment notes as security for a loan will not be held to be a disposition unless it is a disguised sale of the notes. *United Surgical Steel Co.* (1970) 54 TC 1215. If, however, the installment note is pledged as collateral for a loan equal to the face amount of the note at maturity, it may be held to be a disposition requiring recognition of gain under IRC §453B. Rev Rul 65-185, 1965-2 Cum Bull 153.

§5.15   5. Relationship to Buyer's Financing Needs

The seller's desire to limit payments in the year of sale and spread the tax benefits over a number of years may conflict with the buyer's need to release land from the seller's lien as development progresses (see §5.56). Negotiations on deferring payment must take into account factors such as subordination, financing and development needs, partial reconveyances, and release. Forms at §§5.19 and 5.20 offer some suggestions for resolving these competing needs. See also §5.66 regarding substitution of security.

§5.16   B. Deferred Payment Sales

The deferred payment method of reporting gain is available to sellers in rare and extraordinary circumstances as an alternative to installment reporting (§§5.11-5.15). This reporting method has its genesis in case law (*Burnet v Logan* (1931) 283 US 404) rather than statute, does not require an election by the seller, and depends on the seller's accounting system. Under the deferred payment method, the seller reports no gain until payments equal to the basis in the property have been received; all remaining payments must then be reported as gain from the sale. Thus, gain is deferred as under the installment method, but it is not spread proportionately over the period of payment. There is no restriction on the amount of the total payment that can be received in the year of sale.

In the Installment Sales Revision Act of 1980, Congress extended installment reporting to certain sales for a contingent price which had not previously been covered (Act §2(a); IRC §453(i)(2)) although Congress left the formulation of precise rules to the Treasury Department (IRC §453(i)(2)). The Senate Finance Committee Report expressed the intention that deferred payment reporting be "limited to those rare and extraordinary cases involving sales for a contingent price where the fair market value of the purchaser's obligation cannot reasonably be ascertained." SR No. 96-1000, 96th Cong, 2d Sess (1980), reprinted in 1980 US Code Cong & Ad News 8340, 8363. Thus, although the situations in which deferred payment reporting will be permitted remain to be defined by regulations and case law, its use will be limited and confined to those infrequent sales in which the value of buyer's obligation is neither capable of calculation nor given a fixed dollar limit.

In order to qualify for the deferred payment method of reporting gain (1) the agreement must call for payment of installments in one or more future taxable years, and (2) the gain must not be reportable immediately under the seller's usual accounting system. The second requirement requires resolution of two issues. First, generally only a cash basis taxpayer will be able to qualify; qualification will usually be impossible for an accrual basis taxpayer because, under accrual accounting, a note or other obligation containing a fixed dollar amount is reported and taxed when received, not when paid. See, *e.g., Spring City Foundry Co. v Commissioner* (1934) 292 US 182; Rev Rul 79-292, 1979-2 Cum Bull 287. Second, for a cash basis taxpayer, it must be determined whether the sale is for a stated or ascertainable price. Sales for an indeterminate price in which no present fair market value can be ascertained for the buyer's obligation have qualified for installment reporting (*Burnet v Logan, supra,* 283 US 404; *Commissioner v Edwards Drilling Co.* (5th Cir 1938) 95 F2d 719) and should continue to do so under the Installment Sales Revision Act. An indeterminate price contract is not generally used in real property sales, but might be a rare instance in which an accrual basis taxpayer could take advantage of deferred payment reporting.

Transactions in which the current value of the buyer's obligation to make future payments is ascertainable will disqualify the seller from deferred payment reporting, and the price under an installment land contract will lack ascertainability only in rare and extraordinary circumstances. SR No. 96-1000, 96th Cong, 2d Sess (1980), reprinted in 1980 US Code Cong & Ad News 8340, 8363; *In re Steen* (9th Cir 1975) 509 F2d 1398. In *Warren Jones Co. v Commissioner* (9th Cir 1975) 524 F2d 788, the seller was denied deferred payment treatment on an installment land contract which was held to have a fair market value of only 50 percent of face value. See also *Heller Trust v Commissioner* (9th Cir 1967) 382 F2d 675. Because the price under a note secured by a deed of trust is almost always determinable, deferred payment reporting was rarely allowed in transactions in which these conventional financing devices were used even before the Installment Sales Revision Act. See *Phillips v Frank* (9th Cir 1961) 295 F2d 629; *Ruth Iron Co. v Commissioner* (8th Cir 1928) 26 F2d 30. Installment reporting would be required by the act under the facts of any of these cases.

IV. DEFERRING PAYMENTS; FORM PROVISIONS FOR THE PURCHASE AND SALE AGREEMENT

§5.17   A. Form: Cash in Escrow

Form 5.17-1

[*Insert in purchase and sale agreement after provisions in §3.47 or §3.48*]

(2) Buyer's deposit during business hours at least one business day before close of escrow of ____[$ _____]____.

[Continue with provision at §5.19 or §5.20]

Comment: If no payments are to be deferred to the period following close of escrow, this form or the form at §3.49 should be used. If there are deferred payments, this form may be used with §5.19 or §5.20.

§5.18   B. Form: Credit for Existing Encumbrances

Form 5.18-1

[Insert after form at §5.17 if appropriate]

Buyer shall be credited toward the purchase price with the balance of principal due the encumbrancer(s) at the date of the close of escrow ____[*plus any other charges, e.g., interest not prorated to seller or charges asserted by the encumbrancer to reinstate a note with due-on-sale provisions*]____.

Comment: When the buyer acquires title subject to existing encumbrances, the provision at §5.17 should be followed with this provision which gives the buyer credit for principal and interest still due on the continuing encumbrances.

The parties should determine before close of escrow the balance due on prior encumbrances as well as other terms of the notes and security instruments. See §§3.50-3.51. Release provisions of the prior encumbrances should be checked and coordinated with release provisions of the security instrument for the seller's deferred payments. The buyer should not overlook accrued interest on prior encumbrances and should receive a credit for it; otherwise he may find himself paying interest to the encumbrancer at the due date while having it included in the price paid the seller. The agreement should allocate liability for any other charges of the encumbrancer.

For rights of parties on assumption of encumbrances or taking property subject to them, see §§5.23-5.25. For sales in which the existing encumbrance is government-financed or insured (*i.e.*, by the VA, or FHA), see §5.25.

§5.19   C. Form: Note for Balance; First Year Payments Limited

Form 5.19-1

[Precede with provision at §5.17; see alternate provision note for balance at §5.20]

(3) The balance of the purchase price in Buyer's promissory note, in the form attached, bearing interest at _____ percent per year, principal payable in _____ equal ____[annual / monthly]____ installments ____[plus / including]____ interest ____[on the unpaid balance / on the installment due]____, beginning on ____[or before]____, 19__, and continuing on ____[or before]____ the _____ day of _____ thereafter until paid; provided that payments of principal before _____, 19__, shall not exceed $_____.

Buyer's note is to be secured by a ____[e.g., first deed of trust]____ in the form used by ____[name of title company or lender]____ ____[as modified] ____ in the form attached, encumbering ____[specify the property conveyed or describe other property]____.

Comment: Interest may be computed in different ways. The payment amounts may remain constant, with the amounts applied to principal and interest varying according to an amortization schedule. This method is the one usually adopted for purchases of residential property. A second method provides for payment of principal in equal installments plus interest either on the unpaid balance or on the payment due.

The note may permit periodic payments larger than those provided for in the note by (1) specifying periodic payments of a stated amount "or more," or (2) requiring payments to be made "on or before" specified dates. When the first method is used, payments in excess of the stated amount may not be applied to the next succeeding installments when due, although the excess reduces the total amount due. *Smith v Renz* (1954) 122 CA2d 535, 265 P2d 160. If the second method is used, as suggested in the form, excess payments may be directed by the buyer to satisfy succeeding installments. See CC §1479 on specifying application of payments made by a debtor who is under several obligations to the same creditor.

When structuring an installment sale, careful attention must be paid to the provisions of California law concerning prepayment of loans secured by real property. See §5.13.

Because the buyer often expects land to be released as payments are made, the release provisions of the agreement are closely related to installment payment provisions. For release provisions, see §§5.62-5.67.

Forms of the note and deed of trust to be used should be attached to the agreement to avoid later disputes about their terms. Unless the exact form of the note is attached, the note submitted at close of escrow may contain provisions for attorneys' fees, allocation of payments between principal and interest, an acceleration clause (see §5.21), or other terms not contemplated by the parties and not discussed during negotiations. If the deed of trust is not attached, the instrument actually submitted might contain restrictions on the buyer's use of the property, or other uncontemplated provisions, although this is unlikely if the standard title company form is used.

When the security for the buyer's note is property other than that conveyed, the nature of the security (*e.g.*, a first deed of trust) should be stated and an exact list of all prior encumbrances given by reference either to an exhibit or to a preliminary title report. The seller will always wish to obtain a lender's title insurance policy covering the stated priority of the security, together with a statement from the holder or beneficiary of each itemized encumbrance having priority, as provided in CC §2943. If the security instrument encumbers all or part of the property sold, for clarity its priority should be stated, although priority can be determined from other provisions of the agreement.

Forms for notes and deeds of trust are usually available from title companies. The note and deed of trust must be modified to include the special provisions which the parties have negotiated, such as acceleration of principal (see §5.21), subordination (see §§5.39-5.54), and release and reconveyance of land (see §§5.55-5.67). These provisions can be duplicated from the agreement itself as addenda to the deed of trust. The form notes and deeds of trust available from title companies must be substantially modified if used as all-inclusive notes and wraparound deeds of trust although title companies are now providing forms for these instruments as well. All-inclusive notes and wraparound deeds of trust are discussed in §§5.26-5.37.

A seller who is receiving payments over a period of time should endeavor to obtain the right to pay broker's commissions as payments are received. See §2.41.

For forms for notes, see California Mortgage and Deed of Trust Practice §§2.22, 2.24, 2.30, 2.32, 2.47 (Cal CEB 1979). For the statutory statement required with subordination agreements and subordination clauses, see §5.54.

§5.20   D. Form: Note for Balance; Annual Payments Limited

Form 5.20-1

[*May be substituted for provisions for balance due seller at §5.19*]

(3) The balance of purchase price in Buyer's promissory note, in the form attached, bearing interest at _____ percent per year, due _____ years from date of close of escrow.

Buyer's note is to be secured by a ____[e.g., first deed of trust]____ in the form used by ____[name of title company or lender]____ ____[modified as]____ in the form attached, encumbering ____[specify the property conveyed or describe other property]____.

Buyer shall make no further payments on the note until after ____[date of end of calendar year]____. During each calendar year thereafter, buyer shall pay no less than _____ percent and no more than _____ percent of the principal face amount of the note together with accrued interest on the unpaid balance and accrued interest to be paid on its due date. The minimum annual payment shall be made before _____ of each year.

Comment: The seller may want payments spread over as long a period as possible for reporting gain (see §5.10), while the buyer-developer will desire releases as quickly as development permits (see §§5.55-5.58). If the buyer may pay on or before the anniversary date of the note, as in the form at §5.19, the seller may be paid sooner than he wishes. The seller may prefer to limit the payments to the anniversary date. This form is a compromise, with a minimum and maximum payable for each year. Because the buyer may still wish to have land released after he has reached the annual maximum, he may be permitted to substitute other security for the land after the maximum is reached and still receive the benefit of additional partial reconveyances of land. For a form permitting substitution of security, see §5.66. For variations in the method of paying interest, see §5.19.

Civil Code §2954.9 permits prepayment of a loan for residential property of four units or less, secured by a deed of trust, mortgage or other lien on real property, and this form cannot prevent prepayment after the calendar year of sale for sales of such property. See §5.13. Prepayment charges are permitted, but CC §2954.9(b) restricts their amount on loans secured by a mortgage or deed of trust on owner-occupied residential property containing four or fewer units. See California Mortgage and Deed of Trust Practice §§2.46-2.49 (Cal CEB 1979). If the property is not residential property of four or fewer units, the only limitation on the prepayment charge is that it be neither exorbitant nor unconscionable (see §5.13). *Williams v Fassler* (1980) 110 CA3d 7, 167 CR 545.

§5.21 E. Form: Acceleration of Balance on Deferred Payments

Form 5.21-1

[Insert in purchase and sale agreement (chap 3) as appropriate]

The note shall contain the following provision:

Payee may at ____[his / her]____ election accelerate payment of the entire unpaid balance of the note if maker or anyone holding the property through maker does any of the following:

1. Defaults on the payment of any installment under this note when due, or in the performance of any of the agreements contained in the deed of trust securing this note;

'*[Add if there is a prior encumbrance]*

2. Fails to make payments required by any encumbrance having a priority of record to the deed of trust securing this note or to perform any obligation under such encumbrance or otherwise allows any such encumbrance to be in default.

Comment: All installment note forms provide for acceleration of the unpaid balance on default in payment of any installment of principal or interest or performance of any other agreement. If the installment note is attached to the purchase and sale agreement, acceleration provisions should be incorporated in the note and need not be repeated in the agreement. Any changes in a printed form note should be initialed by both parties. The acceleration clause should also appear in the security instrument, which if recorded gives constructive notice to all subsequent purchasers and lien holders. CC §1214.

The proposed provision does not give the seller the right to accelerate if the buyer further encumbers the property, because such due-on-encumbrance clauses are no longer automatically enforceable. *La Sala v American Sav. & Loan Ass'n* (1971) 5 C3d 864, 97 CR 849. Moreover, there is no right to acceleration at all on further encumbrance of a single-family, owner-occupied dwelling. CC §2949. See §5.24 on due-on clauses. This provision also does not permit the seller to accelerate if the buyer is adjudged a bankrupt because such a provision is unenforceable under the Bankruptcy Act. 11 USC §365(b)(2)(A), (e)(1)(A).

A defaulting mortgagor or trustor or his successor may reinstate the obligation by curing most monetary defaults within three months of recording the notice of default under a power of sale, or before entry of judgment of foreclosure. CC §2924c. See California Mortgage and Deed of Trust Practice §6.17 (Cal CEB 1979). The beneficiary under a subordinate deed of trust or a person holding a subordinate lien may also reinstate under CC §2924c by paying the amount in default plus costs and expenses.

§5.22   F. Form: Trustee's Authority To Sign Documents

Form 5.22-1

[Insert in purchase and sale agreement (chap 3) as appropriate]

The deed of trust shall contain the following provision: ____*[Name of trustee]*____ as trustee under this deed of trust is authorized to execute, as directed by trustor ____*[and beneficiary]*____, (a) certificates consenting to the preparation and recording of final or parcel maps subdividing the property subject to this deed of trust, or any portion of it, together with certificates on any such map or separate instruments to make dedications or offers of dedications required as a condition to subdivision approval by the applicable governmental authority, and (b) grants of easements to public or private utility companies required to provide utility services to improvements constructed or to be constructed on the property initially subject to this deed of trust or for other land if such easements are within _____ feet of the perimeter boundary lines of the property or within the right of way of any street shown on a recorded final or parcel map.

Comment: Subject to limited exceptions, a certificate consenting to the preparation and recording of a final or parcel map must be executed by all parties having interests of record in the property. Govt C §§66436, 66445. Frequently, as part of the development approval process, easements must be granted to public or private utility companies for telephone, gas, sewer, or other utility purposes. It also may be appropriate, depending on the type of development, to supplement the proposed form to provide for the trustee's consent to other items that may be required, particularly if the deed of trust will be subordinated to construction financing and will continue in effect during the development period. For example, administrative requirements of the FHA, VA, and other agencies may call for statements from the encumbrancer. Also, it may be necessary to subordinate the deed of trust to covenants, conditions, restrictions and easements required for common-interest subdivisions, shopping centers, or other types of developments.

The seller who wishes some control might require submission of the maps, easement deeds, or other items for his or her approval ten days before submission to the trustee for execution. As an alternative, the seller may reserve the right to direct the trustee to act, following review and approval of the required action. Institutional trustees generally prefer to receive instructions executed by the beneficiary as well as the trustor.

Under some circumstances, it may be necessary to restrict the buyer's power to direct the trustee to act. Absent sufficient restrictions on the buyer's power to require dedications, the value of the real property security may be impaired for the benefit of other properties. For example, if the property will be subdivided and developed as a portion of a larger subdivision project, dedications of the property serving as the seller's security may inure to the benefit of other portions of the project. Similarly, if the deed of trust permits partial releases, dedications of the property serving as security may inure to the benefit of portions of the property previously released from the deed of trust. This prospective unfairness may result in the executory purchase and sale agreement or the above provision in the deed of trust being unenforceable in a specific performance action. CC §3391(2); see §5.42.

In addition to the normal dedications of real property within a subdivision for streets, drainage, and public utility easements, dedications may also be required for park and recreational purposes (Govt C §66477), and for public access to or along public waterways, rivers, or streams (Govt C §§66478.4, 66478.5, 66478.11).

V. RETAINING EXISTING ENCUMBRANCES

A. Buyer's Assumption of, or Sale Subject to, Existing Encumbrances

§5.23   1. General Considerations

Taking title subject to an existing encumbrance may permit buyer and seller to avoid prepayment penalties and refinancing costs and to keep in effect an existing encumbrance with a favorable interest rate. See §3.50. The terms of the underlying deed of trust and the interest rate on the secured promissory note should be examined by the buyer and compared to those available with new financing. The wraparound deed of trust is yet another approach to retaining existing encumbrances (§§5.26-5.37).

A buyer who merely takes subject to an existing encumbrance is not burdened with personal liability for the underlying obligation (*Cornelison v Kornbluth* (1975) 15 C3d 590, 125 CR 557); the property remains as security for payment of the obligation. A nonassuming buyer will, however, be personally liable for waste resulting from intentional or reckless conduct, and in the absence of a CCP §580b defense, possibly for waste resulting from negligent conduct. *Cornelison v Kornbluth, supra;* Leipziger, *The Mortgagee's Remedies for Waste,* 64 Calif L Rev 1086, 1129-1142 (1976). The buyer may also assume an existing loan by written agreement with either the lender or the seller. In the latter case, a specific recital of assumption in the deed constitutes a sufficient writing (CC §1624(7)), and the assuming buyer becomes personally liable to the beneficiary for repayment of the loan under a theory of equitable subrogation (*Braun v Crew* (1920) 183 C 728, 192 P 531). See §3.50 for a more detailed description of assumption of and sale subject to existing encumbrances and their interaction with California antideficiency legislation.

§5.24   2. Due-on-Sale Clauses

A due-on-sale (or due-on) clause in the existing note and deed of trust may restrict the ability of the new buyer to take subject to or to assume the existing obligation. A due-on clause permits the secured lender to accelerate the loan in the event of a sale or other specified transfer or transaction affecting the property. See California Mortgage and Deed of Trust Practice §§2.32-2.45 (Cal CEB 1979). Although the California courts have restricted lenders' rights to automatic acceleration, there are still many situations in which a due-on clause may restrict a potential buyer's ability to assume or take subject to an existing obligation.

Early cases held that due-on-sale provisions were permissible restraints on alienation under CC §711 when reasonably designed to protect the lender's security. *Coast Bank v Minderhout* (1964) 61 C2d 311, 38 CR 505; *Hellbaum v Lytton Sav. & Loan Ass'n* (1969) 274 CA2d 456, 79 CR 9. These cases recognized the lender's interest in the credit strength and character of the borrower, not only to ensure the borrower's ability to repay the loan, but also to avoid the inconvenience and risk of foreclosure and to ensure that the property was properly maintained and protected from waste.

In practice, institutional lenders used the due-on-sale clause not only to approve the buyer and require assumption of the loan, but to exact collateral benefits such as assumption fees and increased interest rates. This practice was approved in *Cherry v Home Sav. & Loan Ass'n* (1969) 276 CA2d 574, 81 CR 135, which held that the lender's interest in maintaining its loan portfolio at current market interest rates justified enforcement of its due-on-sale clause, even in the absence of a showing that the buyer's credit strength or character might adversely affect the lender's security.

In a series of decisions since these cases, however, the California Supreme Court has held enforcement of due-on clauses to constitute unreasonable restraint on alienation, and has limited the situations in which lenders will be entitled to automatic acceleration. In *La Sala v American Sav. & Loan Ass'n* (1971) 5 C3d 864, 97 CR 849, the court ruled that the beneficiary under a deed of trust could not automatically accelerate when the trustor further encumbered the property by imposing a second mortgage on it. See also CC §2949 barring acceleration on further encumbrance of a single-family, owner-occupied dwelling. In *Tucker v Lassen Sav. & Loan Ass'n* (1974) 12 C3d 629, 116 CR 633, the court ruled that a due-on clause does not permit automatic acceleration when the trustor executes an installment land contract for sale of the property. In *Wellenkamp v Bank of America* (1978) 21 C3d 943, 148 CR 379, the court held that automatic acceleration by an institutional lender is not permitted under a due-on clause even when there is an outright sale of the property by the trustor with title passing to the purchaser.

Lenders will probably continue to use due-on clauses because even under *Wellenkamp, supra,* an institutional lender can accelerate the loan if it can show that the security would be impaired by the proposed transfer of the property. Thus, acceleration may be permitted if the sale is to an uncreditworthy buyer or to a buyer who makes no personal investment in the property.

Wellenkamp leaves unclear whether noninstitutional lenders will be entitled to automatic enforcement of due-on clauses. In *Pas v Hill* (1978) 87 CA3d 521, 151 CR 98, it was suggested that *Wellenkamp* should not be extended to a purchase money loan given by a noninstitutional lender, but denied the seller the right to accelerate on foreclosure of a junior encumbrance, relying instead on *La Sala v American Sav. & Loan Ass'n, supra,* 5 C3d 864, 97 CR 849.

Thus, when the seller takes back a second note for all or a portion of the purchase price, automatic enforcement of a due-on-sale provision might be permitted by the courts. See Comment, *The Due-On-Sale Clause in California: A Case for Automatic Enforcement by the Private Lender,* 13 U San Francisco L Rev 639 (1979); Zeller, *The Due-on Clause After Wellenkamp: Unresolved Issues,* 55 Cal SBJ 76 (1980).

Federally chartered savings and loan associations are also permitted automatic acceleration under due-on clauses. On June 8, 1976, the Federal Home Loan Bank Board adopted a regulation authorizing federal associations to enforce due-on clauses. It has been held that this federal regulation preempts state law regarding due-on clauses contained in loan instruments executed after June 8, 1976. *Glendale Fed. Sav. & Loan Ass'n v Fox* (CD Cal 1978) 459 F Supp 903.

§5.25   3. Transferability of Government Financing

Existing encumbrances may include loans guaranteed by the Veterans Administration (VA) (38 USC §§1801-1828), loans insured by the Federal Housing Administration (FHA) (12 USC §§1701-1750(g)), or loans made by the State of California through the Department of Veterans Affairs (Cal-Vet) (Mil & V C §§984-987.93). Typically, VA, FHA, and Cal-Vet loans provide for lower interest rates and downpayments than conventional loans. Loans guaranteed by the VA are transferable, although the original borrower remains liable unless released by the VA. 38 USC §1817. Mortgages insured by FHA are also transferable. 12 USC §1707(b). Written consent of the Department of Veterans Affairs is required to transfer Cal-Vet loans (Mil & V C §987.1), but assumption is rare because a purchaser acceptable to the Department of Veterans Affairs can usually obtain a larger loan in his or her own right, and on assumption the seller loses the right to a second Cal-Vet loan (Mil & V C §987.16).

B. The Wraparound Deed of Trust and All-Inclusive Note

§5.26   1. Definition

The wraparound deed of trust, also referred to as "all-inclusive," "hold harmless," or "overriding," is a real property security device used for secondary financing. The terms "wraparound deed of trust" and "all-inclusive note" will be used in this text to refer to the deed of trust and promissory note used in a wraparound loan. Although a similar device, known as a "blanket mortgage," has been used by Canadian life insurance companies since the 1930s, it has only been since the tight money market of the 1960s that the device has been used frequently in California. Gunning, *The Wrap-Around Mortgage . . . Friend or U.F.O.,* 2 Real Estate Rev 35 (1972); Healey, *A "New" Security Instrument,* 41 Cal SBJ 681 (1966).

When used in seller financing a wraparound deed of trust is similar to a conventional second deed of trust, except that the indebtedness represented by the all-inclusive note includes not only the deferred portion of the purchase price, but also the unpaid balance of a promissory note secured by a prior encumbrance. Under conventional second deed of trust seller financing, the buyer would assume or take subject to the prior encumbrance. For example, if property encumbered by a first deed of trust securing a promissory note with an unpaid balance of $40,000 is to be sold for $60,000, with a downpayment of $10,000, the seller could take back a note for $10,000 secured by a second deed of trust, or an all-inclusive note for $50,000. The wraparound deed of trust will contain the seller's covenant to pay the principal and interest installments accruing on the prior note.

Although the wraparound deed of trust may be used for third party as well as seller financing, the discussion in §§5.27-5.37 is limited to seller financing. For a discussion of the wraparound deed of trust in third party financing, see Lane, *The "Wrap-Around" Mortgage: Tax Problems Related to its Use in Connection with the Refinancing or Sale of Real Estate,* NYU 33rd Inst Fed Tax 1235 (1975); Gunning, 2 Real Estate Rev 35. Unless otherwise indicated, the discussion in §§5.27-5.37 assumes the existence of only one prior encumbrance, although a wraparound deed of trust and all-inclusive note may wrap around and include any number of prior encumbrances and the obligations that they secure.

2. Purposes and Uses

§5.27   a. Higher Effective Interest Rate

The primary reason for using wraparound instruments is for both buyer and seller to take advantage of a lower interest rate on the existing loan. For example, if the interest rate on the existing first deed of trust is 6 percent, a wraparound second deed of trust at 8 percent will generate far more interest for the seller than would a conventional second deed of trust, even at 10 percent, because the wraparound generates interest on the total loan and not just on the additional funds. Although the seller will generally demand a purchase price in excess of the property's cash value as consideration for taking back a conventional second deed of trust, the buyer frequently gets a lower purchase price with wraparound financing because of the higher effective yield. The wraparound arrangement may also result in smaller monthly payments than would be required for independent notes covering two unconsolidated loans. See California Mortgage and Deed of Trust Practice §2.55 (Cal CEB 1979).

§5.28   (1) Reporting Interest for Tax Purposes

It is not clear whether a seller should report the gross interest received under an all-inclusive note or the net after excluding interest on the underlying first deed of trust for income tax purposes. Some authority exists for reporting the gross amount of the interest received. Lane, *The "Wrap-Around" Mortgage: Tax Problems Related to its Use in Connection with the Refinancing or Sale of Real Estate,* NYU 33rd Inst Fed Tax 1235, 1243 (1975). The manner in which interest income is reported may affect an individual seller's basis for charitable contributions and a corporate seller's status as a subchapter S corporation or a personal holding company. NYU 33rd Inst on Fed Tax at 1243. Whether the interest received is reported on a gross or net basis will not affect the seller's taxable income.

§5.29   (2) Usury Considerations

The seller generally need not worry about the possibility of usury even if the effective yield on the wraparound financing exceeds the amount permitted by Cal Const art XV, §1 (as amended by initiative in 1979). See Hyman, *Proposition 2 and the California Usury Law,* 3 CEB Real Prop L Rep 25 (1980). If the seller takes back an all-inclusive note and wraparound deed of trust, the transaction should be exempt from the usury law under the time-price differential doctrine which distinguishes a credit sale of property from a loan or forbearance, freeing the credit sale from the restrictions of Cal Const art XV, §1. *Boerner v Colwell Co.* (1978) 21 C3d 37,

145 CR 380; *Verbeck v Clymer* (1927) 202 C 557, 261 P 1017; *Golden State Lanes v Fox* (1965) 232 CA2d 135, 42 CR 568; see Brown, *The Current Status of the Time-Price Differential Doctrine in California,* 2 CEB Real Prop L Rep 93, 109 (1979).

If wraparound financing is provided by a third party, usury may be a problem. Even in this situation, however, usury limitations might not apply if the beneficiary remains personally liable on the senior indebtedness and agrees to continue to pay on it. The suggested rationale is that the beneficiary is then lending his credit to the buyer and should be entitled to interest on the full amount of the credit extended, not just his equity. See 1 Miller & Starr, Current Law of California Real Estate §3:20 (rev ed 1975); Comment, *The Wrap-Around Mortgage: A Critical Inquiry,* 21 UCLA L Rev 1529 (1974); Comment, *The Wrap-Around Deed of Trust: An Answer to the Allegation of Usury,* 10 Pac L J 923 (1979).

§5.30   b. Seller's Control Over Security

The seller who remains liable for making the payments on the existing senior lien, retains greater control over the security and is assured that payments are made as due. See 1 Miller & Starr, Current Law of California Real Estate §3:20 (rev ed 1975). The buyer incurs a corresponding loss of control, unless the all-inclusive note provides for payments to be made by the buyer to a third party disbursing agent. Use of a third party collection agent, however, may cause the seller to realize taxable gain in a sale in which the encumbrances exceed the seller's adjusted basis in the property because the transaction might be treated as including an assumption of the existing encumbrance by the buyer (see §5.31). See *Floyd J. Voight* (1977) 68 TC 99, aff'd (5th Cir 1980) 614 F2d 94; Comment, *The Wrap-Around Mortgage: A Critical Inquiry,* 21 UCLA L Rev 1529, 1551 (1974).

c. Tax Considerations

§5.31   (1) Installment Reporting

Before enactment of the Installment Sales Revision Act of 1980, Pub L 96-471, 94 Stats 2247 (1980), it was felt that wraparound instruments would enable a seller to qualify for installment reporting for federal income tax purposes (see §5.10) under certain circumstances. Under the previous version of IRC §453, a sale could qualify for installment reporting only if payments in the year of sale did not exceed 30 percent of the total selling price; payments in the year of sale included the amount by which existing encumbrances exceeded the seller's basis in the property. Although specific case authority was lacking, many commentators suggested that if wraparound financing were used, the existing encumbrance would neither be assumed nor taken subject to by the buyer and thus any excess of encumbrance over basis would not have to be counted as part of the initial payment. See Anderson, Tax Factors in Real Estate Operations 164 (6th ed 1980); Lane, *The "Wrap-Around" Mortgage: Tax Problems Related to its Use in Connection with the Refinancing or Sale of Real Estate,* NYU 33rd Inst Fed Tax 1235, 1238 (1975); Prager, *The All-Inclusive Deed of Trust: Can it Save an Installment Sale?,* 7 Bev Hills BJ 31 (1973).

The Installment Sales Revision Act eliminated the requirement that payments in the year of sale be limited to 30 percent of the total selling price. See §5.11. Therefore, any encumbrance on the property, whether or not in excess of basis, will not affect the sellers' ability to qualify for installment reporting, and this particular rationale for wraparound financing is no longer relevant. However, the excess of encumbrances over the seller's adjusted basis will be treated as a cash payment to the seller in the year of sale and the seller may want to use wraparound instruments to be able to report that excess as being received in increments over the term of the obligation.

§5.32 (2) Prepaid Interest

Until 1976, real estate investors were motivated to purchase property under wraparound instruments because of the possibility of prepaying interest on the all-inclusive note in the year of sale and taking a deduction for it. See Anderson, Tax Factors in Real Estate Operations 91-92 (6th ed 1980). The Internal Revenue Service had tightened the rules for prepaid interest in 1968 by allowing deduction of a prepayment only to the extent of interest accruing through the end of the taxable year next following the year of payment, provided that it did not materially distort income. Rev Rul 68-643, 1968-2 Cum Bull 76. In the Tax Reform Act of 1976, however, Congress enacted IRC §461(g) which provides that interest payments can be deducted only in the tax year for which they represent a charge for the use or forbearance of money. See generally Sexton,

Elimination of the Prepaid Interest Deduction by the 1976 TRA Analyzed, 46 J Tax 146 (1977). Thus IRC §461(g) has effectively eliminated the possibility.of deducting prepaid interest as a beneficial feature of wraparound financing for buyers.

3. Drafting Wraparound Instruments

§5.33   a. General Considerations

The wraparound deed of trust and the all-inclusive note must be drafted carefully not only to achieve the benefits discussed in §§5.27-5.32, but to conform to the terms and provisions of the underlying first deed of trust and the note it secures. In addition, the wraparound deed of trust must contain provisions satisfactory to the institutional trustee and to the title company that may be asked to conduct the trustee's sale and to insure title following delivery of a trustee's deed. Standard form deeds of trust customarily used in California are inadequate for this purpose and must be appropriately modified and supplemented. Some title companies have their own forms for the all-inclusive note and wraparound deed of trust, and these might be used after careful inspection and, if needed, modification. The wraparound instruments to be used should be reviewed and approved by the institutional trustee and the title company that may be asked to insure title following foreclosure. For an extensive discussion of drafting considerations, see Caplan, *The Wrap-Around Merry-go-round,* 1 Real Prop News, Summer, 1980, p 1.

The note and deed of trust must be drafted with the needs of the parties to the specific transaction in mind. Because these needs vary so greatly, it is difficult to draft all-purpose wraparound forms. It is possible, however, to pinpoint issues which must be addressed in drafting any wraparound instruments.

§5.34   b. Consistency With Underlying Obligation and
               Encumbrance; Prepayments; Amortization

The wraparound instruments must be consistent with the terms and provisions of the underlying note and deed of trust to ensure that the buyer's obligations and the seller's rights are not less than those of the maker and the payee under the first note. For example, any event that constitutes a default or permits acceleration of the first note should also be a default or permit acceleration under the all-inclusive note. If the underlying note contains a late charge provision, a similar provision should be added to the all-inclusive note and the wraparound deed of trust.

Prepayment restrictions present a separate series of issues to be negotiated. If the underlying debt is a lock-in loan which prohibits prepayment, the all-inclusive note and deed of trust should either prohibit prepayment or specify that prepayment is limited to the seller's equity in excess of the underlying debt. The buyer who does have the right to prepay under the overriding note may want to include a requirement that the seller execute a reconveyance when the unpaid balance of the all-inclusive note equals the balance on the senior note. On the other hand, the seller may want the note to provide that he will continue to realize the interest differential even though his equity has been reduced to zero. If prepayment is to be permitted, the parties must decide how any prepayment is to be allocated between the wraparound and the underlying obligations. They also must decide who is to pay any prepayment charges incurred under the underlying note.

Payment on the all-inclusive note must be established after consideration of amortization schedules for both the wraparound and the included debt, to ensure that the balance on the all-inclusive note will, throughout its life, exceed the balance on the underlying note. If the all-inclusive note is amortized faster than the included note, the amount of the included obligation could eventually exceed the balance on the overriding note.

§5.35   c. Rights in Case of Default

The rights of each party if the other defaults should be clearly spelled out. For example, most all-inclusive notes make the seller's covenant to make payments on the underlying note conditional on the buyer's performance of his obligations under the wraparound instruments. This condition seems an essential protection for the seller, who otherwise might be contractually obligated to continue paying on the first obligation despite the buyer's default on the wraparound. On the other hand, the buyer needs protection against the seller's failure to make payments on the underlying note. Protection of the buyer is frequently accomplished by providing that the buyer may make payments directly to the holder of the first deed of trust when the seller fails to do so, and that those payments will be credited against the next installments due under the all-inclusive note. The buyer might require that the seller submit proof of payment within a specified time after the due date of each installment on the underlying obligation, or simply secure agreement of the holder of the underlying encumbrance to send notice of any default. In any event, the buyer should include in the wraparound deed of trust, or separately record, a request for notice of default and notice of sale under CC §2924b.

§5.36   d. Foreclosure

Provisions regarding foreclosure under wraparound instruments are extremely important because many title companies will neither act as trustee nor insure title unless foreclosure provisions are clearly set forth. Questions arise because the trustor's payments on the all-inclusive note include amounts due on the underlying obligation. Does the holder of the wraparound deed of trust declare a default on both obligations, or only on the installments due on the all-inclusive note? Does he bid the amount of his equity, or the full amount due on the wraparound at the trustee's sale? Because the holder of the wraparound is obligated to pay on the included encumbrance, the wraparound instruments should provide that failure to pay on the wraparound is a default on that obligation only. The documents should provide that the purchaser at the trustee's sale acquires only the seller's equity, and therefore takes title subject to the senior included lien.

§5.37   4. Form: Provision in Purchase and Sale Agreement for Wraparound Financing

Form 5.37-1

[Precede with provision at §5.17]

(3) The balance of the purchase price in an all-inclusive promissory note executed by buyer in the form attached, secured by a wraparound deed of trust in the form attached, and bearing interest at _____ percent per year, principal payable in _____ equal ____[annual / monthly]____ installments, beginning on _____, 19__, and continuing until the principal and interest due have been paid.

The total principal amount of the all-inclusive note shall include the unpaid principal balance of the following underlying promissory note(s) secured by deed(s) of trust:

1. (a) Promissory note:
Maker: _____
Payee: _____
Date: _____
Original amount: _____
Unpaid balance: _____
   (b) Deed of trust:
Beneficiary: _____
Original amount: _____
Recordation date: _____
Document No. _____ Book: _____ Page: _____
Place of recordation: _____, County, California

[Repeat as necessary for each note and deed of trust]

Comment: Drafting a provision for the purchase agreement is obviously simplified if the forms for the wraparound instruments have been agreed on and can be attached. If they are not available, key provisions to be included in the wraparound instruments should be specified in the purchase agreement itself. On drafting considerations, see §§5.33-5.36.

VI. SELLER'S PARTICIPATION IN BUYER'S FINANCING

§5.38   A. Usual Methods

In addition to deferring a portion of the purchase price, the seller may be asked to assist in financing the buyer's development of the property by subordinating his or her purchase money deed of trust to liens for construction and permanent financing, by reconveying portions of the property to the buyer, or both.

By subordinating his or her lien, the seller agrees that it be junior in priority to the encumbrance to which it is subordinated, generally a lien for construction financing. If construction is not completed or the completed project is unsuccessful, the seller may find the security inadequate. Because the seller's security is at the risk of the successful completion and operation of the project, the seller will often require an increased purchase price and larger payments for the release of portions of the property from the subordinated purchase money deed of trust.

Frequently the buyer wants part of the land conveyed at close of escrow free of the seller's lien to an extent commensurate with the amount of the downpayment. If, for example, the buyer pays 29 percent of the price at closing, he may want some fraction of the land conveyed free and clear of liens. The percentages of payment and release are matters to be negotiated, but if the seller is also subordinating his loan to other security, he may be reluctant to reduce his security further by conveying a portion of the land free of liens at close of escrow. It may be important, however, to negotiate releases in addition to the subordination to enable the buyer to sell lots free of encumbrances as they are developed. See §§5.55-5.67.

B. Subordination

§5.39   1. Buyer's Need; Usual Methods ·

When a developer buys acreage for subdivision, he or she is faced with financing both the land purchase and construction. Two factors create a problem: (1) a deed of trust securing a note for the purchase price of the land is given statutory priority over other liens under the recording acts (CC §2898); and (2) institutional lenders which normally furnish construction loans are required to secure those loans by a first lien on the property (Fin C §§1227 (commercial banks), 1560 (trust companies), 7102(a) (savings and loan associations)); federally chartered lenders are also required to be secured by first liens (12 USC §1464).

The buyer-developer can provide the institutional construction lender a first lien by either (a) recording the construction loan deed of trust at the close of escrow before recording the seller's purchase money deed of trust, or (b) obtaining the seller's consent to a provision in the purchase agreement, or in a separate agreement, that priority will be reversed so that the seller's lien will be junior to the construction lien once construction financing is obtained. Only the latter is a true subordination, but both an agreement regarding the priority of recording at close of escrow and an agreement to reverse the record priority after closing may be treated by the courts as subordination agreements and the rights and obligations of the construction lender and the seller may be treated similarly regardless of the manner in which their respective loan priorities are achieved. *Middlebrook-Anderson Co. v Southwest Sav. & Loan Ass'n* (1971) 18 CA3d 1023, 96 CR 338; California Mortgage and Deed of Trust Practice §3.54 (Cal CEB 1979); 2 Miller & Starr, Current Law of California Real Estate §§11:174, 11:181 (rev ed 1977).

The construction loan and the permanent (or take-out) loan which replaces it will normally be recorded after recordation of the seller's deed of trust. In this situation, subordination may be accomplished automatically if the seller's deed of trust includes a provision that subordinates the lien of the deed of trust to those of the construction and permanent loans; subordination may also be achieved by using a separate, recorded agreement. Institutional lenders and title insurance companies require that the change in priority be accomplished by a separate subordination agreement, rather than an automatic subordination provision in a deed of trust. See 2 Miller & Starr, Current Law §11:174; 2 Bowman, Ogden's Revised California Real Property Law §17.37 (TI Corp-CEB 1975).

The buyer should be advised that he or she will lose the antideficiency protection of CCP §580b when the seller's lien is subordinated to a construction financing lien in order to develop the property commercially, and the seller's security is subsequently destroyed by a trustee's sale or judicial foreclosure under the construction deed of trust. *Spangler v Memel* (1972) 7 C3d 603, 102 CR 807.

§5.40   2. Seller's Need for Protection

Sellers will normally agree to accept the risks of subordination only in exchange for some benefit, such as a higher purchase price. In *Spangler v Memel* (1972) 7 C3d 603, 613, 102 CR 807, 813, the court notes that the seller's agreement to subordinate makes it possible to obtain the financing required to realize the commercial potential of the property which, in turn, justifies the higher purchase price. In determining whether or not to subordinate, the seller must consider, in addition to the purchase price, the financial strength and ability of the developer, the economic potential of the proposed development, and the state of the real property market. The seller should also attempt to protect his or her interests by ensuring that the subordination agreement restricts the terms of the construction loan to require that the proceeds be used only to pay for improvements on the property.

Following subordination to a construction loan, the property will generally be over-encumbered during the construction period, because the total amount of the liens will exceed the value of the property until the improvements are completed. The seller receives some protection from the fact that most construction loans are disbursed by the lender in the form of progress payments as improvements are built and the value of the property increases correspondingly. See §§6.14-6.15. See also 2 Miller & Starr, Current Law of California Real Estate §11:173 (rev ed 1977). In case of the buyer's default, few sellers are able either to take over and complete an unsuccessful real property development or to meet the payment obligations on the construction loan in order to prevent foreclosure. If the construction lien is foreclosed, the buyer may be insolvent even though personally liable for repayment of the seller's note. *Spangler v Memel, supra.* Many practitioners disapprove of subordination by a seller who is not a sophisticated real estate developer because the pitfalls for sellers (and their attorneys) are legion. See *Starr v Mooslin* (1971) 14 CA3d 988, 92 CR 583.

Because the seller's security is at the risk of the successful completion and operation of the buyer's development when he subordinates to construction and permanent financing, the courts may treat the relationship between the buyer and the seller as being one of quasi-joint venture. *Miller v Citizens Sav. & Loan Ass'n* (1967) 248 CA2d 655, 56 CR 844.

§5.41   3. Types of Subordination Agreements

Three types of subordination agreements are commonly used.

(1) Automatic subordination occurs when the seller's lien is recorded together with an executed agreement which provides that the lien of the subsequent construction or take-out loan will automatically be senior to the seller's lien. *Carpenson v Najarian* (1967) 254 CA2d 856, 62 CR 687; *Joanaco Projects, Inc. v Nixon & Tierney Constr. Co.* (1967) 248 CA2d 821, 57 CR 48. Title companies usually require execution of an additional agreement subordinating the seller's lien to the particular construction loan obtained. 2 Miller & Starr, Current Law of California Real Estate §11:174 (rev ed 1977). If there is variation between the new and original subordination agreements, the new agreement will be unenforceable unless it is supported by new consideration. *Miller v Citizens Sav. & Loan Ass'n* (1967) 248 CA2d 655, 56 CR 844.

(2) An executory subordination agreement, as in an agreement of purchase and sale, is a promise by the seller to execute a subsequent instrument subordinating the seller's lien to the lien of the

improvement loan (see §5.42). See *Handy v Gordon* (1967) 65 C2d 578, 55 CR 769; *Magna Dev. Co. v Reed* (1964) 228 CA2d 230, 39 CR 284.

(3) A third type, essentially de facto subordination, is created when the seller agrees that the security instrument for the sale price will be recorded after recordation of the lien of the construction lender (see §5.53). Some commentators note that this is not true subordination, because priority is determined solely by the recording date and the seller has no prior lien to subordinate to the improvement lien. 2 Miller & Starr, Current Law §11:175. Courts have characterized this situation as subordination, however, in holding the lender to the same liability for misapplication of funds (§5.47) as would arise under an automatic subordination clause. *Middle-brook-Anderson Co. v Southwest Sav. & Loan Ass'n* (1971) 18 CA3d 1023, 96 CR 338.

Subordination agreements are frequently classified as either executory or executed. An executory agreement (see §§5.42-5.44) is a mere promise by the seller to execute a subsequent subordination instrument. An executed subordination agreement may be either an automatic subordination agreement, as discussed in §5.48, or an executory agreement which has become executed by the seller's actions in signing and recording a subordination instrument. Executed subordination agreements are discussed in §§5.45-5.52.

a. Executory Subordination Agreements

§5.42 (1) Enforceability

The seller's executory promise to subordinate the purchase money lien typically is found either in the purchase and sale agreement (see chap 3) or in an executory subordination agreement recorded along with the seller's deed of trust. The particular problem posed by an executory agreement is whether the buyer will be entitled to specific performance to compel the seller to carry out his promise to subordinate. To be enforceable, an executory subordination agreement must be both certain and reasonable. *Handy v Gordon* (1967) 65 C2d 578, 55 CR 769. If the subordination agreement is unenforceable, the entire purchase and sale agreement is unenforceable, even if the buyer attempts to waive the subordination provisions. *Handy v Gordon, supra*; *Magna Dev. Co. v Reed* (1964) 228 CA2d 230, 39 CR 284.

The detailed terms of the loan to be acquired must be stated if the agreement is to be sufficiently certain to be enforced specifically *(Handy v Gordon, supra)* and the terms of the subordination agreement must be just and reasonable to the seller (CC §3391(2)). In *Handy v Gordon, supra,* the California Supreme Court held that the agreement must define and minimize the risk that the subordinating liens will impair or destroy the seller's security. The court criticized a number of aspects of the purchase and sale agreement including: failure to limit the size and number of lots into which the property was to be subdivided; absence of a restriction on use of loan funds (leaving the possibility that funds might be used for purposes other than improvements, thus depleting the seller's security); the low downpayment ($100, which was insufficient to cushion the seller's position); and deferral of any payment of principal to the seller until three years after close of escrow. Decisions after *Handy* demonstrate the willingness of the courts to deny both specific performance and damages under executory subordination agreements, particularly when enforcement is sought against unsophisticated sellers. *Butcher v Dauz* (1967) 257 CA2d 524, 65 CR 166; *Spellman v Dixon* (1967) 256 CA2d 1, 63 CR 668; *Loeb v Wilson* (1967) 253 CA2d 383, 61 CR 377. In *Woodworth v Redwood Empire Sav. & Loan Ass'n* (1971) 22 CA3d 347, 99 CR 373, specific performance was granted although the terms of the loans were not specified in the subordination provisions, because the seller was an active participant in the financing and development.

§5.43   (2) Required Terms

To meet the test of certainty (§5.42), the subordination agreement must specify maximum principal of the new loan, maximum interest rate, maximum term, and the mode of payment. *Cummins v Gates* (1965) 235 CA2d 532, 45 CR 417. In order to meet the additional test of fairness and reasonableness to the seller *(Handy v Gordon* (1967) 65 C2d 578, 55 CR 769), the agreement should include a number of other provisions limiting the terms of the new loan and the disbursement of its proceeds, including:

(a) The minimum prepayment term, as well as the maximum, in order to avoid a burdensome balloon payment which the buyer might not be able to meet (see 2 Miller & Starr, Current Law of California Real Estate §11:178 (rev ed 1977));

(b) The purpose of the loan, what costs are to be covered out of loan proceeds, and restrictions on use of funds to constructing improvements on the property *(Weiss v Brentwood Sav. & Loan Ass'n* (1970) 4 CA3d 738, 84 CR 736; *Ruth v Lytton Sav. & Loan Ass'n* (1968) 266 CA2d 831, 72 CR 521);

(c) The amount of loan fees and other charges, such as prepayment penalties, and the provisions of the note and deed of trust to be delivered to the lender *(Collins v Home Sav. & Loan Ass'n* (1962) 205 CA2d 86, 22 CR 817); and

(d) A description of the improvements to be constructed on the property *(Handy v Gordon, supra)*.

The seller might also insist on assurances that the buyer has a firm commitment for take-out or permanent financing. *Jones v Sacramento Sav. & Loan Ass'n* (1967) 248 CA2d 522, 56 CR 741. In most instances, the agreement should provide for subordination to take-out financing, as well as construction financing, and specify the terms (see §5.51).

§5.44   (3) Form: Executory Subordination Provision

Form 5.44-1

[Precede with provision at §5.18 or §5.19]

(4) Seller will execute a subordination agreement in the form attached, subordinating the deed of trust described in paragraph (3) above to deeds of trust executed by Buyer to secure construction ____[*and permanent*]____ loans and shall include the following terms and provisions:

(a) The construction loan shall ____[*specify maximum principal, maximum and minimum term of loan, maximum interest rate, mode of payment, purpose of loan, and costs to be included and excluded, amount of loan fees and other charges, terms of the note and deed of trust to the lender, and any other matters considered essential***]____.**

(b) Concurrent with execution of the construction loan documents, Buyer shall obtain a commitment for permanent financing to replace the construction loan. The permanent loan shall ____[*specify terms of loan as in (a) above***]____.**

Comment: This provision is to be included in the purchase and sale agreement. It should specify the terms of the subordinating loans in as much detail as possible in order to provide protection for the seller and to enable the buyer to enforce it if necessary. See §5.42. With modifications, this form could be utilized to draft a separate executory subordination agreement which could be recorded with the seller's deed of trust.

§5.45   b. Executed Subordination Agreements

When a subordinating loan is made in reliance on an automatic subordination agreement, or a previously executory agreement is fully executed and recorded, the legal problems which may arise differ from those encountered with executory agreements (§§5.42-5.43). If the new loan complies precisely with the terms of the subordination agreement, and if the funds are not misapplied, an agreement that when still executory might have been too uncertain to be enforceable becomes a valid executed agreement, and the new loan achieves priority over the seller's lien. If, however, the new loan does not meet the requisites of the subordination agreement, either because of a discrepancy in the loan terms or because loan funds are misapplied, then the lender may not be able to attain the priority sought in the subordination agreement.

§5.46   (1) Discrepancy Between Agreement and Loan

A discrepancy between the loan described in the subordination agreement and that actually entered into may entitle the seller to retain priority. A change in the interest rate or term, or inclusion of other clauses adversely affecting the seller's interests, might be sufficient to alter priority. In *Collins v Home Sav. & Loan Ass'n* (1962) 205 CA2d 86, 22 CR 817, the interest rate charged complied with the subordination agreement, but a 13½-percent loan placement fee did not, and the seller's lien retained its priority.

§5.47   (2) Misapplication of Funds

If the construction lender knows or should know of the buyer's application of loan funds to uses or purposes not permitted by the subordination agreement, the construction lien may lose its priority. *United States Bldg. & Loan Ass'n v Salisbury* (1932) 217 C 35, 17 P2d 140; *Radunich v Basso* (1965) 235 CA2d 826, 45 CR 824. In one decision the court allowed the lender priority to the extent that funds were disbursed in accordance with the subordination agreement, but held that the lender's lien was junior to that of the seller to the extent that funds were misapplied. *Miller v Citizens Sav. & Loan Ass'n* (1967) 248 CA2d 655, 56 CR 844. Note that this holding created three encumbrances rather than two: a lien for the amount of the properly used funds, the seller's subordinated lien, and the lien for the misapplied funds.

Some buyers have attempted to avoid this rule by including in the subordination agreement a conclusive presumption that the construction loan funds have been properly applied. In *Joanaco Projects, Inc. v Nixon & Tierney Constr. Co.* (1967) 248 CA2d 821, 57 CR 48, the court held such a purported presumption ineffective to shelter the buyer from immunity for its own misconduct.

Sellers have had less success in recovering damages for lenders' misfeasance in failing to ensure the buyer's compliance with the conditions of the subordination agreement than in retaining the priority of the sellers' liens, as in the cases cited above. Courts have held that the lender owes no duty of care to the seller because there is no privity of contract between lender and seller. *Weiss v Brentwood Sav. & Loan Ass'n* (1970) 4 CA3d 738, 84 CR 736; *Fries v Broadway Fed. Sav. & Loan Ass'n* (1968) 258 CA2d 119, 65 CR 460; *Gill v Mission Sav. & Loan Ass'n* (1965) 236 CA2d 753, 46 CR 456; *Matthews v Hinton* (1965) 234 CA2d 736, 44 CR 692.

(3) Automatic Subordination Provisions

§5.48   (a) Form: Contents of Note and Deed of Trust

Form 5.48-1

[To be inserted in purchase and sale agreement (chap 3), or separate subordination agreement]

The deed of trust shall contain the following provisions:

[Insert statutory notice provisions; see §5.54]

This deed of trust, provided no unrescinded notice of default under its terms then appears of record, shall be subordinate to deed(s) of trust thereafter executed by trustor

[Choose appropriate statement]

[Land to be subdivided; individual or blanket loans]

covering any lot or group or groups of lots into which the described land then has been subdivided as shown on a map filed for record, the total number of lots not to exceed ____,

[Land already subdivided; individual or blanket loans]

covering any lot or group or groups of lots described in this agreement

[Land to be subdivided; individual loans only]

one on each of the lots into which the land will have then been subdivided, as shown on a map filed for record, the total number of lots not to exceed _____,

[Improved lot or building site]

covering the described land

[Continue]

and securing a ____*[construction]*____ **loan made by** ____*[specify lender by name or specify type of institution, e.g., a bank, savings and loan association, or life insurance company]*____.
The loan shall be evidenced by a promissory note not in excess of

[Choose appropriate statement]

[Land to be subdivided or already subdivided; individual or blanket loans]

an amount arrived at by multiplying the number of lots described in the deed of trust securing the note by ____*[$_____ / ____ percent of the value as appraised by* ____*[FHA / VA / lender]*____ *]*____,

[Land to be subdivided; individual loans only]

____*[$_____ / ____ percent of value as appraised by* ____*[FHA / VA / lender]*____ *]*____,

[Improved lot or building code]

____*[$ _____ / ____ percent of value as appraised by]*____ ____*[FHA / VA / lender]*____,

[Continue]

bearing interest at not more than _____ percent per year. If a construction loan, the loan shall be payable not more than _____ months or less than _____ months from the date of recordation of the loan, and if a permanent loan, principal and interest shall be payable in equal monthly installments sufficient to amortize fully the loan over a period of not less than _____ years nor more than _____ years. If a combination construction and permanent loan, interest only shall be payable during the construction loan period, which period shall not be less than _____ months nor more than _____ months and thereafter on the same terms as though a permanent loan.

[Insert provisions regarding acceleration clauses, late payment charges, prepayment charges, and other loan provisions as appropriate]

The remaining terms and provisions of the loan shall be as required by the lender.

[Continue with form at §5.49]

Comment: The provision provides for automatic subordination if no default appears of record. The seller may prefer permitting subordination only if no default exists under the terms of the deed of trust. For similar language on reconveyance, see §5.62. Title companies usually will not insure the priority of a subordinating loan based on an automatic subordination clause. See §5.41. Instead, a subordination agreement executed by the seller expressly subordinating the purchase money deed of trust to the new loan must be recorded concurrently with the new loan instruments. See §5.52. The provisions at §§5.48-5.51 providing for automatic subordination should be combined with the provision at §5.52 obligating the seller to execute a specific subordination agreement.

A construction loan has been defined as a loan of money to be used for the construction of improvements on the property and incidental expenses (*Pollock v Tiano* (1967) 253 CA2d 183, 186, 61 CR 235, 237) and does not include reimbursement to the purchaser for land acquisition costs (*Ruth v Lytton Sav. & Loan Ass'n* (1968) 266 CA2d 831, 72 CR 521; *Pollock v Tiano, supra*). More detailed provisions concerning the purpose and use of the loan are set out at §5.49, and may be required under the decision in *Handy v Gordon* (1967) 65 C2d 578, 55 CR 769. For the loan terms that must be specifically described in an enforceable subordination agreement, see §5.43. Under *Handy v Gordon, supra,* the terms of the subordinating loan should be stated as specifically as possible in absolute terms or as falling within a permissible range. Other terms that should be specified include restrictions on prepayment, late charges, and terms required to conform to leases or to a permanent loan commitment. Details of the loan may be left to the buyer's negotiations with the lender if the specified lender is an institutional lender active in the relevant loan market, particularly if the seller is familiar with the loan practices of the lender. Under *Handy v Gordon, supra,* however, the transaction will be reviewed as a whole and precise specification of the terms of the subordinating loan may not be sufficient if the transaction is otherwise unfair to the particular seller. See §5.49.

§5.49   (b) Form: Purpose and Use of Loan

Form 5.49-1

[Precede with provision at §5.48]

The loan shall be used for ____[specify purpose of loan]____. The proceeds of the loan shall be disbursed in payment, or in reimbursement for payment, of only the following:

[Specify uses permitted; see Comment below]

[Continue with provision at §5.50]

Comment: The subordination agreement should state clearly what payments may properly be made from the subordinating loan. Disbursements that do not enhance the value of the property increase the encumbrance to which the seller is subordinated without increasing his security, and lack of fairness to the seller prevents specific performance. *Handy v Gordon* (1967) 65 C2d 578, 55 CR 769. The statement of permitted disbursements in the recorded security instrument is constructive notice to later encumbrancers. The lender's priority under an automatic subordination clause in a deed of trust will depend on the loan's provisions' meeting the conditions under which the seller agreed to subordinate. *Middlebrook-Anderson Co. v Southwest Sav. & Loan Ass'n* (1971) 18 CA3d 1023, 96 CR 338. See §5.46., For this reason, the seller may be required to execute an additional subordination agreement specifically describing the subordinating loan. See §5.52.

Terms of the subordinating loan that should be specified include:

(1) *Loan fees and other loan charges.* Charges amounting to 13½ percent of the total loan have been held excessive in the absence of provision for them. *Collins v Home Sav. & Loan Ass'n* (1962) 205 CA2d 86, 22 CR 817. See §5.46. One solution is to specify permitted charges (*e.g.,* all costs of obtaining the loan or discounts, including loan fees, appraisers' charges, escrow and title insurance fees) and set a maximum for them. Interest payments during the construction loan period and other indirect construction costs such as construction bond and insurance premiums, real property taxes during the construction loan period, leasing commissions, and legal expenses are also frequently specified with appropriate limitations as to amount.

(2) *Land improvement costs.* An example of a provision detailing the permitted charges is the following:

(a) Actual costs of construction of the dwelling with the usual appurtenances including garage, patio, driveway, and fencing, but including only the expenditures for labor and materials by buyer or by an entity owned in whole or in part by buyer; (b) a prorata share of aggregate costs of general subdivision improvements, which shall comprise engineering fees, architectural fees, drafting fees, permit and inspection fees, map recording charges, subdivision bond premiums, onsite and offsite grading and excavation costs, and all costs for improvements required by the City of _____ for approval of a subdivision. The prorata share for each item shall be determined by dividing the cost for the item by the number of lots for which the cost is incurred.

(3) *Developer's fee.* If the subordinating construction loan includes a distribution to the buyer-developer for a development or construction supervision fee, it should be stated in the subordination agreement. See *Collins v Home Sav. & Loan Ass'n, supra.* Similarly, if the construction loan borrower will act as the general contractor, specific provision for the payment of a fee to the borrower as general contractor should be included.

(4) *Purchase price of land.* Application of loan proceeds to the purchase price of the land has been held to be improper in the absence of agreement to it. *Radunich v Basso* (1965) 235 CA2d 826, 45 CR 824. See Comment at §5.48.

(5) *Other charges.* In *Ruth v Lytton Sav. & Loan Ass'n* (1968) 266 CA2d 831, 72 CR 521, the interest rate of the construction loan was subject to increase from 6.75 percent to 8.75 percent on default. The court held that the loan did not comply with the conditions of the subordination agreement which limited the interest rate to 7.2 percent.

(6) *Amount of loan.* The loan in *Ruth v Lytton Sav. & Loan Ass'n, supra,* also failed to comply with a condition of the subordination agreement restricting the loan amount to 66.67 percent of the appraised value of the improved property, because the actual loan equaled 68.84 percent of the appraised value of the improved property.

§5.50   (c) Form: Disbursement Method

Form 5.50-1

[*Precede with provisions at §§5.48 and 5.49*]

Buyer shall arrange to receive funds from the lender by a voucher payment plan based on inspection for work completed and submission by buyer of an invoice or voucher for payment of, or reimbursement for payment of, and release of lien in connection with items designated in paragraph ____[see §5.49]____. The priority of the lender's lien shall not be reduced as a result of buyer's misuse of disbursements or the falsity of vouchers or invoices certified and lien releases submitted by buyer.

[*Continue with provision at §5.51 if appropriate*]

Comment: Institutional lenders require title insurance on their lien priority. If the lender's priority is to be insured, the agreement must provide that its lien will retain priority under terms acceptable to the lender. These are matters for negotiation among buyer, seller, and lender. The suggested provision, continuing the clauses starting in §5.48 for inclusion in the security instrument, calls for the voucher system frequently adopted by lenders and retains the lender's lien priority when that system is used. The voucher system is discussed in California Mechanics' Liens and Other Remedies §6.36 (Cal CEB 1972).

A developer not accustomed to working under a voucher system might refuse to accept this provision. In that case, the seller might consider requiring that the buyer furnish a surety bond of which the seller would be an obligee. Opinions differ about the efficacy of a bond in this situation. See Ground Lease Practice §2.63 (Cal CEB 1971). The method used and the extent to which each party's interests will be protected are matters for negotiation. Other methods include: requiring the seller's approval and execution of voucher requests, and employing an independent third party to disburse the construction loan proceeds. Whatever method is used will incur additional costs for the buyer in the form of loan fees, insurance premiums, or other charges. This may be accounted for in the subordination agreement by fixing a maximum for such costs and permitting them to be paid from the proceeds of the subordinating loan.

The seller may wish to reduce the risk further by imposing additional conditions on subordination to a construction loan. These conditions will depend on the circumstances of the transaction, but might include requirements that (1) the buyer obtain a firm commitment for a permanent loan, (2) the buyer enter into satisfactory commercial leases with major tenants for a specified number of square feet of building improvements, (3) the buyer obtain bonding for offsite improvements, (4) the construction lender agree to provide the seller with notice and an opportunity to cure defaults and that noncurable defaults will not be grounds for foreclosure if the seller promptly performs all other provisions of the subordinating note and deed of trust. For forms covering some of the conditions in (1) and (4), see Ground Lease Practice §§2.94, 2.99 (Cal CEB 1971).

§5.51   (d) Form: Subordination to Permanent Loan

Form 5.51-1

[Precede with provisions at §§5.48, 5.49 and 5.50]

After completion of the improvements on the described land, a permanent loan deed of trust may be placed on ____*[the described land / the lot / each of the lots]*____ ____*[described in it]*____ ____*[each]*____ securing a loan made by a bank, a savings and loan association, or an insurance company, to be evidenced by a promissory note not to exceed ____*[$*_____ / ____ *percent of appraised value]*____ on ____*[the described land / the lot / each of the lots]*____ including all costs of obtaining the loan or discounts not in excess of $_____, bearing interest at not more than _____ percent per year, payable at the time and on the terms the lender requires but over a period of not less than _____ years or more than _____ years. The permanent loan deed of trust, when recorded, and when ____*[the described land / the lot / each of the lots]*____ ____*[described in it]*____ has been reconveyed from the contemplated ____*[construction]*____ loan deed of trust to which this deed of trust is subject, shall constitute a lien on ____*[the described land / the lot / each of the lots]*____ ____*[described in it]*____ prior to the lien of this deed of trust.

[Continue with provision at §5.52]

Comment: The construction loan is frequently based on a commitment for a permanent loan after construction is completed (see §6.14), and the seller will want assurance that a commitment for permanent financing has been obtained. See §5.43. The subordination agreement should include the permanent loan; otherwise, if the permanent loan is to have the priority institutional lenders require, the seller's note must be paid when the construction loan matures, usually within 12 to 24 months. The same need for certainty about lender, maximum amount, interest rate, maturity date, and amortization applies for permanent loans as for construction loans. See §5.42.

On developments built for resale, subordination to a permanent loan should permit payment to the seller on sale to the ultimate purchaser. This result might be accomplished either (1) by accelerating the buyer's note on resale to the extent of the release price per lot or (2) by leaving the subject of this aspect of subordination to future negotiations and omitting the provision from the purchase and sale agreement. If left to future negotiations, any new agreement must be supported by its own consideration. CC §1698.

§5.52   (e) Form: Execution of Additional Subordination Agreement

Form 5.52-1

[Precede with provisions at §§5.48, 5.49, 5.50, 5.51]

Seller agrees, on request, to execute and deliver to buyer for recordation a subordination agreement or agreements in the form attached as Exhibit _____, in favor of any loan to which seller's lien is to be subordinated under the terms of this deed of trust. The terms of any such subordination agreement executed by seller shall prevail over the subordination terms provided for in this deed of trust.

Comment: Title insurance companies generally require that a specific subordination agreement be executed by the seller and recorded concurrently with the subordinating loan. See §§5.41, 5.48. The form of the subordination agreement to be attached must be acceptable to the title company insuring the subordinating loan. Subordination agreements satisfactory to title companies have been prepared by the California Land Title Association and are available from most title companies. Any variation from these forms should be approved in advance by the title company that will insure the priority of the subordinating loan.

§5.53   c. De Facto Subordination

Seller and buyer may simply agree that the construction encumbrance will be recorded first and the purchase money encumbrance second to subordinate the purchase money encumbrance to the construction lender's lien. Some commentators contend that such an agreement does not result in reordering the priority of the liens and is thus not a true subordination situation. See 2 Miller & Starr, Current Law of California Real Estate §§11:175, 11:181 (rev ed 1977). For all practical purposes, however, courts have treated this situation as raising the same issues as exist under subordination agreements (see §§5.42-5.43), regardless of the mechanics used. Thus, whether the lender's lien retains priority still depends on whether the construction loan complies with the conditions under which the seller agreed to modify the order of recording (*Middlebrook-Anderson Co. v Southwest Sav. & Loan Ass'n* (1971) 18 CA3d 1023, 96 CR 338), and the construction lender faces the same risk of loss of priority when funds are misused as under any other form of subordination (*Gluskin v Atlantic Sav. & Loan Ass'n* (1973) 32 CA3d 307, 108 CR 318).

§5.54   d. Cautionary Language Required

The Civil Code requires that specific warnings be given in connection with subordination provisions to advise the holder of the lien being made junior of that fact and its implications. Warnings must be included in instruments containing subordination clauses (CC §2953.2) and subordination agreements (CC §2953.3), but need not appear in a purchase agreement in which the seller merely takes back a second deed of trust. The statutory provisions do not apply when the subordination provisions expressly state that the subordinating loan is to exceed $25,000 (CC §2953.5(a)) or when the subordinated loan exceeds $25,000 (CC §2953.5(b)). Although these provisions thus apply to very few real property transactions, many title insurance companies nevertheless insist that the statutory language be inserted in any deed of trust with subordination provisions.

If, under the terms of the instrument creating it, a security interest becomes subordinate to another lien when certain conditions occur, the instrument containing the subordination provision must have the word "subordinated" at its top in at least 10-point bold type if printed or in capital letters and underlined if typewritten. CC §2953.2. The following provision must appear immediately below in at least 8-point bold type if printed or in capital letters if typewritten (CC §2953.2(b)).

NOTICE: This (insert description of real property security instrument) contains a subordination clause which may result in your security interest in the property becoming subject to and of lower priority than the lien of some other or later security instrument.

If the security instrument permits the proceeds of the loan being made senior to be used for purposes other than costs for improvement of the land, CC §2953.2 requires that the following provision appear immediately above the space for the signature of the subordinated lienor in at least 8-point bold type if printed or in capital letters if typewritten (CC §2953.2(c)).

NOTICE: This (insert description of real property security instrument) contains a subordination clause which allows the person obligated on your real property security instrument to obtain a loan a portion of which may be expended for other purposes than improvement of the land.

If an agreement provides that a security interest is made junior to a new loan, either conditionally or otherwise, the agreement must have the words "subordination agreement" at its top in at least 10-point bold type if printed or capital letters underlined if typewritten. CC §2953.3. The following language must appear immediately below in at least 8-point bold type if printed or in capital letters if typewritten (CC §2953.3(b)).

NOTICE: This subordination agreement ("may result" or "results" as appropriate) in your security interest in the property becoming subject to and of lower priority than the lien of some other or later security instrument.

If the agreement permits the proceeds of the loan being made senior to be used for purposes other than actual contract costs for improving the land, the following must appear immediately above the space for the signature of the subordinated lienor in at least 8-point bold type if printed or in capital letters if typewritten (CC §2953.3(c)).

NOTICE: This subordination agreement contains a provision (which "allows" or "may allow" as appropriate) the person obligated on your real property security to obtain a loan a portion of which may be expended for other purposes than improvement of the land.

For those situations in which the lender's subordinating lien achieves priority by being recorded earlier than the seller's subordinated lien, the California Attorney General has declared that the notice provisions of CC §2953.2 are not applicable. 43 Ops Cal Atty Gen 19, 22 (1964). However, if the subordinating or subordinated lien is less than $25,000, the statutory notice must be included in deeds of trust on subordination agreements using the form provisions at §§5.44, 5.48-5.52.

These statutory provisions may be waived by the person whose lien is being subordinated. CC §2953.4(c). However, because the Attorney General has declared that the subordinated lien must be signed and delivered before any steps are taken to sign the waiver (43 Ops Cal Atty Gen 19 (1964)), it is best to include the statutory language rather than to rely on the seller's willingness to waive his rights after the event.

C. Release and Partial Reconveyance

§5.55   1. Agreement Required

Buyer and seller can agree that portions of the property will be released from the lien of the deed of trust on the entire property on payment of specified consideration. The release is accomplished by a partial reconveyance, executed by the trustee, that describes the released portion. Civil Code §2941 requires reconveyance on full satisfaction of the indebtedness, but there are no statutory provisions requiring partial reconveyance or release on partial payment. In the absence of an enforceable agreement between trustor and beneficiary, the trustor is not entitled to a partial release in exchange for partial satisfaction of the obligations secured by the deed of trust. CC §2912; *Bradbury v Thomas* (1933) 135 CA 435, 27 P2d 402.

The preferred practice is to include release clauses in both the purchase and sale agreement and the purchase money deed of trust, although a separately recorded release agreement is enforceable (*Woodward v Brown* (1897) 119 C 283, 51 P 542). The property to be released may be described by lot, by metes and bounds, or by any other means that is sufficiently specific. See §5.59. Property released should be legally severed from the property remaining subject to the deed of trust to comply with the Subdivision Map Act (Govt C §§66410-66499.58). See §5.60.

§5.56   2. Buyer's Needs

A buyer who intends to develop real property in increments, or to subdivide and sell lots separately, may need to be able to release portions of the real property from the lien either when the construction loan is recorded for each increment of the development (in the absence of a subordination agreement), or when the subdivided lots are sold. Subordination agreements are discussed in §§5.39-5.54. The proceeds from the construction loan or sale will probably provide the consideration for the partial release.

At the time the purchase and sale agreement is executed, a developer will seldom have sufficient information to determine exactly how the property will be improved. Many factors, including financing, governmental requirements, the cost and method of providing utilities and road access, soil conditions and drainage, and market demand, will affect the type, design, and schedule of the property's development. Typically, developers are unwilling to determine these factors before entering into the purchase and sale agreement or option for acquisition of the property. As a result, specific legal descriptions for the parcels or lots to be partially released are seldom available when preparing the purchase agreement or option, and the buyer will need a release clause which allows a great deal of flexibility in determining what parcels are to be released, and in what order.

§5.57   3. Seller's Needs

The seller must be assured that the security for the deed of trust will not be impaired by releases made to the buyer. To protect the seller, restrictions must be placed on the buyer's selection of release parcels to ensure that the value of the property remaining subject to the seller's lien after each release will be adequate security for the then unpaid balance of the seller's purchase money note. One device for achieving this protection is to require that releases be made in a stated order, the less valuable first; another is to fix the release price higher than the prorata portion of the purchase price allocable to the released parcel. A purchase and sale agreement providing for partial releases without adequate provisions to protect the seller will be unenforceable either because the agreement lacks the necessary certainty (*White Point Co. v Herrington* (1968) 268 CA2d 458, 73 CR 885) or because the agreement is unfair and unjust to the seller (*Eldridge v Burns* (1978) 76 CA3d 396, 142 CR 845). The requirements of certainty and fairness are discussed at §5.59. The seller may also use release provisions to discourage delinquency by conditioning the right to release on the absence of a default or on the absence of a recorded notice of default. These protections are provided in the forms at §§5.62-5.64.

§5.58   4. Resolving Conflicting Needs

Counsel for buyer and seller must often accommodate the buyer's requirement for flexibility in describing release parcels with the seller's requirements for certainty and fairness necessary to protect his security and to ensure the legal enforceability of the agreement. Resolving these competing needs calls for skilled negotiating and careful drafting.

Usually buyer's and seller's requirements are accommodated by giving the buyer some discretion to define the boundaries of the release parcels, but limiting this discretion to ensure that its exercise will not impair the seller's security. A form limiting the buyer's discretion to determine the boundaries of release parcels is set forth in §5.63; an alternative method of protecting the seller's security by adjusting release prices is set forth in §5.64.

§5.59   5. Requirement of Certainty and Fairness

To be enforceable by the buyer, a release clause must be both certain and fair to the seller. This is an area fraught with pitfalls for the potential buyer, and great care must be taken in drafting release clauses that will withstand judicial scrutiny. If the transaction itself is still executory, an uncertain release clause will deny the buyer specific performance of the entire purchase agreement; if the sale has been consummated and only the release provisions remain executory, the conveyance cannot be rescinded by the seller but the buyer will be denied specific performance of the release clause.

In *White Point Co. v Herrington* (1968) 268 CA2d 458, 73 CR 885, the entire sale was still executory, and the escrow instructions provided that the note would contain a release clause for partial releases at $3000 per acre. The court held this provision to be uncertain and denied the buyer specific performance of the entire agreement stating that when only the broadest guidelines for releases are given, the contract is unfair to the seller because of the many undesirable possibilities that the choice parcels will be released and the seller will be left with land of less value than the balance on the note.

In *Lawrence v Shutt* (1969) 269 CA2d 749, 75 CR 533, the buyer sued for specific performance of the release clause after the property had been conveyed, and the seller cross-complained for rescission of the entire transaction. The release clause was quite detailed, but the court found it uncertain because it provided that each parcel to be released had to be contiguous to the portion previously released, and the term "contiguous" means only having a minimum common boundary without specifying the precise area to be released. Although the uncertainty of the release clause precluded specific performance, it was not a reason to invalidate the otherwise complete conveyance, and the seller was denied rescission.

The decisions in both *White Point Co. v Herrington, supra,* and *Lawrence v Shutt, supra,* relied on *Handy v Gordon* (1967) 65 C2d

578, 55 CR 769, a case pertaining to subordination (see §5.42), for the proposition that enforcement of subordination and release clauses requires certainty and fairness to the seller. The underlying rationale of all three cases seems to be that a seller is not afforded adequate protection unless the subordination and release clauses are sufficiently certain to ensure that the seller's security cannot be impaired. Thus, the test contains an element of subjectivity which calls for extremely careful drafting if buyers are to be able to enforce release clauses.

Although an unfair release clause in a purchase agreement will deny the buyer specific performance, it cannot be used defensively by the buyer in an action by the seller for damages for breach of the purchase agreement. *Yackey v Pacifica Dev. Co.* (1979) 99 CA3d 776, 160 CR 430. In *Yackey* the release clause was similar to that in *White Point Co. v Herrington, supra,* but the fact that its uncertainty could be abused by the buyer to select the best parcels for release could not be used defensively by the buyer who had drafted it. When a seller has accepted substantial payments on an obligation secured by a deed of trust which permits partial releases for such payments, the buyer may be entitled to equitable relief or damages even though not otherwise entitled to enforce the release provisions due to uncertainty or unfairness. *Eldridge v Burns* (1978) 76 CA3d 396, 142 CR 845.

6. Subdivision Requirements

§5.60   a. Subdivision Map Act

If the property to be sold is currently undivided, partial releases will probably constitute division of the property requiring compliance with the Subdivision Map Act (Govt C §§66410-66499.58). The seller might wish to provide in the release clause that the buyer's entitlement to a partial release is conditioned on compliance with the Subdivision Map Act. See form at §5.63.

Under the Subdivision Map Act, local jurisdictions are required to adopt ordinances regulating and controlling subdivisions, and providing for recording of an approved map when land is divided (see §1.42). Govt C §§66411, 66411.1; see *Friends of Lake Arrowhead v Board of Supervisors* (1974) 38 CA3d 497, 113 CR 539. The purposes of the act are to encourage orderly community development by providing for control of the design and improvement of subdivisions

(*Newport Bldg. Corp. v City of Santa Ana* (1962) 210 CA2d 771, 26 CR 797; 56 Ops Cal Atty Gen 496 (1973)), and to permit the imposition of conditions on subdivision approval to prevent the subdivision from becoming an undue burden on the community's taxpayers (*Bright v Board of Supervisors* (1977) 66 CA3d 191, 135 CR 758).

An approved subdivision map must be recorded for any subdivision as defined in the act. Subdivision is defined as the division of improved or unimproved land shown on the latest county assessment roll as a unit or contiguous units, for the purpose of sale, lease, or financing, immediate or future. Govt C §66424. Both tentative and final maps must be approved for a subdivision creating five or more parcels, unless the subdivision comes within one of the exceptions listed in Govt C §66426. Subdivisions of fewer than five parcels or exempted under Govt C §66426 must obtain a parcel map. Govt §66428. Procedures for preparation and approval of tentative, final, and parcel maps are set forth in Govt C §§66433-66463.5. See *Lenney v Board of Supervisors* (1974) 41 CA3d 902, 116 CR 500.

The California Attorney General has interpreted Govt C §§66424 to include within its definition of subdivision the placing of two separate deeds of trust on different portions of a single lot or parcel. 58 Ops Cal Atty Gen 408 (1975). The opinion cites the legislative history to show that the term "financing" was added to Bus & P C §11535 (the predecessor to Govt C §66424) to prevent the circumvention of the act through subdivision by financing. This same reasoning would seem to apply to partial releases from a blanket encumbrance of portions of currently undivided land.

§5.61   b. Subdivided Lands Act

Under the California Subdivided Lands Act (Bus & P C §§11000-11200), an owner or subdivider is prohibited from selling a lot or parcel subject to a blanket encumbrance unless certain conditions are met. Bus & P C §11013.1. The prohibition can be avoided if the blanket encumbrance contains an unconditional release clause. Bus & P C §11013.1. The provisions set forth in §§5.62-5.64 are not unconditional release clauses, and thus do not meet the exception of Bus & P C §11013.1. The subdivider can still sell lots subject to a blanket encumbrance if he complies with one of three methods for protecting the purchaser's deposit: (1) placing the purchaser's funds in an escrow account (Bus & P C §11013.2(a)); (2) conveying the subdivision property in trust (Bus & P C §11013.2(b)); or (3) posting a bond (Bus & P C §11013.2(c)). The subdivider would have to meet one of these exceptions in order to qualify to sell lots under the release clauses provided in §§5.62-5.64.

§5.62   7. Form: Partial Release of Determined Lots

Form 5.62-1

[Insert in purchase and sale agreement (chap 3) as appropriate]

The deed of trust shall contain the following provisions:

Beneficiary shall cause trustee to release and execute partial reconveyances of any one or more of the parcels of real property described in the schedule set forth below from the lien of this deed of trust on satisfaction of each of the following conditions:

(a) No release will be given if a notice of default then appears of record.

(b) No portion of the real property will be released unless all other portions of the real property subject to this deed of trust identified with a lower number than the number identifying the portion sought to be released have been reconveyed.

(c) No release will be given unless trustee holds and is authorized to deliver to beneficiary the release price for the property to be released as set forth in the schedule of release parcels and release prices below.

(d) No release will be given unless trustee holds and is authorized to deliver to beneficiary, in addition to the sum computed under (c) above, an amount equal to the accrued interest on the promissory note secured by this deed of trust through the date of reconveyance.

The portions of the real property described above subject to partial release, the price to be paid for the release of each such portion, under (c) above, and the order of release, are as follows:

Schedule of Release Parcels and Release Prices

Property to be released	Release Price
1. ____[Legal description of lot or parcel]____	$_____
2. ____[Legal description of lot or parcel]____	$_____

[Continue as needed]

Payments for releases under (c) above, except periodic payments required by the note, shall be applied to the ____[next / final]____ payment on the note secured by this deed of trust. Payments under (d) above shall be applied to accrued interest on the note. Principal payments made on the note for which no releases are obtained by trustor shall constitute a credit fund to apply against subsequent releases from the lien of this deed of trust.

Comment: This form is to be used when the lots to be released have already been determined. The forms at §§5.63 and 5.64 suggest two methods of permitting partial release when the agreement is drafted before the property is subdivided.

The release clause must fit the peculiar features of a given transaction in order to ensure that any discretion of the buyer with respect to the property to be released cannot be exercised in a way that might be inequitable to the seller. This form provides one method for limiting the buyer's discretion.

The agreement must specify the extent and manner of application of release payments to the contract balance; lack of clarity may bring about unintended results. *Vilkin v Sommer* (1968) 260 CA2d 687, 67 CR 837; *San Diego Constr. Co. v Mannix* (1917) 175 C 548, 166 P 325. The buyer usually prefers to have payments apply to the next payment due under the note, and to apply all payments, including the downpayment, to the release price. The seller may prefer crediting payments to the last payment due. The manner of crediting payments must be tailored to fit the needs of the parties to the transaction.

Generally, the right to reconveyance is not lost by the buyer's failure to request the release of land when payments are made. Absent a contrary provision in the agreement, the trustor's subsequent default does not extinguish the right to partial reconveyances of land already paid for. *Eldridge v Burns* (1978) 76 CA3d 396, 142 CR 845; *Conley v Poway Land & Inv. Co.* (1965) 232 CA2d 22, 42 CR 636. This form gives the buyer credit on releases for payments previously made for which reconveyances were not received.

For provisions allowing releases even when annual payments by the buyer are limited as in the provision at §5.20, see §5.66.

§5.63   8. Form: Partial Release (Lots Not Determined); Limiting Buyer's Discretion

Form 5.63-1

[Insert in purchase and sale agreement (chap 3) as appropriate]

The deed of trust shall contain the following provisions:
Beneficiary shall cause trustee to release and execute partial recon-

veyances of portions of the real property described above from the lien of this deed of trust on satisfaction of each of the following conditions:

(a) ____[Describe order of reconveyance and any other limitations necessary to prevent impairment of the seller's security; see Comment for examples]_____.

(b) No release will be given if ____[a notice of default then appears of record / trustor is then in default under this deed of trust]_____.

(c) Trustee holds and is authorized to deliver to beneficiary the sum of $_____ for each acre for which release is sought by trustor.

(d) Trustee holds and is authorized to deliver to beneficiary, in addition to the sum required by (c) above, an amount equal to the accrued interest on the promissory note secured by this deed of trust through the date of reconveyance.

(e) Each portion of the real property released from the lien of this deed of trust shall consist of one or more legal lots or parcels as shown on a recorded parcel or final map. Notwithstanding the description of the release parcels in paragraph (a) above, trustor reserves the right, in order to satisfy this condition, to release less than the entire portion of the real property which trustor would otherwise be entitled to release by reason of the payment made. Portions of the real property not included in a partial release under this provision but included in computing the principal payment required to obtain a partial release shall not be included in computing the principal payment required to obtain any subsequent release which includes that portion, or any part of it.

[Continue with last paragraph in provision at §5.62]

Comment: On balancing the needs of buyer and seller in drafting release clauses, see §§5.56-5.57; on the requirements of certainty and fairness, see §5.59; for provisions for the release of determined lots, see §5.62.

The order of reconveyance in the agreement might be provided in a manner such as the following when, for example, the southerly portion of the property is the most valuable, and the property is approximately square:

The first parcel to be reconveyed shall have as its northerly, westerly, and southerly boundaries the northerly, westerly, and southerly boundaries, respectively of the property, and the easterly boundary shall be parallel to the westerly boundary. Subsequent releases shall each have as a westerly boundary the easterly boundary of the previously released parcel, an easterly boundary parallel to the westerly boundary, and as its northerly and southerly boundaries the northerly and southerly boundaries, respectively, of the property. In no event shall any reconveyance be permitted if the property remaining subject to the lien of this deed of trust would contain less than _____ square feet, as a result.

Another way of providing for the order or reconveyance when, for example, the property is rectangular in shape with greater depth than frontage and the southerly portion of the property is most valuable, might be:

The first parcel to be reconveyed shall have as its northerly and westerly boundaries the northerly and westerly boundaries of the property; the length of the westerly boundary shall not exceed the length of the northerly boundary of the land released; the southerly and easterly boundaries shall be parallel respectively to the southerly and easterly boundaries of the property. Subsequent releases shall have as a westerly boundary the easterly boundary of the parcel previously released, the northerly, easterly, and southerly boundaries shall be parallel to the northerly, easterly, and southerly boundaries of the property until the easterly boundary of the property is reached and subsequent releases shall be subject to the above conditions as if the southerly boundary of the land then released is the northerly boundary of the property. In no event shall any such release, other than a release having as its easterly boundary, the easterly boundary of the property, have its easterly boundary closer than _____ feet from the easterly boundary of the property, as measured at right angles from the easterly boundary. In no event shall any such release, other than a release having as its southerly boundary, the southerly boundary of the property, have its southerly boundary closer than _____ feet from the southerly boundary of the property, as measured at right angles from the southerly boundary.

When frontage or other choice land is to be released only after the remainder of the property has been released, and, for example, the southerly portion is frontage, the provision might read:

No partial reconveyance shall be given of any portion of the southerly 150 feet measured at right angles to the southerly boundary until all of the remainder of the property has been partially reconveyed to buyer.

Other limitations might also need to be imposed, *e.g.*, that releases shall be made in parcels of five acres or more and that land not reconveyed and still subject to the seller's lien shall have a specified type of access to a dedicated street or highway. Each parcel has its own demands and peculiarities and the release clause must be shaped to take them into account.

The above release provision conditions the right of the trustor to obtain reconveyance on satisfaction of the requirements of the Subdivision Map Act. This will generally require that a parcel or final map be recorded. See §5.60. For a provision authorizing the trustee to record a map affecting the real property secured by the deed of trust, see §5.22. Because government requirements and the topography of the property may require irregular lot or parcel boundaries, the form permits the trustor to obtain the release of any legal lot or parcel on payment of the release price for the larger permissible release parcel within which the lot or parcel to be released is situated.

§5.64   9. Form: Partial Release (Lots Not Determined); Adjustment of Release Price

Form 5.69-1

[Insert in purchase and sale agreement (chap 3) as appropriate]

Before the close of escrow, buyer may, at buyer's option, submit to seller, for seller's approval, a proposed division of the property into ____*[specify number, give maximum or minimum if desired]*____ parcels, to be released from the lien of the deed of trust. Buyer's proposed division shall include (a) certification of the total number of gross acres, to the nearest 1/1000th of an acre, within each of the proposed release parcels, addressed to seller and executed by a licensed civil engineer or land surveyor, (b) a legal description of each such parcel, (c) the order of release of such parcels, and (d) a proposed release price for each such parcel. Seller agrees to approve the division proposed by buyer, provided that the ratio that the fair market value of the land remaining subject to the deed of trust after each release bears to the maximum unpaid principal balance of the promissory note is equal to or greater than ____*[state a fraction, or specify, e.g., the ratio of the total purchase price to the principal balance of the seller's purchase money note]*____.

If seller disapproves of buyer's proposed division, seller shall give written notice of disapproval to buyer within _____ days of receipt of the proposed division. Seller's notice shall include a proposed new schedule of release prices for each of buyer's proposed release parcels, which in seller's opinion cause the ratio that the fair market value of the land to be subject to the deed of trust after each such release bears to the maximum unpaid principal balance of the promissory note equals ____*[specify ratio of value of land remaining to balance on note]*____. Seller's failure to give written notice of disapproval to buyer within _____ days shall constitute seller's approval of buyer's proposed division of the property and proposed schedule of release prices. If buyer believes that any of the release prices proposed by seller are greater than necessary to cause the ratio to be equal to or greater than _____, buyer shall notify seller of the disagreement, and if buyer and seller are unable to resolve their disagreement within _____ days of receipt of buyer's notice, the matter shall be conclusively determined by submitting the dispute to ____ *[arbitration / appraisal]*____ as follows:

[Insert provisions for arbitration or appraisal]

Fair market value for purposes of this paragraph shall be determined as of
____*[specify, e.g., the date of this agreement]*____.

The release parcels and release prices determined under this paragraph
shall be inserted into the schedule of release parcels and release prices in the
following provision for partial releases which shall be set forth in the deed of
trust:

*[Insert last paragraph in provision at §5.62; if appropriate, add paragraph (e)
from the provision at §5.63 as an additional condition to partial releases]*

Comment: In the absence of unfairness, the parties to a contract
may provide for determination of the consideration by disinterested
third parties. CC §1610. An option to purchase at a price to be
agreed on by the parties was held sufficiently certain to give rise to
an enforceable contract in *Bewick v Mecham* (1945) 26 C2d 92, 156
P2d 757, when the agreement also provided that if the parties could
not agree on the purchase price, the price would be fixed by three
arbitrators, one to be appointed by each party and the third by the
two previously appointed arbitrators. An agreement to surrender
shares of stock in a settlement agreement in exchange for payment
of an amount equal to the "fair evaluation as agreed upon by the
attorneys" for the parties was held sufficiently certain for specific
enforcement in *Forde v Vernbro Corp.* (1963) 218 CA2d 405, 32 CR
577. For a form for the submission of a dispute to arbitration, see
§3.183; a form for the submission of a dispute to appraisal is set forth
in Commercial Real Property Lease Practice §3.27 (Cal CEB 1976).

If buyer and seller are unable to agree on the principal payment
required for each partial release and if the seller refuses to permit,
or otherwise frustrates, resolution of the dispute by appraisal or arbitration, the buyer should be able to have the release prices established by the court in a specific performance or declaratory relief
action, particularly if he has changed his position in reliance on the
enforceability of the partial release provision. In *Bewick v Mecham,
supra,* 26 C2d 92, 156 P2d 757, the tenant had constructed $13,500
worth of building improvements on leased property in reliance on
his option to purchase, and the court determined the purchase price
when the defendant-seller refused to appoint an arbitrator. In this
situation, if equitable considerations support the position of the
party seeking specific performance, the courts tend "to consider
these stipulations for a determination of the price by third persons,

rather as matters of form than of substance; to construe them in such a manner that they become incidental only to the main object of the agreement. (Pomeroy, Specific Performance of Contracts (3d ed.) §151.)" *Bewick v Mecham* (1945) 26 C2d 92, 100, 156 P2d 757, 762.

The form provides for the parties to reach agreement on the release parcels and release prices before the close of escrow. It would also be appropriate to provide that escrow close despite a dispute over the release prices, or to extend the time for closing. The first might be accomplished by including a provision for determination of the release prices by appraisal or arbitration in the deed of trust. The possibility of substantial delay in determining the principal payment required for reconveyance of the release parcels is the primary disadvantage with this form.

Alternative methods of determining the release prices might be used. For example, the release prices might be established by providing that the fair market value of the property to remain subject to the deed of trust must be equal to the maximum unpaid principal balance of the promissory note secured by the deed of trust plus a fixed dollar amount.

Normally, the property should be appraised as of the date the purchase and sale agreement is executed. If, however, subdivision and development will affect the value of different portions of the property, and if the right to obtain releases will be conditioned on subdivision and development, the buyer may want the appraisal to take the different values into account by appraising the property as of a specified later date. In a common interest subdivision, common interest lots will have no independent value, and in other subdivisions, property subject to open space restrictions or required to be dedicated for parks or other public purposes may require different treatment. See §5.22.

§5.65   10. Form: Unencumbered Conveyance at Close of Escrow

Form 5.65-1

[Insert in purchase and sale agreement (chap 3) as appropriate]

At close of escrow and on payment by buyer to seller of the sum of $_____, seller shall convey free of any lien of the seller ____[*describe land*]_____.

Comment: Often, and particularly when the seller is not subordinating the purchase money deed of trust to liens for construction of other loans (see §§5.39-5.54), the buyer requires release of some land from the seller's lien. Consideration for acreage released at closing is a matter to be negotiated by the parties. The seller must keep in mind the risk in releasing part of his margin of security at this point.

When lots already subdivided are sold, describing the property to be conveyed free of the seller's lien is relatively simple. When undivided acreage is sold, however, describing the property to be released at closing is difficult because the exact acreage of the entire parcel may not be known until a survey is completed (see §§5.63, 5.64), and the exact location of those portions the buyer wishes to be conveyed free of any seller's lien cannot be determined until preliminary subdivision maps have been prepared. See §5.60. The land to be conveyed free of any seller's lien should be described in language similar to that employed for partial releases after close of escrow (see §§5.62-5.64), and closing should be conditioned on recordation of a parcel or final map which divides the property in such a way that the portion to be conveyed free of the lien of the purchase money deed of trust is a separate lot or parcel.

§5.66   11. Form: Substituted Security for Releases

Form 5.66-1

[Insert in purchase and sale agreement (chap 3) as appropriate]

The deed of trust shall contain the following provision:

After ____*[end of seller's tax year of sale]*____, and if no notice of default under this deed of trust then appears of record, and after trustor has paid the maximum payment for the year in which the following arrangement is made, trustor may obtain partial reconveyances otherwise permissible only in subsequent years by providing security for release payments for the land reconveyed by either (a) delivering to the trustee security for the payment, adequate in value and of a nature and on terms reasonably approved by beneficiary; or (b) depositing with the trustee under the deed of trust as a pledge and as security for the payment personal property of the following kinds of a face value not less than the balance then due beneficiary, including interest accrued to date of the deposit, plus ____*[specify additional amount]*____:

(1) United States, state, municipal, school or other public district bonds

legal for use as collateral, providing they are then currently selling at not less than face value; or

(2) Deposit books or time deposits of any _____ County branch of a bank whose deposits are insured by an agency of the federal government; or

(3) Passbooks or time certificates of any _____ County branch of a savings and loan association whose deposits are insured by an agency of the federal government; or

(4) Any combination of the above.

The deposit shall be made and held subject to the terms of a pledge agreement executed by trustor, trustee, and beneficiary before recordation of this deed of trust. Subject to the lien of the pledge, trustor shall retain ownership of the pledged property, and any increment of interest on it, and shall not permit or cause the substituted security to be subjected to any impairment, levy, or claim.

Comment: Although the seller may want to limit annual payments in order to spread his tax deferral over as long a period as possible (see §5.10), the buyer may require reconveyances sooner than the payment schedule permits, especially when the development is successful. If other security is substituted for the land reconveyed, the buyer achieves his purpose; if the security is of sufficient value, the right of the seller to ultimate payment is not jeopardized. Substitution of a cash equivalent as security under a pledge agreement may reduce the risk to the seller that he will be considered to have received reportable income. In *J. Earl Oden* (1971) 56 TC 569, however, installment reporting was held not available when the buyer merely deposited certificates of deposit into escrow at the time of sale and the parties intended that the certificates constitute payment rather than security. See also Rev Rul 77-294, 1977-2 Cum Bull 173. For further discussion of constructive receipt problems with cash equivalents held as substituted security, see Greene and Share, *Starker and Beyond: Including the Uncertain Life of the Secured Deferred Exchange,* 58 Taxes 724, 732 (1980).

A title insurance company usually will act as pledge holder, provided it approves the form of the pledge agreement. The terms of the pledge agreement should be agreed on before execution of the purchase agreement and a copy of the pledge agreement attached to the purchase agreement. The pledge agreement should provide that the pledged property is held as security for payment of the unpaid portion of the release price and that the pledgor is personally liable for payment.

§5.67   12. Form: Release on Condemnation Award

Form 5.67-1

[Insert in purchase and sale agreement (chap 3) as appropriate]

The deed of trust shall contain the following provision:

If any award of damages is made for condemnation affecting any part of the property subject to this deed of trust and at the time of the award the trustor has the right to demand reconveyance on payment of a specific sum, trustor shall pay that sum to beneficiary and shall then be entitled to receive the award. If any award of damages is made for any other portion of the property subject to this deed of trust, beneficiary shall receive the proportion of the award that the balance then due beneficiary bears to the market value of the entire parcel subject to the deed of trust at the date of the award. If the market value of the entire parcel cannot be agreed on by trustor and beneficiary, it shall be determined by appraisal as provided in paragraph ____.

Comment: Complications may arise if the property is condemned after close of escrow when the seller's rights in the property are those of an encumbrancer. The agreement and the security instrument should contain provisions for these rights.

If the entire parcel is condemned, there is usually no problem, because the lienholder receives the amount due on his lien from the award, which is generally sufficient for this purpose. See Condemnation Practice in California §10.14 (Cal CEB 1973). The problem is also minimized if a partial taking affects a portion of the property that may itself be reconveyed under other provisions of the instrument (a specific lot, for example, under provisions as at §5.62). Under CCP §1265.225, in a partial taking the lienholder shares in the award only to the extent that the security is impaired. See Condemnation Practice in California §10.14 (Cal CEB 1973). However, the taking under condemnation may include property not yet subject to release because other property must first be released (see Comment at §5.63), or may impair the value of the remaining land because of severance damages, the irregularity of the taking, or other factors. Most standard forms of deeds of trust permit the beneficiary to receive all proceeds of any award, although such a provision might be held to be subject to an implied covenant of good faith on the part of the beneficiary. See *Milstein v Security Pac. Nat'l Bank* (1972) 27 CA3d 482, 103 CR 16. The form divides the award in proportion to the parties' financial interests. As between buyer and seller, such a provision is subject to variations in allocation to suit the particular situation.

6

Edward S. Washburn

Institutional Financing

EDWARD S. WASHBURN, A.B., 1937, Yale University; LL.B., 1941, University of California School of Law (Berkeley). Mr. Washburn is of counsel to the San Francisco firm of Washburn, Kemp & Wagenseil, specializing in real property law, and previously served as counsel for Great Western Savings and Loan Association.

417

Note: As this book went to press (December 1980) a number of lending practices, as well as legal limitations on lending, were in a state of rapid change. The Depository Institutions Deregulation and Monetary Control Act of 1980 (Pub L 96-221, enacted March 31, 1980, 94 Stat 132) should have the effect of reducing the differences in lending practices not only between banks and savings and loan associations but also between federal and state institutions. The Federal Home Loan Bank Board has proposed new regulations that will alter legal limitations by lifting all dollar restrictions on residential loans by federal savings and loan associations; amortize home loans with 40 year terms; lift all geographic limitations on real property loans; and recognize 90-percent loans as the standard instead of the current 80-percent loans. The Federal National Mortgage Association has announced restrictions on the purchase of long term, fixed rate mortgages (see §6.11 for a discussion of the secondary market). A number of institutional lenders are either resisting or refusing to make fixed rate, 30-year loans (see §§6.47-6.52 on alternative mortgage instruments). Because of the rapid changes in this field, the attorney should check the current version of statutes and regulations and check directly with the lending institutions concerning current lending practices.

I. INTRODUCTION

§6.1   A. Financing Real Property Sales

Because acceptable financing is usually indispensable in a real property sales transaction, the buyer should investigate the financing of the purchase before executing a binding agreement, even though he or she does not need a formal or binding commitment from a lender. The purchase agreement is often contingent on the buyer's obtaining acceptable financing. See form at §3.152. Moreover, the information a lender needs to determine the advisability of making a loan may guide the buyer in his own decision, as well as provide the buyer with new information about the transaction. The lender's opinion can also be helpful to the buyer.

Although some seller (see chap 5) and other noninstitutional financing is available, most mortgage money comes from institutional lenders. For example, of the total outstanding mortgage loans at the end of 1975, savings and loan associations accounted for 51 percent, commercial banks for 17 percent, sponsored governmental agencies for 13 percent (investment activities and issues of these agencies include federally sponsored mortgage pools and pool securities), mutual savings banks for 10 percent, and life insurance companies for 4 percent. Individuals and others accounted for only 5 percent. Kaufman, *Variable Rate Residential Mortgages: The Early Experience From California,* Fed Reserve Bank of San Francisco Econ Rev, Summer 1976, p 5.

§6.2   B. Lawyer's Role

Although lawyers rarely play a large role in real property transactions for single-family residences, they can be of invaluable assistance to borrowers, especially in large and complex transactions, and can often influence the structure of the final transaction considerably, even the type of financing and its terms. Attorneys may not be able to negotiate the terms for financing with institutional lenders, particularly in smaller transactions, but they can advise clients on the criteria lenders consider, their procedures, regulations that govern institutions, and which lender may best fit the needs of a particular client. Attorneys can advise clients about the factors the various lending institutions will probably consider and the policies and procedures they follow in making a loan. See §§6.3-6.9 for the general policies and procedures of institutional lenders in making interim and permanent loans. For the legal limitations of institutional lenders, see, *e.g.,* Fin C §1227 (state banks); 12 USC §371 (national banks); Ins C §§1176, 1192.2 (insurance companies); Fin C §§7150-7187 (state savings and loan associations); 12 USC §1464(c) (federal savings and loan associations). For a discussion of the extent to which various loan terms may be subject to negotiation, see §§6.38-6.46.

II. INSTITUTIONAL LENDERS

A. Commercial Banks

§6.3   1. National Banks Versus State Banks

Commercial banks may be organized under either state or federal law. National banks are formed under federal law and are supervised by the Comptroller of the Currency (12 USC §§1-215b). They are also subject to regulation by the Federal Reserve Board (12 USC §§222, 248) and the Federal Deposit Insurance Corporation. 12 USC §1814. State banks are California corporations to which the California Superintendent of Banks has issued a certificate to engage in the banking business (see Fin C §§99-1382) and are supervised by the California Superintendent of Banks (see Fin C §§210-215).

For their lending operations, national banks are subject to state law unless state and federal law conflict, in which case the latter preempts the former. Fin C §100(b); Comment, *Constitutional Law: Federal and State Powers: State Regulation of National Banks*, 13 Calif L Rev 50 (1925). Congress has not enacted comprehensive laws for national banks, as it has for federal savings and loan associations (see §6.5), and in some instances Congress has specifically deferred to state law.

State banks usually are members of the Federal Reserve System in order to take advantage of its services and become stockholders in the Federal Deposit Insurance Corporation to obtain insurance of deposits by the federal government. 12 USC §1814. Concomitant with membership, state banks become subject to regulation by the Federal Reserve Board and the Federal Deposit Insurance Corporation. Fin C §§754-755.

Because the overlapping regulation of state and national banks by state and federal authorities tends to blur distinctions between these two types of commercial banks, they are now basically similar, although the legal loan limitations on national and state banks still differ in some instances. Compare, *e.g.*, Fin C §1227 (state banks) with 12 USC §371 (national banks).

§6.4   2. Lending Practices

Commercial banks are usually not aggressive in the long term (or permanent) residential mortgage lending market. Even though regulations permit such loans, the banks prefer to keep their funds in short term loans. This policy is dictated in part because much of their lendable funds are in checking accounts subject to immediate withdrawal. Commercial loans to business customers for financing business operations are their greatest source of short term loans. Nonetheless, a borrower should not overlook commercial banks as a source for long term residential property loans when seeking the best possible rate and fee for such a loan. Individual bank policies differ considerably, but banks in rural communities and those that have other banking relationships with the potential borrower (*e.g.*, a business customer) are more likely to be receptive to an application for a long term residential loan.

B. Savings and Loan Associations

§6.5   1. Federal Versus State Associations

All savings and loan associations are either chartered by the federal government or incorporated in and licensed by the states where they are located. Other financial institutions similar in character but not so chartered or licensed may not use the term *savings* and loan in their name (Fin C §5004); *e.g.,* "Blank *Thrift* and Loan" by its name indicates it is neither a federally chartered nor a state-licensed savings and loan association. Although the names of federal and state savings and loan associations are confusingly similar, all federally chartered associations must contain the words federal savings and loan in their names, while state-licensed associations are prohibited from using the word federal in their names. 12 CFR §543.1.

Federal associations are governed by the Federal Home Loan Bank Board (FHLBB), an agency established by the Home Owners' Loan Act of 1933 (12 USC §§1461-1470). Until 1975 all federal associations were mutuals. The associations had no stockholders but were owned by their depositors, who automatically became members of the mutual association on depositing funds in the institution. Management of the mutual is selected by vote of the membership, though in practice it tends to be self-perpetuating because individual depositors lack interest in the details of management. In 1975 the FHLBB adopted regulations authorizing and regulating the operation of stock associations chartered under federal law. 12 CFR §§552.1-552.15.

State associations in California are licensed under Fin C §§5000-9717 and are regulated by the Savings and Loan Commissioner, who heads the Department of Savings and Loan in the Business and Transportation Agency. Because all California associations' deposits are now insured by the Federal Savings and Loan Insurance Corporation (FSLIC), these associations are also regulated by the FHLBB, the regulatory agency of the FSLIC. 12 USC §1470; 12 CFR §500.4. Consequently, many state and federal regulations are similar, as are the regulations for banks (see §6.3), although this is truer for savings operations than for lending operations.

In contrast to the regulatory procedures for national banks (see §6.3) which generally defer to state law, the FHLBB, under the Home Owners' Loan Act of 1933, has promulgated detailed and extensive regulations for federal savings and loan associations (12 USC §1464(a) authorizes the FHLBB to regulate their activities). These comprehensive rules and regulations have, in effect, preempted many state laws. See, *e.g., People v Coast Fed. Sav. & Loan Ass'n* (SD Cal 1951) 98 F Supp 311. The extent of this preemption has become an issue with respect to whether the rule enunciated in *Wellenkamp v Bank of America* (1978) 21 C3d 943, 148 CR 379, concerning the enforceability of a due-on clause, applies to federal associations. The federal associations take the position that it does not. In *Glendale Fed. Sav. & Loan Ass'n v Fox* (CD Cal 1978) 459 F Supp 903, the district court held that federal law exclusively governs the validity of due-on clauses in loan instruments of federal associations executed on or after June 8, 1976, the date on which the FHLBB enacted a specific regulation (formerly 12 CFR §545.6-11(f), now in 12 CFR §545.8-3(f)) authorizing federal associations to use due-on clauses. The court specifically refrained from ruling on whether federal law preempted state law in this area before the enactment of the regulation.

To what extent federal associations are subject to various state consumer protection laws, such as the antideficiency prohibitions for purchase money mortgages (CCP §580b) and those following private sale foreclosures (CCP §580d), is not entirely clear. The FHLBB and many federal associations take the position that the federal statutory and regulatory scheme is so complete that it does not permit any application of state law unless federal law has specifically deferred to the former. See, *e.g.,* the advisory opinion of the FHLBB filed in *Schott v Mission Fed. Sav. & Loan Ass'n* (CD Cal July 30, 1975, FHLBB Resolution No. 75-647, CIV-75-366). The preemption argument is not limited to due-on-sale clauses. It has already been advanced with great success in other areas, such as internal management of federal associations (*e.g.,* rules governing solicitation of proxies, voting requirements, and election of directors) and branching. See, *e.g., First Nat'l Bank v Dickinson* (1969) 396 US 122 (branch banking); *People v Coast Fed. Sav. & Loan Ass'n, supra,* 98 F Supp 311 (business practices); and *Central Sav. & Loan Ass'n v Federal Home Loan Bank Bd.* (8th Cir 1970) 422 F2d 504 (mobile facilities).

§6.6   2. Lending Practices

Except for the insignificant differences dictated by their regulatory requirements, federal and state associations' policies on conventional loans for single-family residences (which constitute the major proportion of their loan portfolios) are similar. One reason regulatory requirements tend not to differ is the California Savings and Loan Commissioner's peremptory power granted under Fin C §5500.5. This section provides that whenever, by statute or regulation, a federal association is granted a power that is unauthorized (or even prohibited) by the Financial Code to state associations, the commissioner may grant a similar power to state associations. Any regulation issued under this provision expires on January 1 of the second year after the end of the calendar year in which it was adopted, thus presumably giving the legislature time to consider whether the power should be granted permanently by an appropriate Financial Code amendment.

Both state and federal associations offer loans at an 80 percent of loan-to-value ratio, and their loan fees and interest rates tend to be similar, varying only slightly among individual associations. One exception to this tendency relates to the type of interest rate applicable to the loan. Many state associations offer variable interest rate loans, and particularly when interest rates are low, some offer only these loans. See §6.48. Federal associations, though permitted to make these loans, must also offer each applicant a comparable fixed rate loan (12 CFR §545.6-4(c) (5)), and in general are not aggressively marketing variables. Interest rates for variables are sometimes 1/4 percent lower than for comparable fixed rate loans as an incentive to induce borrowers to select a variable rather than a fixed rate loan. State and federal associations, as well as commercial banks, are also permitted to make renegotiable rate mortgages. See §6.49.

Differences in practices among institutions, regardless of whether they are state or federal, tend to become more substantial for loans other than conventional single-family residential loans. For example, some associations may emphasize government insured or guaranteed loans (FHA, VA, and Cal-Vet) while others do not actively pursue these loans. So-called spot construction loans, in which a property owner borrows to build one single-family dwelling for his or her own use, are not considered profitable by many associations. Under powers authorized by the Financial Institutions Regulatory and Interest Rate Control Act of 1978 (12 USC §504(f)), the FHLBB has approved home improvement loans made by federal associations with no dollar ceilings (other than overall loan-to-value ratio limitations) and with maximum terms of 20 years (12 CFR §545.6-12(b)); there are likewise no ceilings with respect to state licensed associations and commercial banks.

Both federal and state associations make loans on individual condominium units, which for regulatory purposes (*e.g.*, loan limitations) are treated as single-family dwellings. 12 CFR §541.7; Fin C §7153.1(a). Both types of associations are authorized to lend to purchasers of stock cooperative apartments. 12 CFR §545.6-2(a); Fin C §7153.1(b). Here, although the loan is secured by a pledge of the stock of the cooperative issued to each resident, for regulatory purposes it is treated like a lien on the living unit, possession of which is incident to ownership of the stock. This legal fiction is necessary because savings and loan associations generally wish to classify these loans as loans secured by liens on real property; although they can now make consumer and other loans not secured by real property liens, there are a number of restrictions and reserve requirements regarding these.

§6.7 C. Life Insurance Companies

Life insurance companies are regulated by the California Commissioner of Insurance. See Ins C §12921. The extent of supervision and regulation of real property lending activities by life insurance companies is not as great as it is for banks or savings and loan associations. See Ins C §1176.

Life insurance companies, unlike commercial banks, have traditionally been heavily engaged in real property loans. One reason is that their flow of lendable funds, generated by receipt of life insurance premiums and income from security portfolios, is reasonably steady and more predictable than bank deposits. Generally, life insurance companies concentrate on large multifamily and commercial loans, such as large apartment houses and office buildings, and are not active in the single-family residence market.

Before Proposition 2, which amended the usury provisions in Cal Const art XV, §1, was passed in 1979, life insurance companies were limited to a 10-percent interest rate on their loans. This often inhibited them from lending in California during times of high interest rates. The amendment raises this limitation to a rate equal to the federal discount rate plus 5 percent. Although the 1979 amendment does not include life insurance companies in the list of exempt lenders, it does empower the legislature to expand this list by statute and thus to exempt life insurance companies from the usury limitations and to place them on a par with banks and savings and loan institutions, which are constitutionally exempt.

§6.8 D. Pension and Welfare Funds

Pension and welfare funds are playing an increasingly important part in mortgage lending throughout the United States. They actively purchase mortgages in the secondary mortgage market (see §6.11) and also invest directly in large commercial loans. Many of these funds, such as public employee retirement funds, have enormous cash flows. In California the same usury restrictions apply as for the life insurance companies because they are not exempt lenders. See §6.7. Their funds are generally funneled into the market through mortgage brokers. Although not subject to specific regulation of their investments, they are nevertheless conservative in approach, generally emphasizing security rather than high yield in their mortgage loan portfolios.

§6.9 E. Real Estate Investment Trusts

Real estate investment trusts, known as REITs, are unincorporated associations in trust form, with at least 100 beneficial interest holders that invest in real property interests. The organizational form of REITs is that of the Massachusetts business trust, which dates back to the middle of the 19th century.

They are formed primarily for certain income tax advantages. See IRC §§856-858; Corp C §§23000-23005. Their real property investments are in both equity and loan investments. In equity investments, the REIT acquires ownership of real property; in loan investments the REIT lends its funds, which are secured by real property. At one time REITs were a significant factor in the mortgage lending market and invested in large multifamily residential projects and in commercial and industrial developments. For various reasons, including lack of experience and expertise in real estate, many REITs have fallen on evil times and are out of the market, are being liquidated, or are retrenching and attempting to upgrade the quality of their mortgage and real property holdings. There are REITs still active in the field, particularly those that are managed by banks or other financial institutions whose real property expertise has kept their REITs out of the kinds of problems that beset the industry in general, but they have lost much of the significance that they once had as institutional lenders.

§6.10   F. Mortgage Bankers and Mortgage Brokers

As the term is generally used, a "mortgage banker" is an unregulated lender who makes loans secured by a lien on real property; it should not be confused with the statutory mortgage banker as defined in Fin C §18680. Although Fin C §§18680-18705 were enacted in 1973 in an attempt to bring mortgage bankers under the exemption afforded to industrial loan companies from the usury provisions of Cal Const art XV, §1 (see Note, *The Mortgage Banking Act: A New Way Around California's Usury Laws?* Hastings LJ 460 (1974), very few corporations have sought to come under the statutory provisions of mortgage bankers.

The mortgage banker is an indirect source of financing, who typically has an established line of credit with one or more institutions that are used to originate and fund real property loans. These loans vary from single-family residence loans to large commercial loans. Mortgage bankers are very active in originating government-insured (FHA) and government-guaranteed (VA) loans. After origination, the mortgage banker holds the loans for a period of time, thus "warehousing" until a substantial dollar volume is on hand (usually several million dollars—this amount is related to the extent of the mortgage banker's line of credit). The loans are then pooled and sold to an institutional lender, either locally or more often in the secondary mortgage market. The mortgage banker continues to service these loans (*i.e.,* collecting monthly payments, handling payoffs and delinquencies, etc.); the fees for such loan servicing, together with the loan origination fees generated when the loans are made, are a principal source of income for the mortgage banker. Ongoing relationships with particular institutional lenders tend to develop, especially with life insurance companies. Governmental agencies that are active in the secondary mortgage market are sources of funds for mortgage bankers. In 1978 the Federal Home Loan Mortgage Corporation specifically was permitted to purchase mortgages from mortgage bankers, ending a long controversy between savings and loan associations and mortgage bankers. 12 USC §1454(a)(1). See §6.11 for a discussion of the secondary mortgage market.

Mortgage brokers, as distinguished from mortgage bankers, act like real estate brokers in placing individual loans with lenders and must hold a real estate broker's license (Bus & P C §§10130, 10131(d)). Frequently they handle loans more difficult to place and also are often responsible for placing large loans. Their functions may include preparing loan applications, negotiating terms of a loan, and securing appraisals and other information required by lenders. See also Bus & P C §§10240-10248.9 for provisions regulating such loans.

§6.11   G. The Secondary Mortgage Market

There is a secondary mortgage market in which original lenders, such as banks, savings and loan associations, and life insurance companies, may sell off a portion of their loan portfolios. The sale of these loans provides funds for new loans to customers.

The secondary market has been greatly expanded by the operations of several federally sponsored organizations. The three principal organizations are the Federal National Mortgage Association (FNMA, or Fannie Mae), originally a federal agency that has been converted to a publicly held, private corporation whose policies are still influenced by the federal government; the Government National Mortgage Association (GNMA, or Ginnie Mae), which took the place of FNMA as the federal agency when the latter became private; and the Federal Home Loan Mortgage Corporation (FHLMC, or Freddie Mac, or, as it now prefers to be called, The Mortgage Corporation), sponsored by the Federal Home Loan Bank Board (FHLBB). For FNMA and GNMA, see 12 USC §1717, for FHLMC see 12 USC §1454.

In 1970 the FHLBB established the FHLMC to create a secondary mortgage market solely for members of the FHLBB system (see 12 USC §§1451-1459), all of which were federal and state savings and loan associations with their deposits insured by the Federal Savings and Loan Insurance Corporation, another affiliate of the FHLBB. To do business with FHLMC, associations were required to purchase its capital stock. 12 USC §282. Unlike other federally sponsored organizations active in the secondary market, such as FNMA or GNMA, which purchased loans from various institutional lenders (see 12 USC §1717), FHLMC's clientele was limited to savings and loan associations. These associations vigorously opposed the mortgage bankers' efforts to obtain access to the FHLMC market. Effective in 1980 the FHLBB granted mortgage bankers a restricted right to sell to FHLMC (pursuant to prior congressional authorization in 12 USC §1454(a)(1)); this represented a compromise between the no access and the unlimited access desired by the respective antagonists. (Mortgage bankers must pay an extra fee and meet certain minimum net worth requirements to be eligible.)

Each organization requires special documentation for the loans it will purchase; two examples demonstrate this. First, at present all three organizations require that the loan be documented by a fixed rate note. Thus, at present none of the organizations will purchase a variable rate mortgage. They are not prohibited from purchasing such mortgages; they are simply not authorized to do so and purchase of such a mortgage does not fit conveniently into these agencies' present mode of operation. This is so because the agencies raise their funds by selling fixed interest rate bonds secured by pools of mortgages. How to integrate a fixed rate pass through bond with an underlying variable rate mortgage pool has not yet been satisfactorily solved. In 1980, however, the Federal Home Loan Bank Board granted federal savings and loan associations the authority to make variable rate loans (12 CFR §545.6-4(c)), and FHLMC, at least, will probably eventually purchase these loans.

Second, when a loan is secured by a condominium, the covenants, conditions, and restrictions (CC&Rs) governing the operation of that condominium must meet specific FHLMC requirements to make the loan eligible for purchase by FHLMC. If it is an existing condominium project and the CC&Rs do not conform, amendment is the only solution, and this is not always practical. If the condominium is being constructed, and a take-out loan is sought, the developer's attorney should consider FHLMC's requirements in drafting the CC&Rs in order to avoid this potential problem.

In order to make their loans readily salable on the secondary mortgage market, many institutional lenders are using the FNMA or FHLMC uniform instruments for promissory notes and deeds of trust instead of their own forms.

III. TYPES OF LOANS

§6.12   A. Residential Loans

(1) Single Family (One-to-Four Units)

"Single-family residential loan" is a term of art that applies to all residential property with fewer than five units ("one-to-fours") in which the potential borrower intends to reside. The term also includes condominium units and cooperative apartment units. Fin C §7153.1. The credit requirements for borrowers are discussed in §§6.21-6.27. Property standards for such loans are discussed in §6.30. Savings and loan associations are the largest source of funds for these loans, which are usually obtained through the efforts, or at least with the assistance, of the real estate broker. Many larger associations work through their own loan agents, who are paid on a commission basis for the loans they generate and in turn work closely with real estate brokers to obtain loans. Those associations not having loan agents usually maintain loan offices at one of their savings branches in their areas of activity, so that all necessary loan information and loan applications are available locally to the inquiring broker or buyer. Thus, in the typical transaction, either the seller's broker or both the seller's and the buyer's brokers if the latter has one, help the buyer obtain the loan best suited to his or her needs. The brokers, in turn, are in constant contact with loan agents from various savings and loan associations and are thus apprised of their individual rates and fees, as well as of other details about available loans. Often the buyer obtains the application for a loan from the broker.

(2) Multifamily

Multifamily loans are those made to purchase houses or other residential properties of five or more units.

The savings and loan associations are also the largest source of funds for this type of loan, but other institutional lenders, particularly commercial banks, are also active in this field. The credit requirements for borrowers applicable to multifamily residential loans are discussed in §§6.20-6.25, 6.28-6.29. Property standards are discussed in §§6.31-6.32.

§6.13   B. Commercial Loans

The term "commercial loan" in the context of mortgage lending generally describes a loan secured by a lien on nonresidential real property, the income from which is expected to service the loan, although some institutional lenders, particularly savings and loan associations, tend to lump all loans secured by income property, both residential and nonresidential, into the category of commercial loans. Typical examples of commercial loans are those secured by restaurant buildings, office buildings, and motels. The term does not include a loan to a business entity in which business income is the source for loan repayment, even though the loan may have a lien on real property (*e.g.,* the manufacturing plant) as additional security. See §§6.33-6.36 for property considerations in making commercial loans.

Commercial banks and life insurance companies are more active in this area of mortgage lending than in residential lending and are probably the prime source for commercial loans, although savings and loan associations are also active in the field.

C. Construction Loans

§6.14   1. Construction Loans and Permanent Financing

The term "construction loan" describes a loan made to fund the construction of a project that is all due and paid off when the construction is completed. When a straight construction loan is obtained, the borrower generally obtains at the same time a commitment from another lender for a permanent loan (take-out loan) once the project is completed. The latter is a full term conventional amortizing loan, and funds generated from it are used to pay the construction lender. Most institutional construction lenders today insist on the borrower's obtaining a commitment for permanent financing as a condition precedent to making the construction loan.

In contrast to the straight construction loan, the construction take-out (or construction permanent), loan combines the straight construction and permanent loan into two phases of a single loan. The first phase is identical to a straight construction loan, with funds disbursed during the construction period to fund the building of the project. At the end of the construction period, however, it does not become all due, but rather enters into phase two, which is a long term conventional amortizing real property loan to be paid off in equal monthly installments over the full term of the loan, generally 25 years for commercial and 30 years for residential property.

Commercial banks are principally interested in making straight construction loans, often using a floating rule (*e.g.*, "three points above prime"), whereas savings and loan associations are much more receptive to making construction take-out loans. Problems of subordination and release may occur when separate construction loans and permanent loans are used. See §§5.38-5.67 for a discussion of subordination and release.

§6.15   2. Construction Loan Administration

The administration of a construction loan by an institutional lender is fairly standard. As a part of the required documentation for a construction loan application, the borrower must submit a cost breakdown. This is a detailed schedule of all costs incident to the project by category, as well as a chronological order of completion of each category. The cost breakdown will be the master control document for loan disbursements.

The loan funds are deposited in a special account known as a loan in process account (l.i.p.). The lender then disburses funds from the l.i.p. account on the submission of vouchers detailing work and materials and accompanied by lien releases from all subcontractors and materialmen involved. The amounts requested to be disbursed must balance with the cost breakdown, or the borrower must deposit additional funds in the l.i.p. account to cover any cost overruns.

Example:

Suppose the cost breakdown for the rough plumbing is $156,000. When the rough plumbing on the project is completed, the borrower's authorized representative submits vouchers to pay the subcontractors and materialmen for this phase of the project along with lien releases from each. Before honoring the vouchers, the lender usually sends an inspector to the project to verify completion of the rough plumbing. Then the lender disburses the funds to the borrower (if lien releases have been obtained) or directly to the particular subcontractor or materialman. If the total amount of the vouchers for rough plumbing exceeds the cost estimate of $156,000, the lender calls on the borrower for additional funds to cover the shortage.

This rather complex mechanism of loan administration accomplishes several objectives for the lender: (a) it ensures that funds disbursed from the l.i.p. account reach the subcontractors and materialmen for whom they are intended, thus avoiding the filing of mechanics' liens and stop notices; (b) it enables the lender to

1977 (42 USC §§5301-5319) for rehabilitation of housing purposes. See also the Community Redevelopment Law (Health & S C §§33000-33738) which authorizes several housing rehabilitation programs, and deferred payment rehabilitation loans (Health & S C §§50660-50670).

Institutional lenders often participate in these government subsidy programs only as an agent of the municipality or another governmental unit to originate and service loans. The actual funds for the loans come from the government subsidizer. See, *e.g.,* Health & S C §§51300-51311 (neighborhood preservation).

§6.18   b. Conventional Loans

A number of commercial banks and savings and loan associations are actively marketing nonsubsidized conventional home improvement loans, but on a selective basis. One reason for the popularity of these loans is the advantage they provide to the homeowner who desires to make improvements on his or her home and who has an existing first mortgage on the property that is several years old. Because of the relatively steady rise in home mortgage interest rates in recent years, the rate on this existing loan is probably well below current market rate. Rather than refinancing this loan with a new loan at existing rates, the homeowner may be better off by borrowing these funds through a home improvement loan. Even though the rate for the latter generally is one to two percent higher than a conventional single-family residence loan from the same lender, the impact of this higher rate is more than offset by retaining the lower rate on the existing loan.

Loan eligibility is generally determined on the basis of consolidating the proposed home improvement loan with any existing loans. If the proposed home improvement loan, when added to any existing loans secured by liens on the property, meets loan-to-value ratio requirements (usually 80 percent for conventional loan purposes) and monthly payments on all such loans do not exceed a maximum percentage (usually 30-35 percent) of gross monthly income (see §6.26 on income requirements), and if there is no negative credit information, the homeowner will be considered eligible for the loan. Contrary to their practice regarding construction loans, institutional lenders generally do not monitor the disbursement and use of home improvement loan funds because of the loans' small size compared to the cost of administration. Usually the lender disburses the entire loan to the borrower without verifying that the funds are or will be devoted to actual home improvements, but institutional lenders' practices on verification vary widely. Some institutions disburse only jointly to the borrower and the home improvement contractor after receiving satisfactory evidence of completion of the work.

Institutions also differ on their willingness to secure the home improvement loan with a deed of trust, junior to any existing liens. Some will take such a lien, even behind their own first deeds of trust (thus raising possible problems of merger); others do so only when they do not hold the first deed of trust, even though the added value generated by the home improvements enhances the security of the first lien.

§6.19   2. Mobile Home Loans

Like improvement of existing housing, using mobile homes for permanent shelter is becoming increasingly common as the cost of conventional single-family housing continues to escalate. Mobile homes may be located in either mobile home parks or on a single-family lot, where it is essentially the same as a conventional home. The latter use is particularly prevalent in rural communities, where zoning provisions permit such land use and individual lots tend to be widely scattered.

Commercial banks and savings and loan associations are authorized to make mobile home loans (see, *e.g.*, 12 CFR §§545.7-5 through 545.7-8), but they are more commonly used as a source of financing in rural areas where mobile homes are usually located on individual lots. In more urban areas, where the mobile home will probably be located in a park, the mobile home dealer is often the source for financing, as is the case with motor vehicles. Many larger dealers maintain ongoing relationships with one or more financial institutions that either buy the dealer's conditional sales contract or finance the sale directly on reference by the dealer. Some institutional lenders employ agents who solicit business from mobile home dealers, often combining the financing of a dealer's sales with that of the dealer himself, generally through a flooring arrangement similar to that prevalent with automobile dealerships. The functions of these agents are like those of the loan agents used by some savings and loan associations for their single-family residential lending programs.

Under amendments to the Health and Safety Code enacted in 1979, it is now possible for a mobile home to become real property, rather than be considered a motor vehicle even after its adoption for use as a residence, as had been the case. See, in particular, Health & S C §18551. Because state law governs the matter, it appears proper for both federal and state savings and loan associations as well as commercial banks to make a standard real estate loan on a mobile home permanently affixed to a foundation system and in compliance with all code requirements, securing the loan with a standard deed of trust rather than the security agreement required when the mobile home remains a vehicle.

IV. OBTAINING THE LOAN

§6.20   A. Credit Standards

The potential borrower's financial condition and credit worthiness are extremely important to the proposed lender. No matter how great the borrower's equity in the security property is over and above the loan amount, lenders invariably insist that the borrower demonstrate the financial ability to make monthly payments, whether the borrower is one individual, several individuals acting jointly, or some form of business enterprise.

Compelled by disclosure requirements of federal law (Community Reinvestment Act of 1977, 12 USC §§2901-2905) and their own desire to serve the public, banks and savings and loan associations have increased the amount of information they release regarding the types of loans they make and the criteria they use to evaluate loan applications. Many of these lenders distribute brochures detailing their current lending policies.

In judging credit worthiness, standards differ with respect to individual borrowers (§§6.21-6.27), partnership borrowers (§6.28), and corporate borrowers (§6.29).

§6.21   1. Individual Borrowers

For individual borrowers seeking loans on owner-occupied, one-to-four unit residential property, both the federal and state governments have passed antiredlining and other antidiscrimination legislation that has had a significant impact on lending practices of institutional lenders in California. The major statutes are the federal Equal Credit Opportunity Act (15 USC §§1691-1691f) and the state Housing Financial Discrimination Act of 1977 (Health & S C §§35800-35833). Extensive regulations have been promulgated under them. Although federal savings and loan associations are not subject to state antiredlining legislation because of federal preemption (*Conference of Fed. Sav. & Loan Ass'ns v Stein* (9th Cir 1979) 604 F2d 1256), all national and state commercial banks, and state savings and loan associations are subject to both federal and state regulations, and most other institutional lenders are subject to at least state requirements. See §6.37 on redlining.

The federal and state laws and regulations on loans are generally comparable (hereafter they will be jointly referred to as fair lending requirements). They prohibit discrimination based on the applicant's race, color, religion, sex, age, marital status, national origin, or ancestry. 15 USC §1691; 12 CFR §531.8; Health & S C §35811. Federal and state law both prohibit rejecting a loan application because the property is in a declining neighborhood. 12 CFR §531.8(c)(7); Health & S C §35810. In addition, state provisions prohibit denying a loan on the basis of conditions, characteristics, or trends in the neighborhood or geographical area surrounding the property that will secure the loan unless the lender can affirmatively demonstrate that rejecting the loan is necessary "to avoid an unsafe and unsound business practice." Health & S C §35810. Similarly, discounting the spouse's (in the past, generally the wife's) earned income when the joint applicants are both working is now impermissible. See, *e.g.,* 12 CFR §531.8(c)(3). Also, income may no longer be disregarded solely because of its source (*e.g.,* welfare payments, alimony) unless the permanence of continuing receipt may be in question. 15 USC §1691(a) (2), (b) (2).

In addition to prohibiting certain specified discriminatory practices in the underwriting of mortgage loans, the fair lending requirements of these acts and regulations also include provisions requiring institutions to maintain certain specified records. These requirements include maintenance of complete records of all rejected loan applications and adoption of written loan underwriting standards available to the public.

§6.22   a. Payment History

The applicant's payment record is carefully reviewed by the institutional lender to establish whether the applicant has a past record of paying his or her obligations. Almost invariably the lender obtains information about the applicant's paying habits from a credit reporting agency. These records are examined for any evidence of slow payments, written-off loans, late charges, repossessions, judgments, garnishments, bankruptcies, and the like. If the applicant has an existing mortgage loan, his payment record on it is solicited from the mortgage holder. All inquiries about the borrower's credit must be authorized by the applicant. The information from the credit report is generally cross-checked with financial information in the loan application to verify the latter. In using a credit report when applicants are husband and wife, the lender must consider all accounts that an applicant and spouse are permitted to use or for which both are contractually liable.

§6.23   b. Work History

The applicant's employment history is also carefully reviewed. Generally, if current employment has lasted more than two years, it will not be necessary to go to previous employers. Earnings are also verified, as are length of employment, frequency of job changes, and stability of income in the applicant's line of work. The Federal Home Loan Bank Board has issued guidelines for institutional lenders for evaluating an applicant's work history. See 12 CFR §531.8(c)(5).

If the applicant is self-employed, most lenders require verification of income through the last two years' federal income tax returns. Full credit must be given to both spouses' earned incomes, when husband and wife coapplicants are both working. Information regarding childbearing intentions, a subject some lenders formerly considered, may not now be requested. 12 CFR §531.8(c)(3).

§6.24   c. Financial Statements

Most institutional lenders incorporate financial statements in their standard loan application form, and these are invariably in the form of a statement of assets, liabilities, and net worth. The lender looks for information not contained in the credit report, *e.g.,* the source of the applicant's cash downpayment for the security property (when the loan being sought is purchase money). The applicant's financial ability to withstand reverses and the extent of the applicant's savings and other liquid assets are also scrutinized.

Any contingent liabilities, such as lawsuits or obligations as a guarantor, must be evaluated to determine whether the applicant is likely to become financially liable in the future. Net worth is important for its value in cash.

§6.25   d. Fair Credit Reporting Act

Under the fair lending requirements and the Fair Credit Reporting Act (15 USC §§1681-1681t), institutional lenders have a number of responsibilities regarding loan applicants. First, the lender must notify the applicant in writing of the lender's decision on the application within 30 days of receipt of a completed application. 12 CFR §202.9(a). If the loan is denied or is accepted under any terms more onerous than applied for (*e.g.,* lesser amount, higher interest rate, shorter term), the lender must specify the reason for not accepting it as applied for. 15 USC §1681m; 12 CFR §202.9(a)(2).

When a denial is based on the applicant's credit, the Fair Credit Reporting Act requires the lender specifically to inform the applicant whether the adverse credit information leading to declination is based on data furnished by a consumer credit reporting agency. 15 USC §1681m(a). If it is not so based, the details must be spelled out in the denial notice (*e.g.,* insufficient cash shown to make downpayment, or past poor payment record with a mortgage lender or the lender from whom the new loan is sought). 12 CFR §202.9(a)(2). If it is based on information from a consumer credit reporting agency, the denial notice must give the name, address, and telephone number of that agency and must advise the applicant of the right, on written demand, to obtain the sources and other particulars of the adverse credit information from the credit reporting agency. 15 USC §1681m(a).

If the denial is not based on credit considerations, then the other reasons must be specified (*e.g.,* appraisal does not support purchase price or claimed market value, extensive code violations discovered). 12 CFR §202.9(a)(2).

e. Residential Loans

§6.26   (1) Ratio of Home Payments to Income

In underwriting a residential loan, institutional lenders use, as a rule of thumb, a ratio of housing costs to the borrower's gross income. Similar guidelines exist for many government-assisted loans, such as FHA-insured loans or VA-guaranteed loans (see generally 12 USC §1715n). In applying these standards, the institutional lender compares the borrower's total projected monthly housing costs (*i.e.,* payments on the loan being sought, payments on any secondary financing on the property, real property taxes, hazard insurance premiums, and any other property-related expenses, such as homeowners' association dues when the property is in a planned development or condominium project) to the borrower's total monthly gross income. In applying the ratio, the borrower's monthly gross income is reduced by the amount of any monthly payments on long term installment obligations that will not mature or be liquidated within twelve months after the date of the loan application.

At least for conventional, nongovernment-assisted loans, the ratio of home payments to gross income that the lender uses is subject only to the lender's own discretion. However, for ease of application by their lending officers (and to avoid charges of discrimination under equal credit laws), all institutional lenders adopt established income ratio requirements that are applied with general uniformity. This ratio in the past was about 25 percent but has generally been revised upward, in recognition of rapidly escalating housing costs; it is now considered that total housing costs should normally not exceed one third of the borrower's gross income. This ratio may also be increased slightly when the borrower's age and other factors indicate upward mobility and resultant prospective early increase in gross income.

§6.27 (2) Cosigners or Guarantors

If the loan applicant does not have sufficient monthly income to meet the lender's underwriting standards (see §6.26), the lender may still be willing to grant the loan if the applicant can furnish a cosigner or a guarantor. A cosigner (or comaker) of a note differs substantially from an accommodation maker or a guarantor of the obligation. See, *e.g., Caito v United Cal. Bank* (1978) 20 C3d 694, 144 CR 751. These differences exist both with respect to the lender and with respect to the cosigner or guarantor.

Although the law is not clear in this matter, a cosigner or comaker of a note will probably be treated in the same manner and is considered to have the same relationship with the lender as the principal loan applicant. The cosigner, if signing as a comaker rather than as an accommodation party, is probably entitled to the same anti-deficiency protections afforded by CCP §§580b, 580d, and 726 as are given to the principal borrower. In the case of a purchase money note on an owner-occupied, one-to-four family dwelling, the existence of a cosigner gives the lender no additional rights. In any event, the lender's only remedy is foreclosure without the possibility of a deficiency judgment. See CCP §580b. Although in such a case the addition of a cosigner gives the lender no additional remedies in the event of default, the lender may still prefer to have a cosigner if having a cosigner (and with it the additional income available to service the debt) seems to decrease the possibility of default.

A guarantor, on the other hand, gives the lender security in addition to the lien on the real property under the deed of trust. Under a guaranty agreement, the guarantor can, and often does, wave the antideficiency protections. This enables the lender to obtain against the guarantor a deficiency judgment that might otherwise be barred by CCP §580b. The guarantor can also waive the right to require the lender to proceed against the principal borrower first, thus permitting the lender to seek a money judgment against the guarantor without first having to foreclose on the security property. See generally California Mortgage and Deed of Trust Practice §§4.42-4.52 (Cal CEB 1979) on guarantors.

In spite of substantial advantages to the lender in having a guarantor rather than a cosigner, lenders usually prefer a cosigner when the original applicant's income is insufficient to obtain the loan because the lender considers the cosigner's income, as well as the principal borrower's, in determining whether total monthly income is sufficient to justify the amount of the loan requested. However, the lender will consider cosigner's income only if the cosigner has some equity in the property so that he has an incentive to keep the loan current. To a lending officer this usually means that the cosigner's income can be included if the cosigner's name is on the deed conveying title. Often a borrower whose income is insufficient will ask if the loan can be granted if someone else, such as a parent, cosigns the note. The borrower will be told that the cosigner's income will be included only if the cosigner's name is on the deed. As a consequence, buyers may find themselves holding title with their cosigners even though their cosigners do not actually have an interest in the property. Attorneys should be alert to this situation and advise their clients to resist any attempt by a lender to have the deed drawn in a manner that does not reflect the true ownership interests. If a lender insists, as a condition to making the loan, that a cosigner's name appear on the deed as a co-owner, the cosigner should quitclaim his interest to the true owner after the close of escrow.

§6.28   2. Partnership Borrowers

Usually, when the applicant is a partnership, institutional lenders require that all general partners sign the loan documents and be personally liable on partnership loans, at least when the partnership is not in a major syndicated project. Some confusion about this requirement may exist because all of the general partners are personally liable for the partnership obligations, whether or not all sign. The explanation seems to be that because institutional loan officers are unsure of all the ramifications of partnership borrowing and do not have time to review all the details of the partnership agreement, they try to simplify the underwriting of the transaction. Often spouses of general partners are also required to sign.

This becomes difficult when a transaction is large and sophisticated. In this situation the number of partners might inhibit signatures by all (powers of attorney can be substituted). When a syndicated limited partnership is the proposed borrowing entity, the lender may be forced to take a different underwriting approach, because often the sole general partner does not have sufficient financial strength to warrant making the loan, and in any event, the syndicate seeks a nonrecourse loan to take advantage of the tax benefits that flow from such a loan (*i.e.*, the increase of the limited partners' basis over each limited partner's actual capital contribution by the amount of each partner's share of the nonrecourse debts of the limited partnership). Treas Reg § 1.752-1(e). Most often, the loan is for income property; and the lender determines the loan's acceptability based on positive cash flow before debt service and the likely income stream.

§6.29   3. Corporate Borrowers

When the applicant is a corporation, the institutional lender tends to be rather cautious unless the corporation's past financial history and present worth are strong and it is publicly held. When the loan is sought by a solely owned or closely held new corporation (sometimes incorporated only to consummate the proposed real estate transaction that is the subject of the loan), the lender will insist on personal guarantees of the principal stockholders or other persons whose personal net worth is sufficient to justify making the loan. Institutional lenders usually require that audited financial statements and copies of tax returns accompany a loan application from a corporation that is other than newly formed.

B. Property Standards

§6.30   **1. Residential Property (Loan-to-Value Ratio)**

In evaluating loans, institutional lenders use loan-to-value ratios, which are generally mandated by the regulations under which most lenders operate. The ratios vary according to the type of security property and other factors. The standard ratio for single-family, owner-occupied residences is 80 percent, *i.e.*, the amount of the loan cannot exceed 80 percent of the appraised value of the security property. See *e.g.*, Fin C §7153 concerning state-licensed savings and loan associations. When the borrower pays the balance of the purchase price in cash, that is, when there is no secondary financing, the rate for this type of loan is the institutional lender's prime rate, which a particular institution quotes as its mortgage lending rate. Other rates for different kinds of loans are related to this prime rate and are based on differing loan-to-value ratios. For example, when the loan is 80-10-10, which indicates a loan-to-value ratio based on an 80-percent primary loan secured by the institutional lender's first lien, a 10-percent secondary loan secured by a second lien, and a 10-percent cash downpayment, the rate charged by the institutional lender is likely to be 1/4 percent over its prime rate. Similarly, if the institutional lender's loan is a 90-percent loan, which is any loan whose loan-to-value ratio is between 80 percent and 90 percent, the rate will usually be at least 1/2 percent higher than prime (loan fees will also increase comparably). Some lenders will require private mortgage insurance for 90-percent loans and regulatory requirements will limit the maximum permissible amount of the loan (currently $93,750 for 90-percent loans). 12 CFR §545.6-2(a)(2)(iii); 10 Cal Adm C §§235.27-235.28. Private mortgage insurance is written by a number of private (*i.e.*, nongovernmental) insurers, generally covering the top portion of the loan, *e.g.*, 20 percent, so that the private insurer protects the lender against the first 20 percent of any net loss the lender may sustain in the event of foreclosure. The rate for this 20-percent coverage is traditionally an additional 1/4 percent added to the loan interest rate.

For 95-percent loan-to-value ratio loans (those between 90 percent and 95 percent), regulations limit the loan to $60,000 and require private mortgage insurance (12 CFR §545.6-2(a)(3)) and impounds to cover real property taxes (12 CFR §545.6-2(a)(3)(i)). Again, the institutional lender's rate will be a stated increase above its prime rate.

2. Multifamily Residential Property

§6.31 a. Appraisal

Legal limitations on loan-to-value ratio for multifamily residential properties are generally the same as for single-family homes (see, *e.g.*, Fin C §7153 and 12 USC §1464(c)), but in practice lenders will rarely lend as high a percentage of appraised value on multifamily residences as they do on single-family residences.

To establish a loan-to-value ratio limitation for multifamily residential property, appraisers make three separate evaluations and then theoretically base the ratio on the lowest result. First, the replacement value is calculated on the basis of an estimate of the cost to construct a similar building, less depreciation based on the age of the existing building. Second, comparable sales, based on recent sales prices of comparable buildings in the general locality, are determined; and after adjustment for differences between the comparison buildings and the building being appraised, such as number of living units, age, amenities and other matters that would affect the price, a probable selling price for the latter is established (not necessarily the actual sale price for the building). The third evaluation is based on income. The appraiser determines either the actual net rental income that the building has generated in recent years or, if the building is to be constructed, rental income based on the market rents that the developer's feasibility studies indicate will be achieved given the size and configuration of the proposed individual living units (*e.g.*, number of square feet, studio or one or two bedrooms), the location of the building, its amenities, and any other factor likely to influence the level of rents. The appraiser then reduces the rental income by applying the vacancy factor prevalent in rental properties in the locality. The appraiser may further reduce the income tó so-called stabilized rents, *i.e.,* current rent for comparable space in the locality. This may be less than the rents projected by the developer's feasibility study, which tends to be optimistic.

Having determined the rental income, the appraiser then fixes the capitalization (cap) rate. This is theoretically the rate of return that a prudent investor expects to receive if he purchases the building being appraised, given its age, the neighborhood, the total amount of investment, and all other factors of risk likely to influence the rate of return. In practice, the cap rate is arrived at by determining the purchase price for recent sales of comparable income properties in the area and the rental income for such properties and then calculating the rate of return each purchaser is to receive, given the purchase price he paid for the property. The appraiser then applies this cap rate to the net rental income of the building being appraised and arrives at the value of the building. This value equals the total investment in the building that, when the selected cap rate is applied, will yield an annual return equal to the annual net rental income.

§6.32   b. Other Loan Terms

For older buildings, institutional lenders tend to restrict the length of the loan on multifamily residential property to less than the maximum permitted number of years (generally 25). Often this is done by structuring the loan to provide for monthly amortization payments on a 25-year basis but requiring that the balance of the loan is all due and payable in less than 25 years. This results in a balloon payment on expiration of the loan but permits the rental income generated by the building to carry the loan in the meantime, because the monthly payments are kept lower by applying the 25-year amortization schedule.

One other guideline that lenders generally consider is the ratio of operating expenses to gross income. Because the impact of the Jarvis-Gann initiative (Cal Const art XIIIA, enacted June 6, 1978) tends to reduce operating expenses, ratios of less than the traditional 40 percent are insisted on by some lenders.

§6.33   3. Commercial Property

Loan-to-value ratio requirements sometimes are stricter for commercial property than for residential property. See, *e.g.,* Fin C §§7152-7153 (state savings and loan associations). Otherwise, underwriting and appraisal procedures for commercial loans differ little from those for multifamily residential loans, except for some special considerations that apply to commercial loans (discussed in §§6.34-6.36).

§6.34   a. Special-Purpose Property

Often the property being offered as security for a commercial loan is for a special purpose. Although multifamily residential property is also designed for a single purpose (to furnish housing for its tenant occupants), it suits a large demand that is not likely to vary and therefore does not present a problem.

On the other hand, a bowling alley or a racquetball court complex may either produce good income or become a financial burden, depending on a change of circumstances (*e.g.,* loss of public enthusiasm for the particular activity for which the structure was built, innovations in competing facilities making the particular building obsolete, overbuilding of similar facilities in the locality). Many single-purpose designs make conversion to some other purpose extremely expensive if not impossible. For this reason, a lender making a commercial loan examines the applicant's financial condition more critically than is done when making a loan for multifamily residential property and requires that the applicant have sufficient financial strength to carry the proposed loan without using any projected profit that might come from the property securing the loan. By contrast, in multifamily residential properties, realistic projection of sufficient income to service the loan, based on current market conditions, generally is acceptable even though the potential borrower is not particularly strong financially.

§6.35   b. Personal Property

Conduct of the operation for which the commercial property is designed often requires the use of substantial personal property. Convalescent hospitals, which in the past have been popular applicants for commercial loans, provide a good example. The mortgage lender who makes a loan on a convalescent hospital obtains a deed of trust covering the hospital building and the land on which it is built, but operating the hospital requires extensive personal property not covered by the deed of trust, *e.g.*, beds, linen, laundry facilities, kitchen equipment, and medical equipment such as X-ray machines. Personal property is also a consideration, but to a lesser extent, for multifamily residential property when the units are fully or partially furnished.

A security agreement (Com C §9105) and financing statement (Com C §9402) can be used to create a lien on this personal property in favor of the mortgage lender. Then, in the event of a default necessitating take-over of the property either by a receiver or through foreclosure, the personal property will remain in place permitting continued operation of the facility. This solution is often not available because the borrower finances the construction or purchase of the real property through the mortgage lender and finances the purchase of the personal property elsewhere. When the personal property is extensive and costly, the borrower typically finances it through conditional sales contracts or equipment leases. When this occurs for personal property that might become fixtures and thus be subject to the mortgage lender's deed of trust, the equipment lender requires as a condition of the extension of credit that the mortgage lender execute a mortgagee's waiver agreement under which the latter waives any lien he might otherwise have to the installed personal property.

The mortgage lender's only solution is to proceed with a security agreement, even though the lien will be junior to the lien of the equipment lender, and at the same time obtain an agreement from the equipment lender that, on default under the equipment loan, the mortgage lender has the option to take over the borrower's position and make the payments owed by the borrower. In this way, by foreclosing his junior lien on the personal property while continuing to make the payments on the borrower's obligation secured by the senior lien, the mortgage lender can be assured that the personal property will remain in place during any receivership and foreclosure of his mortgage on the real property.

§6.36   c. Credit Loans

A credit loan is used when the conventionally appraised value of the real property being offered as security is not sufficient to warrant the size of the loan requested. Such a loan might be used, for example, when the building has one or more tenants (usually this is a single-tenant situation) on long term leases that do not expire before the maturity of the loan and whose monthly rental payments are more than sufficient to make the monthly loan payments. A typical example would be the construction of a building leased to a major bank for a branch under a 30-year lease. The bank may be willing to pay a premium for occupancy of the building for reasons peculiar to its operation as a bank. The loan being sought is larger than can be justified by conventional appraisal. However, the bank's rental payments are more than the monthly payments on the loan being sought. In this instance, the commercial lender will look to the credit of the tenant bank rather than the appraised value of the property or the financial strength of the lessor-borrower in underwriting the loan; hence the term "credit loan." The lender assures itself of access to the rental payments by requiring an appropriate assignment of rents from the borrower. See §6.55 on assignment of rents.

§6.37   4. Redlining

Both federal and state legislatures have adopted legislation aimed at preventing discrimination in mortgage lending, including redlining. See Civil Rights Act of 1968 (42 USC §§3601-3631); Equal Credit Opportunity Act of 1976 (15 USC §§1691-1691f); Community Reinvestment Act of 1977 (12 USC §§2901-2905) federal; Housing Financial Discrimination Act of 1977 (Health & S C §§35800-35833) state. See also §6.21. The term "redlining" originated because some lending institutions allegedly designated geographical areas within which they would not make loans with a red pencil or crayon outlined on a map. Extensive regulations implementing state and federal statutes have been adopted by the agencies that regulate institutions making mortgage loans. See, *e.g.*, 21 Cal Adm C §§7100-7117 for regulations that apply to state-regulated financial institutions, and 12 CFR §§528, 531.8 for those that apply to all savings and loan associations.

Institutions must report all loans made and rejected in certain specific geographical areas (sometimes called mortgage-deficient areas) and keep copies of such reports on file and available for public inspection at all branches.

C. Negotiating Loan Terms

§6.38   1. Rates and Loan Fees

Real property loans are invariably quoted in terms of the rate and fee. Rate refers to the contract interest rate being charged and fee (also called points) is an additional loan fee representing, in effect, prepaid additional interest, expressed as a percentage of the total loan. For example, a fee of one point on a $50,000 loan means an additional payment of $500 (one percent of $50,000) due when the loan closes. All savings and loan associations and most other institutional lenders charge this loan fee. Loan fees constituting additional interest should be distinguished from fees charged by some institutional lenders for services rendered incident to making the loan, *e.g.,* for appraisals and document preparation.

The particular type of fee should be ascertained because the true loan fee is deductible for income tax purposes as prepaid interest, whereas fees for services must be capitalized. Such prepaid interest must usually be deducted ratably over the life of the loan. Points paid for home mortgages may be deducted in the year of payment if certain conditions are met (IRC §461(g)), but many institutional lenders are beginning to structure loan fees in such a way that for income tax purposes they must be deducted by the borrower over the life of the loan. The true cost of funds, including the loan fee, must be disclosed as an annual percentage rate in those loans subject to the federal Truth in Lending Act (which generally applies to all loans made for nonbusiness purposes). 15 USC §§1601-1681t. Variations in rates and fees are discussed in §6.39; negotiating in §6.40.

§6.39   a. Variations in Rates and Fees

The particular interest rates and fees, as well as length of loan and other pertinent provisions, vary only slightly among different types of institutional lenders and among individual lenders within each type. Although banks and savings and loan associations do not have a real property loan rate comparable to the banks' prime rate for business loans, traditionally interest rates charged by associations are within 1/4 percent of each other and their loan fees vary only slightly. The commercial banks' rates (without a special banking relationship between the borrower and the particular bank) closely follow those of the savings and loan associations. Lenders' rates and loan fees tend to vary more as the size of the loan increases and for large multifamily, commercial, or industrial transactions. The loan-to-value ratio of the proposed loan (total amount of loan as it relates to appraised value or sales price of the property) will affect the rate and fee. If the loan-to-value ratio of the proposed loan exceeds 80 percent, or if the total amount allowed for the proposed loan and any secondary financing exceeds 80 percent, the interest rate will probably be increased by at least 1/4 percent and the fee increased by one-half point over the current market rate for residential property. Many institutional lenders offer variable interest rate loans (see §6.48) and some quote a rate 1/4 percent below that available for a fixed rate conventional loan from the same institution as an inducement to the borrower to opt for the variable rate. However, if acceptance of this type of loan becomes sufficiently widespread, the rate differential may disappear.

Institutional lenders readily quote their current rate and fee for a conventional loan with an 80-percent loan-to-value ratio secured by prime residential property and any variations resulting from increases in loan-to-value ratio, character of security property, or type of loan being sought. Most real estate brokers are aware of the terms available from various lenders, at least for single-family residences.

§6.40 b. Negotiating Rates and Fees

Institutional lenders are generally inflexible on the terms of a proposed loan, particularly for single-family residential financing, but rates and fees on larger loans secured by multifamily, commercial, and industrial property may be negotiable, depending to a certain extent on the current availability of funds to the lender and its loan volume at the time. For commercial business loans, many commercial banks tie the interest rate, particularly on short term and construction loans, to their prime rate, which results in a floating rate that varies as the bank changes its prime rate. On larger loans, the financial institution allows the number of years used to calculate the amortization schedule to extend beyond the number of years before the all due date, particularly when, because of the age of the improvements or for some other reason, the loan term is shorter than the 25 years generally applicable to this type of loan (e.g., a loan all due in 15 years but with an amortization schedule based on 25 years). This results in a balloon payment on maturity (generally handled by refinancing) but reduces the monthly principal and interest payment in the meantime. However, institutional lenders are subject to certain restrictions in making loans that are not fully amortized. See, *e.g.,* 12 USC §371(a)(1) (national banks).

2. Negotiability of Other Loan Provisions

§6.41   a. Form of Note and Deed of Trust

The note and deed of trust are invariably on the lender's pre-printed forms. It is usually not possible to negotiate any changes or amendments to these documents. In those rare instances when a lender may agree to some amendment or modification of the loan terms, it will usually be done by a separate letter agreement varying one or more of the terms of the preprinted note or deed of trust. Even then, the lender's willingness to vary the provisions is usually confined to certain limited areas. See §§6.42-6.46.

§6.42   b. Prepayment

One area in which a lender may be willing to vary strict terms of the note and deed of trust is the provision on the fee or penalty to be charged if the borrower pays all or any portion of the loan before it is due. Many institutional lenders, by policy, are willing to waive all or a substantial portion of a prepayment penalty otherwise due when the loan is being paid off in connection with a sale and the lender can make a new loan to the purchaser. Some lenders will commit themselves to this policy in advance in a side agreement varying the printed provisions in the note regarding prepayment penalties.

When the loan is secured by owner-occupied residential property of four units or less, there are statutory restrictions on the extract-ing of a prepayment fee. CC §2954.9(b). These restrictions provide that such a penalty may be levied only during the first five years of a loan and, further, that the borrower may always prepay up to 20 percent of the original principal amount of the loan in any twelve-month period without penalty. On any excess prepayment over that 20 percent, the lender may not charge more than an amount equal to six-months' advance interest on the excess amount being prepaid. Federal savings and loan associations are limited by the Federal Home Loan Bank Board to charges of six-months' advance interest. 12 CFR §545.8-5(b). See California Mortgage and Deed of Trust Practice §§2.46-2.54 (Cal CEB 1979) for a discussion of prepayment provisions and their legislative regulation. See also §5.13.

§6.43 c. Due-on Clauses

The due-on-encumbrance clause was struck down in *La Sala v American Sav. & Loan Ass'n* (1971) 5 C3d 864, 97 CR 849, in which the court ruled that a lender could not automatically accelerate the loan when the borrower placed a second mortgage on his property. In *Wellenkamp v Bank of America* (1978) 21 C3d 943, 148 CR 379, the court held that an institutional lender could not automatically enforce a due-on-sale clause and accelerate the loan on a sale of the property without a showing that the lender's security was impaired or that the likelihood of default was increased by the sale and transfer of ownership.

In spite of these court decisions, due-on clauses continue to be employed by institutional lenders because they are still free to call in their loans if they can show that their security will be impaired by the transfer of the property.

Federal savings and loan associations take the position that they are not subject to state law in this area because of preemption. See §6.5. The Federal Home Loan Bank Board adopted 12 CFR §545.8-3(f), which specifically authorizes federal associations to use due-on-sale clauses. A lower federal court held that this regulation preempts state law, at least on loans made on or after the effective date of the board's regulation (June 8, 1976). *Glendale Fed. Sav. & Loan Ass'n v Fox* (CD Cal 1978) 459 F Supp 903. Whether federal associations can enforce due-on clauses on loans made before the board adopted its regulation is still unsettled. None of the cases on this subject have yet reached the appellate level. During this hiatus, individual federal associations are taking different positions. Some insist on a right to accelerate in all cases; others do not, particularly when the loan is for a single-family residence. Because state and federal associations' loan terms tend to be identical in all aspects, some pressure may exist on federals to bend on acceleration rights in order to stay competitive. When a lender seems willing to waive acceleration, the borrower should get advance written agreement that the absolute terms of the printed deed of trust will be waived.

See also discussion of due-on clauses in §§3.50, 5.24.

§6.44 d. Tax and Insurance Impounds

Some lenders require impounds for real property taxes and hazard insurance premiums. The annual costs for taxes and insurance are estimated, divided by 12, and the resulting amount is added each month to the principal and interest payment due. When due, the lender pays the taxes and insurance premiums out of this fund. Following a multiplicity of class-action suits claiming that interest was payable to borrowers while such funds were in the hands of the lending institution, the California legislature enacted CC §2954.8 requiring the payment of interest at the rate of 2 percent on all impounds collected for loans secured by one-to-four family residences. The law requiring payment of interest applies only to loans executed after December 31, 1976.

Lenders often will negotiate on impound requirements, except when impounds are required by law or regulation, *e.g.,* for FHA-insured loans (24 CFR §203.73) or for loans whose loan-to-value ratio is 90 percent or greater (see, *e.g.,* 12 CFR §545.6-2(a)(3)). Lenders on occasion will accept, instead of impounds, a savings account pledged in the amount of one year's taxes as additional security for the payment of taxes. They may also be willing to waive enforcement of the impound provision, but without deleting from the note and deed of trust the right to require impounds, as long as the borrower does not default in paying property taxes and hazard insurance premiums.

Civil Code §2954 prohibits impounds when the secured real property is a single-family, owner-occupied dwelling, except when (1) required by a state or federal regulatory authority, (2) a loan is made, guaranteed, or insured by a state or federal governmental lending or insuring agency, (3) a borrower is delinquent in two consecutive tax payments, or (4) a loan is for 90 percent or more of the purchase price or appraised value of the property.

§6.45   e. Hazard Insurance Requirements

The form of deed of trust offered by an institutional lender rarely specifies the lender's hazard insurance requirements. Usually the deed of trust merely states something to the effect that the borrower will maintain fire insurance satisfactory to the lender. Lenders generally will furnish to the borrower, along with the loan documents, specific information stating in detail the lender's hazard insurance requirements. A related clause in the deed of trust deals with the lender's right to receive insurance proceeds and apply them to reduce the indebtedness. *Schoolcraft v Ross* (1978) 81 CA3d 75, 146

CR 57, held that this right to the proceeds was subject to an implied covenant of good faith and fair dealing, and permitted application of the proceeds to rebuilding the property over the lender's demand for its application to the loan. In large commercial loans, lenders will modify their insurance requirements or the provisions in their deeds of trust relating to insurance proceeds.

See §§10.17-10.18 for a discussion of lender's insurance requirements.

§6.46 f. Statutory Restrictions

The Civil Code contains numerous restrictions on loan terms. Many of these restrictions apply only to single-family (one-to-four unit) residential dwellings and often apply only if the property is owner-occupied. In addition to the statutory restrictions on prepayment charges (see §6.42) and impound requirements (see §6.44), statutory restrictions also exist for late charges (CC §§2954.4-2954.5) and due-on clauses (CC §§2924.5-2924.6). Although institutional lenders invariably incorporate these restrictions into their printed forms, a comparison of the form with the applicable statute is advisable.

§6.47 3. Alternative Mortgage Instruments

Financial Code §7153.9, effective January 1, 1978, has authorized a number of alternative mortgage instruments (AMIs), on a four-year experimental basis, for banks and savings and loan associations in California. These instruments are limited to loans secured by one-to-four family residential dwelling units. 10 Cal Adm C §§178.1, 178.4. The Savings and Loan Commissioner has adopted regulations implementing the provisions of this section. 10 Cal Adm C §§178-178.6. The development of these AMIs will give the potential borrower a broader selection of loans. These alternative mortgage instruments offer the attorney advising a prospective borrower a choice and an opportunity to counsel a client even though, within any given loan program, institutional lenders tend to be inflexible about variations of terms applicable to the program selected. The principal characteristics of several of these are discussed in §§6.48-6.52.

These various types of alternative mortgage instruments are designed to attack the two basic problems which in inflationary times have led to skyrocketing housing prices and volatile and escalatory interest rates. The graduated payment mortgages and flexible payment mortgages are addressed to enabling a home buyer to finance (and thus buy) a home he or she could not afford under conventional financing. But both are long term fixed yield (to the lender) instruments and do not touch the problem of the lender who must commit to a fixed rate for as long as 30 years in a market that has seen the cost of fund to loan almost double in the period from 1975 to 1980. Variable rate mortgages and renegotiable rate mortgages attack this latter problem. Additionally, the changes in interest rate yield are so limited (2-1/2 percent to 5 percent over the life of the loan) and move so slowly (1/2 percent per year maximum) (10 Cal Adm C §240.2(b)(1), (5); 12 CFR §545.6-4a) that they are unresponsive to the lender's problem, for whom rates have fluctuated as much as 4 or 5 percent in a year.

In this context, several other alternative mortgage instruments are now being proposed. One is a renegotiable rate mortgage with frequent adjustments (every six months, similar to VRMs) but with no limit up or down. Another is the shared appreciation mortgage (SAM) under which, in return for an initial below market interest rate (though perhaps subject to variable adjustment), the borrower would assign to the lender a portion of any increase in value of his equity in the property securing the loan, so that on sale, the borrower would have to pay this to the lender as additional interest. If the property was not sold within a specified time (*e.g.*, 10 years) the borrower would have to refinance with a conventional loan, including any equity buildup he "owes" the lender, and the latter would be obligated to offer such refinancing. Proposed regulations authorizing SAMs for federally chartered savings and loan associations have been circulated by the Federal Home Loan Bank Board (FHLBB Resolution 80-610) and their adoption is anticipated. (This would be accomplished by amending Part 545 of the Rules and Regulations of the Savings and Loan system by adding a new 12 CFR 545.6-4b.)

§6.48   a. Variable Interest Rate Loans

The variable interest rate loan (called Variable Rate Mortgage or VRM) has been permitted without specific legislative authority, and therefore is not one of the experimental AMIs mentioned in Fin C §7153.9. It is, nonetheless, an alternative to the standard conventional fixed rate mortgage. See CC §§1916.5-1916.6 for statutory regulation of variable rate mortgages.

The variable interest rate loan features an initial stated interest rate that thereafter may vary throughout the life of the loan in accordance with the fluctuations of a predetermined independent index. In California, state savings and loan associations use the cost-of-money index published semiannually by the Federal Home Loan Bank of San Francisco. 10 Cal Adm C §240.2(a),(b)(5). The index is a weighted average of the components that make up the cost of lendable funds to the associations, including interest paid by all California associations on their savings accounts, the current commercial bank prime rate, and the current interest charged by the Federal Home Loan Bank of San Francisco to California associations borrowing funds from it.

Certain statutory and regulatory requirements for VRMs must be met when such a loan is secured by one-to-four unit residential property and has been made to finance the purchase of such property. These are set forth in CC §1916.5 and in accompanying regulations of the Savings and Loan Commissioner (10 Cal Adm C §§240-240.6).

For California state savings and loan associations, changes in the semiannual index that result in a lowering of the interest rate by at least ten basis points (1/10 percent; 100 basis points equals 1 percent) *must* be implemented by the lender (10 Cal Adm C §240.2(b)(2), (7)); changes upward by at least ten basis points may be made. No change, in the case of a note issued under CC §1916.5, can be made more often than once every six months. 10 Cal Adm C §240.2(b)(5). Any change must be made within two months after the publication of the semiannual index triggering the change. 10 Cal Adm C §240.2(b)(6). No change can be greater than 1/4 percent. 10 Cal Adm C §240.2(b)(1). Additional fluctuations unusable because of this restriction may be carried forward and be the basis of a future change. 10 Cal Adm C §240.2(b)(2). The total of all upward changes cannot result in an increase of greater than 2.5 percent in the interest rate during the life of the loan (there is no limitation on the down side). 10 Cal Adm C §240.2(b)(1).

When the interest rate is increased, the borrower may, within 90 days after receiving notice of the increase, repay the loan in full without a prepayment fee regardless of any provision in the loan documents (10 Cal Adm C §240.5). Also, on any such increase, the lender must permit the borrower to elect whether such increase is to be reflected by an increase in monthly loan payments (because of the higher interest rate) or by maintaining the same monthly payments (to the extent possible) and increasing the term of the loan (10 Cal Adm C §240.3). This in effect provides a longer amortization period and enables absorption of at least part of the interest increase in this fashion rather than increasing the monthly payment. The total term of the loan, including any such extension, cannot exceed 40 years (10 Cal Adm C §240.3). Thus, an extension of the loan term will only accommodate a limited increase in the interest rate.

One feature of variable interest rate loans that is designed to make them attractive to borrowers is their assumability, *i.e.,* the absence of any due-on-sale clause. Sellers need no longer negotiate with their lender over the terms under which the latter will permit a potential buyer to assume the existing loan on the property being sold (usually an interest rate adjustment upward).

The advantage of the assumability feature of the variable rate loan has been largely eliminated, however, by the California Supreme Court decision in *Wellenkamp v Bank of America* (1978) 21 C3d 943, 148 CR 379, holding that institutional lenders could not automatically accelerate a loan, under a due-on clause, whenever the property was sold. See §6.43 for a discussion of the due-on clause.

Federal savings and loan associations are also authorized to make variable interest rate loans, but must also offer the borrower a comparable fixed rate loan. 12 CFR §545.6-4(c)(5). Thus federal associations are not extensively marketing the variable rate loans. Federal associations also take the position that they are not bound by the *Wellenkamp* rule restricting enforcement of a due-on clause. See §6.43. Consequently, assumability could be a significant feature if offered on a variable rate loan made by a federal association. However, in order to remain competitive with state associations, many federal associations will bend on the assumability issue, even for fixed rate loans.

§6.49   b. Renegotiable Rate Mortgages

Federal savings and loan associations have been authorized by the Federal Home Loan Bank Board to issue renegotiable rate mortgages (RRMs). 12 CFR §545.6-4a. Under these mortgages the interest rate can be adjusted at prescribed intervals of three, four, or five years. The lender must give the borrower 90 days' notice of the renegotiation date. The borrower is then free to refinance elsewhere and pay the loan off without penalty. If the borrower chooses not to, he will be bound by the new interest rate. The change in the interest rate cannot exceed more than a half percentage point a year nor more than five percentage points, in either direction, over the life of the loan. The change in the interest rate will be based on a government index reflecting residential mortgage rates. There is no requirement that federal associations continue to offer fixed rate mortgages along with the new renegotiable rate mortgages.

In 1977, CC § 1916.6 was enacted to allow California financial institutions to offer a variable interest rate mortgage similar in some respects to the renegotiable rate mortgage now authorized for federal associations. This is also a variation of the variable rate mortgage discussed in §6.48. Under CC § 1916.6, the interest rate may be changed not more frequently than every five years and the adjusted rate may not exceed the original rate by more than 2.5 percentage points. Effective January 1, 1981, state-licensed associations and commercial banks are authorized to issue RRMs identical to those authorized for federal associations (see above) except that the former must offer the prospective borrower the choice of a fixed rate mortgage as well (CC §§ 1916.8-1916.9).

§6.50   c. Graduated Payment Mortgages

Under a graduated payment mortgage (GPM), the monthly payments start out lower than under a comparable fixed rate mortgage but rise during the first few years of the loan to a predetermined level that exceeds payments under a comparable fixed rate loan. The theory behind the GPM is that it reflects the presumed increase in a family's income (particularly that of a young family) throughout the loan term due to upward mobility and inflation.

In underwriting a traditional fixed rate mortgage, the amount of the loan is limited by a predetermined percentage of present total annual family income representing the maximum amount the lender believes the family should devote to housing costs. In the past this was set at 25 percent of gross income. See §6.26. Thus, a family with an annual gross income of $30,000 would, according to lenders, be able to devote at most $7500 annually to housing. This factor, given the current interest rate for the particular loan, limits the total loan available to that family and this, in turn, limits the price the particular family can afford to pay for housing. Under the GPM, the lender uses the lower initial monthly payment in determining the ratio of the loan payment to the borrower's income. Consequently, the borrower is able to obtain a larger loan than would be the case with a traditional fixed rate mortgage.

Although the GPM is a fully amortized loan over its term (*i.e.*, there is no balloon payment), the initial payments usually are insufficient to cover even the interest due. Consequently, there is some capitalization of interest during the first years of the loan. As a result, the principal balance is often larger after the first few years than it was at the beginning of the loan.

The California Savings and Loan Commissioner has issued regulations authorizing GPMs for state associations. 10 Cal Adm C §178.4(c). Even though authorized, very few loans of this type have been made in California. For federal GPMs, see 12 CFR §545.6-4(b). Under FHA regulations (24 CFR §203.45) GPMs have been authorized and made for several years and are known as "sec 245 loans" (12 USC §1715z-10).

§6.51   d. Flexible Payment Loans

The flexible payment loan (FLIP) is another version of the variable payment loan that results in lower payments during the early years of the loan and yet results in full amortization over the life of the loan without a balloon payment at the end. Unlike a graduated payment mortgage loan, a FLIP loan provides for the lender to receive full monthly amortization payments throughout the term of the loan (as in a fixed payment loan). The difference between the lower payment by the borrower and the full fixed-loan-level payment received by the lender is covered by the manner in which the downpayment is handled. In a FLIP loan, the lender can, subject to the limitations of Fin C §7153.2(b)(1), advance up to 95 percent of the sales price or appraised value, whichever is lower. Instead of using all the downpayment to create equity in the property, a major portion is deposited in a savings account that is pledged as additional security for the loan, and out of these funds, plus the interest that they earn while on deposit, come the supplemental monthly payments necessary to make up the difference between the borrower's payments during the early years of the loan and the full level payments received by the lender. This predetermined amount, deducted from the savings account each month, decreases as the borrower's monthly payment increases, and when the savings account is exhausted, the borrower makes monthly payments sufficient to fully amortize the then existing loan balance within the term of the loan.

The California Savings and Loan Commissioner has issued regulations authorizing FLIPs for state-licensed associations. 10 Cal Adm C § 178.4(b). Very few, if any, loans of this type have yet been made in California.

§6.52   e. Reverse Annuity Mortgages

The reverse annuity mortgage (RAM) is designed for elderly and retired homeowners who may have a substantial equity in their homes and wish to raise cash by borrowing against that equity rather than selling the home. The RAM may take various forms. Those authorized by regulation for state savings and loan associations are illustrative of the general approach of RAM loans. See 10 Cal Adm C § 178.4(d). Federal savings and loan associations are also permitted to make such loans, but each particular plan must be submitted in advance for approval by the Federal Home Loan Bank Board. If no action is taken within 60 days of submission, the plan is considered to be approved. There are a number of disclosure requirements. 12 CFR § 545.6-4(d). Because RAMs are not used in financing the purchase of real property, a detailed discussion of the various forms of a RAM is not included here.

D. The Loan Application

§6.53   1. Preliminary Material

The amount and character of preliminary material required to be submitted to an institutional lender before the lender will issue a commitment to make a loan will vary substantially, depending on the type of loan. When the loan is sought to finance the purchase of a single-family residence, the required documentation is rather simple. The basic instrument is a loan application, on a form furnished by the institution, that contains the terms and amount of the loan being sought and detailed personal information about the applicant (or all applicants, if more than one) including a financial statement. The application is accompanied by several related documents, generally including authorizations for the lender to verify any employment and wages listed on the application and any bank balances or other financial data included in the financial statement. For applicants who are currently borrowers, there will also be written permission for present mortgage lenders or other creditors to release information regarding their payment record.

The second basic document is a preliminary title report covering the property that will secure the loan, usually obtained by a real estate broker, if one is participating in the transaction.

The third document that an institutional lender will require is a copy of the purchase and sale agreement or, as local practice dictates, the escrow instructions or any other document that the parties use to spell out the terms of the sale.

§6.54   2. Documenting the Multifamily or Commercial Loan

If the loan sought is to finance the purchase of multifamily residential or commercial property, the preliminary material will be considerably more extensive; it will vary with the particular type of loan and will be subject to requirements on an individual basis. When the loan is to finance existing income property, operating statements and other financial data relating to the property over recent years will invariably be required. When a construction loan is sought, a cost breakdown will certainly be required, as well as a copy of the proposed construction contract. All applicable required regulatory permits, such as approved subdivision maps, will have to be submitted before the lender's final consideration of the loan. More detailed financial information will also probably be required and will include audited statements if the applicant is a business entity (see §6.57), or recent tax returns if the applicant is one or more individuals. Larger and more complex loans require substantially more preliminary documentation because the requirements vary, depending on the type and size of the loan, and on the particular lender.

When the loan sought is for existing rental property, most lenders require a special set of documents for existing tenancies on the property. Therefore, copies of any long term leases (when there are more than one or two years left on the term of the lease) and estoppel certificates from each tenant in occupancy must be furnished. An estoppel certificate is the tenant's recital of the details surrounding the tenancy, including the amount of the monthly rent, the date to which it has been paid, any provisions for rent escalation, and a certification (when there is a written lease) that the lease being submitted to the lender is a true copy, that no defaults by either landlord or tenant exist, and that there are no amendments or other documents, such as renewal options, except those submitted. The estoppel certificate will also include a statement of any special conditions to be furnished by the landlord and verify the amount of any deposits (for cleaning, security, last month's rent, and the like) that the tenant has made to the landlord. See §3.112 for a form of estoppel certificate.

§6.55 a. Assignment of Rents

If the loan is for rental income property, many lenders require a separate assignment of rents (or leases), although the deed of trust almost certainly will contain an assignment of rents clause. One reason the lender may wish a separate document is because of a distinction the courts have made between an assignment of rents as additional security (the typical language used in a deed of trust) and an absolute assignment of rents, conditional on the borrower's default. The typical assignment of rents as additional security creates only an inchoate lien and requires the lender to take some sort of action to perfect its lien on the rents. By taking an absolute assignment conditional on default, the lender hopes to obtain the rents and profits in preference to junior lienholders and trustees in bankruptcy, without the necessity of perfecting the lien through possession or appointment of a receiver. See *Kinnison v Guaranty Liquidating Corp.* (1941) 18 C2d 256, 115 P2d 450; *Malsman v Brandler* (1964) 230 CA2d 922, 41 CR 438. See also California Mortgage and Deed of Trust Practice §7.10 (Cal CEB 1979) for a discussion of this distinction.

§6.56 b. Personal Property Security

If there is any substantial personal property located on the secured real property, whose continued presence is vital to the business purpose of the property, the lender will usually insist on a security agreement covering this personal property as well as the deed of trust covering the real property. Examples are ranges, ovens, and other furniture, including rugs, when the security property consists of furnished apartments; kitchen equipment, when the security property is a restaurant; and hospital equipment, when it is a hospital. When the value of the personal property is extensive, thus forcing the borrower to finance its acquisition, and no part of the real estate lender's loan funds is to be used to acquire such personal property, the borrower can often get the real property lender to take a junior security interest in the personal property behind the primary financing (e.g., conditional sales contract, or equipment lease) with a provision that the real property lender may take over the borrower's position on assuming his obligation on the primary financing if the borrower defaults. This arrangement leaves the borrower free to obtain initial financing of the personal property, and at the same time ensures the real property lender that, in the event of foreclosure of its deed of trust, it can keep the necessary personal property in place, enabling continued operation of the property as a business.

§6.57   3. Business Entity as Borrower

When the business borrower is a business entity, rather than an individual, documentation of the organization's capacity to make the loan and the authority of individuals in the organization to act on behalf of the business entity will be required. The documentation may be a corporate resolution, or a copy of the general partnership agreement, or evidence of the recording of the certificate of limited partnership. See also §§6.28-6.29.

§6.58   4. Refinancing Loans; Documentation

If a loan is to replace a current loan (i.e., to refinance), is for the same borrower, is secured by the same real property, and the property is intended to be the borrower's principal residence, the federal Truth in Lending Act requires that the borrower receive notice when refinancing that he has until midnight of the third business day after the loan is consummated to rescind the transaction. 15 USC §1635(a). The notice must be on a form prescribed by the regulations of the Board of Governors of the Federal Reserve System. 15 USC §1635(a). The right to rescind can be waived only in an emergency. 12 CFR §226.9(e). Failure to comply with all of the statutory requirements results in a loan that continues to be rescindable at the borrower's option, subject to the three-year statute of limitations. 15 USC §1635(f). If rescission is elected, any property or money the borrower has given to lender must be returned within 20 days; no costs or expenses incident to the making of the loan may be charged. 15 USC §1635(b). Effective March 31, 1982, refinancing transactions by the original lender are exempt if no additional advance is made. Pub L 96-221, 94 Stat 132 (1980).

§6.59   5. Real Estate Settlement Procedures Act (RESPA)

The Real Estate Settlement Procedures Act (RESPA) of 1974 (12 USC §§2601-2617) applies to all lenders who make federally related mortgage loans on one-to-four-family residential dwellings. 12 USC §2602(1)(A). A federally related mortgage loan includes any loan made by a lender whose accounts are federally insured, by either the Federal Deposit Insurance Corporation or the Federal Savings and Loan Insurance Corporation. 12 USC §2602(1)(B). Thus, the law in effect applies to most mortgages and deeds of trust granted for residential property by institutional lenders.

The purpose of RESPA is to provide more effective advance disclosures on closing costs to home buyers and sellers, to eliminate kickbacks or referral fees, and to impose limitations on the amount of impound accounts for the payment of taxes, insurance, and other similar costs. 12 USC §2601(b).

Under RESPA, a financial institution, on receipt of a written loan application, must mail a brochure to the applicant describing the general nature of a real property loan. Although the brochure may appear to be that of the lending institution concerned, in fact the entire text is prescribed by the Secretary of Housing and Urban Development and may not be varied. 12 USC §2604.

Concurrently, the lender must furnish the borrower with a RESPA good faith estimate of settlement services. 12 USC §2604(c); 24 CFR §3500.7. This document is the lender's estimate of the amount of all closing costs that the borrower will be charged for closing the loan in the event it is made. The costs include not only the loan origination fee and any other charges that the lender may levy, such as appraisal fees, credit report costs, inspection fees, and private mortgage insurance application fees, but also all charges attendant on closing, such as recording and escrow fees, title insurance premiums, and transfer taxes.

The person conducting the settlement (usually the title or escrow company) is required by RESPA to furnish the seller and the buyer with a settlement statement, in prescribed detail, setting forth the actual closing costs. See 12 USC §2603 and 24 CFR §§3500.8-3500.10. See also §§11.85-11.89 for a discussion of RESPA.

§6.60 E. Written Commitment

Most institutional lenders will verify the acceptance of a loan application by issuing a written loan commitment that sets forth all the conditions of the loan, including amount, rate, loan fee, and term. If the proposed loan is not a standard conventional type (*e.g.*, it has a variable interest rate), lenders often supply a brochure explaining in detail the nonstandard feature.

There are several types of loan commitments, ranging from unenforceable verbal commitments by a lender to formal, written commitments signed by both the borrower and the lender, for which the borrower pays a fee and which constitute a binding contract between the lender and borrower, obligating the lender to make the loan under the terms of the commitment. See §6.61 on commitment fees and §6.62 on take-out commitments.

§6.61 1. Commitment Fees

Lenders often issue written commitments for loans to purchase single-family residences and existing multifamily residential or commercial property when the loan must close within a short time (60 to 90 days), without charging a commitment fee. There is some question whether the buyer can enforce a commitment issued without a fee.

For a large loan, institutional lenders usually require the deposit of a nonrefundable commitment fee (a standby fee) when the commitment is issued. The fee is retained by the lender if the loan is never funded and is applied against the loan origination fee if the loan is funded. This arrangement has been held valid and does not constitute a penalty, even if the deposit is refunded to the borrower if the loan is actually made. *Lowe v Massachusetts Mut. Life Ins. Co.* (1976) 54 CA3d 718, 127 CR 23. Commitment fees are particularly prevalent when the lender does not charge separately for the activities it must undertake to fund the loan, such as appraising the property and preparing all the loan documents. These expenses are covered by the loan origination fee if the transaction is consummated and are compensated by the commitment fee if the transaction is not completed. Nonrefundable commitment fees also tend to discourage further "shopping," and encourage the applicant to shop for the best loan available before obtaining a firm commitment from the lender. Lenders incur certain expenses and administrative actions to issue a commitment (*e.g.,* cash management planning to ensure funds are available to meet the commitment) and, therefore, try to discourage further shopping.

The amount of the commitment fees varies among lenders and, within one institution, according to the length of time that the commitment remains in effect. Institutional lenders dislike long term commitments to specified rates and fees and generally limit their commitments to no more than 90 days. The usual fee for the commitment is about one quarter of a point (*i.e.,* 1/4 percent) of the total loan.

§6.62   2. Take-Out Commitments

Most commonly, borrowers obtain take-out commitments for the long term financing of projects at the same time they obtain their short term loans, *e.g.,* their construction loans. See §6.14. The long term financing will be used to pay off the interim construction loan.

The take-out loan commitment is also used by residential subdivision developers who wish to establish a working relationship with a particular lender in order to offer loans to individual purchasers of houses or units. In this situation the lender will usually make a commitment for a longer period (12 or 18 months), which represents the time the developer estimates is needed to complete the project. The typical commitment fee for this type of loan is one half a point (1/2 percent). The commitment does not specify a particular rate but indicates a lender's willingness to make loans to qualified buyers at its then current market rate for the particular type and quality of housing being constructed. There is no obligation on the part of the developer to use all or any portion of the total commitment.

Although this kind of arrangement seems illusory and of little benefit to the developer, there are in fact several distinct advantages. First, it assures the developer of continuing availability of loan funds to finance sales at current market rates. Second, these commitments often contain other arrangements favorable to the developer, *e.g.,* the lender may commit itself to make loans at specified loan-to-value ratios or to permit secondary financing behind its loans in specified cases. Third, because the houses or units tend to fall into a few general uniform types (*e.g.,* three-bedroom, two-bath, studio), with similar values within a given type, having a single lender active on the project who is thoroughly familiar with it tends to minimize appraisal and other potential loan origination problems and to expedite the consummation of individual loans. This is particularly true when the take-out lender is also the developer's construction lender.

7

Deeds

This chapter was originally published as chapter 15 in California Real Estate Sales Transactions (Cal CEB 1967), by Joseph C. Mascari. It has been revised and updated by the CEB legal staff.

I. REQUISITES OF DEEDS

§7.1   A. Legal Definitions

A deed is a written instrument that conveys or transfers title to real property. *Brusseau v Hill* (1927) 201 C 225, 256 P 419; *Hellman v Howard* (1872) 44 C 100. It is an executed conveyance and acts as a present transfer of title to the property. *Alferitz v Arrivillaga* (1904) 143 C 646, 77 P 657. On the essential elements of deeds, see §7.6.

A transfer is an act of the parties, or of law, by which title to property is conveyed from one person to another. CC §1039. Property of any kind can be transferred (CC §1044), but a mere possibility not coupled with an interest cannot be transferred (CC §1045). If title to real property is transferred by a writing, the transfer is called a grant or conveyance. CC §1053. In general, the word "grant" includes transfers by operation of law (*White v Rosenthal* (1934) 140 CA 184, 35 P2d 154) and voluntary conveyances whether by quitclaim or grant deed (*MacFarland v Walker* (1919) 40 CA 508, 181 P 248), and must be distinguished from use of the word "grant" in the body of the conveyance to embody the covenants specified in CC §1113 (see §§7.2, 9.5).

B. Types of Deeds

1. Grant Deed

§7.2   a. Features

A grant deed is characterized by use of the word "grant" as the operative word of conveyance. CC §1092. It contains implied covenants that the grantor has not conveyed the same estate to anyone other than the grantee, and that the property is free of encumbrances placed on the property or suffered by the grantor (see §§9.5-9.7). CC §1113; 1 Bowman, Ogden's Revised California Real Property Law §3.4 (TI Corp-CEB 1974). If the grantor acquires title to the property after executing a grant deed to it, title passes to the grantee by operation of law. CC §1106.

§7.3   b. Statutory Form, CC §1092

The following grant deed form is prescribed by CC §1092:

I, A B, grant to C D all that real property situated in ____[insert name of county]____ County, State of California, bounded (or described) as follows: ____[here insert description, . . .]____

Witness my hand this ____[insert day]____ day of ____[insert month]____, [19]____.

A B.

This statutory form need not be used; even a badly worded instrument can operate to convey property if the intention to make a present transfer of real property is evident from it. See *Olson v Cornwell* (1933) 134 CA 419, 25 P2d 879. However, in order for the writing to be given effect as a deed, it must satisfy the requisites listed in §7.6.

§7.4   2. Quitclaim Deed

The quitclaim deed, frequently used in California, is derived from the common law release and is characterized by the operative words "remise, release, and quitclaim" or merely "quitclaim." It transfers only whatever interest the grantor has at the time of its execution, without any implied covenants concerning title or encumbrances. *Southern Pac. Co. v Dore* (1917) 34 CA 521, 168 P 147. Therefore, a quitclaim deed, unlike a grant deed conveying the fee interest, usually does not pass afteracquired title to the grantee by operation of law. *Taylor v Coachella Valley County Water Dist.* (1952) 108 CA2d 743, 239 P2d 454. The grantee of a quitclaim deed can be a bona fide purchaser and thus protected from unrecorded instruments affecting title. *Beach v Faust* (1935) 2 C2d 290, 40 P2d 822.

§7.5   3. Warranty Deed

Warranty deeds contain express covenants, such as covenants against encumbrances and of quiet enjoyment. They are rarely used in California because a grant deed combined with a title insurance policy is generally considered sufficient protection for buyers. See 2 Miller & Starr, Current Law of California Real Estate §14:9 (rev ed 1977).

§7.6   C. Necessary Elements of Deeds

To be valid, a deed of any type must contain each of the following requisites: (1) a sufficient writing (see CC §1091) bearing the names of the grantor and grantee (see §§7.14-7.21, 7.23-7.30), operative words of conveyance (see §7.22) and a sufficient description of the property (see §7.31); (2) competent parties (see §§7.14, 7.23); (3) property interests that may be legally transferred (see §7.1); (4) proper execution (see §§7.49-7.58); and (5) delivery and acceptance (see §§7.63-7.64).

Generally, consideration is not essential to the validity of a deed (see §7.13). Recording is not essential to a deed's validity as between grantor and grantee and against those with notice of its existence. *Chaffee v Sorensen* (1951) 107 CA2d 284, 236 P2d 851. Acknowledgment is necessary if the deed is to be recorded but is not essential to the deed's validity, except in the case of a conveyance of a married person's homestead. See §§7.59-7.62 for a discussion of acknowledgments.

II. COMPONENTS ANALYZED

§7.7   A. Form: Illustrative Grant Deed

Form 7.7-1

RECORDING REQUESTED BY

    [see §7.8]

WHEN RECORDED MAIL TO

    [see §7.9]

MAIL TAX STATEMENTS TO

    [see §7.10]

GRANT DEED

The undersigned grantor(s) declare(s):   [see §§7.11-7.12]
Documentary transfer tax is $ _____
( ) computed on full value of property conveyed, or
( ) computed on full value less value of liens and encumbrances remaining at time of sale.
( ) Unincorporated area: ( ) City of _____, and

FOR A VALUABLE CONSIDERATION, receipt of which is hereby acknowledged,   [see §7.13]

[names of grantors; see §§7.14-7.21]

hereby GRANT(S) to   [see §7.22]

[names of grantees; see §§7.23-7.30]

the following described real property in the ____[name of city if incorporated area]____

County of   , State of California:

[See §7.31 on property descriptions]

[See §7.33 on "subject to" clauses]

[See §§7.34-7.48 on special recitals]

Dated [see §7.49] _____   ___[Execution; see §§7.50-7.58]___

[Acknowledgment; see §§7.59-7.62]   _____

_____   _____

[Notarial stamp or seal]

MAIL TAX STATEMENTS AS DIRECTED ABOVE [see §7.10]

Comment: This form is an example of available form deeds. Grant deed forms are available from title companies and stationery stores, and may be adequate for simple transfers of real property. The various components of deeds are discussed in the sections that follow, as cross-referenced in the body of the illustrative deed.

Form clauses in §§7.15-7.48 are set out and discussed to assist the drafter in meeting specific problems, and might be included either in a separately drafted deed or by amending a form deed if space permits.

B. Recording Information

§7.8   1. "Recording Requested By"

Government Code §27320 requires that the name of the person at whose request the document is recorded be noted. "Grantee," "beneficiary," and "vendee," in place of the name of a person, are not sufficient. "Recording requested by" or its equivalent and the name of the requesting person must appear on the face of the document.

The space in the upper left-hand corner of the document, measuring 2½ inches vertically by 3½ inches horizontally, must be reserved to show the name of the person requesting recordation and the return name and address discussed in §7.9. Govt C §27361.6.

§7.9   2. Return Name and Address

The recorder must mail (or deliver if specified) each instrument to the person named in the instrument, and if no person is named, to the person leaving it for recording. Govt C §27321. To enable the recorder to comply, a return name and address should appear on each document to be recorded. On the location of this information, see §7.8. If the instrument effects a change of ownership, a change of ownership statement (Rev & T C §480) should accompany the recorded document. Govt C §27321.

§7.10   3. Tax Statements

Before acceptance for recording, every deed or instrument executed to convey fee title to real property must have across the bottom of the first page the name and address to which future tax statements may be mailed.

There are four acceptable ways to comply with Govt C §27321.5.

(1) The bottom of the first page may be worded as follows:

Mail tax statements to ____[name]____, ____[address]____.

(2) The tax name and address may be located below the recording address, with the wording across the bottom of the first page as follows:

Mail tax statements as directed above.

(3) When the return name and address (see §7.9) is the same as that to which future tax statements are to be mailed, the following wording may be used across the bottom of the first page:

Mail tax statements to the return address above.

(4) If the deed does not convey fee title to real property, the tax information is not required. Govt C §27321.5. In this event, "does not convey fee title" must appear either in the heading or the body of the deed.

If a life estate, estate for years, or estate at will is conveyed, the deed must recite "does not convey fee title," because these are not estates of inheritance (CC §761) and therefore are not fee estates under CC §762.

4. Documentary Transfer Tax

§7.11   a. Statutory Requirements

Under the Documentary Transfer Tax Act (Rev & T C §§11901-11934), cities and counties may by ordinance impose a tax on each deed or other instrument by which real property is transferred. Subject to certain exemptions (Rev & T C §§11921-11926), the tax is imposed on deeds when the value of the interest or property conveyed, less any liens or encumbrances remaining on it at the time of sale, exceeds $100. Rev & T C §11911. The maximum allowable tax rate is $.55 per $500 of the property's value, less remaining liens and encumbrances, and if the land is within a city that has enacted a tax, one half of that amount goes to the city and the rest goes to the county, if it has enacted a tax. Rev & T C §11911. The tax is collected by the county recorder, who allocates it between county and city (Rev & T C §11931), and the tax must be paid before the instrument will be recorded (Rev & T C §11933). The face of a deed submitted for recordation must show the amount of the tax due and the location of the real property, except that the party submitting the document may provide that information on a separate document to be attached to the deed after recording and before return to the party.

Rev & T C §11932. See §7.12 for a form for a separate document providing the documentary transfer tax information.

§7.12   b. Form: Separate Statement of Documentary Transfer Tax

Form 7.12-1

____[Name]____, County Recorder
____[Name of county]____
____[Address]____
Dear _____:

In accordance with Revenue and Taxation Code section 11932, it is requested that this statement of documentary transfer tax due not be recorded with the attached deed but be affixed to the deed after recordation and before return as directed on the deed.

The deed names _____ as grantor and _____ as grantee. The property being transferred is located in ____[name of city; specify if an unincorporated area of the county]____.

The amount of documentary transfer tax due on the attached deed is $_____, computed on the full value of the property ____[less any encumbrances remaining on the property]____.

Comment: Because the documentary transfer tax varies with the value of the property, its disclosure on the deed enables third parties to calculate the amount paid for the property. If the buyer wishes to avoid disclosing the price paid, this procedure may be followed. When this form is used, the deed should contain a statement that the amount of tax due is shown on a separate writing and is not for public record.

C. Body of Deed

§7.13   1. Consideration

Consideration is not necessary for a voluntary transfer. CC §§1040. A written instrument is presumptive evidence of consideration. CC §1614. "For a valuable consideration" is superfluous language. *Goad v Moulton* (1885) 67 C 536, 8 P 63. In deeds made by administrators, executors, guardians, trustees, and receivers who are conveying property under court order, title insurers require that the deeds recite the exact amount of consideration received. Some title insurers require consideration to be recited in deeds made by trustees not acting under court order, attorneys-in-fact, municipal corporations, or other public agencies.

Whether there was consideration for a conveyance may, however, have important consequences for the parties.

(a) A conveyance without a fair consideration that leaves the grantor insolvent is fraudulent toward creditors. If there is no purchaser, encumbrancer, or successor in interest for a fair consideration and without knowledge of the fraud, the creditors can have the deed set aside. CC §§3439.04-3439.09. See *Kirkland v Risso* (1979) 98 CA3d 971, 159 CR 798; *Stearns v Los Angeles City School Dist.* (1966) 244 CA2d 696, 53 CR 482.

(b) A deed without consideration may be considered a gift deed and may be subject to federal or state gift taxes (IRC §2512(b); Rev & T C §15106), federal estate taxes (IRC §2035), or state inheritance taxes (Rev & T C §§13641-13642).

(c) The law will not imply a covenant against encumbrances from a gift deed. *Estate of Porter* (1903) 138 C 618, 72 P 173.

(d) In addition to good faith, valuable consideration is necessary to give a recorded deed priority over an earlier unrecorded deed. CC §1214.

(e) Both valuable consideration and lack of notice are necessary for a purchaser to take good title free of any claim that an earlier transaction, although absolute on its face, was a mortgage. CC §2925.

(f) A deed, absolute on its face, may be shown to be only a mortgage. *Munger v Moore* (1970) 11 CA3d 1, 89 CR 323; *Rickless v Temple* (1970) 4 CA3d 869, 84 CR 828.

(g) There may be a resulting trust in favor of the grantor. *Lehmann v Kamp* (1969) 273 CA2d 701, 77 CR 910.

(h) The estate conveyed may be determined to comprise merely an easement rather than a fee. *Warren v Atchison T. & S.F. Ry.* (1971) 19 CA3d 24, 96 CR 317.

§7.14 2. Grantor Recitals

The body of the deed must contain the grantor's name or other description sufficient to identify him. "I, the undersigned," is permissible. See *Childs v Newfield* (1934) 136 CA 217, 28 P2d 924. See §§3.10-3.14 on the capacity of grantors. For a discussion of discrepancy between the grantor name in the body of the deed and the execution name, see §7.50.

§7.15   a. Form: Grantor's Name Different From Record Owner's

Form 7.15-1

____[Name(s) of grantor(s)]____, **also known as** ____[name under which title held]____

Form 7.15-2

____[Name of grantor]____, **being the same person who acquired title as** ____[name under which title held]____

Form 7.15-3

____[Name of grantor]____, **who acquired title to the property described below under** ____[his / her]____ **former name of** ____[name under which title held]____

Comment: If a person has record title to real property in one name and later changes his or her name, whether by court action (CCP §§1275-1279) or otherwise, the name in which he or she derived title to the property must be stated. If this is not done, the conveyance, though recorded, does not impart constructive notice; it is valid, however, between the parties. CC §1096. Unless there is substantial identity between the name of the grantor in the deed and the name of the record owner (creating presumption of identity of person) the title is not marketable. *Benson v Shotwell* (1890) 87 C 49, 25 P 249.

A longer statement is sometimes used: "*AB*, being the person formerly known as *CD*, her name having been changed by a final judgment of the Superior Court of the State of California, County of Los Angeles, in Case No. 00000. . . ." This is objectionable because reference to a case by court and number increases the hazard of error in dictating or transcribing.

§7.16   b. Form: Unincorporated Association

Form 7.16-1

____[Name of organization]____, ____[a lodge / a branch]____ **of** _____, **an unincorporated** ____[specify: society, association, labor organization]____

Comment: Traditionally, in California, the property of an unincorporated association belongs to its members. *Grand Grove of United Ancient Order of Druids v Garibaldi Grove No. 71* (1900) 130

C 116, 62 P 486; *County of Trinity v Rourke* (1969) 275 CA2d 628, 79 CR 209. Because the property was considered to belong to members, the association itself could not hold title to or convey real property. This rule has been ameliorated by statutes which now provide that an unincorporated society, association, or labor organization (Corp C §20001), and certain medical associations (Corp C §21200), may acquire title to real property. See §3.25. A conveyance of real property by an unincorporated association must be executed by its presiding officer and recording secretary under its seal after a resolution has been duly adopted by the association authorizing the conveyance. Corp C §20002.

If an unincorporated association does not fall within the purview of Corp C §§20001 and 21200, its trustees can convey title for it if title is recorded in their names. See §7.18. Otherwise, the individual members should be named as grantors. Therefore, reference in the deed to the association is unnecessary and serves no useful purpose except identification.

§7.17   c. Form: Partnership

Form 7.17-1

____[Name of partnership]____ , **a partnership,**

Comment: An estate in real property, acquired in the partnership name, can be conveyed only in the partnership name. Corp C §15008(3). Title companies usually require recordation under Corp C §15010.5 of a statement of a general partnership, and will not insure title in a purported limited partnership or its successors unless the certificate of partnership required by Corp C §15502 is recorded. See §§3.22-3.23.

§7.18   d. Form: Trustee

Form 7.18-1

____[Name(s) of trustee(s)]____, **as trustee(s)** ____[for _____, under the will of _____, deceased / under the trust agreement dated _____, 19__, between _____ and _____]____,

Comment: This form is suitable for naming a trustee, under a will or by inter vivos trust, as grantor. See §3.17 regarding trustees' authority to hold and convey real property.

In a testamentary trust, the order for distribution must be recorded in the county where the property is located when it covers real property. Prob C §1222. If the order has been recorded and the property is properly described in it, the trustee's deed need not recite the probate case number or the place where the order is recorded.

The recital of the date of the trust agreement and of the names of the trustors of an inter vivos trust is also unnecessary if the transfer to the trustee is of record. However, it is common practice to make these recitals because trustees feel more comfortable referring to the source of their authority.

§7.19   e. Form: Corporation

Form 7.19-1

____[Name of corporation]____, a ____[name of state of incorporation]____ corporation,

Comment: California corporations have the power to acquire and convey real property (see §3.26). Corp C §207(d), (e), (g). Foreign corporations can also acquire and convey California real property. Corp C §208.

Naming the place of incorporation is customary to identify the grantor corporation, although it is not necessary if the property is of record in the name of the grantor. Some lawyers even recite the principal place of business. This kind of recital multiplies the opportunities for error in dictating or transcribing, and therefore increases the chances for ambiguity in the deed.

If the corporation has changed its name after acquiring title to real property, when it conveys the property it is subject to CC §1096. See Comment at §7.15. See also *Puccetti v Girola* (1942) 20 C2d 574, 128 P2d 13. In that event, the grantor should be further identified as:

Form 7.19-2

successor by ____[manner of succession]____ to ____[name of predecessor corporation]____

On title company policy regarding CC §1096, see Comment at §7.15.

There is no statutory provision prohibiting or invalidating acquisitions or conveyances of real property made by an unqualified foreign corporation, but there are penalties against such a corporation for transacting intrastate business. Corp C §§2203(c), 2258.

§7.20   f. Form: Joint Venture

Form 7.20-1

____*[Names of joint venturers]*____ , constituting all the joint venturers in ____*[name of joint venture]*____ , a joint venture,

Comment: See §3.24 for a discussion of legal aspects of joint ventures and their impact on ownership and conveyance of real property by joint venturers. For the most part, the designation "joint venture" should simply be avoided because of uncertainties surrounding the legal consequences of the designation. Both partnerships (see §§3.22, 7.17) and unincorporated associations (see §§3.25, 7.16) can hold and convey real property in their own names, and most joint ventures can also be characterized as either of those entities.

If the joint venture format is used, conveyances to the joint venture should be in the names of the joint venturers, not that of the joint venture, and the joint venture name should not be used except for identification.

§7.21   g. Other Grantor Clauses

For discussion of sales by administrators and executors, and a form for executor's deed, see 1 California Decedent Estate Administration §§14.1, 14.3, 14.51 (Cal CEB 1971). See also Prob C §786 for legal requirements. On legal requirements for deeds executed by guardians and conservators, see Prob C §§2109, 2111.

The name and official capacity of an officer acting under court order or authority (*e.g.,* sheriff, marshall or constable, court commissioner, receiver, or referee in partition) should be stated in a deed from that person. This type of deed often contains a reference to the proceedings authorizing the conveyance, but the recital is not essential.

In describing cities, some lawyers add "a municipal corporation of the State of California" or similar language; in describing counties, "a body corporate and politic" is sometimes seen. It is sufficient to say "the City of Los Angeles, California" or "Contra Costa County, California."

§7.22   3. Words of Conveyance

The operative words of conveyance used will generally determine the type of deed with all the legal consequences that flow from the characterization. For example, use of the word "grant" will make the deed a grant deed (CC §1092) and invoke the implied covenants that the grantor has not conveyed the same estate to anyone other than the grantee, and that the property is free of encumbrances placed on it by the grantor (CC §1113). See §7.2. Use of the words "assign," "remise, release, and quitclaim," or merely "quitclaim," will characterize the instrument as a quitclaim deed without any implied covenants concerning title or encumbrances. See §7.4.

If the buyer intends that covenants stated in the purchase and sale agreement (other than those implied in the deed as covenants) are to survive delivery of the deed, the agreement should provide for their survival, and the deed should recite the covenants. See §9.4. For a discussion of survival, see §§3.66-3.67.

To "waive" or "renounce" title, or to say that it "shall go to" the buyer, will not pass title. *Davis v McGrew* (1889) 82 C 135, 23 P 41; see *Litten v Warren* (1936) 11 CA2d 635, 54 P2d 39.

4. Grantee

§7.23   **a. Requirement of Capacity**

To take title, a grantee must be (1) a natural person (see CC §671); (2) a partnership or corporation (see §§7.17, 7.19); or (3) an unincorporated association authorized by law to take title to real property (see §7.16). See §§3.9-3.26 on capacity to hold title to real property. See Pen C §§2600-2604 on the rights of prisoners.

Infants and incompetent or insane persons are capable of taking title because the law presumes their acceptance of a beneficial conveyance (see §3.11). *Estate of Yano* (1922) 188 C 645, 206 P 995; see *Estate of Kalt* (1940) 16 C2d 807, 813, 108 P2d 401, 404. See §3.13 for a discussion on the requirement of a guardianship to convey property for persons under disability.

§7.24   **b. Requirement of Certainty**

The grantee must be so named or designated that his or her identity is absolutely certain. This requirement can be met without naming the grantee if a means of identification can be inferred from the language of the deed. For example, a quitclaim of an easement to "the record owners of all lots in the tract described below, in severalty, on the same tenures as their respective interests appear of record at the time of recording this deed" might be sufficient. See CC §§681 (severalty), 761 (tenures of estates). Another example is "the heirs or devisees of *A*, deceased, subject to the administration of his estate." See *Schade v Stewart* (1928) 205 C 658, 272 P 567 (language upheld).

Examples of deeds void for uncertainty are deeds to:

(1) "*A* or *B*." See *Schade v Stewart, supra* (dictum). See §§3.19-3.21 for a discussion of the problems presented when the purchase and sale agreement requires the deed to recite the grantee as "*A* or nominee."

(2) "The inhabitants of the City of Los Angeles" (except for dedication of an easement of public use). See Note, 14 Calif L Rev 135 (1925).

(3) A deed to a fictitious person is void (*Copeland v Fairview Land & Water Co.* (1913) 165 C 148, 162, 131 P 119, 124), but a deed to an actual person under an assumed name is good (*Wilson v White* (1890) 84 C 239, 24 P 114).

§7.25 c. Status of Grantee

It is customary to show the marital status of a grantee and the marital relationship of grantees who are husband and wife. See CC §5110 on the community property presumption when a husband and wife are so described in a deed. Title insurers require that deeds describe the status of grantees to increase certainty of identification. See also §§3.30, 7.26.

Common status designations are: an unmarried man or woman, husband and wife, a married man or woman, his or her spouse, a minor, an incompetent person, and an administrator, trustee, or executor. A deed to a minor or incompetent person should run directly to that person rather than to the guardian or conservator, but deeds often name the guardian as grantee and add a recital of guardianship. A conveyance to heirs or devisees of the deceased can run either to the heirs or devisees or to the administrator or executor. However designated, it is customary to include a recital that the conveyance is subject to administration of the estate.

§7.26 d. Estate, Nature of Ownership, and Proportion of Interest

In addition to the name and status of the grantee or grantees, three other elements of the grant are necessary, if applicable:

(1) *Nature of estate.* If the nature of the estate is not otherwise stated, the deed is presumed to pass an estate in fee. CC §1105. Other kinds are estates for life, estates for years, and estates at will.

CC §761. The intent to pass an estate other than fee title must be expressed in the deed.

The grant should make clear whether the estate passed is one of full ownership (a fee) or merely of some more limited interest (such as an easement). See *Johnson v Ocean Shore R.R.* (1971) 16 CA3d 429, 94 CR 68. See also *Warren v Atchison T. & S.F. Ry.* (1971) 19 CA3d 24, 96 CR 317. Estates may be divided into present and future interests. Future interests are discussed in California Will Drafting chap 14 (Cal CEB 1965).

(2) *Nature of ownership.* Multiple ownership may be in joint tenancy, tenancy in common, community property, or partnership interests. CC §§682-687. All real property in California and all personal property wherever located that is acquired during marriage is community property (CC §5110), with some exceptions (CC §§5107, 5108). However, real or personal property acquired by a married woman by written instrument before January 1, 1975, is presumed to be her separate property. CC §5110. The deed should express the buyers' wishes about the nature of ownership. On multiple ownership generally, see §§3.28-3.30.

(3) *Proportion of interest.* A grant, for example, "to A and B as tenants in common" gives the grantees undivided equal shares. See 1, 2 Bowman, Ogden's Revised California Real Property Law (TI Corp-CEB 1974, 1975). The shares may be made unequal by express provision in the deed or may be shown to be unequal by parol evidence (*Anderson v Broadwell* (1931) 119 CA 150, 6 P2d 267). To avoid litigation, the proportions should be expressed in the deed, even when they are equal, *e.g.,* by specifying "undivided equal shares."

A single grant may entail questions concerning each of these elements. For example, "to the following as tenants in common: A and B, husband and wife, as joint tenants, an undivided one half; C and D, husband and wife, as community property, an undivided one third; and E, a married woman, as her separate property, an undivided one sixth."

e. Grantee Recitals

§7.27   (1) Form: Joint Tenancy

Form 7.27-1

____[Names of grantors]____ ____[state words of conveyance]____ **to** ____[names of grantees]____ **as joint tenants**

Comment: Because a joint tenancy conveyance is made to two or more people in equal shares (CC §683), the proportions of the respective interests need not be specified. See §7.26. The salient characteristic of joint tenancies, of course, is the right of survivorship in remaining joint tenants, which removes the property from the estate of the decedent. Prob C §§1170-1175. Features of joint tenancies are discussed in §3.28.

A joint interest in property can be created by any of the following as grantor: (1) a sole owner to himself or herself and others; (2) from tenants in common or joint tenants to (a) themselves or some of them, and (b) themselves or any of them and others; (3) from husband and wife, when holding title as community property or otherwise, to (a) themselves, (b) themselves and others, (c) one of them and to another or others. CC §683.

§7.28   (2) Form: Tenancy in Common

Form 7.28-1

____[*Names of grantors*]____ ____[*state words of conveyance*]____ **to** ____[*names of grantees*]____ **an undivided** ____[*e.g., one-half*]____ **interest and to** ____[*names of grantees*]____ **an undivided** ____[*e.g., one-third*]____ **interest,** ____[*state any other interests*]____ **as tenants in common**

Comment: Tenants in common may hold their interests in disproportionate shares (CC §685), but if the shares are not specified, it will be presumed that they are equal. See §3.28 concerning other features of tenancies in common.

§7.29   (3) Form: Community Property

Form 7.29-1

____[*Names of grantors*]____ ____[*state words of conveyance*]____ **to** ____[*names*]____ **husband and wife, as their community property**

Comment: A deed to the grantees as husband and wife without specification of the form of ownership will be presumed to convey title as community property (CC §5110), but it may be that this presumption can be overcome by tracing contributions to the purchase of the property back to separate property sources. See *Marriage of Lucas* (1980) 27 C3d 808, 166 CR 853. If the parties specify that the form of ownership is community property, the presumption can be overcome only by proof of an agreement to allow the separate property contributor to recoup the separate property investment on dissolution, or to devise it. *Marriage of Lucas, supra.* Thus, if the parties intend that the property be treated as community property, it is best to state that intention expressly in the deed.

§7.30   (4) Form: Changing Title From Joint Tenancy to Community Property

Form 7.30-1

____*[Names of husband and wife; see Comment below]____ ____[words of conveyance]____* to ____*[names of husband and wife]____,* husband and wife, as their community property

Comment: Although it is common practice for brokers and title companies to suggest that married couples who acquire real property take title as joint tenants, ownership in community property is preferable to joint tenancy for federal tax purposes. On the death of a joint tenant, one half of the basis of the property is stepped up to the time of death (IRC §1014(b)(9)), but the entire basis is stepped up on the death of a spouse if the property is held as community property (IRC §1014(b)(6)). The parties could also execute an independent agreement that the property will be treated as community property if they do not wish to execute a new conveyance. See §7.29. A conveyance from husband and wife as joint tenants to themselves as their community property will not trigger a reappraisal of the property for property tax purposes under Cal Const art XIIIA. Rev & T C §63. The names used by husband and wife in filling in the grantor portion of the deed must be the same as they appear in the joint tenancy deed by which they took title.

§7.31   5. Description

Real property can be transferred only by a writing that describes the property (*Craig v Zelian* (1902) 137 C 105, 69 P 853), with sufficient clarity that it can be identified and located (*Best v Wohlford* (1904) 144 C 733, 78 P 293; *Podd v Anderson* (1963) 215 CA2d 660, 30 CR 345). No particular form of description is required (see, *e.g.,* CC §1092) as long as the description permits identification of the property. If the description is omitted or not sufficiently certain, however, the conveyance is void. *Edwards v City of Santa Paula* (1956) 138 CA2d 375, 292 P2d 31.

The description generally follows directly the designation of the grantee. See, *e.g.,* the illustrative grant deed at §7.7. On descriptions generally, see chap 8.

"Subject to" clauses (see §7.33) and special recitals (see §§7.34-7.48) follow the description and may be inserted in the space for description if there is enough room. If not, it is generally better to type the entire deed than to attach an exhibit to a printed form.

§7.32   6. Exhibits and Riders

If, for any reason, an exhibit is to be attached to the deed, recorders prefer that it be attached as a second page rather than pasted to the front of the deed and folded.

Some recorders take the position that a rider covering provisions other than the description is not "legible" and may require the person presenting it for record to prepare a substitute for the "illegible" original. Govt C §27361.7.

§7.33   7. "Subject to" Clauses

Grant deeds are often restrained by conditions or qualifications, agreed on by grantor and grantee, that negate the grantor's liability under implied covenants. See CC §1113. These conditions or qualifications are the "subject to" clauses of grant deeds. For a discussion of the restrained grant deed and for examples of "subject to" clauses, see §9.7. These clauses are not to be confused with contractual conditions commonly introduced by similar words. See §3.68.

§7.34   8. Special Recitals

When appropriate, various special recitals should be incorporated in a deed to explain its purpose, show the interest and intent of the parties, and incorporate by reference other recorded documents. Some common recitals are presented as illustrations and discussed individually in §§7.35-7.48. Special recitals should be used liberally because they clarify the intent of the parties and eliminate the effect of legal presumptions that may operate contrary to the intentions of the parties (see, *e.g.,* CC §§5110 (presumption of community property), 686 (presumption of tenancy in common)). On the conclusive presumption of recitals in written instruments, other than recitals of consideration, see Evid C §622.

§7.35 a. Form: Recital of Separate Property; Spouse to Spouse

Form 7.35-1

This deed is given to carry out the mutual desire and agreement of the parties that the property shall become vested in the grantee as ____[his / her]____ sole and separate property.

Comment: Either spouse may enter into any property transaction with the other that either might if unmarried. CC §5103. However, because both are controlled by the rules relating to confidential relations as defined by the code provisions on trusts (CC §§2215-2289), they should state their intentions explicitly. In a deed from one to the other, when the intent is to vest title in the grantee as his or her separate property, this form is a useful recital.

Despite the recital of separate property, either spouse can show against the other that there was no intention to change the property from community to separate. Compare *Salveter v Salveter* (1929) 206 C 657, 275 P 801, with *Donze v Donze* (1928) 88 CA 769, 264 P 294. If the wife was the grantee of an interest acquired before January 1, 1975, the presumption of separate property is conclusive in favor of a third party who dealt with her in good faith and for value. CC §5110. When the husband is the grantee and a third party deals with him in good faith and for value, the wife is estopped from denying the separate property recital in the deed. *MacKay v Darusmont* (1941) 46 CA2d 21, 115 P2d 221.

Some title companies require this recital in deeds between husband and wife as a condition to insuring title as separate property or to insuring a subsequent conveyance from the grantee spouse.

§7.36 b. Form: Consent to Joint Tenancy Between One Spouse and Another Person

Form 7.36-1

____[Name of grantee spouse]____, named above as a grantee, and ____ [name of consenting spouse]____, ____[his / her]____ ____[wife / husband]____, consent to the creation in the grantees of a joint tenancy in the property described in this deed.

____[Execution and acknowledgment by consenting spouse]____

Comment: In *Yeoman v Sawyer* (1950) 99 CA2d 43, 221 P2d 225, a husband contributed half the purchase price of property from community funds and took title, without his wife's consent, under a joint tenancy deed with a single woman who contributed the other half of the purchase price. The court regarded the interests under the deed as being one-quarter vested in the husband, one-quarter in the wife (giving her one half of the community property), and the other half in the single woman. Because the interests were unequal, the joint tenancy was defeated, and a tenancy in common was held to have been created.

Before insuring title in grantees as joint tenants when one of the grantees is married, title companies, to remove doubt regarding the state of title to the property, require a recital in the deed similar to those presented above, the consenting spouse's signature on the deed, and its acknowledgment. As an alternative, title insurers will accept as evidence of consent escrow instructions signed by the consenting spouse authorizing the joint tenancy. However, it is better to have the consent in the deed because off-record evidence may be unavailable, lost, or destroyed. On execution, see §§7.49-7.58. On acknowledgments, see §§7.59-7.62.

§7.37   c. Form: Deed in Lieu of Foreclosure

Form 7.37-1

This deed is an absolute conveyance, grantor(s) having sold the property to grantee(s) for a fair and adequate consideration. The consideration is ____[the sum of $_____ and]____ full satisfaction of all obligations secured by the ____[mortgage / deed of trust]____ securing the obligation of ____[name] ____ in favor of ____[name]____ recorded on _____, 19__, as Instrument _____in book_____, page _____ of ____[official book]____, the Office of the County Recorder of _____ County. This conveyance is freely and fairly made, and there are no agreements other than this deed between grantor(s) and grantee(s) with respect to the property.

Comment: Civil Code §2889 declares void all contracts for the forfeiture of property subject to a lien in satisfaction of the obligation secured, as well as contracts in restraint of the right of redemption. The code section applies only to contracts of forfeiture or restraint made as part of the original transaction or concurrent with it (*Graves v Arizona Cent. Bank* (1928) 205 C 715, 272 P 1063; *Bradbury v Davenport* (1896) 114 C 593, 46 P 1062). Because the equity of redemption is a favored right, however, the courts often view subsequent transactions with suspicion, unless the transfer represents a bona fide sale based on sufficient consideration. *Graves v Arizona Cent. Bank, supra.* Therefore, when a deed in lieu of foreclosure is given to satisfy a preexisting debt, a recital to that effect should be in the deed.

If a monetary consideration is given in addition to satisfaction of the secured indebtedness, the amount paid to the grantor should be included in the recital. Title insurers recommend that any monetary consideration be stated in order to indicate the fairness of the amount, but it need not be stated precisely (*e.g.,* "over $100").

The recital states that the conveyance is absolute in order to negate any inference that it is merely further security to the lender. See *Beeler v American Trust Co.* (1944) 24 C2d 1, 147 P2d 583. The recital also states that there are no other agreements between the parties concerning the property in order to make it clear that the conveyance is not made under a contract voided by CC §2889.

Some title companies prefer an estoppel affidavit to a recital in a deed, and some require both. However, a deed recital should always be used because a title insurer may refuse to insure without the recital even if there is an estoppel affidavit and a recorded reconveyance of the deed of trust or a cancellation of the mortgage. See California Mortgage and Deed of Trust Practice §§6.29-6.37 (Cal CEB 1979) for discussion of deeds in lieu of foreclosure and title company practices in handling them.

d. Correcting, Removing, and Releasing Recitals

§7.38   (1) Form: Correcting or Clarifying Description

Form 7.38-1

This deed is given to ____[*correct the erroneous* / *clarify the indefinite*]____ description of the property contained in the deed recorded on _____, 19__, as Instrument _____ in book _____, page _____ of ____[*official book*] ____, in the Office of the County Recorder of _____ County, and is in lieu of that deed.

Comment: Erroneous descriptions in deeds fall into two categories:

(1) The description is sufficient despite the errors because the property intended to be conveyed can be ascertained; and

(2) The description is not sufficient because the exact property intended to be conveyed cannot be ascertained. If the description

falls into this category, the deed is void. *Saterstrom v Glick Bros. Sash Co.* (1931) 118 CA 379, 5 P2d 21.

A grant is interpreted in favor of the grantee. CC §1069. To interpret the description in favor of the grantee, the court will reject what is apparently false in the description and uphold the deed if the remainder of the description is applicable to the property intended to be conveyed. See *Podd v Anderson* (1963) 215 CA2d 660, 30 CR 345. See §8.10 on erroneous and indefinite descriptions. Despite the new deed, intervening interests may have priority unless the erroneous or unclear description can be upheld as sufficient.

§7.39   (2) Form: Removing Cloud

Form 7.39-1

This deed is given to clear the records of any interest grantor may have in the property described in this deed because of any statement of any purported interest of grantor included by error in the deed recorded on _____, 19__, as Instrument _____ in book _____, page _____ of ___[official book] ____ , in the Office of the County Recorder of _____ County.

Comment: An erroneous conveyance of property not owned by the grantor creates a cloud on the title to that land. The title company will discover the cloud when the true owner orders a title search in connection with a contemplated sale or encumbrance. To obtain title insurance, the owner must remove the cloud.

The problem can be eliminated by having the grantee execute a deed to the true owner. This could be in the form of a quitclaim. The owner, however, may prefer a grant deed with its implied covenants (see chap 9) that the grantee has not encumbered the property. If a grant deed is given, it should negate any implied covenants of title (see §§9.5-9.7) by containing a recital like the one above.

If the grantee is unwilling to execute and deliver a deed removing the cloud, the true owner should promptly commence an action to quiet title to remove the cloud, and file a lis pendens (see §§12.86-12.92) to cut off the rights of intervening third parties.

§7.40   (3) Form: Release of Exception or Reservation

Form 7.40-1

This deed is given to relinquish and release all interest that the grantor may have in the property described in this deed because of any exceptions or reservations contained in the deed recorded on _____, 19__, as Instrument _____ in book _____, page _____ of ____[official book]____, in the Office of the County Recorder of _____ County.

Comment: A grant of real property passes a fee unless it is clear from the grant that a lesser estate was intended. CC §1105. The grant carries with it the following incidents and appurtenances unless clearly excepted:

(a) A permanent building and its fixtures (see *Fratt v Whittier* (1881) 58 C 126);

(b) Deposits, *i.e.,* minerals and other substances of the land (*Moore v Smaw* (1861) 17 C 199);

(c) Water rights necessary for the use of the land (*Stanislaus Water Co. v Bachman* (1908) 152 C 716, 93 P 858);

(d) Rents not yet due from an existing lease on the land (*Fahrenbaker v E. Clemens Horst Co.* (1930) 209 C 7, 284 P 905);

(e) Award money from a pending condemnation proceeding (*Security Co. v Rice* (1932) 215 C 263, 9 P2d 817);

(f) Landowner's royalty from oil produced on the land conveyed (*Tanner v Title Ins. & Trust Co.* (1942) 20 C2d 814, 129 P2d 383);

(g) An easement for a road over adjoining lands that benefits the land conveyed (*Elliott v McCombs* (1941) 17 C2d 23, 109 P2d 329);

(h) Title to the center of an adjoining highway (CC §1112).

For general principles of law on the passing of incidents and appurtenances, see CC §§1084, 1104, 3522.

This form is commonly used to release incidents and appurtenances excepted from the original conveyance. It may also be used to eliminate problems created by thoughtless reiteration of reservations or exceptions in copying prior deeds. See §§3.91, 8.34, 8.57 for a discussion of reservations and exceptions; see §8.48 on reservations and exceptions in successive deeds.

e. Compliance With Obligation Recitals

§7.41 (1) Form: Conveyance in Performance of Sales Agreement

Form 7.41-1

This deed is given in full satisfaction of an agreement to convey executed by grantor(s) to ____[assignor(s) of]____ grantee(s), recorded on _____, 19__, as Instrument _____ in book _____, page _____ of ____[official book]____, in the Office of the County Recorder of _____ County.

Comment: The purpose of this provision is to remove the lien of a purchaser under a recorded purchase agreement or installment land contract (CC §3050), and it may be used in a deed to either the buyer named in the agreement or the buyer's assignee.

See Evid C §642 for the presumption that a person having a duty to convey real property actually conveyed when the presumption is necessary to perfect title.

§7.42   (2) Form: Conveyance on Exercise of Option

Form 7.42-1

This deed is given and accepted in compliance with an option to purchase contained in a lease recorded on _____, 19__, as Instrument _____ in book _____, page _____ of the ____[*official book*]____, in the Office of the County Recorder of _____ County, and as a cancellation of the lease and full release of all parties to the lease and their respective successors in interest, from all other obligations under the lease.

_____[*Execution and acknowledgment by grantee*]_____

Comment: Many leases include a provision permitting the lessee to purchase the property on the exercise of an option. Good practice requires that a lease containing an option be recorded. The lease must be acknowledged by the lessor as a condition to recordation. Govt C §27287. If the lease is not recorded, however, the tenant's possession of the property may be sufficient to put a buyer on notice of the tenant's option rights.

When the option is exercised, this provision should be used in the deed to evidence the intention of canceling the recorded lease. The form contemplates both an acceptance by the grantee and a general release between the parties. The grantee's signature must be acknowledged.

§7.43   (3) Form: Conveyance on Distribution of Trust

Form 7.43-1

The grantee having attained the age of majority, this deed is executed and delivered under the trust contained in the deed to the grantor recorded on ____, 19__, as Instrument _____ in book _____, page _____ of ____[*official book*]____, in the Office of the County Recorder of _____ County.

Comment: See Evid C §642 on the presumption applied to a trustee or other person having a duty to convey real property to a particular person.

If a trust in relation to real property is not stated in the deed to the trustee or in an instrument signed by the trustee and recorded in the same office with the deed, a conveyance by the trustee is absolute in favor of a buyer without notice and for value. CC §869. Should the deed to the trustee fail to name or indicate the beneficiary, even though the grantee is described as trustee, the trustee holds title free from any trust. CC §869a.

When the trust is expressed in the deed to the trustee, every conveyance by the trustee in contravention of the trust is absolutely void. CC §870.

f. Termination Recitals

§7.44 (1) Form: Termination of Recorded Lease

Form 7.44-1

This deed is given and accepted for the purpose of terminating the lease recorded on _____, 19__, as Instrument _____ in book _____, page _____ of ____[official book]____, in the Office of the County Recorder of _____ County.

_____[Execution and acknowledgment by tenant]____

Comment: A lease creates both contractual and property rights in the tenant. *City of Pasadena v Porter* (1927) 201 C 381, 257 P 526. The lease may be terminated by surrender of the premises and unconditional acceptance by the lessor. *Flynn v Mikelian* (1962) 208 CA2d 305, 25 CR 138. It is good practice to evidence the termination of a recorded lease, even if the lease itself reveals the termination, by a deed from the tenant to the lessor containing the above recital.

§7.45 (2) Form: Elimination of Covenants, Conditions, and Restrictions

Form 7.45-1

This deed is given to cancel and annul all the covenants, conditions, restrictions, and reservations contained in the deed recorded on _____, 19__, as Instrument _____ in book _____, page _____ of ____[official book] ____, in the Office of the County Recorder of _____ County, and to release the property described in this deed from any effect of all the above covenants, conditions, restrictions, and reservations.

Comment: This provision is designed as a recital in a quitclaim deed given to eliminate covenants, conditions, and restrictions. For a discussion of covenants, conditions, and restrictions, see 2

Bowman, Ogden's Revised California Real Property Law chap 23 (TI Corp-CEB 1975); Guide to California Subdivision Sales Law §§4.4, 4.5(2), 4.6, 4.22 (Cal CEB 1974).

§7.46 (3) Form: Removal of Power of Termination

Form 7.46-1

This deed is given to convey all rights and powers to terminate the estate described in this deed, vested, conditional, or contingent, that grantor has now, or may acquire later because of the conditions, restrictions, or reservations contained in the deed recorded on _ _ _ _ _ _ _ _, 19_ _, as Instrument _ _ _ _ _ _ _ _ in book _ _ _ _ _ _ _ _, page _ _ _ _ _ _ _ _ of _ _ _ _[official book]_ _ _ _ , in the Office of the County Recorder of _ _ _ _ _ _ _ _ County,

[Add if relinquishment is only partial]

but only to the extent _ _ _ _[state rights relinquished, e.g., they purport to establish setback lines from the front lines of the lots described in the recorded deed]_ _ _ _. Except as above released, the conditions, restrictions, and reservations contained in the deed described above are to remain in full force and effect.

Comment: A grantor can impose a condition subsequent in a conveyance, which is a power to terminate the estate by appropriate action if there is a breach of the condition. *Boughton v Socony Mobil Oil Co.* (1964) 231 CA2d 188, 41 CR 714. The breach must be proved in an action to compel a reconveyance or quiet title. See *Parsons v Smilie* (1893) 97 C 647, 32 P 702.

The deed should be executed by the grantor who imposed the restrictions or by his or her heirs, and it should be recorded.

g. Reservation Recitals

§7.47 (1) Form: Mineral Rights

Form 7.47-1

[Insert after description of property conveyed; §7.31]

Reserving all oil, mineral, gas, and other hydrocarbon substances below a depth of 500 feet under the real property described in the deed, without the right of surface entry.

Comment: For a discussion of reservations and exceptions, see §§3.91, 8.34, 8.57; on the creation of easements, see §§8.56-8.59.

This provision is designed for use by a buyer who intends to develop the property using institutional financing. Many institutional lenders will lend money on property when the borrower is not the owner of the mineral rights, if the mineral rights are more than 500 feet below the surface and do not include the right of surface entry.

§7.48 (2) Form: Life Estate

Form 7.48-1

Grantor reserves the exclusive possession and the use and enjoyment in ____[his / her]____ own right of the rents, issues, and profits of the property described in this deed for the term of ____[his / her]____ lifetime.

Comment: For a discussion of reservations and exceptions, see §§3.91, 8.34, 8.57. Elderly grantors often convey their property, reserving for their support a life estate in the rents, issues, and profits of the property. The recital in this section was upheld in *Tennant v John Tennant Memorial Home* (1914) 167 C 570, 140 P 242. Reservation of a life estate can be coupled with a power of disposal. See *Estate of Wood* (1973) 32 CA3d 862, 875, 108 CR 522, 531.

Even though the owner of a life estate has the right to all the rents, issues, and profits of the property during his or her lifetime (CC §818), when the life estate is created by a reservation in a conveyance of the fee, the right to the rents, issues, and profits should be expressly recited.

The owner of a life estate must keep the buildings in repair and must pay taxes and other annual charges, an equitable proportion of special assessments (CC §840), and interest on encumbrances (see *Boggs v Boggs* (1944) 63 CA2d 576, 147 P2d 116).

D. Execution

§7.49 1. Date of Execution

A deed's validity is not affected by the lack of a date of execution or an erroneous date. However, the date of execution may be evidence in determining priority among conflicting deeds, as a duly executed grant is presumed to have been delivered when executed. CC §1055. The presumption applies only to the time and not to the fact of delivery. *Blackburn v Drake* (1963) 211 CA2d 806, 27 CR 651. The date in the body of the deed gives rise to the CC §1055 presumption, although the presumption can be overcome by extrinsic evidence. *Gordon v City of San Diego* (1895) 108 C 264, 41 P 301. The presumption arises from the deed's date even if the date of acknowledgment is later. *Gordon v City of San Diego, supra.* If the date of acknowledgment is earlier, it has been held sufficient to overcome the presumption arising from the later date. *Merle v Meagher* (1870) 1 CU 644.

§7.50   2. Definition and Requirements

In a strict sense execution consists of both the signing and delivery of an instrument. CCP §1933. The term "execution" is often used to indicate only the signing of the instrument, however, as in CC §§1185, 1189-1192 (acknowledgment). See *Le Mesnager v Hamilton* (1894) 101 C 532, 35 P 1054.

The deed must be signed by the grantor or his authorized agent. CC §1091. A deed not signed by the grantor is sufficiently executed if it is signed by a person in the grantor's presence, at his request, and with his authorization *Knaugh v Baender* (1927) 84 CA 142, 257 P 606. The grantor may adopt and ratify his signature made by another without previous authority. *Blaisdell v Leach* (1894) 101 C 405, 35 P 1019.

If property is subject to a marital homestead, any deed or voluntary encumbrance must be executed and acknowledged by both husband and wife, or they may execute and acknowledge separate instruments conveying or encumbering the homestead to the same party or to the party's successor in interest. CC §1242. Execution by either spouse under a power of attorney does not comply with CC §1242. *Katsivalis v Serrano Reconveyance Co.* (1977) 70 CA3d 200, 138 CR 620.

When property is held jointly or in common, the signature of only one owner may be sufficient to convey his interest in the property. This is so, even though the owner who signed intended that the other owners also sign the deed, unless the parties intended that one signature would not be effective until the others were added. See *Gonzales v Gonzales* (1968) 267 CA2d 428, 73 CR 83.

The signature on the deed should conform exactly to the name shown as grantor. A deed signed and acknowledged by persons not named in the body of the deed as grantors does not pass their title. *Cordano v Wright* (1911) 159 C 610, 115 P 227. The rule in *Cordano* originated in the fact that common law deeds were not signed, but sealed, and identification of the grantor was therefore required in the body of the deed, but it is no longer given a mechanical application. *Strong v Strong* (1943) 22 C2d 540, 544, 140 P2d 386, 388. Although the name signed to the deed differs from the grantor's name, the conveyance is valid if the name in the acknowledgment conforms to the grantor's name in the body of the deed. *Middleton v Findla* (1864) 25 C 76.

Grantees and title insurers may require a spouse to join in the conveyance of the other spouse's separate property if they lack knowledge of the true character of the property. By signing the deed, however, the accommodating spouse becomes exposed to potential personal liability for breach of covenants in the deed. See *Evans v Faught* (1965) 231 CA2d 698, 711, 42 CR 133, 141. See §3.19 for suggested language to avoid the personal liability of the nonowning spouse. On implied covenants, see chap 9. Nevertheless, to avoid disputes and possible litigation, care should be taken to ensure that the signatures conform to the grantors named in the deed.

3. Particular Executions

§7.51 **a. Form: Mark**

Form 7.51-1

[Mark of executing party]

____[Name of executing party written by a witness]____

____[Name of executing party]____, being unable to write, made____ [his / her]____ mark in my presence and I signed ____[his / her]____ name at ____[his / her]____ request and in ____[his / her]____ presence.

[Signature of witness]

____[Typed name below]____

[Signature of additional witness]

____[Typed name below]____

Comment: The mark of a person who cannot write has the same legal effect as his signature, provided his name is written near it by a person who writes his own name as a witness. If the signature is to be acknowledged, it must be witnessed by two persons both of whom must subscribe their own names as witnesses. CC §14; Govt C §16.

§7.52 **b. Form: Attorney-in-Fact**

Form 7.52-1

____[Name of executing party written by attorney-in-fact]____ by ____ [signature of attorney-in-fact,]____ ____[his / her]____ attorney-in-fact.

Comment: Civil Code §1095 authorizes an attorney-in-fact to execute an instrument transferring an estate in real property, provided he or she subscribes the name of the principal to it and his or her own name as attorney-in-fact. "*A,* attorney-in-fact of *B,*" does not comply with §1095.

The importance of compliance with CC §1095 was discussed in *Hodge v Hodge* (1967) 257 CA2d 31, 64 CR 587, in which a deed executed by an authorized agent, who signed her principal's name and typed in her own name (as agent) but then failed to sign her own name, was declared invalid. The case contains a helpful review of previous California decisions on execution of deeds by an agent.

Civil Code §1091 requires that the power of attorney be in writing. Govt C §27322 permits the power of attorney to be recorded; most title insurance companies require its recordation. A recorded power of attorney affecting real property can be revoked only by recording the revocation in the same office in which the power of attorney was recorded. CC §1216. On revocation by death or incapacity, see CC §2356.

§7.53 c. Form: Trustee

Form 7.53-1

[Signature of trustee]
____[Typed or printed name of trustee]____
as trustee of ____[name of trust]____

Comment: Failure to indicate the representative capacity of the execution may be overcome by recitals in the deed or other record evidence indicating that the execution is actually in a representative capacity. For a form of recital for a trustee as grantor, see §7.18. Even when there is a representative capacity recital in the deed, failure to indicate that execution is made in that capacity can create problems. In *Estate of Conroy* (1907) 6 CA 741, 93 P 205, the deed named the grantor as "A (Administrator of the Estate of B)," and the deed was signed and acknowledged by *A.* The court disregarded the words in parentheses and held the deed was that of *A,* individually.

§7.54 d. Form: Guardian or Conservator

Form 7.54-1

[Signature of guardian / conservator]
____[Typed name of guardian or conservator]____

as ____[guardian / conservator]____ of ____[name of
ward]____, a ____[minor / an incompetent person]____

Comment: On guardians and conservators, see §7.21; on the consequences of failing to indicate that the execution was in a representative capacity, see §7.53

§7.55   e. Form: Executors and Administrators

Form 7.55-1

___[Signature of representative]___
____[Typed or printed name of representative]____
as ____[executor / administrator / administrator with
will annexed]____ of the ____[will / estate]____ of
____[name of decedent]____, deceased

Comment: On the consequences of failing to indicate that the
execution was in a representative capacity, see §7.53. For a form of
executor's deed suitable for administrators and administrators with
the will annexed, see 1 California Decedent Estate Administration
§14.51 (Cal CEB 1971). The deed must refer to the order confirming
sale and directing execution of the conveyance. Prob C §786. A certified copy of the order confirming the sale must be recorded in the
office of the recorder of the county in which the land or any portion of
it lies. Prob C §§786, 1222.

§7.56   f. Form: Partnership

Form 7.56-1

____[Name of partnership]____
By ___[signature]___
____[Typed name]____
By ___[signature]___
____[Typed name]____
Being all the partners

Comment: Corporations Code §15010 permits any partner to convey title to real property held in the partnership name, and Corp C
§15009 obligates the partnership if one partner executes a deed in
the partnership name. However, all the general partners should
sign a conveyance of partnership in real property. One partner may
lack authority to act or may have exceeded his or her authority, and
the partnership might be able to recover the property unless it was
conveyed to a bona fide purchaser for value without knowledge that

the partner executing the conveyance had exceeded his authority. Corp C §15010. For a more detailed discussion of partnerships, see §§3.22-3.23.

Rather than subjecting the deed to the risk of attack, the grantee should insist that the deed be executed by all the partners. Alternatively, the partnership might authorize one or more partners to execute the deed under the partnership agreement or other recorded documents.

Title insurers require that the statement of partnership be recorded under Corp C §15010.5. Conveyances in the name of a limited partnership signed by all the general partners or, if so authorized, by less than all, will be insured if the partnership agreement permits the partnership to deal in real property, or a resolution signed by all the limited partners authorizes the transaction.

§7.57   g. Form: Corporation

Form 7.57-1

____[Name of corporation]____

[Seal]   By __[signature]__

____[Typed name]____

____[Official capacity]____

Comment: The name of the corporation should appear in the signature, but corporate misnomers are not detrimental if the identity of the intended corporation is clear. See *Sixth Dist. Agricultural Ass'n v Wright* (1908) 154 C 119, 97 P 144.

Unless execution is acknowledged in accordance with CC §1190.1, title insurers require a certified copy of a resolution authorizing the conveyance. Some title insurers may waive the certified copy of the resolution when (1) a bank or financial institution with a responsible reputation executes the instrument and the corporate act is routine and does not affect its own property; or (2) the president or vice-president and secretary or assistant secretary execute the instrument on behalf of the corporation, the transaction is clearly within the ordinary scope of the business of the corporation, and the possible loss if execution is unauthorized would not exceed an amount the insurer feels is reasonable. See Corp C §313. See §3.26.

§7.58   h. Form: Joint Venture

Form 7.58-1

[Signature of joint venterer]
____[Typed name of joint venturer]____
[Signature of joint venturer]
____[Typed name of joint venturer]____
**constituting all the joint venturers
in** ____[name of joint venture]____,
a joint venture

Comment: For discussion of joint ventures, see §§3.24, 7.20. Consistent with the practice recommended in §7.20 (_i.e.,_ that conveyances to joint ventures be avoided, and if made, be in the names of the joint venturers, not in the name of the joint venture, and that the joint venture name need not be used except for identification), the execution form provides for the individual joint venturers to execute the deed. Although reference is made to the joint venture, it is only for identification and is not required.

If the deed to the joint venture is in the form "to _X,_ a joint venture, composed of _A, B,_ and _C,_" or "to _X,_ a joint venture, and _ABC,_" title insurers may require a deed from the joint venture executed by all the joint venturers and the joint venture, even though it may not be a legal entity capable of taking title.

The provision in §7.56 (partnership) or §7.57 (corporation) must be included in the provision in this section if any of the joint venturers is a partnership or corporation.

The title company should be consulted on whether the spouses of the joint venturers must sign.

E. Acknowledgment

§7.59   1. Legal Requirements

Unless excepted by statute, a document's execution must be either acknowledged or proved, and the acknowledgment or proof certified, before it can be recorded. Govt C §§27287-27288. Acknowledgment is essential to the validity of a deed conveying the homestead of a married person. CC §1242. On exceptions, see §7.60; on procedures for proving unacknowledged documents, see §7.62. An acknowledgment is a statement that the person who appears to have signed the document did in fact sign it (see, *e.g.*, CC §1189), and must be distinguished from a verification, which is a sworn statement that the contents of a document are true (see CCP §446).

Blank acknowledgment forms can readily be obtained from most title companies and stationery stores. These forms need only be filled out and stapled to the document that is going to be recorded. Acknowledgments can be made before a number of specified public officials (CC §§1181, 1182), but the most common practice is to have a notary public execute the acknowledgment. The Civil Code specifies the form of acknowledgment to be used when documents are executed by the following: individuals (CC §1189); corporations (CC §1190); partnerships (CC §1190a); public agencies (CC §1191); and attorneys-in-fact (CC §1192).

§7.60   2. Documents That Need Not Be Acknowledged

The following documents may be recorded without being acknowledged or proved:

(a) Judgments affecting real property (Govt C §27282(a)(1));

(b) Certain certificates, extensions, and releases related to taxes (Govt C §27282(a)(3));

(c) Certain documents relating to mining claims and leases (Govt C §§27282(a)(2); 27283-27285; CC §1219);

(d) Letters patent, mineral leases in which the United States is the lessor, certain copies of interdepartmental communications of the Department of the Interior, and certain copies of documents filed with the General Land Office (Govt C §27285);

(e) Certain documents related to letters patent (Govt C §§27285-27286);

(f) Fictitious mortgages or deeds of trust (CC §2952; Com C §9401);

(g) Lis pendens (no requirement in CCP §409, the enabling statute);

(h) Duplicate certificates of sale of real property sold under execution or under a court order (*Foorman v Wallace* (1888) 75 C 552, 17 P 680);

(i) Federal tax liens (Govt C §27330);

(j) Notices of lien for postponed property taxes (Govt C §27282(a)(4)).

§7.61   3. Effect of Acknowledgment

A certificate of acknowledgment is prima facie evidence of the execution of the document to which it is attached. Evid C §1451. A person who properly acknowledges that he or she has executed an instrument cannot deny execution against subsequent innocent parties after the certificate of acknowledgment is attached to the instrument. This is true even if he or she did not freely execute the document. *Bryan v Ramirez* (1857) 8 C 461. But see *Mentry v Broadway Bank & Trust Co.* (1912) 20 CA 388, 129 P 470 (rule inapplicable to encumbrance such as a mortgage).

§7.62   4. Proof of Unacknowledged Documents

An unacknowledged document that does not come under any of the exceptions listed in §7.60 may still be recorded if it is proved by one of the following:
   (a) The party executing the document (CC §1195);
   (b) A subscribing witness (CC §1195);
   (c) Proof of handwriting (CC §§1195, 1198);
   (d) Court action (CC §§1203-1204).

§7.63   F. Delivery

A basic requirement for validity of a deed is its delivery (see §7.6). CC §1054; *Hademan v Dodson* (1932) 215 C 3, 7 P2d 997. It is delivery that passes title. *Pellissier v Title Guar. & Trust Co.* (1929) 208 C 172, 280 P 947. Besides physical transfer of the deed and acceptance by the grantee, the grantor must intend to pass title for delivery to be complete. *Henneberry v Henneberry* (1958) 164 CA2d 125, 330 P2d 250. The intent of the grantor is a question of fact to be determined from all the circumstances surrounding the transaction. *Blackburn v Drake* (1963) 211 CA2d 806, 27 CR 651.

Delivery to the grantee or the grantee's agent cannot be conditional if the grantor intended to pass title. CC §1056. For example, if the grantor intended to pass title but delivers the deed to the grantee on the condition that the grantee execute an agreement to pay money, or that the conveyance take effect only in the event of the grantor's death, delivery is absolute, and title passes immediately to the grantee. *Bias v Reed* (1914) 169 C 33, 44, 145 P 516, 520; *Estate of Pieper* (1964) 224 CA2d 670, 687, 37 CR 46, 58. However, if the grantor believes, even though erroneously, that the condition is necessary for the deed to be effective, the delivery may fail for lack of the required intention, *i.e.,* there may be no delivery notwithstanding the physical transfer of the documents. *Hotaling v Hotaling* (1924) 193 C 368, 224 P 455. To convey property subject to a condition effectively, the grantor should deliver the deed to a third party who is not solely the grantee's agent. See CC §1057.

There are a few rebuttable presumptions affecting the burden of producing evidence on the issue of delivery:

(1) When the deed is in the possession of the grantee, delivery is presumed. See *Podd v Anderson* (1963) 215 CA2d 660, 30 CR 345.

(2) When the deed is in the possession of the grantor, nondelivery is presumed. *Miller v Jansen* (1943) 21 C2d 473, 132 P2d 801.

(3) Recordation of a deed at the request of the grantor is prima facie proof of delivery with the intention on the part of the grantor to convey title. *Osterberg v Osterberg* (1945) 68 CA2d 254, 156 P2d 46. If a recorded deed is found in the grantor's possession, however, there is a conflict of presumptions. *Hill v Donnelly* (1941) 43 CA2d 47, 110 P2d 135.

Delivery can be constructive if (1) by agreement of the parties at the time of execution, it is understood that the deed is to be delivered, and the grantee is entitled to immediate delivery; or (2) the deed is delivered to a stranger for the benefit of the grantee, and his assent is shown or may be presumed. CC §1059.

For what appear to be rather special considerations regarding delivery of deeds that create or terminate joint tenancies, see *Rebmann v Major* (1970) 5 CA3d 684, 85 CR 399; *Meyer v Wall* (1969) 270 CA2d 24, 75 CR 236; *Gonzales v Gonzales* (1968) 267 CA2d 428, 73 CR 83; *Clark v Carter* (1968) 265 CA2d 291, 70 CR 923; *Burke v Stevens* (1968) 264 CA2d 30, 70 CR 87.

See *Kish v Bay Counties Title Guar. Co.* (1967) 254 CA2d 725, 62 CR 494, on the right to waive ineffective delivery.

§7.64   G. Acceptance

For a deed to be effective, it must be accepted by the grantee. See *Green v Skinner* (1921) 185 C 435, 195 P 60. If the grantee has knowledge of the beneficial grant, acceptance is presumed. See *Boye v Boerner* (1940) 38 CA2d 567, 101 P2d 757. If the grant is beneficial, the grantee's acceptance is presumed. *Kropp v Sterling Sav. & Loan Ass'n* (1970) 9 CA3d 1033, 88 CR 878. Knowledge as well as acceptance is presumed unless lack of knowledge is clearly proved. See *Marshall v Marshall* (1956) 140 CA2d 475, 479, 295 P2d 131, 133; *Steitz v Irwin* (1949) 94 CA2d 871, 211 P2d 919; *Herman v Mortensen* (1945) 72 CA2d 413, 164 P2d 551. On the presumption of acceptance by minors and incompetent or insane persons, see §7.23.

When the grantee is a corporation, its intention to accept can be shown by its acts or words (*e.g.*, acts of ownership generally, retention of the deed, or execution of a mortgage). See *Canal Oil Co. v National Oil Co.* (1937) 19 CA2d 524, 66 P2d 197.

III. VALIDITY OF DEEDS

§7.65   A. Void Deeds

A deed is void if the grantor is a person judicially declared incompetent (CC §40; see §3.12) or a minor under 18 (CC §33; see §3.11) or if it is executed in blank with the grantee's name later inserted without the grantor's authorization (*Trout v Taylor* (1934) 220 C 652, 32 P2d 968). An undelivered deed, such as one stolen from the grantor or delivered by an escrow holder in violation of the grantor's instructions, is also void. *Hildebrand v Beck* (1925) 196 C 141, 236 P 301; *Gould v Wise* (1893) 97 C 532, 32 P 576, 33 P 323.

A deed to "*A* or *B*" is void for uncertainty (see §7.24). See *Schade v Stewart* (1928) 205 C 658, 272 P 567. On the use of "*A* or nominee" language, see §§3.19-3.21. A deed expressly intended to operate on the death of the grantor or in contemplation of death is purely testamentary in character and therefore void unless executed with the formalities required of wills (*Van Core v Bodner* (1947) 77 CA2d 842, 176 P2d 784) or delivered on a condition to a third party (see 1 Bowman, Ogden's Revised California Real Property Law §3.52 (TI Corp-CEB 1974)). A deed may also be declared void if it has been materially altered. *Jay v Dollarhide* (1970) 3 CA3d 1001, 84 CR 538.

Void deeds do not pass title even in favor of innocent purchasers unless estoppel is present. See *Blaisdell v Leach* (1894) 101 C 405, 35 P 1019; *Crittenden v McCloud* (1951) 106 CA2d 42, 234 P2d 642.

§7.66   B. Voidable Deeds

Some examples of voidable deeds are:

(1) A fraudulently procured deed (*Seeger v Odell* (1941) 18 C2d 409, 115 P2d 977);

(2) A deed containing a mistake about the quantity of land conveyed (see *Danielson v Neal* (1913) 164 C 748, 130 P 716);

(3) A deed procured by undue influence (*Cox v Schnerr* (1916) 172 C 371, 156 P 509);

(4) A deed procured by duress or menace (*Campbell v Genshlea* (1919) 180 C 213, 180 P 336);

(5) A deed from a grantor of unsound mind whose incapacity has not been judicially determined (*Hughes v Grandy* (1947) 78 CA2d 555, 177 P2d 939).

On deeds obtained by confidential relationships, see generally CC §§1566-1575, 1689.

If the deed is voidable, a bona fide purchaser from the grantee obtains good title as against the grantor. *Duff v Randall* (1897) 116 C 226, 48 P 66.

8

Descriptions of Property

This chapter was originally published as chapter 8 in California Real Estate Sales Transactions (Cal CEB 1967), by Jerrald K. Pickering. It has been revised and updated by the CEB legal staff.

I. INTRODUCTION

§8.1   A. Nature and Purpose of Descriptions

The description of property covered by a purchase and sale agreement or instrument of transfer must delineate the property so precisely that the parcel can be located unquestionably and distinguished from all other parcels of land on this earth. Any failure to adhere to strict standards of precision may result in expense, litigation, and distortion or defeat of the purposes of either the transferor or the transferee. This is true whether the description is found in a deposit receipt, escrow instructions, or a more formal agreement. See *Beverage v Canton Placer Mining Co.* (1955) 43 C2d 769, 278 P2d 694 (deposit receipt); *Salmons v Jameson* (1956) 144 CA2d 698, 301 P2d 431 (option). On descriptions generally, see 3 Witkin, Summary of California Law, *Real Property* §§103-108 (8th ed 1973); 3 American Law of Property §§12.98-12.123 (A.J. Casner ed 1952). See also 1 Bowman, Ogden's Revised California Real Property Law, chap 14 (TI Corp-CEB 1974).

In addition to land, personal property may be part of the sale or exchange. On describing personal property that is to be transferred as part of the transaction, see §8.64.

§8.2   B. The Lawyer's Responsibilities

To carry out the purposes of both transferor and transferee, it is not enough simply to copy into the new deed the description that appears on the transferor's deed. Many circumstances may require a different description from the one by which the transferor acquired title. The original description may be erroneous (see §8.47). Subsequent events may have deprived the record owner of all or part of his land (see §8.38), or may have enlarged the transferor's holdings (see §8.40). The record itself may reveal changes in the client's ownership (see §8.9), or the transferor may desire to part with only a portion of the land described in his documents (see §8.23).

To meet these situations, the lawyer—whether counsel for buyer or seller—must know how to find correct descriptions (see §§8.5-8.9), read them (see §§8.13-8.24), determine their accuracy (see §§8.10-8.11, 8.25-8.43) and correct them if necessary (see §§8.44-

8.49), and draft descriptions that will carry out the intentions of the parties (see §§8.50-8.62).

In addition, the lawyer must know how to describe any personal property that is to be transferred as part of the transaction. On descriptions of personal property, see §8.64.

§8.3   1. Limitations on Lawyer's Function

While the lawyer has a responsibility in connection with accurate descriptions, he does not have absolute responsibility, nor can he discharge it alone. Sections 8.7-8.9 suggest a number of problems in which the help of surveyors, engineers, and title companies should be employed.

Once the lawyer has employed the proper assistance, he should (a) help in furnishing the proper information on which the reports of surveyors and others are to be based; (b) insist that the reports be rendered promptly; and (c) examine them critically, since error is always possible.

Still, the lawyer is entitled to rely to a large extent on information furnished by other experts. In title searches, for example, he may rely on the title company and cannot be held responsible for the title company's errors if he has performed his own function according to the standards prevailing among lawyers practicing in his community. On attorneys' liability and standard of care generally, see §1.12. On title company services, see §1.36.

Surveyors or engineers (referred to in this section simply as surveyors) should be called on to determine whether metes and bounds are correct and whether the property is subject to unrecorded defects such as encroachments, shifting water boundaries, tendency to earth slide, or structural defects. If the attorney has properly performed his function, he is not responsible for errors in the surveyor's report. When appropriate, however, he should (a) counsel clients on the need for a surveyor, (b) state the problem correctly to the surveyor, (c) check the complete report, and (d) question the surveyor about aspects of the report that appear incorrect to the lawyer.

In drafting subdivision and survey maps, the law requires employment of a licensed surveyor. See §8.8. In using the California Coordinate System (explained in §8.14), the difficulty of understanding and interpreting the calls makes a surveyor indispensable. In describing the effects of nonrecord matters affecting descriptions (see §§8.25-8.43), prudence often dictates the employment of a professional surveyor; and the same is true of area or quantity transfers such as condominiums, cooperative apartments, and reservations.

§8.4   2. Lawyer's Exclusive Function

One of the services that only a lawyer should perform is describing estates and form of ownership. For example, whether an estate is to be a fee, a life estate, an estate for years, or an estate at will, and whether it is to be held as separate or community property or in some other form of cotenancy is to be determined by the client (with the attorney's advice) and effectuated by the lawyer's competent drafting. The title company will determine for itself whether it will insure the title as the kind of estate that the attorney and the client intend (that determination should be ascertained in advance), but the lawyer and not the title company is responsible for proper draftsmanship.

Similarly, the lawyer is solely responsible for drafting a transfer so that a strip of land intended as an easement will not be construed as a fee, and vice versa. He may need a surveyor to provide the information he needs in describing the land included in the strip, but setting out the nature of the estate in the land is the lawyer's responsibility alone.

The same is true of restrictions on use, whether these appear as deed restrictions, zoning ordinances, or in some other form. A title company may warn of the existence of these restrictions, a surveyor may (and often should) define the boundaries of land to which the restrictions are applicable, and municipal engineers may help in finding ordinances and indicating the interpretation given to them by the administering authorities; but the lawyer must draft and interpret the restrictions or uses properly. If, for example, there is to be a uniform setback requirement, the lawyer alone must make certain that the restriction is a limit on use and not on ownership. Similarly, in drafting deed restrictions, title companies may help in a number of ways (e.g., descriptions of land to which the restrictions apply, examples of other well-drafted declarations, consultation about the insurability of the lawyer's proposals), but the lawyer bears the ultimate responsibility for drafting restrictions that will do what the client expects them to do.

II. FINDING CORRECT DESCRIPTIONS

A. From Client's Documents

§8.5   1. Deed

Ordinarily the seller should be able to produce the deed, judgment, or other document by which he acquired title to the property. This document cannot always, however, be relied on as an accurate description of the property to be conveyed: The seller may be parting with only a fraction of the property described in his documents of title, or the description may have been changed by subsequent matters of record, such as condemnation or partial conveyances, or by events that do not show of record, such as easements, adverse possession, prescription, implied dedication, etc. See §§8.25-8.43.

§8.6   2. Title Insurance Report or Policy

The seller's lawyer should ask to see his client's title insurance policy but should not rely on it. It may help in drafting the description, but it will not show matters that may have altered or affected the description since the policy was issued. Some of these matters are discussed in §§8.25-8.43. To discover possible changes in the description, both parties should obtain the additional information enumerated from inspections, surveys, and title services (see §§8.7-8.9).

As part of this information, it is customary and prudent to order a preliminary title report. The report generally includes a copy of the map of record. If it does not include a map, it is prudent to request one so that the parties may ascertain that the description refers to the particular property that they are considering.

Because the preliminary report does not ensure the description, buyers should protect themselves by conditioning the purchase and sale agreement on delivery of title in conformity with the title report or as expressly required in the agreement. Forms for this purpose are offered in §§3.55, 3.79-3.80. See California Title Insurance Practice §§5.27-5.30 (Cal CEB 1980) on abstracter's liability.

Title insurance policies, too, have their limitations. They are contracts and should be approached with the same skepticism as any other contract; they may be in error, and the remedies they afford may be inadequate or vigorously contested by the title company. See *J.H. Trisdale, Inc. v Shasta County Title Co.* (1956) 146 CA2d 831, 304 P2d 832.

Neither title policies nor preliminary reports give evidence of off-record information, such as availability of transportation, schools, or churches. They may also fail to reveal important matters discoverable by inspection or survey (see §§8.7-8.8).

§8.7   B. Inspection of Premises

Some experienced real property lawyers insist that an attorney cannot give proper advice concerning a transfer unless he personally inspects the premises. While this attitude is not uniformly reflected by the prevailing practice in this state, personal inspection by the attorney may be of great advantage to the client: It may result in the discovery of nonrecord matters discussed in §§8.27, 8.38-8.43; it could reveal the existence of physical hazards, such as slides or floods; or it could suggest such problems as zoning, transportation, or access. The buyer is charged with notice of matters discoverable by inspection even if he does not actually make an inspection. See CC §19.

The cost to the client of the lawyer's time spent in a personal inspection may be small or large, depending on the size and location of the property (see §§1.23-1.25 on compensation for real estate services), but the discoveries made in this inspection could result in considerable net savings to the client in both time and money.

§8.8   C. Surveys and Engineering Studies

Some problems are discoverable only by engineers and surveyors. If the seller has a recent survey, he may make it available to the buyer. If not, the attorney's failure to advise employment of an engineer or surveyor in a proper case is a disservice to the client.

Ideally, qualified engineers or surveyors should draft all new descriptions. They are required by law to do so in drafting subdivision and survey maps. Govt C §§66495-66496. Their services should also be employed when there is any question of encroachment, structural defects, uncertain boundaries, possible landslides, or similar defects.

Sometimes, however, surveyors assume without question that a fence or line between adjacent buildings correctly marks a boundary. When the assumption is open to question, the lawyer may have to insist that the line be accurately measured.

Some title services require and use the services of surveyors. If these title services are to be used, additional engineering and surveying services may be a needless duplication of expense.

§8.9   D. Title Services

Title services may, at times, be the only adequate protection against inaccurate descriptions or against discrepancies between a description and the actual land that the seller can convey. Title officers and "title engineers" can help lawyers in the following tasks:

(1) Read complicated descriptions and indicate or identify property as described on a plat (which, however, must yield to survey marks "on the ground" if the two conflict);

(2) Determine whether the property owned by the seller is the same as the property to be conveyed or encumbered;

(3) Prepare or approve legal descriptions, acceptable for title insurance purposes, from record information or from an approved survey or both, the source of information being dependent on the title service rendered;

(4) Determine that the bearings and distances shown in a metes and bounds description (see §§8.16-8.22) are mathematically correct and that the complete description is sufficient to enclose and identify a particular parcel;

(5) In conjunction with extended coverage title insurance, verify and correlate survey and record information to determine if discrepancies exist that indicate the necessity for remedial action;

(6) Prepare a plat from a given description to illustrate the property's relation to known objects and to show its accessibility by road, highway, or easement, or other physical matters of interest to the parties.

California title companies do not, however, offer surveying services as such. Moreover, their liability for these reports and services is limited.

See California Title Insurance Practice §§5.26-5.32 (Cal CEB 1980).

III. READING DESCRIPTIONS

A. Determining Sufficiency of Description

§8.10   1. Requirement of Certainty

The cardinal rule in construing descriptions is to discover and effect the parties' intentions. *County of Los Angeles v Hannon* (1910) 159 C 37, 112 P 878. A description of real property is generally sufficient if it identifies the land or furnishes the means of designating the property sought to be conveyed. This general rule has been elaborated on by a holding that if a competent surveyor can take the description and locate the land with or without the aid of extrinsic evidence, the description is sufficient. *Daluiso v Boone* (1969) 269 CA2d 253, 262, 75 CR 287, 294. If the description is not sufficiently certain, the conveyance is void. *Mesick v Sunderland* (1856) 6 C 297; *Saterstrom v Glick Bros. Sash Co.* (1931) 118 CA 379, 5 P2d 21.

In the purchase and sale agreement, the description must be certain enough to satisfy the statute of frauds (CC §1624(4); CCP §1971) and be specifically enforceable (CC §3390). While less certainty is required in a contract to convey land than in the conveyance itself, the description must be sufficient, without parol evidence to supply it, to locate the property. *Calvi v Bittner* (1961) 198 CA2d 312, 17 CR 850. But see §8.11.

§8.11   2. Ambiguity

Mere ambiguity is not fatal if it can be cured by parol or extrinsic evidence. *Fudickar v East Riverside Irr. Dist.* (1895) 109 C 29, 41 P 1024. The intent must be discovered according to statutory and judicial rules of construction. See CCP §§1857, 1866, 2077; CC §§830-831, 1069, 1112; Govt C §§23071-23076; *White v California* (1971) 21 CA3d 738, 766, 99 CR 58, 77; 1 Bowman, Ogden's Revised California Real Property Law §§14.28-14.29 (TI Corp-CEB 1974).

Although parol evidence is admissible to allow the description to be identified with its location on the ground (*Calvi v Bittner* (1961) 198 CA2d 312, 17 CR 850), it is not admissible to supply a description when the writing does not furnish the means to make it certain (*Vezaldenos v Keller* (1967) 254 CA2d 816, 823, 62 CR 808, 814). See *Finn v Goldstein* (1927) 201 C 605, 258 P 85 (description by address sufficient when it includes entire property); *Brudvig v Renner* (1959) 172 CA2d 522, 342 P2d 276 (description by address insufficient when undescribed portion excluded); *Roberts v Lebrain*

(1952) 113 CA2d 712, 248 P2d 810 (description by street alone insufficient when seller owned two residential properties on same street).

If the parties' intentions are ascertainable from the instrument itself, parol evidence is inadmissible. *Joerger v PG&E* (1929) 207 C 8, 276 P 1017. However, an additional concept has developed that concerns the effect of oral conversations or understandings related, but extrinsic, to a written agreement that is unambiguous on its face. In *PG&E v G.W. Thomas Drayage & Rigging Co.* (1968) 69 C2d 33, 69 CR 561, the court held that extrinsic evidence is admissible to prove a meaning to which the language of a written agreement is reasonably susceptible, even though on its "four corners" the instrument appears to the court to be clear and unambiguous. This rule does no more than allow extrinsic evidence of the parties' understanding and intended meaning of the words used in their written agreement.

An agreement may be sufficiently certain to permit damages for breach but not sufficiently certain for specific performance. See *Brudvig v Renner, supra,* 172 CA2d 522, 342 P2d 276. On damages for seller's breach, see §§12.13–12.18.

§8.12   3. Acreage Problems

A statement of acreage as part of a description may help either to create ambiguity or to resolve it. For example, since a government survey section may not be exactly one mile square (see §8.13), the addition of the language "consisting of 640 acres" may create ambiguity. For this reason, the words "more or less" are generally added if acreage is given at all. On a plat, more or less may be expressed by the symbol ± (as in Figure 1; see §8.13). On the other hand, a statement of exact or approximate acreage may help in resolving an otherwise fatal ambiguity, such as in a metes and bounds description that does not close. See §8.22. Net acreage may be different from gross acreage when, for example, usable land is diminished by a new road. The difference to the parties may be substantial, particularly if the value of the land is high and the price is to be based on acreage (see §3.48). Moreover, not even the terms "net" and "gross" may be sufficient. For example, does "net" exclude a surface utility easement or an encroachment about to ripen into a prescriptive right?

To resolve these uncertainties, it is best to refer specifically in the description to each potential ambiguity revealed by the record or an inspection. If the entire fee is to be conveyed, but the price is to be computed on less than the gross area, two different descriptions will be used in the same transaction.

B. Types of Descriptions

§8.13   1. Reference to Government Surveys

Lawyers commonly encounter descriptions based on United States government surveys, particularly in large parcels of rural land. These surveys have been applied generally to public lands in all states north of the Ohio River and all states west of the Mississippi except Texas. They have also been used in Alabama, Mississippi, and Florida. The surveys divide the land into rectangular units as outlined in Bureau of Land Management, Manual of Instructions for the Survey of the Public Lands of the United States (1973). For assistance in reading these descriptions, see Wattles, Land Survey Descriptions (rev ed 1964).

A typical description based on these rectangular surveys is: Southwest 1/4 of southwest 1/4 of southwest 1/4, section 36, township 2 north, range 4 east, Mount Diablo base and meridian. The land described by this formula is the shaded plot near the lower right-hand corner of Figure 1. Sometimes the description is abbreviated. Thus, the above description may appear as SW 1/4 of SW 1/4 of SW 1/4 S 36 T2N R4E MDB&M or as SW 1/4 of SW 1/4 of SW 1/4, Sec 36, Twp 2N, Range 4E, Mount Diablo B&M. Generally, although abbreviations are desirable on maps, authorities recommend that descriptions be spelled out in conveyances and agreements to avoid inadvertent errors. See Brown & Eldridge, Evidence and Procedures for Boundary Location 430 (1962).

Potential ambiguity results from the omission of "of" in a description containing a series of quarter sections. For example, if the description is SE 1/4 SW 1/4, does this mean both the southeast quarter and the southwest quarter or only the southeast quarter of the southwest quarter?

In reading a description based on reference to a government rectangular survey, the best way to locate the land on a map is to read the description backwards. This is explained step by step below.

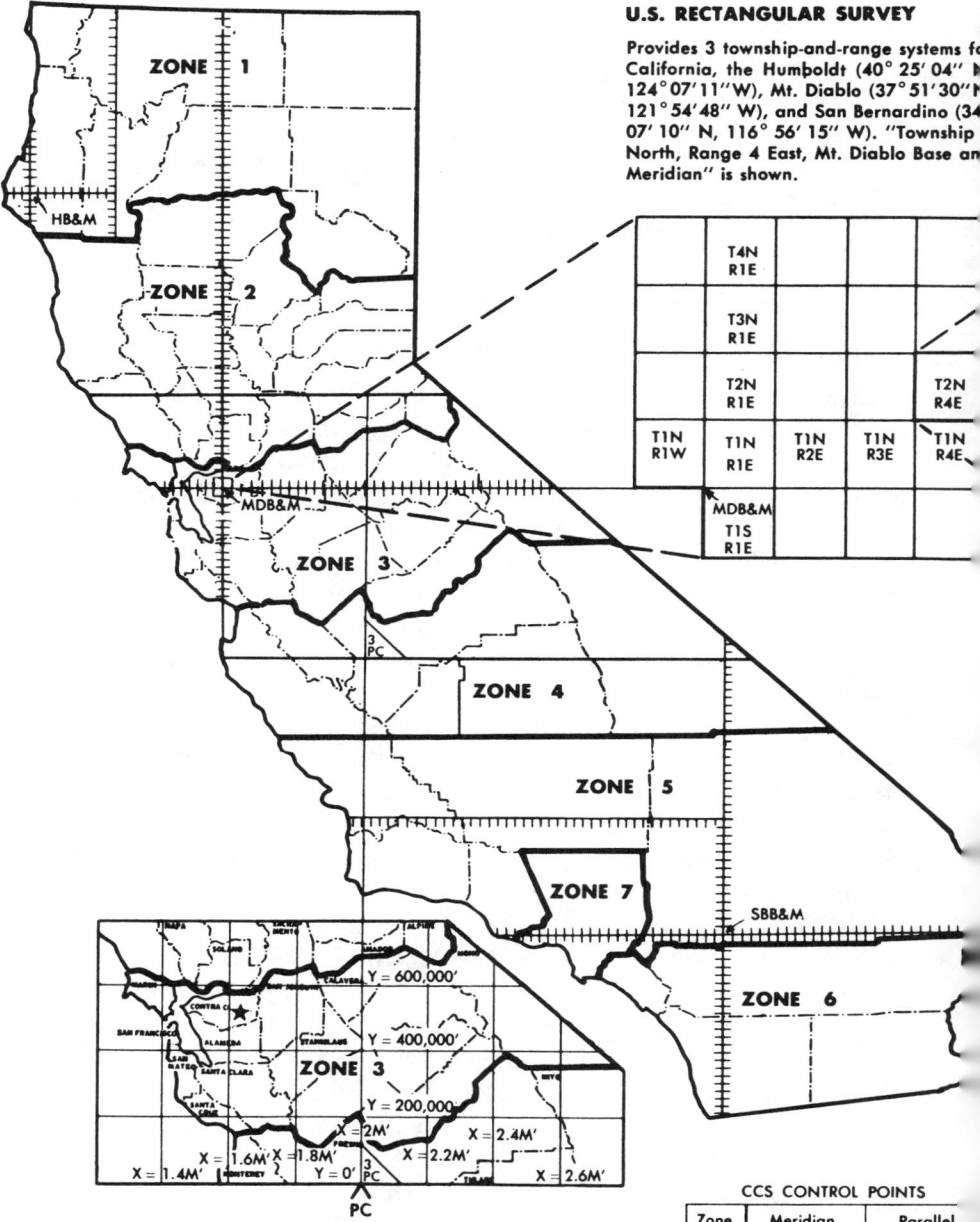

U.S. RECTANGULAR SURVEY

Provides 3 township-and-range systems for California, the Humboldt (40° 25′ 04″ N, 124°07′11″W), Mt. Diablo (37° 51′30″N, 121° 54′48″ W), and San Bernardino (34° 07′ 10″ N, 116° 56′ 15″ W). "Township 1 North, Range 4 East, Mt. Diablo Base and Meridian" is shown.

CALIFORNIA COORDINATE SYSTEM

Divides state into 7 zones and prescribes a point of control (PC) for each (Pub Res C §§8801–8816). A point of control is the intersection of a meridian (for Zone 3, 120° 30′ W) given the value X (East) = 2,000,000 feet, and a parallel (for Zone 3, 36° 30′ N) at which Y (North) = 0 feet. Adjustment factor commonly shown converts sea level distances of system to ground level. Coordinates of this point ★ are X = 1,675,000, Y = 525,000, CCS, Zone 3, Factor 1.0000546.

CCS CONTROL POINTS

Zone	Meridian	Parallel
1	122° W	39°20′ N
2	122° W	37°40′ N
3	120°30′ W	36°30′ N
4	119° W	35°20′ N
5	118° W	33°30′ N
6	116°15′ W	32°10′ N
7	118°20′ W	34°08′ N

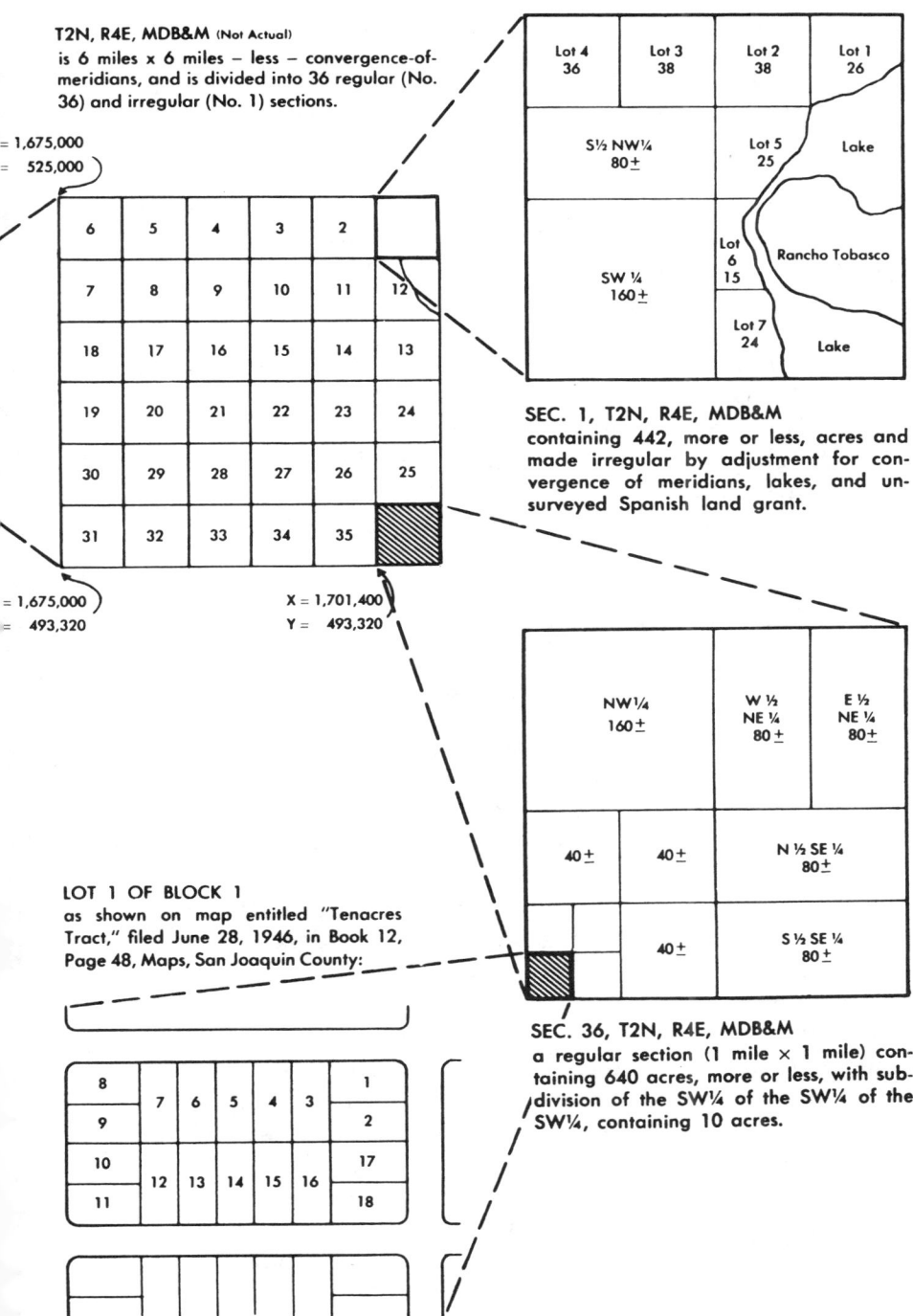

T2N, R4E, MDB&M (Not Actual)
is 6 miles x 6 miles – less – convergence-of-meridians, and is divided into 36 regular (No. 36) and irregular (No. 1) sections.

X = 1,675,000
Y = 525,000

6	5	4	3	2	
7	8	9	10	11	12
18	17	16	15	14	13
19	20	21	22	23	24
30	29	28	27	26	25
31	32	33	34	35	

X = 1,675,000
Y = 493,320

X = 1,701,400
Y = 493,320

Lot 4
36

Lot 3
38

Lot 2
38

Lot 1
26

S½ NW¼
80±

Lot 5
25

Lake

SW ¼
160±

Lot
6
15

Rancho Tobasco

Lot 7
24

Lake

SEC. 1, T2N, R4E, MDB&M
containing 442, more or less, acres and made irregular by adjustment for convergence of meridians, lakes, and unsurveyed Spanish land grant.

NW¼
160±

W ½
NE ¼
80±

E ½
NE ¼
80±

40±

40±

N ½ SE ¼
80±

40±

S ½ SE ¼
80±

LOT 1 OF BLOCK 1
as shown on map entitled "Tenacres Tract," filed June 28, 1946, in Book 12, Page 48, Maps, San Joaquin County:

8	7	6	5	4	3	1
9						2
10	12	13	14	15	16	17
11						18

SEC. 36, T2N, R4E, MDB&M
a regular section (1 mile × 1 mile) containing 640 acres, more or less, with subdivision of the SW¼ of the SW¼ of the SW¼, containing 10 acres.

FIGURE 1

(a) Base and Meridian

The initials "MDB&M" in the description refer to the Mt. Diablo base and meridian. Mount Diablo is one of three geographic centers established in California by United States government surveys. The others are Humboldt and San Bernardino. All are shown on the map of California in Figure 1. Humboldt (HB&M) covers the northwest corner of the state to the coast; Mt. Diablo (MDB&M) covers central California; and San Bernardino (SBB&M) covers southern California.

The rectangular system takes a number of known geographic centers (*e.g.*, Mt. Diablo) and runs north-south meridians and east-west bases through them. The Mt. Diablo base is the east-west line running through Mt. Diablo; the Mt. Diablo meridian is the north-south line running through the same point. Thus, MDB&M describes the point at which those two lines cross.

(b) Range and Township

In the description southwest 1/4 of southwest 1/4 of southwest 1/4, section 36, township 2 north, range 4 east, Mt. Diablo base and meridian, the element range 4 east refers to the fourth range east of the Mt. Diablo meridian. Each range is approximately six miles wide (subject to variations due to the convergence of meridians as they go northward); the ranges are numbered consecutively, east or west from the applicable meridian. For example, the first range to the west of the meridian would be range 1 west.

Township lines occur at six-mile intervals north and south of bases. Thus, the designation township 2 north in the above description refers to a township in the second tier north of the Mt. Diablo base in the specified range (range 4 east), and describes an area of approximately 36 square miles. As a matter of convention, township always precedes range in descriptions.

(c) Section

The element preceding the designation of township and range is usually a section number. In the example given, the section described is section 36. A township ordinarily consists of 36 sections, each approximately one mile square, *i.e.*, approximately 640 acres. The numbering of these sections is explained in 1 Bowman, Ogden's Revised California Real Property Law §14.4 (TI Corp-CEB 1974).

In the same way that meridians and range boundaries converge as they approach the North Pole, the north-south lines separating sections also converge. As a result, sections rarely measure a perfect square mile. For this reason, the words "more or less" should be used if the area or acreage of a section is given at all. On the question whether to add acreage to the description, see §8.12.

(d) Quarters

Sections are commonly subdivided into quarters or halves, and this quartering may be carried down into further quarters or halves. In the description (southwest 1/4 of southwest 1/4 of southwest 1/4, section 36), the quarter reference preceding the section number refers to the southwest quarter of section 36. That is the quarter consisting of the three 40-acre squares, more or less (±), in Figure 1 that contain the number 40 ± plus the square that is further subdivided; a total of 160 acres more or less. The middle "southwest 1/4" refers to the southwest quarter of the 160-acre quarter. And the first "southwest 1/4" describes the shaded 10-acre parcel in the diagram of section 36 in Figure 1. As indicated in the illustration, that parcel may be further subdivided (e.g., into lots, quarters, halves, or parcels described by metes and bounds).

§8.14   2. California Coordinate System

An optional system of describing land is the California Coordinate System (CCS) provided by Pub Res C §§8801-8816. It is "the system of plane coordinates which has been established by the United States Coast and Geodetic Survey for defining and stating the positions or locations of points on the surface of the earth within the State of California." Pub Res C §8801. (The rectangular system discussed in §8.13 is based not on the Coast and Geodetic Survey, but on Bureau of Land Management surveys.)

In drafting a description, CCS coordinates are superfluous in most instances: To constitute constructive notice, which is at the very heart of the recording statutes (see §§11.90-11.98), the description must contain data sufficient to identify the property without recourse to the coordinates; in case of conflict between the two descriptions, the coordinates yield to the other description. Pub Res C §8814; see MacEllven, *Coordinate Surveying System*, California Land Title Association Proceedings, 32 (1958).

In reading a CCS description, lawyers who care about accuracy and potential liability will not rely solely on their own skill. The location of a point consists of a measurement in feet, east or west from a north-south axis parallel to a stated meridian and north or south from an axis at right angles to that meridian. An example of this kind of description is shown at the lower left of Figure 1 (see §8.13).

The system is primarily an aid to surveyors (especially the Division of Highways in taking land for freeway purposes) but is of little value in describing land for conveyances. See 1 Bowman, Ogden's Revised California Real Property Law §14.26 (TI Corp-CEB 1974) for a discussion of the California coordinate system.

§8.15   3. Reference to Recorded Maps or Other Recorded Instruments

Property may be described by reference to a recorded map (*McCullough v Olds* (1895) 108 C 529, 41 P 420) or another recorded instrument, such as a previously recorded deed (*Central Pac. R.R. v Beal* (1873) 47 C 151). The two requirements for the validity of this type of description are that (1) the document can be produced and identified and the land located from the descriptive data (see §§8.10-8.12); and (2) the map or other instrument is properly recorded. A transfer by reference to a map that is not properly recorded is voidable at the option of the grantee or his successor in interest within one year after the discovery of the irregularity. Govt C §66499.32. (Before 1929, however, a conveyance based on an improperly recorded map was void. See 1 Bowman, Ogden's Revised California Real Property Law §14.11 (TI Corp-CEB 1974).)

The requirements for recordation of maps are set out in Govt C §§66410-66499.37 (Subdivision Map Act; see also 10 Cal Adm C §§2790-2819.96); Bus & P C §§11650-11658 (official maps of cities, towns, counties, etc.); Bus & P C §§8762-8771.5 (record of survey maps; see also 16 Cal Adm C §465); Rev & T C §327 (assessors' maps); Health & S C §§8550-8557 (cemeteries); and CC §§1350-1359 (condominiums).

Descriptions should not be drafted with reference to assessors' maps, since the distances and courses on these maps are not always accurate. Moreover, these maps change from year to year, and the map needed may not be available at the time it must be examined.

See §§8.51-8.54 for forms showing how to draft descriptions referring to recorded maps and other proper documents.

4. Metes and Bounds

§8.16   a. Kinds of Metes and Bounds Descriptions

Land boundaries may be described by reference to natural and artificial monuments, courses and distances, adjoining lands, quasi metes and bounds, combinations, and designation of north. These elements are described in §§8.17-8.21.

A description by metes and bounds may combine two or more of the kinds of references described in §§8.17-8.20. It may be combined with descriptions other than metes and bounds, as in the second example in §8.20.

§8.17   (1) Natural Monuments and Artificial Monuments

Natural monuments include rivers, trees, and rocks. Generally, reference to natural monuments is less desirable than surveyors' calls: The course of a river may change, the point of a hill may be eroded, a tree may die, a rock may give way to the work of the highway commission.

Artificial monuments include walks, fences, buildings, railroads, stakes, streets, and the like. Artificial monuments are generally regarded as the least desirable reference points for descriptions since they are too easily removed or destroyed.

Several cases have made it clear that land can be described by reference to railroad right-of-way easements as borders. These descriptions imply ownership to the center of the easement. See *Millyard v Faus* (1968) 268 CA2d 76, 73 CR 697; *Freeman v Affiliated Property Craftsmen* (1968) 266 CA2d 723, 72 CR 357; *Faus v Nelson* (1966) 241 CA2d 320, 50 CR 483. These cases are applications of the long-established monument doctrine, which presumes an intent to grant to the middle of the monument when it is used to describe a property boundary. *Freeman v Bellegarde* (1895) 108 C 179, 41 P 289. The same rule applies when land is sold with reference to a recorded map that shows a street or railroad right-of-way easement as bounding the property. *Freeman v Affiliated Property Craftsmen, supra,* 266 CA2d 723, 72 CR 357.

In *Millyard v Faus, supra,* the rule of *Faus v Nelson, supra,* was carefully limited to easements for railroad rights-of-way and was not extended to include an easement for a railroad depot.

§8.18   (2) Courses and Distances

Bearings due north or south or east or west require no numbers (but see §8.21 on identifying north bearings). Bearings that deviate from those four directions require numbers to indicate the angle of deviation. Between, for example, north and west, the difference in angle is ninety degrees (90°). One-ninetieth of that angle is one degree. Each degree is divided into sixty minutes (60') and each minute into sixty seconds (60"). Thus, the angle between north and west is divisible into 324,000 angles of one second each. (At a distance of ten miles from the point of angle, a deviation of one second results in a difference of about three inches; a deviation of one minute makes a difference of about 14 feet.)

Figure 2 illustrates the meaning of descriptions by surveyors' courses.

In Figure 2, the bearing S 79° E indicates an angle 79 degrees to the east of due south; S 52° W indicates an angle 52 degrees to the west of due south; N 10° W indicates an angle 10 degrees west of due north.

Curves are described by three elements: radius, angle, and arc length. A short radius indicates a tight curve, while a long radius indicates a shallow curve. The angle indicates the amount of change in direction (a full circle being 360°); thus an angle of 90° means that the direction at the end of the curve will be at right angles to the direction at the beginning of the curve. The arc length supplies the actual distance traveled by the curve. The symbols R=50', $\triangle$=120°, L=104.72' indicate a curve having a radius of 50 feet, turning 120° in direction, through an arc 104.72 feet long. (The radius of a curve is sometimes described in degrees. Thus a one-degree curve has a radius of practically 5730 feet, a two-degree curve has a radius of 5730÷2=2865 feet.)

Although symbols for feet ('), inches ("), and degrees (°) are conventionally used on maps, title companies frown on their use in written descriptions because they are too easy to misread or mistranscribe and their meaning is too easily lost in the event of even slight damage to the document. For the same reasons it is better to spell out minutes ('), seconds ("), and angle ($\triangle$) in written descriptions. Spelling out directions instead of abbreviating them also avoids error; for example, copying machines sometimes make N look like W.

For further discussion,see 1 Bowman, Ogden's Revised California

Metes and Bounds

BEARINGS

Are given, commonly clockwise, as easterly or westerly from North or South to a maximum of 89°59'59". Thus "North 10° West . . . , thence South 79° East . . . , thence South 52° West . . . ."

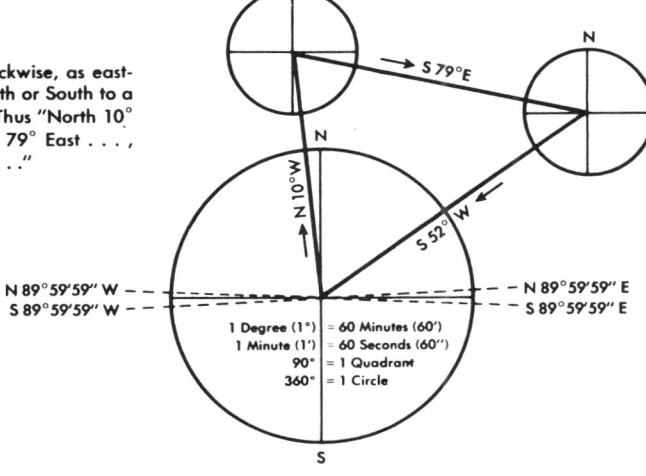

1 Degree (1°)	= 60 Minutes (60')
1 Minute (1')	= 60 Seconds (60")
90°	= 1 Quadrant
360°	= 1 Circle

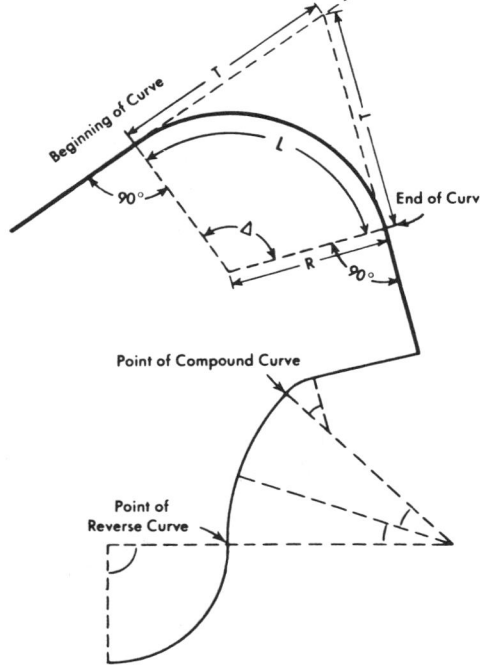

CURVES

Simple, compound, or reverse, are analyzed and described as arcs of specified circles. Thus ". . . thence along a tangent curve to the right having a radius of 50 feet, through an angle of 120 degrees, an arc length of 104.72 feet" or R = 50', Δ = 120°, L = 104.72'.

FIGURE 2

Real Property Law § 14.8 (TI Corp-CEB 1974); Bowman, Real Estate Law in California (5th ed 1978).

§8.19 (3) Adjoining Lands

An example of a description by reference to adjoining lands is:

... bounded on the north and west by the lands of A. R. Smith per deed recorded at book 9, page 2, Misc. Records, and on the south and east by the Gonzalez Ranch per decree of distribution recorded at book 14, page 112 of Judgments, office of County Recorder, County of Nevada, State of California.

Good draftsmanship requires that a description by reference to adjoining lands consist of more than just the names of the properties or their owners. In the above illustration, the description is supported by references to recorded instruments. The requirements of descriptions by reference to recorded instruments are discussed in §8.15. For an example of a description by reference to names only, see *McKeon v Millard* (1874) 47 C 581.

§8.20 (4) Quasi Metes and Bounds

Two examples will serve to illustrate a description by quasi metes and bounds. One is a strip description:

... a strip of land extending easterly from Baker Road measuring 50 feet in width, the boundary lines of which are perpendicularly distant northerly 20 feet and southerly 30 feet, respectively, from the following described line...

The other example is a recital of boundaries by reference to matters of record or dimensions or both:

...beginning at the southeast corner of lot 6 in the map described above, then

(a) Northeasterly to the West corner of land of Charles Abel per deed recorded at book 4, page 5, Official Records, office of County Recorder, Tulare County; then

(b) Northeasterly along the northwest line of Charles Abel's land to the south line of Doe Lane as shown on subdivision map recorded at book 7, page 6 of Maps, office of County Recorder of that county; then

(c) 50 feet in a westerly direction along that south line; then

(d) Southwesterly, parallel to the northwest line of Charles Abel's land to the south line of lot 6; then

(e) Easterly to the point of beginning.

In each of these quasi metes and bounds descriptions, courses and distances are given, but the reference points are located by reference to deeds or maps rather than physical monuments or surveyors' points.

In the strip description, notice that the distance of the boundary lines is measured perpendicularly to the controlling line. This is to prevent ambiguity that would result if the controlling line did not run due east and west. In that situation, measuring 20 and 30 feet respectively due north and south would result in a strip less than 50 feet wide, as shown in Figure 3.

Similar problems arise from descriptions of the north (or any other) "half" of an irregularly shaped lot. See §8.23.

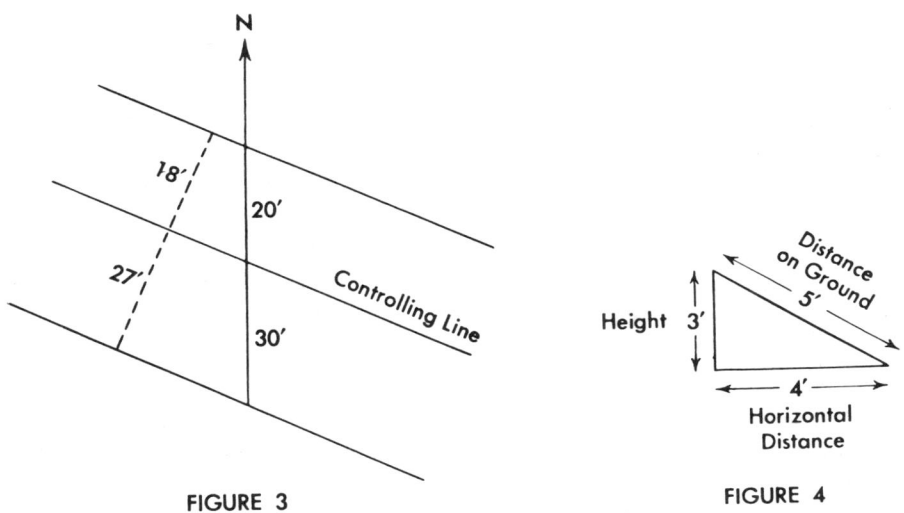

FIGURE 3   FIGURE 4

§8.21   (5) Designation of North

The most commonly used designations of north are grid, magnetic, and astronomic.

The direction of grid north lies along a line formed by the two geographic poles. The north-south lines of the United States rectangular survey system indicate grid north.

Magnetic north shifts about the geographic pole and is only intermittently in line with grid or astronomic north. Since magnetic north shifts, plats based on it should bear a date. See Brown & Eldridge, Evidence and Procedures for Boundary Location 385 (1962).

Astronomic north also shifts (see Brown & Eldridge 201-212) but much more slowly. It is common in survey-located descriptions.

If plats or maps indicate which designation of north is used and are included in the recorded document containing the description, north need not be further identified in the description itself. The same is true of descriptions that refer to other recorded maps. Otherwise, the description should clearly state which north is used.

§8.22   b. Using Metes and Bounds Descriptions

A metes and bounds description must describe a boundary line that (1) is continuous, (2) has a definite and stable starting point, (3) returns to the starting point, and (4) forms a closed area. A failure to close is fatally defective. *Adams v Hopkins* (1904) 144 C 19, 43, 77 P 712, 721. Courts may, however, supply a missing course on evidence that it was intended. *Serrano v Rawson* (1873) 47 C 52. On the use of a statement of acreage to resolve ambiguities, see §8.12.

If any points or boundaries are variable (a river's course may shift) or perishable (a tree may rot or burn), litigation may result and the intentions of the parties may be defeated. All physical monuments should therefore be verified by inspection and, preferably, by survey. The results should be compared with recorded evidence of the boundaries of the property in question and adjoining properties. The assistance of an experienced title officer may be helpful.

For the accuracy of these descriptions, lawyers are almost entirely dependent on surveyors and engineers. It is therefore important that these agents be skilled, careful, and financially responsible. On erroneous surveys, see §8.49. In the event of error, the injured party must ordinarily look to the surveyor or title company for damages. On title insurance coverage, see California Title Insurance Practice chap 3 (Cal CEB 1980).

Lawyers should not overlook the possibility that they too may be held accountable by damaged clients. For this reason, the nature of the lawyer's responsibility should be clearly stated by the lawyer in his agreement with the client or in the report that he makes on the results of his examination of the description. On lawyers' liability generally, see §1.12.

Measurements commonly encountered in descriptions:
1 chain = 66 feet = 4 rods.
1 rod = 16 1/2 feet.

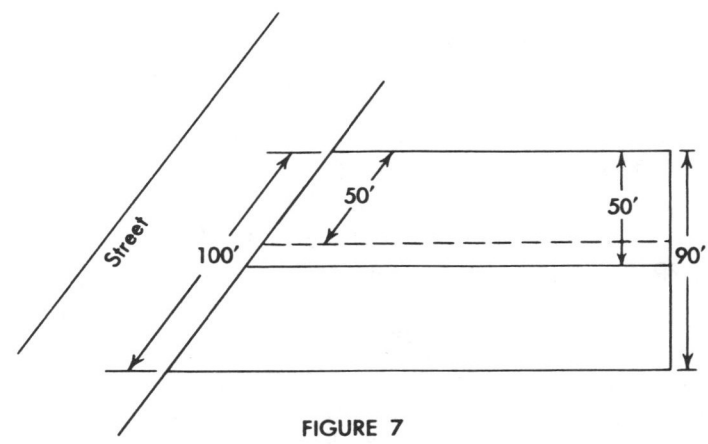

FIGURE 7

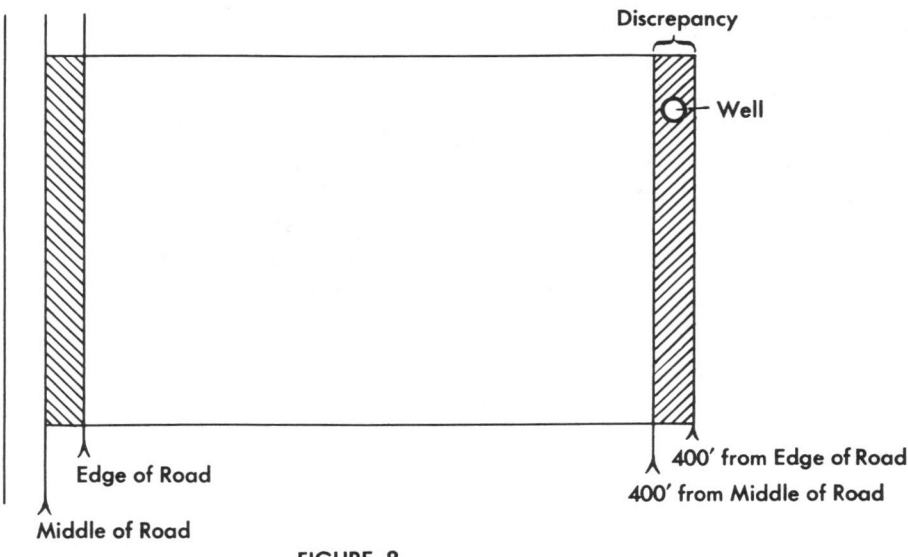

FIGURE 8

In the example shown in Figure 7, is the "northerly 50 feet of Lot 9" to be measured along the 100-foot frontage on the street or across the 90-foot width?

To avoid litigation and the frustration of intent that may result from these ambiguities, lawyers for sellers as well as for buyers should insist on absolute clarity in the description. Some guidelines are:

(a) Avoid fractional descriptions unless clarified by metes and bounds or by clear statement of how to measure the fractional parts.

(b) Specify the directions of all measurements, bearing in mind the discussion in §8.21 on indicating direction.

(c) Supplement all descriptions of area with clear descriptions of boundaries and location.

(d) If the parcel adjoins a street or road (particularly if any measurement is from or along the street or road), declare whether the grantor's interest, if any, in the road is included, and whether the measurement is from or along the center or the edge of the road. See Figure 8 for an example of the difference this could make. On counseling seller concerning lot splits, see §1.28.

§8.24   6. General or Common Description

General descriptions are divided into five types: (1) a blanket description ("all the lands belonging to the grantor in Black County"), (2) description of all "unsold" or "unconveyed" lots of grantor, (3) description by name (all of "Blackacre"), (4) description by street number ("159 South Lincoln Street"), and (5) description by ownership ("my lot in Shasta County"). See 1 Bowman, Ogden's Revised California Real Property Law §14.21 (TI Corp-CEB 1974).

Each of these descriptions presents problems of proof. On proper evidence many of them have been sustained (see Bowman §14.21) but none can be supported as examples of conscientious drafting if more precise descriptions are possible.

§8.25   C. Matters Altering or Affecting Descriptions

Matters outside the record may substantially affect title and may either augment or diminish the estate. Examples appear in §§8.32, 8.43-8.48 and may not appear in title reports unless previously established by judgments.

A lawyer reading a description for the purpose of advising his client on its effect cannot give an adequate opinion without knowledge of the existence and effect of these off-record elements.

1. Easements

a. Problems With Easements

§8.26   (1) Benefit or Burden

Property may be affected by easements in two ways: It may be subject to an easement and be called the servient tenement, or it may enjoy the benefit of an easement over other land and be called the dominant tenement. CC §803. Easements that benefit nearby land are often called augmenting or appurtenant easements; they lie outside the augmented land but generally connect with it. Encumbering easements (easements to which land is subject) lie within the boundaries of that land or within easements augmenting that land. On easements of both types, see 3 Witkin, Summary of California Law, *Real Property* §§340-380 (8th ed 1973).

§8.27   (2) Off-Record Easements

Examination of the record is not sufficient for discovering an easement, whether it augments or encumbers, since easements may be created by means not shown on the record. This possibility emphasizes the necessity for inspecting the parcel to determine if any easements exist or may come into being and for making explicit in the agreement and grant their extent and use. See §§3.92-3.94. Some of the off-record easements that may arise are:

(a) *Easements by implication.* A grant may imply the existence of an easement for the benefit of the grantee, to carry out the intent of the parties, as shown by all the facts and circumstances. *Sierra Screw Prods. v Azusa Greens, Inc.* (1979) 88 CA3d 358, 151 CR 799. When an owner sells a portion of his land, the buyer obtains the same right to use the unsold portion for the benefit of the portion sold as the seller obviously and permanently enjoyed before the sale. CC §1104. In *Fristoe v Drapeau* (1950) 35 C2d 5, 215 P2d 729, subsequent grantees of the original owner of the dominant tenement had an implied easement over a roadway, constructed by the original owner on the servient tenement and used by the original owner and his grantees for 25 years. An implied easement need only be reasonably necessary; the manner of its use is determined by future use reasonably contemplated by the parties, rather than the actual use at the time of its creation. In *Fristoe,* the easement included use for access to residences, although originally it was used to service fruit groves. For similar easements arising from wills, see *Cheda v Bodkin* (1916) 173 C 7, 158 P 1025.

Although prior use is usually a factor, an implied easement may arise from the conduct of the parties. Examples are: a grant containing reference to a map showing an easement (*Norcross v Adams* (1968) 263 CA2d 362, 365, 69 CR 429, 432), representations by the seller or his agent about the existence of easements (*Kytasty v Godwin* (1980) 102 CA3d 762, 162 CR 556), or construction blueprints showing easements, which are exhibited by the lessor to the lessee (*Owsley v Hamner* (1951) 36 C2d 710, 227 P2d 263). Easements acquired this way are sometimes referred to as easements by estoppel. *Metzger v Bose* (1960) 183 CA2d 13, 6 CR 337.

(b) *Easements by implied reservation.* Just as an easement may arise by implication for the buyer's benefit, it may arise to his detriment. Although an easement is less readily implied in favor of a grantor (*Jordan v Henck* (1958) 166 CA2d 321, 325, 333 P2d 117, 120), a sale of a portion of land with irrigation ditches on it imposes a burden on the buyer to permit the water to flow through the ditches to the land retained by the seller. *Palvutzian v Terkanian* (1920) 47 CA 47, 190 P 503. The preexisting use by the grantor must be open, visible, and continuous at the time of the conveyance. *People v Bowers* (1964) 226 CA2d 463, 38 CR 238.

(c) *Easement of necessity.* Unlike an implied easement under CC §1104, an easement of necessity does not depend on prior use but arises by operation of law. If at the time of the conveyance the dominant and servient tenements are owned by the same person and there is an absolute necessity for the easement because it is the only access (*e.g.,* when the land sold is otherwise landlocked), an easement of necessity is created. Availability of other access at the time of the conveyance bars an easement of necessity over more convenient access (*Reese v Borghi* (1963) 216 CA2d 324, 30 CR 868), and if other access later becomes available so that the necessity disappears, the easement ceases (*Irvin v Petitfils* (1941) 44 CA2d 496, 112 P2d 688). The easement's use is limited by the necessity for the easement itself.

(d) *Easement by prescription.* To acquire an easement by prescription, the claimant must make open and notorious use of it that is hostile to the owners of present estates, and this use must continue for five uninterrupted years under a claim of right. CCP §321; *Cleary v Trimble* (1964) 229 CA2d 1, 39 CR 776; *Zunino v Gabriel* (1960) 182 CA2d 613, 6 CR 514. If separate taxes are assessed against the easement (normally not the case), apparently the claimant must pay them. See *Glatts v Henson* (1948) 31 C2d 368, 188 P2d 745. A prescriptive easement cannot arise if the use is with the owner's permission or if it is an easement of necessity, flowing from the grant and the circumstances then existing.

The rule that the use of a prescriptive easement is fixed and determined by the manner of use in which it originated, and cannot be extended or increased, has been modified to allow such increased use if the change is one of degree, not kind. In ascertaining whether a particular use is permissible under such an easement, consideration must be given to the needs that result from the normal development in the use of the dominant tenement as well as the increased burden on the servient tenement. *Cushman v Davis* (1978) 80 CA3d 731, 145 CR 791. Any claim for the enlargement of easement rights must be exercised openly, notoriously, continuously, and adversely during the period of prescription. *Security Pac. Nat'l Bank v San Diego* (1971) 19 CA3d 421, 97 CR 61. For statutory provisions allowing the fee owner to post notice of permission, which precludes prescriptive easements, see CC §1008. See §8.38 on adverse possession, prescription and implied dedication.

§8.28   (3) Termination of Easements

Easements may exist on or off the record; they may also be terminated by means that may or may not appear on the record. CC §811. Easements may be terminated in the following ways:

(a) *Termination by release or merger.* If the owner of an easement affirmatively releases his rights to the owner of the servient tenement (defined in §8.26) or if both dominant and servient parcels come into the same ownership, the easement is extinguished. CC §811(1). On releases, see §8.60. The effect of bringing both parcels into one ownership is to merge the easement into the fee; an owner cannot have an easement over his own property.

(b) *Termination by destruction of the servient tenement.* An easement is terminated when the servient tenement is destroyed (CC

§811(2)) either involuntarily (*Cohen v Adolph Kutner Co.* (1918) 177 C 592, 171 P 424), or through depreciation or obsolescence, which is tantamount to destruction (*Walner v City of Turlock* (1964) 230 CA2d 399, 41 CR 29). This is of particular importance in buildings, for example, for staircases or supports that have deteriorated.

(c) *Termination by incompatible use.* An easement may be extinguished by its owner's acts, or by his assent to acts, that are incompatible with the nature or exercise of the easement. CC §811(3). See, *e.g., Crimmins v Gould* (1957) 149 CA2d 383, 308 P2d 786 (extinguishment by improper use).

(d) *Termination by abandonment.* Abandonment (nonuse with the intention of relinquishing) terminates the easement. For acts showing abandonment, see *Ocean Shore R.R. v Doelger* (1960) 179 CA2d 222, 3 CR 706; *Flanagan v San Marcos Silk Co.* (1951) 106 CA2d 458, 235 P2d 107. Consent of the servient owner is not necessary. See 5 Restatement of Property §§500, 504 (1944). See also §8.39.

(e) *Termination by nonuse.* Although an easement acquired by grant is not terminated by mere nonuse (*Wilson v Abrams* (1969) 1 CA3d 1030, 82 CR 272), an easement by prescription (see §8.27) is extinguished by nonuse for the prescriptive five-year period (*People v Ocean Shore R.R.* (1948) 32 C2d 406, 419, 196 P2d 570, 579). CC §811(4); *Zimmer v Dykstra* (1974) 39 CA3d 422, 114 CR 380.

(f) *Termination by adverse possession.* Just as an easement may be acquired by prescription (see §8.27), it likewise may be terminated by the adverse possession of the owner of the servient tenement. In *Glatts v Henson* (1948) 31 C2d 368, 188 P2d 745, the owner of the servient tenement erected a building on part of his lot over which an easement existed for road purposes; the buildings remained undisturbed for more than five years. The part of the easement on which the building stood was held extinguished.

§8.29   (4) Dominant Tenement; Change in Burden on Servient Tenement

Though an easement may be of record, it may not show the dominant tenement (the property benefited by the easement) since the easement encumbers the servient property of record, not the dominant property. A search of the record back to the creation of the easement may be necessary. On occasion, a covenant or warranty in favor of the party to be served by the easement may make it possible to close the transaction.

Parol evidence is admissible to show what land comprises the dominant tenement. In *Continental Baking Co. v Katz* (1968) 68 C2d 512, 67 CR 761, the supreme court rejected the servient owner's contention that because a deed conveyed one parcel plus an easement over an adjacent parcel, the benefit of the easement was limited to the parcel conveyed. Instead, the court permitted the dominant tenant to offer parol proof that other adjacent land owned by him was also intended to share the benefit of the easement. See also *Welch v Kai* (1970) 4 CA3d 374, 84 CR 619.

A common law rule that no easement could be reserved in a stranger has been abolished by the decision in *Willard v First Church of Christ, Scientist* (1972) 7 C3d 473, 102 CR 739. The court held that because there had been no reliance on the old rule, the doctrine could not be used to defeat the grantor's intent. Thus, the dominant tenement of an easement created by reservation need no longer be land held by the grantor. (This more liberal approach should pose no problem for the title searcher, however, because any effective reservation in a stranger would obviously require some description of the stranger or of his property.)

If denial of an easement seriously impaired access to a dominant tenement, the dominant tenant's right to possession would be affected. Therefore, a lis pendens recorded against the dominant tenement in an action by the servient tenant will not be expunged by the court, because CCP §409.1(a) forbids expungement if the action affects the possession of that real property. *Kendall-Brief Co. v Superior Court* (1976) 60 CA3d 462, 131 CR 515.

Traditionally, once an easement has been established by prescription, the scope of that easement is fixed. *Bartholomew v Staheli* (1948) 86 CA2d 844, 195 P2d 824. The dominant owner could not thereafter materially increase the burden on the servient tenement or impose new kinds of use on the easement. This approach has been eroded in recent years.

The current rule, as set forth in *Cushman v Davis* (1978) 80 CA3d 731, 145 CR 791, permits change in the use of an easement if the change is one of degree and not kind (see *Gaither v Gaither* (1958) 165 CA2d 782, 332 P2d 436) or if the increase is a reasonably foreseeable, normal development "consistent with the pattern formed by the adverse use by which the prescriptive easement was created" (*Hill v Allan* (1968) 259 CA2d 470, 484, 66 CR 676, 686).

§8.30   (5) Appurtenant or In Gross

A difficulty in advising clients on easements is the difference between "appurtenant" easements (which pass with the fee to the dominant tenement whether mentioned in the conveyance or not) and easements "in gross" (which exist without a dominant tenement and cannot pass unless expressly transferred). See 1 Bowman, Ogden's Revised Real Property Law §§13.7-13.9 (TI Corp-CEB 1974). If the easement was created to benefit the easement holder in his use of particular land, it is appurtenant. See 5 Restatement of Property §453 (1944). If the easement was created independently of the holder's ownership or possession of any specific land, it is in gross. See 5 Restatement of Property §454 (1944).

The following considerations distinguish appurtenant easements from easements in gross:

(a) The nature of the right and the intention of the parties creating it are determinative. *Eastman v Piper* (1924) 68 CA 554, 568, 229 P 1002, 1007; *Schofield v Bany* (1959) 175 CA2d 534, 346 P2d 891.

(b) The right is not personal (in gross) if it can fairly be construed to be appurtenant to land. *Eastman v Piper, supra.* For examples, see 3 Witkin, Summary of California Law, *Real Property* §342 (8th ed 1973).

(c) An intended easement will never be construed as personal when it may fairly be construed as appurtenant. *St. Louis v DeBon* (1962) 204 CA2d 464, 22 CR 443.

(d) The use in the grant of one designation or the other is not necessarily determinative; the designation must be in accordance with the intended uses.

Although easements in gross have been said to be personal and not capable of transfer, they can be transferred if expressly referred to in the grant (*Collier v Oelke* (1962) 202 CA2d 843, 21 CR 140), and they are inheritable (*Le Deit v Ehlert* (1962) 205 CA2d 154, 166, 22 CR 747, 755). An appurtenant easement may be transferred to a person receiving only a very limited interest in the dominant estate. See *Franceschi v Kuntz* (1967) 253 CA2d 1041, 61 CR 810, in which the court held that the easement holder who had timber and access rights could contract with other persons to do logging and use the access roads.

On drafting to eliminate ambiguity in easements, see §§8.56-

8.59; Kratovil, *Easement Draftsmanship and Conveyancing,* 38 Calif L Rev 426, 437 (1950).

§8.31 (6) Ambiguous Description

In general, the land subjected to an easement must be described with sufficient certainty to locate it. *PG&E v Crockett Land & Cattle Co.* (1924) 70 CA 283, 233 P 370. However, a right of way for road purposes has been upheld even though its location was not fixed in the reservation; the grantee of the right may locate it reasonably, and, if he does not do so, the grantor may do it. *Collier v Oelke* (1962) 202 CA2d 843, 21 CR 140. Acquiescence in a particular use may fix not only the location of the easement but also the nature of its use. *Snodgrass v Crane* (1943) 57 CA2d 565, 134 P2d 862.

The great virtue of a precise description of land location is that it prohibits any future variation based on arguments of reasonableness. See *Wilson v Abrams* (1969) 1 CA3d 1030, 82 CR 272, in which the easement holder tried unsuccessfully to have a parking lot agreement construed to permit construction of an automobile service station. See also *Keith v Superior Court* (1972) 26 CA3d 521, 103 CR 314, in which great inconvenience to the servient tenant was held insufficient to permit him unilaterally to relocate a described right-of-way over the objection of the dominant tenant.

§8.32 (7) Uncertain Duration

If an easement is terminated in one of the ways provided by CC §811 (see §8.28), its extinction may not appear of record. Equally troublesome are ambiguous termination provisions in the document creating the easement. An example is: "to *A*, an easement 12 feet wide as long as he needs it for a wagon road." When does *A*'s need terminate? How is his need determined? Duration should be stated without ambiguity. If that cannot be done, it is generally better simply to state the purpose, as in §§8.56-8.59.

Railroad easements create special problems. It is often difficult to determine whether fee title or only an easement to a strip has been conveyed. Furthermore, abandonment of the railroad line creates its own problems about the existence of any further rights in the land below the tract. See *Johnson v Ocean Shore R.R.* (1971) 16 CA3d 429, 94 CR 68, for a discussion of both issues.

§8.33   (8) Failure To Designate as Easement

A problem with easements arises from failure to describe them as easements. A grant or reservation of a strip of land, if not expressly qualified as an easement, may result in ownership in fee.

In *Murphy Slough Ass'n v Avila* (1972) 27 CA3d 649, 104 CR 136, a document conveying "a strip of land" along a river was held, under the circumstances, to grant an easement rather than a fee. The grantor therefore retained his riparian rights.

A document may be construed to grant an easement even though the word "easement" never appears in it. *Maywood Mut. Water Co. No. 2 v City of Maywood* (1972) 23 CA3d 266, 100 CR 174.

See also §8.32 on related problems.

§8.34   (9) Exception or Reservation

Sometimes in transferring property, a grantor withholds an estate, or a use less than a fee (*e.g.,* a life estate or easement), or a portion of the property in fee. The words generally used for these purposes are "excepting" and "reserving." "The difference between the two terms is so slight and shadowy that in common parlance they are used interchangeably." *Van Slyke v Arrowhead Reservoir & Power Co.* (1909) 155 C 675, 680, 102 P 816, 818. Historically, in this country, a reservation amounted to a grant back to the grantor by the grantee. The question whether a particular provision in a deed is an exception or reservation is not conclusively determined by the use of the terms alone but depends on the real intention of the parties as ascertained from the whole conveyance. *Main v Legnitto* (1964) 230 CA2d 667, 41 CR 223. To avoid any implication that matters affecting the grantee might impair the grantor's easement rights, the word "exception" appears to be preferable. For further discussion, see §8.48.

On abolition of the common law rule prohibiting reservation of easements in a stranger, see §8.29.

§8.35   (10) Failure To State All Purposes and Limitations

Whether the easement is to be exclusive or nonexclusive should be stated expressly in the instrument creating it. If the easement is nonexclusive, it is important to fix responsibility for maintenance.

Sometimes, the statement of purpose is not sufficiently explicit. For example, the phrase "for utility purposes" gives no guidance on whether the utilities are to be underground or above ground. Similarly, a statement that an easement is "for driveway purposes" does not resolve disputes about whether the driveway may be raised or fenced in or improved with planting. See *Faus v City of Los Angeles* (1967) 67 C2d 350, 62 CR 193, in which the court held that the holder of a municipal electric railway easement could convert from streetcars to buses without forfeiting its easement.

For further discussion, see 1 Bowman, Ogden's Revised California Real Property Law §13.62 (TI Corp-CEB 1974).

§8.36   b. Precautions for Buyers

Buyers should be protected against easements that encumber the land they are buying and should be assured of the benefit of easements that they need to augment the usefulness and value of that land.

To protect against encumbering easements, the buyer's attorney should (1) make provision against them in the agreement and (2) investigate to discover evidence of existing easements. For provisions against impairments of title, see §§3.78-3.115, 9.4-9.12. On the duty to inspect and the constructive notice provided by matters that might have been discovered, see §§11.4, 11.22. Easements may also be revealed by a preliminary title report. These reports are discussed in §1.36. Existence of easements that do not appear of record are discussed in §8.27.

If an undesired easement is discovered, a properly drawn agreement will give the buyer his choice of avoiding the agreement or waiving the defect and buying the property at a reduced price. Provisions for achieving this result are offered and discussed in §§3.72-3.75. If the buyer elects to acquire the property even though it is subject to an easement, he may still be able to eliminate the encumbrance. One way to do this is by agreement with the owner of the easement. In the alternative, the buyer may be able to quiet his title or obtain a declaratory judgment against the easement if it has been terminated in one of the ways discussed in §8.28. Sometimes a title company, on presentation of an affidavit conforming to its requirements, will insure against questionable easements. However, this may not assure the buyer of ability to convey marketable title when he decides to sell. Easements of record and those evidenced by physical indications on the land should be removed by judgment, agreement, or deed, and the document should be recorded.

The same remedies are applicable if, by reason of ambiguity, it cannot be determined whether an easement exists or where it is located. In addition, reformation may be proper. On reformation, see §3.38.

If the problem is that the buyer's lawyer cannot determine from the language creating the easement whether it is appurtenant (and therefore transferable) or in gross (personal to the holder of the easement and open to questions discussed in §8.30), the remedies applicable to other ambiguities are generally proper.

If the boundaries of the easement are not clear, a survey may be required. If the location of the easement is not fixed (*i.e.*, the easement holder has the right to move it), an attempt should be made to fix its location by agreement.

To secure the benefit of augmenting easements, the buyer's lawyer may avail himself of the same kinds of remedies as those discussed above for encumbering easements. Under proper circumstances, he may even be able to use the right of eminent domain under CC §1001. See *Linggi v Garovotti* (1955) 45 C2d 20, 286 P2d 15.

Sometimes an easement, as distinguished from a fee interest in a strip of land, does not satisfy local regulations. Typical of these are setback ordinances and regulations that require denial of building permits unless access roads between lot and street are held in fee by the applicant and are of a minimum width. In these situations, counseling the buyer requires more than just an accurate description of an easement.

§8.37   c. Precautions for Sellers

To protect the seller against easement problems, his lawyer should (1) make sure that the seller has a right to grant the easement that he intends to pass with the land being sold; (2) help the seller determine whether an intended easement over the land he will retain after the transfer is consistent with his own intended use of that land; (3) make sure that there are no encumbering easements over the land being sold that would constitute a breach of the seller's obligation (see §3.78 on marketable title); and (4) describe the easement as an easement, locate it precisely, fix its duration, and specify its purpose (see §§ 8.57-8.59).

§8.38   2. Adverse Possession, Prescription, and Implied Dedication

Adverse possession, prescription, and implied dedication may affect all or part of the record owner's title. Prescription refers to the creation of easements by adverse use over a period of time; adverse possession refers to the acquisition and extinguishment of possessory interests. See 5 Restatement of Property 2922 (distinction between prescription and adverse possession), 2903 (corporeal and incorporeal interests) (1944). For a thorough discussion of the elements and requisites of a claim under the doctrine of adverse possession and the related subject of "agreed boundaries," see *Finley v Yuba County Water Dist.* (1979) 99 CA3d 691, 160 CR 423; *Kunza v Gaskell* (1979) 91 CA3d 201, 154 CR 101. "Implied dedication" is appropriation of land to some public use implied by law from the acts of the owner.

Code of Civil Procedure §§321-325 set out the requirements for acquiring title by adverse possession. Civil Code §1007 calls this a "title by prescription."

In *Gion v City of Santa Cruz* (1970) 2 C3d 29, 84 CR 162, the California Supreme Court made it easier for privately held land to be declared subject to public easements under a doctrine of implied dedication. In response to *Gion,* the 1971 legislature amended CC §813 and added CC §1009, clearly prescribing how the public may acquire rights in land and how owners may best protect themselves against such claims of public rights. See *County of Los Angeles v Berk* (1980) 26 C3d 201, 161 CR 742; *City of Long Beach v Daugherty* (1977) 75 CA3d 972, 142 CR 593; *County of Orange v Chandler-Sherman Corp.* (1976) 54 CA3d 561, 126 CR 765; *Richmond Ramblers Motorcycle Club v Western Title Guar. Co.* (1975) 47 CA3d 747, 121 CR 308.

If an owner's efforts to exclude the public or discourage public use effectively put the public on notice that its use of property was not authorized, the owner can defeat the accrual of a public easement. In *County of Los Angeles v Berk, supra,* 26 C3d 201, 216, 161 CR 742, 752, the court held that defendants and the former property owners had not fulfilled the burden of putting the public on notice.

Compare *Gion, supra,* with *Kaiser Aetna v U.S.* (1979) 444 US 164, in which the federal government was required to compensate a private land owner when it allowed free public access to "navigable waters" on the private land.

§8.39   3. Abandonment and Vacation

Except for titles held in fee, lawyers should not assume that interests appearing of record or revealed by inspection are as they appear to be. They may have been abandoned or vacated.

Abandonment of a right in land requires that the owner of the right (a) intends to abandon it and (b) gives evidence of his intent by acts or omissions that are clear, unequivocal, and decisive. See 3 Witkin, Summary of California Law, *Real Property* 374-376, 508-509 (8th ed 1973).

The doctrine of abandonment is not applicable to a fee simple interest in real property. However, certain fee interests such as perpetual easements and perpetual profits derived from land, including oil and gas interests, can be abandoned. *Gerhard v Stephens* (1968) 68 C2d 864, 69 CR 612.

If an interest has been abandoned, the description of the property may be affected. Thus if an appurtenant easement has been abandoned, its description as part of the transfer will not pass the right to the buyer (except as the rights of a bona fide purchaser apply as discussed in §11.90). Generally, the abandonment should be established by agreement, deed, or judgment.

On vacation of street easements and the closing of streets and highways to public use, see Str & H C §§8300-8363.

§8.40   4. Effect of Water on Land

Physical changes resulting from the action of water on real property raise many questions. Other problems arise out of the imprecise use of water monuments as points or boundaries in descriptions. While some of these problems may be eliminated by careful drafting (see §8.62), others may occur even after the most careful draftsmanship. Among the most common of these problems are:

(a) *High-water mark, low-water mark.* In the absence of contrary evidence of intent in the grant, land bordering tidewaters extends to the high-water mark. On inland waters (including Monterey Bay), see *U.S. v California* (1965) 381 US 139. Land on a navigable lake or stream extends to the low-water mark. CC §830; CCP §2077. These marks may shift as the water deposits sand or soil (alluvion), thus augmenting the land on the bank (accretion), or as it recedes (reliction) or encroaches on the land. If the change is gradual and of natural causes, the owner's land is augmented or diminished by the shifting of the water boundary. CC §1014; *Raglan v Johnston Rock Co.* (1942) 50 CA2d 705, 123 P2d 883. The shifting of tides, however, makes the determination of high-water marks extremely difficult. See the discussion in *People v William Kent Estate Co.* (1966) 242 CA2d 156, 51 CR 215, and its use of the expression "neap" tides. For a discussion of the history of California sea boundary disputes and engineering methods for determining those boundaries, see Shalowitz, U.S. Department of Commerce, Coast and Geodetic Survey, Shore and Sea Boundaries (2 vols, 1962, 1964). Public Resources Code §§6357-6360 provide a complete procedure for establishing boundaries on tidal and submerged lands by agreement and by quiet title.

(b) *Thread or middle of lake or stream.* The owner of land bordering on a nonnavigable lake or stream is presumed to take to the thread or middle of the lake or stream (CC §830; CCP §2077) unless otherwise expressed in the instrument. Accretion, reliction, erosion, or encroachment may change the location of the thread.

(c) *Islands.* Islands may be formed by accretion, by the recession of the water, or by a new water course isolating land that was formerly part of the mainland. Islands in navigable streams belong to the state if there is no title to the contrary. CC §1016. This is true even if the water between the island and the bank is not navigable. *Packer v Bird* (1886) 71 C 134, 11 P 873. An island in a nonnavigable stream belongs to the owner of the shore: If the island lies entirely on one side of the thread, it belongs to the owner of the shore on that side; if it bestrides the thread, the owners on the opposite banks own it up to the midstream dividing line. CC §1017. If a new channel forms an island by separating a portion of the land from the property to which it was attached, it continues to belong to the owner of that land. CC §1018.

(d) *Formerly navigable waters.* If the waters cease to be navigable, two important rights arise: (1) The state may sell to abutting owners the underlying land thus made available or may exchange an abandoned navigable river or slough for lands having equal or greater value (Pub Res C §6210.8); and (2) persons claiming an interest in property lying in the former bed may bring quiet title actions against the state to determine ownership (Pub Res C §6461).

(e) *Avulsion.* Avulsion, as distinguished from the gradual processes of accretion, reliction, or erosion, is the sudden removal of land from the estate of one owner of the shore or bank to that of another as a result of the action of the water. See Title Insurance & Trust Company Title Handbook for Title Men (22nd ed 1980). The owner of a distinguishable part of a bank that is suddenly carried away may reclaim it within one year. CC §1015.

§8.41　　5. Inverse Condemnation

Inverse condemnation is an action brought by a holder of an interest in real property against the state or an authority with the power of eminent domain to recover compensation for a taking or damaging of his property rights without just compensation. See Condemnation Practice in California §13.1 (Cal CEB 1973). The term is also used to characterize the acts that deprive the owner of the use or value of his land, thereby giving rise to the cause of action.

Although this deprivation or damage will not be revealed in a title search unless it is described in a judgment of record awarding compensation for the taking, it may have a substantial effect on the value of the property. Therefore, both sellers and buyers should exercise care to discover the existence of conditions that may have an effect on value. The seller is concerned because of potential liability for failing to deliver what he impliedly agreed to deliver (see chap 9), and the buyer does not wish to pay for property that has been diminished in value.

§8.42　　6. Doctrine of Agreed Boundaries

If owners of adjoining property are uncertain of the true boundary line, they may fix it by agreement (or acquiescence). See *Cosgrave v Donovan* (1921) 52 CA 625, 199 P 808. The requirements for an agreed boundary are:

(a) Uncertainty about the true boundary. *Janes v LeDeit* (1964) 228 CA2d 474, 39 CR 559. It is not essential that the true location be absolutely unascertainable, that an accurate survey from the calls in the deed be impossible, or that the uncertainty should appear from the deeds. The line may also be founded on a mistake. *Janes v*

LeDeit, supra. The boundary, however, is definite when by survey it can be made certain from the deed. *Kraus v Griswold* (1965) 232 CA 2d 698, 706, 43 CR 139, 145.

The requirement of uncertainty has been made less strict by some later cases. In *Vella v Ratto* (1971) 17 CA3d 737, 95 CR 72, the court declared that this element may be proven by circumstantial evidence, shown in that case by long acquiesence in the existing boundary line. In *Roman v Ries* (1968) 259 CA2d 65, 66 CR 120, the court held that the requisite uncertainty existed when one party was uncertain but the other was certain, although wrong, about the location of the true line. In a third case, *Zachery v McWilliams* (1972) 28 CA3d 57, 104 CR 293, both parties were certain but wrong when they set the boundary line; nevertheless, their agreement was upheld in court.

(b) An agreement, express or implied from the facts and circumstances of the case, between the coterminous owners fixing the line. Such agreement may be inferred from the long-standing acceptance of a fence as a boundary between their lands. *Kunza v Gaskell* (1979) 91 CA3d 201, 154 CR 101.

(c) Actual designation of the line on the ground and occupation in accordance with the line. (This element is not included in all expressions of the rule by California courts, however.) See *Janes v LeDeit* (1964) 228 CA2d 474, 481 n8, 39 CR 559, 564 n8.

(d) Acquiescence for a period equal to the statute of limitations or under circumstances in which a change of boundary would cause substantial loss. *Aborigine Lumber Co. v Hyman* (1966) 245 CA2d 938, 54 CR 371. On estoppel, see §8.43.

If one of the adjoining owners acquires more by the agreed boundary than he formerly held, he owns the excess under the original tenure; no writing or words of conveyance are necessary. *Young v Blakeman* (1908) 153 C 477, 95 P 888.

A seller who is a party to an agreed boundary, either express or implied, may own more or less than the record description of his land. Both his lawyer and the buyer's lawyer should be alert to the possibility of a discrepancy.

§8.43   7. Estoppel

A boundary may be changed by estoppel. *Helm v Wilson* (1888) 76 C 476, 26 P 1103. This occurs when adjoining owners recognize a dividing line and one makes such valuable improvements on the basis of this recognized line that it would be inequitable to require him to remove or abandon them.

IV. ELIMINATING DEFECTS IN DESCRIPTIONS

A. Solutions to Typical Problems

§8.44   1. Overlapping Descriptions

If a seller owns a rectangular lot measuring less than 100 feet in width but conveys "to *B* the easterly 50 feet measured perpendicularly to the easterly boundary" and "to *C* the westerly 50 feet measured perpendicularly to the westerly boundary," there is an overlapping description, since the total width conveyed is 100 feet although the width of the lot is less than 100 feet. How can the defect be cured?

B and *C* could execute and record a mutual quitclaim deed describing precisely the boundary line between the two parcels. This solution, however, leaves unresolved the questions of effective date and rights of innocent parties, *e.g.,* lenders, whose interests attached between the original deeds and the corrective deed.

To eliminate these questions, or if overlapping owners cannot agree, either of the grantees could bring a quiet title action against the other. In such an action, the one who first recorded his deed would be in a preferred position. See §11.90 on priority. The other grantee has an action against the seller for breach. His choice of actions is discussed in §§12.6, 12.12. He may also have an action against the title insurance company if his title is insured. See California Title Insurance Practice §5.25 (Cal CEB 1980).

§8.45   2. Failure To Close Metes and Bounds Description

The requirements of a metes and bounds description are enumerated in §§8.16-8.21. One requirement is that it close, *i.e.,* that no gap be left in the boundaries. If a description of record is found to contain a gap, an engineer or surveyor should be retained to draft a proper description unless the needed element is obvious from the face of the document. Often the grantor in whose instrument the gap first appeared can be found and induced to execute a new deed. If there are intervening owners, the deed from the first grantor should conform to the requirements of afteracquired title (see §9.10), if possible. In other situations, it may be necessary to rely on adverse possession.

If a grantor will not cooperate, the choice may be whether to buy the necessary cooperation or to seek a judicial solution.

The two judicial solutions are quiet title or reformation. In this context, declaratory relief is treated as a variant of quiet title.

On quiet title actions, see 2 Bowman, Ogden's Revised California Real Property Law §§27.52-27.59 (TI Corp-CEB 1975); 2 Chadbourn, Grossman & Van Alstyne, California Pleading §§1053-1055 (1961); 3 Witkin, California Procedure, *Pleading* §§522-534 (2d ed 1971).

On reformation, see §3.38; 2 California Pleading §1083; 3 Witkin, Procedure, *Pleading* §§661-673.

§8.46 3. Incomplete or Confusing Descriptions

A description may be incomplete in itself (*e.g.,* it fails to state county or tract number) or become incomplete as a result of an event (*e.g.,* a monument has disappeared). Similarly, although a description is apparently complete, it may be contradictory, *e.g.,* contain an incorrect legal description followed by a correct street address.

Sometimes the defect is easily cured by agreement between the buyer and the seller. This can be accomplished by a quitclaim deed giving the correct description and reciting that it is given for the purpose of correcting the deed (described by book and page number) containing the misdescription.

In many cases, however, the time has long passed for an easy cure. In some instances, the lawyer must first procure a valid description from a competent engineer or surveyor and then seek relief by agreement with the property owner's predecessors in interest. If agreed relief is not available for any reason, the solution lies in action for reformation or quiet title. See §8.45 for references to works on the subject of quiet title and reformation actions.

If the error is contained in a judgment, ex parte relief may be available. See 4 Witkin, California Procedure, *Judgment* §§72-73 (2d ed 1971). See also 1 California Decedent Estate Administration §§5.29-5.32 (Cal CEB 1971) on decree of distributions.

§8.47 4. Erroneous Description of Other Property

If a parcel other than the one intended has been described, the lawyer must not only obtain the correct description of the intended property but also undo the damage, if any, to the property actually described.

Obtaining the correct description is discussed in §§8.5-8.9. Undoing the damage to the property described probably requires a reconveyance (by quitclaim) of the property incorrectly described and a new deed to the intended property. But see §11.90 on interests that may intervene before the new deed is recorded.

§8.48 5. Reservation or Exception in Successive Descriptions

If B is the owner under a deed that excepts (or reserves) an estate less than fee or a described strip of land or subsurface mineral rights, he may be tempted to insert the same exception when he conveys the property to C. This repeating of exceptions in successive descriptions may create ambiguities about the ownership of the excepted interest. For example, A grants to B, reserving an easement in favor of A's adjacent land; B grants to C, "reserving" the same easement. Has B clouded A's title to the easement by ostensibly reserving it for himself? Or has B attempted to indicate that he, too, expects to use the easement for the benefit of another parcel of adjacent property, rather than merely excluding A's reserved interest? To eliminate ambiguity, B's deed should state clearly the property for the benefit of which he makes the exception if it is a parcel other than A's, or he should make his deed "subject to the easement reserved in deed from A to B recorded at. . . ."

A common law rule that no easement could be reserved in a stranger has been abolished by the decision in *Willard v First Church of Christ, Scientist* (1972) 7 C3d 473, 102 CR 739. The court held that because there had been no reliance on the old rule, the doctrine could not be used to defeat the grantor's intent. Thus, the dominant tenement of an easement created by reservation need no longer be land held by the grantor. (This more liberal approach should pose no problem for the title searcher, however, because any effective reservation in a stranger would obviously require some description of the stranger or of his property.)

§8.49 6. Fraudulent or Erroneous Surveys

In the early days of California, some surveys made under contract to the government misplaced such markers as rivers, mountains, and section corners. For instance, in *Schwartz v Dibblee* (1921) 51 CA 451, 197 P 125, the question turned on the fact that the surveyor of section 30 had discovered that the south line of adjacent section 19 was ten chains too far north.

Even though these official surveys are erroneous, they benefit from the presumption that official duty has been properly performed. *Southern Pac. Land Co. v Meserve* (1921) 186 C 157, 198 P 1055. However, public lands may be resurveyed if the resurvey would not impair the bona fide rights or claims of any owner or claimant. 43 USC §772; Bureau of Land Management, Manual of Instructions for the Survey of the Public Lands of the United States §§387, 409, 428 (1973).

If a survey is private and unofficial, the presumption that official duty has been properly performed does not apply; a correct survey is admissible to show the error of a prior survey. The remedy is then by agreement, reformation, or quiet title.

B. Drafting To Eliminate Defects

§8.50   1. Drafting Principles

The following principles apply to descriptions generally.

(a) Avoid double calls and nonessential descriptions except when necessary to prevent uncertainty or as a precaution against error. For example, if the southwest quarter is assumed to consist of 160 acres, but the exact area is not a substantial factor in the deal, the addition of the information "consisting of 160 acres" opens the possibility of conflicting calls and litigation. For a comparison of merits and hazards in adding acreage to descriptions, see §8.12.

(b) If more than one call or description is helpful, specify which is to control. The two may turn out to be inconsistent. In case of inconsistency, CCP §2077 supplies certain rules of construction, but these may be contrary to the intent of the parties.

(c) Appurtenances (*i.e.,* augmenting easements, additional rights, personal property, and similar elements transferred in addition to the principal property) should be described with the same care as is necessary for the property itself. Easements, for example, being interests in real property, bring into play all the principles discussed in this chapter. Easements are more fully discussed in §§8.26-8.37, and forms are presented in §§8.57-8.59. When personal property is being transferred with real property, it should be identified with particularity in the agreement and in a bill of sale separate from the deed. A vague description, such as "all the living room furniture," may lead to later disputes and even to attempted circumvention of the intent of the parties. Generally, an agreed and initialed inventory, describing the goods precisely, is the most satisfactory method. On occasion, equipment may be photographed and the photographs made part of the agreement.

§8.51   2. Drafting Particular Descriptions

Many principles discussed under reading descriptions (see §§8.10-8.43) apply equally to drafting descriptions. For instance, the draftsman must know about nonrecord elements (see §§8.25-8.43) so that they may be either confirmed (by including necessary provisions in the agreement or deed) or removed (by clearing the record before the transaction is consummated).

Forms for the kinds of descriptions most commonly encountered in California practice are set out in §§8.52-8.61. The elements in the forms apply whether the description is part of a deposit receipt, escrow instructions forming a bilateral contract, or a more formal purchase and sale agreement. See *Beverage v Canton Placer Mining Co.* (1955) 43 C2d 769, 278 P2d 694. The drafting principles discussed in §8.50 apply in drafting the particular descriptions that follow.

§8.52   a. Form: Description by Reference to Subdivision Map

Form 8.52-1

The real property in the ____[*City of* _____, / *City and*]____ County of _____, State of California, described as ____[*lot, tract, block, or other designation used on map*]____ per map recorded at book _____, page(s) _____ of Maps, Office of County Recorder of _____ County.

Comment: This provision describes property by reference to a recorded subdivision map. Absence of the name of the state may be crucial in documents. The recorder may record in a book of subdivision maps, a book of parcel maps, or a book of cities and towns. Govt C §66466. Either way, the word "Maps" in the form is sufficient. If the property lies in the same county as that in which the map is recorded, it is sufficient to identify the recorder as "County Recorder of that county"; otherwise the county in which the map is recorded should be named at the end of the form to distinguish it from the county names at the beginning of the form as the location of the property.

Statutory authority for description by reference to a subdivision map is given in §8.15, which also cites code sections that permit the recording of maps and warns of consequences flowing from improperly recorded maps.

For marketing purposes, subdivisions sometimes bear names instead of or in addition to numbers. If the name is shown on the recorded map it is a proper part of the description. If it is the only designation of the subdivision (*i.e.*, there is no tract number), the name is a necessary part of the description.

On descriptions for transfers of less than all of the parcel shown on the map, see forms and Comments at §§8.53-8.54.

§8.53 b. Form: Description by Reference to Rectangular Survey Map

Form 8.53-1

The real property in the ____[*City of* _____, / *City and*]____ **County of** _____, **State of California, described as** ____[*e.g., SW quarter*]____, **section** _____, **township** _____, **range** _____, ____[*Humboldt / Mt. Diablo / San Bernardino*]____ **base and meridian,** ____[*per survey dated* _____, *19*____]____.

Comment: This provision describes property by reference to a United States government rectangular survey, discussed in §8.13. The Comment in §8.52 emphasizes the importance of naming the state. If there has been more than one survey or plat (see §8.49), the date of the one to which reference is made must be given; if it is not known whether there was more than one, inserting the date is a simple precaution.

If an oddly shaped parcel is being transferred (*e.g.*, Lot 1, section 1 as shown in Figure 1 (see §8.13), or the property cannot be described as a quarter or half, the form should be modified to read:

described as ____[*that / those*]____ portion(s) of ____[*specify: e.g., quarters or section*]____ ____[*state other qualifications*]____ ____[*describe*]____.

An example of a description of an oddly shaped parcel is:

"described as that portion of section 30, township 2 north, range 4 east, San Bernardino base and meridian lying southerly of the lands described in deed from R. Quinn to B. Quinn recorded at book. . . ."

If, instead, a transfer is to be described in terms of lands excluded, the following should be added:

EXCEPT ____[that / those]____ portion(s) ____[specify parts not included in transfer]____.

"Except" has a precise legal meaning and is defined in §8.34. It is capitalized in this form because it is customary to do so in descriptions. For additional elements in descriptions, see §8.50.

§8.54   c. Form: Description by Reference to Deed or Other Instrument

Form 8.54-1

The real property in the ____[City of _____, / City and]____ County of _____, State of California, described as ____[that / those]____ portion(s) of the property described in ____[specify document, e.g., deed, judgment, or other]____ dated _____, 19__, in which ____[name]____ ____[is / are]____ ____[specify designation in document, e.g., grantor, plaintiff, or other designation]____ and ____[name]____ ____[is / are]____ ____[specify designation, e.g., grantee, defendant, or other designation]____, recorded on _____, 19__, as Instrument _____ in book _____, page _____ of ____[official book]____, of the Office of the County Recorder of _____ County.

Comment: Land may be described by reference to another instrument. See §8.15. However, the description will be improper if (1) the description in the previously recorded instrument is faulty, or (2) the reference to that instrument in the present document is faulty. To protect against either pitfall, the attorney should examine the map or other instrument or obtain adequate assurance from the title company, and carefully compare that information with the reference in the new instrument. Copies of maps can usually be obtained from title companies, assessors' offices, city or county engineers, or zoning offices, though title company maps are generally preferable.

It is prudent never to describe by reference to an instrument that is not of public record. The instrument referred to need not be of record to assure validity of the new conveyance (*Saunders v Schmaelzle* (1874) 49 C 59, 66), but if it is not recorded, serious problems of proof and constructive notice may arise.

The importance of including the name of the state and determining the correct city and county is discussed in §8.52. The document to which reference is made should be described by date, parties, designation of the parties in the document, and any recording data.

For other elements in descriptions, see §8.50. If any part of the property described in the other document is to be excluded from the present transfer, the exclusion or exception should be clearly shown. See §8.34.

§8.55   d. Description by Metes and Bounds

Descriptions by metes and bounds are so diverse that they do not lend themselves to a single form. In general, the rules for reading these descriptions (see §§8.16-8.22) are the rules for drafting them. For rules of construction, see CCP §2077. With experience in drafting descriptions, other rules will become apparent. For example, the courses of parallel lines in a single description use the same numbers but opposite directions (*e.g.,* S 79° 12' 10" E is parallel to N 79° 12' 10" W).

If the metes and bounds consist of bearings, angles, arcs, and distances, the drafter should use only those calls that have been certified by a qualified surveyor or engineer. These experts may not be necessary for metes and bounds descriptions based entirely on physical monuments; but because of difficulty in identifying both natural and artificial physical monuments, description by surveyors' courses is generally preferable.

Only the most recent survey should be used; all surveys should be read critically to make certain the area is closed and should be compared with other pertinent data (including record title to prevent record gaps or overlaps). For an example of discrepancies to be avoided, see *Schwartz v Dibblee* (1921) 51 CA 451, 197 P 125.

If water, streets, or mountains are boundaries, it is wise not to rely on the rules of construction in CC §§830-831, 1112; CCP §2077(4); and Govt C §§23073-23076. It is best to specify *thread* of river, *center* of road, *middle* of lake, *ridge* of mountain, etc., if that is what is meant. On waters, see §8.40. For additional drafting principles, see §8.50. On railroad easements, see *Faus v Nelson* (1966) 241 CA2d 320, 50 CR 483.

Successive numbering of the calls (see example in §8.20) contributes to easy reading and to the drafter's accuracy.

§8.56   e. Easements

Problems concerning easements are discussed in §§8.26-8.35, and precautions for buyers and sellers are listed in §§8.26-8.37. Many of the problems discussed in those sections can be eliminated by proper drafting. Forms for that purpose are set out in §§8.57-8.59.

§8.57   (1) Form: Reservation of Easement in Grant

Form 8.57-1

____[Describe parcel conveyed]____ excepting from that property ____ [describe the property covered by the easement]____ as an easement ____ [personal and in gross to grantor / appurtenant to ____[describe dominant tenement]____]____ ____[describe purpose, e.g., providing ingress to and egress from the dominant tenement]____ for ____[specify duration, e.g., until the dominant tenement shall abut on a public road or street]_____.

Comment: This provision creates an easement in favor of the grantor out of land conveyed by the grantor in the same instrument. Provisions for the separate creation and transfer of easements are set out in §§8.58-8.59.

Instead of "excepting," as used in this provision, many lawyers use "reserving." The distinction is defined in §8.34.

The exception in this provision is expressly referred to as an easement to negate its construction as an estate in fee. On the difference between easements that are personal (in gross) and those that are appurtenant, see §8.30. On problems with easements generally, see §§8.26-8.35.

§8.58   (2) Form: Transfer of Appurtenant Easement

Form 8.58-1

____[Describe property conveyed]____ , together with an easement appurtenant to that property ____[described as/as described in]____ ____[describe property covered by easement or instrument in which it is described]____.

Comment: This provision transfers an appurtenant easement together with the land that it serves. Matters to consider with easements are discussed in §§8.31-8.37. Express transfer of an appurtenant easement is not necessary in a transfer of the dominant tenement; the easement passes by operation of law. See §8.30. Some lawyers nevertheless make express reference to the easement as a precaution. This express reference, however, may raise an inference that other appurtenances not included in the grant are intentionally excluded (see CC §3534; Bader v Coale (1942) 48 CA2d 276, 119 P2d 763), particularly against the party who drafted the instrument (see *Steven v Fidelity & Cas. Co.* (1962) 58 C2d 862, 27 CR 172).

The physical boundaries of easements may be described in as many ways as are possible for interests in fee. See §§8.13-8.24.

§8.59 (3) Form: Creation of Easement

Form 8.59-1

____[Name of transferor]____ ____[grants / quitclaims]____ **to** ____[name of transferee]____ ____[describe property covered by easement]____ **as an easement** ____[in gross, personal to transferee / appurtenant to ____[describe dominant tenement]____]____ **for** ____[describe purpose]____ **for** ____[state duration, e.g., in perpetuity, so long as used for road purposes] ____.

Comment: As distinguished from the provision in §8.57 (reservation of easement in favor of grantor) and §8.58 (transfer of easement with property to which it is appurtenant), this provision is for use in creating a new easement.

On matters affecting the description of easements, see §§8.26-8.35.

§8.60 (4) Release of Easement

An easement may be extinguished by a written release given by the owner of the easement to the owner of the servient tenement. *Westlake v Silva* (1942) 49 CA2d 476, 121 P2d 872. However, the concurrence of both owners is required. See 5 Restatement of Property §500 (1944). In this bilateral aspect it is distinguished from abandonment. See 5 Restatement §504; see also §8.28. The owner of the servient tenement should not concur in the release without first making certain that he is fully protected, *e.g.,* that unwanted structures erected by the easement owner are first removed or that the releasing owner will indemnify against claims that the easement continues in force. The owner's attorney should advise examination of a current title report and inspection of the premises.

§8.61 f. Form: Describing Multiple Parcels

Form 8.61-1

In addition to the foregoing property,

[*In a deed*]

grantor conveys

[In an agreement]

seller will convey

[Continue]

____*[all his right, title, and interest in / marketable fee title to / (other agreed state of title)]*____ **all other property, if any, contained within the exterior boundaries of the area containing the several parcels described above:** ____*[describe exterior boundaries]*____.

Comment: Sometimes the transfer of adjacent parcels presents problems in description. For example, each parcel may have been transferred to the present seller by separate metes and bounds descriptions, but a gap may have been left between boundaries that should have formed a common boundary. As another example, two properties sharing a common alley may have been described as bounded by that alley with no clear indication whether the boundary is intended to be the center or the edge of the alley.

To meet these problems, experienced practitioners suggest following the separate descriptions of the parcels with an overall statement of intent to convey all the property included within the exterior boundaries of the area containing those parcels except for portions that the grantor cannot convey, such as dedicated streets, or gaps actually intended. This provision makes such a statement.

Sellers may prefer to express the provision in the form of a quitclaim, as a protection against liability for matters that they cannot convey. Buyers should ordinarily insist on assurance of good title.

§8.62   g. Eliminating Water Problems

Problems in describing lands bordered by water (lakes, streams, tidewaters, slough channels) are extremely difficult to recognize and solve. (The effect of water on land is discussed in §8.40; this section is concerned with drafting.) Generally these descriptions should be the joint product of lawyer, engineer, and title officer.

The seller should not purport to grant more than he has; the buyer should make certain that the description gives him all that the seller can convey, if that is the intention of the parties. Different kinds of water present various drafting problems. The most common kinds of water are discussed below. Underlying all of them are these basic cautions: Before drafting the description, investigate to determine whether any changes have taken place since the previous transfer; and draft the description to secure for the appropriate party the benefits that may flow from these changes.

(1) *Tidewaters.* To eliminate doubt, the conveyance to buyer should specify to what line the grant is made even if the intent coincides with the statutory rule discussed in §8.40. In most cases, however, there should be no attempt to substitute surveyors' or other measurements for the intended water boundary. Such a description could deprive the buyer of accretions accruing before close of escrow and create ambiguity about later accretions. For the definition of accretions, see CC §1014. See also 1 Bowman, Ogden's Revised California Real Property Law §15.4 (TI Corp-CEB 1974).

(2) *Navigable lake.* In the absence of other circumstances, the rights of the grantor to the low-water mark are considered to be included in the conveyance. CCP §2077. To negate "other circumstances," low-water mark should be specified in the description if that is what is intended. As with tidewaters, however, an attempt to define the low-water mark by substituting surveyors' courses may deprive the buyer of accretions or compel him to go to court to establish his right to them.

(3) *Nonnavigable stream or lake.* Except when the grant indicates a different intent, the abutting owner takes to the middle or thread of the lake or stream. See §8.40. As in the case of tidewaters and navigable waters, it is better to express the intent of the parties than to leave the description to statutory interpretation. However, the expressed intent should leave open to the buyer the benefit of the statutory provisions discussed in §8.40. See 1 Ogden's Real Property Law §§15.3-15.10 for a discussion of boundary rules and problems affected by water; 2 Ogden's Real Property §§26.54-26.57 for a discussion of tidelands boundaries.

§8.63 3. Contract Provision for Expressing Covenants in Deed

Certain covenants, although expressed in the purchase and sale agreement, are merged in the deed and become unenforceable when the deed is recorded unless they are stated in the deed itself. See §3.66. To prevent the omission of these covenants from the deed, it is prudent to make, in both the agreement and the escrow instructions, an express requirement that the covenants be included in the deed. The best place for this provision is directly following the description. There it serves as a flag to the drafter when the description is copied in preparing the deed. A form for the contractual clause appears in §3.67.

§8.64 V. DESCRIBING PERSONAL PROPERTY

Transfers of real property commonly include personal property on the premises. For instance, residences are often sold with carpets, drapes, and appliances; sales of furnished apartment houses or other commercial properties may include elaborate inventories of furniture, fixtures, merchandise, and accounts receivable; and farm properties may be sold with livestock, harvested crops, or stock in mutual water companies.

If there are only a few items of personal property, they may be listed in the purchase and sale agreement itself. Longer lists are commonly attached as exhibits. If the inventories are so extensive that they cannot be readily determined or valued by a visual inspection, the parties often agree that an inventory will be taken in the future by their representatives. In this event, the total price is left open, but a method of computing the price (such as book value) must be agreed on. For a form for describing personal property in the purchase and sale agreement, see §3.171. For a form of agreement transferring the assets of a going business, see Drafting Agreements for the Sale of Businesses, chap 4 (Cal CEB 1971).

In any event, the need for certainty in describing personal property is as great as it is in describing the real property. On uncertainty as rendering a contract illusory, see §12.98. If the property itself is not described in the agreement, the method by which it can be ascertained and located must be clear. For examples of proper descriptions of specific goods, see 3 California Commercial Law §2.22 (Cal CEB 1966).

Some kinds of personal property present special problems. For example, the seller's interest in a neon sign may be no more than a leasehold interest; the buyer should check with the manufacturer or lessor whose name is on the sign. Vehicles may be subject to encumbrances, as shown on registration slips. On public notice of other security instruments, see 3 Commercial Law chap 5. To prevent substitution of goods after taking inventory, some buyers insist on possession of the goods as soon as inventory is completed; others place an indelible mark (*e.g.*, by means of a steel die) on each item. This is generally unnecessary for equipment that can be described by serial number. On bulk transfers without change of possession, see CC §3440.

On the transfer of guaranties and warranties see §3.169.

9

Covenants of Title

This chapter was originally published as chapter 16 in California Real Estate Sales Transactions (Cal CEB 1967), by George H. Whitney. It has been revised and updated by the CEB legal staff.

I. COVENANTS AND WARRANTIES

§9.1 A. Need for Title Covenants

In a transfer of real property, it is not enough for the buyer to receive whatever interest the seller has; he must receive what he has bargained for or receive compensation if his expectations are not fulfilled. One device for protecting the buyer is the seller's covenant of title. Another method is through title insurance. See §§3.55, 3.79-3.80 for provisions making a sale contingent on the issuance of a title insurance policy. These methods are often used concurrently.

In 1974 the California Supreme Court followed the lead of several other states and held that in the sale as well as in the manufacture of new housing, an implied warranty exists that the building was designed and constructed in a reasonably workmanlike manner. *Pollard v Saxe & Yolles Dev. Co.* (1974) 12 C3d 374, 115 CR 648. This warranty of merchantability should not be confused with covenants of title. See also *Avner v Longridge Estates* (1969) 272 CA2d 607, 77 CR 633; *Kriegler v Eichler Homes, Inc.* (1969) 269 CA2d 224, 74 CR 749.

B. Covenants and Warranties Distinguished

§9.2 1. Types of Covenants

In real property sales and exchanges, covenants may be roughly divided into three groups:

(1) *Contractual covenants.* An example is the seller's promise in the agreement of sale that he will not increase the height of a party wall. It is not a title covenant even though it may run with the land. Contractual covenants are discussed in §9.4.

(2) *Covenants concerning the use of property.* These are typified by declarations of covenants, conditions, and restrictions (CC&R's) commonly used by subdividers to protect economic value by restricting use. These are discussed in §§3.96-3.99. For further discussion of

covenants, conditions, and restrictions, see 2 Bowman, Ogden's Revised California Real Property Law, chap 23 (TI Corp-CEB 1975); Guide to California Subdivision Sales Law §§4.4-4.6, 4.22 (Cal CEB 1974).

(3) *Title covenants.* These are assurances that the grantee is getting the estate that the grantor purports to convey. The six kinds in California are: (1) of seisin and good title, (2) against encumbrances, (3) of warranty, (4) for quiet enjoyment, (5) of the right to convey, (6) for further assurance. See Comment, *Covenants of Title Running With the Land in California,* 49 Calif L Rev 931 (1961). These covenants are treated separately in §§9.6-9.10. Some of them run with the land; others do not. None applies unless expressed in the deed or implied by law from words used in the deed.

§9.3   2. Warranties

"Warranty" has two legitimate uses in the context of conveyances in California. Its use as part of the term "covenant of warranty" is of minor importance in actual practice. Its use in the contractual sense (*i.e.,* a promise made by the seller about the quantity, quality, character, or condition of the property) is found in practically every transaction for the transfer of real property. See *Hackett v Lewis* (1918) 36 CA 687, 173 P 111; *Morris v Fiat Motor Sales Co.* (1916) 32 CA 315, 162 P 663.

A "covenant of warranty" is a term of art used in deeds to signify a continuing promise that the covenantor will compensate the covenantee if the title to any part of the estate fails because of superior title in a third party at the time of the conveyance. See *Tropico Land & Improvement Co. v Lambourn* (1915) 170 C 33, 38, 148 P 206, 208; Comment, *Covenants of Title Running With the Land in California,* 49 Calif L Rev 931, 936 (1961). It runs with the land. See 49 Calif L Rev at 936. A warranty deed is one that contains a covenant of warranty. For further discussion of this covenant, see §9.8.

The purely contractual warranty is, for example, a contract provision in which the seller assures the buyer that the property is zoned for the kind of structure the buyer intends to build, or a judicially implied warranty of fitness or condition. See, *e.g.,* provisions in §§3.121, 3.137. For a discussion of these warranties, see Comment, *Buyer's Remedies in the Sale of Real Property in California,* 53 Calif

L Rev 1062, 1072 (1965). See also §§3.65-3.67 for a discussion of warranties. A contractual warranty exists only when the seller intends his affirmation as a promise (*Miller v Germain Seed & Plant Co.* (1924) 193 C 62, 75, 222 P 817, 822), and the purchaser buys in reliance on this promise (*McLennan v Ohmen* (1888) 75 C 558, 561, 17 P 687, 688). Affirmations that merely express the seller's opinion, belief, judgment, or estimate do not constitute warranties. *Corporation of the Presiding Bishop v Cavanaugh* (1963) 217 CA2d 492, 32 CR 144.

"Warranty," used in the contractual sense, is a promise just as a covenant is a promise. In California, practitioners and some cases (*e.g., Liberty Bldg. Co. v Royal Indem. Co.* (1960) 177 CA2d 583, 589, 2 CR 329, 333) use the two words interchangeably. However, legal writers still adhere to the word "covenants" in referring to affirmations respecting title, and this chapter will do likewise.

An action for breach of warranty sounds in contract, whereas an action for misrepresentation sounds in tort. See 1 Witkin, Summary of California Law, *Sales* §52 (8th ed 1973).

II. COVENANTS IMPOSED BY DEED OR CONTRACT

§9.4 A. Contractual Covenants

Once a buyer has accepted a deed to the property covered by a purchase agreement, he may not generally rely on covenants of title contained in the agreement unless they are also contained in the deed. This general rule does not apply if there is mistake, fraud, or invalidity affecting the deed, nor does it affect matters collateral to the deed. *Palos Verdes Corp. v Housing Auth.* (1962) 202 CA2d 827, 21 CR 225. Otherwise, however, contractual covenants are merged in the deed (*i.e.,* lost unless expressed in the deed). See *Szabo v Superior Court* (1978) 84 CA3d 839, 148 CR 837.

This chapter assumes, therefore, that the title covenants under discussion are contained in deeds. This does not negate the utility of covenants in the agreement. On the contrary, the agreement should contain all the title covenants that the parties expect the deed to contain. In addition, however, because all covenants are merged in the deed, they must be expressed there unless the law implies them without express provision. On covenants implied by use of "grant," see §§9.5-9.7; on contractual provisions for covenants and warranties to survive deed, see §3.67.

§9.5 B. California Statutory Grant Deed

Civil Code §1113 provides:

From the use of the word "grant" in any conveyance by which an estate of inheritance or fee simple is to be passed, the following covenants, and none other, on the part of the grantor for himself and his heirs to the grantee, his heirs, and assigns, are implied, unless restrained by express terms contained in such conveyance:

1. That previous to the time of the execution of such conveyance, the grantor has not conveyed the same estate, or any right, title, or interest therein, to any person other than the grantee;

2. That such estate is at the time of the execution of such conveyance free from encumbrance done, made, or suffered by the grantor, or any person claiming under him.

Such covenants may be sued upon in the same manner as if they have been expressly inserted in the conveyance.

The covenants implied by CC §1113 are discussed in §§9.6-9.7. These covenants are implied only if the conveyance (1) contains the word "grant," (2) passes an estate of inheritance or fee simple, and (3) contains no express terms of "restraint" (*i.e.*, a limitation or qualification of the covenant that would otherwise be implied). For further discussion of restraints, see §9.22.

The word "grant" is not sufficient to raise the implication if the deed is a gift deed (*Estate of Porter* (1903) 138 C 618, 72 P 173) or a quitclaim deed (*i.e.*, a deed passing whatever interest the grantor has, even a fee, but without any representation that he has any interest). *Southern Pac. Co. v Dore* (1917) 34 CA 521, 168 P 147. See §9.21 on quitclaim deeds. On actions for breach of covenant, see §§9.13-9.20.

§9.6 1. Covenant of Seisin and Good Title

One of the covenants of title implied by the word "grant" in the conveyance of an estate of inheritance or fee simple is "that previous to the time of the execution of such conveyance, the grantor has not conveyed the same estate, or any right, title, or interest therein, to any person other than the grantee." CC §1113; see §9.5.

This is a special covenant of seisin against prior conveyances that is somewhat similar to the special covenant defined below. See Comment, *Covenants of Title Running With the Land in California,* 49 Calif L Rev 931, 934 (1961). A general covenant of seisin is a covenant that the grantor is the owner of the property. See *McCor-*

mick v Marcy (1913) 165 C 386, 388, 132 P 449, 450. A special covenant of seisin is a covenant that the grantor owns the property and has not sold it himself. The California statutory covenant is narrower: The grantor covenants not that he owns the property or ever did own it, but only that he himself has not previously conveyed the estate.

If the buyer wants the benefit of a covenant of seisin, either special or general, he must see that it is inserted in his deed. A provision for this covenant appears in §9.12. On negating the covenant, see §§9.21-9.22.

The covenant does not run with the land (*Lawrence v Montgomery* (1869) 37 C 183); only the covenantee may bring action for its breach.

The statute of limitations begins to run on a covenant of seisin, whether general or special, when the instrument is executed. *Hotaling v Hotaling* (1924) 193 C 368, 379, 224 P 455, 459; *McCormick v Marcy, supra.*

Covenants of seisin are rarely relied on in California, much less expressly provided for in deeds. One of the principal reasons is that purchasers have come to rely on title insurance for proof of title. See 1, 2 Bowman, Ogden's California Real Property Law (TI Corp-CEB 1974, 1975). In most instances, the title company issuing the policy is assumed to have greater financial responsibility than the grantor in the event of a defect of title. On occasion, however, the grantor's covenant in addition to the title company's responsibility may be of advantage to the buyer. On remedies for breach of covenant of seisin, see §§9.13, 9.17-9.20.

§9.7   2. Covenant Against Encumbrances

The second of the covenants of title implied under CC §1113 by the word "grant" in the conveyance of an estate of inheritance or fee simple is "that such estate is at the time of the execution of such conveyance free from encumbrances done, made, or suffered by the grantor, or any person claiming under him." See §9.5.

Like the covenant of seisin (see §9.6), this is a special covenant assuring only that the grantor himself has not encumbered the property or suffered it to be encumbered; it is not a covenant that the property is free of encumbrances. See Comment, *Covenants of Title Running With the Land in California,* 49 Calif L Rev 931, 934

(1961). The provision in §9.12 broadens the covenant.

"The term 'encumbrances' includes taxes, assessments, and all liens upon real property." CC §1114. The implied covenant against the lien of taxes is potentially hazardous to the seller unless the deed contains appropriate words of restraint. This arises because the lien attaches during the first day of March for the following fiscal year, but the second installment for the current year is not delinquent until April 10. See §§3.56, 3.83. In view of this overlap, few properties are ever free of tax liens. Therefore, a grant deed to encumbered property without words of restraint breaches this covenant. The seller may not defend on the ground that the buyer had notice from the preliminary title report or otherwise; the action is on breach of contract and does not require a showing of reliance or misrepresentation. *Evans v Faught* (1965) 231 CA2d 698, 42 CR 133. But see *Babb v Weemer* (1964) 225 CA2d 546, 553, 37 CR 533, 537 on damages.

The covenant is breached, if untrue, when the instrument is executed. *Evans v Faught, supra.*

Preferred practice is to insert words of restraint in both the agreement and the deed unless the escrow holder is instructed to pay all taxes that would otherwise be a lien. The "subject to" clauses in §§3.55, 3.80 are appropriate words of restraint if they appear in the deed. See also provision in §9.22. Making the title subject to stated encumbrances leaves the covenant applicable to other encumbrances not expressly excluded. *Mains v City Title Ins. Co.* (1949) 34 C2d 580, 585, 212 P2d 873, 876.

In addition to the matters enumerated in CC §1114, "encumbrances" include mortgages, deeds of trust, judgment liens, attachments, leases, water rights, easements, restrictions on use, or any right in a third party that diminishes the value or limits the use of the property. See 3 American Law of Property §12.128 (A. J. Casner ed 1952); Hill, *Grant and the Obvious Encumbrance,* 41 LA B Bull 231 (1966). The implied covenant against encumbrances under CC §1113 does not include visible easements or physical burdens on the land, even though they may also be of record. *Sisk v Caswell* (1910) 14 CA 377, 112 P 435.

The covenant is a promise to indemnify the grantee against loss; hence the grantee cannot recover until he has sustained a loss. *Wright v Boggess* (1914) 24 CA 533, 141 P 1082. This is true even though the statute of limitations begins to run when the covenant is made, *i.e.,* on delivery of the deed, and may well run before any loss has occurred. See *McPike v Heaton* (1900) 131 C 109, 63 P 179.

The covenant implied by CC §1113 does not accompany a quitclaim conveyance (discussed in §9.21) or a devise or gift (see 49 Calif L Rev at 935), nor does it run with the land *(Babb v Weemer* (1964) 225 CA2d 546, 37 CR 533).

§9.8   C. Warranty Deed; Covenant of Quiet Enjoyment

A warranty deed is one that contains a covenant of warranty. Black's Law Dictionary 1759 (4th ed 1957). A covenant of warranty is a promise that the covenantor will compensate the covenantee if the title to any part of the estate fails because of an outstanding paramount title in a third party. See *Tropico Land & Improvement Co. v Lambourn* (1915) 170 C 33, 38, 148 P 206, 208. It is sometimes called a covenant of "non-claim." *Gee v Moore* (1859) 14 C 472, 473. The compensation may be in damages or in other lands of equal value. See Black's Law Dictionary 1757. As distinguished from covenants of seisin (see §9.6) and against encumbrances (see §9.7), covenants of warranty run with the land, but only when (1) contained in a deed and (2) made for the direct benefit of the property or some part of it then in existence. CC §§1462-1463.

The covenant of quiet enjoyment is in effect the same as the covenant of warranty; both are intended to secure compensation to the buyer for a disturbance of his quiet and peaceable possession if he is evicted from the premises. See 3 American Law of Property §12.129 (A. J. Casner ed 1952). In contrast with the covenants of seisin and right to convey and against encumbrances, which refer to the state of title and are broken if the defects exist, the covenants of warranty and for quiet enjoyment deal with the enjoyment of possession and are broken only when that is disturbed. See 3 American Law of Property §12.129.

Warranty deeds are rarely used in California, although they are common in other parts of the country. Title insurance, which gives recourse against the title company, has largely supplanted the warranty deed, which gives recourse against the grantor. See 1 Bowman, Ogden's Revised California Real Property Law §3.6 (TI Corp-CEB 1974).

This express covenant makes a warranty deed of the instrument of conveyance. There is no provision of law in California for a covenant of warranty except by express provision in the instrument. For a provision, see §9.12.

From a buyer's point of view, it is usually better to rely on a secure title insurance company than on the seller's ability to respond in damages. A buyer can, however, have the benefit of both if he negotiates for that protection as part of his purchase transaction.

From a seller's point of view, a covenant of warranty should explicitly set forth the encumbrances to which the title is subject, in much the same manner as a title policy. For this purpose, the seller's attorney should be guided by a reliable and current title report, but he should add all unrecorded encumbrances of which he or his client is aware. See Freshman, *The Warranty Deed: Where and When to Use It,* 51 LA BJ 186 (1975).

D. Other Covenants

§9.9   1. Covenant of Right To Convey

The covenant of right to convey, although often held to be the equivalent of the covenant of seisin (see Comment, §9.12), is nevertheless a separate covenant. It may be used when the grantor does not own the property but still has the right to convey it, *e.g.,* an attorney in fact for the owner. See Comment, *Covenants of Title Running With the Land in California,* 49 Calif L Rev 931, 934 (1961).

This covenant is not among those implied from the word "grant" under CC §1113. See §9.5. It is included in the provision in §9.12. It does not run with the land. See 49 Calif L Rev at 934. If the covenant is false, it is broken when made. *Salmon v Vallejo* (1871) 41 C 481.

§9.10   2. Covenant for Further Assurance

A covenant for further assurance is an undertaking on the part of the seller to do any further acts for the purpose of perfecting the buyer's title that the buyer may reasonably require. See Comment, *Covenants of Title Running With the Land in California,* 49 Calif L Rev 931, 935 (1961). It carries with it a covenant against encumbrances. 49 Calif L Rev at 936. Under CC §1463 it runs with the land in California if it otherwise complies with the requirements of CC §§1462-1464.

The covenant for further assurance generally requires the grantor to convey afteracquired title to the grantee to give him what he bargained for, but an express covenant for further assurance is not always necessary to protect the grantee. Thus, a grant in fee simple without express covenant is sufficient to pass, by operation of law, the grantor's afteracquired title. CC §1106. A quitclaim deed transfers only such interest as the transferor has in the land at the date of its execution, and hence does not carry an afteracquired title. *Taylor v Coachella Valley County Water Dist.* (1952) 108 CA2d 743, 239 P2d 454. Since a quitclaim deed passes whatever legal or equitable interest the grantor possesses at the time of the grant, this includes the passing of rights only inchoate at the time of the grant but which later ripen into a vested estate. *Soares v Steidtmann* (1955) 130 CA2d 401, 278 P2d 953. Even afteracquired title may pass under a quitclaim deed on estoppel principles if the parties intended that a particular interest be conveyed. See *Estate of Wilson* (1940) 40 CA2d 229, 104 P2d 716.

§9.11   3. Lineal and Collateral Warranties

Civil Code §1115 purports to abolish "lineal and collateral warranties," but provides that the heirs and devisees of a person who has made a covenant or agreement in reference to the title of any real property are answerable to the extent of the land descended or devised to them.

"The whole doctrine of collateral warranty seems repugnant to plain and unsophisticated reason and justice; and even its technical grounds are so obscure that the ablest legal writers are not agreed upon the subject." See Black's Law Dictionary 1220 (2d ed 1910). Lineal warranties are also rooted in old conveyancing, and their modern meaning, if any, is obscure. The abolition of the two principles by CC §1115 makes further consideration unnecessary.

However, in holding the heirs and devisees of a grantor liable on a title covenant to the extent of land descended or devised to them, the statute gives modern protection to the buyer and his assigns. If an owner conveys land with a covenant of title, either expressed in a warranty deed or implied by the terms of CC §1113, and title fails in breach of the covenant, the heirs and devisees of the covenantor are liable for the payment of any loss suffered by the covenantee or his assigns as a result of the breach, to the extent of any land descended or devised to them, even though they may not be estopped from claiming title to the land itself. *Tropico Land & Improvement Co. v Lambourn* (1915) 170 C 33, 46, 148 P 206, 211; *Foote v Clark* (Mo 1890) 14 SW 981.

§9.12   E. Form: Comprehensive Title Covenant

Form 9.12

Grantor, for ____[himself / herself]____ and ____[his / her]____ heirs, representatives, and assigns, covenants with the grantee and ____[his / her]____ heirs, representatives, and assigns, as follows:

[Covenant of seisin]
(1) That grantor is lawfully seised ____[specify, e.g., in fee simple]____ of the described property;

[Covenant of right to convey]
(2) That grantor has the right to convey it;

[Covenant of warranty and quiet enjoyment]
(3) That grantor warrants and will defend the title and quiet enjoyment of the property against the lawful claims and demands of all persons;

[Covenant of further assurance]
(4) That grantor will do any further acts for the purpose of perfecting the title that the covenantees may reasonably require; and

[Covenant against encumbrances]
(5) That the estate is free from all liens and encumbrances except ____ [state matters excepted]____.

Comment: This provision contains all the title covenants enumerated in §9.2 and defined in §§9.5-9.10.

The first is a covenant of seisin. It is for use when the special covenant of seisin implied under CC §1113 is considered insufficient. The differences are explained in §9.6. This covenant may state that the grantor is lawfully seised or has good sufficient seisin. See 3 American Law of Property §12.127 (A. J. Casner ed 1952). However, because the rule in some states is that the simple covenant of seisin is not a representation or guaranty of the grantor's right or title (3 American Law of Property §12.27), the form makes the assurance explicit by stating that the grantor owns what he purports to convey.

The second is a covenant of the right to convey. This is generally held to be the exact equivalent of a covenant of seisin, but used for a different purpose. However, they are sometimes distinguished; therefore both have been expressed in this provision. The difference is explained in §9.9.

The third combines the covenants of warranty and quiet enjoyment. These covenants are discussed and contrasted in §9.8.

The fourth is a covenant for further assurance. For discussion, see §9.10.

The fifth is the covenant against encumbrances discussed in §9.7. If the parties are satisfied with the special covenant provided by CC §1113, no broader covenant is required and this provision is unnecessary. If a general covenant is desired, a form like this may be used. In either case, liens or encumbrances to which the property will remain subject at the close should be expressly excluded from the operation of the covenant. Unrecorded leases that an inspection would reveal limit the buyer's title, but, despite the buyer's knowledge, breach the seller's implied covenant against encumbrances under CC §1113. *Evans v Faught* (1965) 231 CA2d 698, 42 CR 133. The need for making the transfer subject to the lien of taxes or assessments is discussed in §9.7. Other exclusions frequently required are (1) mortgages or deeds of trust to which the property remains subject, (2) utility easements, (3) leases, and (4) deed restrictions (CC&Rs), although others (such as the impairments of marketable title discussed in §3.78) may be called for by the particular situation. An example of how to list these exceptions is provided in §9.22.

Covenants in the purchase and sale agreement that are to survive the deed should also be contained in the deed. Although the agreement's provision against merger (see §§3.66-3.67) preserves the buyer's rights, inclusion of the covenants in the deed permits subsequent purchasers to enforce them in an appropriate case either as covenants running with the land or as equitable servitudes (see §3.99).

III. REMEDIES FOR BREACH OF TITLE COVENANTS

A. What Constitutes Breach

§9.13   1. Of Covenant of Seisin

If the failure of title is due to an act of someone other than the grantor, the statutory covenant against prior conveyance is not breached. *Gaffey v Welk* (1920) 46 CA 385, 189 P 300. See, however, the broader covenant in §9.12 and discussion at §9.6 on general covenants of seisin, which are breached by any failure to have title.

The covenant refers only to prior transfers of estates in the land; a license does not breach the covenant, because it is not an estate in land. See *Shaw v Caldwell* (1911) 16 CA 1, 115 P 941. A water right, however, is an interest in land. *Lyles v Perrin* (1901) 134 C 417, 66 P 472. The covenant refers not only to the land itself but also to all property appurtenant to it. 3 American Law of Property §12.127 at 461 (A. J. Casner ed 1952). Because the covenantee's knowledge of defects in the covenantor's title does not bar an action for breach of the covenant, all limitations on title affecting the property should be enumerated in the grant and the covenant.

§9.14   2. Of Covenant Against Encumbrances

The existence of a lien for property taxes or assessments is a breach of the implied covenant against encumbrances, even if the payment is not delinquent. See §9.7. A mortgage or lien is also a breach of the covenant. The same is true of judgment liens (*Waggle v Worthy* (1887) 74 C 266, 15 P 831), restrictions on use (*Fraser v Bentel* (1911) 161 C 390, 119 P 509), building restrictions (*Tandy v Waesch* (1908) 154 C 108, 97 P 69), easements (*Goldstein v Hensly* (1906) 4 CA 444, 88 P 507), and unrecorded leases (*Evans v Faught* (1965) 231 CA2d 698, 42 CR 133). For other encumbrances under CC §1113, see *Evans v Faught, supra,* 231 CA2d at 706, 42 CR at 137.

A distinction must be made between encumbrances that affect title and those that affect only the physical condition of the land. The latter, such as a visible right of way, do not come within the implied covenant of CC §1113 because the parties are considered to have contracted with regard to visible physical encumbrances. An unrecorded lease, in contrast, constitutes a breach of the covenant, even if the grantee took with knowledge of its existence. *Evans v Faught, supra,* 231 CA2d 698, 42 CR 133.

§9.15   3. Of Covenant for Further Assurance

The covenant for further assurance requires the covenantor to take any further action to perfect the buyer's title that the buyer may reasonably require. See §9.10. Failure to do so within a reasonable time constitutes a breach. *Vance v Pena* (1871) 41 C 686. In contrast with covenants of warranty and of quiet enjoyment, which require only that the seller compensate the buyer if a third party has a superior title (see §9.8), the covenant for further assurance requires the seller to take affirmative action against the third party and makes failure to do so a breach. See *Zabriskie v Baudendistel* (NJ Ch 1890) 20 A 163, aff'd (1892) 50 NJ Eq 453, 26 A 455.

§9.16   4. Of Covenant of Warranty

The covenant of warranty is not breached until the buyer is evicted under paramount title. *Blackwell v Atkinson* (1859) 14 C 470. This occurs when there is actual eviction by process of law (*Norton v Jackson* (1855) 5 C 262; *Fowler v Smith* (1852) 2 C 39, 2 C 568) or the buyer or his successor is compelled to yield possession or to buy the superior title (*McCormick v Marcy* (1913) 165 C 386, 389, 132 P 449, 450).

§9.17   B. Damages

Civil Code §3304 provides:

The detriment caused by the breach of a covenant of "seisin," of "right to convey," of "warranty," or of "quiet enjoyment," in a grant of an estate in real property, is deemed to be:

1. The price paid to the grantor; or, if the breach is partial only, such proportion of the price as the value of the property affected by the breach bore at the time of the grant to the value of the whole property;

2. Interest thereon for the time during which the grantee derived no benefit from the property, not exceeding five years;

3. Any expenses properly incurred by the covenantee in defending his possession.

Additional damages may be awarded to cover costs and attorney fees paid by the buyer in a prior action to recover the possession of which he was deprived by the seller's breach. *Levitzky v Canning* (1867) 33 C 299.

Civil Code §3305 provides:

The detriment caused by the breach of a covenant against encumbrances in a grant of an estate in real property is deemed to be the amount which has been actually expended by the covenantee in extinguishing either the principal or interest thereof, not exceeding in the former case a proportion of the price paid to the grantor equivalent to the relative value at the time of the grant of the property affected by the breach, as compared with the whole, or, in the latter case, interest on a like amount.

Under CC §3305, unless the buyer alleges that he actually paid the encumbrance, he may recover only nominal damages. See *Woods v Bennett* (1919) 40 CA 34, 180 P 25. See also *Wright v Boggess* (1914) 24 CA 533, 141 P 1082, holding that no cause of action arises until the grantee pays the encumbrance.

Section 3305 applies only to encumbrances that may be satisfied by money payments. The damages recoverable for other encumbrances (*e.g.,* restrictions or leases) are determined under breach of contract rules and are measured by the reduction in market value resulting naturally and proximately from the existence and the continuance of the encumbrance. CC §3300; *Fraser v Bentel* (1911) 161 C 390, 119 P 509; *Evans v Faught* (1965) 231 CA2d 698, 42 CR 133. But see *Babb v Weemer* (1964) 225 CA2d 546, 553, 37 CR 533, 537, indicating in dictum that no damages were recoverable when the grantee knew of the encumbrance, and it was taken into account in determining the price.

C. Parties

§9.18   1. Who May Claim

Who may recover for breach of a title covenant depends in part on whether the covenant runs with the land.

Covenants of seisin and good title, of the right to convey, and against encumbrances do not run with the land; only the buyer may bring action for their breach. See Comment, *Covenants of Title Running With the Land in California,* 49 Calif L Rev 931 (1961). There have been some judicial attempts to extend the benefits of covenants of seisin and against encumbrances beyond the immediate buyer. See *Soderberg v Holt* (Utah 1935) 46 P2d 428; *Post v Campau* (Mich 1879) 3 NW 272; *Schofield v Iowa Homestead Co.* (Iowa 1871) 32 Iowa 317; 49 Calif L Rev at 943.

Covenants of warranty, for quiet enjoyment, and for further assurance run with the land; not only the buyer but also his successors may bring action. CC §§1462-1463. Moreover, CC §1463 appears to say that the buyer's covenant for the payment of taxes or assessments runs with the land, although it is likely that the framers of the statute had in mind only covenants made by lessees. The remote grantee's damages appear to be determined under CC §3304 and limited to the price paid the original grantor, plus interest and expenses incurred. *McCormick v Marcy* (1913) 165 C 386, 390, 132 P 449, 451.

§9.19 2. Parties Liable

The covenantor is liable to the covenantee on his title covenant whether or not the covenant runs with the land. *Barrows v Jackson* (1952) 112 CA2d 534, 247 P2d 99. He is also liable to anyone to whom the buyer expressly assigns the benefits of the covenant. CC §§954, 1458. He is liable to remote grantees if the covenant runs with the land, even in the absence of express assignment. CC §1460.

Aside from the covenantor, the only persons who are liable on his covenant are those who acquire the whole estate of the covenantor in all or some part of the property (CC §1465), provided the covenant runs with the land (see CC §1460), and the heirs and devisees of the covenantor to the extent of the land descended or devised to them (CC §1115).

The rules are different for covenants concerning the use of property covenants, conditions, and restrictions (CC&R's).

For a discussion of CC&Rs, see 2 Bowman, Ogden's Revised California Real Property Law, chap 23 (TI Corp-CEB 1975); Guide to California Subdivision Sales Law §§4.4-4.6, 4.22 (Cal CEB 1974).

§9.20 D. Statute of Limitations

Actions for breach of title covenants are contract actions subject to the four-year statute of limitations provided for by CCP §337. The time when the statute begins to run depends on the nature of the covenant. The times for the respective covenants are stated in §§9.6-9.10. For convenience, they are summarized here.

Covenant	*Time Begins When*
Of seisin and good title	Covenant is made
Against encumbrances	Covenant is made
Of warranty	Buyer or successor is evicted or compelled to buy the superior title, whichever occurs first
Of quiet enjoyment	Buyer or successor is evicted or compelled to buy the superior title, whichever occurs first
Of right to convey	Covenant is made
For further assurance	Buyer or successor is evicted or covenantor or his successor fails to comply with a reasonable demand, whichever occurs first

IV. AVOIDING EFFECT OF TITLE COVENANTS

§9.21   A. Quitclaim Deed

A seller wishing to avoid liability under title covenants may deliver the buyer a quitclaim deed. This deed contains no express or implied warranties about the seller's title; it simply passes whatever title he has. *Graff v Middleton* (1872) 43 C 341; *Klamath Land & Cattle Co. v Roemer* (1970) 12 CA3d 613, 91 CR 112. These deeds, however, may arouse suspicion that the seller is hiding something. Consequently, buyers sometimes do not want to accept a quitclaim, even when a title policy gives almost all the assurance needed. On the effect of a quitclaim deed on afteracquired title, see §9.10.

The deed obtained on a judicial sale is similar to a quitclaim and does not carry the covenants implied under CC §1113. See *Mains v City Title Ins. Co.* (1949) 34 C2d 580, 212 P2d 873. A probate sale, however, is not a judicial sale; the order is a confirmation, not an order for judicial sale, and the buyer may rely on the implied covenants. *Mains v City Title Ins. Co., supra.*

§9.22   B. "Restrained" Grant Deed

A grant deed without express covenants carries with it no covenants other than the two that are implied from the word "grant." CC §1113; see §9.5. Even recognizing that the implied covenants are of scant protection to the buyer in most situations, the seller may nonetheless want to negate even that much personal liability. He can do so by giving a "restrained" grant deed. The most common way to accomplish this restraint is to set out in the grant deed the matters to which the title is subject as in the following example.

A grants to *B* the following described property subject to:

(1) The lien of general and special city and county taxes for the fiscal year July 1, 1981–June 30, 1982;

(2) Covenants, conditions, and restrictions of record;

(3) Easement granted to The Pacific Telephone and Telegraph Co. by deed recorded at _____;

(4) Deed of trust to XYZ Title Company as Trustee, in which Charles White is beneficiary, recorded at _____; and

(5) Unrecorded lease to National Stores, dated January 1, 1980, for a term from January 1, 1980, to December 31, 1989, containing an option for renewal for a term ending December 31, 1999, to be exercised before

January 1, 1989, and an option to purchase the leased premises to be exercised before January 1, 1988.

Another way is to incorporate in the grant deed a general disclaimer of covenants:

A grants to *B*, but without warranty or covenant of any kind, express or implied, the following described property:

If the restraints consist of enumerating matters to which the title is subject, they need only list items that would otherwise constitute breach under the implied covenants of CC §1113. These implied covenants are discussed at §§9.5-9.7. For example, covenants, conditions, and restrictions of record need not be listed unless the seller himself, or any person claiming under him, subjected the property or suffered it to be subjected to those restrictions. This is because CC §1113 implies only a limited or special covenant.

Delinquent taxes or taxes for periods before close of escrow are usually prorated and charged to the seller, as discussed in Comment at §11.51. On the correct way to describe matters of record, see §8.15.

Making the deed subject to a lease containing an option to purchase will cloud the title for at least the period prescribed by CC §1213.5. The option will be shown as an exception in all title reports and policies unless the title company is satisfied that CC §1213.5 protects it or the tenant releases the option or is barred by judgment from exercising it. See §4.36. For a recital to be used in removing a cloud created by inadvertence, see §7.39.

§9.23   C. Title Insurance

Because title insurance ordinarily provides more comprehensive and financially secure protection for the buyer than any of the usual seller's covenants, most buyers are willing to forgo any title covenants if this insurance is provided.

Title insurance and title covenants can be combined. Suppose a property owner named as the insured under a title policy conveys property to a buyer by means of a full warranty deed, but no new title insurance is obtained in connection with the transaction. The new owner then suffers a loss because of a title defect that breaches the covenant and that preexisted the seller's acquisition of the property but was not disclosed in the title policy. If suit is brought against the seller on the covenant, it appears that the seller is covered under his own title insurance policy. Paragraph 2(b) of the conditions and stipulations in the California Land Title Association standard coverage policy provides for continuation of coverage after conveyance of title as long as the insured has liability by reason of covenants of warranty. See California Title Insurance Practice, Appendix B (Cal CEB 1980) for a form of CLTA standard coverage policy.

Title insurance does not negate covenants that are expressed in the deed or implied from it; the covenants constitute protection in addition to the title insurance. In practice, however, the buyer looks to his insurance protection rather than to the seller and conditions his obligation to purchase on title acceptable to him, evidenced by title insurance. For a proposed form for that purpose, see §3.55. If the title policy excludes an element on which the buyer has conditioned his obligation, he usually calls off the transaction.

10

Risk of Loss - Property Insurance

This chapter was originally published as chapter 13 in California Real Estate Sales Transactions (Cal CEB 1967), by Bert W. Levit and John B. Hook. It has been revised and updated by the CEB legal staff.

I. CALIFORNIA RULE ON RISK OF LOSS

§10.1   A. Uniform Vendor and Purchaser Risk Act

The Uniform Vendor and Purchaser Risk Act (CC §1662), adopted in 1947, was meant to eliminate doubt about when the risk of loss shifted from seller to buyer in California. See Comment, *Uniform Vendor and Purchaser Risk Act: Effect on California Law,* 36 Calif L Rev 476, 477 (1948). See also *Risk of Loss in Executory Land Sales Contracts,* 14 Colum J L & Soc Prob 453, 464 (1979). Civil Code §1662 provides:

Any contract hereafter made in this State for the purchase and sale of real property shall be interpreted as including an agreement that the parties shall have the following rights and duties, unless the contract expressly provides otherwise:

(a) If, when neither the legal title nor the possession of the subject matter of the contract has been transferred, all or a material part thereof is destroyed without fault of the purchaser or is taken by eminent domain, the vendor cannot enforce the contract, and the purchaser is entitled to recover any portion of the price that he has paid;

(b) If, when either the legal title or the possession of the subject matter of the contract has been transferred, all or any part thereof is destroyed without fault of the vendor or is taken by eminent domain, the purchaser is not thereby relieved from a duty to pay the price nor is he entitled to recover any portion thereof that he has paid.

This section shall be so interpreted and construed as to effectuate its general purpose to make uniform the law of those states which enact it.

The act specifies the circumstances under which the seller can enforce the purchase and sale agreement against the buyer or the buyer can recover what he has paid; neither "risk" nor "risk of loss" is mentioned. However, if the seller cannot enforce the agreement, he cannot expect the buyer to pay for a material loss. Therefore, under CC §1662, unless the agreement provides otherwise, the party in possession bears the risk of loss before the transfer of legal title. *Long v Keller* (1980) 104 CA3d 312, 163 CR 532. After transfer of legal title, if the seller is without fault, the risk is on the buyer no matter who is in possession. However, several problems of interpretation remain. See §§10.2-10.11.

Problems arise under the act most frequently when the buyer takes possession before title passes. See §10.6.

B. Material Loss Under CC §1662(a)

§10.2   1. Law in Absence of Agreement

Civil Code §1662(a) states that the seller cannot enforce the purchase agreement if all or a "material part" of the property is destroyed when neither title nor possession has been transferred. The act fails, however, to define "material."

To avoid the uncertainties and expenses of litigation over what constitutes a material loss, the purchase and sale agreement should include a definition.

The amount of damage that will make the loss material is best expressed in a dollar amount rather than as a percentage of loss or destruction. The amount of damage from destruction should be stated as the cost of repairing or replacing. Because the amount of damage could vary if depreciation is considered, it is preferable to specify in the agreement whether depreciation will be used in making the determination.

In determining whether a loss by eminent domain is material, it is not practical to use the cost of repairing or replacing. Reduction in market value is a better measure, because it takes into account inverse condemnation and other factors that affect the value of the remaining parcel.

The risk of loss by destruction can be covered by insurance. The insured may reduce premiums by taking deductible amounts at his own risk.

§10.3   2. Form: Definition of Material Loss

Form 10.3-1

[Insert in purchase and sale agreement, chap 3]

For the purposes of this agreement and for the application of California Civil Code section 1662(a) to the extent that it applies, a destruction is material if the cost of repairing or replacing it, without deduction for depreciation, exceeds the sum of $ _____, provided that, if the applicable building codes or other laws or regulations require work exceeding the repair or replacement of the actual damage, the cost shall be considered to include all the work. A taking by eminent domain is material if the diminution in market value exceeds the sum stated above.

Comment: The purposes and effects of this provision are discussed in §10.2.

C. Who Bears Risk of Nonmaterial Loss Under CC §1662(a)

§10.4   1. Law in Absence of Agreement

Civil Code §1662(a) applies only to situations in which all or a material part is destroyed or taken by eminent domain. What happens if there is a nonmaterial loss? The subsection implies that the seller can still enforce the contract. If he does, however, who must pay for the damage?

Under CC §1662(a) the seller bears the risk of a material loss; it would seem therefore the seller should also bear the risk of a nonmaterial loss as long as he is in possession and presumably has control over the property. See Comment, *Uniform Vendor and Purchaser Risk Act: Effect on California Law,* 36 Calif L Rev 476, 481 (1948). See also *Risk of Loss in Executory Land Sales Contracts,* 14 Colum J L & Soc Prob 453, 470 (1979). This approach was adopted in the New York version of the uniform act. In the New York act if the loss is nonmaterial, the buyer, although compelled to perform the contract, is entitled to a reduction of the purchase price to the extent of the loss. New York General Obligation Law §5-1311.

Because interpretation of the act is intended to be uniform, the courts might interpret CC §1662(a) to achieve the same result as provided expressly by the New York act. See 7 Williston, Contracts 975 n7 (3d ed 1963). However, it is best to insert in the purchase and sale agreement a clause expressly providing that the seller bears the risk of a nonmaterial loss and that the purchase price be reduced to the extent of the loss.

§10.5   2. Form: Risk of Nonmaterial Loss

Form 10.5-1

[Insert in purchase and sale agreement, chap 3]

If, when neither legal title nor possession of the subject matter of this contract has been transferred, a nonmaterial part of the subject matter is destroyed or is taken by eminent domain, neither Seller nor Buyer is thereby deprived of the right to enforce the contract; but if the nonmaterial part is destroyed without the fault of the Buyer or is taken by eminent domain, the Buyer is entitled to a reduction of the purchase price to the extent of the cost of repairing or replacing the damage from destruction or the diminution in value resulting from eminent domain.

Comment: The need for this provision is explained in §10.4. See the saving clause in §10.10.

D. Buyer's Assumption of Risk or Agreement To Insure

§10.6   1. Buyer's Possession Before Transfer of Title

The transfer of either title or possession shifts the risk of loss to the buyer. CC §1662(b); see §10.1. The point at which the risk of loss shifts can, however, be altered by the terms of the purchase and sale agreement. See §§10.7-10.8. In the usual transaction, the buyer's insurance coverage, whether obtained by taking over the seller's insurance or by acquiring his own, does not take effect until close of escrow. In this case the buyer is unprotected against the risk of loss that shifts to him if he takes possession before title passes or if agreement provisions place the risk on him before closing. See *Long v Keller* (1980) 104 CA3d 312, 163 CR 532. If he is to take possession before title passes, he should make certain that insurance coverage becomes effective on the date he takes possession rather than at the close of escrow. If the risk shifts to him as a result of a provision in the agreement, the insurance should be made effective when the agreement is executed or as soon after that as possible.

If the buyer is to take over the seller's insurance, he should require the seller to have the buyer named as an additional insured in the seller's existing policy and to furnish a certificate of insurance within a specified time. The certificate should show the extent of the coverage and the fact that the buyer has been named as an additional insured. If the insurer resists adding the buyer or if the coverage is inadequate, the buyer should obtain his own coverage. In most situations he may be better advised to obtain his own coverage anyway to make certain that it is tailored to his own needs.

The seller, too, must be concerned because his insurance may not protect him if the risk shifts to the buyer before the close of escrow. See Ins C §300; *Mackintosh v Agricultural Fire Ins. Co.* (1907) 150 C 440, 89 P 102; *Finkbohner v Glens Falls Ins. Co.* (1907) 6 CA 379, 92 P 318. When the buyer is to take possession before title passes, agreements sometimes require the buyer to insure. See §10.9.

§10.7   2. Form: Buyer's Assumption of Risk

Form 10.7-1

Buyer shall not, by reason of eminent domain or the destruction of all or any part of the property without Seller's fault, be relieved of the obligation to complete the purchase. Buyer shall bear the risk of all losses by destruction without fault of Seller or by eminent domain.

Comment: This provision requires the buyer to purchase not-withstanding any loss covered by CC §1662(a). Its utility is discussed in §10.6. For an additional caveat, see §10.10.

§10.8   3. Effect of Buyer's Agreement To Insure

Does a requirement that the buyer maintain insurance constitute an "express" provision under CC §1662 (see §10.1) and therefore shift the risk to the buyer? This question has not yet been decided by the California courts.

Cases decided before the enactment of CC §1662 indicate that an agreement to insure is evidence of an intent to assume the risk of loss. See *Ware v Security-First Nat'l Bank* (1936) 7 C2d 604, 61 P2d 936; *Kelly v Smith* (1933) 218 C 543, 24 P2d 471. In both cases, the buyer had the right of possession, but the court placed equal emphasis on the existence of the agreement to insure as evidence of an intent to assume the risk of loss. See 4 Witkin, Summary of California Law, *Equity* §§119-120 (8th ed 1973); Comment, *Risk of Loss Occurring Between Date of Contract to Sell Real Estate and Transfer of Legal Title,* 22 Calif L Rev 427 (1934).

If the courts decide that an insurance clause is an express provision shifting the risk of loss under CC §1662, the decision may have an important effect on the rights of the buyer who agrees to maintain insurance. For example, if the loss exceeds the insurance coverage, the buyer may then be required to pay the difference between the proceeds received from the insurance and the agreed price of the property. See Comment, *Uniform Vendor and Purchaser Risk Act: Effect on California Law,* 36 Calif L Rev 476, 478 (1948). Some risks (*e.g.,* earthquake and flood) are covered only at prohibitive rates. Moreover, the insurer may resist the buyer's claim on the ground that he lacks an insurable interest. See Ins C §286.

§10.9   4. Negotiating Buyer's Agreement To Insure

In addition to the problems discussed in §10.8, a provision requiring the buyer to insure is extremely difficult to draft. The advice of a competent insurance broker or counselor may be helpful, and the requirements of the lender or prospective lender should be ascertained.

One problem arises in deciding what perils are to be covered. It is seldom possible to anticipate every risk, the premiums for some of them may be considered prohibitive, and the descriptive names given to various policies or risks may confuse persons outside the field. See §10.14.

The amount of coverage is another problem. A fixed dollar amount may be appropriate in some situations; in others, it may be better to require coverage "for the full undepreciated value of the improvements" (or variations of that language).

Some lawyers specify that the insurance must be carried by companies with certain circulated ratings, such as those contained in Best's Insurance Reports. Best has two ratings. One shows assets (from Class I with assets of less than $250,000 to Class XV with $100,000,000 or more). The policy holders' ratings give evaluations based on success in underwriting, economy of management, adequate reserves, adequate resources, and sound investments. On the latter scale there are six ratings: A+ (excellent and above the average of all the companies in the excellent rating group), A (excellent), B+ (very good), B (good), C+ (fairly good), and C (fair).

Disposition of the proceeds in the event of loss may also be difficult to negotiate or draft. If title has not yet passed, the seller may be reluctant to see the proceeds go outright to the buyer. The buyer, on the other hand, may be eager to commence restoration before escrow closes. If the parties agree to entrust the funds to a trustee or escrow holder, the agent's requirements must be ascertained and all contingencies must be anticipated (*e.g.*, disposition of the proceeds if the buyer defaults or exercises a permitted disapproval in the agreement).

§10.10   E. Form: Code Governs Except as Expressly Agreed

Form 10.10-1

[*Insert in purchase and sale agreement, chap 3*]

Except as expressly provided in ____[*designate provisions relating to risk of loss or right to enforce after destruction or condemnation*]____ **, this agreement shall be governed by the provisions of California Civil Code section 1662 in effect at the date of this agreement.**

Comment: At least one court has held that any provision relating to risk of loss makes the entire Uniform Vendor and Purchaser Risk Act inapplicable in that the parties had provided otherwise. *World Exhibit Corp. v City Bank Farmers Trust Co.* (App Div 1946) 61 NYS2d 889, 893 (construing a statute similar to CC §1662). To meet this problem, it is desirable to state that the act will apply to the extent it is not in conflict with the provisions of the contract.

§10.11   F. Effect of Material Loss After Breach by Buyer

Civil Code §1662(a) leaves unspecified the effect of a material loss during a period when the buyer is in default. *Tinker v McLellan* (1958) 165 CA2d 291, 331 P2d 464, although not directly based on CC §1662(a), indicates that the buyer in default may not be able to avoid his obligation when the property is destroyed.

§10.12   II. TRANSFER OF SELLER'S PROPERTY INSURANCE TO BUYER

In addition to protection against loss pending the transfer of title (see §§10.1-10.11), the buyer needs protection against loss from destruction of the property after title passes to him. He may protect himself by purchasing his own insurance (see §§10.13-10.16) or by taking an assignment of the seller's insurance. Generally, it is better for the buyer to obtain his own insurance.

If the buyer expects to take over the seller's insurance, an express transfer of the policy is necessary because an insurance policy covering real property does not pass with the title on the sale of the property insured. *Alexander v Security-First Nat'l Bank* (1936) 7 C2d 718, 62 P2d 735. Under Ins C §305, "the mere transfer of subject matter insured does not transfer the insurance, but suspends it until the same person becomes the owner of both the insurance and the subject matter insured."

Even when the insurance policy does not expressly limit its assignability, the courts have held that the consent of the insurer must be obtained for an express assignment of the policy. *Bergson v Builders Ins. Co.* (1869) 38 C 541, 543.

The courts will not invalidate a policy of hazard insurance despite an assignment of the policy without the insurer's consent before the loss if the insurer has suffered no prejudice from lack of notice and would have consented if notice had been given, and if invalidation of the policy would result in a forfeiture. *University of Judaism v Transamerica Ins. Co.* (1976) 61 CA3d 937, 132 CR 907.

Fire insurance policies covering California property must be written on the California Standard Form Fire Insurance Policy. Ins C §2070. A policy which includes coverage against other perils need not use the standard form if the policy in its entirety is substantially equivalent to the standard form. Ins C §2070. The provisions of the required policy are prescribed by Ins C §2071. The form provides that assignment of the policy is not valid except with the written consent of the insurance company. However, the insurer may waive consent (*Limsky v Scottish Union & Nat'l Ins. Co.* (1924) 68 CA 688, 229 P 1017; *Lewis v Reed* (1920) 48 CA 742, 192 P 335) or estop itself to deny that consent was given (*Tucker v American Ins. Co.* (1932) 123 CA 316, 11 P2d 55). Express consent is better assurance to the buyer.

Ordinarily the details of obtaining consent from the insurance company are handled through the real estate broker or insurance broker. Insurance companies use a standard form providing for the assignment.

The requirement of the insurer's consent to an assignment does not apply to assignments after loss; any right of the insured to insurance proceeds resulting from loss may be assigned without the consent of the insurer. Ins C §520; *Greco v Oregon Mut. Fire Ins. Co.* (1961) 191 CA2d 674, 12 CR 802; *Vierneisel v Rhode Island Ins. Co.* (1946) 77 CA2d 229, 175 P2d 63.

III. COUNSELING BUYER ON PURCHASE OF PROPERTY INSURANCE

§10.13   A. Need To Examine Available Coverage

Property and casualty insurance companies sell insurance and service their policies through a variety of representatives, such as salaried employees, agents who represent one company exclusively, independent agents who represent several companies, and insurance brokers.

Because of the changing and increasingly complex nature of the insurance business, a property owner should seek the services of a competent insurance broker or agent. The lawyer should encourage this and may, in addition, look through the policy, raise questions about it, and consult with the broker to point out important aspects of the transaction and to ask about the effects of insurance clauses that are not clear. The lawyer should, for his or her own protection, make clear the limits of an attorney's competence and functions concerning the insurance aspects of the transaction. A letter to this effect is less disputable evidence than oral communication.

On independent insurance counselors, see §10.16.

B. Coverage Available

§10.14　1. Perils Covered

Coverage for a great many perils is readily available through "package" or "multiple peril" policies. "Homeowner" policies commonly cover fire, windstorm, hail, lightning, water damage, theft, liability, damage to glass or contents, and cost of housing during reconstruction. "All risks" policies, although broader, exclude certain perils. Particular business risks are beyond the scope of this chapter.

§10.15　2. Dollar Limits

With the present trend of increased litigation and exposure to liability, all homeowners should obtain liability insurance with substantial limits. The basic liability limit on most "homeowner" policies is low, and for a small increase in premium, liability limits can be raised substantially.

To be able to realize enough from the insurance proceeds after a loss to rebuild the property, the property owner should consider insuring for replacement cost rather than actual cash value. This coverage is more expensive but it precludes subtracting depreciation when adjusting a loss.

When the sale closes, the limits that the client may need at the time of the casualty are often unknown. Therefore, the coverage should be reviewed from time to time as costs and experiences change.

§10.16　C. Independent Insurance Counselors

Independent insurance consultants or analysts are a result of the size and complexity of the insurance business. Unlike insurance brokers, the consultants do not sell or receive any commissions from the sale of insurance. Instead, they are paid a fee by the insured. As a rule, these consultants can be used effectively and economically only by large organizations that carry substantial portfolios of insurance.

The consulting firm makes an audit of the insurance presently held by the client, including an inspection of buildings, equipment, and merchandise, and a review of leases and other agreements to determine exposure to loss. Consultants look for errors in rates, overlapping coverages, overinsurance and underinsurance, hidden exposure to risks assumed in leases and other agreements, and inadequate records preventing special rating advantages. Sometimes their advice is valuable in drafting leases.

IV. COUNSELING HOLDERS OF SECURED INTERESTS

§10.17   A. Protecting the Secured Lender

The interest of the secured lender should be protected by insurance on the property by which the debt is secured. Lending institutions always require that sufficient insurance be maintained by the borrower to cover the amount of the obligation, and that the insurance proceeds be payable to the lender to the extent of its interest. This protection is especially important in a California purchase money deed of trust because the value of the property represents the lender's sole security and source of repayment in the event of default. CCP §580b; *Krone v Goff* (1975) 53 CA3d 191, 127 CR 390; 3 Witkin, Summary of California Law, *Security Transactions in Real Property* §117 (8th ed 1973); California Mortgage and Deed of Trust Practice, chap 4 (Cal CEB 1979).

Although a lender may obtain its own policy covering its separate insurable interest in the property, a single policy is usually written covering the owner and containing a clause in favor of the lender. In this way, the interests of both parties are protected under one policy at a lower cost, as no charge is made for the lender's coverage.

Commercial lenders customarily require the borrower to insure the property as a condition of the loan, and failure to maintain the insurance in force places the borrower in default under the deed of trust. The lender keeps the original policy, and the borrower gets a copy.

Most deeds of trust provide that insurance proceeds either be used to repair the property or be applied to the unpaid loan balance, at the lender's option. In *Schoolcraft v Ross* (1978) 81 CA3d 75, 146 CR 57, the court held that the lender must exercise its option in good faith, and to the extent the security has not been impaired, the proceeds must be used to repair the property.

§10.18   B. Loss Payable Clauses

The usual loss payable clause in an insurance policy does not adequately protect the interest of a secured lender because any act of the owner that would void the insurance also voids the rights of the lender. See Ins C §171.

To avoid this problem lenders usually require a further lender's loss payable provision or endorsement, also known as a mortgage clause. A commonly used lender's loss payable endorsement is Board of Underwriters of the Pacific Form 438 BFU NS. Such a provision constitutes a separate contract between the lender and the insured (see, *e.g., Seccombe v Glens Falls Inc. Co.* (1920) 45 CA 611, 188 P 305) and offers greater protection to the lender than the loss payable clause because the insurer cannot interpose defenses to liability against the secured lender on the ground that some act or neglect of the owner invalidated the policy. The insurer is not precluded by the clause from raising defenses against the owner's claim.

Institutional lenders often obtain special provisions or endorsements that give lenders certain additional protections not provided for in the more commonly used lender's loss payable endorsement. Some carry separate protection against a borrower's failure to insure.

11

C. Darrell Sooy

Escrow and Closing the Sale

C. DARRELL SOOY, B.S., 1966 University of California (Berkeley); J.D., 1969, Hastings College of the Law. Mr. Sooy, of the San Francisco law firm of Charles D. Sooy & C. Darrell Sooy Law Corporation, specializes in real estate lending.

I. ELEMENTS OF ESCROW

§11.1   A. Definition

The word "escrow" is derived from the Old French *escroe* or *escroue* meaning a roll of writings. The modern English counterpart of *escroe* is "scroll."

Common law attached two conditions to the scroll or other writing, usually a deed, for it to be termed an escrow. First, the writing had to be in the possession of a third party, being deposited there by the grantor, promisor, or obligor, and secondly, the future delivery of the writing to the grantee, promisee, or obligee by the third party had to be subject to the performance of a condition. California codified the common law definition in 1872 as Civil Code § 1057.

Today the term "escrow" generally applies to the entire transaction of depositing a writing with a third party to be delivered on the performance of a condition, and not just to the writing itself. Fin C § 17003.

The discussion of escrow in this chapter is limited to transfers of title to real property. (An escrow can be utilized to transfer tangible or intangible personal property, and must be used to transfer liquor licenses. Bus & P C § 24074.)

§11.2   B. Reasons for Escrow

The parties to a transfer of real property require assurance that they will receive what they have bargained for when they part with their respective considerations. The buyer will not be willing to pay the purchase price until he is guaranteed he will receive satisfactory title, and the seller will not transfer his title until the purchase price is paid. Moreover, the financing arrangements usually require that the purchase price be paid before the transfer of title because the money is needed to pay off the existing loan on the property. At the same time, the lender will want a senior lien against the buyer's property when it advances the loan funds, which may represent the bulk of the purchase price.

This apparent impasse is resolved by the use of escrow which has conditional delivery features; all parties can deposit their respective considerations with instructions to the escrow holder to deliver only on performance of the other party's obligations. This allows the escrow holder concurrently to perform all the conditions required to consummate the sale, or sale and loan transaction. The use of an escrow holder also provides someone reliable to perform the necessary clerical tasks entailed in a real property sale, such as obtaining title insurance, securing pay-off demands from existing lien holders, and prorating taxes, interest, and rents.

C. Legal Requirements for a Valid Escrow

§11.3   1. Enforceable Contract Between the Parties

An essential element of escrow is the irrevocability of the deposit of both the deed and the purchase money. Under common law this irrevocability was assumed in the escrow transaction. However, early in California legal history, the deposit with a third person, with directions to that person to deliver only on performance of a condition, without an underlying agreement between the parties to convey title, was held to be a revocable offer and not an escrow. *Fitch v Bunch* (1866) 30 C 208. This decision judicially created the need for an enforceable contract betweeen the parties to render an escrow irrevocable in California.

§11.4   a. Escrow Instructions as Underlying Contract

The deposit of a deed or money into escrow is irrevocable only if there is an enforceable underlying contract between the buyer and seller. See §11.3. In the typical situation, the underlying contract supporting the escrow will be escrow instructions signed by the buyer and seller and delivered to the escrow holder. These may be either separate instructions signed by buyer and seller respectively, or they may be joint escrow instructions signed by both buyer and seller as is common in Southern California. *Caras v Parker* (1957) 149 CA2d 621, 309 P2d 104. If separate (or unilateral) escrow instructions are given, as is the practice in Northern California, both sets must be substantially identical in their terms before they can support a valid escrow. *Neher v Kauffman* (1925) 197 C 674, 242 P 713.

Insofar as the escrow holder is concerned, the escrow instructions signed by the buyer and seller and delivered to the escrow holder become the underlying contract making the deposit of the deed and money irrevocable. This is true even if, as is usually the case, the buyer and seller have first executed an enforceable purchase and sale agreement, because the escrow holder is not concerned with any agreement that is outside of escrow and not evidenced by the escrow instructions. *Schaefer v Manufacturers Bank* (1980) 104 CA3d 70, 163 CR 402; *Contini v Western Title Ins. Co.* (1974) 40 CA3d 536, 115 CR 257; *Lee v Title Ins. & Trust Co.* (1968) 264 CA2d 160, 70 CR 378. In the absence of an underlying purchase and sale agreement, matching escrow instructions signed by both buyer and seller may independently form a purchase and sale agreement subject to specific performance. See *Spangler v Castello* (1956) 147 CA2d 49, 304 P2d 752. On the effect of inconsistencies between the escrow instructions and the purchase and sale agreement, see §11.39.

§11.5   b. Purchase and Sale Agreement as Underlying Contract

The purchase and sale agreement, even in the absence of escrow instructions, can support a valid escrow. If the seller, for example, deposits a deed with a third party as escrow holder, the deposit is irrevocable if an enforceable purchase and sale agreement has been entered into. As far as the escrow holder is concerned, however, the deposit is not irrevocable unless joint or matching escrow instructions have been signed and deposited or the purchase and sale agreement has itself been deposited with the escrow holder. The reason for this is that the escrow holder is not concerned with any agreements that are outside the escrow. See §11.4. A distinction thus must be made between the rights of the buyer and seller as evidenced by the purchase and sale agreement and the duties and responsibilities of the escrow holder as evidenced by the escrow instructions (although the purchase and sale agreement may also serve as escrow instructions if deposited with the escrow holder for that purpose). For example, mutual cancellation of an escrow will not necessarily terminate the parties' rights and duties under the purchase and sale agreement. *Cohen v Shearer* (1980) 108 CA3d

939, 167 CR 10. See §11.34 on the distinction between the purchase and sale agreement and escrow instructions.

Option agreements can also support a valid escrow as long as the option agreement is irrevocable (an option agreement given for a valid consideration is such). See, *e.g., Caras v Parker* (1957) 149 CA2d 621, 309 P2d 104. Option agreements unsupported by consideration, and therefore revocable, if made irrevocable by being exercised before revocation, can also be used as the foundation to support a valid escrow. See §4.10. Any lack of mutuality of remedy in option agreements is not a bar to their use as the underlying contract. *Feisthamel v Campbell* (1921) 55 CA 774, 205 P 25.

§11.6   2. Conditional Delivery

To constitute an escrow, documents (*e.g.*, a grant deed) or funds must be deposited with a third party (see §11.7), the escrow holder, to be delivered on the performance of a condition or conditions. CC §1057. It is the satisfaction of the condition that triggers the delivery by the escrow holder.

§11.7   3. Relinquishment of Control

No valid escrow exists unless the parties relinquish all control and dominion over the respective items, typically the grantor's deed and the grantee's purchase money, which they deposit with the escrow holder. *Kenney v Parks* (1899) 125 C 146, 57 P 772. A reservation of control over a deposited instrument, whether or not exercised, will negate the existence of an escrow and any later delivery on performance of the specified condition will be ineffective to transfer title. *Kenney v Parks, supra.*

D. Parties to Escrow

§11.8   1. Buyer and Seller

The primary parties to a real property sale escrow are always the buyer of the property and its current owner, the seller. There may be other parties to the escrow. See §§11.9-11.12.

§11.9   2. Lender

Most real property sales involve third party financing, thus making lenders additional parties to the escrow. Typically, there will be two lenders concerned with a sales escrow: the buyer's lender, who is supplying the bulk of the purchase money, and the seller's lender, whose loan is being paid off. Escrow instructions of the seller's lender are customarily only a pay-off demand letter sent to the escrow holder specifying the amount required to pay off the loan, while the buyer's lender will prepare more formal escrow instructions. See §11.76 for form. See chap 6 on practices of financial institutions.

3. Escrow Holder

§11.10   a. Relationship to Buyer and Seller

After escrow has opened (see §11.13 on opening of escrow) but before all the conditions for the close of escrow have been met, the escrow holder is a dual agent for both the buyer and the seller. *Riff v Mayhew* (1949) 90 CA2d 712, 203 P2d 812. After the conditions of the escrow have been complied with, the role of the escrow holder changes from being a dual agent for both of the parties to being an agent for each of the parties with respect to their particular aspect of the escrow (*i.e.*, agent for the seller regarding the funds and agent for the buyer regarding the deed). *Shreeves v Pearson* (1924) 194 C 699, 230 P 448.

The status of the escrow holder is a limited agency, rather than a general agency. Normally, the obligations of the escrow holder are only to comply with the instructions of the parties. *Axley v Transamerica Title Ins. Co.* (1978) 88 CA3d 1, 151 CR 570; *Lee v Title Ins. & Trust Co.* (1968) 264 CA2d 160, 70 CR 378; *Blackburn v McCoy* (1934) 1 CA2d 648, 37 P2d 153. Because the escrow holder's obligations are those of a limited agent, there is no liability for his failure to do something not required by the escrow instructions, or for a loss incurred while obediently following the instructions. *Lee v Title Ins. & Trust Co., supra.*

The escrow holder is under no duty to inform either principal regarding the other party's documents or instructions. *Gordon v D & G Escrow Corp.* (1975) 48 CA3d 616, 122 CR 150. (No information concerning the existence or terms of an escrow should be given to persons not parties to the escrow.) It is not settled that each of the principals to the escrow has a right to see the instructions of the other party. In practice many escrow holders refuse to disclose the instructions or documents to the other party. See *Shiver v Lib-*

erty Building-Loan Ass'n (1940) 16 C2d 296, 308, 106 P2d 4, 10 (dissenting opinion). Because there is no duty of disclosure regarding the other party's documents or instructions, the contents of such instructions and documents are generally not imputed to the other party. *Rice v Taylor* (1934) 220 C 629, 32 P2d 381.

The limited agency status of the escrow holder does produce a limited imputation to his principals of knowledge possessed by the escrow holder, and a limited duty of disclosure by the escrow holder to his principals. Generally, a principal is charged only with notice of the facts appearing from the papers contained in his escrow file, with certain exceptions in fraud situations. *Kroeker v Hurlbert* (1940) 38 CA2d 261, 101 P2d 101. The escrow holder's duty to disclose cannot be generalized sufficiently to define it because it varies with the facts of the situation. Compare *Amen v Merced County Title Co.* (1962) 58 C2d 528, 25 CR 65, with *Lee v Title Ins. & Trust Co.*, *supra*, 264 CA2d 160, 70 CR 378. See also 2 Miller & Starr, Current Law of California Real Estate §§11:50, 12:103 (rev ed 1977).

§11.11   b. Who Can Act as Escrow Holder

The majority of real property escrow transactions are handled by title companies in Northern California and by title companies or by independent escrow companies in Southern California. The third most common group handling escrows are institutional lenders who use their own escrow department or a subsidiary service corporation when they are financing the purchase. Attorneys and real estate brokers may also act as escrow holders subject to certain limitations.

Independent escrow companies are corporations licensed and regulated by the Commissioner of Corporations under the escrow law. Fin C §§17000-17654. The commissioner has adopted numerous regulations covering the activities of independent escrow companies. See 10 Cal Adm C §§1700-1753. The escrow law requires licensed escrow companies to maintain records (Fin C §17404), supply an audit report to the Commissioner of Corporations (Fin C §17406), keep escrow funds in a separate trust account (Fin C §17409), and to obtain fidelity bonds on officers and employees having access to funds (Fin C §17203.1). A violation of any of these requirements constitutes a misdemeanor (Fin C §17011) except for certain acts of fraud which are considered felony offenses (Fin C §17414).

The Commissioner of Corporations has the power to enforce the escrow law by ordering discontinuance of business operations (Fin C §17415), revoking or suspending the escrow company's license (Fin C §17608), taking possession of the property and business of an escrow company (Fin C §17621), or seeking a liquidation of the business (Fin C §17635).

Banks, savings and loan associations, insurance companies, title companies, real estate brokers, and attorneys may also act as escrow holders without being licensed or regulated as independent escrow companies because they are exempt from the provisions of the escrow law. Fin C §17006. The exemption for attorneys applies only to those not actively engaged in conducting an escrow agency, and real estate brokers can act only while performing acts in the course of or incidental to their real estate business. See §2.13. The exemption scheme was upheld in *Escrow Instit. of Cal. v Pierno* (1972) 24 CA3d 361, 100 CR 880. No other persons or entities can handle escrows for compensation. Fin C §17200.

§11.12   4. Attorneys and Brokers

Normally, unless acting as the escrow holder, neither the buyer's nor seller's attorney is a party to the escrow. This is also true of the real estate broker involved in the sale. Consequently, neither the broker nor the attorneys for the parties are entitled to give instructions to the escrow holder or to amend the buyer's or seller's instructions unless specifically authorized to do so by a party to the escrow. *Moss v Minor Properties, Inc.* (1968) 262 CA2d 847, 69 CR 341. Attorneys drafting escrow instructions may sometimes provide in the instructions to be signed by their client that the attorney is authorized to sign amendments to the instructions.

Neither the broker nor the attorneys are entitled to copies of the parties' instructions except as authorized by the parties.

II. CONSEQUENCES OF ESCROW

§11.13   A. When Escrow Opens; When Escrow Closes

The escrow holder's duties and the consequences of escrow depend on whether escrow has been opened, is proceeding, or has been closed. Although brokers, in Northern California in particular, may refer to escrow as being opened when a preliminary title report has been issued and an escrow number assigned by the title company, escrow is not actually opened until there has been an irrevocable deposit of documents and funds with the escrow holder to be delivered on the occurrence of a condition. CC §1607. The existence of an enforceable underlying purchase and sale agreement may make the deposit irrevocable (at least as between the buyer and seller, see §11.5), however, escrow generally is not opened until either joint escrow instructions or matching separate escrow instructions have been signed by both the buyer and the seller and deposited with the escrow holder. See, *e.g., Montgomery v Bank of America* (1948) 85 CA2d 559, 193 P2d 475.

The close of escrow is generally when all of the conditions to the transfer of the documents and the funds have occurred. At common law, this was when the conditions for the delivery of the seller's deed and the disbursement of the buyer's funds had occurred. Close of escrow is often now defined as the recording of the grant deed, thus changing somewhat the common law rule. See §11.84.

Before the opening of escrow, the escrow holder is the agent of only the party who has deposited documents or funds; during escrow, the escrow holder is the limited agent of both the buyer and the seller (see §11.10); after the close of escrow, the escrow holder is the seller's agent with respect to the funds and the buyer's agent with respect to the deed.

B. Effect on Title and Possession

§11.14   1. Before Performance of Conditions

It is often necessary to determine who has title to the items deposited in escrow at some point during an escrow transaction. Before the conditions specified in the escrow instructions are performed, title to any item deposited in escrow remains in the party who deposited it; the buyer retains title to the purchase money and the seller retains title to and possession of the property. *Love v White* (1961) 56 C2d 192, 14 CR 442; *Heney v Pesoli* (1895) 109 C 53, 41 P 819. Title is important in determining who bears the risk of loss if property is destroyed (CC §1662) and when a creditor can acquire a lien on money or property a debtor will receive at the close of escrow. See chap 10 on risk of loss. In the latter situation, a creditor of the buyer cannot acquire a lien on the property and the seller's creditor cannot reach the purchase money before performance of the escrow conditions. *Whitney v Sherman* (1918) 178 C 435, 173 P 931.

§11.15   a. Effect of Premature Delivery or Return to Depositor

Because a depositor retains title to what he deposits in escrow until performance of the escrow conditions, any premature delivery by the escrow holder to the other party is a void transfer, which does not pass title to the recipient. *Greenzweight v Title Guar. & Trust Co.* (1934) 1 C2d 577, 36 P2d 186. The seller can quiet title to the property if his deed was delivered to the buyer before performance, and the buyer can recover the purchase money from the seller if it has been delivered prematurely. *Kish v Bay Counties Title Guar. Co.* (1967) 254 CA2d 725, 62 CR 494.

Even though the depositor retains title, the other party has an equitable interest in the other's deposit, subject to performance of the escrow conditions. *Osborn v Osborn* (1954) 42 C2d 358, 267 P2d 333. The return of a deposit to the depositor before termination of the escrow will not prevent the other party from acquiring title to the deposit after performance of the conditions.

§11.16   b. Embezzlement or Loss of Funds

The risk of loss on embezzlement of a deposit in escrow by acts of the escrow holder falls on the party who held title at the time of loss. *Pagan v Spencer* (1951) 104 CA2d 588, 232 P2d 323; *Crum v City of Los Angeles* (1930) 110 CA 508, 514, 294 P 430, 432. Before performance of conditions specified in the escrow instructions, the buyer suffers from the loss of his purchase money deposit; he cannot rely on an embezzled or lost payment into escrow as his performance and compel the seller to convey title to the property. *Shreeves v Pearson* (1924) 194 C 699, 230 P 448.

The rule on who has title to deposits in escrow changes on performance of the escrow conditions (see §11.17); after performance the seller bears the risk of loss of the purchase money. See *Greenzweight v Title Guar. & Trust Co.* (1934) 1 C2d 577, 36 P2d 186.

The rule regarding risk of loss assumes that both the buyer and seller are innocent parties. If either party's negligence is the direct or proximate cause of the loss, then that party must bear the risk of loss. *Majors v Butler* (1950) 99 CA2d 370, 221 P2d 994. If negligence by both parties causes the loss, then the rules of comparative negligence apparently will apportion the loss, but there is no case law on this point.

2. On Performance of Conditions

§11.17   a. Delivery Immaterial to Title

The depositor's title to what he had deposited in escrow passes to the other party when the conditions specified in the escrow instructions have been performed. This transfer of title is automatic: actual physical delivery by the escrow holder is immaterial on the issue of title. *Hagge v Drew* (1945) 27 C2d 368, 165 P2d 461; *Andover Land Co. v Hoffman* (1968) 264 CA2d 87, 70 CR 38. (This is the true close of escrow, and subsequent delivery of the deed, and money, etc., is merely a ministerial act of the escrow holder as agent.)

§11.18   b. Waiver of Conditions

Determining whether the escrow conditions have or have not been performed, in order to know when title has been transferred, is resolved by examining the particular escrow instructions.

A waiver of condition can be a substitute for its performance. It has been held that a transfer of title occurs when all the conditions to be performed by the transferee have been performed, and the escrow holder makes an actual delivery, despite the fact the conditions to be performed by the other party have not been performed. *Kish v Bay Counties Title Guar. Co.* (1967) 254 CA2d 725, 62 CR 494 (title passed despite failure to create security interest for protection of grantee when grantee was content to keep title despite condition's nonoccurrence). The basis for this rule is that a party to an escrow may waive a condition created for his protection.

§11.19   c. Doctrine of Relation Back

An exception to the general rule regarding transfer of title in escrow is the equitable doctrine of relation back. This doctrine provides that, when great hardship will be suffered by a party to an escrow by application of the rule that title does not pass until performance of the escrow conditions, the actual delivery by the escrow holder "relates back" to the date of the original deposit in escrow.

The doctrine of relation back is usually applied in favor of the buyer to defeat interests in the property acquired during the escrow period by third parties who had knowledge or notice of the escrow or the rights of the grantee. *McDonald v Huff* (1888) 77 C 279, 19 P 499. The doctrine, being equitable in nature, is not applied against third parties who acquired interests without knowledge or notice. *Hibberd v Smith* (1885) 67 C 547, 4 P 473.

C. Escrow Holder's Duties

§11.20   1. Fiduciary Responsibilities

An escrow holder assumes the duties and responsibilities of a fiduciary to the parties to the escrow. *Common Wealth Ins. Systems, Inc. v Kersten* (1974) 40 CA3d 1014, 115 CR 653. The escrow holder is bound to use good faith in dealing with the parties and exercise ordinary skill in the performance of his duties. The escrow holder's primary duty is to comply strictly with the terms and conditions of the escrow instructions, notwithstanding any unilateral attempt to change or revoke instructions. But see §11.22. The doctrine of substantial performance does not apply. *Todd v Vestermark* (1956) 145 CA2d 374, 302 P2d 347.

§11.21   2. Time for Performance

One problem escrow holders may face in performing their duties is the effectiveness of performance tendered after the time for performance specified in the instructions has lapsed. Ordinarily, the escrow holder is not authorized to act on a late performance and must return the funds and documents on demand to the party depositing them. This reflects the right of a party to terminate a contract not performed on time by the other party, if time is of the essence. However, *Williams Plumbing Co. v Sinsley* (1975) 53 CA3d 1027, 126 CR 345, casts some doubt on this right to terminate. But see *Nash v Superior Court* (1978) 86 CA3d 690, 150 CR 394. Escrow instructions should specify the duty of the escrow holder with respect to time for performance. See §11.62.

§11.22   3. Inconsistent Demands; Interpleader

When an escrow holder is faced with apparently conflicting instructions or claims by the parties to an escrow, he can initiate an action (or cross-complain in an existing action) to interplead the conflicting claimants and deposit with the court the money and documents in his possession. Subject to the court's discretion, the escrow holder can recover his costs and reasonable attorney's fees in such an action. CCP §386.6.

This situation should be distinguished from one in which claims are made by one *not* a party to the escrow. The escrow holder's duty is to comply strictly with the instructions of his principals; he acts at his peril if he interpleads funds because of a third party claim instead of following the instructions of the party to the escrow. (A typical example would be the claim or demand of a broker against funds of the seller when the seller refuses to instruct the escrow holder to pay that claim. The duty of the escrow holder is to follow the seller's instructions; an interpleader is neither called for nor proper.)

An escrow holder, put on notice of a possible error in the instructions by one party, should hold up the close of escrow until the apparent error is clarified when the instructions authorize the holder to stop the escrow. *Diaz v United Cal. Bank* (1977) 71 CA3d 161, 139 CR 314.

§11.23   4. Liability

Liability of the escrow holder for the actual damages suffered by either party to the escrow proximately caused by the escrow holder is based on either of two theories: breach of contract or negligent performance of its duties as a fiduciary. *Common Wealth Ins. Sys., Inc. v Kersten* (1974) 40 CA3d 1014, 115 CR 653. Actual damage may be a party's costs and attorney's fees incurred to correct a clerical error of the escrow holder. *Cook v Redwood Empire Title Co.* (1969) 275 CA2d 452, 79 CR 888.

The statute of limitations on the breach of contract cause of action is four years if the instructions are written, and two years if oral. CCP §§337, 339. The statute of limitations on the negligent performance of fiduciary duties is two years. *Amen v Merced County Title Co.* (1962) 58 C2d 528, 25 CR 65.

The escrow holder will incur liability to any injured parties for intentional tortious conduct, such as conversion when the escrow holder embezzles escrow funds.

The escrow holder may also be held liable for actual damages to nonparties in an escrow transaction. Such causes of action against an escrow holder generally follow a third-party beneficiary theory.

They can arise when a third party, typically a creditor of the seller, is granted an interest in the proceeds held in escrow by an agreement outside of the escrow of which the escrow holder is informed, but the escrow holder fails to pay over the proceeds to the creditor on the close of escrow. *Builders' Control Serv. of N. Cal., Inc. v North Am. Title Guar. Co.* (1962) 205 CA2d 68, 22 CR 712.

§ 11.24   5. Provisions Limiting Liability of Escrow Holder

Escrow holders who have their own printed form of escrow instructions (see §11.35) often include various exculpatory clauses. Some escrow holders might insist that these clauses be incorporated in any individually prepared escrow instructions submitted to them. Exculpatory clauses required by an escrow holder must be analyzed carefully by the party's attorney to see if any important protections or rights are being waived. Typical exculpatory provisions are discussed in §§11.25-11.28.

§11.25   a. Right of Escrow Holder To Commingle Funds

Institutional escrow holders do not want to maintain individual bank accounts for each escrow transaction they handle; their instructions therefore provide that any funds received may be deposited to their general escrow accounts and be transferable between such accounts. If the escrow holder is financially stable, the parties should have no objection to this clause.

§11.26   b. Correctness of Documents and Identity of Signers

Escrow holders do not want to make decisions regarding the effectiveness of documents encountered in processing an escrow and will want a clause protecting them from liability for the correctness, genuineness, sufficiency, or validity of any document handled or the authority, identity, or right of any person executing the document. Declining to judge the validity of documents not prepared by the escrow holder or the proper execution of documents executed outside the presence of escrow officers is an understandable position of the escrow holder. The parties, however, should require the escrow holder to take responsibility for any documents prepared by the escrow holder and for the proper execution of documents signed in the presence of escrow officers.

§11.27 c. Liability Limited to Willful Neglect or Gross Misconduct

Most business entities naturally desire to limit their exposure to liability as much as possible. Common general exculpatory clauses attempt to limit liability only to willful neglect or gross misconduct and excuse any act done or omitted in good faith. A prudent buyer or seller should avoid clauses attempting to limit an escrow holder's liability to less than that imposed by law. An exculpatory clause by which an escrow holder attempts to avoid liability for its own negligence has been held contrary to public policy. *Akin v Business Title Corp.* (1968) 264 CA2d 153, 70 CR 287.

§11.28 d. Attorney's Fees in Third Party Actions

Escrow holders typically want an agreement that any party bringing an action to which the escrow holder is joined must reimburse the escrow holder for any expenses, costs, and attorney's fees incurred. Many such clauses grant the escrow holder a lien on escrow funds for such expenses. Normally, a party forced to accept an attorney's fee clause gains some equality under CC §1717, which allows either party, if it is the party in whose favor final judgment is rendered, its reasonable attorney's fees. A distinction must be made, however, between the typical attorney's fees clause that come within CC §1717 and the indemnity clause more frequently sought by escrow holders protecting them against costs and expenses incurred in defending an action brought against them. In the latter case the indemnity (which includes the escrow holder's attorney's fees) is only in favor of the escrow holder. Civil Code §1717 does not cause such an indemnity to run in favor of a party who brings an action and includes the escrow holder.

§11.29 D. Duties of Buyer and Seller

The buyer and seller must perform those conditions that are specified in the instructions to be performed by them respectively and that are the conditions precedent to the delivery to each party of the money or documents deposited by the other party. Performance must comply strictly with terms of the escrow instructions because any material deviation will prevent the consummation of the escrow transaction. *Altadena Escrow Corp. v Beebe* (1960) 181 CA2d 743, 5 CR 530.

III. ESCROW PROCEDURE

§11.30 A. Usual Steps in Escrow

Numerous steps must be taken to open, process and close an escrow transaction. In practice, the timing and the party performing each step may differ between northern and southern California. The following list contains the steps common to most simple single-family residence sale escrows.

(1) Pertinent information needed to prepare the escrow instructions must be obtained from the parties, or from their deeds, title policies, preliminary title reports, or the purchase and sale agreement.

(2) A preliminary title report on the property must be ordered.

(3) A pay-off demand from the current lender on the property must be requested and full reconveyance of the deed of trust must be ordered, unless the loan is to be assumed or to remain a lien against the property.

(4) Escrow instructions and loan documents must be obtained from the buyer's new lender. See §11.76.

(5) Any initial deposits must be received and a receipt for funds issued.

(6) All documents must be prepared and executed by the proper parties.

(7) The buyer's and seller's escrow instructions must be prepared and signed.

(8) Prorations must be computed.

(9) The funds needed to close the escrow must be estimated and received.

(10) A uniform settlement sheet must be prepared. See §11.99.

(11) A title insurance policy should be ordered to reflect the state of title at the time of recording.

(12) All documents that require recordation must be recorded. (Escrow instructions commonly provide that this event is the close of escrow, *i.e.*, the transfer of record title to the property sold from seller to buyer.) See §11.62.

(13) Disbursement of funds, and delivery of documents, including the uniform settlement sheet, must be made to the respective parties.

§11.31   B. Variations Between Northern and Southern California Practices

The majority of real property escrows in California, in the number of transactions if not also in the dollar amount, are handled without the services of an attorney. Consequently, various common practices have been developed throughout the state by real estate brokers, title companies, and escrow companies with regard to the handling of escrows. Some differences exist between northern and southern California practice in these nonattorney situations.

In southern California, in small, nonattorney transactions, the parties normally meet, shortly after a purchase and sale agreement has been signed, at the office of the escrow holder to open their escrow. At this time an escrow officer obtains the necessary information from the parties, which is often entered on a work sheet form used by many escrow holders. The escrow instructions are prepared from the work sheet and are signed by the parties at the beginning of the escrow transaction. Thereafter the escrow holder orders the preliminary title report and takes the other steps necessary to close the escrow. If the original instructions do not cover some problem encountered in processing the escrow, amended or supplemental instructions must be obtained. When the escrow appears almost ready to close, the escrow holder will estimate the amount of money that will be needed from the buyer and will send a letter requesting the funds.

In nonattorney transactions in northern California, the real estate broker plays a greater role in helping to process an escrow than he does in southern California. The broker in northern California will ordinarily obtain much of the data needed to process the escrow and will also act as an intermediary between the escrow holder and the parties, who often have no direct contact at all with the escrow holder. A second difference is that escrow instructions are usually prepared and executed at a later stage in the transaction in northern California than in southern California. It is not uncommon in northern California for the buyer to sign his instructions, plus any promissory note or deed of trust, at the conclusion of the transaction when he deposits the balance of his funds due, shortly before the close of escrow. In southern California, the buyer and seller usually sign joint escrow instructions shortly after the purchase and sale agreement (often called a "deposit receipt") has been signed.

Another major difference is that in southern California independent escrow companies licensed by the Commissioner of Corporations under the Escrow Law are available to act as escrow holders (see §11.11), as well as title companies and institutional lenders. Independent escrow companies are rarely located in northern California.

These apparent differences in practice between northern and southern California are relatively unimportant in transactions in which an attorney represents a party. The discussion in this chapter assumes, of course, that an attorney is representing at least one of the parties. The attorney will generally supervise the closing (a role that might be assumed by a broker if there is no attorney) and will structure it in a way that best meets the needs of the client without particular regard for the practices that are common to the nonattorney closings. Generally speaking, northern California escrow practices can be followed in southern California without difficulty. The converse is not true with respect to at least two southern California practices. First is the use of the independent escrow company; such companies rarely do business in northern California. Second is the not uncommon practice in southern California of presenting the entire purchase and sale agreement to the escrow holder; title companies in northern California generally resist this practice and require escrow instructions limited to those matters with which the escrow holder need be concerned.

§11.32 C. Selection of Escrow Holder

The choice of escrow holder can be subject to the agreement of the parties, but is often in effect made for the parties either by their acquiescence to a recommendation made by the real estate broker handling the sale or to the suggestion of a lender that its escrow department be used. The attorney negotiating and drafting the purchase and sale agreement should discuss this matter with the client; the agreement should name the escrow holder. See §3.53. The attorney may wish to suggest to the client an escrow holder with which the attorney has previously dealt. The broker's suggestion on the selection of escrow holder should not necessarily be followed. From the standpoint of the attorney's working relationship with the escrow holder, an escrow holder selected by the attorney will probably be more cooperative than one who feels that the choice was a result of the broker's recommendation.

Sellers may often have some connection with or a business incentive for dealing with a particular title company, *e.g.*, a discount given to tract developers, or a reissue discount given to owners who sell within a short time after their purchase and want that title company to act as the escrow holder. (But sellers cannot require, as a condition to selling the property, that title insurance covering the property be purchased by the buyer from any particular title company when the sale is subject to the Real Estate Settlement Procedures Act of 1974 (RESPA). 12 USC §2608. See §§11.85-11.89 for a discussion of RESPA.)

Real estate developers cannot require the use of an escrow holder in which the developer has a financial interest as a condition for the transfer of property containing a single-family dwelling. CC §2995.

Factors to consider in making the choice of escrow holder are those common to any choice between competing business entities: price, location and availability, financial stability, managerial expertise, integrity, and experience. The information required to make this decision can be gathered from other members of the real estate community (brokers, lenders, and attorneys) and records on file with the public agencies (Department of Corporations for independent escrow companies and Department of Insurance for title companies). See §11.11 on who can act as an escrow holder.

§11.33   D. Role of the Attorney

Although many real property transactions are closed without any involvement by an attorney, the importance of the attorney in such matters of consequence and the need for both buyer and seller to be represented by knowledgeable, independent counsel should be obvious. Although a buyer and seller may receive some advice and assistance from other parties, *e.g.*, brokers, salespeople, lenders, title and escrow company employees, many of these persons have some interests that are potentially in conflict with those of the buyer and seller.

Probably as a result of the lack of involvement by attorneys in many California real property closings, real estate brokers and escrow personnel sometimes resent an attorney's involvement in a sale they are trying to close. These people see the deliberateness employed by attorneys in protecting their client as ultratechnical legalese designed to kill a sale. Certainly it is understandable why parties whose entire compensation depends on a completed sale may become uneasy when attorneys for the buyer, seller, and lender spend considerable time negotiating and drafting documentation satisfactory to all parties. However, attorneys should not be put off by these negative feelings concerning their involvement and must always bear in mind their duties toward advancing and protecting their client's interests. Attorneys must remember that they alone are authorized to provide legal advice and to draft legal documents.

On the other hand, other parties can be helpful if used by the attorney in a spirit of cooperation and with a proper recognition of the services they render as well as their shortcomings. A real estate broker, for example, can be very useful in expediting matters essential for the closing, such as the execution of necessary documents prepared by the attorney, and in obtaining certain documents and information, such as rent statements, tenant estoppel certificates, and income statements. Title or escrow companies can be helpful in advising on commonly used escrow procedures. Title companies, of course, can provide necessary information on the requirements to insure title or to issue special endorsements. Attorneys should not, however, necessarily rely on statements from title or escrow officers about the correct procedures or about the legal consequences of a transaction. The attorney's own knowledge, judgment, and responsibility cannot be replaced by that of a title or escrow company. Attorneys should also resist any efforts by brokers and title or escrow officers to advise the parties on the legal consequences of the transaction.

§11.34 E. Drafting Escrow Instructions

Escrow instructions may be drafted by an attorney (see forms at §§11.42-11.77) or contained in a printed form supplied by the escrow holder either with or without a rider (see §11.35). The distinction between the purchase and sale agreement on the one hand and escrow instructions on the other hand should be kept in mind. The purchase and sale agreement defines the agreement and understanding between the buyer and the seller; the escrow instructions define the relationship of the escrow holder to the buyer and to the seller and, in essence, constitute directions to the escrow holder on closing the sale. As a result of these distinct purposes, the purchase and sale agreement of necessity contains much that is not needed (and perhaps even unwise) in the escrow instructions, and the escrow instructions may often need to contain information that would not be in the purchase and sale agreement (e.g., instructions to the escrow holder on the method of clearing title by removal of liens and encumbrances).

Escrow instructions may be given separately to the escrow holder by both the buyer and the seller, or the buyer and seller may sign joint escrow instructions (see §11.37). Notwithstanding the difference in function between the purchase and sale agreement and the escrow instructions, these two documents are sometimes combined. See §11.38. It is even possible to go into escrow without an underlying purchase and sale agreement; the escrow instructions then serve as the contract between the buyer and seller. See §11.4. It is also possible to deposit the purchase and sale agreement with the escrow holder in lieu of escrow instructions. See §11.5.

An attorney must take care to draft instructions which can be easily followed by the escrow holder and which accurately and fully embody the agreement between the parties. Attorneys cannot avoid liability by relying on any alleged custom or usage of escrow holders to correct deficiencies in the escrow instructions they have drafted. *Starr v Mooslin* (1971) 14 CA3d 988, 92 CR 583.

Beyond employing the skill, prudence, and diligence required of them as attorneys, real property attorneys are cautioned to give some study to the economics of any real property sale they are retained to handle, since there is possible liability for allowing a client to be defrauded. See *Starr v Mooslin, supra* (concurring opinion).

§11.35   1. Printed Form Escrow Instructions

For their own convenience, most escrow holders try to use their own printed form escrow instructions, although this practice should generally be resisted by an attorney. These forms are intended for use in the simpler real estate transactions, particularly those involving sale of single-family residences.

In northern California, separate printed instructions are often used for the buyer and seller. Conversely, southern California uses joint escrow instructions (*i.e.*, a single set signed by both buyer and seller). The printed forms used in southern California tend to be more detailed and complete than those forms used in northern California, which are often little more than a preliminary closing statement.

An attorney representing a buyer or seller will find little use for the printed forms of escrow instructions. The nature of the sale transaction commonly requires escrow instructions beyond the scope of those in printed forms. While the printed forms can be supplemented by amendments, the recommended practice is to prepare complete escrow instructions as one document.

Even for simple transactions, an attorney will probably find the use of printed form escrow instructions less than satisfactory. The printed forms often fail to state all the necessary conditions precedent to the delivery of documents or the disbursement of funds (relying instead on the custom and practice in the industry), and fail to state with sufficient specificity the method of proration. Some even fail to detail correctly the state of title the buyer is to receive, stating instead that buyer will take title subject to "covenants, conditions, restrictions, rights of way, easements and reservations of record." Certain general provisions, including exculpatory clauses, which an attorney may find unsatisfactory, are often part of the printed form. See §11.24 for a discussion of common exculpatory clauses.

Although some attorneys may feel that, in a simple real property sale, the cost of the transaction to the client cannot justify the fee for preparing escrow instructions, the additional cost and time needed to prepare instructions should not be significant when compared to the time needed to review printed instructions and to make necessary corrections and additions. Once an attorney has created his or her own format for buyer's and seller's instructions (see buyer's form at §§11.42-11.65; seller's form at §§11.66-11.75), the time and cost of tailoring them to a particular transaction is not great and the result far more satisfactory than with the use of printed forms.

§11.36 2. Unilateral Escrow Instructions

Although escrow instructions are sometimes combined with the purchase and sale agreement (see §11.38) and even when separately drafted, the buyer's and seller's instructions may be combined in a single set (see §11.37), the forms in this chapter contemplate that the escrow instructions will be separate from the purchase and sale agreement and that séparate (unilateral) instructions will be prepared for the buyer and for the seller. Separate instructions are the simplest and easiest to draft and thus should be considered over the use of combined instructions unless practice dictates or the attorney has some compelling reason to combine the buyer's and seller's instructions or to combine the purchase agreement with the escrow instructions. See §§11.37 and 11.38 for a discussion of the pros and cons of combined forms.

§11.37   3. Joint Escrow Instructions

In southern California it is common, when printed forms are used (see §11.35), to combine the buyer's and seller's instructions in one document. The advantage to this format is that it eliminates the possibility of an inconsistency between the buyer's and the seller's instructions. The problems of inconsistency are usually resolved, though, with little difficulty even when separate instructions are used. See §11.39.

The disadvantages to the use of joint escrow instructions are that a more complex document must be drafted than would be needed if the attorney were only drafting separate instructions for his own client. The attorney who undertakes the task of drafting the joint instructions, in effect, drafts not only his own client's instructions but those of the other party as well. One of the parties may also need to furnish certain information, such as the method of clearing title, to the escrow holder that he does not wish disclosed to the other party. The use of joint instructions eliminates any such confidentiality. (Even with the use of separate instructions, an escrow holder can (but is not required to) furnish copies of one party's instructions to the other parties to the escrow. See §11.10.)

§11.38   4. Escrow Instructions Combined With Purchase and Sale Agreement

In southern California attorneys frequently combine the purchase agreement and escrow instructions in one document. The advantage to this practice is that it eliminates not only any possibility of conflict between the buyer's and seller's separate instructions but also any conflict between the purchase agreement and the escrow instructions. But see §11.39 on resolving conflicts and inconsistencies. A second advantage to this practice is that escrow can be opened immediately after the purchase and sale agreement is executed because the buyer's and seller's instructions are already prepared and signed.

The combined purchase agreement and escrow instructions contains all the disadvantages of joint escrow instructions. See §11.37. Additional disadvantages are that, since the instructions are prepared at such an early stage, amended and supplemental instructions are usually necessary. From the standpoint of the escrow holder, the use of instructions combined with the purchase agreement may be less than satisfactory. The combined form provides the escrow holder with much information with which it is not concerned and may create some confusion regarding the actual duties and responsibilities of the escrow holder since these two documents normally serve two distinct purposes. See §11.34. Some attorneys attempt to resolve this problem by indicating those portions of the document that are matters between the buyer and seller with which the escrow holder need not be concerned. Nonetheless, the possibility exists that the escrow holder could be charged with this knowledge. Consequently, title companies in northern California when acting as escrow holders usually refuse to accept the purchase agreement as part of the escrow instructions.

§11.39   5. Inconsistencies Between Agreement and Escrow Instructions

Concern is sometimes expressed that, unless the purchase agreement is combined with joint escrow instructions, a problem may arise because of inconsistencies between the purchase agreement and the escrow instructions or between the buyer's and seller's separate instructions. Inconsistencies may occasionally arise, but such problems are usually not difficult to resolve. The attorney should have a copy of the purchase and sale agreement and, with that, should be able to draft instructions that are consistent with the agreement. Therefore, both buyer's and seller's instructions should themselves be consistent with each other and with the purchase and sale agreement.

When inconsistencies do occur they are usually either due to an error in drafting the instructions, or because one party's interpretation of the agreement is at a variance from the other's, or because the parties have orally modified the agreement after its execution. Inconsistencies in the buyer's and seller's instructions as the result of a drafting error can generally be resolved without difficulty. Inconsistencies as the result of conflicting interpretations of the agreement may require further negotiation before the transaction can close.

In resolving inconsistencies between the agreement and the instructions, the general rule of construction is that when more than one document between the same parties pertains to the same subject matter, both documents are to be interpreted together to the extent they are not inconsistent. CC §1642; *Katemis v Westerlind* (1953) 120 CA2d 537, 261 P2d 553.

These rules generally apply when resolving inconsistencies between a sales agreement and escrow instructions. An exception is when the inconsistency results from the omission of sales agreement provisions in the escrow instructions, in which case the instructions are held to be merely supplemental to the sales agreement and both are interpreted together, the sales agreement controlling when the instructions are silent. *Keelan v Belmont Co.* (1946) 73 CA2d 6, 165 P2d 930. Because of the different purpose served by the agreement and the escrow instructions, the latter, being essentially closing instructions to the escrow holder, will seldom cover all the matters set forth in the purchase agreement. See §11.34.

When separate escrow instructions are employed, subsequent to an executed sales agreement, any inconsistency between the buyer's and seller's instructions which arises because one set of instructions or the other attempts to modify the prior agreement of sale is of no effect, for one party cannot bind the other party without his consent.

§11.40 6. Information Needed Before Drafting Instructions

In drafting escrow instructions, the two most important sources of the necessary data are the purchase and sale agreement (sometimes called "deposit receipt"; see §3.40) and the preliminary title report. A preliminary closing statement obtained from the escrow holder is also helpful; it will show the escrow holder's estimate of costs and prorations and can be used as a checklist in drafting instructions. Other relevant data include the current tax bill, leases, maintenance contracts, utility bills, prior deeds, structural pest control reports, and loan commitments.

It is often advisable for the attorney to draft proposed instructions and have them reviewed by the escrow holder before the document is signed by the client and deposited. The escrow holder's review can identify any problems arising from the closing procedures as contemplated in the proposed instructions and may suggest an easier or more expeditious method of solving particular problems.

The following information should be known before the attorney drafts even simple escrow instructions:

(a) Name and address of escrow holder;

(b) Names and addresses of parties;

(c) Manner of vesting title to the property (see §§3.27-3.31);

(d) Nature of underlying transaction and purpose of escrow;

(e) Time for opening escrow;

(f) Documents, money, and other items to be deposited with the escrow holder;

(g) Conditions for delivery of documents, money, and other items deposited in escrow to the party entitled to them;

(h) Items the buyer's title will be subject to;

(i) Legal description of real property;

(j) Personal property included in the sale;

(k) Structure of financing;

(l) Prorations and payment of expenses of escrow; and

(m) Time limit for close of escrow.

§11.41   7. Format of Unilateral Escrow Instructions

Unilateral escrow instructions can be divided into six parts.

(1) The identification of the parties, the reference to the contract or escrow number, and the list of documents and money the party is depositing. See §11.66 on seller's instructions; §§11.42-11.43 on buyer's instructions.

(2) The conditions precedent to the close of escrow, *i.e.*, each item that must be accomplished before the delivery of a document or the disbursement of funds. See §§11.44-11.49 on buyer's instructions; §11.67 on seller's instructions.

(3) The instruction on prorations and costs. The instructions should list the items to be prorated, followed by an enumeration of the costs that the party submitting the instructions will pay. See

§§11.51-11.57 on buyer's instructions; §§11.69-11.70 on seller's instructions.

(4) Instructions on other charges that the party submitting the instructions agrees to pay. See §§11.58-11.60 on buyer's instructions; §11.71 on seller's instructions.

(5) Instructions on forwarding the documents at the close of escrow. See §§11.61-11.64 on buyer's instructions; §§11.72-11.74 on seller's instructions.

(6) The acceptance of the instructions by the escrow holder. See §11.65 on buyer's instructions; §11.75 on seller's instructions.

F. Buyer's Separate Escrow Instructions

§11.42   1. Form: Introductory Clause

Form 11.42-1

Buyer's Escrow Instructions

Date:_____

To: ____[name of escrow holder]____   Your Escrow No._____

____[address of escrow holder]_____

Sale: ____[name of seller]____ to ____[name of buyer]____

Property address: _____

In order to complete the purchase by ____[name of buyer]____ from ____ [name of seller]____ of the real property described in ____[your / Title Company's]____ preliminary report dated _____, 19__, Order No. _____, ____[I / we]____ enclose the following:

1. Cashier's check, payable to your order, in the amount of $_____;

[Add if third party financing]

2. Promissory note in the principal sum of $ _____, payable to ____ [name of lender]____;

3. Deed of trust in favor of ____[name of lender]____

[Add if seller financing]

__ Promissory note in the principal sum of $ _____, payable to ____ [name of seller]____;

__ Deed of trust in favor of ____[name of seller]____.

Comment: The opening clause, directed to the escrow holder, sets forth the information used by the escrow holder to reference the escrow: the date and the escrow holder's file number. In northern California, when a title company acts as escrow holder, the escrow number will be the number of the preliminary title report. The escrow number will have no relevance for the parties, their attorneys, and the real estate broker; the clause therefore sets out the names of the parties and address of the property, and of course may include the attorney's file reference number.

The moneys and documents deposited by the buyer are specified in this clause. The buyer may be required to deposit documents in addition to those mentioned in the form. In the case of institutional financing, the buyer may have to sign and deposit certain disclosure statements and other certifications. All documents deposited should be mentioned in this clause.

The buyer's deposit normally consists of money paid by cashier's check, although occasionally by cash. The attorney should check with the escrow holder concerning the acceptability of out-of-state cashier's checks if their use is contemplated. Large transfers of money should be carefully planned in advance with the escrow holder and the buyer's banker to avoid closing delays. The total purchase price, and any money previously paid to the seller, escrow holder, or real estate broker as a deposit, are referred to in the provision on conditions precedent to closing. See §11.44. The escrow holder should be instructed to place the buyer's funds in an interest-bearing account if the buyer anticipates there may be any significant delay from the time the deposit is made until close of escrow.

The promissory note and deed of trust in favor of a third party lender will have been submitted previously to the escrow holder by the lender under its own escrow instructions (see §11.76). The escrow holder will then deliver these documents to the buyer, along with any other documents required by the lender, who is to execute them and return them with the buyer's instructions. A seller taking back a purchase money deed of trust will follow essentially the same procedure. The note and deed of trust in favor of the seller are usually prepared by the seller's attorney, and are submitted to the escrow holder with the seller's instructions. See seller's form at §11.66. See California Mortgage and Deed of Trust Practice, chaps 2-3 (Cal CEB 1979) for a discussion of the note and deed of trust and how to protect a seller-lender.

The parties may be referred to throughout the escrow instructions as buyer and seller. Additional clarity may be gained by referring to them by their last names (if individuals) or by a short title if some other entity. (The use of last names or short titles is particularly useful in exchange transactions in which there are multiple parties.)

§11.43   2. Form: Buyer's Additional Deposit of Money

Form 11.43-1

If additional money is necessary to close this escrow, buyer shall deposit such sum with you no later than _____ day(s) before close of escrow provided that you give buyer _____ days notice of the amount due.

Comment: In northern California, the escrow instructions are signed close to the end of the entire sales transaction and usually the escrow holder has computed the amount of funds required of the buyer and knows what documents are needed to close the escrow. Consequently, there is normally no additional deposit of moneys or documents required. In southern California, the instructions often are signed before the escrow holder has fully determined what needs to be deposited, and additional deposits are customary. This clause provides a manner for the escrow holder to request necessary future deposits.

§11.44   3. Form: Conditions Precedent to Disbursement of Funds and Delivery of Documents

Form 11.44-1 (Introductory Clause)

Please obtain and record a grant deed, conveying to ____[*state name of buyers and manner of holding title*]____ that real property described in ____ [*your* / _____ *Title Company's*]____ preliminary report dated _____, Order No. _____. You shall note across the bottom of the grant deed the following:

"All future tax statements may be mailed to ____[*name and address for sending tax statements*]____."

[*Add if personal property included in sale*]

Please obtain a bill of sale to ____[*the following items of personal property* / *the personal property listed on Exhibit* _____ *attached*]____ and included with the sale: ____[*list all personal property included with sale*]____ .

[*Add if third party financing*]

You are authorized to deliver the promissory note and deed of trust to ____ [*name of third party lender*]____ when you are willing to credit buyer's account with the loan proceeds of $_____.

[*Continue*]

The purchase price of the real property is $_____,

[*Add if prior deposit made*]
of which $_____ has already been ____[*deposited with you as escrow holder / deposited with* ____*[name of broker]*____ */ paid to seller outside of escrow]*____ to be credited against the purchase price.

Form 11.44-2 (Specific Conditions Precedent)

You are authorized to pay the purchase price of $_____ subject to the adjustments provided for in these instructions to____[*name of seller]*____ , or to seller's order, and to charge the amount so paid to buyer's account

[*Add if seller financing*]
and to deliver to ____[*name of seller]*____ the promissory note payable to seller and the deed of trust securing that note when:

[*Continue*]
1. You have recorded the grant deed;

2. ____[*You are willing to issue your /* _____ *Title Insurance Company has confirmed to you its willingness to issue its]*____ California Land Title Association standard coverage policy of title insurance in the amount of $ _____, insuring that title to the real property is vested in ____[*names of buyers and manner of holding title]*____ , free and clear of all title defects, liens, encumbrances, deeds of trust, mortgages, rights of way, and restrictive covenants and conditions, except for:

[*List all exceptions to appear in schedule B Part II of the title insurance policy, including lien for current taxes, exceptions shown on the preliminary title report which buyer is willing to accept, and any deeds of trust executed by the buyer*]

[*Add if third party financing*]
3. You have credited buyer's account with the above-mentioned loan proceeds of $ _____ ____[*state amount of any third party financing]*____ ; and

[*Add if personal property included in sale*]
4. You have obtained a bill of sale for the personal property referred to above.

[*Continue*]
Disbursement of the funds in buyer's account shall obligate you to ____[*issue / obtain]*____ the above-mentioned title insurance policy.

Comment: The primary condition precedent which the buyer desires fulfilled before the escrow closes and his funds are delivered to the seller is issuance of a title insurance policy insuring his title subject only to those exceptions to which the buyer has agreed. This provision directs the escrow holder to issue, if it is a title insurer, or obtain, if it is another entity, a CLTA standard coverage policy in a specified amount. This amount normally is the purchase price of the property. For other forms of title insurance coverage, see California Title Insurance Practice §§3.2-3.5, 3.10 (Cal CEB 1980). The provision also provides for the manner of vesting title to the property. See §§3.27-3.31 for a discussion of the manner of holding title.

It is a requirement of Govt C §27321.5 that the name and address to which all future tax statements be mailed appear in any deed conveying fee title. See §7.10.

The exceptions included in the preliminary title report, which the buyer accepts, are usually listed in the escrow instructions by their title report number. Any deed of trust executed by the buyer must also be included as a permitted exception. Often the promissory note will be submitted undated with instructions to the escrow holder to date the note as of the close of escrow. When a preliminary title report is not available at the time the instructions are drafted, the exceptions must be described sufficiently in the instructions and the instructions must contain a correct legal description of the property. Attempting to draft escrow instructions for either buyer or seller without a current preliminary title report is obviously fraught with difficulty if not danger and should be avoided.

4. Other Conditions Precedent

§11.45   a. Form: FHA Appraisal as Condition

Form 11.45-1

> [*Add, if appropriate, as a numbered item to list*
> *of conditions precedent in Form 11.44-2*]

You shall have received a written appraisal of the real property issued by the Federal Housing Administration, or its successor, stating the value to be not less than $_____. In the event the appraised value is less than that amount, you shall notify buyer in writing. Buyer shall have _____ days after such notification in which to notify you in writing of his election to accept the lower appraised value and proceed as though this condition had been satisfied.

Comment: When the loan obtained by the buyer of a single- or two-family residence, which he will occupy, is to carry mortgage insurance under the National Housing Act (12 USC §1701), the seller must deliver an FHA approved appraisal to the buyer. 12 USC §1715q. This provision establishes the issuance of such an appraisal in an amount acceptable to the buyer as a condition precedent to the close of escrow.

b. Pest Control

§11.46 (1) Form: Pest Control Report as Condition; No Work Required

Form 11.46-1

[Add, if appropriate, as a numbered item to list of conditions precedent in Form 11.44-2]

You have received a written report ____[approved by buyer]____ by a licensed structural pest control operator selected by____[buyer / seller]____ covering the ____[describe improvements, e.g., house and garage]____ situated on the property showing them to be free from infestation of wood-destroying pests or organisms, and that no corrective work is required. ____ [Buyer / Seller]____ shall pay the cost of the written report.

Comment: This provision conditions the close of escrow on the issuance of a report from a licensed operator selected by either the buyer or seller showing no infestation in, or work required on the improvements to the real property. The improvements should be listed so that there is no confusion over whether a freestanding garage or other structure is included.

Some escrow holders contend that such a provision requires them to make a decision about what the report says and will therefore refuse to accept such a provision unless the report is "to be approved by the buyer." This is probably the better practice anyway. See §§3.125-3.127 for a discussion of structural pest control provisions in the purchase agreement. For a provision covering the required work, see §11.47.

§11.47 (2) Form: Pest Control Report as Condition; Work Required

Form 11.47-1

[Add, if appropriate, as a numbered item to list of conditions precedent in Form 11.44-2]

All corrective, but not preventive, work required to be performed under the terms of a structural pest control report dated _____, 19__, furnished by ____[name of structural pest control operator]____ and approved by buyer shall have been performed before the close of escrow as evidenced by a completion report approved by buyer, or you shall hold in escrow from the funds otherwise due and payable to seller the cost of performing such work as stated in the report. Any funds so withheld are to be paid to ____[name of operator] ____ when you have received a clearance certification and notice of work completed in accordance with Business and Professions Code section 8519(b) and you have been informed in writing by buyer that the work has been completed to buyer's satisfaction.

Comment: Some infestation is usually found and reported in the pest control report. The report then lists two types of work to be performed: corrective work to remedy the current infestation, and preventive work recommended to prevent possible future or threatened infestation. The report usually also quotes a price to perform the work. A buyer will normally condition the close of escrow on completion at seller's expense of all corrective work; preventive work is not usually at seller's expense, although this can be subject to negotiation between the parties. See §§3.125-3.127.

It is customary in northern California for the pest control report to have been obtained before escrow instructions are submitted. When the report has not been issued at the time escrow instructions are submitted, as may be the case in southern California, the clause must be modified to provide for the future approval of the report.

Often the parties do not wish to delay closing until after termite work is performed; in that event the buyer will condition closing, not on completion of the work, but on the escrow holder's withholding sufficient funds from the seller to perform the work pursuant to the price quoted in the report. This clause provides for such withholding as an alternative to work completion. In practice a buyer may prefer merely to receive credit on the selling price for the cost of the work; he can then elect to seek a lower bid, or even omit having the work done. An institutional lender may, however, insist that the work be completed.

§11.48   c. Form: Assignment of Lease as Condition

Form 11.48-1

> [*Add, if appropriate, as a numbered item to list
> of conditions precedent in Form 11.44-2*]

You hold for buyer the original lease, dated _____, 19__, in which ____ [*name*]____ is lessee, which lease buyer has examined and approved, and an assignment of the lease in form approved by buyer, executed by seller to buyer.

Comment: When the real property to be transferred to the buyer is subject to an existing lease or leases, the buyer should provide for delivery of the original lease or leases to him since he may require the original lease as evidence in some future judicial proceeding, and a lender might require the original lease if it is assigned to the lender as part of the loan transaction. The buyer should also require the seller to assign the lease or leases to him in writing (he should give notice of such assignment to the lessees). See §3.111. Escrow holders do not want any responsibility concerning the validity or effectiveness of documents such as a lease and assignment of lease, and may desire a provision specifying that they are responsible only for delivery of the documents. See §11.26 for a discussion of exculpatory clauses concerning the correctness of documents. See also §11.54 for a discussion of other tenant related matters.

§11.49   d. Form: Provision for Assumption of or Taking Subject to Existing Deed of Trust

Form 11.49-1

[Add to exceptions to title which buyer will accept, Form 11.44-2, item 2]

Existing deed of trust in favor of ____*[name of lender]*____ recorded _____, 19__, and listed as item _____ in ____*[your /_____ Title Company's]*____ preliminary title report dated _____, 19__, Order No. _____.

You are requested to obtain a beneficiary's statement paid for by ____ *[buyer / seller]*____ showing an unpaid balance of $_____ with nondelinquent payments of $_____ per month and an interest rate of _____ percent and to adjust the ____*[cash due seller / face amount of note to seller]*____ accordingly if the unpaid balance is different. The beneficiary's statement is to be approved by buyer as a condition to closing.

Comment: As an alternative to the buyer's obtaining a new loan in order to purchase the subject real property, he may, if allowed by the existing lender, or if otherwise allowable under current law (see generally §§3.50, 5.24, 6.43), assume or take subject to the seller's obligations under the existing loan. Loan assumptions are explained at §§3.50, 5.23. This provision is intended to be listed as an exception to title in the provision appearing in item 2 of Form 11.44-2 in place of listing a new deed of trust.

This clause instructs the escrow holder to obtain a beneficiary's statement from the existing lender to verify the unpaid balance and other terms of the loan. Beneficiary's statements are required to be made by lenders on written request of certain persons. CC §2943.

The statement must list the unpaid balance of the loan, the interest rate, any delinquencies, the amount of monthly payments, and other loan terms. If the deed of trust so provides, the lender may charge a fee of $15 for furnishing the statement. CC §2943.

The buyer's attorney should have obtained and carefully examined copies of the promissory note and deed of trust evidencing and securing the loan the buyer is assuming or taking subject to. This examination will reveal whether the loan documents contain provisions for late charges, due-on-sale clauses, prepayment fees for loan prepayments, and provisions permitting the lender to require tax and insurance reserve account payments. None of these matters would necessarily appear in an ordinary beneficiary's loan statement.

If the buyer's attorney has not yet examined the existing loan documents, the clause should reserve the right to examine and approve the documents as a condition to the close of escrow.

If the buyer is to assume the seller's obligations under the note and deed of trust, instead of merely taking subject to the existing debt, an assumption agreement will be prepared to be executed by the buyer. This agreement may be between the buyer and the lender or between the buyer and the seller. More commonly, the agreement is with the lender who will provide the form the buyer is to sign. Although an assumption by the buyer does not necessarily relieve the seller of the obligations, the practice of institutional lenders, when agreeing to an assumption, is to release the seller from further liability. When an assumption is part of the transaction, the instructions should make reference to the assumption agreement in the list of documents deposited with the escrow holder (see §11.42) and include the assumption agreement among the documents whose delivery is subject to the conditions set forth in the clause in Form 11.44-2.

§11.50 5. Prorations

The ownership of real property gives rise to certain items of expense, which are either direct burdens or liens on the real property, such as real property taxes, and expenses, which are necessarily incurred by an owner, such as premiums for fire and hazard, and public liability and property damage insurance, and monthly utility and maintenance charges. (Some or all of these items may have been shifted to a lessee under the terms of a lease.) These items can be either prepaid by the seller, necessitating a credit due him for the period of time the buyer will own the property, or be paid after the sale, necessitating a credit due the buyer for the period of time the seller owned the property, but for which the buyer will eventually pay the item of expense. The adjustment of these credits and debits between the buyer and the seller is proration.

Escrow instructions covering proration must specify the date on, or as of which, the computation of the adjustment is to be made, and the source of information on which the escrow holder must rely to obtain the figures to be used in making the adjustments.

The most common date chosen on which to compute the adjustments is the close of escrow, which for specificity is usually defined as the date the documents are recorded and record title passes from seller to buyer. See §11.84. This date is generally chosen because the right to possession between buyer and seller changes on this date in the absence of an agreement to the contrary. When the buyer takes possession before the close of escrow, the date of possession is often chosen as the date on which to base the computations.

§11.51   a. Form: Introduction and Proration of Taxes

Form 11.51-1

Prorate the following items on the basis of a 30-day month as of ____[state date of close of escrow or other agreed date]____:

(1) Real property taxes for the tax fiscal year 19__–19__ based on the most recent official information available in the office of the taxing entity;

Comment: The proration of real property taxes is commonplace in real property sale escrows in California. Whether the proration results in a credit or debit to the buyer depends on the date chosen on which to make the computation. This results from the law in California that taxes are payable on a fiscal-year basis (July 1-June 30) in two equal installments on dates which do not relate to the start or end of the first and second halves of the fiscal year. The first installment is due and payable on November 1 and becomes delinquent on December 10; the second installment is due and payable on February 1 and becomes delinquent on April 10. Rev & T C §§2605, 2606, 2617, 2618.

For convenience, and because of the lack of better information, the prior year's tax bill is often used as a basis for proration of the next fiscal year's taxes. The actual tax bill is not available until November 1. Thus, for sales closing on October 1, before the tax bills are available, the proration would often be based on the prior year's tax bill. The form in this provision, however, requires that the proration be based on "the most recent official information." If the current tax bill is not available, all information needed to determine the current taxes should still be available to the escrow holder by October 1. The county assessor must complete the equalized assessment roll by July 1. Rev & T C §616. The legislature has, in effect, set the maximum 1 percent of full value allowed by Cal Const art XIIIA, §1 as the tax rate in all counties and has prohibited local governments from levying any property taxes except for amounts necessary to make annual payments on bonded or other indebtedness approved by the voters before July 1, 1978. Rev & T C §93. Unless instructed otherwise, most escrow holders will prorate based on the latest available tax bill rather than obtaining the information, even when available, to compute the amount of the current year's taxes.

It should also be noted that, under Cal Const art XIIIA, property is generally not reassessed to full cash value except following a change of ownership or new construction. If the seller recently acquired the property being sold, or undertook new construction on the property, it is possible that the most recent assessment might not reflect this. In such cases it is possible that an escape assessment will be made when the facts become known to the assessor. Rev & T C §531. In that case, a supplemental tax bill could be issued. How this amount is to be prorated (which would have to be outside of escrow) depends on which party is liable for the supplemental tax. See Rev & T C §531.2. See also California Taxes §§4.70-4.74 (Cal CEB 1978) for a discussion of escape assessments. Any provision on the allocation of any supplemental tax bill for the year of the sale will have to be contained in the purchase and sale agreement. See comment to §3.56.

In addition to the lien for current taxes, there may be a lien for special assessments. If the buyer is to take subject to a special assessment, rather than requiring the seller to pay it off (see §3.87), the interest on the assessment will also have to be prorated by the escrow holder and should be provided for in this clause. In this situation the lien of the assessment bond will have to be included in the list of title exceptions in the clause in item 2 of Form 11.44-2.

§11.52   b. Form: Proration of Interest on Existing Loan

Form: 11.52-1

> [*Add, if appropriate, as a numbered item to list*
> *of items for proration in Form 11.51-1*]

(2) Interest on the note secured by the recorded deed of trust in favor of ____[*name of beneficiary*]____ in accordance with figures furnished in beneficiary's statement and approved by buyer before close of escrow;

Comment: When the buyer has either assumed or taken subject to an existing loan (see §11.49) the interest must be prorated on the loan. In California, interest on real property loans is usually paid monthly in arrears, so that the buyer will be credited and the seller debited for that portion of the month the seller owned the property prior to the close of escrow. Some lenders in California and elsewhere charge interest monthly in advance, in which case the buyer would be debited and the seller credited for that portion of the month the buyer owned the property after the close of escrow. The escrow holder will have to analyze the beneficiary's statement to determine whether interest is prepaid.

§11.53   c. Form: Proration of Maintenance Charges

Form 11.53-1

> [*Add, if appropriate, as a numbered item to list*
> *of items for proration in Form 11.51-1*]

(3) Monthly maintenance fee prepaid to ____[*date*]____ based on the rate of $ _____ per month.

Comment: In condominiums, planned developments, and other types of real property ownership in which some form of homeowners' association dues or fees are assessed against the individual units for common expenses, the proration of such maintenance charges must be made. This form accomplishes such proration for prepaid charges payable monthly. These charges are generally prepaid monthly, but are sometimes paid quarterly or even less frequently. If so, a corresponding change must be made in this form.

§11.54   d. Form: Proration of Rents

Form 11.54-1

*[Add, if appropriate, as a numbered item to list
of items for proration in Form 11.51-1]*

(4) Rentals based on ____*[tenant estoppel certificates / seller's rent statement]*____ approved by buyer and deposited in escrow by seller. The balance remaining from any payments to secure rental agreements after lawful deductions previously made by seller and approved by buyer shall be transferred to buyer. You ____*[shall / shall not]*____ be responsible for notification to tenants of this transfer of security deposits.

Comment: Rentals that are customarily paid in advance by agreement are prorated. This provision is directed to the proration of rentals and the transfer of security deposits and refundable key and cleaning deposits with regard to the sale of real property containing rental dwelling units.

For residential property, CC §1950.5, applying to rental security deposits on dwellings made on or after January 1, 1971, requires a landlord, on termination of his interest in a dwelling unit, to transfer the balance of the security deposit "remaining after any lawful deductions" (*i.e.*, rent defaults, damage repairs, cleaning charges) to either the tenant or the landlord's successor in interest, in which case the landlord must notify the tenant personally or by certified mail of the transfer and of the transferee's name, address, and telephone number. (Sometimes these letters, signed by seller, are deposited with the escrow holder.)

See §3.115 for a discussion of the various methods of handling delinquent rent, as between the buyer and the seller. See §3.112 for a discussion of tenant estoppel certificates and for a form.

§11.55   e. Form: Proration of Hazard Insurance Premiums

Form 11.55-1

*[Add, if appropriate, as a numbered item to list
of items for proration in Form 11.51-1]*

(5) Premium on seller's hazard insurance, which is to be assigned to buyer.

Comment: The seller's hazard insurance on the property can often be assigned to the buyer if the buyer agrees to this. The advantage to the seller of an assignment of the policy is that the seller will receive a prorata credit for the premium paid. If, instead, the seller cancels the policy, and the buyer takes out a new policy, the seller will receive a premium refund based on a short-rate table rather than a prorata refund. See §§3.174, 10.12-10.18 for a discussion of hazard insurance.

§11.56   f. Form: Other Prorations (Outside of Escrow)

Form 11.56-1

____[State items to be prorated outside of escrow, e.g., utility and service charges, operating expenses]____ shall be prorated outside of escrow unless you are provided with a proration statement covering these items, approved in writing by both seller and buyer, before the close of escrow.

Comment: Adjustment of charges, in addition to those discussed in §§11.51-11.55, are often necessary, but are minor in amount or not easily calculated; for this reason the parties may choose to make the necessary adjustments themselves outside of escrow. This clause provides for such adjustments outside of escrow, but allows an option to have these charges prorated in escrow if the parties so elect.

In a sale of a home or other modest property, the usual solution is for the seller to terminate all normal utility services and obtain closing bills, and for the buyer to make his own arrangements for reconnection and installation of telephone, gas, electric, water, and renewal of garbage collection services. (In leased property, the lessee is usually required to pay for these services or most of them.)

§11.57   6. Form: Handling Balance in Lender's Impound Account

Form 11.57-1

The amount of any funds held by ____[name of lender]____ as advance payments for real property taxes and hazard insurance premiums as of ____ [specify, e.g., closing date]____ plus interest, if any, shall be credited to seller and debited to buyer in full.

Comment: If a buyer takes title subject to or assumes an existing mortgage or deed of trust and the seller has been required to or has elected to make monthly advance payments to the lender for real property taxes and hazard insurance premiums, a balance of such funds in a book account to the credit of seller (commonly referred to in California as an impound account and in other states as an escrow account) usually exists on the closing date. Therefore, regardless of whether real property taxes are prorated, the seller must be given credit for these amounts he has prepaid and which the buyer will benefit from under the continuing loan. (If the buyer takes subject to the existing loan, rather than entering into a formal assumption agreement with the lender, the buyer should obtain an assignment from the seller of the impound account balance in order to receive credit from the lender for any impound account balance remaining when the loan is paid off.)

The proration of real property taxes which are a lien on the real property should not be confused, however, with the transfer of the impound account balance from the seller to the buyer. These are two separate and distinct matters. The impound account balance is not prorated; it is merely transferred from the seller to the buyer through a debit and credit in escrow in the same manner that tenants' security deposits are transferred.

When an existing loan is paid off, the lender credits the impound account to the amount owing on the loan, or refunds it to the seller so that no adjustment in escrow is necessary.

7. Authorized Disbursements (Buyer and Seller)

§ 11.58   a. Closing Costs; Chart of Customary Division

The fees and charges, in addition to the prorations discussed in §§11.51-11.55, associated with the sale of real property are customarily paid from the funds deposited in escrow and are often referred to as settlement or closing costs. The escrow instructions should specify which party is to pay which expenses by authorizing the escrow holder to disburse these amounts and debit the account of the paying party.

Customs have developed in most counties of California that dictate whether the seller or buyer is typically charged with certain items or whether there is a division between them. However, these customs are not rigid, and the parties are free to negotiate who will pay which item. Some charges are the direct liability of one party because of contractual agreements with a third party, *e.g.*, a seller's duty to pay his broker, embodied in a listing agreement. The obligation of one party to pay these charges is seldom shifted to the other party by their agreement of sale or the escrow instructions.

The following chart lists common closing costs and indicates who typically pays such charge, by county.

CHART OF CUSTOMARY DIVISION

Closing costs	Paid by	
1. Real estate broker's sales commission	Seller	
2. Title charges Escrow settlement fee	Buyer in counties of Alameda, Contra Costa, Lake, Marin, Mendocino, Modoc, Napa, San Francisco, San Mateo, Solano, Sacramento, and city of Davis	Seller in city of Chico and counties of Del Norte, Humboldt (sometimes buyer in southern part of county), Monterey, Sacramento, San Benito, Santa Clara, Sutter, Yolo (except city of Davis), Yuba.
	In other counties the fee usually is divided between buyer and seller. There is no strong custom in Nevada and Sierra counties.	
3. Title insurance premium	Buyer in counties of Alameda, Amador, Contra Costa, Lake, Marin, Mendocino, Napa, San Francisco, San Mateo, Solano, Sonoma, and city of Davis.	Seller in city of Chico and counties of Del Norte, Fresno, Humboldt (sometimes buyer in southern part of county), Inyo, Kern, Kings, Los Angeles, Madera, Modoc, Monterey, Orange, Placer, Riverside, Sacramento, San Benito, San Bernardino, San Diego, San Luis Obispo, Santa Barbara, Santa Clara, Stanislaus, Sutter, Tehama, Tulare, Ventura, Yolo (except city of Davis), Yuba.
	In other counties the fee usually is divided between buyer and seller. There is no strong custom in Nevada and Sierra counties.	
4. New financing expenses Credit report fee	Buyer	

Hazard insurance premium	Buyer	
Loan appraisal fee	Buyer	
Loan origination fee (points)*	Buyer	
Tax service fee	Buyer	
5. Seller's loan expenses		
Assumption fee	Buyer	
Prepayment loan fee		Seller
Reconveyance fee		Seller
6. Other charges		
Documentary transfer tax		Seller
Local transfer taxes	Varies, *e.g.,* in Oakland and San Jose, divided between buyer and seller	
Notary fee on deed		Seller
Notary fee on new deed or trust	Buyer	
Pest inspection report	Buyer	
Pest report work**		Seller
Recording fee for deed and deed of trust	Buyer	
Recording fee for reconveyance		Seller
7. Attorneys' fees	Party employing council, or as agreed.	

---

*On HUD-insured or VA-guaranteed loans there is a limit on the amount the buyer-borrower is permitted to pay. The seller often agrees to pay any "points" charged by lender in excess of that maximum.

**Seller usually agrees to pay for corrective work but not preventive work.

§11.59   b. Form: Buyer's Statement Regarding Seller's Closing Costs

Form 11.59-1

The seller is to pay all costs and expenses of clearing title, preparing, executing, acknowledging, and delivering the above-mentioned grant deed, and any real estate commissions incurred in this transaction.

Comment: This provision sets forth those costs that are invariably borne by the seller. Although even without this provision the escrow holder would have no authority to charge any of these costs to the buyer, its incorporation in the instructions may avoid any misunderstanding.

§11.60   c. Form: Payment of Closing Costs

Form 11.60-1

As of the close of escrow and not before, you are also authorized to disburse for the account of buyer from funds deposited with you the following:

[*Add appropriate statements*]

1. The recorder's fee for recording the above-mentioned grant deed____ [*and deed(s) of trust*]____;

2. Loan origination fee of $_____, loan appraisal fee of $_____, credit report fee of $_____, and tax service fee of $_____ to ____ [*name of lender*]____;

3. Prepaid interest to____[*name of lender*]____ from date of disbursement of loan proceeds to _____, 19__;

4. Hazard insurance premium for one year of $_____to____[*name of insurance agency or company*]____;

5. Title insurance premium of $_____ to ____[*name of title insurance company*]____;

6. Escrow fee of $_____ to ____[*name of escrow agent*]____;

7. Your fee for any notary services performed for buyer.

8. ____[*Specify other, e.g., pest control report*]____.

Comment: This provision authorizes the payment of the closing costs agreed to be paid by the buyer. The items listed are those customarily paid by the buyer in most San Francisco Bay Area counties except Santa Clara.

The closing costs paid to the lender include the loan origination fee, usually stated in points (a point equals 1% of the loan amount; see §6.38) or points plus a fixed amount, which compensates the lender for the expenses of preparing documents and other related work in originating the loan, *i.e.*, the loan appraisal fee (for making an appraisal of the property), the credit report fee (for obtaining a credit report on the buyer), and a tax service fee (to obtain current information on the status of real property tax payments on the subject real property during the life of the loan). Not all of these fees are charged by every lender; occasionally additional fees are charged. Some prepayment of interest may be required.

The title insurance charge normally will include the premium for the buyer's title insurance (CLTA policy) and the premium for the lender's title insurance (ALTA policy). See California Title Insurance Practice chap 3 (Cal CEB 1980) for discussion of title insurance. In northern California, most title insurance companies acting as escrow holders now charge a separate fee for their services as escrow holder, although some still follow the former practice of including the escrow fee in their title insurance premium.

See provision and Comment at §11.71 for seller's closing costs.

§11.61   8. Form: Notice to Parties

Form 11.61-1

Except for any notice required under applicable law to be given in another manner, any notice given by one party to the other(s), including the escrow holder, shall be in writing, signed by the party giving notice and sent by certified or registered mail, return receipt requested, postage prepaid, to the other party(ies) at the last address the party(ies) ____[has / have]____ designated by notice as provided herein, and a copy of the notice shall be filed with the escrow holder. Notice shall be considered to have been given at the time of deposit in the United States mail when given in the manner here designated.

Comment: Conflicts can arise when escrow instructions provide only that "notices be given in writing." Such a clause does not define what is a proper giving of notice and does not cover situations when the notice is never received.

This provision attempts to meet these problems by specifying how the notice must be sent; it defines the giving of notice as deposit in the mails, not the filing of a copy of the notice with the escrow holder.

9. Concluding Provision

§11.62   a. Form: Time for Close of Escrow

Form 11.62-1

This escrow is to be completed and closed____[on or before]____ _____, 19__, at the hour of _____ o'clock__.m. After that date and time, buyer reserves the right to demand the return of all documents and money deposited by buyer in this escrow. On being reimbursed for all your charges and expenses in connection with this escrow, you shall comply with such demand and terminate this escrow. If no such demand is made, this escrow shall be closed as soon as possible.

Comment: The consequences to the real property sales transaction of either party's failure to perform on time is discussed in §§3.177, 11.21, and 12.8. The principal objective of this clause is to provide for a date and time after which the parties may demand return of their respective deposits. Clauses that provide for automatic termination as of a specific date are too inflexible for general use because the parties, while desiring to close by that date, will often want an escrow to continue past that date if necessary to complete performance of all conditions.

Some clauses condition the return of a party's deposit on the fulfillment of all performance required of that party. The idea behind such a clause is sound, but unfortunately many escrow holders will not attempt to judge whether a party has fully performed and will interplead the deposit into court if the parties cannot mutually agree to a return of the respective deposits. The suggested clause tries to avoid this problem by withdrawing any need for judgment by the escrow holder. Escrow holders are still reluctant to return deposits on unilateral demand; therefore some difficulty in obtaining a return without the consent of the other party can be expected.

Including the phrase "time is of the essence" in these instructions is contradictory to a provision worded as in this form in which the escrow can be closed after the specified event if no party demands return of his deposit and, in any event, will be narrowly applied by the courts. Compare *Williams Plumbing Co. v Sinsley* (1975) 53 CA3d 1027, 126 CR 345, with *Nash v Superior Court* (1978) 86 CA3d 690, 150 CR 394.

§11.63　　b.　Form: Approval Required of Documents

Form 11.63-1

The approval by buyer of any report, statement, form, or other document required by these escrow instructions shall be considered given if buyer has not given notice of disapproval to you of any such items within _____ days after you notify him of receipt of the item and you furnish buyer with a copy of the item.

Comment: When escrow instructions require that a party approve a particular document, such as the pest control report (see §11.47) or assignment of lease (see §11.48), a provision such as this should be included to define the giving of approval, and to set a time limit within which it must be done. This provision puts the burden on the party to disapprove a specific document within the time limit or he will be considered to have approved it. This type of affirmative disapproval clause avoids the problems involved in affirmative approval clauses in which the party's approval is delayed beyond the time limit set.

§11.64 c. Form: Forwarding of Documents After Closing

Form 11.64-1

On completion of this transaction, please send to ____[state name and address of buyer or buyer's attorney]____ the following:

1. Title insurance policy;
2. Your itemized statement of the costs charged to buyer's acount;
3. Your check for the balance of buyer's deposit, if any, or your bill for the amount due you for buyer's account;

[Add if applicable]

4. Bill of sale to personal property;

[Add if applicable]

5. ____[List any other documents, e.g., leases, assignments, estoppel certificates to be delivered to buyer at close of escrow]____.

Please instruct the recorder to send the recorded grant deed to ____[name and address of buyer or buyer's attorney]____.

Comment: This provision sets out the final duties of the escrow holder to deliver documents and funds at the close of escrow. The escrow holder will indicate on the grant deed the name and address of the party to whom it is to be returned after recordation. The other documents are delivered by the escrow holder at the close of escrow, or, in the case of the title insurance policy, issued a short time later. It is advisable to have all documents, including the grant deed, sent to the buyer's attorney. The attorney can then check and review the documents to make certain that they comply with the escrow instructions before sending them on to the buyer.

§11.65 d. Form: Buyer's Signature; Escrow Holder's Acknowledgment and Acceptance

Form 11.65-1 (Buyer's Signature)

Please acknowledge receipt of these instructions and the accompanying documents by signing the acceptance below and returning to ____[specify if to buyer or give name and address of buyer's attorney]____ a copy of these instructions. Buyer's address for purposes of notice is:

____[Address of buyer or buyer's attorney]____

[Signature of buyer]
____[Typed name of buyer]____

Form 11.65-2 (Escrow Holder's Acknowledgment and Acceptance)

____[Name of escrow holder]____ acknowledges receipt of buyer's escrow instructions dated _____ 19__, of which the foregoing is a copy, and acknowledges receipt of the money and documents referred to and agrees to act as escrow holder and to comply with the terms and conditions of your escrow instructions.
Dated: _____

____[Typed name of escrow company]____
By__[signature of officer]__
____[Typed name of officer and title]____

Comment: This provision requests the escrow holder to acknowledge receipt of the instructions and the deposit by executing the form and returning a copy to the buyer or the buyer's attorney.

Most escrow holders have printed receipt forms, especially for the deposit of funds, and will send these to the respective parties in addition to signing this form.

By signing this clause, the escrow holder also agrees to act as the escrow holder pursuant to the terms of the instructions.

G. Seller's Separate Escrow Instructions

§11.66   1. Form: Introductory Clause

Form 11.66-1

Seller's Escrow Instructions

Date: _____
To:____[name of escrow holder]____   Your Escrow No. _____
    ____[address of escrow holder]____
Sale: ____[name of seller]____ to ____[name of buyer]____
Property address: _____

In order to complete the sale by ____[name of seller]____ to ____[name of buyer]____ of the real property described in ____[your / _____ Title Company's]____ preliminary title report dated _____, 19__, Order No. _____,____[I / we]____ enclose the following:

1. Grant deed conveying the real property to____[name of buyer and manner of holding title]____ ;

[Add if personal property included in sale]

2. Bill of sale to____[name of buyer]____ of certain personal property included with the sale;

[Add if seller financing]

3. Unsigned promissory note in the amount of $_____payable to ____*[name of seller]*;

4. Unexecuted deed of trust securing the promissory note; and

[Add if income property]

5. Rent statement.

Comment: The grant deed is often prepared by the escrow holder. The seller's attorney should always review the grant deed and, preferably, should draft it. Grant deeds prepared by escrow holders almost invariably fail to list exceptions to title that would otherwise fall under the implied covenant of title in CC §1113. See chap 7 on deeds and chap 9 on covenants of title.

Title and escrow companies usually have printed forms available for promissory notes and deeds of trust. Quite often the seller's attorney will find it preferable to draft the note. A title company form of deed of trust is often satisfactory, although sometimes a rider may be needed. See California Mortgage and Deed of Trust Practice chaps 2, 3 (Cal CEB 1979) for a discussion of the note and deed of trust and a checklist of steps necessary to protect the seller-lender.

The note and deed of trust in favor of the seller must always be approved by the seller before they are given to the buyer for execution. This may be done by enclosing the unexecuted note and deed of trust with the seller's instructions (as provided here) or by the seller's separately approving the form of the note and deed of trust. After the seller's approval, the escrow holder will deliver these documents to the buyer, who will execute them and return them with the buyer's instructions.

Often it will also be necessary to instruct the escrow holder on the details of completing the note, such as entering dates for payments to begin, for interest to accrue, and for final payment when such dates depend on the date escrow closes.

Any additional documents deposited, such as the insurance policy if assigned to the buyer, leases, assignments of leases, and rent statements, should be included in the list.

See also Comment in §11.42 on buyer's form.

§11.67   2. Form: Conditions Precedent to Delivery of Deed

Form 11.67-1

The purchase price is $_____,____*[of which buyer has paid $_____ outside of escrow to be applied to the purchase price]*____ .

You are authorized to deliver and record the grant deed____[*and to deliver the bill of sale*]____ when:

1. You shall have received and hold for seller's account, in available funds, the sum of $_____ ____[*compute and insert purchase price less any deposits paid outside of escrow and less amount of any note given to seller*] ____ less the disbursements which you are authorized by these instructions to make on behalf of seller, plus or minus the balance due on the prorations as enumerated below.

[*Add if seller financing*]

2. The enclosed promissory note and deed of trust have been executed by buyer without amendment or deletion and returned to you;

3. You are ready to record the deed of trust securing the promissory note;

4. You____[*are willing to issue / can obtain from _____Title Insurance Company*]____ a California Land Title Association joint protection policy in the amount of $_____insuring title vested in ____[*name of buyer*]____ and insuring the deed of trust to ____[*name of seller*]____ subject only to: ____[*list all prior liens and encumbrances of record including tax liens and the liens of any prior deeds of trust*]____ .

5. You have received and hold for delivery to seller a standard form policy of fire and extended coverage hazard insurance, in an amount not less than $____[*amount of seller's note plus amount owing on prior liens*]____ with lender's loss payable endorsement naming seller as ____[*designate, e.g., first*]____ loss payee.

Comment: The major concern of a seller is that before his deed is recorded the buyer has paid the purchase price and the escrow holder holds the purchase price due the seller. This clause established such concern as a condition precedent on the seller's behalf to closing the escrow. The provision requires that the escrow holder have possession of the sums due the seller "in available funds" and necessitates the negotiation and collection of any personal or third-party check deposited by the buyer in payment of the purchase price before the escrow may close. In this way the seller avoids the problems associated with dishonored checks.

A seller taking back a promissory note for part of the purchase price will usually agree to accept a California Land Title Association (CLTA) joint protection policy. Such policies insure both the buyer and the seller-lender and are issued at no additional charge over the cost for the buyer's policy alone. An institutional lender will invariably require the more extensive coverage afforded by the American Land Title Association (ALTA) lender's policy. See California Title Insurance Practice §§3.2-3.5 (Cal CEB 1980). See also chap 5 on seller financing.

§11.68   3. Form: Request for Notice

Form 11.68-1

Please record a request pursuant to Civil Code section 2924b for a copy of any notice of default or notice of sale under the deed of trust(s) in favor of ____[names of beneficiaries under any prior deeds of trust]____.

Comment: If the seller is to take back a note and deed of trust, and that deed of trust is junior to other deeds of trust, then the escrow holder should be instructed to record a request for notice under CC §2924b.

§11.69   4. Form: Payoff of Existing Encumbrance

Form 11.69-1

You are authorized to pay to ____[name of beneficiary under existing deed of trust]____ and charge to seller's account, the remaining principal balance of $_____ (less loan trust fund balance of $_____), a prepayment charge of $_____, and interest at the rate of $_____ per day from ____[date interest paid to at time of last installment]____ to the close of escrow when you have received:

1. Cancellation and return of the promissory note given to ____[name of beneficiary]____;
2. The original deed of trust securing the note; and
3. Reconveyance of deed of trust securing the note.

Comment: This provision should be included in the instructions whenever an existing loan is to be paid off at the close of escrow. The amount to be paid to the lender will be the remaining principal balance, less the amount remaining in any impound account for taxes and insurance, plus any prepayment charge. If the interest has been paid in arrears, the seller will owe interest at the daily rate from the date paid until the close of escrow (when the loan is paid off). If interest was paid in advance, the form will have to be modified to reflect that the seller will be entitled to a credit at the daily interest rate from close of escrow to the date interest has been paid.

Under CC §2941 the seller is entitled to the return of the note and the original deed of trust when the loan is fully paid. The escrow holder should be specifically instructed to arrange for the return of these documents. Institutional lenders, and title companies acting as trustees, tend to keep these documents, even after the loans have been fully paid, unless the borrower insists on their return. See California Mortgage and Deed of Trust Practice §3.57 (Cal CEB 1979).

§11.70   5. Form: Prorations

Form 11.70-1

Prorate the following items on the basis of a 30-day month as of ____[state date of close of escrow or other agreed date]____:

Form 11.70-2 (Real Property Tax)

(1) Real property taxes for the tax fiscal year 19__–19__ based on the most recent official information available in the office of the taxing entity;

Form 11.70-3 (Existing Loan To Be Assumed or Taken Subject to)

(2) Interest on the note secured by the recorded deed of trust in favor of ____[name of beneficiary]____ in accordance with figures furnished in beneficiary's statement;

Form 11.70-4 (Maintenance Charges)

(3) Monthly maintenance fee prepaid to____[date]____ based on the rate of $_____ per month;

Form 11.70-5 (Rents)

(4) Rentals based on the enclosed rent statement. Security deposits of $_____ and prepaid rent of $_____ shall be credited to buyer's account and charged to seller's account.

Form 11.70-6 (Hazard Insurance)

(5) Premium on seller's hazard insurance, which is to be assigned to buyer.

Form 11.70-7 (Impound Account Transferred to Buyer)

The amount of any funds held by____[name of lender]____ as advance payments as of____[date]____ plus interest, if any, shall be credited to seller and debited to buyer in full.

Comment: See comments and discussion in §§ 11.51-11.57 on buyer's instructions. See also § 11.56 for a provision for prorations outside of escrow.

§11.71   6. Form: Payment of Closing Costs

Form 11.71-1

You are also authorized to pay and charge to seller's account:

[Add appropriate statements]

1. From funds held for seller's account at close of escrow, a real estate broker's commission to ____[*state name of broker, amount of commission, and how divided if more than one broker*]____;

2. Documentary transfer tax;

3. ____[*Apportionment of local transfer tax if applicable*]____;

4. Your fee for any notary services performed for seller;

5. Fees for recording reconveyance of existing deed of trust;

6. Any reconveyance fee charged by____[*name of trustee*]____ as trustee under existing deed of trust; and

7. The sum of $_____ to ____[*name of structural pest control operator*]____ for termite work.

Comment: This clause is similar to the one for payment of the buyer's closing costs (see §11.60) and lists costs usually paid by the seller in northern California. See §§2.29, 3.62 for a discussion of the broker's commission. This form conditions payment of the commission on the close of escrow. If any existing deed of trust is to be reconveyed, the seller will pay the fee for recording the reconveyance and any prepayment fee. Under some deeds of trust the trustee is entitled to charge a fee for executing the reconveyance. See Comments to forms at §§11.46 and 11.47 for a discussion of structural pest control work.

A number of California communities now charge a tax or fee in addition to the documentary transfer tax of $.55 per $500 of net value of property transferred after deducting existing encumbrances, charged by each county in California. See Rev & T C §11911. Among the cities collecting additional taxes are San Francisco ($2.50 per $500 of full sales price), Albany ($1.65 per $1000 of net value), and Oakland (0.5% of total sales price). The counties of Calaveras, Ventura, and Santa Barbara charge an additional survey monumentation fund fee of $10 for recording certain types of deeds when the property description is other than an entire lot or lots created by a recorded subdivision map. This fee was authorized by Govt C §§27584-27585, enacted in 1976, and it is anticipated that many more counties will soon start to charge this fee. The seller is liable for the documentary transfer tax (Rev & T C §11912), but the local transfer taxes are generally made the joint and several liability of the buyer and seller, although both are subject to negotiation between buyer and seller.

See also discussion of closing costs at §§11.58-11.60 on buyer's instructions.

§11.72 7. Notice to Parties

Form 11.72-1

Except for any notice required under applicable law to be given in another manner, any notice given by one party to the other(s), including the escrow holder, shall be in writing, signed by the party giving notice and sent by certified or registered mail, return receipt requested, postage prepaid, to the other party(ies) at the last address the party(ies)____[has / have]____ designated by notice as provided herein, and a copy of the notice shall be filed with the escrow holder. Notice shall be considered to have been given at the time of deposit in the United States mail when given in the manner here designated.

Comment: See Comment at §11.61.

8. Concluding Provisions

§11.73 a. Time for Close of Escrow

Form 11.73-1

This escrow is to be completed and closed____[on or before]____ _____, 19__, at the hour of _____o'clock__.m. After that date and time, seller reserves the right to demand the return of all documents and money deposited by buyer in this escrow. On being reimbursed for all your charges and expenses in connection with this escrow, you shall comply with such demand and terminate this escrow. If no such demand is made, this escrow shall be closed as soon as possible.

Comment: See Comment at §11.62.

§11.74 b. Form: Forwarding of Documents After Closing

Form 11.74-1

On completion of this transaction, please send to ____[state name and address of seller or seller's attorney]____ the following:

[*Add appropriate statements*]

1. Cancelled note given to ____[name of lender]____;
2. The original deed of trust securing the above note;
3. California Land Title Association joint protection policy;
4. Promissory note in favor of ____[name of seller]____ ;
5. Copy of insurance policy naming ____[name of seller]____ as loss payee;
6. Your itemized statement of the costs charged to seller's account; and

[*Choose appropriate statement*]

7. Check for the balance due to seller.

Seller will pick up the check for the balance due seller at your office on the date escrow closes.

[Continue]

Please instruct the recorder to send the recorded reconveyance to the seller____[in care of seller's attorney at ____[address]____]____ .

Comment: The cancelled note and deed of trust are to be returned if an existing lien is paid off. See § 11.69. The CLTA joint protection policy, new promissory note, and insurance policy are to be delivered to the seller if the seller takes back a note as part of the purchase price. The original of the deed of trust securing the note given to the seller will be returned to the seller by the recorder after recordation if the seller's name and address (or that of seller's attorney) is shown on the form. (This information should be completed by the seller's attorney before submitting the approved form to the escrow holder for the buyer's signature.)

See also Comments to the buyer's forms at § 11.64.

§11.75   c. Seller's Signature; Escrow Holder's Acknowledgment and Acceptance

Form 11.75-1 (Seller's Signature)

Please acknowledge receipt of these instructions and the accompanying documents by signing the acceptance below and returning to____[*specify if to seller or give name and address of seller's attorney*]____ a copy of these instructions. Seller's address for purposes of notice is:

____[*Address of seller or of seller's attorney*]____

[Signature of seller]
____[Typed name of seller]____

Form 11.75-2 (Escrow Holder's Acknowledgment and Acceptance)

____[*Name of escrow holder*]____ acknowledges receipt of buyer's escrow instructions dated _____ 19__, of which the foregoing is a copy, and acknowledges receipt of the money and documents referred to and agrees to act as escrow holder and to comply with the terms and conditions of your escrow instructions.

Dated: _____

____[Typed name of escrow company]____
By__[signature of officer]__
____[Typed name of officer and title]____

Comment: See Comment at § 11.65.

§11.76   H.   Form: Lender's Printed Form Escrow Instructions

San Francisco *Federal Savings and Loan Association*

DATE:
RE: YOUR NUMBER:
DATE OF YOUR REPORT:
OUR NUMBER:
TRUSTOR:
PROPERTY:

GROSS LOAN AMOUNT: $
CC:

Gentlemen:

Please find enclosed the following:

☐ Deed of Trust Note for execution;
☐ Deed of Trust for execution and recordation;
☐ Regulation Z Disclosure Statement for execution and date in duplicate (original to borrower—return copy);
☐ Notice to Customer of Right of Rescission in duplicate (original and copy to borrower);
☐ Title Company Certification for execution and date in duplicate (retain copy—return original);
☐ Our Loan Application for execution or re-execution to acknowledge corrections as indicated thereon;
☐ Tax Service Application; ☐ will follow with Loan Proceeds;
☐ Statement of Fees and Charges in duplicate for completion, date and execution (copy to borrower—return original);
☐ Pest Control Withhold Instructions for execution;
☐ Certificate of One Borrower (Borrower must attest to completeness of Exhibit B and execute);
☐ Agreement to Make Payments to Tax and Insurance Liability Account for completion and execution:
☐ Affidavit of Purchaser and Vendor for execution and acknowledgment;

EXECUTED LOAN DOCUMENTS TOGETHER WITH CERTIFIED COPIES OF THE GRANT DEED (IF SALE) AND DEED OF TRUST ARE TO BE RETURNED TO SAN FRANCISCO FEDERAL SAVINGS AND LOAN ASSOCIATION AT LEAST 24 HOURS PRIOR TO REQUEST OF LOAN FUNDS. DIRECT ALL DOCUMENTS AND REQUESTS FOR FUNDS TO THE LOCAL BRANCH OFFICE INDICATED ON PAGE 2 OF THESE INSTRUCTIONS.

1. The following amounts will be deducted from the loan proceeds and only the net discounted loan proceeds will be paid into escrow when this loan is closed:

A. Interest at $ _____ per day from the date of our check to
    (No interest will be deducted when disbursement is after said date.)

B. Assn. Loan Fee . . . . . . $ _____
C. Credit Report . . . . . . $ _____
D. Withhold . . . . $ _____
E. Tax Reserve . . . . $ _____

F. Insurance Reserves . . . . . $ _____ (2 months + expired portion)
G. Payoff Loan No. _____ . . . $ _____
H. PMI Premium . . . . $ _____

2. Each of the following conditions precedent must be met prior to disbursement of any part of the gross loan proceeds:

A. The Deed of Trust Note, the Loan Application if enclosed, Statement of Fees and Charges and Pest Control Withhold Instructions shall have been executed by the Trustor without deletion or amendment and delivered to you as agent without condition or restriction for our account.

B. You shall be able, by recording the Deed of Trust enclosed herewith, to issue a ALTA form of Title Insurance Policy in favor of this Association in the amount of our Note, with CLTA endorsements form 100 and 116 (116.2, if a condominium) identifying the property, insuring this Association, the beneficiary under said Deed of Trust, as the holder of a valid first deed of trust lien upon the real property described therein and showing title thereto vested in our Trustors, named above and in the Deed of Trust, except as may be permitted by our specific written amendment to these instructions, said title to be free from all liens and encumbrances prior or superior to the lien of our Deed of Trust, except only the following as shown on your preliminary report bearing a vesting date and number as set forth above.

Taxes, Bonds and Assessments, Homeowner Association Dues: All that are liens on the property must be paid in full or paid to date as checked below.

1. ( ) Pay all prior years taxes.
2. ( ) Pay first installment all taxes due and payable.
3. ( ) Pay both installments of taxes.

4. ( ) Pay all bonds in full.
5. ( ) Pay bonds payments and/or assessments to date;
        ALTA Policy to so state.
6. ( ) Pay HOA dues to date; ALTA Policy to so state.

If your escrow closes on or after October 15, you must pay a minimum of first installment of county and city taxes due and payable November 1st; deduct such payment from our tax impounds request, if any.

INSTRUCTIONS RE: TRUTH IN LENDING (only box checked applies): ☐ You must deliver the Regulation Z Disclosure Statement to our borrowers at the time they execute the loan documents and obtain the written receipt of our borrowers for such Disclosure Statement on a copy thereof. ☐ The conditions precedent set forth in Addendum B attached hereto which relate to Truth in Lending Law and regulations shall be fully performed prior to close of the loan escrow and recordation of the loan documents.

THE DATE OF CONSUMATION OF THIS LOAN TRANSACTION SHALL BE THE DATE THE LOAN DOCUMENTS ARE SIGNED BY THE BORROWER(S) AND THE REGULATION Z DISCLOSURE STATEMENT, IF APPLICABLE, IS DELIVERED TO THE BORROWER(S).

LP-18-1 (Rev. 8/80)

(Continued on Page 2)

You are further advised and instructed that it has been expressly agreed between Borrower(s) and San Francisco Federal Savings and Loan Association, hereinafter Lender, that the Lender shall finance and deduct from the proceeds of the loan the Association Loan Fee (Item 1-B above) and Lender will disburse only the net discounted amount of the loan proceeds on closing through your escrow, after deducting said Association Loan Fee and the other deducted loan fees and costs specified in paragraph 1 herein.

You are further instructed that Borrower(s) are not obligated to pay, nor shall they pay, such financed and deducted loan costs and fees from their own cash funds either directly or indirectly, actually or constructively, and your Borrower's and Lender's Loan Closing statements shall accurately reflect that the cash deposited by the Borrower(s) in escrow, if any, in excess of the net discounted loan amount and the amount of any secondary financing permitted by Lender, is paid to the Seller or other party entitled thereto other than Lender.

In the event our loan is being made to finance the purchase of real property by Borrower(s), the balance of the purchase price of the property being encumbered over and above such net discounted loan proceeds to be funded by Lender and the amount of any secondary financing permitted by Lender must be provided and paid by the Borrower(s) to the Seller from their own funds or sources other than the proceeds of Lender's loan.

C. PEST CONTROL. We hold a copy of a pest control inspection report dated

No.   from

You are to advise us prior to recordation if other than the named inspection report is accepted by our trustor(s).

D. Collect the tax service fees of $ and forward to the Tax Agency along with their form.

E. Trustor shall deposit cash to escrow in payment of the sales price of the property due Seller, plus closing costs payable through escrow, less the sum of (1) the net discounted loan amount to be funded by Lender and (2) the amount of any secondary financing permitted by Lender as herein specified.

Secondary financing is permitted in the amount of $ for a term of   years and a payment of $ per month. Selling price is not to be less than $

F. Provide this Association with an itemized copy of trustor's closing statement and a duplicate copy of the note covering any secondary financing allowed above.

G. In the event your report does not include an examination of municipal assessments, you are hereby instructed to make such an examination and to insure this Association that all assessments are paid in full prior to the recording of our Deed of Trust.

H. You are to comply with all fire insurance requirements as shown in Addendum A attached hereto and made a part hereof by reference.

3. We hereby instruct you to hold the said enclosed documents exclusively for the benefit and account of San Francisco Federal Savings and Loan Association. Our written approval is required in the event of any change or alteration. Subject to our order, you are not to deliver or record the same, or any of them, unless or until each and every one of the above conditions precedent shall have been fully performed.

4. As we will charge interest from the date of our disbursement of loan proceeds, please call for the loan funds stated below ONLY when receipt of the funds will permit our loan to be then recorded. Your request for disbursement will be under-

stood as your assurance that you are able to record under the provisions of these instructions. Fire insurance information will be required at this time.

5. We further require that junior mortgages and deeds of trust which are recorded prior to our Deed of Trust and are subordinated, or are recorded subsequently to our Deed of Trust but as a part of the same escrow or shortly after the close thereof, and of which you have knowledge, be set forth in a letter to this Association as junior liens with the address of each lienholder where available.

6. When each and every one of said conditions has been fully performed, you are hereby authorized and directed to record our Deed of Trust. It is to be understood that your closing of this transaction constitutes a certification on your part that all the conditions stated above have been complied with and an agreement that all documents will be forwarded in accordance with these instructions as soon as possible.

7. You are hereby further advised that these instruction are expressly made revocable and may be withdrawn, amended or supplemented at any time and from time to time by letter, or wire, or telephone message confirmed by letter or wire, and the enclosures may be withdrawn at any time prior to the recordation of the enclosed Deed of Trust. We will expect to recall our papers and instructions for redrawing when our loan will not be recorded at least fifteen (15) days prior to the first monthly loan payment due date.

We are to be at no expense in connection with this transaction.

Very truly yours,

SAN FRANCISCO FEDERAL SAVINGS & LOAN ASSOCIATION

By...

Escrow Officer

LP-1B-2 (Rev. 8/80)

SAN FRANCISCO FEDERAL SAVINGS AND LOAN ASSOCIATION

A D D E N D U M   A

Insurance

1. We require an original policy of insurance to be in effect and held for delivery
   to us on the close of escrow; the policy is to be for a minimum term of three (3)
   years or Continuous and shall include:

   a. If the loan security is one to four residential units - - Fire with Special
      Form Coverage equivalent to Standard Form 188DDNS - 8/67 in at least the
      amount of our loan.
   b. If the loan security is anything other than the above - - Fire with Extended
      Coverage with Vandalism and Malicious Mischief endorsements in at least the
      amount of our loan.
   c. Premium prepaid for a minimum of either ONE YEAR or the remaining policy term,
      whichever is least. Receipt to be furnished if premium is paid outside of
      escrow.
   d. With remaining term of at least SIX (6) MONTHS as of the date of the close of
      escrow.
   e. As of Issue or by endorsement issued, or by order of endorsement with evidence
      thereof, naming our Trustor-title owners as insured and this Association as
      first lender loss payee, Post and Kearny Streets, San Francisco, California,
      94104 (Standard Form 438BFU).
   f. Deductible: Not to exceed $250.00.
   g. The insurance company shall:
      (i) Be licensed to do business in California.
      (ii) Have a Class VI rating in the current edition of Best's Insurance
           Guide, or the policy shall contain the following reinsured notice
           statement: "This risk is reinsured in compliance with Insurance
           Commissioner's Regulation. If such reinsurance is not maintained
           or is terminated, then written notice will be mailed or delivered
           by the primary insurer to the lender at its office or branch   ·
           described on the first page of the policy."

2. If insurance required above exists, but cannot be delivered without undue delay,
   you may submit full description of such insurance coverage offered in satisfaction
   of our requirements. You are not to consider this insurance requirement to be met,
   however, until an original insurance policy has been delivered to this office.

PLEASE HAVE THIS INFORMATION FOR US AT THE TIME YOU REQUEST OUR LOAN FUNDS.

LP 78 (Rev. 10-76)

ADDENDUM B   (TRUTH IN LENDING)

Prior to closing this loan escrow, the following conditions precedent shall be fully performed:

1. You must deliver the Regulation Z Disclosure Statement to our borrowers at the time they execute the loan documents and obtain the written receipt of our borrowers for such Disclosure Statement on a copy thereof.

2. You shall insert the date of execution of the loan documents and delivery of the Disclosure Statements in the first line of the Notice of Right of Recission and insert the date of the third business day following such date of execution and delivery in the fourth line from the end of said Notice of Right of Recission. No date will be inserted in the blank opposite the borrower's signature unless the borrower in fact elects to cancel this loan transaction and signs the space provided for his signature.

3. You must deliver to each borrower two copies of the Notice of Right of Recission at the time our borrowers execute the loan documents and acknowledge receipt of the Disclosure Statement.

4. You must immediately return to this Association:

   A. Receipted Disclosure Statement

   B. The certification that you have delivered to each borrower two copies of the said Notice of Right of Recission.

5. You may call for our loan funds to be mailed not earlier than the fourth business day following the date the Disclosure Statement is executed and/or the Notice of Right of Recission is given to our Borrower(s) whichever is later.

6. Under no circumstances will loan funds be transmitted by this Association until the items called for under paragraph 4A and 4B above have been received by our Loan Processing Department and the four day waiting period described in paragraph 5 above has elapsed.

LP 89

Comment: Third party lenders who finance a real estate sale submit their own escrow instructions to the escrow holder. Most institutional lenders use a printed form of escrow instructions because of the volume of loans they make. This printed form is typical of most institutional lenders' escrow instructions.

All lenders, whether institutional lenders or private parties, such as a seller financing the sale, normally require at least three conditions precedent to the close of escrow.

The first condition is the execution by the buyer of the loan documents, usually a promissory note and deed of trust, but possibly also a loan application (as in this form; necessary for recordkeeping purposes of institutional lenders under the Equal Credit Opportunity Act, 12 CFR §202.12), statement of fees and charges, and pest control withhold instruction (when pest control work is to be performed after the close of escrow).

The second condition is the issuance of an American Land Title Association (ALTA) lender's title insurance policy with any desirable endorsements or, more commonly, a CLTA joint protection policy in the case of seller financing (see California Title Insurance Practice §§3.2-3.27 (Cal CEB 1980) for a discussion of lender's title insurance) insuring the lender's security interest in the amount of the loan. The clause in the printed form is intended for use in northern California, where a title insurance company acts as escrow holder and the preliminary title report is available to the lender before it submits its instructions.

The third condition is the existence of hazard insurance, in at least the amount of the loan, covering the real property security. The printed form contains an addendum explaining the lender's requirements for insurance.

In addition to these basic conditions precedent, institutional lenders require that their borrowers execute a Regulation Z Disclosure Statement, if necessary, under the Truth in Lending Act, 15 USC §§1601-1665a, and that the disclosure statement be delivered by the escrow holder to the borrower on the date of consummation of the loan.

Institutional lenders will not deposit the loan proceeds when they submit their escrow instructions. They will disburse the loan proceeds only immediately before the escrow is to close and their deed of trust or other security interest is to be recorded. The printed instructions inform the escrow holder that interest will accrue on the loan proceeds from the date of disbursement and instruct the escrow holder to call for the funds only after all other steps have been completed and the documents are ready to be recorded.

§11.77 I. Form: Amendment to Escrow Instructions

Form 11.77-1

Date: _____

To: ____[name of escrow holder]____   Your Escrow No.: _____
____[address of escrow holder]____
Sale:____[name of seller]____ to____[name of buyer]____
Property: ____[street address or legal description if short]____
____[Name of party]____ , hereafter____[buyer / seller / or last name]____
submits the following amendments, which supersede any contrary provisions in and constitute part of those escrow instructions dated _____, 19__, submitted to you by the undersigned.
1. ____[List amendments]____

[Signature of party]
____[Typed name of party]____

Comment: This clause may be utilized either to amend escrow instructions that have already been submitted to the escrow holder, or to add or change instructions in an escrow holder's printed form instructions. When amendments are made to printed escrow instructions, a provision should be added to the printed form referring to the attached amendments, incorporating them in the printed instructions and specifying that the amendments supersede any contrary provisions in the printed form.

On the right of one party to amend instructions unilaterally, see §11.39.

IV. TERMINATION OF ESCROW

§11.78 A. Without Performance of Conditions

An escrow can be terminated by mutual consent of the parties or by the parties' failure to perform or to satisfy the escrow conditions within the time specified.

Most escrow instructions provide that either party may cancel the escrow by notice to the escrow holder on failure of the other party to perform on time. See §11.62. This right to cancel exists even when the escrow instructions are silent. However, a defaulting party may not cancel against a nondefaulting party. *Diamond v Huenergardt* (1959) 175 CA2d 214, 346 P2d 37. Although an escrow may be cancelled because of a failure to perform on time, such failure, even when time is made the essence of the agreement, will not deprive a party of the right to specific performance unless his failure to perform was unlawful, grossly negligent, or intentional. Compare *Williams Plumbing Co. v Sinsley* (1975) 53 CA3d 1027, 126 CR 345, with *Nash v Superior Court* (1978) 86 CA3d 690, 150 CR 394.

Methods of termination are discussed in §§11.79-11.83.

§11.79   1. Unilateral Revocation

Because irrevocability is an essential element of an escrow, a party may not unilaterally revoke or withdraw from an escrow before expiration of the time set for performance of the escrow conditions. *Wood Bldg. Corp. v Griffitts* (1958) 164 CA2d 559, 330 P2d 847; *Deming v Smith* (1937) 19 CA2d 683, 66 P2d 454.

§11.80   2. Mutual Cancellation

The parties to an escrow can agree to cancel it just as any two contracting parties may mutually terminate their contractual relationship, although a mutual cancellation of an escrow does not necessarily terminate the parties' rights and duties under the purchase and sale agreement. *Cohen v Shearer* (1980) 108 CA3d 939, 167 CR 10. Such cancellation, however, cannot affect any vested rights of third parties, such as real estate brokers or creditors who are assignees of any escrow proceeds. See *Warington Lumber Co. v Fullerton Mortgage & Escrow Co.* (1963) 222 CA2d 706, 35 CR 423.

§11.81   B. Form: Cancellation of Escrow Due to Failure To Perform

Form: 11.81-1

Due to the failure of ____[buyer / seller]____ to perform those terms and conditions required of the ____[buyer / seller]____ under the escrow instructions pursuant to your Escrow No. _____ within the time limit specified in those instructions, you are notified by the undersigned to cancel Escrow No. _____ and return all papers executed and all funds deposited by the undersigned.
Dated:_____

[Signature]

Comment: This form serves as a notice by one of the parties to the escrow holder cancelling the escrow due to a default by the other party. Most escrow instructions require such a notice. A copy of the notice should be sent to the defaulting party (many escrow instructions also require notice to the defaulting party before cancellation). See §11.62 for a provision in escrow instructions concerning cancellation and discussion of problems encountered in obtaining a return of the deposit from the escrow holder.

If cancellation is based on default other than failure to perform on time, a suitable provision should be drafted.

V. CLOSING THE SALE

§11.82   A. On Performance of Conditions

An escrow is terminated and the sale closed when the parties have performed their respective conditions as set forth in the escrow instructions. Unless the escrow instructions specify a certain time when the escrow shall be considered terminated (see §11.84), the termination, and its effect on title and possession, occurs automatically on the completion of the last condition to be performed, or waiver by the party entitled to demand performance.

Termination of an escrow on the performance of the escrow conditions is commonly referred to as the close of escrow, even though many ministerial acts must still be completed by the escrow agent before documents and money are delivered to the parties entitled to them.

§11.83   1. Substantial Performance

Generally, only strict compliance with the escrow instructions will qualify as performance of the escrow conditions that permit the escrow to close. The doctrine of substantial performance, often available in other contractual situations, is inapplicable to escrow agreements. *Love v White* (1961) 56 C2d 192, 14 CR 442. The possible harsh results of such inapplicability are often tempered by the use of the doctrines of waiver or estoppel.

§11.84   2. Form: Defining Close of Escrow

Form 11.84-1

The term "close of escrow" shall mean the date the instrument(s) transferring title ____[is / are]____ recorded.

Comment: This provision simplifies the determination of when an escrow closes by stating a specific date (date of recordation), which is easily discoverable by reference to the dated recording stamp; and is a change from the common law rule (when all conditions have been performed).

B. Real Estate Settlement Procedures Act

§11.85   1. Act of 1974 and 1975 Amendments

The Real Estate Settlement Procedures Act of 1974 (12 USC §§2601-2617), commonly referred to as RESPA, as originally enacted, was intended to control real estate settlement costs on a national basis. Understandably, such an act necessarily affected various real estate practices, including the escrow transaction.

Effective June 20, 1975, RESPA required nearly all lenders to provide a HUD-prepared information booklet to their loan applicants; to make an advance disclosure of settlement costs 12 days before settlement, using a prescribed form; and to issue a uniform settlement statement on settlement, which is generally the close of escrow. 12 USC §§2603-2604. Institutional lenders insisted that the escrow agent prepare the uniform settlement statement and, in some cases, the advance disclosure statement. The 1974 RESPA also required a disclosure of the property's previous selling price by the seller in certain situations, prohibitions on kickbacks, unearned fees and title insurance referrals, limits on advance deposits in tax and insurance impound accounts, and required future studies, including the establishment of a demonstration model land parcel recordation system.

Because of negative reactions to RESPA from nearly all concerned in a real property sales transaction, Congress passed the Real Estate Settlement Procedures Act Amendments of 1975 (RESPA amendments; Pub L 94-204, 89 Stat 1157 (1975)), which almost totally changed the requirements of the 1974 RESPA.

The RESPA amendments, effective January 2, 1976, narrowed the coverage of RESPA (see §11.86), eliminated the provisions for advance disclosure of previous selling prices, and modified the kickback and unearned fees and impound account requirements. The amendments created a new RESPA, which requires lenders to provide estimates of closing costs at the time a loan application is made to them (see §11.87) and allows a borrower-buyer to inspect the uniform settlement statement one day before settlement (see §11.88). (RESPA now refers to the 1974 act as amended.)

§11.86　2. Transactions Covered

The Real Estate Settlement Procedures Act (RESPA) is applicable to what is termed "federally related mortgage loans." A federally related mortgage loan is a loan used in whole or in part to finance the purchase or transfer of title of a one-to-four-family structure (including individual condominium or cooperative units) or a mobile home. 12 USC §2602(1); 24 CFR §3500.5(b). The loan must be secured by a first lien or other first security interest covering the real property and must be made by a specified class of lenders. Nearly all institutional lenders fit into the class delineated in RESPA. 24 CFR §3500.5. (The RESPA regulations are referred to as Regulation X.)

Certain transactions are exempted from RESPA coverage by 24 CFR §3500.5(d). Among the exemptions are loans made to finance or purchase property consisting of 25 acres or more, loans on vacant land, and assumptions or sales subject to a preexisting loan, except for the conversion of a construction loan to a permanent loan by the first user.

§11.87　3. Estimates of Closing Costs

The 1974 RESPA provided for advance disclosure of settlement costs (broker's commission, lender's charges, title charges, and government charges); this enabled borrowers to seek the lowest costs, thereby ostensibly controlling these costs. However, the added delays and paperwork required for advance disclosure apparently outweighed the limited investigating borrowers did. Consequently, Congress tried a different approach with the new RESPA.

Since June 30, 1976, RESPA requires lenders to provide their loan applicants with a good faith estimate of the amount or range of charges for specific settlement services the borrower is likely to incur in connection with the settlement, together with the HUD-prepared special information booklet. 12 USC §§2603-2604. See also 24 CFR §3500.7. The intent is that the borrowers' knowledge of estimates, coupled with their capability of inspecting the uniform settlement statement one day prior to settlement (see §11.88), will enable them to obtain the lowest costs.

§11.88   4. Advance Inspection of Uniform Settlement Statement

The most direct impact of RESPA on the escrow phase of a real estate sales transaction arises from the requirements that the person conducting settlement, which in California is the escrow holder when an escrow is used, use the Uniform Settlement Statement (HUD Form 1, see §11.99) as the settlement statement and, on request of the borrower, allow him to inspect the Uniform Settlement Statement, which must be as complete as possible, on the business day immediately preceding the day of settlement. However, an exception exists to this advance inspection when the borrower-buyer or his or her agent does not attend the settlement or when the person conducting the settlement does not require a meeting of the parties. In such cases, the Uniform Settlement Statement need only be mailed as soon as possible after the settlement. 24 CFR §3500.10. This exception will apply to most California settlements.

§11.89   5. Incidental Provisions

Other provisions in RESPA include a prohibition against kickbacks and unearned fees (12 USC §2607), a prohibition against forcing a buyer to use a particular title company (12 USC §2608), limitations on the amount collectible per month by a lender for a tax and insurance impound account (12 USC §2609), a prohibition against charging a fee for preparation of the Uniform Settlement Statement (12 USC §2610), and directions for future study, including the National Land Parcel Recordation System (12 USC §2611).

The 1974 RESPA provided for civil recovery by a buyer or seller of actual damages or $500, whichever is greater, plus court costs and reasonable attorneys' fees for a RESPA violation by a lender (the lender was ultimately responsible for RESPA under the 1974 act). This civil recovery provision was contained, however, in the advance disclosure requirement section of the 1974 RESPA (later repealed). Pub L 94-205, 89 Stat 1157 (1975). There is no specific authority under the 1975 amended RESPA for private civil action by an injured party, except for a statement that violators of the kickback and unearned fee provision and the provision requiring a specific title company are liable for treble damages. 12 USC §§2607(d)(2), 2608(b). Severe criminal penalties are also possible for violation of the kickback and unearned fees provision. 12 USC §2607(d).

The civil actions allowable under RESPA must be brought within one year of the violation in the United States District Court where the property is located, or any other court of competent jurisdiction. 12 USC §2614.

C. Recordation

1. General Considerations

§11.90   a. Purpose of Recording Acts

The basic California recording laws, for purposes of real property transfers, appear in CC §§1169-1220 and Govt C §§27201-27383.

The recording statutes were enacted to protect buyers and encumbrancers of real property from the adverse effects of any unknown prior interests in the property. In transfers and encumbrances of real property, recording has two principal effects:

(1) It gives constructive notice of the contents of the instrument to subsequent purchasers and encumbrancers. CC §1213 (notice is more fully discussed in §11.97).

(2) It gives priority over conveyances and encumbrances that are recorded later, even though the execution of the latter may have been prior in time. Civil Code §1214, which creates this priority, excepts leases for a term not exceeding one year and requires that the subsequent conveyance be in good faith (*i.e.*, without notice of the prior conveyance) and for valuable consideration. Judgment creditors are not considered bona fide purchasers or encumbrancers under CC §1214. *Wells Fargo Bank v PAL Invests., Inc.* (1979) 96 CA3d 431, 157 CR 818.

This is termed a race-notice type of recording statute. The "race" part refers to the race for the recorder's office encouraged by the "first duly recorded" provision of CC §1214. The "notice" part of the phrase recognizes that mere priority in recording is not enough to confer priority of interest if the first to record had notice of an interest before his in time; he must take his interest "in good faith and for a valuable consideration." CC §1214. Notice may be actual or constructive and is discussed in §11.97.

§11.91   b. Types of Documents Entitled to Recordation

"Any instrument or judgment affecting the title to or possession of real property may be recorded. . . ." Govt C §27280(a). The statute raises two questions pertinent to escrow: (1) What is an "instrument"? (2) What may be said to "affect" title to or possession of real property?

The California Supreme Court defines an instrument as a document "signed and delivered by one person to another, transferring the title to or creating a lien on property, or giving a right to a debt or duty." *Hoag v Howard* (1880) 55 C 564.

"Affecting" real property has never been specifically defined, but in addition to such obvious instruments as deeds and mortgages, the term has been held to include instruments that declare restrictions (*Cornbleth v Allen* (1926) 80 CA 459, 251 P 87) and that declare a conveyance to be rescinded (*Dreifus v Marx* (1940) 40 CA2d 461, 104 P2d 1080).

In addition to documents recordable as affecting real property under the general provision of Govt C §27280, a number of documents are specifically made recordable by other statutes and case law. Some of these are certified copies of judgments or decrees of court (Govt C §§27282, 27326), notices of completion (CC §3093), declarations of homestead (CC §1262), and record of survey maps (Bus & P C §8762). For an extensive, but not exhaustive, list of the types of documents that may be recorded, see 2 Miller and Starr, Current Law of California Real Estate §11:8 (rev ed 1977).

The most common instruments recorded in a simple real estate sale include the grant deed from seller to buyer, the mortgage or deed of trust of the buyer's lender, and the reconveyance of the deed of trust or release of the mortgage of the seller's lender.

§11.92   c. Defective Documents

The priority gained by recordation of an instrument depends on the "constructive notice" (see §11.97) the recorded instrument gives to the world. An instrument affecting real property, although entitled to be recorded, may be defective in some way so that its recording does not impart constructive notice of its existence.

Such a defect may be the failure of the instrument to be properly recorded or indexed (see §§11.93-11.95), or the invalidity or defectiveness of the instrument itself. Thus, a deed that contains an incorrect description of the land it is intended to convey does not give constructive notice of the transfer of that land (*Davis v Ward* (1895) 109 C 186, 41 P 1010), nor would the recording of a forged instrument give any constructive notice of its existence (*Hopkins v Fresno County Abstract Co.* (1918) 36 CA 699, 173 P 106). With respect to defects in the execution of an instrument, or in the certificate of acknowledgment, or lack of such certificate, CC §1207 provides generally that, if otherwise properly recorded, such instruments give constructive notice one year after recordation, notwithstanding the defect.

2. Recording Procedures

§11.93   a. Form of Instruments

Government Code §27361.6 specifies that printed forms, intended to be recorded, reserve the top right two and one-half (2½) inches of the first page for recording information, the left three and one-half (3½) inches to be used to show the name and address of the person requesting recordation and return of the document, and the remaining space to be used by the recorder. (When the document is a deed conveying fee title, the name and address of the person to whom future tax statements are to be mailed must be stated, although lack of such statement does not affect constructive notice. Govt C §27321.5.) Additionally, the document must have one-half (½) inch margins on each side. Govt C §27361.6. See also §§7.7-7.11 on deeds.

Because recorded documents are usually copied by a photographic or microphotographic process, they must be sufficiently legible themselves, and on a quality of paper that will reproduce legibly when such copying processes are used. Govt C §27361.6.

As for the content of the document, the only major requirements for recording purposes are that it be written in English unless a certified translation is attached (Govt C §27293), and that the real property affected be sufficiently described, either by a legal description contained in the document, or by reference to another recorded document that contains such a description. It is important to note that, when an instrument, such as a deed granting an easement, affects two parcels of real property, both the benefited and burdened properties must be described. CC §1468.

Government Code §27288.1 provides that certain information regarding names of record owners be contained in specific types of documents, including those transferring or encumbering any interest in real property.

§11.94   b. Acknowledgment of Instruments

To be recorded, most documents must contain a certification of acknowledgment or other acceptable proof. CC §§1195, 1213. The acknowledgment, which is a statement that the person purporting to have signed the document did in fact sign it, must be that of the person or persons whose real property is affected or alienated (Govt C §27288), *i.e.*, the grantor, lessor, or mortgagor, not the grantee, lessee, or mortgagee. When there are two or more persons whose acknowledgment is required, each signature must be acknowledged, for no constructive notice is given of the interest of nonacknowledging parties (*DuRoss v Trainor* (1932) 122 CA 732, 10 P2d 763), except to the extent that a curative act such as CC §1207 may apply.

Government Code §27287 imposes a general requirement that all instruments be acknowledged before they can be recorded, but excepts certain instruments from this requirement by reference to other statutes. Documents that are not "instruments" need not be acknowledged to be recorded. *U.S. Hertz, Inc. v Niobrara Farms* (1974) 41 CA3d 68, 116 CR 44 (notice of default under deed of trust not an "instrument").

The lack of a required acknowledgment for recording purposes does not alter the enforceability of the document between the parties or one having actual knowledge of its contents. *Johndrow v Thomas* (1947) 31 C2d 202, 187 P2d 681. Some documents, however, must be acknowledged in order to be valid. In real property transactions, a homestead (CC §1262) or conveyance or encumbrance of homesteaded property (CC §1242) is not valid unless it is acknowledged. Under CC §1207 a recorded instrument, otherwise valid, imparts constructive notice one year after it has been recorded, notwithstanding any defect in the acknowledgment.

The form of the certificate of acknowledgment depends on the status of the party executing it. Civil Code §§1183.5, 1189, 1190, 1190a, 1191, and 1192 prescribe forms for various classes of acknowledgments. When the statute applies, the acknowledgment must be substantially in the form set forth in the statute. CC §1188. All acknowledgments must state that the executing party acknowledges his or her signature and must contain the state and county where the acknowledgment is made, the name and capacity of the acknowledging party, and a statement that the executing party appeared before a notary public and is either personally known to the notary or that another person has identified him or her under oath. See also §§7.59-7.62 on acknowledgments.

§11.95   c. Place of Recording

Documents are recorded in the office of the county recorder at the county seat. Govt C §24250. When a document to be recorded affects real property, it must be recorded in the county (or counties, if the land is located in more than one) where the real property is situated in order to impart constructive notice. There is authority that when a portion of land is in one county, recording a document affecting land in that county will give constructive notice about the land in the county of recordation regardless of the failure to record in other counties where the land is situated. *Votypka v Valentine* (1919) 41 CA 74, 182 P 76.

When a document is required to be recorded in more than one county, a certified copy of the document recorded in one county can be recorded in the other counties and will have the same force and effect as the original document. CC §1213.

§11.96   d. Recorder's Procedure

Before the county recorder may act on a document presented for recordation, the fee required by Govt C §27361 must be tendered or paid, and all county recorders also insist that other fees, such as the documentary transfer tax, be paid before recordation. On payment of the fees, and assuming the document is entitled to be recorded, the recorder must enter the next filing number in order, the year, month, day, hour, and minute of reception, and the amount of fees on the document and then without delay record it in the proper book of records. Govt C §27320.

In most California counties, documents affecting real property are recorded in a master set of books called the "official records," although statutory authority exists for maintaining separate sets of books for different classes of documents. Govt C §27323. Generally, the only documents affecting real property, which are recorded in separate books, are subdivision maps and tax liens.

The actual recording process today consists of either making a photocopy of the original document and placing the copy in a permanently bound book, or microfilming the original and storing the microfilm record.

After recordation, the recorder endorses on the document the book and page number in which the document has been recorded, and returns the original document to the party whose name and address appear in the upper lefthand corner of the first page. Govt C §27321.

Perhaps the most important task of the recorder is the indexing of the document so that the public can locate a particular document without the necessity of searching the entire official records of a county.

If a recorder keeps separate sets of records for different types of documents, he must index the document according to the document's title (Govt C §27324), or as he determines if there is no title (Govt C §27325). Because a recorder can be held liable for an incorrect indexing (Govt C §27203), most recorders keep only the master official records books (Govt C §27323), in which case only two indexes are required, one for grantors and one for grantees. The grantor index includes anyone conveying or losing an interest in property, *i.e.,* grantors, mortgagors, lessors, and judgment debtors. The grantee index includes those receiving or claiming an interest in property, *i.e.,* grantees, mortgagees, lessees, and judgment creditors.

3. Effectiveness of Recording

§11.97   a. Legal Effectiveness Versus Constructive Notice

Most documents affecting interests in real property do not depend on the fact of being recorded for their validity. These documents are valid as between the parties and those who have notice of them or who have knowledge of facts which would prompt a reasonable person to inquire, regardless of recordation. The recordation of these documents affects only the priority between the grantee or mortgagee and subsequent purchasers or encumbrancers who pay a valuable consideration in good faith and without notice or knowledge of the prior interest. Recording constitutes constructive notice to such bona fide purchasers and bona fide encumbrancers, and the subsequent recordation of the document transferring an interest to them will not gain priority over that of the original grantee or mortgagee. In the absence of recordation of prior interests, subsequent bona fide purchasers and bona fide encumbrancers who do record gain priority over all unrecorded prior interests.

There are classes of documents affecting real property which must be recorded to be valid. The important ones are homestead declarations (CC §§1264 and 1268) and claims of mechanics' liens (CC §§3115, 3117). Such documents have no legal effect until recorded, and must often be recorded within a limited period of time.

§11.98 b. Time of Recording

An instrument is considered recorded when it is deposited for recordation in the recorder's office with the proper officer. CC §1170. A recorded document is considered constructive notice of the conveyance "from the time it is filed with the recorder for record." CC §1213. Nevertheless, many courts have held that a document must be physically copied in the proper book and indexed before it is "recorded," and that it gives only the constructive notice apparent from the physical record. See *Dougery v Bettencourt* (1931) 214 C 455, 6 P2d 499; *Cady v Purser* (1901) 131 C 552, 63 P 844. On constructive notice, see §11.97.

Various courts have attempted to reconcile these apparently conflicting rules by stating that a recording intended to comply with a statutory requirement or that is an essential step in completing some act of the party constitutes a recording when the instrument is filed, but documents intended to give notice to a third party must be physically recorded before they are considered recorded. See *Dougery v Bettencourt, supra; Cady v Purser, supra*.

The law has been interpreted to mean that the grantee or mortgagee must act as though the recorder were his agent (see 13 Ops Cal Atty Gen 185, 187 (1949)) and check to make certain that the recording has been done properly.

§11.99 D. Form: Uniform Settlement Statement

The Uniform Settlement Statement is reproduced on pages 670-673.

Form Approved OMB NO. 63-R-1501

U.S. DEPARTMENT OF HOUSING AND URBAN DEVELOPMENT
SETTLEMENT STATEMENT

A.

B. TYPE OF LOAN

1. □ FHA　　2. □ FMHA　　3. □ CONV. UNINS.

4. □ VA　　5. □ CONV. INS.

6. FILE NUMBER:　　7. LOAN NUMBER:

8. MORT. INS. CASE NO.:

C. NOTE: This form is furnished to give you a statement of actual settlement costs. Amounts paid to and by the settlement agent are shown. Items marked "(p.o.c.)" were paid outside the closing; they are shown here for informational purposes and are not included in the totals.

D. NAME OF BORROWER:

E. NAME OF SELLER:

F. NAME OF LENDER:

G. PROPERTY LOCATION:

H. SETTLEMENT AGENT:

PLACE OF SETTLEMENT:

I. SETTLEMENT DATE:

J. SUMMARY OF BORROWER'S TRANSACTION:		K. SUMMARY OF SELLER'S TRANSACTION:	
100. GROSS AMOUNT DUE FROM BORROWER		400. GROSS AMOUNT DUE TO SELLER	
101. Contract sales price		401. Contract sales price	
102. Personal property		402. Personal property	
103. Settlement charges to borrower (line 1400)		403.	
104.		404.	
105.		405.	
Adjustments for items paid by seller in advance		Adjustments for items paid by seller in advance	

106.	City/town taxes	to	406.	City/town taxes	to
107.	County taxes	to	407.	County taxes	to
108.	Assessments	to	408.	Assessments	to
109.			409.		
110.			410.		
111.			411.		
112.			412.		
120.	**GROSS AMOUNT DUE FROM BORROWER**		420.	**GROSS AMOUNT DUE TO SELLER**	
200.	**AMOUNTS PAID BY OR IN BEHALF OF BORROWER**		500.	**REDUCTIONS IN AMOUNT DUE TO SELLER**	
201.	Deposit or earnest money		501.	Excess deposit (see Instructions)	
202.	Principal amount of new loan(s)		502.	Settlement charges to seller (line 1400)	
203.	Existing loan(s) taken subject to		503.	Existing loan(s) taken subject to	
204.			504.	Payoff of first mortgage loan	
205.			505.	Payoff of second mortgage loan	
206.			506.		
207.			507.		
208.			508.		
209.			509.		
	Adjustments for items unpaid by seller			Adjustments for items unpaid by seller	
210.	City/town taxes	to	510.	City/town taxes	to
211.	County taxes	to	511.	County taxes	to
212.	Assessments	to	512.	Assessments	to
213.			513.		
214.			514.		
215.			515.		
216.			516.		
217.			517.		
218.			518.		
219.			519.		
220.	**TOTAL PAID BY/FOR BORROWER**		520.	**TOTAL REDUCTION AMOUNT DUE SELLER**	
300.	**CASH AT SETTLEMENT FROM OR TO BORROWER**		600.	**CASH AT SETTLEMENT TO OR FROM SELLER**	
301.	Gross amount due from borrower (line 120)		601.	Gross amount due to seller (line 420)	
302.	Less amounts paid by/for borrower (line 220)	( )	602.	Less reduction amount due seller (line 520)	( )
303.	**CASH (□ FROM) (□ TO) BORROWER**		603.	**CASH (□ TO) (□ FROM) SELLER**	

HUD 1A REV. 5/76

U.S. DEPARTMENT OF HOUSING AND URBAN DEVELOPMENT
SETTLEMENT STATEMENT
PAGE 2

L. SETTLEMENT CHARGES	PAID FROM BORROWER'S FUNDS AT SETTLEMENT	PAID FROM SELLER'S FUNDS AT SETTLEMENT
700. TOTAL SALES/BROKER'S COMMISSION based on price $ @ % =		
Division of commission (line 700) as follows:		
701. $ to		
702. $ to		
703. Commission paid at Settlement		
704.		
800. ITEMS PAYABLE IN CONNECTION WITH LOAN		
801. Loan Origination Fee %		
802. Loan Discount %		
803. Appraisal Fee to		
804. Credit Report to		
805. Lender's Inspection Fee		
806. Mortgage Insurance Application Fee to		
807. Assumption Fee		
808.		
809.		
810.		
811.		
900. ITEMS REQUIRED BY LENDER TO BE PAID IN ADVANCE		
901. Interest from to @ $ /day		
902. Mortgage Insurance Premium for mo. to		
903. Hazard Insurance Premium for yrs. to		
904. yrs. to		
905.		
1000. RESERVES DEPOSITED WITH LENDER FOR		
1001. Hazard insurance mo. @ $ /mo.		
1002. Mortgage insurance mo. @ $ /mo.		
1003. City property taxes mo. @ $ /mo.		
1004. County property taxes mo. @ $ /mo.		
1005. Annual assessments mo. @ $ /mo.		
1006. mo. @ $ /mo.		
1007. mo. @ $ /mo.		
1008. mo. @ $ /mo.		

1100. TITLE CHARGES

1101.	Settlement or closing fee	to		
1102.	Abstract or title search	to		
1103.	Title examination	to		
1104.	Title insurance binder	to		
1105.	Document preparation	to		
1106.	Notary fees	to		
1107.	Attorney's fees	to		
	(includes above items No.: *)*			
1108.	Title insurance	to		
	(includes above items No.: *)*			
1109.	Lender's coverage $			
1110.	Owner's coverage $			
1111.				
1112.				
1113.				

1200. GOVERNMENT RECORDING AND TRANSFER CHARGES

1201.	Recording fees: Deed $; Mortgage $; Releases $		
1202.	City/county tax/stamps: Deed $; Mortgage $		
1203.	State tax/stamps: Deed $; Mortgage $		
1204.			
1205.			

1300. ADDITIONAL SETTLEMENT CHARGES

1301.	Survey	to		
1302.	Pest inspection	to		
1303.				
1304.				
1305.				

1400. TOTAL SETTLEMENT CHARGES *(enter on lines 103 and 502, Sections J and K)*

HUD 1B REV. 5/76·

Comment: While the close of escrow is typically defined as the date of recording the necessary documents, the escrow process is not completed on that date. The escrow holder must distribute the funds and documents held in escrow to the parties entitled to them under the escrow instructions. Often, because the recordation does not occur on the date originally estimated by the escrow holder, the prorations must be recomputed. The buyer and seller are notified of the final debits and credits when they receive an escrow statement, which, when RESPA applies (see §11.86), is this uniform settlement statement.

In RESPA transactions, the uniform settlement statement must be mailed or personally delivered to the borrower (the buyer) and the seller at or before settlement, unless the escrow holder does not require the parties to meet on the settlement date or the borrower or his or her agent does not attend the settlement, or waives immediate delivery, in which cases the form shall be delivered as soon as practicable after settlement. 24 CFR §3500.10.

The details of how to complete this form are explained in Appendix A to Regulation X (24 CFR §§3500.1-3500.14, App A). The blanks which relate only to one party's transactions may be deleted from the copy of the uniform settlement statement delivered to the other party. 24 CFR §3500.8.

§11.100 E.   Change in Ownership Statement

Every transferee of an ownership interest in real property must file with the county recorder or assessor a "change in ownership statement" setting forth certain required information. Rev & T C §480.

The penalty for failure to file the statement within 45 days after receipt of a written request to do so by the assessor is the greater of $100 or 10 percent of the current year's taxes on the real property (or mobile home if subject to local property taxation). Rev & T C §480.

12

Burch Fitzpatrick

Remedies

BURCH FITZPATRICK, B.S., 1961, University of California, Berkeley; LL.B., 1965, University of California, Berkeley. Mr. Fitzpatrick is a member of the Oakland firm of Miller, Starr & Regalia.
Portions of this chapter are adapted from chapters 11 and 12 of California Real Estate Sales Transactions (Cal CEB 1967), which were written by Roger Bernhardt.

I. INTRODUCTION

§12.1   A. Scope of Chapter

This chapter discusses remedies for breach of the purchase and sale agreement (see chap 3) as distinguished from remedies of creditors holding security interests in real property. Judicial and nonjudicial remedies available under mortgages and deeds of trust are discussed in detail in California Mortgage and Deed of Trust Practice, chaps 4-6 (Cal CEB 1979). Because use of installment land contracts is not recommended (see §5.5), remedies for their breach are not discussed. See generally the discussion in §§5.4-5.7. The attorney must carefully distinguish the purchase agreement (or "marketing contract") from the installment land contract because the respective remedies for breach differ greatly. See §12.2.

The remedies discussed in this chapter apply to both the failure to form a valid agreement through lack of mutual assent and the failure to perform under a valid agreement (breach). Failure to form a binding agreement may arise from mistake, lack of consideration, fraud, undue influence, or duress (see §§12.94-12.103). 1 Miller & Starr, Current Law of California Real Estate §§5:1-5:5 (rev ed 1975). Remedies for failure to form an agreement include damages for fraud (§§12.31-12.38), rescission (§§12.58-12.76), and reformation (§§12.77-12.85). Remedies for breach include damages (§§12.13-12.30), specific performance (§§12.39-12.57), and rescission (§§12.58-12.76). An action for either damages or specific performance may include a cause of action for reformation (§§12.77-12.85) as well.

§12.2   B. Purchase Agreement and Installment Land Contract Distinguished

If the contract is treated as a purchase and sale agreement (see chap 3), traditional contract remedies apply; if it is treated as an installment land contract, the seller's remedies are those of a secured creditor, and debtor protections applicable to mortgages and deeds of trust are available to the buyer. In an installment land contract, the buyer agrees to make installment payments for the property over a substantial period of time and the seller retains title until the purchase price is fully paid. See generally California Mortgage and Deed of Trust Practice §1.7 (Cal CEB 1979). Because the seller's retention of title functions like a security interest, the installment land contract is usually treated like a mortgage or deed of trust. See, *e.g., Venable v Harmon* (1965) 233 CA2d 297, 43 CR 490.

Although many agreements for the purchase of real property clearly fall into one category or the other, those that fall into the borderline area between the two can be difficult to categorize. See, *e.g., Cain v Hunter* (1958) 161 CA2d 808, 327 P2d 583.

In distinguishing between a purchase agreement and an installment land contract, courts consider the intent of the parties as manifested by their conduct. *Venable v Harmon, supra,* 233 CA2d 297, 43 CR 490. This standard requires analyzing the facts of a particular transaction to discern the purpose of the contract. Facts to be considered include:

(1) Who has possession during the contract period? If possession changes from seller to buyer, leaving the seller with only title as security, the contract is more likely to be treated as a security device.

(2) Who will pay current and recurring expenses of the property? Charging the buyer with them is more consistent with an installment land contract.

(3) How many payments must the buyer make before receiving a deed, and how regular are they to be? If there are many periodic payments, and if they cover a long period of time (see CC §2985), the agreement looks like an installment land contract.

(4) Will the contract be fulfilled by delivery of a deed without further financing, or will it be replaced by a deed and deed of trust? The true purchase agreement is replaced at close of escrow by a deed

of trust or similar security instrument. An installment land contract is itself the security device and it endures until the buyer has paid the number of installments that entitle him to a deed.

§12.3　　C. Early Consideration of Remedies

The practical problems of enforcing a purchase and sale agreement should be considered when the agreement is at the drafting stage. Because the remedies actually available for breach are often contrary to the expectations of the parties, the agreement should be drafted with an eye to existing rules for breach and should include alternative remedies when appropriate. See chap 3 on drafting considerations. The seller should be advised that he or she may not be entitled to keep the deposit on the buyer's default (see §§12.26-12.30) and that title may be clouded by a recorded lis pendens if a dispute arises over performance (§§12.86-12.92). The buyer should be advised that the damage remedies available may not give him the benefit of the bargain (§§12.13-12.18) and an action for specific performance will require proof of adequate consideration and fairness to the seller (see §§12.40-12.41).

After breach, the nondefaulting party must select the remedy that best meets his or her particular needs and avoid taking actions that might prejudice the right to that remedy. See §§12.5-12.12.

§12.4　　D. Inadequacy of Remedies

There are drawbacks to all available remedies when either party breaches a purchase and sale agreement. If the buyer breaches, the seller receives what seems to be an inadequate measure of damages, precluding recovery in any situation but a declining market (§§12.19-12.25) and may be unable to retain the buyer's deposit (§§12.26-12.30). Although the seller may obtain specific performance (§§12.48-12.53), the judgment may be ineffective to compel the buyer's performance, and the seller will be forced to hold the property off the market while the lawsuit is pending. Even if the seller wants to forget the matter and sell to someone else, he or she may find that the breaching buyer has clouded title with a lis pendens (§§12.86-12.92).

The picture from the buyer's side is not much brighter. The damage remedy is inadequate unless he or she can establish the seller's bad faith. See §12.14. Seeking specific performance may keep the buyer from acquiring other property, because he or she may feel compelled to retain the purchase price on hand to be able to obtain the seller's performance if he is successfull in obtaining a specific performance decree. See §12.45. A buyer who seeks damages as an alternative to specific performance may be caught in a costly contradiction. See §12.12. Moreover, even if the buyer is entitled to recover the deposit, the seller can make it difficult to recover it from the escrow holder (and it earns no interest in the meantime unless the buyer requested when making the deposit that it be put into an interest-bearing account). See §§3.47, 12.26.

II. ESTABLISHING BREACH

§12.5   A. Breach Defined

Wrongful failure to perform a contract or a material promise or covenant of a contract is a breach. *Woodard v Glenwood Lumber Co.* (1915) 171 C 513, 153 P 951; *Sterling v Gregory* (1906) 149 C 117, 85 P 305. If the failure to perform is excused or legally justified, *i.e.*, not wrongful, there is no breach. *Goudal v DeMille Pictures Corp.* (1931) 118 CA 407, 5 P2d 432. Nonperformance of a condition, as distinct from a covenant, is not a breach; it excuses the injured party from further performance, but it does not give rise to damages. *Britschgi v McCall* (1953) 41 C2d 138, 257 P2d 977.

Any breach, partial or total, entitles the injured party to damages. CC §3300. A total breach also excuses further performance by the nonbreaching party, but a partial breach excuses performance only if it is material. See *Karz v Department of Professional & Vocational Standards* (1936) 11 CA2d 554, 54 P2d 35; *Axis Petroleum Co. v Taylor* (1941) 42 CA2d 389, 108 P2d 978.

An anticipatory breach may occur if a party expressly or impliedly repudiates the contract before his or her performance is due. See §12.11.

B. First Steps After Breach

§12.6   1. Seller's Breach

When the buyer first learns that the seller has breached (or will breach), he or she should be advised about the available choices of remedies and his or her conduct in the meantime. The buyer's actions will depend on (a) the remedy selected, (b) the nature of the breach (whether the seller has repudiated, announced an inability to perform, or merely failed to perform so far), (c) the duties of each party (whether the seller was the party obliged to perform next, or the buyer's performance or some other event was to occur first), and (d) what the buyer has done so far (*e.g.*, whether he or she has performed fully or has waived any conditions).

Because the buyer typically does not deposit the balance into escrow until the last moment, there is frequently doubt whether the buyer should still tender payment after the seller has breached or indicated intent to breach. If the agreement is silent, payment and conveyance will be treated as concurrent conditions—each party must perform or tender to put the other in default. *Diamond v Huenergardt* (1959) 175 CA2d 214, 346 P2d 37. Therefore, a buyer who does nothing may be unable to enforce his or her remedies. See *Katemis v Westerlind* (1953) 120 CA2d 537, 261 P2d 553, appeal after new trial (1956) 142 CA2d 799, 299 P2d 383.

If the breach consists of the seller's repudiation of the agreement, the buyer need not tender the price. CC §1440; *Beverage v Canton Placer Mining Co.* (1955) 43 C2d 769, 278 P2d 694. The buyer is also excused if the seller cannot perform, because tender would be an idle act. *Weneda Corp. v Dispalatro* (1964) 225 CA2d 187, 37 CR 267. If the price is not yet due under the agreement, the buyer need not tender it. *Lifton v Harshman* (1947) 80 CA2d 422, 182 P2d 222. The buyer must tender, however, to claim successfully that the seller has breached by failing to perform by the closing date. Without the buyer's tender and demand for the seller's performance, the seller is not in breach. *Baird v Barton* (1958) 163 CA2d 502, 329 P2d 492. See §12.8 regarding the effect of a time of the essence clause.

§12.7   2. Buyer's Breach

Ordinarily the buyer's basic obligation under a purchase agreement is to pay the purchase price, and breach consists of failure to pay the price when due. Most purchase agreements make the buyer's performance conditional (*e.g.*, on obtaining financing) and excuse the buyer's performance if the condition does not occur. If the condition fails without fault on the buyer's part, nonperformance is not a breach, and he or she is entitled to recover the deposit regardless of the language in the agreement. *Rodriguez v Barnett* (1959) 52

C2d 154, 338 P2d 907. The seller must stay alert to see that conditions do not fail solely because the buyer wants to back out. Thus, if performance is contingent on the buyer's obtaining financing, the seller should try to find the buyer a loan to block this potential avenue of escape. See, *e.g., Fry v George Elkins Co.* (1958) 162 CA2d 256, 327 P2d 905. The seller may also claim that the buyer has waived a condition through inactivity if the buyer has the exclusive power to make a condition (such as sale of his own house) occur, but fails to do so. See *Noel v Dumont Builders, Inc.* (1960) 178 CA2d 691, 3 CR 220.

A seller who decides on rescission is free to sell the property in the meantime (see §12.58); a seller who seeks specific performance must retain title to the property throughout the litigation (see §12.49). If the seller chooses to pursue damages, the decision about resale depends on the real estate market: resale when values are rising will hurt the seller's legal position; resale during a downward trend may not (see §12.22). A considered choice should be made as soon as possible to avoid an inadvertent election of remedies. See §12.12.

To put the buyer in default, the seller must be in a position to perform; he or she must tender performance and demand timely payment from the buyer. *Baird v Barton* (1958) 163 CA2d 502, 329 P2d 492. Tender and demand for performance are necessary for any remedy selected unless the buyer repudiates the agreement. *McKinley v Lagae* (1962) 207 CA2d 284, 24 CR 454. The seller must also waive any conditions that benefit him. *Tibbets v Robb* (1958) 158 CA2d 330, 322 P2d 585. The buyer may attempt performance at a later date despite the seller's tender and demand for timely performance. Unless irrevocably committed to rescission, the seller should accept the buyer's belated performance because this late attempt to perform may seriously diminish the seller's damages. See §12.8. Moreover, the buyer will be in a position to sue for specific performance (and record a lis pendens), contending that the seller could not insist on strict time limits for payment. *Katemis v Westerlind* (1953) 120 CA2d 537, 261 P2d 553, appeal after new trial (1956) 142 CA2d 799, 299 P2d 383.

§12.8   C. Time for Performance

A time of the essence clause cannot be relied on to establish a breach when a party fails to perform by a specific date. See §3.178 for a time of the essence provision. Although many cases hold that a time of the essence clause in a purchase agreement or escrow instructions requires that the buyer deposit the purchase price by the specified date (see, *e.g., Pothast v Kind* (1933) 218 C 192, 24 P2d 771; *Weisberg v Ashcraft* (1963) 223 CA2d 793, 36 CR 188), courts have fashioned many exceptions to this rule. For example, if the transaction is still pending after the date specified in the agreement, without objection by the seller, the time of the essence clause is considered waived. *Chan v Title Ins. & Trust Co.* (1952) 39 C2d 253, 246 P2d 632. To avoid a forfeiture of the buyer's rights (CC §3275), a court might permit the buyer to obtain specific performance if the failure to make timely payment was not unlawful, grossly negligent, or intentional. *Williams Plumbing Co. v Sinsley* (1975) 53 CA3d 1027, 126 CR 345. See also *MacFadden v Walker* (1971) 5 C3d 809, 97 CR 537, for a similar result involving an installment land contract. The buyer may be entitled to perform late, despite a time of the essence clause, if the seller has not demanded that the escrow agent terminate the escrow. *McCown v Spencer* (1970) 8 CA3d 216, 87 CR 213; *Andover Land Co. v Hoffman* (1968) 264 CA2d 87, 70 CR 38. When the seller is also the builder, the completed structure must be consistent with the original plans for the seller to be able to invoke the time of the essence clause to defeat the buyer's specific performance action. *Kossler v Palm Springs Devs. Ltd.* (1980) 101 CA3d 88, 161 CR 423.

Despite these limitations, a time of the essence clause should be included in the purchase agreement because its omission will allow either party to perform merely within a "reasonable period of time." CC §1657; *Kersch v Taber* (1945) 67 CA2d 499, 154 P2d 934; *Walsh v Walsh* (1940) 42 CA2d 287, 108 P2d 765. Including the clause permits a party to reject late performance after making a tender and demanding timely performance.

Courts have held that a clause allowing the broker to extend the escrow indicates that time is not of the essence, despite inclusion of a time of the essence clause. *Katemis v Westerlind* (1953) 120 CA2d 537, 261 P2d 553, appeal after new trial (1956) 142 CA2d 799, 299 P2d 383. Some older deposit receipt forms contained such a clause. A party wanting timely performance should delete any clause giving the broker or escrow agent the right to extend the closing date. Similarly, the party seeking timely performance should avoid any statements or conduct that would evidence intent to waive the time of the essence clause. See §§12.9, 12.74. Both the purchase agreement and the escrow instructions should contain a specific time of the essence clause, a recital of why time is of the essence, and provisions for the automatic termination of escrow and return of documents and funds after the closing date. The party seeking timely performance should notify the other party shortly before the closing date of his or her intent to rely on the time provisions.

§12.9 D. Waiver of Conditions

Neither party is obliged to perform under a purchase and sale agreement until all conditions have been fulfilled or waived. See, e.g., *Weneda Corp. v Dispalatro* (1964) 225 CA2d 187, 37 CR 267; *Pease v Brown* (1960) 186 CA2d 425, 8 CR 917. An unfulfilled condition can be waived by the party for whose benefit it was inserted in the contract. *Crescenta Valley Moose Lodge v Bunt* (1970) 8 CA3d 682, 87 CR 428; *Wesley N. Taylor Co. v Russell* (1961) 194 CA2d 816, 15 CR 357. Most conditions are for the buyer's benefit, and if the buyer waives the condition, its failure will not excuse the seller's performance. *Weneda Corp. v Dispalatro, supra*; *Wesley N. Taylor Co. v Russell, supra*. The buyer should promptly notify the seller of the satisfaction or waiver of any financing, inspection, or approval condition contained in the agreement, and the seller should promptly notify the buyer of the satisfaction of any condition, such as subdivision or lot split approvals or removal of an unacceptable title defect.

If a condition benefits both parties to the agreement, it cannot be waived by only one party, and its failure will therefore excuse performance. *Britschgi v McCall* (1953) 41 C2d 138, 257 P2d 977 (defective title could expose seller to personal liability); *Spangler v Castello* (1956) 147 CA2d 49, 304 P2d 752 (financing condition benefited seller because it affected seller's secondary financing); *Isaacson v G. D. Robertson & Co.* (1948) 85 CA2d 71, 192 P2d 486 (rezoning condition benefited seller, who owned property in the vicinity).

§12.10 E. Tender of Performance

Normally, the seller's conveyance and the buyer's payment of the purchase price are treated as concurrent conditions, so that one party cannot place the other in default without himself performing or tendering performance. CC §§1437, 1439; *Diamond v Huenergardt* (1959) 175 CA2d 214, 346 P2d 37; *Groobman v Kirk* (1958) 159 CA2d 117, 323 P2d 867. See §12.6. Tender creates more of a problem for the buyer than the seller. The seller can deposit a deed in escrow with instructions to deliver it only on the buyer's performance by a certain date. Even if the escrow agent fails to return the deed, the seller's ability to use the property will not normally be affected during any subsequent litigation. However, a buyer who deposits funds in escrow may not be able to recover from the escrow holder pending litigation and must demand that the escrow holder deposit the funds in an interest-bearing account. A buyer can avoid having these funds tied up in escrow during litigation by making the tender conditional on the seller's delivery of a valid deed. CC §1498; *Groobman v Kirk, supra.* A conditional tender is an offer to perform if the other party performs, and the buyer must be willing and able to perform for the tender to be valid. CC §§1486, 1495. Thus, if financing is contemplated, the buyer must be able to demonstrate the availability of financing. If the buyer's conditional tender is made and rejected, there is no need to keep it in effect until the other party is ready to perform. *Hunt v Mahoney* (1947) 82 CA2d 540, 187 P2d 43. Although a valid conditional tender must be for performance under the exact terms of a contract, if the tender is defective the other party must promptly state his objections or they are considered waived. CC §1501, CCP §2076; *Riverside Fence Co. v Novak* (1969) 273 CA2d 656, 78 CR 536; *Hunt v Mahoney, supra.*

§12.11 F. Anticipatory Breach or Repudiation

The obligation to perform is excused if the other party expressly repudiates the agreement by giving notice that he or she will not perform. CC §1440; *Beverage v Canton Placer Mining Co.* (1955) 43 C2d 769, 278 P2d 694. Although the statement repudiating a contract can be oral (*Daum Dev. Corp. v Yuba Plaza, Inc.* (1970) 11 CA3d 65, 89 CR 458), an oral repudiation may be difficult to prove. Accordingly, the party intending to rely on the repudiation should obtain the statement in writing or send the repudiating party a letter confirming and indicating reliance on the oral repudiation. Without a written statement evidencing the repudiation, the party relying on the oral repudiation should make a conditional offer of performance. See §12.10. An anticipatory breach also occurs if a party impliedly repudiates by putting it out of his power to perform. *Zogarts v Smith* (1948) 86 CA2d 165, 194 P2d 143; *Poirier v Gravel* (1891) 88 C 79, 25 P 962.

§12.12   G. Selection of Remedies

On default or repudiation, the nondefaulting party should immediately determine the remedy to be pursued and act consistently with that remedy. For example, the buyer who wants specific performance should avoid conduct and statements evidencing intent to rescind. *Cook v Nordstrand* (1948) 83 CA2d 188, 188 P2d 282, held that the buyer's demand for and receipt of his deposit constituted rescission of the purchase agreement.

Although specific performance and damages may be pleaded as alternative remedies, a party seeking both faces a practical dilemma. To obtain specific performance, the complaint must allege that the contract price was fair, but to recover an adequate award of damages, the contract price must be shown to have differed markedly from market value at the time of breach. If the contradiction is too great, the entire action may fail on that ground alone. See *Baran v Goldberg* (1948) 86 CA2d 506, 194 P2d 765. This dilemma may be avoided at the pleading stage by omitting allegation of a specific amount in the damages cause of action and simply alleging on information and belief that the value of the property exceeded the price on the date of the breach. Because the complaint seeks specific relief, it should survive a demurrer based on CCP §425.10 for failure to allege damages.

A seller under economic pressure to sell is in a particularly vulnerable position after the buyer's breach. If the seller cancels the escrow and attempts to resell the property, the original buyer may record a lis pendens (see §§12.86-12.92) in connection with a suit for specific performance alleging waiver of the time conditions or seeking relief from forfeiture under the holding in *Williams Plumbing Co. v Sinsley* (1975) 53 CA3d 1027, 126 CR 345. The seller must always be cautious in reselling the property to avoid getting caught between suits brought by both the defaulting buyer and the subsequent purchaser. When a seller is under economic or time pressure, the best course of action is often to return the original defaulting buyer's deposit, reserving the right to recover damages after resale.

III. DAMAGES

A. Seller's Breach

§12.13   1. General Damages; CC §3306

The buyer's damages for breach are limited by CC §3306 to the price paid plus certain costs and expenses, essentially the same recovery that would be available if the buyer rescinded (see §12.72). Civil Code §3306 provides:

The detriment caused by the breach of an agreement to convey an estate in real property, is deemed to be the price paid, and the expenses properly incurred in examining the title and preparing the necessary papers, with interest thereon; but adding thereto, in case of bad faith, the difference between the price agreed to be paid and the value of the estate agreed to be conveyed, at the time of the breach, and the expenses properly incurred in preparing to enter upon the land.

In an action for breach of a real property purchase and sale agreement, this specific statutory provision supersedes CC §3300, the general contract measure of damages. *Crag Lumber Co. v Crofoot* (1956) 144 CA2d 755, 301 P2d 952.

A breach compensable in damages under CC §3306 may occur by the seller's repudiation any time after formation of the agreement and before closing. Breach may also consist of failure to convey title within the time specified in the agreement; inability to convey before the time specified is never a breach. *Fara v Wells* (1957) 156 CA2d 322, 319 P2d 394. Defective performance, *i.e.,* an attempt to convey less than the agreed title, may also constitute a breach. See *Levy v Wolff* (1956) 46 C2d 367, 294 P2d 945.

Expenses incurred in examining title and preparing the necessary papers are considered special damages and must be specifically pleaded. *Moore v Fredericks* (1914) 24 CA 536, 141 P 1049. Section 3306 limits the buyer's recovery of special or consequential damages for a good faith breach to the expenses of a title search and preparation of documents, and does not permit recovery for preparations to enter onto the land. See, *e.g., Crag Lumber Co. v Crofoot, supra,* 144 CA2d 755, 301 P2d 952 (damages for building access roads denied); *Smith v Schrader* (1926) 80 CA 478, 251 P 967 (damages for increased rent paid for other premises denied); *Bernesen v Fish* (1933) 135 CA 588, 28 P2d 67 (award of damages did not include reasonable value of avocado trees that could not be transplanted). The limitations of CC §3306 may be avoided if the buyer's recovery is based on the seller's breach of an obligation other than to convey real property, such as breach of a warranty or collateral covenant. See §12.15.

§12.14 2. Bad Faith

A buyer who can prove that the seller breached in bad faith is entitled to recover the difference between the contract price and actual value of the property at the time of breach. CC §3306. Bad faith is a question of fact and must be pleaded and proved by the buyer. *Wheeler v Oppenheimer* (1956) 140 CA2d 497, 295 P2d 128; *Robertson v Bogert* (1955) 130 CA2d 639, 279 P2d 572. Bad faith does not require proof of malice or fraud, and if a seller's only reason for refusing to perform is that he or she could make a better deal elsewhere, he or she will probably be held to have breached in bad faith. See *Collins v Marvel Land Co.* (1970) 13 CA3d 34, 91 CR 291; *Kahn v Lischner* (1954) 128 CA2d 480, 275 P2d 539; *Cushing v Levi* (1931) 117 CA 94, 3 P2d 958. If the buyer's efforts have caused property to appreciate, the breaching seller's bad faith may be easy to prove. See, *e.g., Tancredi v Garrett* (1962) 210 CA2d 818, 27 CR 52. Because bad faith is a question of fact, the seller may avoid liability for bad faith damages by showing that the buyer's conduct has been less than honorable. See *Robertson v Bogert, supra* (buyer knew contract price was far under market value and seller did not). An inexperienced seller may also be excused from a claim of bad faith if he was induced by a real estate broker to refuse to convey (*Chalmers v Raras* (1962) 200 CA2d 682, 19 CR 531) or relied on the advice of counsel (*Fox v Aced* (1957) 49 C2d 381, 317 P2d 608).

§12.15 3. Breach Other Than Failure To Convey Title

A buyer's claim for damages for breach of a warranty or other convenant of the agreement is not subject to the limitations of CC §3306. Consequently, if title is conveyed to the buyer but the seller breaches a warranty or other duty that survives the closing, the buyer may recover all amounts that will compensate him or her for the damage proximately caused by the breach under CC §3300. For example, in *Christensen v Slawter* (1959) 173 CA2d 325, 343 P2d 341, the buyer accepted late delivery of the deed, and then recovered damages incurred from a work stoppage caused by the delay. See also *Williams v Graham* (1948) 83 CA2d 649, 189 P2d 324 (rental for property used to conduct buyer's business allowed with interest because failure to convey was part of a fraud); *Evans v Faught* (1965) 231 CA2d 698, 42 CR 133 (buyer recovered cost of removing title defects); *Coughlin v Blair* (1953) 41 C2d 587, 262 P2d 305 (buyer awarded damages under CC §3300 for seller's breach of covenant to install improvements).

§12.16 4. Interest

Recovery of prejudgment interest on the price paid and special damages is expressly authorized by CC §3306 (*Vineland Homes, Inc. v Barish* (1956) 138 CA2d 747, 292 P2d 941), but not on any damages awarded for the seller's bad faith (CC §3306; *Crag Lumber Co. v Crofoot* (1956) 144 CA2d 755, 301 P2d 952; *Boshes v Miller* (1953) 119 CA2d 332, 259 P2d 447).

§12.17 5. Attorneys' Fees

Notwithstanding the limitations of CC §3306, the buyer may recover attorneys' fees if the agreement contains an attorneys' fees clause. *Vineland Homes, Inc. v Barish* (1956) 138 CA2d 747, 292 P2d 941. Attorneys' fees are not recoverable without an express provision in the agreement. CCP §1021. If the agreement provides for an award of attorneys' fees to one party on the other's breach, the provision is reciprocally enforceable, and either party who prevails in an action on the agreement can recover attorneys' fees. CC §1717.

§12.18 6. Punitive Damages

If the seller's conduct is oppressive, fraudulent, or malicious, and the measure of damages under CC §3306 is inadequate, the buyer may want to plead a cause of action for tortious failure to deal in good faith or intentional infliction of emotional distress. Punitive damages are not recoverable for breach of contract per se. CC §3294; *Crogan v Metz* (1956) 47 C2d 398, 303 P2d 1029. It might be possible to argue successfully, however, that the seller's breach constituted a tort as well as a breach of contract. See, *e.g., Johansen v California State Auto. Ass'n* (1975) 15 C3d 9, 123 CR 288 (insurer's failure to settle within policy limits constituted breach of implied convenant of good faith and fair dealing, a cause of action sounding in both tort and contract); *Jarchow v Transamerica Title Ins. Co.* (1975) 48 CA3d 917, 122 CR 470 (title insurer's failure to clear easement constituted breach of covenant of good faith and fair dealing, and negligent infliction of emotional distress). Note, however, that the buyer must establish malice, oppression, or fraud, as well as a tort cause of action to recover punitive damages under CC §3294. *Jarchow v Transamerica Title Ins. Co., supra*. See §12.34 on punitive damages for fraud.

B. Buyer's Breach

§12.19 1. General Damages; CC §3307

The seller's measure of damages is the difference between the contract price and the property's value at the time of breach, whether or not the buyer breaches in bad faith. CC §3307. The seller can also recover some special or consequential damages. See §§12.23-12.25. However, the seller will be unable to recover a significant damage award unless the property has depreciated sharply between the agreement date and the time of the breach, or the seller has incurred substantial additional expenses in holding and reselling the property after breach. See §§12.21-12.22.

Unlike its counterpart, CC §3306 (see §12.13), CC §3307 does not distinguish between good and bad faith defaults by the buyer. See *Royer v Carter* (1951) 37 C2d 544, 233 P2d 539. Whether the default is willful or innocent may have some significance, however, under CC §3275 (relief from forfeitures) and CC §3369 (penalties and forfeitures) if the defaulting buyer seeks affirmative relief against the seller.

Sellers have been permitted to recover damages from buyers who breach purchase agreements despite the antideficiency provisions of CCP §580b (*Royer v Carter, supra*; *Kerrigan v Maloof* (1950) 98 CA2d 605, 221 P2d 153); apparently §580b is limited in its application to sales agreements that can be classified as security devices (*Venable v Harmon* (1965) 233 CA2d 297, 43 CR 490; see §§5.4, 12.2).

The seller's primary problem is proving that the property decreased in value from the contract date to the date of breach. If the property's value increases or remains constant, damages are not recoverable. See §12.22.

§12.20 2. Discounting Price to Cash Equivalent

In assessing damages under CC §3307, the value of the property should be estimated on a cash basis. In *Abrams v Motter* (1970) 3

CA3d 828, 83 CR 855, the court held that the contract price in a credit sale must be discounted to reflect its cash equivalent. Thus, when the seller takes back a note and deed of trust, the contract price is discounted on the basis of various factors such as the value of the real property securing the note, the amount of senior encumbrances, the provisions of the note, the risk of economic changes during the term of the note, the risk and expense of foreclosure, and the risk of changing interest rates. This discounting in a credit sale could eliminate any excess of the purchase price over the value of the property at the date of breach.

§12.21   3. Proof of Damages

Though not an expert, the seller may testify regarding his or her opinion of the property's market value on the date of breach. *Fleischer v Cosgrove* (1956) 145 CA2d 14, 301 P2d 911. The seller should do more than guess at its value, however, or no finding can be based on this testimony. *Newhart v Pierce* (1967) 254 CA2d 783, 62 CR 553. Expert testimony can and should be elicited from either a broker (*Fleischer v Cosgrove, supra)* or an appraiser (*Newhart v Pierce, supra*).

Opinions of value at the date of breach may be based on subsequent events. The resale price is relevant evidence, but adjustments must be made for subsequent changes in market conditions (*Royer v Carter* (1951) 37 C2d 544, 233 P2d 539; *Bouchard v Orange* (1960) 177 CA2d 521, 2 CR 388) and subsequent improvements added by the seller (*Mathews v MacArthur* (1953) 119 CA2d 196, 258 P2d 1068). The resale price is not controlling, however, and may be ignored by the trial court if it is an inappropriate indicator of value under the circumstances. *Fleischer v Cosgrove, supra,* 145 CA2d 14, 301 P2d 911; *Major-Blakeney Corp. v Jenkins* (1953) 121 CA2d 325, 263 P2d 655. If no resale has actually occured, the seller may testify about the highest offer received to corroborate his or her own opinion of value. *Bouchard v Orange, supra.*

The seller always faces the problem of explaining a differential between price and market value, while avoiding exposure to charges of fraud, when the breach occurs only a short time after execution of the contract. One way to overcome this problem is to have experts testify about the chilling effects of the buyer's breach on the resale market after the property has had its initial exposure.

Abrams v Motter (1970) 3 CA3d 828, 83 CR 855; *Bouchard v Orange, supra.*

§12.22   4. Effect of Market

In an era of rising property values, the property will probably be resold for a higher price after the buyer defaults. Even though the seller may be able to show that market value was less than the contract price at the time of the breach, the fact that a profit was made on resale means that the seller was not damaged by the first buyer's default. *Freedman v The Rector* (1951) 37 C2d 16, 230 P2d 629; *Silver v Boyd* (1961) 196 CA2d 790, 16 CR 865.

If the market is declining, the longer the time period between execution of the contract and breach, the greater will be the buyer's liability. See *Bouchard v Orange* (1960) 177 CA2d 521, 2 CR 388. Once the breach occurs, however, the buyer's liability is fixed by the market value as of that date and cannot be increased. Thus, if it takes a considerable time to resell and the resale is at a substantial loss because of the continued downward trend of prices, the seller cannot recover any increment of this downward trend beyond the date of breach. *Royer v Carter* (1951) 37 C2d 544, 233 P2d 539.

If the market is stable, market value on the date of breach will probably be the same as the contract price, and the seller will be unable to recover damages. See *Fleischer v Cosgrove* (1956) 145 CA2d 14, 301 P2d 911.

5. Special Damages

§12.23   a. Resale Expenses

In addition to general damages under CC §3307 (see §12.19), the seller may recover expenses incurred in reselling the property after the breach. *Royer v Carter* (1951) 37 C2d 544, 233 P2d 539. When the market value of the property increases or remains constant (see §12.22), resale expenses will be the only damages the seller can recover. *Allen v Enomoto* (1964) 228 CA2d 798, 39 CR 815. If there is no second sale, a court may conclude that the wasted expenses of the first sale are roughly equivalent to the expenses of a hypothetical second sale. See *Royer v Carter, supra.*

In *Yackey v Pacifica Dev. Co.* (1979) 99 CA3d 776, 160 CR 430, the sale was at less than market value because of a lis pendens against the property, which the defaulting buyer had agreed to clear. Although the sellers later resold the property at a higher price, they were permitted to recover additional attorneys' fees incurred because of the lis pendens, property taxes paid after the date of breach, and interest on amounts due but not paid by the buyers. See the discussion of *Yackey* in 3 CEB Real Prop L Rep 77 (1980).

§12.24   b. Other Expenses

Courts have permitted sellers to recover some other categories of expenses. See, *e.g., Yackey v Pacifica Dev. Co.* (1979) 99 CA3d 776, 160 CR 430, discussed in §12.23. If the seller evicts a tenant because of the sale agreement, he is entitled to the rental value until the date of resale along with any broker's fees he is obligated to pay. *McKinley v Lagae* (1962) 207 CA2d 284, 24 CR 454. Some courts have permitted recovery of various operating expenses after the breach. *Jensen v Dalton* (1970) 9 CA3d 654, 88 CR 426 (sellers recovered cost of commuting between new and old houses to take care of latter); *Allen v Enomoto* (1964) 228 CA2d 798, 39 CR 815 (fire insurance premiums, mortgage payments, and property taxes recovered by seller). *Sutter v Madrin* (1969) 269 CA2d 161, 74 CR 627, however, held that recovery of operating expenses is allowed only when the court finds that the seller resold the property with reasonable diligence. The court in *Abrams v Motter* (1970) 3 CA3d 828, 83 CR 855, ruled that to recover operating expenses the seller must show that they were incurred in connection with resale and not for continued use of the property. These cases indicate that the seller will be able to recover at least some of the expenses incurred in purchasing a new home in reliance on an agreement for the sale of the old one.

§12.25   c. Broker's Commission

One element of the seller's damages for the buyer's breach is the amount of any commission that the seller pays or owes to a broker; the seller, not the buyer, is entitled to the benefit of any savings made by reselling without the assistance of a broker. *Caplan v Schroeder* (1961) 56 C2d 515, 15 CR 145. If the property has not been resold, the seller is entitled to a broker's commission based on a hypothetical resale at the market price at the time of breach, but from this must be subtracted whatever the seller saved by paying less than the full commission due on the first sale. *Royer v Carter*

(1951) 37 C2d 544, 233 P2d 539. For example, as a result of the buyer's breach, the seller might have had to pay only half of the retained deposit instead of the full commission, or perhaps no commission at all if it was contingent on closing. See §§2.37, 2.42. On retention of the deposit, see the discussion of liquidated damages at §§12.26-12.30.

Example: If the first sale was to have been for $50,000, with a six-percent commission ($3000) to a broker, and the market value on the date of breach was $40,000, the commission on the hypothetical resale would be $2400 (six percent of $40,000). However, if the broker accepted half of a $5000 deposit made on the first agreement instead of a full commission of $3000, the seller saved $500. This $500 subtracted from the hypothetical commission of $2400 leaves special damages of $1900. This rule was confirmed in *Barton v White Oak Realty, Inc.* (1969) 271 CA2d 579, 76 CR 587, which also established the corollary that when the seller sues the buyer for damages, the broker cannot intervene to claim the full commission from the buyer. See also *Bay Shore Homes, Inc. v San Diego Trust & Sav. Bank* (1969) 276 CA2d 108, 80 CR 849.

The rights of the parties in this situation will depend primarily on the language of the listing agreement and the purchase agreement. If the commission is earned when the broker produces a ready, willing, and able buyer, the seller could be liable for two commissions if the first buyer defaults. See §2.35. A prudent seller can avoid this problem by conditioning the commission on consummation of the transaction. See §2.37. If the parties have initialed the liquidated damages provision in the sale agreement, the broker may be entitled to half of the deposit if retained by the seller, less expenses. See §§12.26-12.30 on liquidated damages; see §2.42 on the broker's right to a portion of the deposit on the buyer's default. The California Association of Realtors (CAR) deposit receipt form currently in use (see §3.40) provides that on the buyer's default, the broker is entitled to half of any damages the seller collects from the buyer, less title, escrow, and collection expenses.

6. Disposition of Deposit

§12.26   a. General Considerations

A seller who wants to retain the buyer's entire deposit should insist on including in the purchase and sale agreement a liquidated damages provision that complies with CC §§1675-1681. Depending on the amount of the deposit, however, the seller may be able to obtain a larger recovery by leaving the damage remedy open in the purchase and sale agreement. See §3.179. Without such a clause, the seller may be unable to retain all, or even a part of, the deposit if the sale is not completed. See §§12.27-12.28. If an agreement executed after July 1, 1978, contains a valid liquidated damages provision, the seller should have some assurance of being able to retain the deposit; at least under CC §§1675-1681, effective that date, the buyer now has the burden of proving that the provision is unreasonable. See §12.30.

b. Without a Liquidated Damages Clause

§12.27 (1) Failure of Condition

If the sale is not consummated because of failure of a condition, rather than because of any default by the buyer, the buyer is entitled to the return of the entire deposit. *Rodriguez v Barnett* (1959) 52 C2d 154, 338 P2d 907. The courts reason that the seller may retain the deposit in these circumstances only if it can be considered a separate consideration paid for an option. In the usual purchase agreement, however, the deposit is part of the consideration, so that when a condition of the agreement fails, each party is entitled to the return of what was deposited into escrow. *Caplan v Schroeder* (1961) 56 C2d 515, 15 CR 145. Using an option as an alternative to a purchase agreement is discussed in chap 4.

Even if the agreement cannot be completed because of the buyer's default, the seller cannot automatically retain the deposit. See §12.28. If the seller elects to rescind the agreement (see §§12.58-12.76), all consideration received from the buyer must be returned, less any special loss the seller is entitled to recover. *Royer v Carter* (1951) 37 C2d 544, 233 P2d 539.

§12.28 (2) Buyer's Breach

Without benefit of a valid liquidated damages clause (see §§12.29-12.30), the seller may retain the deposit only to the extent that actual damages have been suffered. See §§12.19-12.25 on the measure of the seller's damages. The deposit can serve as a fund from which the seller obtains whole or partial reimbursement for actual loss sustained. See *Beason v Griff* (1954) 127 CA2d 382, 274 P2d 47. To take more than is needed for compensation amounts to unjust enrichment of the seller, and the seller must refund the excess over actual damages to the buyer, whether the breach was innocent or willful. *Freedman v The Rector* (1951) 37 C2d 16, 230 P2d 629. Even if the buyer paid the deposit directly to the seller rather than into escrow, the seller still cannot retain more of it than the actual loss sustained. *Caplan v Schroeder* (1961) 56 C2d 515, 15 CR 145. The deposit, however, does give the seller the practical advantage of shifting to the buyer the burden of proving that the seller's retention constitutes unjust enrichment. *Baffa v Johnson* (1950) 35 C2d 36, 216 P2d 13.

c. Liquidated Damages Provisions

§12.29   (1) Agreements Executed Before July 1, 1978

In the past, sellers had difficulty enforcing liquidated damages clauses in real property purchase agreements because they had a heavy burden of establishing the validity of such clauses. For agreements executed before CC §1671 was amended in 1978, the proponent of a liquidated damages clause has the burden of proving the foundational facts: an agreement between the parties, impracticability or extreme difficulty of fixing actual damages, and a reasonable endeavor to agree on an amount bearing a reasonable relationship to actual damages. See, *e.g., Barbera v Sokol* (1980) 101 CA3d 725, 161 CR 843. Including recitals of these facts in the liquidated damages provision itself is insufficient; the seller must still prove the difficulty of ascertaining damages and the reasonableness of the amount. *Cook v King Manor & Convalescent Hosp.* (1974) 40 CA3d 782, 115 CR 471. Thus, a provision inserted by one party, but never negotiated with the other party, is invalid because the seller cannot show a reasonable effort by the parties to establish these elements. *United Sav. & Loan Ass'n v Reeder Dev. Corp.* (1976) 57 CA3d 282, 129 CR 113. Although liquidated damages clauses are intended to prevent litigation altogether, under the rule for agreements executed before July 1, 1978, they merely shift the facts that the seller must prove from the actual damages to the content of the parties' negotiations.

§12.30   (2) Agreements Executed on or After July 1, 1978

Effective July 1, 1978, the legislature amended CC §1671, and added CC §§1675-1680, which now govern the validity of liquidated damages provisions in real property purchase and sale agreements.

See generally, Guggenhime, *California's New Liquidated Damages Law,* 1 CEB Real Prop L Rep 17 (1978). These new rules do not apply to installment land contracts as defined in CC §2985. CC §1681. Under this statutory scheme, the seller should find it easier to enforce a liquidated damages clause than under the former statute.

A liquidated damages provision in any real property purchase and sale agreement must be separately initialed by each party, and a provision in a printed agreement must be set out in 10-point bold type or contrasting red 8-point bold type. CC §1677.

Civil Code §1675 governs liquidated damages provisions in agreements for purchase and sale of residential property, which is defined to include dwellings of not more than four residential units, at least one of which the buyer intends, when the agreement is executed, to occupy as his or her residence. CC §1675(a). To be valid, the clause must meet the following tests: (a) the payment to be kept by the buyer as liquidated damages must actually have been made in cash or by check (including postdated check) and (b) the amount paid must not exceed three percent of the purchase price unless the seller can establish that the amount was reasonable. CC §1675(b)-(d). If the deposit is less than three percent, the buyer can still invalidate the clause by showing that the amount is unreasonable (CC §1675(c)), but in this situation the burden is on the buyer. If the deposit exceeds three percent, however, the burden is on the seller to prove that the amount is reasonable, and if he fails, the entire clause is invalid; the seller cannot keep as liquidated damages even that part of the payment that does not exceed three percent. CC §1675(d).

The reasonableness of the amount actually paid as liquidated damages is to be determined by (a) the circumstances at the time the agreement was executed and (b) the price and other terms and circumstances of any subsequent sale or sale agreement that is made within six months of the buyer's default. CC §1675(e).

If the agreement calls for the buyer to make more than one payment that will constitute liquidated damages, any amount beyond the first payment may validly be retained as liquidated damages only if (a) the total of all such payments satisfies the three-percent requirement of §1675 and (b) a separate liquidated damages provision satisfying the requirements of §1677 is initialed by each party for each subsequent payment. CC §1678.

In agreements for the purchase and sale of real property other than "residential property," liquidated damages provisions are governed by CC §§1676-1677, 1671(b). If the liquidated damages clause in such an agreement meets the requirements that it be separately initialed by each party and be set out in specified type (CC §1677), it is valid unless the person seeking to invalidate it establishes that it was unreasonable under the circumstances at the time the agreement was made (CC §1671(b)).

The provisions of CC §§1675-1678 regarding sales of residential and other real property apply only to breach of the buyer's obligation to complete the purchase. CC §1679. All other breaches are governed by the rule that a liquidated damages clause is valid unless the party seeking to invalidate it proves it was unreasonable when the agreement was made. CC §1671(b). Moreover, the provisions of CC §§1675-1681 do not affect the right of any party to obtain specific performance of a purchase and sale agreement. CC §1680.

C. Fraud

§12.31   1. Basic Out-of-Pocket Measure; CC §3343

The basic measure of damages to which a defrauded party is entitled is the difference between the actual value of that with which he parted and the actual value of what he received, frequently referred to as the out-of-pocket measure of damages. CC §3343. In the past, this out-of-pocket measure of damages was all the defrauded party could recover (see, *e.g., Garrett v Perry* (1959) 53 C2d 178, 346 P2d 758; *Ach v Finkelstein* (1968) 264 CA2d 667, 70 CR 472), but 1971 amendments to CC §3343 added additional elements of recovery, some of which codified exceptions the courts had fashioned to mitigate the sometimes harsh consequences of the out-of-pocket rule. The actual value the defrauded party received and parted with is determined as of the date the fraud occurred, usually the date of sale. *McCue v Bruce Enterprises, Inc.* (1964) 228 CA2d 21, 39 CR 125; *Graf v Sumpter* (1962) 207 CA2d 391, 24 CR 590. Under this rule, a defrauded party may be entitled to no recovery at all if the property was worth the price paid at the time of sale. *Bagdasarian v Gragnon* (1948) 31 C2d 744, 192 P2d 935. The recovery is not reduced, however, because the defrauded buyer later resells the property at a profit. *Burkett v J. A. Thompson & Sons* (1957) 150 CA2d 523, 310 P2d 56. The cost of repairs caused by misrepresentations about the condition of the property is not an element of recoverable damages but may be introduced to show the value of the property. *Central Mut. Ins. Co. v Schmidt* (1957) 152 CA2d 671, 313 P2d 132. Some courts have permitted defrauded buyers to recover the entire purchase price paid, despite the out-of-pocket measure, because use of the property was effectively denied the buyers by misrepresented or undisclosed conditions. *Garrett v Perry, supra* (foreclosure as result of misrepresented income); *Buist v C. Dudley DeVelbiss Corp.* (1960) 182 CA2d 325, 6 CR 259 (property had no value because of landslide problem).

In 1971, the legislature amended CC §3343 by adding four items of "additional damage arising from the particular transaction" that could also be recovered by the defrauded party: reliance damages (CC §3343(a)(1)); damages for loss of use and enjoyment of the property (CC §3343(a)(2)); seller's lost profits (CC §3343(a)(3)); and buyer's lost profits (CC §3343(a)(4)). Profits lost by either buyer or seller are discussed in §12.32.

Civil Code §3343(a)(1) apparently codifies previous decisions allowing reliance damages. *Ward v Taggart* (1959) 51 C2d 736, 336 P2d 534; *Sixta v Ochsner* (1960) 187 CA2d 485, 9 CR 617; *Buist v C. Dudley DeVelbiss Corp., supra*. Reliance damages are recoverable only if they have a causal connection with the fraudulent misrepresentation or nondisclosure for agreements executed before and after the 1971 changes. *Gagne v Bertran* (1954) 43 C2d 481, 275 P2d 15; *Walters v Marler* (1978) 83 CA3d 1, 147 CR 655. Civil Code §3343(a)(2) apparently codifies previous decisional law pertaining to loss of use and enjoyment of property. *Channell v Anthony* (1976) 58 CA3d 290, 129 CR 704; *Williams v Graham* (1948) 83 CA2d 649, 189 P2d 324.

§12.32   2. Lost Profits; CC §3343(a)(3)-(4)

The 1971 amendments to CC §3343 added two items of recovery not previously found in case law interpreting CC §3343. Under §3343(a)(3), a defrauded seller can recover for profits or other gains that might have been earned if the property had been retained. In *Channell v Anthony* (1976) 58 CA3d 290, 129 CR 704, the sellers recovered for loss of income from a management agreement promised them by the buyers as an inducement to sell the property.

Civil Code §3343(a)(4) provides for recovery by a defrauded buyer of the loss of profits and other gains that could have been earned if the property had been as represented, provided the property was acquired for resale at a profit (CC §3343(a)(4)(i)), the buyer reasonably relied on the fraud in buying the property and anticipating profits (CC §3343(a)(4)(ii)), and the lost profits were proximately caused by the fraud and the buyer's reliance on it (CC §3343-(a)(4)(iii)). Under the 1971 amendment the court in *Hartman v Shell Oil Co.* (1977) 68 CA3d 240, 137 CR 244, awarded $20,000 to the plaintiff, who had been induced to lease a small gas station in reliance on the defendant's representations that it would remodel that station or move the plaintiff into a larger one.

These loss-of-profits provisions give CC §3343 some aspects of a benefit-of-the-bargain measure of damages, but the amended section itself declares that it does not authorize recovery of the difference between the value of the property as represented and actual value. CC §3343(b)(1). In *Stout v Turney* (1978) 22 C3d 718, 150 CR 637, the California Supreme Court analyzed the 1971 amendments to CC §3343 and concluded that they do not include a benefit-of-the-bargain measure of damages for fraud, although the loss-of-profits standard may approximate that measure when property is purchased in reasonable anticipation of gain or profit. As the court pointed out, the section does not authorize a benefit-of-the-bargain recovery for a purchase of residential property or for any purchase in which the buyer does not intend to use or sell the property for profit.

§12.33   3. Fraud by Fiduciary; CC §3333

If a misrepresentation or nondisclosure is committed by one who stands in a fiduciary relationship to the defrauded party, recovery is governed not by CC §3343, but by the somewhat broader standards of CC §§1709 and 3333. See *Stout v Turney* (1978) 22 C3d 718, 150 CR 637. Authority for the recovery formula that is to be applied under CC §3333 is divided. Some courts have held that the measure of damages for breach of fiduciary duty is the benefit-of-the-bargain standard applicable to breach of contract actions under CC §3300. *Pepitone v Russo* (1976) 64 CA3d 685, 134 CR 709; *Walsh v Hooker & Fay* (1963) 212 CA2d 450, 28 CR 16; *Simone v McKee* (1956) 142 CA2d 307, 298 P2d 667. See also *Stout v Turney, supra.* Other courts have held that CC §3333 limits the defrauded principal's recovery to the extent of the financial injury actually sustained and does not authorize the plaintiff to recover the benefit of his bargain. *Ward v Taggart* (1959) 51 C2d 736, 336 P2d 534; *Walters v Marler* (1978) 83 CA3d 1, 147 CR 655; *Overgaard v Johnson* (1977) 68 CA3d 821, 137 CR 412. See §2.104 for a discussion of damages for brokers' fraud. See also California Attorney's Damages Guide §2.33 (Cal CEB 1974).

§12.34   4. Punitive Damages; CC §3294

A court may award punitive damages in an action for breach of an obligation not arising from a contract if the defendant's conduct was oppressive, fraudulent, or malicious. CC §3294. Punitive damages may be awarded in addition to the damages authorized by CC §3343 (*Hartman v Shell Oil Co.* (1977) 68 CA3d 240, 137 CR 244; *Channell v Anthony* (1976) 58 CA3d 290, 129 CR 704), or restitution after rescission of the purchase agreement (*Mahon v Berg* (1968) 267 CA2d 588, 73 CR 356; *Millar v James* (1967) 254 CA2d 530, 62 CR 335).

Although fraud as defined in CC §§1572 and 1710 includes negligent misrepresentation or nondisclosure (see §§1.67-1.78), recovery of punitive damages under CC §3294 requires proof of willful or intentional misconduct. *Simmons v Southern Pac. Transp. Co.* (1976) 62 CA3d 341, 133 CR 42; *Ebaugh v Rabkin* (1972) 22 CA3d 891, 99 CR 706. Punitive damages cannot be awarded unless actual damages are suffered and awarded. *Esparza v Specht* (1976) 55 CA3d 1, 127 CR 493. Although a defrauded party may not recover for emotional distress as an element of damages under CC §3343, or as consequential damages incident to rescission (*O'Neil v Spillane* (1975) 45 CA3d 147, 119 CR 245), emotional distress may constitute an element of punitive damages under CC §3294 (*James v Public Fin. Corp.* (1975) 47 CA3d 995, 121 CR 670; *Sierra Nat'l Bank v Brown* (1971) 18 CA3d 98, 95 CR 742).

§12.35   5. Attorneys' Fees

Attorneys' fees are not recoverable unless provided for by statute or contract. CCP §1021; *D'Amico v Board of Medical Examiners* (1974) 11 C3d 1, 112 CR 786; *LeFave v Dimond* (1956) 46 C2d 868, 299 P2d 858. If the purchase and sale agreement (or any other contract) provides that one party may recover attorneys' fees incurred in enforcing the agreement, the provision is treated as being reciprocal; any party who prevails in an action to enforce the agreement can recover attorneys' fees. CC §1717; *Reynolds Metal Co. v Alperson* (1979) 25 C3d 124, 158 CR 1. An action for fraud is treated as a tort action and not an action on the contract, and attorneys' fees may therefore not be recovered in a fraud action under a provision in the purchase and sale agreement. *Schlocker v Schlocker* (1976) 62 CA3d 921, 133 CR 485. However, a defendant in a fraud action who successfully cross-complains to enforce the agreement can recover attorneys' fees if provided for in the agreement. *Shannon v Northern Counties Title Ins. Co.* (1969) 270 CA2d 686, 76 CR 7.

§12.36   6. Interest

Under CC §3288, a defrauded party may recover prejudgment interest in an action for damages, within the trial court's discretion. *Pepitone v Russo* (1976) 64 CA3d 685, 134 CR 709; *Conger v White* (1945) 69 CA2d 28, 158 P2d 415. Interest runs from the date of sale (*Pavlovich v Neidhardt* (1954) 128 CA2d 559, 275 P2d 836; *Williams v Graham* (1948) 83 CA2d 649, 189 P2d 324), except that interest runs from the date payments were made in reliance on the fraud in the case of additional items of damages (*Sixta v Ochsner* (1960) 187 CA2d 485, 9 CR 617). Civil Code §3288 commits recovery of interest to the discretion of the trier of fact, and a trial court's award or denial is unlikely to be overturned on appeal. See *Nathanson v Murphy* (1955) 132 CA2d 363, 282 P2d 174; *Conger v White, supra.*

7. Comparison of Damages and Rescission as Remedies for Fraud

§12.37   a. Measure of Recovery

The recovery available to a defrauded buyer may vary significantly, depending on whether he or she seeks damages under CC §3343 or restitution after rescission under CC §1692 (see §§12.58-12.76). The buyer who affirms the purchase agreement and sues for damages retains the property and is entitled to a judgment for the difference between the consideration paid and the actual value of the property. If the buyer rescinds, the recovery is the purchase price less an offset for rent for the period he or she was in possession of the property. *Kent v Clark* (1942) 20 C2d 779, 128 P2d 868. If the rescinding buyer was forced to remain in possession to protect the property because the seller refused to reassume possession, the court may relieve the buyer of a rent offset. *Smith v Rickards* (1957) 149 CA2d 648, 308 P2d 758. In a damage action, there is no rent offset because the buyer retains possession of the property, but the seller can offset payments in arrears against the buyer's damages. *Bagdasarian v Gragnon* (1948) 31 C2d 744, 763, 192 P2d 935, 942.

Example: Assume a buyer pays $100,000 for property actually worth only $80,000, on the basis of the seller's misrepresentation that it can be subdivided into four parcels and resold for $120,000. The buyer has lived on the property for a year when he discovers the fraud. If the property has a rental value of $1000 per month and the buyer rescinds, the recovery is $88,000 (the purchase price less the rental value of $12,000), and the buyer must restore the property to the seller. A buyer who sues for damages retains the property and the basic measure of damages under CC §3343 is $20,000 (price paid less actual value at time of sale). If the property was purchased for resale, the buyer may be able to recover an additional $20,000 as lost profits under CC §3343(a)(4). See §12.32.

§12.38 b. Election of Remedies

Because the remedies for fraud in a real property transaction (damages and rescission) are inconsistent, an election must be made by the defrauded party, but it need not be made before the complaint is filed or even during the course of trial. *Williams v Marshall* (1951) 37 C2d 445, 235 P2d 372; *Stockton v Newman* (1957) 148 CA2d 558, 307 P2d 56. Merely giving the notice of rescission required by CC §1691 will not bind the defrauded party to that remedy (*Karapetian v Carolan* (1948) 83 CA2d 344, 350, 188 P2d 809, 815), but the damage remedy will be lost if the offer to rescind is accepted by the other party (*Evans v Rancho Royale Hotel Co.* (1952) 114 CA2d 503, 250 P2d 283). Notice of rescission may be given by service of a pleading in an action seeking relief based on rescission. CC §1691. Thus, a defrauded party who is primarily interested in recovering damages for breach should be cautious about joining a cause of action for rescission. If the defendant agrees to accept rescission and restore the consideration, the damage cause of action may be lost.

IV. SPECIFIC PERFORMANCE

A. Seller's Breach

§12.39   1. General Considerations for Buyer

On the seller's failure to perform under the purchase and sale agreement, the buyer may sue for specific performance, either instead of or in addition to damages. CC §§3384, 3387. If the buyer successfully sues for specific performance, the result is a decree ordering conveyance of the property and an accounting. See §12.45. The buyer may prefer specific performance because of the limited measure of damages available for breach under CC §3306. See §12.13.

Specific performance is harder to obtain than damages because of more stringent statutory requirements (CC §§3386-3395), and it may force the buyer to forgo purchasing other property in order to remain ready to purchase the property in question if the specific performance action is successful. These drawbacks may induce the buyer to seek damages instead. Moreover, the buyer seeking specific performance and damages must walk a tightrope to avoid pleading self-defeating inconsistent theories (see §12.12). *Baran v Goldberg* (1948) 86 CA2d 506, 194 P2d 765.

Although the right to specific performance generally depends on the inadequacy of damages as a remedy (*Thayer Plymouth Center, Inc. v Chrysler Motors Corp.* (1967) 255 CA2d 300, 63 CR 148), CC §3387 contains a presumption that monetary compensation cannot adequately relieve the seller's breach of a real property purchase and sale agreement. Moreover, a liquidated damages clause in the agreement (see §§12.29-12.30) will not defeat specific performance. CC §3389. If the seller alone has signed the purchase agreement, the buyer can still obtain specific performance if he has performed or tendered performance. CC §3388.

2. Legal Requirements

§12.40   a. Adequacy of Consideration

The buyer seeking specific performance must plead and prove that the consideration to be paid the seller under the purchase agreement is adequate. CC §3391(1); *Gilbert v Mercer* (1960) 179 CA2d 29, 3 CR 456. To prove adequate consideration, an expert must testify to the value of the property. The seller, as property owner, is permitted to testify concerning its value. *Paratore v Perry* (1966) 239 CA2d 384, 48 CR 682; *Fleischer v Cosgrove* (1956) 145 CA2d 14, 301 P2d 911. The buyer may also be permitted to testify to his opinion of value (*Meyer v Benko* (1976) 55 CA3d 937, 127 CR 846), but whether the testimony will be admitted over the seller's timely objection is not clear. In any event, the prudent buyer should be prepared to present corroborating evidence of adequate consideration in the form of testimony from an appraiser, broker, or other person who can be qualified as an expert. In *Meyer v Benko, supra,* the court reversed the trial court's finding that consideration was inadequate in a case in which the sale price was $23,500, and the sellers testified that the market value was $30,000.

§12.41 b. Agreement Must Be Just and Reasonable

The purchase agreement must be just and reasonable to the party against whom enforcement is sought (CC §3391(2)), and the burden of proof on this issue is on the party seeking specific performance (*Gilbert v Mercer* (1960) 179 CA2d 29, 3 CR 456). A complaint that merely pleads the language of §3391(2) but states no supporting facts, fails to state a cause of action for specific performance. *Salisbury v Yawger* (1921) 184 C 783, 199 P 682; *Foley v Cowan* (1947) 80 CA2d 70, 181 P2d 410. Civil Code §3391(2) creates a real dilemma for the buyer seeking both specific performance and damages. See §12.12. For example, in *Paratore v Perry* (1966) 239 CA2d 384, 48 CR 682, the court denied specific performance of an agreement for the sale of real property for $36,000, basing its decision on the owner's testimony that the reasonable value of the property when the agreement was executed was $50,000.

§12.42 c. Performance of Conditions Precedent

To obtain specific performance, the buyer must allege and prove performance, or an offer of performance, or an excuse from performance of all conditions precedent to the seller's obligation. CC §3392; *Reyburn v Young* (1936) 11 CA2d 476, 54 P2d 87. The buyer's duty to perform or tender performance may be excused by the seller's anticipatory repudiation. *Am-Cal Invest. Co. v Sharlyn Estates, Inc.* (1967) 255 CA2d 526, 63 CR 518. See §§12.9-12.11. Although specific performance will be denied a tardy party when time has been made of the essence (see *Glock v Howard & Wilson Colony Co.* (1898) 123 C 1, 55 P 713; and see §12.8) even under a time of the essence clause, the buyer's failure to perform in a timely manner cannot be relied on to defeat a specific performance action unless the seller has taken steps to terminate the escrow. *Chan v Title Ins. & Trust Co.* (1952) 39 C2d 253, 246 P2d 632; *Williams Plumbing Co. v Sinsley* (1975) 53 CA3d 1027, 126 CR 345; *McCown v Spencer* (1970) 8 CA3d 216, 87 CR 213.

§12.43   d. Certainty of Act To Be Performed

Specific performance will be denied if the contract terms are so uncertain that the precise act to be performed is not clearly ascertainable. CC §3390(5). Courts have frequently stated that specific performance requires a higher degree of certainty than an action for damages requires. See, *e.g., Lawrence v Shutt* (1969) 269 CA2d 749, 75 CR 533; *Brudvig v Renner* (1959) 172 CA2d 522, 342 P2d 276. Uncertainty sufficient to defeat specific performance has been found in various provisions of purchase agreements, *e.g.,* the form of the security device (*Mueller v Chandler* (1963) 217 CA2d 521, 31 CR 646); the interest rate and amortization period (*Bruggeman v Sokol* (1954) 122 CA2d 876, 265 P2d 575); the terms of a release clause (*Lawrence v Shutt, supra;* see §§5.55-5.67); the terms of a subordination provision (*Spellman v Dixon* (1967) 256 CA2d 1, 63 CR 668; see §§5.39-5.54); and the failure to designate a price (*Harder v Allred* (1923) 61 CA 394, 214 P 1017).

§12.44   3. Parties

The buyer should join as defendants in the specific performance action any persons besides the seller who claim interests in the property or are subsequent purchasers or encumbrancers. Civil Code §3395 provides that a specific performance decree may be enforced against anyone claiming an interest in the property except a good faith purchaser or encumbrancer for value and without notice.

The seller's inability to convey perfect title is no reason to deny specific performance if the buyer is willing to take whatever title the seller actually has. See §12.45. Accordingly, the buyer should join any persons having liens that can be discharged by application of the purchase money. See *Grant v Beronio* (1893) 97 C 496, 32 P 556. The buyer can also challenge the validity of the claimed liens by joining the claimants. *Greenstone v Claretian Theological Seminary* (1958) 158 CA2d 493, 322 P2d 482.

If the seller has subsequently sold the property to some other party, the right to specific performance depends on the other party's knowledge. It cannot be granted against a subsequent good faith purchaser for value (CC §3395), but a second grantee who took with notice can be made subject to the decree. *Caras v Parker* (1955) 131 CA2d 141, 280 P2d 226.

If the seller has only a contract right to buy the land, then the record owner who is under contract to the seller should be joined. *Miller v Dyer* (1942) 20 C2d 526, 127 P2d 901.

Co-owners (such as joint tenants, tenants in common, spouses, or partners) who have not bound themselves to the purchase and sale agreement or ratified it or estopped themselves, cannot be held to its terms, and the buyer can get only as much as the seller has to convey. *O'Banion v Paradiso* (1964) 61 C2d 559, 39 CR 370; *Ellis v Mihelis* (1963) 60 C2d 206, 32 CR 415.

The buyer can join to the specific performance action against the seller a tort cause of action against any persons who induced the seller not to sell. Even though the buyer obtains specific performance against the seller, he may also recover damages from these third parties. *Duff v Engelberg* (1965) 237 CA2d 505, 47 CR 114. If the buyer loses the specific performance action against the seller, however, the action against the third parties may be adversely affected. *Boys Town USA v World Church* (1963) 221 CA2d 468, 34 CR 498.

§12.45   4. Nature of Buyer's Relief

Under a specific performance decree, the seller must execute and deliver a deed to the buyer within a specified time. The decree may be enforced by appointing a trustee to convey the land if the seller refuses to execute the conveyance (*Love v Watkins* (1871) 40 C 547), or the court may direct the clerk to execute a deed on the seller's behalf (*Dennis v Overholtzer* (1961) 191 CA2d 791, 13 CR 110). Contempt proceedings may also be initiated against a seller who fails to deliver a deed under the decree. *Goldsworthy v Dobbins* (1952) 110 CA2d 802, 243 P2d 883. If the seller cannot convey the kind of title the buyer seeks, the court cannot compel the seller to obtain good title, and specific performance becomes impossible. *Weisberg v Ashcraft* (1961) 194 CA2d 225, 14 CR 817.

If the seller's title is less than complete but the buyer wants it anyway, the court can order the seller to convey what the seller does own with an abatement in the price. CC §3386; *Johnson v Lehtonen* (1957) 151 CA2d 579, 312 P2d 35. See §12.47. Alternatively, the court can direct the application of some of the purchase money to clear title. *Grant v Beronio* (1893) 97 C 496, 32 P 556.

The decree will also provide that the buyer perform his obligations under the agreement. This usually consists of paying the purchase price within a specified time. *Groobman v Kirk* (1958) 159 CA2d 117, 323 P2d 867. Any other obligations to be performed by the buyer will also be spelled out. *Schomaker v Osborne* (1967) 250 CA2d 887, 58 CR 827; *Burrow v Timmsen* (1963) 223 CA2d 283, 35 CR 668. Because the decree must direct that the buyer pay the purchase price, a judgment creditor of the seller may impose a lien on any monetary recovery that might result from a buyer's specific performance action. CCP §688.1; *Abatti v Eldridge* (1980) 103 CA3d 484, 163 CR 82; 3 CEB Real Prop L Rep 86 (1980). As part of the specific performance decree, the buyer may recover damages, including prorata rents, offset by interest accrued on the purchase obligation. *Ellis v Mihelis* (1963) 60 C2d 206, 32 CR 415. The buyer of a home may recover its fair rental value calculated from the date conveyance should have occurred as part of the specific performance decree. *Meyer v Benko* (1976) 55 CA3d 937, 127 CR 846. The buyer may also recover expenses necessarily incurred as a result of the seller's breach (*Ellis v Mihelis, supra*), and attorneys' fees if provided for in the purchase agreement (*Gates v Green* (1907) 151 C 65, 90 P 189).

§12.46   5. Mutuality of Remedies Not Required

In the past, a party could not compel specific performance if the other party would not have been entitled to the same relief under the mutuality of remedy doctrine. For example, when title was defective, the seller could not obtain specific performance against the buyer, which meant that the buyer could not obtain specific performance either. See 1 Miller & Starr, Current Law of California Real Estate §5:18 (rev ed 1975). In 1969, the legislature substantially altered the mutuality of remedy doctrine by amending CC §3386 to provide that specific performance may be compelled if the agreed counterperformance has been substantially performed, is assured, or can be secured. See §12.47 on securing the buyer's counterperformance.

§12.47   6. Amount Due From Buyer

If the seller's title is defective, the buyer's payment is reduced (or abated) accordingly. *Johnson v Lehtonen* (1957) 151 CA2d 579, 312 P2d 35; *Milkes v Smith* (1949) 91 CA2d 79, 204 P2d 419.

Because the decree comes long after entitlement to a deed under the purchase agreement, the buyer is entitled to an accounting and can recover compensation for the delay. *Ellis v Mihelis* (1963) 60 C2d 206, 32 CR 415. The accounting usually amounts to an abatement in the amount the buyer must pay: the decree awards the profits that the buyer would have earned if the conveyance had taken place in timely fashion, minus the seller's expenses in operating the property and interest on the funds the seller would have received from the buyer. *Ellis v Mihelis, supra*; *Simmons v Dryer* (1963) 216 CA2d 733, 31 CR 199. If all or part of the purchase price was already in escrow, however, the seller cannot recover interest on it from the buyer. *Ellis v Mihelis, supra;* see *Behrendt v Abraham* (1966) 64 C2d 182, 49 CR 292.

The plaintiff in *D-K Inv. Corp. v Sutter* (1971) 19 CA3d 537, 96 CR 830, held an option to purchase property, a portion of which was conveyed for $70,000 to an innocent third person whose improvements increased its value to $93,500. Plaintiff-buyer exercised his prior option and sought to compel the seller to convey the property left at a reduced price. The court held that the proper amount to abate the purchase price was $70,000 rather than $93,500. The court also held that the buyer could recover rents and profits collected by the seller during the period of delay, offset by interest on the price and expenses, and that the seller was entitled to reimbursement for taxes even if no rents and profits had been collected. In *Meyer v Benko* (1976) 55 CA3d 937, 127 CR 846, the buyers were awarded the fair rental value of residential property from the date conveyance should have occurred.

B. Buyer's Breach

§12.48   1. General Considerations for Seller

Although specific performance is theoretically available to the seller as an alternative to damages (see, *e.g., Goldsworthy v Doins*

(1952) 110 CA2d 802, 243 P2d 883), it is generally unsatisfactory because of the drawbacks discussed in §§12.49-12.53. Because specific performance does no more than award the seller money, it is not as attractive a remedy for the seller as it is for the buyer. The differences between the seller's action for specific performance and a legal action for the purchase price are purely technical. See *Hollypark Realty Co. v MacLoane* (1958) 163 CA2d 549, 329 P2d 532; *Ratterree Land Co. v Security First Nat'l Bank* (1938) 26 CA2d 652, 80 P2d 102.

§12.49   2. Seller Must Retain Property

The seller must retain the property during the entire course of a specific performance action and must be ready to convey it whenever the buyer is ordered to perform. A disposition of the property ends the seller's right to specific performance. *Hollypark Realty Co. v MacLoane* (1958) 163 CA2d 549, 329 P2d 532. In a rising market, the seller loses the property's appreciation while litigating the specific performance action and could realize a greater gain simply by reselling the property. In a declining market, a specific performance decree presumably benefits the seller, but if the suit is ultimately unsuccessful, the seller must sell at a greatly depressed price. One court denied specific performance because of the length of time between execution of the agreement and trial and a substantial decline in price. *Pasteur Realty Corp. v La Fleur* (1957) 154 CA2d 5, 315 P2d 374.

§12.50   3. Seller Must Retain Good Title

The seller must retain title in good order throughout the specific performance action because the buyer may insist on strict compliance with the terms of the purchase agreement. *Schmidt v Callero* (1950) 97 CA2d 582, 218 P2d 80. In some instances of impaired title, the seller may be granted relief subject to an abatement in the purchase price. *Goldsworthy v Dobbins* (1952) 110 CA2d 802, 243 P2d 883.

§12.51   4. Waiver of Conditions

A seller seeking specific performance must waive any conditions the buyer cannot perform or is not obligated to perform. *Laske v Lampasona* (1948) 89 CA2d 284, 200 P2d 871. Waiver may be implied from the seller's conduct. *Laske v Lampasona*.

§12.52   5. Greater Risk That Seller Will Lose

A seller who holds the property during the specific performance action (see §§12.49-12.50) risks denial of the requested relief. This risk is greater in an equitable action for specific performance than in an action for damages, because of the more stringent requirements in a specific performance action that the agreement being enforced be both certain and fair. CC §§3390(5)-3391(2); see *Store Properties, Inc. v Neal* (1945) 72 CA2d 112, 164 P2d 38.

§12.53   6. Enforcement Problems

Even if specific performance is granted, the decree is unlikely to meet the seller's needs. Generally, the decree against the buyer will be cast in alternative terms, ordering the buyer to pay the purchase price and providing for a judicial sale if the buyer fails to pay. See *Laske v Lampasona* (1948) 89 CA2d 284, 200 P2d 871. Under this form of decree, if the buyer does not pay the seller may be worse off than before, because the judicial sale will probably result in a distress-sale price that will not cover the original purchase price. A form of decree more advantageous to a seller under some circumstances directs the buyer to pay the purchase price but gives the seller a judgment for the price as damages if the buyer fails to pay. See *Goldsworthy v Dobbins* (1952) 110 CA2d 802, 243 P2d 883.

There is some doubt whether the seller can recover the difference between the unpaid balance of the purchase price and the amount realized from a judicial sale. The courts may treat the attempt to collect the difference as a deficiency judgment barred by CCP §580b, although they have generally distinguished cash sales under court order from the credit sales contemplated by CCP §580b. See *Kerrigan v Maloof* (1950) 98 CA2d 605, 221 P2d 153; *Goldsworthy v Dobbins, supra.* If the seller is to be denied recovery of the difference between the contract price and the judicial sale price because of the antideficiency laws, then it would also be plausible to deny the seller damages under CC §3307 for the buyer's breach, because damages also bear a resemblance to recovery of a deficiency. The seller has always been permitted to recover CC §3307 damages, however, despite CCP §580b. See *Royer v Carter* (1951) 37 C2d 544, 233 P2d 539.

The buyer who refuses to pay the price as ordered in a specific performance decree may be entitled to redeem the property for less than the purchase price after a judicial sale. *Tilley v Bonney* (1898) 123 C 118, 55 P 798; *Bessinger v Grotz* (1944) 66 CA2d 947, 153 P2d 369. See 1 Miller & Starr, Current Law of California Real Estate §5:27 (rev ed 1975). Property purchased at a judicial sale is generally subject to redemption by the defaulting buyer within one year after the sale. CCP §702. The redemption price is only the judicial sale price plus interest and enumerated expenses (CCP §702), and the smaller the judicial sale price, the more tempting it is for the buyer to redeem.

C. Defenses

§12.54   1. Agreement Unjust or Unreasonable

An agreement will not be enforced if its terms are unjust and unreasonable to the party against whom enforcement is sought or if the consideration for it was inadequate (see §§12.40-12.41). CC §§3391(1)-(2); *Lucientes v Bliss* (1958) 157 CA2d 565, 321 P2d 526. If the buyer seeks specific performance, the seller is permitted to testify that the price was too low (*Paratore v Perry* (1966) 239 CA2d 384, 48 CR 682), but will probably need independent evidence of the property's value. If the price is inadequate, the buyer will be denied specific performance. *Stafford v Ballinger* (1962) 199 CA2d 289, 18 CR 568.

§12.55   2. Difficulty of Framing a Decree

A specific performance decree requires counterperformance by the party seeking to enforce the agreement. See §§12.42, 12.47. Although lack of mutuality by itself is not a defense (CC §3386; *Ellis v Mihelis* (1963) 60 C2d 206, 32 CR 415; see §12.46), the plaintiff's counterperformance may be so complicated or difficult that the court will refuse to grant specific performance because the task of supervising the counterperformance would be too difficult (*Boys Town USA v World Church* (1963) 221 CA2d 468, 34 CR 498; *Moklofsky v Moklofsky* (1947) 79 CA2d 259, 179 P2d 628). A buyer with an option for a series of incremental purchases of parcels may find himself saddled with this problem. See, *e.g., Ganiats Constr., Inc. v Hesse* (1960) 180 CA2d 377, 4 CR 706.

§12.56 3. Statutory Defenses

A real property purchase and sale agreement is not specifically enforceable if it is coupled with an obligation to render personal services (CC §3390(1)), to employ another in personal service (CC §3390(2)), to perform an act that the defendant does not have the legal power to perform (CC §3390(3)), or to procure the act or consent of the defendant's wife or a third person (CC §3390(4)). In addition, as discussed in §12.43, the agreement will not be specifically enforced if its terms are not sufficiently certain to make the act that is to be done clearly ascertainable. CC §3390(5). See, *e.g., Lawrence v Shutt* (1969) 269 CA2d 749, 75 CR 533. The defendant may also defeat a specific performance action by proving that his assent to the agreement was obtained by misrepresentation, concealment, circumvention, or unfair practices (CC §3391(3)), or was given under the influence of mistake (unless the agreement provides for compensation in case of mistake), misapprehension, or surprise (CC §3391(4)). *Meyer v Benko* (1976) 55 CA3d 937, 127 CR 846, however, held that a unilateral mistake would not prevent specific enforcement of the agreement without a showing that the plaintiff was aware of the mistaken belief and unfairly took advantage of it. *Boulenger v Morison* (1928) 88 CA 664, 264 P 256, held that when a real estate broker acting as the seller's agent secretly became the buyer's agent, the agreement was entered into through concealment, and the buyer would be denied specific performance.

§12.57 4. Equitable Defenses

Because specific performance is an equitable remedy (CC §§3384-3395), other defenses generally available in equity may also be available to the defendant. Note that some equitable defenses, such as inequity to the defendant or unclean hands, closely parallel the statutory defenses of unfairness and inadequacy of consideration provided for in CC §3391. Equitable defenses held available in specific performance actions include (a) impossibility (see *Miller v Dyer* (1942) 20 C2d 526, 127 P2d 901); (b) inequity to defendant (see *Crittenden v Hansen* (1943) 59 CA2d 56, 138 P2d 37); and (c) laches (*Gatley v Shockley* (1932) 215 C 604, 12 P2d 436). Mere lapse of time will not constitute laches unless it is accompanied by circumstances showing prejudice to the defendant. *Beverage v Canton Placer Mining Co.* (1955) 43 C2d 769, 278 P2d 694.

V. RESCISSION

§12.58 A. Nature of Remedy

Rescission relates back to the formation of the agreement and dissolves it as though it had never been made. *Long v Newlin* (1956) 144 CA2d 509, 301 P2d 271. Thus, the rescinded agreement becomes a nullity and its terms cease to exist and are not enforceable against the other party. *Holmes v Steele* (1969) 269 CA2d 675, 75 CR 216.

In the past, rescission was accomplished by an action to have a rescission adjudged. Former CC §§3406-3408. In 1961 the action to adjudge a rescission was abolished and CC §1691 was amended to provide that a party to a contract may rescind unilaterally by giving notice of rescission and offering to restore the consideration received. *Runyan v Pacific Air Indus.* (1970) 2 C3d 304, 85 CR 138.

B. Grounds

§12.59 1. Mistake

A purchase and sale agreement may be rescinded if the consent of the rescinding party was given by mistake. CC §1689(b)(1); *Crocker-Anglo Nat'l Bank v Kuchman* (1964) 224 CA2d 490, 36 CR 806. In the past, a mistake of fact or law had to be mutual to constitute grounds for rescission. *Hannah v Steinman* (1911) 159 C 142, 112 P 1094; *Williams v Puccinelli* (1965) 236 CA2d 512, 46 CR 285. The modern tendency, however, is to allow rescission for a unilateral mistake not known to the other party when the equities favor the rescinding party. *White v Berrenda Mesa Water Dist.* (1970) 7 CA3d 894, 87 CR 338.

The mistake must be material and may not be the result of the rescinding party's neglect of a legal duty. *White v Berrenda Mesa Water Dist., supra; Roller v California Pac. Title Ins. Co.* (1949) 92 CA2d 149, 206 P2d 694. Mistakes in value and quantity are usually held not material because the parties assume these risks in entering into the agreement. *Vickerson v Frey* (1950) 100 CA2d 621, 224 P2d 126.

§12.60 2. Fraud

Fraud, either actual or constructive, is a ground for rescinding a purchase agreement. CC §1689(b)(1). Constructive fraud arises from a confidential relationship and is discussed in §§2.89-2.99 in the context of the broker-principal relationship. Actual fraud arises from a contractual relationship (CC §1572) and may include:

(a) Affirmative misrepresentation: the suggestion of a fact as true by one who does not believe it to be true (CC §1572(1); *Snelson v Ondulando Highlands Corp.* (1970) 5 CA3d 243, 85 CR 806; *Hale v Wolfsen* (1969) 276 CA2d 285, 81 CR 23);

(b) Negligent misrepresentation: assertion of a fact as true without a reasonable basis for believing it to be true (CC §1572(2); *Doran v Milland Dev. Co.* (1958) 159 CA2d 322, 323 P2d 792);

(c) Concealment, or nondisclosure: suppression of a fact by one with knowledge of, or belief in, the fact (CC §1572(3); *Herzog v Capital Co.* (1945) 27 C2d 349, 164 P2d 8; *Lingsch v Savage* (1963) 213 CA2d 729, 29 CR 201);

(d) Promissory fraud: a promise made without any intention to perform (CC §1572(4));

(e) Any other conduct "fitted to deceive" (CC §1572(5)).

An innocent misrepresentation, made in good faith and with reasonable belief in its truth, is not actionable fraud but may give rise to a right to rescind on the ground of mistake (§12.59). *Wood v Kalbaugh* (1974) 39 CA3d 926, 114 CR 673.

To obtain rescission (or damages) for fraud, the defrauded party must plead and prove that (a) the defendant misrepresented or concealed a material fact, (b) the representation was false and the defendant knew or should have known of its falsity, (c) the misrepresentation or nondisclosure was committed with intent to induce the plaintiff to enter into the transaction, (d) the plaintiff reasonably relied on the representation or his lack of knowledge of the concealed fact, and (e) the plaintiff suffered injury as a result of this reliance. *Gonsalves v Hodgson* (1951) 38 C2d 91, 237 P2d 656; *Ach v Finkelstein* (1968) 264 CA2d 667, 70 CR 472. See generally, §§1.67-1.78.

§12.61 3. Undue Influence

An agreement may be rescinded if the consent of the rescinding party was obtained through duress or undue influence. CC §1689(b)(1); *Leeper v Beltrami* (1959) 53 C2d 195, 1 CR 12. Factors that may be considered in determining the existence of undue influence include (a) whether the consideration was adequate

(*McDougall v Roberts* (1919) 43 CA 553, 185 P 483), (b) whether the plaintiff acted with a free mind (*Anderson v Nelson* (1927) 83 CA 1, 256 P 294), (c) whether the transaction took place at arms' length (*Mills v Kopf* (1963) 216 CA2d 780, 31 CR 80), and (d) whether a confidential relationship existed between the parties (*Kloehn v Prendiville* (1957) 154 CA2d 156, 316 P2d 17).

§12.62   4. Mental Incapacity

Rescission is available if the rescinding party was not mentally competent to understand the subject matter at the time the agreement was entered into. *Deasy v Taylor* (1918) 39 CA 235, 178 P 538.

§12.63   5. Failure of Consideration

An agreement may be rescinded by one of the parties if the consideration for the obligation of the rescinding party (a) fails, in whole or in part, through the fault of the other party (CC §1689(b)(2)), (b) becomes entirely void for any reason (CC §1689-(b)(3)), or (c) fails in a material respect before being rendered to the rescinding party (CC §1689(b)(4)).

Thus, if the purchase agreement fails without fault by either party, rescission may be the only appropriate remedy. CC §1689(b)(3); *Rodriguez v Barnett* (1959) 52 C2d 154, 338 P2d 907. The failure of consideration must be material. See, *e.g., Fountain v Semi-Tropic Land & Water Co.* (1893) 99 C 677, 34 P 497; *Integrated, Inc. v Alec Fergusson Elec. Contractor* (1967) 250 CA2d 287, 58 CR 503.

Failure of the buyer to pay the first installment entitles the seller to rescission (*Smith v Blandin* (1901) 133 C 441, 65 P 894), and failure to tender marketable title when the purchase and sale agreement matures entitles the buyer to rescission (*Post v Palpar, Inc.* (1960) 184 CA2d 676, 7 CR 823).

§12.64   6. Mutual Consent

An agreement may be rescinded with the consent of all parties, regardless of the express terms of the contract. CC §1689(a); *Rackliff v Coronet Constr. Co.* (1958) 157 CA2d 419, 321 P2d 50.

Mutual cancellation of executory rights under a written agreement constitutes consideration for mutual rescission. *Honda v Reed* (1958) 156 CA2d 536, 319 P2d 728. Consent to mutual rescission need not be written (*Martin v Butter* (1949) 93 CA2d 562, 209 P2d 636; *San Roque Property, Inc. v Pierce* (1937) 18 CA2d 379, 63 P2d 1198), and may be implied from the parties' conduct (*Bush v Vernon* (1955) 135 CA2d 33, 286 P2d 903).

7. Special Statutory Grounds

§12.65   a. Home Solicitation Contracts

Civil Code §1689.6 allows a buyer to cancel a home solicitation contract or offer until midnight of the third business day after the buyer signs the contract or offer.

§12.66   b. Subdivided Lands

Under Bus & P C §11028, an agreement to purchase or lease a lot in a land project within the purview of the Subdivided Lands Act (as defined in Bus & P C §§11000.5-11000.6) may be rescinded by the buyer or lessee, without cause, by delivering written notice by midnight of the 14th day after execution of the agreement.

§12.67   c. Subdivision Map Act

Government Code §66499.32 authorizes a grantee, buyer, or person contracting to buy, to rescind any sale, deed of conveyance, or agreement to sell real property that has been divided in violation of the Subdivision Map Act (Govt C §§66410-66499.37), as long as rescission is effected within one year after the date the violation is discovered.

§12.68   d. Interstate Land Sales

The buyer may revoke an agreement to purchase or lease a lot in a subdivision covered by the Interstate Land Sales Full Disclosure Act (15 USC §§1701-1720) until midnight of the seventh day after its execution. 15 USC §1703(b). If the property report required by the act has not been given to the buyer before or at the time of signing, the buyer may revoke the agreement within two years after the date of signing. 15 USC §1703(c).

C. Procedure

§12.69   1. Notice of Rescission

Under CC §1691, unilateral rescission is effected when one party gives notice to the other party and offers to restore everything received under the agreement. The notice need not be in any particular form, but it must clearly indicate to the defaulting party that the injured party considers the agreement terminated. *Whitney Inv. Co. v Westview Dev. Co.* (1969) 273 CA2d 594, 78 CR 302. Filing and service of a pleading seeking relief based on rescission is considered both notice and an offer to restore. CC §1691. Notice is unnecessary when there has been a total failure of consideration. *Holcomb v Long Beach Inv. Co.* (1933) 129 CA 285, 19 P2d 31.

Promptness in giving notice is not a condition to the right to rescind, and rescission may be denied only if the delay amounts to laches, *i.e.,* prejudices the other party. CC §§1691, 1693. See §12.76. The following have been held to be justifiable delays:

(a) The facts would not have put a reasonable person on inquiry concerning the legal right to rescind (*Hannah v Steinman* (1911) 159 C 142, 112 P 1094);

(b) Attempts were made to settle the dispute arising out of facts justifying rescission (*Gist v Security Trust & Sav. Bank* (1933) 218 C 581, 24 P2d 153); and

(c) Delay resulted from the indulgence of the defaulting party (*Wilson v Rigali & Veselich* (1934) 138 CA 760, 33 P2d 455).

§12.70   2. Offer To Restore

Under CC §1691(b), the party seeking rescission must offer to restore everything received under the agreement to the other party but need not specify in detail what items of consideration will be restored. *Smith v Rickards* (1957) 149 CA2d 648, 308 P2d 758. If restoration is impossible through no fault of the plaintiff, then it is not required. *Farina v Bevilaqua* (1961) 192 CA2d 681, 13 CR 791. When the plaintiff has received nothing of value, the restoration requirement does not apply. *Realty Co. v Burton* (1958) 160 CA2d 178, 325 P2d 171. If the plaintiff is entitled to retain whatever consideration was received, an offer to restore is unnecessary. *Shaffer v Security Trust & Sav. Bank* (1935) 4 CA2d 707, 41 P2d 948; *Norton v Rosenkranz* (1923) 62 CA 226, 216 P 380.

D. Actions for Relief

§12.71   1. Form of Action

Although CC §§1688-1693, governing rescission, do not expressly state whether an action based on rescission sounds in law or in equity, it has been held that the rescinding party may seek any relief warranted by the circumstances, whether legal or equitable. When the gist of the action is recovery of money received by the defendant, for example, the action is legal in nature and the plaintiff is entitled to a jury trial. *Paularena v Superior Court* (1965) 231 CA2d 906, 42 CR 366. On the other hand, when the defendant denies the existence of any basis for rescission, the award of monetary damages is ancillary to the equitable determination whether plaintiff had a basis for rescission. *Snelson v Ondulando Highlands Corp.* (1970) 5 CA3d 243, 84 CR 806.

Having rescinded, the plaintiff is generally entitled to restitution, and a cause of action of the lawsuit will be to recover any consideration paid. CC §1692; *Utemark v Samuel* (1953) 118 CA2d 313, 257 P2d 656. An action following rescission might also include causes of action to quiet title (CCP §§760.010-772.060), for declaratory relief (CCP §1060), to cancel an instrument clouding title (CC §3412), and for ejectment (*Francis v West Virginia Oil Co.* (1917) 174 C 168, 162 P 394).

§12.72 2. Damages Recoverable

The goal of rescission is to restore the parties to the status they had before the transaction, and accordingly CC §1692 grants the courts broad discretion to fashion relief by awarding compensation to either party to adjust the equities. Thus, the rescinding party can conceivably be required to reimburse the other party. See, *e.g., Utemark v Samuel* (1953) 118 CA2d 313, 257 P2d 656. For example, a rescinding buyer's recoverable expenses might be less than the reasonable rental value of the premises during the buyer's period of occupancy, so that the defaulting seller would be entitled to a recovery. See 1 Miller & Starr, Current Law of California Real Estate §5:3 (rev ed 1975).

Civil Code §1692 authorizes the aggrieved party's recovery of "consequential damages." Under this language, a rescinding party may be able to recover out-of-pocket expenses incurred in the course of the transaction. *Tampico v Wood* (1963) 222 CA2d 211, 34 CR 885. Items of recovery may include (a) the value of any improvements made on the property (*Soderling v Tomlin* (1959) 170 CA2d 169, 338 P2d 946); (b) payments made by a rescinding buyer on a mortgage imposed by the seller (*Arthur v Graham* (1923) 64 CA 608, 222 P 371); and (c) attorneys' fees, if provided for in the agreement being rescinded (*Kass v Weber* (1968) 261 CA2d 417, 67 CR 876). When rescission is based on fraud, the rescinding party may recover additional expenses, and possibly punitive damages (*Mahon v Berg* (1968) 267 CA2d 588, 73 CR 356). In actions for restitution after rescission for fraud, interest from the date of rescission may be recovered under CC §3288. *Wilson v Rigali & Veselich* (1934) 138 CA 760, 33 P2d 455.

Note that CC §1692 seems to provide a greater measure of recovery for the buyer in some situations than is available under CC §3306 in an action for breach. See §12.13.

§12.73   3. Purchaser's Lien

If the seller fails or refuses to perform and the buyer rescinds, the buyer is entitled to a purchaser's lien on the land as security for reimbursement of any consideration paid, including the downpayment and consequential expenditures for improvements, taxes, and insurance. CC §3050; *Montgomery v Meyerstein* (1921) 186 C 459, 199 P 800. The rescinding buyer may sue both for restitution and to establish and foreclose the statutory lien. *Harder v Allred* (1923) 61 CA 394, 214 P 1017. Such an action affects title to real property, and the buyer may record a lis pendens (see §§12.86-12.92), making the lien enforceable against a subsequent purchaser. See *South San Bernardino Land & Improvement Co. v San Bernardino Nat'l Bank* (1889) 127 C 245, 59 P 699. The purchaser of a leasehold is not entitled to a purchaser's lien, however, because CC §3050 applies only to real property sales. *Weaver v Superior Court* (1949) 93 CA2d 729, 209 P2d 830.

E. Defenses

§12.74   1. Waiver

A party who accepts benefits under an agreement with full knowledge of facts warranting rescission waives the right to rescind. *Chan v Title Ins. & Trust Co.* (1952) 39 C2d 253, 246 P2d 632; *Schmidt v Callero* (1950) 97 CA2d 582, 218 P2d 80. Waiver may also be found if the aggrieved party affirms the agreement by suing for damages or specific performance. See *Price v McConnell* (1960) 184 CA2d 660, 7 CR 695. Delay in bringing the action without sufficient justification may also constitute waiver of the right to rescind.

Leeper v Beltrami (1959) 53 C2d 195, 1 CR 12. See also § 12.76 regarding laches.

Waiver is an affirmative defense that must be pleaded and proved by the party asserting it. *Williams v Marshall* (1951) 37 C2d 445, 235 P2d 372.

§12.75   2. Estoppel

A party may be estopped from rescinding an agreement if he has defaulted in performance of an obligation under the agreement (*Integrated, Inc. v Alec Fergusson Elec. Contractor* (1967) 250 CA2d 287, 58 CR 503) or has given the other party assurances that he will perform and the assurances have been relied on to the other party's detriment (*McCown v Spencer* (1970) 8 CA3d 216, 87 CR 213). Estoppel is also an affirmative defense that must be pleaded and proved by the party asserting it. *Frank Pisano & Assocs. v Taggart* (1972) 29 CA3d 1, 105 CR 414.

§12.76   3. Laches

Under CC § 1693, relief based on rescission will not be denied for delay in giving notice of rescission unless the delay has substantially prejudiced the other party. Mere lapse of time will not suffice. *Beverage v Canton Placer Mining Co.* (1955) 43 C2d 769, 278 P2d 694; *Ulrich v San Jacinto Estates* (1952) 109 CA2d 648, 241 P2d 262. See also § 12.69.

On the statute of limitations for rescission, see § 12.104.

VI. REFORMATION

§12.77   A. Nature of Remedy

In granting reformation, the court issues a judgment correcting an instrument or contract to reflect the true agreement of the parties. CC §§ 3399-3402. The remedy contemplates a continuing contractual relationship between the parties, unlike rescission, which is a retroactive termination of the agreement. See §§ 12.58-12.76. The grounds on which reformation will be granted are discussed in § 12.78. In general, for reformation to be an available remedy, the parties must have reached a mutual understanding on all essential terms. *Lemoge Elec. v County of San Mateo* (1956) 46 C2d 659, 297

P2d 638; *Shupe v Nelson* (1967) 254 CA2d 693, 62 CR 352. If the written agreement actually conforms to the parties' oral understanding, reformation is not available even though performance has proved to be more onerous than the parties suspected. *Bailard v Marden* (1951) 36 C2d 703, 227 P2d 10; *Ellison v City of San Buenaventura* (1975) 48 CA3d 952, 122 CR 167.

Reformation may be sought in conjunction with other remedies so that complete relief may be obtained in one action. For example, specific performance and reformation may be sought in the same action (CC §3402), and money damages may be awarded along with reformation (*Landis v Superior Court* (1965) 232 CA2d 548, 42 CR 893). On the other hand, reformation is generally inconsistent with rescission, and the attorney should consider whether rescission is the more appropriate remedy, especially if there seems to be disagreement about what the parties intended.

§12.78   B. Grounds

Reformation may be granted when an agreement does not express the true intent of the parties because of fraud or mistake. CC §3399.

Mistake provides a basis for reformation if it occurs when the agreement is executed (*Murray v Dake* (1873) 46 C 644), is material to the agreement (*Cottle v Gibbon* (1962) 200 CA2d 1, 19 CR 82), and its correction is material to the rights of the parties (*Auerbach v Healy* (1916) 174 C 60, 161 P 1157). If the mistake is truly innocent and is made by only one party to the agreement or if there is no fraud, reformation is generally not available. *Perry v Bedford* (1965) 238 CA2d 6, 47 CR 461. Situations on which reformation may be based include:

(1) Mutual mistake. Reformation lies if the agreement fails to express the parties' intent because of the inadvertence of both parties or a shared misconception. CC §3399; *Lemoge Elec. v County of San Mateo* (1956) 46 C2d 659, 297 P2d 638; *Jefferson v Pietroroia* (1936) 5 C2d 222, 54 P2d 7. A mistake regarding a document's legal effect can constitute mutual mistake under CC §3399. *Stafford v California Canning Peach Growers* (1938) 11 C2d 212, 78 P2d 1150.

(2) Unilateral mistake. Reformation is also appropriate when the agreement fails to express the parties' intent because one party acted under a mistake known or suspected at the time by the other party. CC §3399; *Stare v Tate* (1971) 21 CA3d 432, 98 CR 264; *Baines*

v Zuieback (1948) 84 CA2d 483, 191 P2d 67. If the aggrieved party fails to establish the other party's knowledge or suspicion of a unilateral mistake, reformation will not be granted. *Moore v Vandermast, Inc.* (1941) 19 C2d 94, 119 P2d 129; *Petersen v Ridenour* (1955) 135 CA2d 720, 287 P2d 848. When the aggrieved party has received no consideration, the requirement of knowledge or suspicion may be relaxed. See *Tyler v Larson* (1951) 106 CA2d 317, 235 P2d 39.

(3) Mistake of a third person. When a third person acting for both parties causes the mistake, a court may reform the agreement. *Martinelli v Gabriel* (1951) 103 CA2d 818, 230 P2d 444; *Mills v Schulba* (1950) 95 CA2d 559, 213 P2d 408.

§12.79   C. Matters Subject to Reformation

When the test for mistake under CC §3399 (see §12.78) has been met, reformation can be granted to alter an agreement in a variety of respects. For example, a written document can generally be reformed (1) to insert the appropriate date (*Waratah Oil Co. v Reward Oil Co.* (1914) 23 CA 638, 139 P 91), (2) to fill in blanks in a printed form (*Calhoun v Downs* (1931) 211 C 766, 297 P 548), and (3) to correct misspellings (*Oatman v Niemeyer* (1929) 207 C 424, 278 P 1043).

An erroneous description may be corrected to express the true intention of the parties as long as the rights of innocent third parties will not be prejudiced. *California Pac. Title Co. v Moore* (1964) 229 CA2d 114, 40 CR 61; *Tyler v Larson* (1951) 106 CA2d 317, 235 P2d 39. When needed to implement the parties' intent, a description completely omitted from a deed may be inserted. *Oatman v Niemeyer, supra; Mills v Schulba* (1950) 95 CA2d 559, 213 P2d 408.

A written instrument that incorrectly reflects the character or extent of the estate or interest intended to be conveyed may be reformed. *Cleghorn v Zumwalt* (1890) 83 C 155, 23 P 294 (incorrect description of fractional interest); *Berendsen v McIver* (1954) 126 CA2d 347, 272 P2d 76 (incorrect statement of nature of cotenancy interests); *Roeder v Roeder* (1953) 118 CA2d 572, 258 P2d 581 (incorrect characterization of estate conveyed).

Reformation of a usurious loan provision will be allowed if the parties did not intend to create a usurious transaction. *First Am. Title Ins. & Trust Co. v Cook* (1970) 12 CA3d 592, 90 CR 645.

§12.80 D. Who May Obtain Reformation

An aggrieved party within the meaning of CC §3399 need not be an actual party to the agreement; any person who has been prejudiced or has suffered pecuniary loss due to a mistake in the agreement may maintain an action for reformation. *Shupe v Nelson* (1967) 254 CA2d 693, 62 CR 352. Usually a party who can recover as a third party beneficiary can also maintain a reformation action. For example, a broker may be able to reform a real property purchase and sale agreement under appropriate circumstances. *Calhoun v Downs* (1931) 211 C 766, 297 P 548.

An escrow holder or title insurer may bring an action to reform an instrument that it erroneously prepared for a real property sales transaction between two other parties. *First Am. Title Ins. & Trust Co. v Cook* (1970) 12 CA3d 592, 90 CR 645 (note prepared by escrow holder included usurious interest rate that was not in escrow instructions); *California Pac. Title Co. v Moore* (1964) 229 CA2d 114, 40 P2d 61 (title insurer erroneously included wrong description in deed).

The personal representative of an estate, or a devisee, may seek reformation of an instrument to which the testator was a party. *Tyler v Larson* (1951) 106 CA2d 317, 235 P2d 39; *Ferguson v Ash* (1915) 27 CA 375, 150 P 657.

§12.81 E. Persons Subject to Reformation

A cause of action for reformation may be maintained against the original parties to an agreement and those claiming under the original parties. *Oatman v Niemeyer* (1929) 207 C 424, 278 P 1043 (administrator); *Stonesifer v Kilburn* (1898) 122 C 659, 55 P 587 (subsequent grantee); *Holt v Holt* (1898) 120 C 67, 52 P 119 (subsequent mortgagee).

Reformation will not be granted when to do so would prejudice rights acquired by third persons in good faith for value. CC §3399. Thus, reformation may not be obtained against a bona fide purchaser who acquires an interest after the instrument sought to be reformed was executed. *Baines v Zuieback* (1948) 84 CA2d 483, 191 P2d 67. A third person who takes with actual or constructive notice of the plaintiff's claim will not be protected. *Shupe v Nelson* (1967) 254 CA2d 693, 62 CR 352. When a corporation that was an original party to an agreement merges with another corporation, the resulting corporation is not a third person subject to protection under CC §3399. *Treadaway v Camellia Convalescent Hosps., Inc.* (1974) 43 CA3d 189, 118 CR 341.

F. Defenses

§12.82 1. Waiver

An executed agreement cannot be reformed when the aggrieved party knew of the mistake and accepted performance under the terms of the unreformed agreement. *Vantress Farms, Inc. v Sydenstricker* (1970) 11 CA3d 943, 90 CR 251; *Burnand v Nowell* (1948) 84 CA2d 1, 189 P2d 796.

§12.83 2. Void or Illegal Contract

Generally, an agreement wholly void for illegality cannot be reformed. *Ainsworth v Morrill* (1916) 31 CA 509, 160 P 1089. However, the fact that the instrument as mistakenly written results in invalidity does not defeat the right to reformation if the agreement as reformed will be valid. *Oatman v Niemeyer* (1929) 207 C 424, 278 P 1043.

§12.84 3. Lack of Consideration

An agreement or conveyance made without consideration will generally not be reformed on behalf of the donee against the donor. *Enos v Stewart* (1902) 138 C 112, 70 P 1005. Reformation may be allowed under these circumstances, however, to carry out the donor's probable intent or when equities favor the donee over those asserting some adverse interest. *Reina v Erassarret* (1951) 103 CA2d 258, 229 P2d 92; *Parker v Hardisty* (1921) 54 CA 628, 202 P 479.

§12.85 4. Plaintiff's Negligence

The aggrieved party's negligence will generally not preclude reformation unless it is so gross as to be inexcusable. *Los Angeles & Redondo R.R. v New Liverpool Salt Co.* (1906) 150 C 21, 87 P 1029; *Voge, Inc. v Rose* (1962) 205 CA2d 534, 23 CR 87; *Mills v Schulba* (1950) 95 CA2d 559, 213 P2d 408. Whether the negligence is sufficiently inexcusable to bar relief is a question of fact. *Hanlon v Western Loan & Bldg. Co.* (1941) 46 CA2d 580, 116 P2d 465.

Reformation based on mistake may be denied if the plaintiff is negligent (*Johnson v Sun Realty Co.* (1934) 138 CA 296, 32 P2d 393), but contributory negligence is not a defense to a reformation action based on fraud if the plaintiff's reliance on the defendant's misrepresentation is justified. *Security-First Nat'l Bank v Earp* (1942) 19 C2d 774, 122 P2d 900.

Failure to read the written document or understand its contents does not necessarily preclude reformation. Whether reformation will be granted in this situation depends on the circumstances (*California Trust Co. v Cohn* (1932) 214 C 619, 7 P2d 297; *Tomas v Vaughn* (1944) 63 CA2d 188, 146 P2d 499) and is a question of fact (*Sparks v Richardson* (1956) 141 CA2d 286, 296 P2d 892). Failure to read the agreement will probably be excused when the aggrieved party justifiably relied on the other party's misrepresentations. *Baines v Zuieback* (1948) 84 CA2d 483, 191 P2d 67; *Nelson v Meadville* (1937) 19 CA2d 68, 64 P2d 1116.

VII. LIS PENDENS

§12.86   A. Effect

When a plaintiff files an action affecting title to or possession of real property, he or she can record a notice with the county recorder that the action is pending. CCP §409. This notice is commonly called a lis pendens, and it gives constructive notice to subsequent purchasers and encumbrancers that the lawsuit is pending. CCP §409. *Rose v Knapp* (1957) 153 CA2d 379, 314 P2d 812; *Harris v Whittier Bldg. & Loan Ass'n* (1936) 18 CA2d 260, 63 P2d 840.

If the plaintiff eventually prevails in the action, the judgment will take its priority from the date the lis pendens was recorded and will have seniority over interests acquired after that date, even if acquired before entry of the judgment. CC §1214; *D-K Inv. Corp. v Sutter* (1971) 19 CA3d 537, 546, 96 CR 830, 835. If the defendant files a cross-action seeking affirmative relief, a lis pendens may be recorded on the cross-action as well. CCP §409. Regarding the right to record a lis pendens, and procedure for doing so, see 1 California Civil Procedure Before Trial, chap 21 (Cal CEB 1977).

§12.87   B. Creation

A lis pendens is created by recording, in an action concerning real property or affecting title to or possession of real property, notice that the action is pending. CCP §409. The notice must be recorded in the county in which the real property is situated (normally also the county in which the action is pending; CCP §392(1)(a)) and must state the names of the parties to the action, the object of the action or defense, and a description of the property. CCP §409.

The range of actions that have been held to affect title to or possession of real property for the purpose of filing a lis pendens is quite broad. For example, a lis pendens may be filed against adjoining property in an action challenging the owner of that property's claim to an access easement across the plaintiff's property. *Kendall-Brief Co. v Superior Court* (1976) 60 CA3d 462, 131 CR 515. Other actions in which a lis pendens can be recorded include actions

(1) to quiet title (CCP §§760.010-762.060); *Moore v Schneider* (1925) 196 C 380, 238 P 81; *Larkin v Bank of America Nat'l Trust & Sav. Ass'n* (1949) 93 CA2d 594, 209 P2d 801);

(2) to foreclose a mortgage or deed of trust (*Johnson v Friant* (1903) 140 C 260, 73 P 993; *Bolton v Logan* (1938) 30 CA2d 30, 85 P2d 546);

(3) to foreclose a street assessment lien (Str & H C §6619; *Page v W. W. Chase Co.* (1904) 145 C 578, 79 P 278);

(4) for eminent domain (CCP §1250.130; *Roach v Riverside Water Co.* (1887) 74 C 263, 15 P 776);

(5) to foreclose a mechanics' lien (CC §3146);

(6) for ejectment (*McLean v Baldwin* (1902) 136 C 565, 69 P 259);

(7) to rescind an agreement for the purchase and sale of real property (*Wilkins v Oken* (1958) 157 CA2d 603, 321 P2d 876);

(8) for partition (CCP §872.250); and

(9) to set aside a fraudulent conveyance of real property (*Putnam Sand & Gravel Co. v Albers* (1971) 14 CA3d 722, 92 CR 636).

A lis pendens recorded in an action that does not come within the terms of CCP §409 does not impart constructive notice of the pending action (*Brownlee v Vang* (1962) 206 CA2d 814, 24 CR 158) and may be expunged (see §12.88). For example, recording a lis pendens does not give effective notice of an action concerning personal property (*MacDermot v Hayes* (1917) 175 C 95, 170 P 616), or of a nonjudicial trustee's sale (*Carpenter v Smallpage* (1934) 220 C 129, 29 P2d 841). It has been held in California that a lis pendens is not effective in a marital dissolution action in which title to real property is in issue (*Mayberry v Whittier* (1904) 144 C 322, 78 P 16), but it has been suggested that the result might be different today (2 Miller & Starr, Current Law of California Real Estate §11:121 n18 (rev ed 1977)). A party having actual knowledge of a dissolution action affecting real property is bound by the decree. *Rotea v Rotea* (1949) 93 CA2d 827, 209 P2d 963.

§12.88. C. Expungement

The lis pendens is a necessary tool to protect the plaintiff with a legitimate claim to real property, but a plaintiff whose claim is not in good faith can also abuse it to try to compel settlement. After the lis pendens is recorded, it is difficult for the owner to sell or refinance the property, and the owner may be forced to settle a nonmeritorious suit to avoid foreclosure. See, *e.g., Howden-Goetzl v Superior Court* (1970) 7 CA3d 135, 86 CR 323. To avoid this problem, the owner can follow the procedure established in CCP §409.1 or §409.2 to remove the lis pendens from the records, while the action is still pending. On motion, the court can order the lis pendens expunged if it finds that (1) the action does not affect title to or possession of real property (CCP §409.1(a); see §12.87); (2) the action was commenced or prosecuted for an improper purpose and not in good faith (CCP §409.1(b); see §12.89); or (3) an undertaking can adequately secure relief to the party who recorded the lis pendens (CCP §409.2; see §12.90).

§12.89   1. Improper Purpose and Bad Faith; CCP §409.1

Under a 1976 amendment to CCP §409.1, the party filing the lis pendens has the burden of showing that the action was filed for a proper purpose and in good faith if the other party files a motion for expungement. Previously, the party seeking expungement had the burden of proving improper purpose and bad faith. *United Prof. Planning, Inc. v Superior Court* (1970) 9 CA3d 377, 88 CR 551.

An action has been brought in bad faith if the court finds that it was begun primarily because of hostility or ill will, solely to deprive the defendant of a beneficial use of the property or to force a settlement not related to the merits of the claim. *United Prof. Planning, Inc. v Superior Court, supra.*

If the court finds that expungement is proper under CCP §409.1(a) or (b), it can require the expunging party to post an undertaking to indemnify the other party if he ultimately prevails in the main action. CCP §409.1.

§12.90   2. Undertaking; CCP §409.2

The court can also order the lis pendens expunged if it finds that the party recording it can be adequately protected by an undertaking. CCP §409.2. In setting the amount of the bond, the trial court can consider all relevant factors, including the likelihood that the plaintiff will prevail and the probable amount of the potential recovery. *Howden-Goetzl v Superior Court* (1970) 7 CA3d 135, 86 CR 323. The undertaking need not cover the full amount claimed in the complaint. *Howden-Goetzl, supra.* If the property in question is commercial or the plaintiff's interest is primarily monetary, an undertaking will probably be found adequate to protect the plaintiff. See, *e.g., Trapasso v Superior Court* (1977) 73 CA3d 561, 140 CR 820; *Empfield v Superior Court* (1973) 33 CA3d 105, 108 CR 375. On the other hand, the adequacy of the protection afforded by an undertaking is within the trial court's discretion and expungement may be denied under CCP §409.2, even when commercial property is involved, if the court finds that the property's uniqueness renders an undertaking inadequate. *Stewart Dev. Co. IV v Superior Court* (1980) 108 CA3d 266, 166 CR 450; *Sheets v Superior Court* (1978) 86 CA3d 68, 149 CR 912.

§12.91   3. Procedure

A motion for expungement under CCP §409.1 must be made on 20 days' notice. Section 409.2 does not contain a 20-day requirement, and presumably the normal 10-day notice requirement for motions (CCP §1005) applies to motions made under CCP §409.2. An order granting or denying a motion made under either §409.1 or §409.2 may direct payment of reasonable attorneys' fees to the prevailing party. CCP §409.3. The purpose of such an award is to control misuse of the lis pendens procedure. *Trapasso v Superior Court* (1977) 73 CA3d 561, 140 CR 820. An order granting or denying an expungement motion is not appealable, but may be reviewed in a mandamus proceeding. CCP §409.4. A petition for writ of mandate may be filed with the reviewing court within 20 days after service of written notice of the order unless extended by the trial court up to a maximum of 60 days after entry. CCP §409.4. An expungement order is not effective and cannot be recorded during this review period. CCP §409.5. After a certified copy of the expungement order is recorded, the lis pendens neither constitutes actual or constructive notice of its contents nor creates a duty of inquiry. CCP §§409.1-409.2.

§12.92   D. Liability for Recording Lis Pendens

A notice of lis pendens is a republication of pleadings filed in a judicial proceeding, and as such is absolutely privileged (CC §47), so that a party filing a lis pendens cannot be liable for slander of title. *Albertson v Raboff* (1956) 46 C2d 375, 295 P2d 405; *Sheets v Superior Court* (1978) 86 CA3d 68, 149 CR 912. However, the privilege will not protect a party filing a lis pendens from liability in a subsequent action for malicious prosecution. *Albertson v Raboff, supra.*

VIII. DEFENSES COMMON TO ALL ACTIONS

§12.93   A. General Considerations

Real property sales agreements may be particularly vulnerable to general contract defenses because they are often prepared by brokers or salespersons rather than attorneys; normally include a variety of covenants and conditions; and are frequently modified before close of escrow. General contract defenses are discussed in §§12.94-12.107; defenses peculiar to specific performance actions are discussed at §§12.54-12.57; defenses to rescission actions are discussed at §§12.74-12.76; and defenses to reformation are discussed at §§12.82-12.85.

Actions for breach can be defended against by alleging the invalidity or nonexistence of the agreement for lack of capacity (see §12.94), lack of assent (see §§12.95-12.98), lack of consideration (§§12.99-12.102), or noncompliance with the statute of frauds (§12.103). In addition, the defendant's performance may be excused by nonoccurrence of conditions (§12.105), by failure of consideration (§12.106), impossibility (§12.107), or the action may be barred by the statute of limitations (§12.104).

B. Invalid or Nonexistent Agreement

§12.94   1. Lack of Capacity

The defendant's minority or incompetence is a defense to contract actions in general and to suits for breach of real property sales agreements. CC §§33, 38, 39, 1556; see generally, §§3.10-3.13. A conveyance of community real property may be challenged if not executed by both spouses. CC §5127; see §3.15. Lack of capacity may also be a defense to an action arising from a transaction with a partnership or corporation. See §§3.22-3.26. A particular partner or corporate officer may lack capacity to bind the partnership or corporation. Parties dealing with general or limited partnerships are charged with notice of the limitations of the partners' authority if a statement of partnership (Corp C §15010) or certificate of limited partnership (Corp C §15010.5) has been recorded. See §§3.22-3.23. Similarly, corporate officers may lack the capacity to sell corporate real property. See §3.26. Corporations Code §1001 requires shareholder approval of the sale of all or substantially all the corporate assets.

2. Lack of Assent

§12.95   a. No Acceptance

Frequently real property sales agreements are formed through exchange of an original offer and a number of counteroffers and acceptances. To form a binding agreement there must be an unqualified acceptance. CC §§1565-1566. If acceptance is qualified, the result is a counteroffer which, if unaccepted, creates no binding agreement. CC §1585; *Krasley v Superior Court* (1980) 101 CA3d 425, 161 CR 629; *Smith v Holmwood* (1965) 231 CA2d 549, 41 CR 907.

§12.96   b. Duress, Mistake, and Undue Influence

A real property purchase and sale agreement, like any other contract, is not enforceable if the defendant's apparent consent was obtained through duress, menace, undue influence, or mistake. CC §1567. Consequently, if the defendant's consent was induced by one of these factors this may be asserted as both a defense and a cross-complaint for rescission. An answer seeking rescission should be sufficient notice to comply with CC §§1691-1692. See §§12.58-12.76 on rescission.

§12.97   c. Fraud

Fraud vitiates the contract, and thus is available as a defense to action brought on a real property purchase and sale agreement. CC §§1566-1567; *Kaluzok v Brisson* (1946) 27 C2d 760, 167 P2d 981; *Rodes v Shannon* (1963) 222 CA2d 721, 35 CR 339. Therefore, if the fraud is discovered before escrow closes, the defrauded party should be able to withdraw and escape liability for breach.

§12.98   d. Uncertainty

The agreement may be so uncertain in some material term that there is no contract at all. On basic contract elements see §§3.8-3.38. Uncertainty is particularly effective as a defense to a specific performance action (see §12.43), for which greater certainty is required than for damage actions. See *Gorges v Johnson* (1959) 167 CA2d 349, 334 P2d 621.

The purchase agreement must include the identities of buyer and seller, the price, the time and manner of payment, and the specific location of the property. *King v Stanley* (1948) 32 C2d 584, 197 P2d 321; *Wolf v Price* (1966) 244 CA2d 165, 52 CR 889. Additional terms necessary to carry out the agreement need not be specified. Without express provisions, incidental terms, such as opening the escrow, furnishing deeds, title insurance, and proration of taxes, may be determined on the basis of custom. *King v Stanley, supra.*

The test for determining the sufficiency of the property's legal description is whether a competent surveyor would have difficulty locating the land and establishing its boundaries from the description. *Leider v Evans* (1962) 209 CA2d 696, 26 CR 123. Courts are very liberal, however, in construing executory agreements for the sale of real property, to give effect to the parties' intent; an agreement is considered sufficiently certain when it furnishes the means to determine the property's description and location. *McKinley v Lagae* (1962) 207 CA2d 284, 24 CR 454.

Release clauses and subordination agreements are material terms of real property sales agreements, and their uncertainty bars specific enforcement of the entire agreement. *White Point Co. v Herrington* (1968) 268 CA2d 458, 73 CR 885 (releases); *Handy v Gordon*

(1967) 65 C2d 578, 55 CR 769 (subordination). See generally, §§5.39-5.54 on subordination, and §§5.55-5.67 on releases. In *Yackey v Pacifica Dev. Co.* (1979) 99 CA3d 776, 160 CR 430, however, the seller was permitted to recover damages on the buyer's default despite an uncertain release clause that would have barred the buyer from obtaining specific performance.

§12.99 3. Lack of Consideration

Consideration for a real property purchase agreement is normally found in the seller's promise to convey and the buyer's promise to pay. Adequacy of consideration must be pleaded and proved by the plaintiff in a specific performance action. CC §3391; *Lucientes v Bliss* (1958) 157 CA2d 565, 321 P2d 526; *Balance v Parlato* (1955) 132 CA2d 816, 283 P2d 288. See §12.40. Courts will generally not weigh adequacy of consideration in an action at law for damages. See *Rice v Brown* (1953) 120 CA2d 578, 261 P2d 565; *Taylor v Taylor* (1944) 66 CA2d 390, 152 P2d 480. Lack of consideration may be available, however, as a defense in an action for damages if one party is not obligated at all under the agreement. See §§12.100-12.101.

§12.100 a. Illusory Agreement

If mutuality of obligation is lacking, the agreement is illusory and may not be enforced by either party while still executory. When the buyer retains an unfettered right to withdraw, the agreement will be held to be illusory. *Kowal v Day* (1971) 20 CA3d 720, 98 CR 118. In the past, if the buyer's performance under a purchase agreement was subject to conditions within his or her control, the buyer's promise was considered illusory and the contract unenforceable for lack of mutuality of obligation. See *e.g., Shortell v Evans-Ferguson Corp.* (1929) 98 CA 650, 277 P 519; *J.C. Millett Co. v Park & Tilford Distillers Corp.* (ND Cal 1954) 123 F Supp 484. In *Mattei v Hopper* (1958) 51 C2d 119, 330 P2d 625, however, the California Supreme Court held a real property purchase and sale agreement enforceable because the buyer had a duty to exercise his rights under the conditions in good faith. The court held that conditions involving personal satisfaction and judgment subject the buyer to a duty to act in good faith, while conditions involving commercial value or quality impose on the buyer a duty to accept or reject reasonably. In

Mattei v Hopper, supra, the sale was conditioned on obtaining leases satisfactory to the buyer. The court held that the buyer had to exercise this condition in good faith. *Kadner v Shields* (1971) 20 CA3d 251, 97 CR 742, held that the buyer's approval under a condition concerning financing terms was subject to a reasonableness standard, and including a prepayment penalty and acceleration clause in the note did not afford the buyer an excuse to withdraw from the transaction.

§12.101   b. Agreement To Agree

If the parties leave a material element of a contract for further negotiation, neither party is obligated to perform, and the contract is unenforceable as an agreement to agree. *Ablett v Clauson* (1954) 43 C2d 280, 272 P2d 753 (price to be determined later); *Bonk v Boyajian* (1954) 128 CA2d 153, 274 P2d 948, and *Burgess v Rodom* (1953) 121 CA2d 71, 262 P2d 335 (failure to specify any installment payments).

§12.102   c. Agreement Enforceable as Option

A purchase agreement with no restriction on the buyer's right to withdraw lacks mutuality of obligation and fails for lack of consideration (see §12.100). A buyer who has given the seller consideration for entering into the agreement, however, may be able to enforce it as an option, despite his or her limited right to withdraw. See chap 4 on options. In *Kowal v Day* (1971) 20 CA3d 720, 98 CR 118, the buyer had the unfettered right to withdraw within 45 days, but the court held the agreement enforceable as an option because the buyer's transfer of an automobile to the seller was sufficient consideration for an option.

§12.103   4. Statute of Frauds

Under the statute of frauds, the essential terms of an agreement for the sale of real property must be stated in writing. CC §1624(4); CCP §1971. The essential terms include identification of seller and buyer, price to be paid, manner and time of payment, and description of the property. *Corona Unified School Dist. v Vejar* (1958) 165 CA2d 561, 332 P2d 294; see §§3.36-3.38. Without express provisions, other terms can be determined by reference to custom or extrinsic evidence. *King v Stanley* (1948) 32 C2d 584, 197 P2d 321. The writing itself need not be a formal contract but may be an informal, written memorandum or a letter or telegram. *King v Stanley, supra.* The agreement must be signed by the party against whom it is to be enforced, but need not be signed by the party seeking enforcement. CC §§1624, 3388; *Steel v Duntley* (1931) 115 CA 451, 1 P2d 999.

The statute of frauds is an affirmative defense that is waived if not raised by the defendant. *Howard v Adams* (1940) 16 C2d 253, 105 P2d 971. The defense may be avoided under the doctrine of partial performance, which in a real property transaction might consist of the buyer's possession with the seller's consent (CCP §1972; *Engasser v Jones* (1948) 88 CA2d 171, 198 P2d 546). Estoppel doctrine may sometimes be invoked to defeat a statute of frauds defense. *Wilk v Vencill* (1947) 30 C2d 104, 180 P2d 351. On the statute of frauds, see §§3.36-3.38. See also 1 Miller & Starr, Current Law of California Real Estate §§1:41-1:64 (rev ed 1975).

§12.104 C. Statute of Limitations

The four-year statute of limitations for actions on written contracts (CCP §337(1)) should govern an action for damages for breach of a real property purchase and sale agreement, although there are no cases so holding.

Authority is divided on whether the limitation period for a rescission action is two years (CCP §339) or four years (CCP §337). Contrast *d'Artenay v Hansen* (1934) 138 CA 39, 31 P2d 460 (two years) with *Boudreay v Ibbetson* (1932) 123 CA 721, 12 P2d 120 (four years). The rationale for applying a two-year statute of limitations to a real property rescission action is that it is essentially an action on an implied contract for recovery of the consideration and not on the written agreement itself. *d'Artenay v Hansen, supra.* See also *Leeper v Beltrami* (1959) 53 C2d 195, 1 CR 12, holding that the three-year period of CCP §338 applies when a rescission action is based on duress. See §12.60 on rescission for fraud.

The statute of limitations for a specific performance action is four years. CCP §337(1); *McAuliffe v Foglesong* (1961) 193 CA2d 525, 14 CR 397 (seller's action); *Reiner v Hermann* (1947) 79 CA2d 543, 180 P2d 385 (buyer's action). In a buyer's action, the statute will not begin to run while the buyer is in possession and continues to perform. See *Fleishman v Woods* (1901) 135 C 256, 67 P 276.

§12.105 D. Nonoccurrence of a Condition

A party may be excused from performance under a purchase agreement if all conditions precedent to his obligation to perform have not occurred. CC §§1436, 1439; *Rubin v Fuchs* (1969) 1 C3d 50, 81 CR 373. Contract provisions will be construed as mutually dependent promises rather than conditions precedent if not plainly designated as conditions. *Rubin v Fuchs, supra* (provision containing words "subject to" held a condition precedent); *Berry v Kettle* (1967) 256 CA2d 252, 63 CR 804 (buyer's obligation to pay absolute because no words of condition used); *Sosin v Richardson* (1962) 210 CA2d 258, 26 CR 610 (provision using words "in the event of" and "then, in such event" held to create condition precedent). Conditions within the control of a party include an implied covenant to use diligence to cause the condition to occur. *Abrams v Motter* (1970) 3 CA3d 828, 83 CR 855 (buyer obligated to use diligence to obtain financing). As discussed in §12.9, the party for whose benefit a condition is inserted in the agreement may waive it. See also §12.8 on time for performance, §12.10 on tender of performance, and §12.11 on anticipatory breach.

If a condition is also one of a party's obligations, he cannot take advantage of its nonoccurrence to excuse his own performance. See *Eastwood Homes, Inc. v Hudson* (1958) 161 CA2d 532, 327 P2d 29.

If a party deliberately leads the other party to believe a condition will not be enforced, and the other relies on this conduct to his detriment, the first party may be estopped from asserting failure of the condition as a defense. See *McCown v Spencer* (1970) 8 CA3d 216, 87 CR 213 (seller estopped from asserting time condition).

§12.106 E. Failure of Consideration Without Fault

Material failure of consideration is a ground for rescission of a purchase agreement (CC §1689(4)) and may be asserted as a defense to an action for damages for breach. See *Mussler v Nash* (1953) 118 CA2d 494, 258 P2d 108, in which the performance of a party to an exchange agreement was excused for failure of consideration when bankruptcy prevented the third party from completing the exchange. The Uniform Vendor and Purchaser Risk Act, adopted in California as CC §1662, covers failure of consideration due to the destruction of the property. Unless the purchase agreement provides to the contrary, CC §1662 excuses the buyer's performance and entitles him or her to recover any portion of the purchase price paid if the property was destroyed before the transfer of title or possession. If title or possession has passed, the seller may enforce the agreement. See chap 10 on risk of loss.

§12.107 F. Impossibility

There is no liability for breach of a contract whose performance is made impossible by operation of law, irresistible superhuman cause, or act of public enemies of the state or the United States. CC §1511(1)-(2); see *Baird v Wendt Enterprises, Inc.* (1967) 248 CA2d 52, 56 CR 118 (purchase of leasehold estate excused because building code changes prevented seller from delivering building permits); *Carey v Cusack* (1966) 245 CA2d 57, 54 CR 244 (conveyance excused because property condemned).

TABLE OF
STATUTES AND REGULATIONS

CALIFORNIA

Constitution

Art XI, 7
    1.44
Art XIIIA
    3.20, 3.29, 3.56, 6.32, 7.30,
    11.51
Art XIIIA, 1
    11.51
Art XV, 1
    2.3, 5.29, 6.7, 6.10

Statutes

Business and Professions Code

490
    2.110
6125–6126
    1.2
8516
    3.126
8519(b)
    3.126, 11.47
8614
    3.125
8762
    11.91
8762–8771.5
    8.15
10000–10602
    2.1, 2.86
10017
    2.11
10071
    2.110
10081
    2.111

10086
    2.111
10100
    2.111
10130
    2.1, 2.4, 2.11, 2.29, 2.111, 6.10
10131
    2.2, 2.4, 2.7
10131(a)
    2.2
10131(b)
    2.2, 2.7
10131(c)
    2.2
10131(d)
    2.2, 2.3, 6.10
10131(e)
    2.2
10131.01
    2.7
10131.1
    2.2, 2.7
10131.2
    2.2
10131.3
    2.6
10131.6
    2.2
10131.7
    2.2
10132
    2.11
10133(a)
    2.7
10133(b)
    2.7
10133(c)
    2.7

UNITED STATES

3500.5(d)
    11.86
3500.6
    1.52
3500.7
    6.59, 11.87
3500.8
    1.52, 11.99
3500.8–3500.10
    6.59
3500.10
    11.88, 11.99

Treasury Regulations

1.212–1(k)
    1.24
1.453–4(c)
    5.12
1.752–1(e)
    6.28
1.761–1(a)
    3.29

1.1031(a)–1(c)
    1.60
301.6323(i)–1(c)
    3.85
301.6325–1(c)
    3.85

Revenue Rulings

79–292
    5.16
78–365
    2.12
77–294
    5.66
71–595
    5.11
69–462
    5.11
68–643
    5.32
65–185
    5.14
55–79
    3.160

TABLE OF CASES

Bay Shore Homes, Inc. v San Diego
Trust & Sav. Bank (1969) 276
CA2d 108, 80 CR 849: §§2.94,
12.25

Beach v Faust (1935) 2 C2d 290, 40
P2d 822: §7.4

Beason v Griff (1954) 127 CA2d 382,
274 P2d 47: §12.28

Beazell v Kane (1954) 127 CA2d 593,
274 P2d 224: §§1.32, 2.36, 2.42,
2.71

Beazell v Schrader (1963) 59 C2d 577,
30 CR 534: §§2.41, 2.51–2.52,
2.55

Beeler v American Trust Co. (1944)
24 C2d 1, 147 P2d 583: §7.37

Beeler v West Am. Fin. Co. (1962) 201
CA2d 702, 20 CR 190: §§2.18,
2.87–2.88

Behrendt v Abraham (1966) 64 C2d
182, 49 CR 292: §12.47

Benson v Shotwell (1890) 87 C 49, 25
P 249: §§3.102, 7.15

Berendsen v McIver (1954) 126 CA2d
347, 272 P2d 76: §12.79

Bergson v Builders Ins. Co. (1869) 38
C 541: §10.12

Bernesen v Fish (1933) 135 CA 588,
28 P2d 67: §12.13

Berry v Kettle (1967) 256 CA2d 252,
63 CR 804: §12.105

Berverdor, Inc. v Salyer Farms (1950)
97 CA2d 459, 218 P2d
138: §3.112

Berzon v U.L.C. Corp. (1969) 274
CA2d 690, 79 CR 277: §2.59

Bessinger v Grotz (1944) 66 CA2d
947, 153 P2d 369: §12.53

Best v Wohlford (1904) 144 C 733, 78
P 293: §§4.6, 7.31

Beverage v Canton Placer Mining Co.
(1955) 43 C2d 769, 278 P2d
694: §§8.1, 8.51, 12.6, 12.11,
12.57, 12.76

Beverly Crest Convalescent Hosp.,
Inc., In re (9th Cir 1976) 548
F2d 817: §1.14

Bewick v Mecham (1945) 26 C2d 92,
156 P2d 757: §§4.17–4.18, 5.64

Biakanja v Irving (1958) 49 C2d 647,
320 P2d 16: §2.100

Birch v Ciria (1962) 205 CA2d 1, 22
CR 798: §1.73

Birkhofer v Krumm (1935) 4 CA2d
43, 40 P2d 553: §3.50

Black Light Corp. v Ultra-Violet
Prods., Inc. (1961) 195 CA2d
473, 15 CR 852: §3.35

Blackburn v Drake (1963) 211 CA2d
806, 27 CR 651: §§7.49, 7.63

Blackburn v McCoy (1934) 1 CA2d
648, 37 P2d 153: §11.10

Blaisdell v Leach (1894) 101 C 405,
35 P 1019: §§7.50, 7.65

Blank v Borden (1974) 11 C3d 963,
115 CR 31: §§2.31, 2.37–2.38,
2.58–2.59, 2.101

Block, Lawrence, Co. v Scholer (1958)
166 CA2d 608, 333 P2d
396: §§2.39, 2.53

Boerner v Colwell Co. (1978) 21 C3d
37, 145 CR 380: §5.29

Boggs v Boggs (1944) 63 CA2d 576,
147 P2d 116: §7.48

Bohannon v City of San Diego (1973)
30 CA3d 416, 106 CR
333: §3.134

Bolton v Logan (1938) 30 CA2d 30, 85
P2d 546: §12.87

Bonaccorso v Kaplan (1963) 218 CA2d
63, 32 CR 69: §2.24

Bonk v Boyajian (1954) 128 CA2d
153, 274 P2d 948: §12.101

Bookout v Local Agency Formation
Comm'n (1975) 49 CA3d 383,
122 CR 668: §3.142

Boshes v Miller (1953) 119 CA2d 332,
259 P2d 447: §12.16

Bouchard v Orange (1960) 177 CA2d
521, 2 CR 388: §§12.21–12.22

Boudreay v Ibbetson (1932) 123 CA
721, 12 P2d 120: §12.104

Boughton v Socony Mobil Oil Co.
(1964) 231 CA2d 188, 41 CR
714: §7.46

Boulenger v Morison (1928) 88 CA
664, 264 P2d 256: §12.56

Bourdieu v Baker (1935) 6 CA2d 150,
44 P2d 587: §4.29

Bovo v Abrahamson (1929) 100 CA
373, 280 P 191: §4.6

Bowen, Truman (1949) 12 TC
446: §5.8

Bowers, People v (1964) 226 CA2d
463, 38 CR 238: §8.27

Boye v Boerner (1940) 38 CA2d 567,
101 P2d 757: §7.64

Boys Town USA v World Church
(1963) 221 CA2d 468, 34 CR
498: §§12.44, 12.55

Bradbury v Davenport (1896) 114 C
593, 46 P 1062: §7.37

Bradbury v Thomas (1933) 135 CA
435, 27 P2d 402: §5.55

Bradner v Vasquez (1954) 43 C2d 147,
272 P2d 11: §1.14

Brady v Carman (1960) 179 CA2d 63,
3 CR 612: §§1.70, 2.100

Brady v Fowler (1920) 45 CA 592, 188
P 320: §4.19

Braun v Crew (1920) 183 C 728, 192
P 531: §§3.50, 5.23

Bright v Board of Supervisors (1977)
66 CA3d 191, 135 CR
758: §5.60

Briles v Paulson (1915) 170 C 408,
149 P 804: §4.22

Brink v Allegro Builders, Inc. (1962)
58 C2d 577, 25 CR 556: §3.183

Britschgi v McCall (1953) 41 C2d 138,
257 P2d 977: §§3.70, 3.177,
12.5, 12.9

Broadmoor Improvement Ass'n v Stan
Weber & Assoc. (5th Cir 1979)
597 F2d 568: §2.116

Broadway, Laguna, Vallejo Ass'n v
Board of Permit Appeals (1967)
66 C2d 767, 59 CR 146: §3.133

Brown v Critchfield (1980) 100 CA3d
858, 161 CR 342: §1.14

Brown v Gordon (1966) 240 CA2d
659, 49 CR 901: §2.102

Brown v IAC (1917) 174 C 457, 163 P
664: §2.12

Brown v Jenson (1953) 41 C2d 193,
259 P2d 425: §3.50

Brown Derby Hollywood Corp. v
Hatton (1964) 61 C2d 855, 40
CR 848: §3.118

Brownlee v Vang (1962) 206 CA2d
814, 24 CR 158: §12.87

Brudvig v Renner (1959) 172 CA2d
522, 342 P2d 276: §§8.11, 12.43

Bruggeman v Sokol (1954) 122 CA2d
876, 265 P2d 575: §§3.151,
12.43

Bruner v Van's Mkts. (1951) 103
CA2d 135, 229 P2d 56: §§2.49,
2.52

Brusseau v Hill (1927) 201 C 225, 256
P 419: §7.1

Bryan v Ramirez (1857) 8 C
461: §7.61

Bryan v Swain (1880) 56 C 616: §3.66

Buckaloo v Johnson (1975) 14 C3d
815, 122 CR 745: §2.44

Buckley v Savage (1960) 184 CA2d
18, 7 CR 328: §§2.18, 2.86,
2.111

Builders' Control Serv. of N. Cal., Inc.
v North Am. Title Guar. Co.
(1962) 205 CA2d 68, 22 CR
712: §11.23

Buist v C. Dudley DeVelbiss Corp.
(1960) 182 CA2d 325, 6 CR
259: §12.31

Burch v Argus Properties Inc. (1979)
92 CA3d 128, 154 CR
485: §2.102

Burgess v Rodom (1953) 121 CA2d 71,
262 P2d 335: §12.101

Burk v Municipal Court (1964) 229
CA2d 696, 40 CR 425: §3.134

Burke v Stevens (1968) 264 CA2d 30,
70 CR 87: §7.63

Burkett v J.A. Thompson & Son
(1957) 150 CA2d 523, 310 P2d
56: §§1.69, 2.118, 2.121, 12.31

Burlingham v Gray (1943) 22 C2d 87,
137 P2d 9: §2.12

Burnand v Nowell (1948) 84 CA2d 1,
189 P2d 796: §§3.38, 3.66, 12.82

Burnet v Logan (1931) 283 US
404: §§5.7, 5.16

Burrow v Timmsen (1963) 223 CA2d
283, 35 CR 668: §12.45

Burrows v State (1968) 260 CA2d 29,
66 CR 868: §3.117

Bush v Vernon (1955) 135 CA2d 33,
286 P2d 903: §§3.37, 12.64

Butcher v Dauz (1967) 257 CA2d 524,
65 CR 166: §5.42

C

Cady v Purser (1901) 131 C 552, 63 P
844: §11.98

Cain v Hunter (1958) 161 CA2d 808,
327 P2d 583: §12.2

Caine v Briscoe (1926) 78 CA 660,
248 P 774: §2.36

Caito v United Cal. Bank (1978) 20
C3d 694, 144 CR 751: §6.27

Calhoun v Downs (1931) 211 C 766,
297 P 548: §§12.79–12.80

Cleary v Trimble (1964) 229 CA2d 1,
39 CR 776: §8.27

Cleghorn v Zumwalt (1890) 83 C 155,
23 P 294: §12.79

Cline v Atwood (1966) 241 CA2d 108,
50 CR 233: §3.18

Cline v Yamaga (1979) 97 CA3d 239,
158 CR 598: §2.30

Coast Bank v Minderhout (1964) 61
C2d 311, 38 CR 505: §5.24

Coast Fed. Sav. & Loan Ass'n, People
v (SD Cal 1951) 98 F Supp
311: §6.5

Cochran v Ellsworth (1954) 126 CA2d
429, 272 P2d 904: §§2.35–2.37

Cohen v Adolph Kutner Co. (1918)
177 C 592, 171 P 424: §8.28

Cohen v Citizens Nat'l Trust & Sav.
Bank (1956) 143 CA2d 480, 300
P2d 14: §2.121

Cohen v Shearer (1980) 108 CA3d
939, 167 CR 10: §§11.5, 11.80

Coid Hurlbut, Estate of (1956) 25 TC
1286: §5.7

Coldwell, Banker & Co. v Pepper Tree
Office Center Assoc. (1980) 106
CA3d 272, 165 CR 51: §2.61

Coleman v Mora (1968) 263 CA2d
137, 69 CR 166: §§2.58, 2.79,
2.101

Collier v Oelke (1962) 202 CA2d 843,
21 CR 140: §§8.30–8.31

Collins v Home Sav. & Loan Ass'n
(1962) 205 CA2d 86, 22 CR
817: §§5.43, 5.46, 5.49

Collins v Marvel Land Co. (1970) 13
CA3d 34, 91 CR 291: §12.14

Collins v Vickter Manor, Inc. (1957)
47 C2d 875, 306 P2d
783: §§2.34, 2.37

Colonial Sav. & Loan Ass'n v
Redwood Empire Title Co.
(1965) 236 CA2d 186, 46 CR
16: §2.14

Commissioner v Edwards Drilling Co.
(5th Cir 1938) 95 F2d
719: §5.16

Common Wealth Ins. Systems, Inc. v
Kersten (1974) 40 CA3d 1014,
115 CR 653: §§11.20, 11.23

Conference of Fed. Sav. & Loan Ass'ns
v Stein (9th Cir 1979) 604 F2d
1256: §6.21

Conger v White (1945) 69 CA2d 28,
158 P2d 415: §12.36

Conley v Fate (1964) 227 CA2d 418,
38 CR 680: §1.80

Conley v Poway Land & Inv. Co.
(1965) 232 CA2d 22, 42 CR
636: §5.62

Conroy, Estate of (1907) 6 CA 741, 93
P 205: §7.53

Contant v Wallace (1923) 62 CA 768,
217 P 1081: §2.35

Continental Baking Co. v Katz (1968)
68 C2d 512, 67 CR 761: §8.29

Contini v Western Title Ins. Co.
(1974) 40 CA3d 536, 115 CR
257: §11.4

Cook v King Manor & Convalescent
Hosp. (1974) 40 CA3d 782, 115
CR 471: §§3.179, 12.29

Cook v Nordstrand (1948) 83 CA2d
188, 188 P2d 282: §12.12

Cook v Redwood Empire Title Co.
(1969) 275 CA2d 452, 79 CR
888: §11.23

Copeland v Fairview Land & Water
Co. (1913) 165 C 148, 131 P
119: §7.24

Corbett v Otts (1962) 205 CA2d 78, 22
CR 849: §1.73

Cordano v Wright (1911) 159 C 610,
115 P 227: §7.50

Cormac v Murphy (1922) 58 CA 366,
208 P 360: §1.35

Cornbleth v Allen (1926) 80 CA 459,
251 P 87: §11.91

Cornelison v Kornbluth (1975) 15 C3d
590, 125 CR 557: §§3.50, 5.23

Corona Unified School Dist. v Vejar
(1958) 165 CA2d 561, 332 P2d
294: §§3.36, 12.103

Corporation of the Presiding Bishop v
Cavanaugh (1963) 217 CA2d
492, 32 CR 144: §9.3

Corwin, Estate of (1882) 61 C
160: §4.17

Cosgrave v Donovan (1921) 52 CA
625, 199 P 808: §8.42

Cottingham v Smith (1938) 28 CA2d
345, 82 P2d 479: §2.34

Cottle v Gibbon (1962) 200 CA2d 1,
19 CR 82: §12.78

Coughlin v Blair (1953) 41 C2d 587,
262 P2d 305: §12.15

Fitzpatrick v Underwood (1941) 17
    C2d 722, 112 P2d 3: §2.32
Flanagan v San Marcos Silk Co.
    (1951) 106 CA2d 458, 235 P2d
    107: §8.28
Fleischer v Cosgrove (1956) 145 CA2d
    14, 301 P2d 911: §§12.21–12.22,
    12.40
Fleishman v Woods (1901) 135 C 256,
    67 P 276: §12.104
Fleming v Dolfin (1931) 214 C 269, 4
    P2d 776: §§2.57, 2.61
Flickenger v IAC (1919) 181 C 425,
    184 P 851: §2.12
Floyd J. Voight (1977) 68 TC 99: §5.30
Flynn v Mikelian (1962) 208 CA2d
    305, 25 CR 138: §7.44
Foley v Cowan (1947) 80 CA2d 70,
    181 P2d 410: §12.41
Foorman v Wallace (1888) 75 C 552,
    17 P680: §7.60
Foote v Clark (Mo 1890) 14 SW
    981: §9.11
Foote v Posey (1958) 164 CA2d 210,
    330 P2d 651: §2.47
Ford v Cournale (1973) 36 CA3d 172,
    111 CR 334: §2.100
Ford v Palisades Corp. (1950) 101
    CA2d 491, 225 P2d 545: §2.55
Forde v Vernbro Corp. (1963) 218
    CA2d 405, 32 CR 577: §5.64
Fountain v Semi-Tropic Land & Water
    Co. (1893) 99 C 677, 34 P
    497: §12.63
Fowler v Smith (1852) 2 C 39: §9.16
Fox v Aced (1957) 49 C2d 381, 317
    P2d 608: §12.14
Frabotto v Alencastre (1960) 182
    CA2d 679, 6 CR 536: §3.78
Franceschi v Kuntz (1967) 253 CA2d
    1041, 61 CR 810: §8.30
Francis v West Virginia Oil Co.
    (1917) 174 C 168, 162 P
    394: §12.71
Frank Lyon Co. v U.S. (1978) 435 US
    561: §5.8
Frank Pisano & Assocs. v Taggart
    (1972) 29 CA3d 1, 105 CR
    414: §12.75
Franklin v Hansen (1963) 59 C2d
    570, 30 CR 530: §2.49
Fraser v Bentel (1911) 161 C 390, 119
    P 509: §§9.14, 9.17

Fratt v Whittier (1881) 58 C
    126: §7.40
Freedman v The Rector (1951) 37 C2d
    16, 230 P2d 629: §§5.5, 12.22,
    12.28
Freeman v Affiliated Property
    Craftsmen (1968) 266 CA2d
    723, 72 CR 357: §8.17
Freeman v Bellegarde (1895) 108 C
    179, 41 P 289: §8.17
Friedberg v Weissbuch (1955) 135
    CA2d 750, 287 P2d 785: §1.77
Friedman v Jackson (1968) 266 CA2d
    517, 72 CR 129: §2.44
Friends of "B" Street v City of
    Hayward (1980) 106 CA3d 988,
    165 CR 514: §1.43
Friends of Lake Arrowhead v Board
    of Supervisors (1974) 38 CA3d
    497, 113 CR 539: §§1.42, 3.143,
    5.60
Fries v Broadway Fed. Sav. & Loan
    Ass'n (1968) 258 CA2d 119, 65
    CR 460: §5.47
Fristoe v Drapeau (1950) 35 C2d 5,
    215 P2d 729: §8.27
Fry v George Elkins Co. (1958) 162
    CA2d 256, 327 P2d 905: §§3.69,
    3.151, 12.7
Fudickar v East Riverside Irr. Dist.
    (1895) 109 C 29, 41 P
    1024: §8.11
Fugate v Cook (1965) 236 CA2d 700,
    46 CR 291: §3.36
Fujita, People v (1932) 215 C 166, 8
    P2d 1011: §3.11

G

Gaffey v Welk (1920) 46 CA 385, 189
    P 300: §9.13
Gagne v Bertran (1954) 43 C2d 481,
    275 P2d 15: §§2.104, 2.118,
    12.31
Gaine v Austin (1943) 58 CA2d 250,
    136 P2d 584: §2.28
Gaither v Gaither (1958) 165 CA2d
    782, 332 P2d 436: §8.29
Ganiats Constr., Inc. v Hesse (1960)
    180 CA2d 377, 4 CR 706: §§4.6,
    12.55
Gardner v Murphy (1975) 54 CA3d
    164, 126 CR 302: §§2.100, 2.117

Garrett v Perry (1959) 53 C2d 178, 346 P2d 758: §12.31

Gates v Green (1907) 151 C 65, 90 P 189: §12.45

Gatley v Shockley (1932) 215 C 604, 12 P2d 436: §12.57

Gee v Moore (1859) 14 C 472: §9.8

Gerhard v Stephens (1968) 68 C2d 864, 69 CR 612: §8.39

Gilbert v Corlett (1959) 171 CA2d 116, 339 P2d 960: §1.70

Gilbert v Mercer (1960) 179 CA2d 29, 3 CR 456: §§12.40–12.41

Gilford v Commissioner (2d Cir 1953) 201 F2d 735: §3.29

Gill v Mission Sav. & Loan Ass'n (1965) 236 CA2d 753, 46 CR 456: §5.47

Gion v City of Santa Cruz (1970) 2 C3d 29, 84 CR 162: §§1.11, 8.38

Gipson v Davis Realty Co. (1963) 215 CA2d 190, 30 CR 253: §§2.12, 2.114

Gist v Security Trust & Sav. Bank (1933) 218 C 581, 24 P2d 153: §12.69

Gladstone, Realtors v Bellwood (1979) 441 US 91: §2.116

Glatts v Henson (1948) 31 C2d 368, 188 P2d 745: §§8.27–8.28

Glendale Bd. of Realtors v Hounsell (1977) 72 CA3d 210, 139 CR 830: §§2.26, 2.41

Glendale Fed. Sav. & Loan Ass'n v Fox (CD Cal 1978) 459 F Supp 903: §§3.50, 5.24, 6.5, 6.43

Glock v Howard & Wilson Colony Co. (1898) 123 C 1, 55 P 713: §12.42

Gluskin v Atlantic Sav. & Loan Ass'n (1973) 32 CA3d 307, 108 CR 318: §5.53

Goad v Moulton (1885) 67 C 536, 8 P 63: §7.13

Godbey & Sons Constr. Co. v Deane (1952) 39 C2d 429, 246 P2d 946: §3.37

Gold v Greenwald (1966) 247 CA2d 296, 55 CR 660: §1.14

Golden v Anderson (1967) 256 CA2d 714, 64 CR 404: §2.44

Golden State Lanes v Fox (1965) 232 CA2d 135, 42 CR 568: §5.29

Goldfarb v Virginia State Bar (1975) 421 US 773: §1.2

Goldstein v Hensley (1906) 4 CA 444, 88 P 507: §9.14

Goldsworthy v Dobbins (1952) 110 CA2d 802, 243 P2d 883: §§12.45, 12.48, 12.50, 12.53

Gonsalves v Hodgson (1951) 38 C2d 91, 237 P2d 656: §§1.68, 12.60

Gonzales v Gonzales (1968) 267 CA2d 428, 73 CR 83: §§7.50, 7.63

Gordon v City of San Diego (1895) 108 C 264, 41 P 301: §7.49

Gordon v D & G Escrow Corp. (1975) 48 CA3d 616, 122 CR 150: §11.10

Gorges v Johnson (1959) 167 CA2d 349, 334 P2d 621: §12.98

Goudal v DeMille Pictures Corp. (1931) 118 CA 407, 5 P2d 432: §12.5

Gould v Wise (1893) 97 C 532, 32 P 576: §7.65

Graf v Sumpter (1962) 207 CA2d 391, 24 CR 590: §12.31

Graff v Middleton (1872) 43 C 341: §9.21

Granberg v Turnham (1958) 166 CA2d 390, 333 P2d 423: §2.27

Grand v Griesinger (1958) 160 CA2d 397, 325 P2d 475: §2.11

Grand Grove of United Ancient Order ᐧof Druids v Garibaldi Grove No. 71 (1900) 130 C 116, 62 P 486: §7.16

Grant v Beronio (1893) 97 C 496, 32 P 556: §§12.44–12.45

Grant v Woods (1977) 71 CA3d 647, 139 CR 533: §2.12

Graves v Arizona Cent. Bank (1928) 205 C 715, 272 P 1063: §7.37

Greco v Oregon Mut. Fire Ins. Co. (1961) 191 CA2d 674, 12 CR 802: §10.12

Green v Skinner (1921) 185 C 435, 195 P 60: §7.64

Greene v Municipal Court (1975) 51 CA3d 446, 124 CR 139: §§1.65, 5.5

Greenstone v Claretian Theological Seminary (1958) 158 CA2d 493, 322 P2d 482: §12.44

Hicks v Wilson (1925) 197 C 269, 240
P 289: §§2.28, 2.70

Hildebrand v Beck (1925) 196 C 141,
236 P 301: §7.65

Hill v Allan (1968) 259 CA2d 470, 66
CR 676: §8.29

Hill v Citizens Nat'l Trust & Sav.
Bank (1937) 9 C2d 172, 69 P2d
853: §2.22

Hill v Donnelly (1941) 43 CA2d 47,
110 P2d 135: §7.63

Hill, J.B. v Pinque (1922) 56 CA 245,
204 P 1097: §3.109

Hillman v Koch (1949) 92 CA2d 163,
206 P2d 434: §2.51

Hiltbrand v Hiltbrand (1936) 13 CA2d
330, 56 P2d 1292: §3.28

Hoag v Howard (1880) 55 C
564: §11.91

Hoar v Tuley (1970) 12 CA3d 344, 90
CR 559: §§2.11, 2.30

Hobson v Hunt (1922) 59 CA 679, 211
P 242: §2.40

Hocking v Title Ins. & Trust Co.
(1951) 37 C2d 644, 234 P2d
625: §3.78

Hodge v Hodge (1967) 257 CA2d 31,
64 CR 587: §7.52

Hodgeson v Brant (1958) 156 CA2d
610, 319 P2d 684: §1.72

Holcomb v Long Beach Inv. Co. (1933)
129 CA 285, 19 P2d 31: §12.69

Holland v McCarthy (1916) 173 C
597, 160 P 1069: §2.28

Holland v Morgan & Peacock
Properties Co. (1959) 168 CA2d
206, 335 P2d 769: §2.47

Holloway v Thiele (1953) 116 CA2d
68, 253 P2d 131: §§2.71, 2.102

Hollypark Realty Co. v MacLoane
(1958) 163 CA2d 549, 329 P2d
532: §§12.48–12.49

Holmes v Steele (1969) 269 CA2d 675,
75 CR 216: §12.58

Holt v Holt (1898) 120 C 67, 52 P
119: §12.81

Honda v Reed (1958) 156 CA2d 536,
319 P2d 728: §12.64

Hopkins v Fresno County Abstract
Co. (1918) 36 CA 699, 173 P
106: §11.92

Horn v County of Ventura (1979) 24
C3d 605, 156 CR 718: §1.42

Horton v Kyburz (1959) 53 C2d 59,
346 P2d 399: §3.35

Hotaling v Hotaling (1924) 193 C 368,
224 P 455: §§7.63, 9.6

Houston v Williams (1921) 53 CA
267, 200 P 55: §2.61

Howard v Adams (1940) 16 C2d 253,
105 P2d 971: §12.103

Howden-Goetzl v Superior Court
(1970) 7 CA3d 135, 86 CR
323: §§12.88, 12.90

Hughes v Grandy (1947) 78 CA2d
555, 177 P2d 939: §7.66

Hughes v Heffner (1938) 29 CA2d
382, 84 P2d 540: §§4.27, 4.35

Humes v Walker (1931) 116 CA 599, 3
P2d 33: §3.72

Hunt v Mahoney (1947) 82 CA2d 540,
187 P2d 43: §12.10

Hunter v Vernon (1948) 85 CA2d 525,
193 P2d 139: §2.43

Hurlbut, Coid, Estate of (1956) 25 TC
1286: §5.7

Huttlinger v Far W. Enterprises, Inc.
(1955) 131 CA2d 808, 281 P2d
554: §§2.42, 2.75

I

In re New York Investors Mut. Group,
Inc. (SD NY 1956) 143 F Supp
51: §4.21

In re San Francisco Indus. Park, Inc.
(ND Cal 1969) 307 F Supp
271: §5.8

In re Steen (9th Cir 1975) 509 F2d
1398: §5.16

Integrated, Inc. v Alec Fergusson
Elec. Contractor (1967) 250
CA2d 287, 58 CR 503: §§12.63,
12.75

Irvin v Petitfils (1941) 44 CA2d 496,
112 P2d 688: §8.27

Isaacson v G.D. Robertson & Co.
(1948) 85 CA2d 71, 192 P2d
486: §§3.136, 12.9

Iusi v Chase (1959) 169 CA2d 83, 337
P2d 79: §§2.29, 2.47

J

J.B. Hill v Pinque (1922) 56 CA 245,
204 P 1097: §3.109

L

Landis v Superior Court (1965) 232 CA2d 548, 42 CR 893: §12.77

Larkin v Bank of America Nat'l Trust & Sav. Ass'n (1949) 93 CA2d 594, 209 P2d 801: §12.87

La Sala v American Sav. & Loan Ass'n (1971) 5 C3d 864, 97 CR 849: §§3.50, 5.21, 5.24, 6.43

Laske v Lampasona (1948) 89 CA2d 284, 200 P2d 871: §§12.51, 12.53

Lathrop v Gauger (1954) 127 CA2d 754, 274 P2d 730: §2.36

Lawrence v Montgomery (1869) 37 C 183: §9.6

Lawrence v Shutt (1969) 269 CA2d 749, 75 CR 533: §§5.59, 12.43, 12.56

Lawrence Block Co. v Scholer (1958) 166 CA2d 608, 333 P2d 396: §§2.39, 2.53

LeBlond v Wolfe (1948) 83 CA2d 282, 188 P2d 278: §2.57

Le Deit v Ehlert (1962) 205 CA2d 154, 22 CR 747: §8.30

Lee v Helmco, Inc. (1962) 199 CA2d 820, 19 CR 413: §2.22

Lee v O'Hara (1962) 57 C2d 476, 20 CR 617: §2.116

Lee v Title Ins. & Trust Co. (1968) 264 CA2d 160, 70 CR 378: §§11.4, 11.10

Leeper v Beltrami (1959) 53 C2d 195, 1 CR 12: §§12.61, 12.74, 12.104

LeFave v Dimond (1956) 46 C2d 868, 299 P2d 858: §12.35

Lehmann v Kamp (1969) 273 CA2d 701, 77 CR 910: §7.13

Leider v Evans (1962) 209 CA2d 696, 26 CR 123: §12.98

Le Mesnager v Hamilton (1894) 101 C 532, 35 P 1054: §7.50

Lemoge Elec. v County of San Mateo (1956) 46 C2d 659, 297 P2d 638: §§12.77–12.78

Lenney v Board of Supervisors (1974) 41 CA3d 902, 116 CR 500: §5.60

Leno v YMCA (1971) 17 CA3d 651, 95 CR 96: §§2.18, 2.20

Leonard v Fallas (1959) 51 C2d 649, 335 P2d 665: §§2.40, 2.77

Levitzky v Canning (1867) 33 C 299: §9.17

Levy v Wolff (1956) 46 C2d 367, 294 P2d 945: §12.13

Lewis v Foppiano (1957) 150 CA2d 752, 310 P2d 658: §2.39

Lewis v Reed (1920) 48 CA 742, 192 P 335: §10.12

Lewis & Queen v N.M. Ball Sons (1957) 48 C2d 141, 308 P2d 713: §2.67

Liberty Bldg. Co. v Royal Indem. Co. (1960) 177 CA2d 583, 2 CR 329: §9.3

Lifton v Harshman (1947) 80 CA2d 422, 182 P2d 222: §12.6

Limsky v Scottish Union & Nat'l Ins. Co. (1924) 68 CA 688, 229 P 1017: §10.12

Lindsay v King (1956) 138 CA2d 333, 292 P2d 23: §3.93

Linggi v Garovotti (1955) 45 C2d 20, 286 P2d 15: §8.36

Lingsch v Savage (1963) 213 CA2d 729, 29 CR 201: §§1.69, 1.72, 2.113, 2.117, 2.119–2.120, 3.122–3.123, 12.60

Lipton v Johansen (1951) 105 CA2d 363, 233 P2d 648: §2.42

Lisenby v Newton (1898) 120 C 571, 52 P 813: §4.19

Litten v Warren (1936) 11 CA2d 635, 54 P2d 39: §7.22

Loeb v Wilson (1967) 253 CA2d 383, 61 CR 377: §5.42

Long v Keller (1980) 104 CA3d 312, 163 CR 532: §§10.1–10.6

Long v Newlin (1956) 144 CA2d 509, 301 P2d 271: §12.58

Los Angeles & Redondo R.R. v New Liverpool Salt Co. (1906) 150 C 21, 87 P 1029: §12.85

Loughlin v Idora Realty Co. (1968) 259 CA2d 619, 66 CR 747: §§2.63, 2.96–2.97

Love v Watkins (1871) 40 C 547: §12.45

Love v White (1961) 56 C2d 192, 14 CR 442: §§11.14, 11.83

Lowe v Loyd (1949) 93 CA2d 684, 209 P2d 851: §§2.59, 2.67

Lowe v Massachusetts Mut. Life Ins. Co. (1976) 54 CA3d 718, 127 CR 23: §6.61

R

Roland v Hubenka (1970) 12 CA3d
215, 90 CR 490: §1.76
Roller v California Pac. Title Ins. Co.
(1949) 92 CA2d 149, 206 P2d
694: §12.59
Roman v Ries (1968) 259 CA2d 65, 66
CR 120: §8.42
Rose v Hunter (1957) 155 CA2d 319,
317 P2d 1027: §2.32
Rose v Knapp (1957) 153 CA2d 379,
314 P2d 812: §12.86
Rosebrook, U.S. v (9th Cir 1963) 318
F2d 316: §3.29
Rosenaur v Pacelli (1959) 174 CA2d
673, 345 P2d 102: §4.35
Rosenthal v Rosenthal (1963) 215
CA2d 140, 30 CR 49: §3.30
Rotea v Rotea (1949) 93 CA2d 827,
209 P2d 963: §12.87
Rothstein v Janss Inv. Corp. (1941) 45
CA2d 64, 113 P2d 465: §2.119
Roven v Miller (1959) 168 CA2d 391,
335 P2d 1035: §4.6
Royer v Carter (1951) 37 C2d 544,
233 P2d 539: §§12.19,
12.21–12.23, 12.25, 12.27, 12.53
Rubin v Fuchs (1969) 1 C3d 50, 81
CR 373: §12.105
Rule, Estate of (1944) 25 C2d 1, 152
P2d 1003: §2.51
Runyan v Pacific Air Indus. (1970) 2
C3d 304, 85 CR 138: §12.58
Rupp v Kahn (1966) 246 CA2d 188,
55 CR 108: §3.28
Russell v Ramm (1927) 200 C 348,
254 P 532: §2.33
Rustigan v Phelps (1923) 190 C 608,
213 P 957: §3.93
Ruth v Lytton Sav. & Loan Ass'n
(1968) 266 CA2d 831, 72 CR
521: §§3.17, 5.43, 5.48–5.49
Ruth Iron Co. v Commissioner (8th
Cir 1928) 26 F2d 30: §5.16
Rylander v Karpe (1976) 60 CA3d
317, 131 CR 415: §2.99
Rylee v DeFini (1955) 134 CA2d Supp
877, 285 P2d 115: §2.34

S

Sackett v Los Angeles City School
Dist. (1931) 118 CA 254, 5 P2d
23: §3.96
Sain v Silvestre (1978) 78 CA3d 461,
144 CR 478: §3.96

St. James Armenian Church v
Kurkjian (1975) 47 CA3d 547,
121 CR 214: §§2.99, 2.105
St. Louis v DeBon (1962) 204 CA2d
464, 22 CR 443: §8.30
Salisbury v Yawger (1921) 184 C 783,
199 P 682: §12.41
Salmon v Vallejo (1871) 41 C
481: §9.9
Salmons v Jameson (1956) 144 CA2d
698, 301 P2d 431: §8.1
Salvati v Cusolito (1950) 98 CA2d
582, 220 P2d 800: §1.77
Salveter v Salveter (1929) 206 C 657,
275 P 801: §7.35
San Diego Constr. Co. v Mannix
(1917) 175 C 548, 166 P
325: §5.62
San Francisco Indus. Park, Inc., In re
(ND Cal 1969) 307 F Supp
271: §5.8
San Roque Property, Inc. v Pierce
(1937) 18 CA2d 379, 63 P2d
1198: §12.64
Sanders v Magill (1937) 9 C2d 145, 70
P2d 159: §3.50
Sanguinetti v Rossen (1906) 12 CA
623, 107 P 560: §1.14
Santos v Wing (1961) 197 CA2d 678,
17 CR 457: §2.100
Saporta v Barbagelata (1963) 220
CA2d 463, 33 CR 661: §§2.113,
2.117
Sarten v Pomatto (1961) 192 CA2d
288, 13 CR 588: §§2.24, 2.28,
2.71
Saterstrom v Glick Bros. Sash Co.
(1931) 118 CA 379, 5 P2d
21: §§7.38, 8.10
Saunders v Schmaelzle (1874) 49 C
59: §8.54
Savage v Mayer (1949) 33 C2d 548,
203 P2d 9: §§2.71, 2.99, 2.105
Save El Toro Ass'n v Days (1977) 74
CA3d 64, 141 CR 282: §1.43
Scarbery v Bill Patch Land & Water
Co. (1960) 184 CA2d 87, 7 CR
408: §§4.1, 4.7, 4.35
Schade v Stewart (1928) 205 C 658,
272 P 567: §§7.24, 7.65
Schaefer v Manufacturer's Bank
(1980) 104 CA3d 70, 163 CR
402: §11.4

V

Vance v Pena (1871) 41 C 686: §9.15

Van Core v Bodner (1947) 77 CA2d 842, 176 P2d 784: §7.65

Van Sicklen v Browne (1971) 15 CA3d 122, 92 CR 786: §§3.133–3.134

Van Slyke v Arrowhead Reservoir & Power Co. (1909) 155 C 675, 102 P 816: §§3.91, 8.34

Vantress Farms, Inc. v Sydenstricker (1970) 11 CA3d 943, 90 CR 251: §12.82

Vargas v Hampson (1962) 57 C2d 479, 20 CR 618: §2.116

Vargas v Ruggiero (1961) 197 CA2d 709, 17 CR 568: §2.20

Vella v Ratto (1971) 17 CA3d 737, 95 CR 72: §8.42

Venable v Harmon (1965) 233 CA2d 297, 43 CR 490: §§5.4–5.5, 12.2, 12.19

Verbeck v Clymer (1927) 202 C 557, 261 P 1017: §5.29

Vezaldenos v Keller (1967) 254 CA2d 816, 62 CR 808: §8.11

Vickerson v Frey (1950) 100 CA2d 621, 224 P2d 126: §12.59

Vidler v De Bell (1954) 125 CA2d 326, 270 P2d 120: §2.32

Vierneisel v Rhode Island Ins. Co. (1946) 77 CA2d 229, 175 P2d 63: §10.12

Vigli v Davis (1947) 79 CA2d 237, 179 P2d 586: §§2.22, 2.92

Vilkin v Sommer (1968) 260 CA2d 687, 67 CR 837: §5.62

Vincent v Garland (1936) 14 CA2d 726, 58 P2d 1320: §3.50

Vineland Homes, Inc. v Barish (1936) 138 CA2d 747, 292 P2d 941: §§12.16–12.17

Voge, Inc. v Rose (1962) 205 CA2d 534, 23 CR 87: §12.85

Voight, Floyd J., (1977) 68 TC 99: §5.30

Votypka v Valentine (1919) 41 CA 74, 182 P 76: §11.95

W

Waggle v Worthy (1887) 74 C 266, 15 P 831: §9.14

Wagner v O'Bannon (1969) 274 CA2d 121, 79 CR 44: §2.116

Walbridge v Richards (1931) 212 C 408, 248 P 971: §3.36

Waldteufel v Sailor (1944) 62 CA2d 577, 144 P2d 894: §2.53

Walner v City of Turlock (1964) 230 CA2d 399, 41 CR 29: §8.28

Walsh v Hooker & Fay (1963) 212 CA2d 450, 28 CR 16: §§2.104, 2.108, 12.33

Walsh v Walsh (1940) 42 CA2d 287, 108 P2d 765: §12.8

Walter G. Reese Co. v House (1912) 162 C 740, 124 P 442: §4.20

Walters v Marler (1978) 83 CA3d 1, 147 CR 655: §§2.27, 2.104, 12.31, 12.33

Walton v Broglio (1975) 52 CA3d 400, 125 CR 123: §1.14

Waratah Oil Co. v Reward Oil Co. (1914) 23 CA 638, 139 P 91: §12.79

Ward v DeOca (1898) 120 C 102, 52 P 130: §3.50

Ward v Taggart (1959) 51 C2d 736, 336 P2d 534: §§2.86, 2.104, 2.107, 2.112, 12.31, 12.33

Ware v Security-First Nat'l Bank (1936) 7 C2d 604, 61 P2d 936: §10.8

Warington Lumber Co. v Fullerton Mortgage & Escrow Co. (1963) 222 CA2d 706, 35 CR 423: §11.80

Warner Bros. Pictures Inc. v Brodel (1948) 31 C2d 766, 192 P2d 949: §4.1

Warren v Atchison T. & S.F. Ry. (1971) 19 CA3d 24, 96 CR 317: §§7.13, 7.26

Warren Jones Co. v Commissioner (9th Cir 1975) 524 F2d 788: §§5.7, 5.16

Warshauer v Bauer Constr. Co. (1960) 179 CA2d 44, 3 CR 570: §§2.70, 2.118

Weaver v Superior Court (1949) 93 CA2d 729, 209 P2d 830: §12.73

Weber v Ross (1958) 159 CA2d 77, 323 P2d 465: §2.36

Weber v Tonini (1957) 151 CA2d 168, 311 P2d 132: §2.20

Weidner v Zieglar (1933) 218 C 345, 23 P2d 515: §4.19

Weiner v Mullaney (1943) 59 CA2d 620, 140 P2d 704: §3.36

58 Ops Cal Atty Gen 408
(1975): §5.60
56 Ops Cal Atty Gen 496
(1973): §5.60
54 Ops Cal Atty Gen 13 (1971): §2.13
53 Ops Cal Atty Gen 196
(1970): §2.116

44 Ops Cal Atty Gen 105
(1964): §2.13
43 Ops Cal Atty Gen 284
(1964): §2.13
43 Ops Cal Atty Gen 19 (1964): §5.54
13 Ops Cal Atty Gen 185
(1949): §11.98

TABLE OF REFERENCES

Advising California Partnerships (Cal CEB 1975): §§*3.22–3.23.*
3 American Law of Property. A. James Casner, editor. Boston, Little,
    Brown & Co., 1952: §§*3.95, 8.1, 9.7–9.8, 9.12–9.13.*
Anderson, Paul Edward. Tax Factors in Real Estate Operations. 6th ed.
    Englewood Cliffs, N.J., Prentice-Hall, 1980: §§*5.7, 5.14,
    5.31–5.32.*
Belsheim, Edmund O. Modern Legal Forms. Kansas City, Mo., and St.
    Paul, Minn., Vernon Law Book and West Publishing, 1963:
    §*3.95.*
Best's Insurance Reports: Property/Casualty Division. Oldwich, N.J.,
    A.M. Best. Published annually: §*10.9.*
1 Bowman, Odgen's Revised California Real Property Law. Vol. 1. (TI
    Corp-CEB 1974): §§*3.18, 3.22, 3.24, 7.2, 7.26, 7.65, 8.1, 8.11,
    8.13–8.15, 8.18, 8.24, 8.30, 8.35, 8.62, 9.6, 9.8.*
2 Bowman, Ogden's Revised California Real Property Law. Vol. 2. (TI
    Corp-CEB 1975): §§*3.96, 3.99, 5.39, 7.26, 7.45, 8.45, 8.62,
    9.8–9.9, 9.19.*
Bowman, Arthur G. Real Estate Law in California. 5th ed. Englewood
    Cliffs, N.J., Prentice-Hall, 1978: §*8.18.*
Brown, Curtis M. & Winfield H. Eldridge. Evidence and Procedures for
    Boundary Location. New York, John Wiley & Sons, 1962: §*8.13,
    8.21.*
Bureau of Land Management. Manual of Instructions for the Survey of
    the Public Lands of the United States. Washington, D.C., U.S.
    Gov't Printing Office, 1973: §§*8.13, 8.49.*
Business Buy-Out Agreements (Cal CEB 1976): §*3.160.*
California Administrative Mandamus (Cal CEB 1966): §*2.111.*
California Attorneys' Damages Guide (Cal CEB 1974): §§*2.104, 12.33.*
1 California Civil Procedure Before Trial (Cal CEB 1977): §*12.86.*
1 California Commercial Law (Cal CEB 1966): §*3.160.*
2 California Commercial Law (Cal CEB 1965): §*3.20.*
3 California Commercial Law (Cal CEB 1966): §*8.64.*
California Conservatorships (Cal CEB 1968): §*3.13.*
1 California Decedent Estate Administration (Cal CEB 1971): §§*3.9,
    7.21, 7.55.*
California Eviction Defense Manual (Cal CEB 1971): §*3.107.*

California Marital Termination Settlements (Cal CEB 1971): §*3.30*
California Mechanics' Liens and Other Remedies (Cal CEB 1972): §§*3.103, 5.50.*
California Mortgage and Deed of Trust Practice (Cal CEB 1979): §§*3.9, 3.50, 3.100, 5.5, 5.9, 5.13, 5.19–5.21, 5.24, 5.27, 5.30, 5.39, 6.27, 6.42, 6.55, 7.37, 10.17, 11.42, 11.66, 11.69, 12.1–12.2.*
California Taxes (Cal CEB 1978): §§*3.56, 11.51.*
California Title Insurance Practice (Cal CEB 1980): §§*1.3, 1.28, 1.36–1.37, 1.76, 2.78, 3.55, 3.78, 3.92, 3.102–3.103, 3.161, 8.6, 8.9, 8.22, 8.44, 9.23, 11.44, 11.60, 11.67, 11.76,*
California Will Drafting (Cal CEB 1965): §§*3.27, 7.26.*
California Zoning Practice (Cal CEB 1969): §§*1.42–1.46, 1.48, 3.132–3.134.*
2 Chadbourn, James H., Harvey M. Grossman & Arvo Van Alstyne. California Pleading. Vol. 2. St. Paul, Minn., West Publishing, 1961: §*8.45.*
Commercial Real Property Lease Practice (Cal CEB 1976): §§*1.61, 3.109, 5.8, 5.64.*
Condemnation Practice in California (Cal CEB 1973): §§*5.67, 8.41.*
Drafting Agreements for the Sale of Businesses (Cal CEB 1971): §§*3.157, 3.160, 8.64.*
Friedman, Milton R. Contracts and Conveyances of Real Property. 3d ed. New York, Practicing Law Institute. 2 vols: §*3.69.*
Ground Lease Practice (Cal CEB 1971): §§*1.61, 3.109, 5.50.*
Guide to California Subdivision Sales Law (Cal CEB 1974): §§*1.53, 3.97, 5.6, 7.45, 9.2, 9.19.*
1 Miller, Harry D. & Marvin B. Starr. Current Law of California Real Estate. Rev ed. San Francisco, Bancroft-Whitney, 1975: §§*2.10, 2.12, 2.27, 2.37, 2.40, 2.71, 2.120, 3.47, 3.78, 4.7, 5.29–5.30, 12.1, 12.46, 12.53, 12.72, 12.103.*
2 ———. Rev ed. 1977: §§*3.83, 3.103, 5.39–5.41, 5.43, 5.53, 7.5, 11.10, 11.91, 12.87.*
3 ———: §*3.91.*
5 Powell, Richard R. The Law of Real Property. Albany, N.Y., Matthew Bender, 1968: §*3.95.*
5 Restatement of the Law of Property. St. Paul, Minn., American Law Institute, 1944: §§*8.28, 8.30, 8.38, 8.60.*
Shalowitz, Aaron L. Shore and Sea Boundaries. Washington, D.C., U.S. Dep't of Commerce, Coast and Geodetic Survey, 1962. 2 vols. 1964: §*8.40.*
Title Insurance & Trust Company. Title Handbook for Title Men. 22d ed. Los Angeles, Title Insurance & Trust Co., 1980: §§*1.18, 8.40.*
Wattles, William C. Land Survey Descriptions. Rev ed. Los Angeles, Title Insurance & Trust Co. 1964: §*8.13.*
7 Williston, Samuel A. A Treatise on the Law of Contracts. Walter H. E. Jaeger, editor 3d ed. Mount Kisco, N.Y., Baker, Voorhis, 1963: §*10.4.*

Witkin, B.E. California Evidence. 2d ed. San Francisco, Bancroft-Whitney, 1966: §*3.186.*

2 ———. California Procedure. 2d ed. San Francisco, Bancroft-Whitney, 1970: §§*3.182, 8.45.*

3 ———. 2d ed. 1971: §§*3.8, 8.45.*

4 ———. 2d ed. 1971: §*8.45.*

1 ———. Summary of California Law. 8th ed. San Francisco, Bancroft-Whitney, 1973: §§*2.21, 3.20, 3.36, 3.38, 3.65, 3.182, 3.188, 9.3.*

2 ———: §*3.65.*

3 ———: §§*1.18, 3.28, 8.1, 8.26, 8.30, 8.39, 10.17.*

6 ———. 8th ed. 1974: §§*3.22–3.23.*

7 ———: §§*2.57, 3.118, 10.8.*

Wydick, Richard C. Plain English for Lawyers. Durham, N.C., Carolina Academic Press, 1979: §*3.5.*

INDEX